Promotional Strategy

Promotional Strategy

JAMES F. ENGEL
Graduate School, Wheaton College (Illinois)

HUGH G. WALES
Roosevelt University

MARTIN R. WARSHAW
The University of Michigan

THIRD EDITION · 1975

RICHARD D. IRWIN, INC.   Homewood, Illinois   60430
Irwin-Dorsey International, London, England   WC2H 9NJ
Irwin-Dorsey Limited, Georgetown, Ontario   L7G 4B3

Third Edition

First Printing, January 1975

ISBN 0-256-01636-4
Library of Congress Catalog Card No. 74–12923
Printed in the United States of America

Preface

As a basic text, *Promotional Strategy* differs somewhat from many similar works. It builds on a rigorous base of consumer psychology and then proceeds to treat advertising, reseller stimulation, personal selling, and other communication tools as part of an overall promotional mix. In other words, various communication methods are treated as variables for use alone or in combination to communicate the want-satisfying attributes of products and services. The approach throughout is to develop fundamental considerations as background and then to focus on managerial issues and problems. Much of the usual descriptive content in books on advertising and promotion has been condensed and integrated into a discussion of the theory and rationale of the various topics that are covered.

Problems are viewed through the eyes of the promotion manager, and major emphasis is placed on understanding the factors that affect his decisions and mold managerial strategy. Rarely are "cookbook" answers given to problems which defy simple rule-of-thumb solutions. No attempt is made to build this degree of certainty into the discussion when, in fact, such certainty seldom exists in the "real" world.

In short, it is our belief that a keen understanding of the variables affecting decisions, an awareness of sources of information pertaining to these variables, a knowledge of the strengths and limitations of methods and strategies, and a grasp of the fundamentals of managerial decision making should be the basic subject matter in a modern marketing textbook. Actual decision rules and practices usually are unique to specific problems within the firm, and it is a futile exercise, for the most part, to document endless lists of possible strategies that usually have only a relatively limited application. It would be wishful thinking to maintain that this or any other text can cover all that needs to be known about communication methods in marketing. An attempt has been made, instead, to provide a balanced overview of pertinent topics and thereby provide sufficient background for the student to perform well in advanced courses and on the job as he gains experience and insight.

For those who have had a prior course in consumer behavior, Part Two of the text may be covered rapidly or perhaps omitted altogether. Without a background in this area, however, it has been our experience that students cannot comprehend the deeper issues of promotional strategy.

Some schools retain separate courses in advertising and sales management. Although we have integrated appropriate topics in this text, the material is readily adaptable to a more limited course in advertising through omission of Part Five. We strongly encourage that the integrated point of view be taken whenever possible, however, for it is becoming increasingly common in promotional practice.

Cases always prove to be a useful teaching tool. The book *Cases in Promotional Strategy* by James F. Engel, W. Wayne Talarzyk, and Carl M. Larson complements this text, and the varied cases can be of significant value in developing the reader's ability to apply what has been learned.

This edition contains much new material as previous users will quickly observe. A separate chapter has been added on the subject of supplemental communications because of the suggestions of many users. In addition, we have not hesitated to express ourselves freely on broader social issues. We have a united concern that irresponsible business practice all too often contributes to the problems of a strife-torn world. We feel that there are now too many instances where the economic system, by permitting continuation of a "business as usual" attitude, is failing to meet its obligations. In this sense that authors are not antibusiness; rather we feel that it is no longer possible to remain silent when so many abuses exist. It is hoped that our faculty colleagues and students alike will be stimulated to think through these pressing issues.

Once again we would like to acknowledge our many colleagues and friends who have contributed criticisms and comments in response to the first two editions. Rather than name them, we are thanking them as a group. Certainly the third edition is a stronger book because of their time and efforts. We especially wish to acknowledge the help of W. Meredith Long of the Wheaton Graduate School who assisted at many points in this revision. We also continue to be grateful to our colleagues on the staff at Ogilvy & Mather, Inc., especially Kenneth

Roman, Jr., Vice President, who have generously provided both cases and media data since the first edition. In addition, we wish to thank Tim Powers and Howard Gulley.

Finally, our thanks once again go to our patient families who continue to put up with the hectic home life which seems inevitable around book revision time. None acknowledged here, of course, are responsible for any errors or omissions in the manuscript. The blame is entirely ours, although each author continues to assign the blame to the others.

December 1974   JAMES F. ENGEL
                                   HUGH G. WALES
                                   MARTIN R. WARSHAW

Contents

Reconciliation of Divergences between Built-Up Costs and Percentage of Sales Figures. Payout Planning. Modification of Estimates in Terms of Company Policies. Specification of When Expenditures Will Be Made. Building in Flexibility. Comments on the Suggested Approach. Budgeting for New Porducts: *Payout Planning. New-Product Models.* Appendix: Application of Quantitative Methods.

On-the-Air-Tests. Recognition Tests. Recall Tests. Association Measures. Combination Measures.
Product-Related Measures under Real-World Conditions: *Pre-Post Tests. Sales Tests. Mini-Market Tests.*

Personal Selling—A Communication Process: *Modified Interpersonal Communication Model. Implications of the Communication Process.* The Nature of the Personal Selling Task: *Functions of the Salesman. Basic Sales Tasks. Determining the Proper Sales Tasks.* Building the Sales Force: *Job Descriptions and Recruitment. Selecting Salesmen. Training Salesmen.* Sales Force Management—Compensation and Motivation: *Compensating Salesmen. Motivating Salesmen. Methods of Communication. Patterns of Organization for Sales.*

Purposes of Evaluation. Information Needs. The Evaluation and Control Process: *Developing Performance Standards. Standards of Measurement of Performance. Comparing Salesmen's Performance to Standards.* Corrective Action. Reallocation of Effort: *A Case History.*

The Channel of Distribution: *Channel Length. Intensity of Distribution. Channel Control.* Wholesalers as Promotional Resources: *Classification of Wholesalers. Wholesaler Performance of the Selling Function. Factors Influencing Wholesaler's Ability to Sell. Economic Role of the Wholesaler. Factors Influencing Wholesaler's Allocation of Selling Effort.* Retailers as Promotional Resources: *Classification of Retailers. Selling Effort at Retail. Factors Affecting Retailer Ability to Sell. Factors Affecting Retailer Willingness to Sell.* Conclusion.

The Promotional Role of Resellers: *Adjustment of the Promotional Mix. Product Evolution. Implications of Resellers' Promotional Role.* Distribution Policies and the Problem of Reseller Competition: *Market Segregation. Selective Distribution.* Price and Margin Policies: *Channel Pricing. Pricing to Reduce Channel Overlap. Intrachannel Effects of Pricing Policy. Setting Reseller Discounts. Implications of Price and Margin Policies.* Inventory Policies: *Stock-Level Policies. Returned-Goods Policies.*

Improving Reseller Performance: *Training Reseller Salesmen. Quotas for Resellers. Advertising and Sales Promotion Assistance.* Supplementing Re-

part one

Overview

Part One is devoted to introductory concepts in order to provide a foundation and framework for the chapters to follow. Chapter 1 reviews the subject of marketing management and clarifies the role of promotion within the marketing mix. To many readers, these topics will be quite familiar. Taking promotion as the communication function of marketing, Chapter 2's analysis of the nature of communication discusses various theoretical perspectives and draws a sharp distinction between the problems presented in face-to-face communication and those arising from the use of mass media. Chapter 3 gives an overview of promotional strategy through an actual case history and provides an outline of the stages in promotional planning and strategy which serves as the rationale for the organization of succeeding chapters.

1

Introduction

ANN LEONARD was more perplexed than she usually was Monday morning. As she was putting the last of the breakfast dishes into the dishwasher her thoughts kept straying to that overly strained family budget. Just last week eggs were up another 10 cents, and the month's food bill was $11 higher than last month's. She and Fred had stayed up late the night before trying to find a way to just survive financially. Fred's raise for next year would only be 5 percent, and there did not seem to be any way to stay even.

When Ann turned on the TV, thinking that might be a way to escape for awhile, her attention was courted by the "Tidy Bowl Man" in the toilet tank. She was told that "all aspirin is not alike," that her marriage could be saved if those "horrible hands" could be made soft and smooth with the magic formula suggested by "Madge," the friendly manicurist. In disgust, Ann turned off the television and picked up the paper, and her eye was caught by the headline "Nader says that industry is ripping off the consumer." She agreed 100 percent. "Here I am trying to make ends meet," she said to herself, "and there they are trying to con me into buying more. What in the world has gone wrong with life in this country?"

Fred Leonard was having his own Monday morning dilemma. As advertising manager for a candy manufacturer, he had been forced to cancel all advertising indefinitely because the production manager had just told an emergency meeting of the corporate planning group that the last of the sugar inventory was being used up, and there was no assurance that additional sugar would be forthcoming for the next month. Furthermore, prices of paper boxes had been raised 45 percent,

3

and a truck strike meant that all retail shipments had ground to a halt. What does an advertising manager do now, Fred wondered.

It is a very changed world, for both the consumer and the manufacturer. Pressures are coming from all sides which would not have been dreamed of a few years ago. Who would have guessed that affluent North America could move so rapidly from an economy of surplus toward an economy of shortage? Who would have dreamed that consumer discontent would reach the point that response to consumerist pressure would become one of the greatest concerns of the businessman? What has happened to the "good old days"?

Yet life must go on in this world of future shock and rapid change. People have legitimate desires for consumer goods. Business must produce, advertise, and sell. The basic functions of life remain, but the rules of practice are undergoing dramatic modification. The authors of this book propose to examine carefully and *critically* the role of promotion—persuasive communication with the consumer—from the perspective of both the producer and the consumer. It is our goal to help the reader to take his or her role as a *responsible* citizen who will be equipped to be a part of the solution, rather than a part of the problem. Old ways must change, and rapidly, because the survival of a comfortable way of life is being threatened. These are hardly times for business as usual.

It is our conviction that the business system of the Western world is a legitimate object of criticism. There are numerous areas where it has failed significantly to adapt to a changing environment. Nevertheless we retain the belief that the situation is not without hope, provided management assumes its responsibility to pursue business practices based on moral and ethical foundations. We invite the reader to join us in exploring the subject of promotional strategy from this perspective. Such an inquiry can contribute answers to the pressing economic and social problems of our time.

WHAT THIS BOOK IS ALL ABOUT

"Promotion" is a term which has assumed many meanings over the years. Its original connotation in Latin was "to move forward." More recently the meaning has narrowed, so it now refers to communication undertaken to persuade others to accept ideas, concepts, or things. The term "strategy" refers to the planning and adjustment of efforts to attain a specified objective. For the business firm, therefore, the subject of *promotional strategy* is the planning and implementation of persuasive communication with customers or prospective customers.

More specifically, promotional strategy is a *controlled, integrated program of communication methods and materials designed to present a company and its products to prospective customers; to communicate need-satisfying attributes of products toward the end of facilitating sales and thus contributing to long-run profit performance.* The tools available for this purpose include:

1. *Advertising*—any paid form of nonpersonal presentation of ideas, goods, or services by an identified sponsor, with predominant use made of the media of mass communication.
2. *Personal selling*—the process of assisting and persuading a prospect to buy a good or service or to act upon an idea through use of person-to-person communication.
3. *Selling support by resellers in a channel of distribution*—any form of effort undertaken by a wholesale or retail middleman with the intent of persuading a prospective customer to act favorably upon the goods or services offered by a manufacturer or other seller.
4. *Publicity*—any form of nonpaid commercially significant news or editorial comment about ideas, products, or institutions.

In addition, under the heading of advertising is included a variety of incentives for immediate buyer action such as coupons, premiums, and price reductions. The term "sales promotion" is sometimes used to describe activities involving use of these incentives.

No single textbook can adequately treat all these topics in detail. The discussion in this book is confined largely to communication with ultimate consumers through advertising and to the stimulation of wholesale and retail selling support. Much of the latter task requires use of the personal selling resources of the manufacturer, so it is also necessary to give consideration to basic topics in management of a field sales force. Public relations and its most frequently used tool, publicity, are discussed in the concluding chapter in Part Five under the title "Supplemental Communications."

It is important to recognize at the outset that promotion is only one of a number of marketing efforts undertaken in most business firms. Therefore we will discuss first the nature of marketing management, in order to provide background for a realistic assessment of the role of promotion in marketing. Chapter 2 discusses the nature of the communication process, and Chapter 3 provides an overview of promotional strategy in the business firm, thus completing the establishment of the framework of ideas and concepts on which this book rests.

MARKETING MANAGEMENT

Marketing has been defined as "the process in society by which the demand structure for economic goods and services is anticipated or en-

FIGURE 1–1

Marketing Management

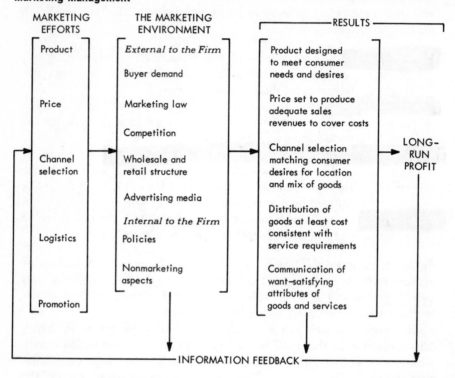

larged and satisfied through the conception, promotion, exchange, and physical distribution of such goods and services."[1] This definition is global, and the underlying philosophy is that marketing is a significant activity in the economy as well as in the firm. It captures the essence of the managerial aspects of marketing which can be referred to as "adaptation of a firm to a changing environment through changes in the marketing program," thereby enabling the organization to survive in a competitive world. In other words, the environment defines and shapes *marketing opportunity*, which is then capitalized on through skillful use of marketing efforts.

These concepts can be grasped more clearly in the form of the diagram presented as Figure 1–1. This shows: (1) the elements of the environment, (2) the mix of marketing efforts, and (3) both short-term and long-term results.

---

[1] "Statement of the Philosophy of Marketing of the Marketing Faculty of The Ohio State University," Bureau of Business Research of The Ohio State University, Columbus, 1964, p. 2.

The Environment for Marketing Efforts

Certain factors must be accepted more or less as given in that they are beyond the immediate and direct control of the firm through managerial action. Most of these uncontrollable factors are external to the firm; among these are demand, competition, marketing law, the wholesale and retail structure, and the advertising media. Other factors which are deemed to be uncontrollable by marketing management are internal to the firm; these include overall business policies as well as non-marketing cost.

A brief discussion of these environmental factors follows. Each is also considered in greater detail where it exerts an influence on specific promotional decisions.

Demand. The aggregate demand for goods and services in any market is the sum of the demands expressed by all of the individual buying units in that market. In its most basic sense demand is not created by marketing effort. Rather, it is the resultant of a variety of consumer needs and the willingness and ability of consumers to fill these needs. Sometimes, however, demand is latent and consumers cannot even articulate what their needs might be. Marketing research can suggest the existence of latent demand and indicate ways in which such demand can be made effective for certain types of goods or services.

Several critics of the American social and economic system have assigned great powers to marketing and have suggested that marketing and especially advertising are tools by which management manipulates the consumer.[2] Although the psychology of consumer behavior is discussed in detail later in the text, it should be made clear at this point that the buyer, as a rule, cannot be persuaded to make a purchase if he or she does not want or need the product. Discussions with executives who tried to persuade people to buy the Edsel or the thousands of other heavily promoted product failures of the past several years would support the view that the powers attributed to marketing in general and advertising in particular are highly exaggerated.

A purchase occurs, by and large, only if the product, package, price, selling appeals, retail outlets, services offered, and all other aspects of marketing efforts are geared to factors which motivate the buyer's behavior. A sale will not take place, for example, if the price is thought to be too high, regardless of how hard management tries to convince the buyer otherwise. To manipulate the customer requires full control over his destiny, including rewards and punishment. It is obvious that the business firm does not have this degree of control.

---

[2] See Vance Packard, *The Hidden Persuaders* (New York: David McKay Co., 1957), and John Kenneth Galbraith, *The New Industrial State* (Boston: Houghton Mifflin Co., 1967).

Marketing activity can, admittedly, modify demand and channel it toward the offerings of specific producers. Attempts to make changes in basic demand on the part of individual firms or even entire industries can be very costly. Given the goal of long-run profit maximization, the most efficient marketing strategy would appear to be the one that treats demand as an uncontrollable environmental variable to which the firm must adapt.

Demand may also be analyzed from the point of view of the size of flows of income available for buyer spending. It is well known, for example, that purchases of automobiles and other durable goods often are deferred during a recession. In such instances the individual firm is powerless to change these economic circumstances, and little can be done but to adjust output accordingly.

Competition.   The marketing manager seldom can directly control the actions of competitors in a given year, short of outright collusion. Yet the actions of competitors cannot be disregarded; a competitor with a superior product, to mention only one example, poses a serious threat. Therefore it becomes necessary to assess the firm's strengths and weaknesses relative to competitors to remedy any weaknesses, while capitalizing on points of strength. Similarly, the likelihood of certain actions by competitors must be evaluated so that a counterattack can be made if necessary. A price reduction, for instance, may have to be met, to avoid losing important customers.

Marketing Law.   Various legal constraints can never be disregarded. The framework of laws pertinent to marketing defines the playing field, so to speak. The Robinson-Patman Act specifies, for example, that an advertising allowance made to one retailer must also be made available to competitive retailers on proportionally equal terms. Failure to meet this provision can have serious lasting repercussions for the firm. Thus the legal framework places real boundaries on marketing action.

The Wholesale and Retail Structure.   The wholesale and retail structure refers to the array of available middlemen. The majority of wholesalers, retailers, or other middlemen are independent businessmen who are not in any way directly owned by manufacturers. The manufacturer must, as a rule, use these resources to make his products available to consumers. He must therefore adapt to this structure and build channels of distribution through selection of middlemen who best suit his purposes. On occasion a company may establish its own wholesale and retail outlets, but a wholly owned channel of distribution of this type tends to be the exception rather than the rule.

Middlemen also play an important role in the promotion of a manufacturer's product through retail advertising, display, personal selling, or other means. Thus the availability and quality of reseller promotional support can be an important determinant of marketing success. Indeed, the stimulation of wholesale and retail support often presents major problems.

Advertising Media. The available types and number of advertising media (the physical vehicles for delivering communication messages to a mass market) also are beyond the direct control of the firm. Adaptation to available resources requires a selection process similar in many ways to that necessary to construct a channel of distribution. This subject is treated in considerable depth.

Factors Internal to the Firm

The factors discussed above all operate in the external environment within which the firm must function. The marketing manager also must adapt his actions to the policies and resources of his own firm. It could be argued that marketing, in turn strongly influences company policy, financial resources, production facilities, and available manpower in the long run, through its success or failure in generating sales revenue. For purposes of short-run decisions, however, these facilities and resources are, for the most part, fixed. Of special importance are financial, production, and managerial capabilities.

Financial and Production Constraints. The marketing budget is generally bounded on the upper end by the available financial resources. At times, of course, additional funds are procured from outside sources, but financial capabilities usually must be accepted as given by the marketing manager.

Production facilities also can be vitally important because marketing efforts can be *too* successful, given limitations on capacity. For example, a dramatically new line of air conditioners was marketed by a well-known manufacturer, and strong consumer demand was generated. The entire plant output was sold prior to the peak selling period, and additional production capacity could not be achieved in sufficient time to meet market opportunity. Disappointment of both buyers and dealers could have been avoided if production had been given more central consideration in marketing planning.

Managerial Failure. Internal constraints may also be the result of managerial failure. Nonprogressive management attitudes, misconceived policies, faulty execution of policy, and a general misunderstanding of the nature of marketing all may lead to what has been termed a hardening of the profit arteries. Figure 1–2 portrays what one company has called internal profit inhibitors. The presence of these inhibitors can prevent marketing from making its potential contribution to company profitability.

FIGURE 1–2

Internal Profit Inhibitors

1. Absence of customer-oriented thinking.
2. Inexact or inadequate marketing objectives.
3. Internal communication failure.
4. Inadequate distribution planning.
5. Lack of innovation in production, packaging, and so on.
6. Budget deficiencies in communication.
7. Misunderstanding of consumer motivation.
8. Inadequate picture of the market and consumer opinion.
9. Failure to merchandise or follow through.
10. Overpromoting (dealing) or too much concern with price.
11. Information loss from company management to point of sale.
12. Giving advertising jobs it cannot do.
13. Placing management responsibility for marketing too low in the organization structure.
14. Absence of built-in measuring systems in all plans and programs.
15. Failure to define and manage the corporate image.
16. Imbalance between promotion tools.
17. Copying competition in marketing planning.
18. Failure to build extra benefits or quality image of the product.
19. Failure to update the marketing organization.
20. Entanglement in decentralization.
21. Inflexibility of policy.
22. Inadequate knowledge of competition.

Source: Reproduced in modified form with special permission from the "Systems Approach to Marketing Communications" published by the ITSM Division of the Interpublic Group of Companies, Inc.

The list of profit inhibitors in Figure 1–2 is not exhaustive, each reader could no doubt add to it. The point is that in every business enterprise there are certain human failings that tend to retard progress or cause other problems which affect profits adversely. Martin Bell has described some of these internal constraints, including inertia, overconfidence, and lack of creativity, as "human forces of resistance."[3] A brief resumé of his thinking follows.

INERTIA. The concept of inertia is, of course, borrowed from the physical sciences. When used to describe certain human traits of behavior, inertia may mean resistance to change. The marketing executive who falls prey to this frailty fails to adapt his strategies to new requirements in the marketplace. This type of inertia can be the result of failure to spot new trends or new opportunities, but more often it is the force that counsels no change in spite of market dynamics.

Inertia on the part of marketing management can be caused by poor training as well as a lack of commitment to customer-oriented thinking. Especially at middle-management levels, inertia might be the result of

---

[3] See Martin L. Bell, *Marketing Concepts and Strategy* (Boston: Houghton Mifflin Co., 1966), pp. 46–49.

poor organization in which the key marketing decisions are made at higher levels and executed at lower levels and the chain of command is very long.

Another cardinal rule of inertia is that a body in motion tends to remain in motion. In a marketing context the analogy might be that a marketing program once initiated tends to continue. Unfortunately, because of the changing nature of the market, the original program might be badly misdirected after a period of time. Doing a job the same way as in the past even though conditions change may be worse than not doing the job at all. Henry Ford's commitment to the Model T for so long a period that competitors were able to make considerable inroads stands as a classic example of management inertia.[4]

In a famous article Theodore Levitt discussed some of the reasons marketing people stay too long with old products and old strategies. He calls this tendency "marketing myopia."[5] Mentioning, among others, the railroads, certain textile companies, motion picture producers, and so forth, he makes the point that lack of foresight and initiative on the part of management led to the replacement of products and services produced by these firms with substitutes produced by others. Thus shortsightedness with respect to the market leads very quickly to inertia and subsequent misdirection of effort.

OVERCONFIDENCE. A management characteristic which differs considerably from inertia but which has the same profit-inhibiting effects is overconfidence. Marketing programs and promotional strategies must be developed in an environment of uncertainty, and the marketing executive must be able to weigh the risks involved in a given course of action against the rewards to be gained. A profit-inhibiting situation exists when overconfidence on the part of management leads to a failure to engage in risk-benefit analysis.

LACK OF CREATIVITY. Creativity is another essential requirement in the formulation of promotional strategy and in the overall development of marketing programs. Lack of this trait on the part of management creates a serious handicap for marketing. Creativity is more than inspiration or artistry; it is the process by which new ideas are developed and brought to the point where there is a product or service which can be marketed with a high expectation of success.

The Marketing Mix

To adapt to the opportunities and limitations imposed by the environment requires the use of certain variables, including: (1) product

---

[4] Ibid., p. 47.

[5] Theodore Levitt, "Marketing Myopia," *Harvard Business Review,* July–August 1960, pp. 45–56.

policy, (2) price policy, (3) channel selection, (4) logistics, and (5) promotion. In effect, these variables are the working tools of the marketing manager.

The overall objective is to unite these tools into an organized and integrated program of action. The goal is to maximize long-run return on company investment, and this is achieved through a mix of marketing efforts which requires the most profitable allocation of company resources. Each variable contributes in unique fashion to this overall objective.

Each area of marketing policy, in itself, is a *submix* of efforts within the broader program. The firm usually will produce more than one product, and the entire product line is often referred to as the *product mix*. Similarly, the use of a variety of different retail outlets (say discount stores, department stores, drugstores, and grocery stores for a packaged drug item) represents a *mix of outlets*.

Product Policy. The purpose of product policy is to adapt to the internal and external environment through design of a product which successfully satisfies the needs, desires, attitudes, and other influences which motivate buyers. Moreover, the product must be created and marketed with full awareness of competing brands, legal restrictions such as laws prohibiting product adulteration, and probability estimates that economic circumstances will facilitate an adequate level of demand to provide a profit over the product life cycle. Available production facilities, labor availabilities, managerial talents, and a host of related internal considerations also affect product planning.

Price Policy. The tangible product or service must be offered to the buyer at a price which will produce an acceptable return on investment. A target return may be established by appropriate company officers, and this guideline then serves as the objective of pricing policy.

The price chosen must be carefully tuned to buyer willingness to pay, or the resulting revenues will be insufficient to provide the necessary return on investment. Competitors' actions also assume crucial importance, especially when a limited number of firms offer highly similar products. A price change by one is certain to be matched by others, and a price war can be an ever-present danger. Moreover, marketing law is quite specific as pertains to pricing; the Robinson-Patman Act and the Federal Trade Commission Act, among others, provide rigorous constraints on pricing policy. Finally, economic conditions frequently affect the buyer's willingness to pay a premium price for certain products. All of these factors interact with company policy and nonmarketing resources to influence the expected return on investment.

Channel Selection. Products must be made available when and where the buyer dictates. With such products as refrigerators or other major appliances, the buyer may be willing to travel a considerable distance to shop and make the "best buy." On the other hand, bread, milk, cigarettes, and *convenience items* of all types must be provided in nearly all possible outlets to satisfy demands for ready product availability. In other instances the buyer may wish to see products made available in combination with a variety of goods so that shopping time is minimized. The planned shopping center is an outgrowth of this desire for a variety of products in one convenient location. Whatever the situation, management is virtually powerless to disregard these desires. The objective of channel selection is to adapt to buyer requirements for product availability.

Logistics. Logistics is a relatively new and more precise term applied to activities required to assemble, store, and ship products to middlemen in the channel of distribution. It has been described this way: "Logistics creates place and time utility in goods and services. Place utility is created primarily by transportation, time utility primarily by the storage of goods and present availability of services. In these terms, logistics does indeed translate customer demands for time and place utility in goods and services into a supply of these same types of utility."[6]

Logistics management is concerned basically with two activities: (1) movement of goods from one place to another, including storage when necessary; and (2) coordination of customer demand with the supply of goods which can be made available to meet it. Transportation, inventory control, warehousing, and supply scheduling are all integral components of a logistics system, the guiding objective of which is to provide the correct variety of goods to wholesalers and retailers at the proper time for the least cost commensurate with customer service requirements. The unique contributions of the logistics concept are the wedding of cost considerations with service requirements and the utilization of the resources of the firm to accomplish this goal.

Promotion. A final major item in the program of marketing efforts is promotion. As has been pointed out above, this function focuses on a system of communication tools designed to present a company, its products, and its services to consumers. It contributes uniquely to overall profit objectives through communicating those product features that satisfy buyer needs and desires.

Comparative Marketing Strategies

The development of a marketing strategy is more of an art than a science. Creativity and timing are vital ingredients in any marketing mix or strategy, and such inputs are the result of experience and intuition rather than of some mathematical formula. Yet basic forces in the

---

[6] J. L. Heskett, Robert M. Ivie, and Nicholas A. Glaskowsky, Jr., *Business Logistics,* 2d ed. (New York: Ronald Press Co., 1973), p. 11.

environment which are beyond the control of marketing management still play their parts as constraining influences on strategy development. Foremost among these influences is, of course, demand. The nature of the market for any given type of product or service will have a considerable effect on the basic strategy that will be chosen to market the product or service. The marketing programs of different manufacturers that are producing essentially similar goods for sale in similar market situations involve certain basic strategy patterns. For example, in the marketing of health and beauty aids on a national basis in the United States, the basic pattern of marketing is one in which a "pull" strategy is used, with consumer advertising as the major promotional input. In the marketing of automotive parts, on the other hand, the pattern utilizes channel strategy to get broad market coverage and personal selling to implement a "push" type of strategy.

FIGURE 1–3

Marketing Strategy Profile: Automobiles

Controllable Variables	Importance Values
Product	5
Price	2
Channels	2
Logistics	3
Promotion	4

Within each strategy pattern there are, of course, opportunities for variation by individual firms. These variations result because each firm attempts to develop a better way of approaching the market or because some of the more desirable strategy alternatives have been preempted by pioneering firms in the industry. It is important to note, however, that the greater the restrictions imposed on strategy development by the uncontrollables such as demand, the less will be the variation in strategies over an array of firms in a given industry.

Strategy Profiles.[7] Basic patterns of marketing strategy can be classified and described by means of a profile. For a given product-market situation a profile can be developed by weighting the strategy variables in terms of their relative importance in the marketing mix. For example, a strategy profile for automobiles being sold to the domestic market might look like the one illustrated in Figure 1–3, in which a rating scale of 5 for most important and 0 for no importance is used.

Our purpose is not to discuss how these weights might be assigned;

---

[7] This section relies heavily on Stewart H. Rewoldt, James D. Scott, and Martin R. Warshaw, *Introduction to Marketing Management,* rev. ed. (Homewood, Ill.: Richard D. Irwin, 1973), ch. 1.

this has been done in some detail by others.[8] Figure 1–3 indicates rather how a profile of a basic marketing strategy might be described in terms of simple weights. In like manner it is possible to analyze any of the controllable variables broken down into subelements. For example, promotion might be analyzed in terms of its subelements: advertising, personal selling, and other forms of sales promotion. A sample breakdown is shown in Figure 1–4 for the promotion element for automobiles shown in Figure 1–3. Note that the importance-value scale in this example adds up to 4, which is the importance value assigned promotion in the overall strategy profile for this particular product-market situation.

In Figure 1–4 advertising is listed as being the most important of the three promotional subelements, while personal selling and other means of sales promotion receive lesser emphasis. This might be explained by the fact that advertising is quite important to the establish-

FIGURE 1–4

Promotional Mix Profile: Automobiles

Controllable Variables	Importance Values
Advertising..............................	2
Personal Selling.........................	1
Sales Promotion.........................	1

ment of a favorable product image. Because even a very extensive and skillful advertising campaign cannot compensate for poor product design, advertising in particular and promotion in general do not rank as important as product in the basic strategy profile as illustrated in Figure 1–3. Nevertheless, given a good product, competitive channel, logistics, and pricing strategy, advertising can do a great deal to stimulate selective demand for a specific brand of automobile. The Cadillac experience is one example of how skillful advertising reinforced product image and created a strong selective demand for the product.

Personal selling is rated much lower in importance than advertising as a strategy variable. Even though personal selling effort has been extensively applied in the selling of automobiles at the retail level, the general quality of the effort has been low. Because sales have risen over the years in spite of the poor quality of personal selling, the importance of the subelement cannot be too great. As one source suggests, however, "we have little real evidence of what personal selling can do, because it has so rarely been used effectively in the sale of automobiles."[9]

---

[8] Ibid.

[9] Ibid., p. 15.

Sales promotion efforts such as dealer incentives, trade shows, and so forth also rate well below advertising in importance in the submix for the promotion of automobiles.

Implications of Comparative Marketing Strategies. Marketing strategy profiles could be developed for a wide range of product and market situations, and the promotional element in each strategy could be analyzed in terms of its composition. Such is not the purpose here, however. What is important is recognition that marketing strategies and promotional strategies vary and that these variations are caused in large part by the demand aspect of the environment. Unfortunately, demand is the one uncontrollable element that management knows the least about. Rapid change, unpredictability, and latent demand discovered by marketing research all combine to make the principal tasks of marketing management to find out what demand is like and to develop a product and communication strategy to meet the needs of the individual buying units in the market.

Results

The nature of the environment, the working tools available for use by the marketing manager, and the concepts of marketing and promotional strategies and how they might vary given certain product-market combinations are all directed at achieving the goals of marketing management, as outlined in Figure 1–1. Each element of the marketing mix, for example, is managed to attain objectives specific to that policy area. The goal of pricing policy is to set a price to produce sales revenues sufficient to cover costs and contribute to return on investment. These and other goals are also summarized in Figure 1–1. Long-run profit is the final result of the proper blending of all marketing efforts into an integrated and coordinated marketing program.

Profit thus far has been referred to only as long-run earnings. Short-run profit can be a meaningless criterion of marketing success, for it is possible to make a quick profit while threatening long-run survival. To take an example, a well-known food processing company could capitalize on its name, long the leader in the industry, and sell a stock of adulterated cranberries which otherwise would be discarded at a loss. Immediate losses could be averted and profits enhanced, but it goes without saying that an adverse consumer reaction to such an ill-advised decision would damage the company's hopes of continuing in business on a profitable basis. Most large firms today are publicly owned corporations which must be managed to assure long-term survival, and marketing efforts can be justified only to the extent that a positive contribution is made to this objective.

Information Feedback

The feedback of information among all elements of marketing management is indicated by the arrows in Figure 1–1. Information is needed for two important purposes: (1) to determine basic facts about the environment for marketing action and (2) to measure the effectiveness of marketing performance.

Information on the Environment. Management cannot adapt to the environment without information on the opportunities and limitations that will be faced. Imagine the difficulties, for example, in designing a new product without information on consumer needs and desires, the availability of similar products by competitors, and the capabilities of the firm to produce and market the item. Feedback of this type is indispensable, and it receives attention throughout much of this book.

Information on Performance. Management also must know the results when marketing action is undertaken. A record of success or lack of success is essential to avoid repeating previous mistakes and to permit further capitalization on actions that have worked in the past.

The Danger of Viewing Promotion in Isolation

To illustrate the dangers inherent in failure to recognize linkages between marketing efforts, assume that the advertising manager has reported that a strong surge of purchases of a dishwashing detergent has resulted from an offer of a premium. Assume further that this rise of buyer interest is reflected in increased orders from retailers and strongly optimistic reports from salesmen that the sales year looks to be one of the best in history.

While it would appear that advertising has indeed been unusually successful, it also is possible that some severe problems have been created. Buyers may have redeemed the coupons in large numbers and purchased the product sooner than they would have without the additional stimulus. The advertising thus may have *borrowed sales from the future,* without a substantial gain in new users. Retailers may have been urged by salesmen to build inventories in anticipation of consumer demand, so that a surge of orders is received at the plant. Meeting the orders may, in turn, have required the addition of new shifts of workers, substantial overtime, and changes in prices or margins.

Once buyers have redeemed the coupons, if few new users actually have been added a sales slump inevitably will result from the fact that consumer demands are satisfied for the time being. In turn, retailers must of necessity cut back on inventories, and the resources added by the manufacturer to meet the surge in orders, such as additional production workers, must be withdrawn. In this case advertising has accomplished basically only one thing: *a disruption of normal flows* of sales revenues, dealer orders, capital investment, production scheduling, and work force planning.[10]

In this example, admittedly somewhat limited in that it is explicitly assumed that advertising primarily borrowed sales from the future, the false success of advertising management has created disequilibriums and has disrupted the functioning of the entire firm. The advertising manager was guilty of *suboptimization*—maximization of response to one activity without regard to others. Advertising response was sought with little or no consideration of its effects on other elements of the marketing or production programs of the firm. A basic point emerges which cannot be emphasized too frequently: promotion efforts do not exist in a vacuum—they strongly *affect* and *are affected by* the other marketing and nonmarketing activities of the firm.

SUMMARY

The nature of marketing management has been reviewed briefly to provide a perspective for realistic consideration of the role of promotion in the marketing mix. While it is necessary to abstract promotion from the total program in order to study it in detail, long-run profit can be maximized only when all types of marketing efforts are undertaken, with full realization of the interdependent relationships which exist in the marketing program.

REVIEW AND DISCUSSION QUESTIONS

1. Compare and contrast promotion and marketing. How does promotion differ from advertising? From personal selling?

2. What is the task of marketing management? What is meant by the term "marketing mix"? Describe and discuss the major elements of the marketing mix, stressing the nature of the interrelationships involved.

3. Consumer demand is cited as a factor to which marketing efforts must be adapted. To what extent can demand be regarded as a *constraint* or limitation on the marketing program? To what extent can it be regarded as presenting an *opportunity* for marketing?

4. Discuss the other factors which comprise the marketing environment, showing the manner in which they define the opportunities and limitations for feasible marketing action.

---

[10] This example is similar to one discussed by Jay Forrester to illustrate the application of industrial dynamics to advertising problems. See "The Relationship of Advertising to Corporate Management," *Proceedings: Fourth Annual Conference* (New York: Advertising Research Foundation, 1958), pp. 75–92.

5. What is a marketing strategy? How might one go about comparing different marketing strategies?

6. What is a promotional strategy? How does it compare with a marketing strategy? How might one describe a specific type of strategy?

7. What types of information feedback are needed for successful management of the marketing function?

8. What is meant by the term "suboptimization"? Why is the danger of subobtimization so great in the management of the promotional efforts of the firm? Can suboptimization be eliminated in designing promotional strategies?

9. The goal of marketing activity is often stated as being to maximize long-run profit. Why is short-run profit not emphasized? Should the marketing goal always be long-run profit maximization?

10. Why is an understanding of consumer behavior so vital to the development of an effective marketing and promotional strategy?

2

The Nature of Communication

THE DISCUSSION OF marketing management in the preceding chapter should lead to the understanding that promotion, although important in its own right, is only one component of the marketing mix. Promotion is the *communication function* of marketing, and knowledge of the fundamentals of the human communication process is necessary for understanding the promotion function.

This chapter begins with an analysis of interpersonal and mass communication and then centers on communication in marketing. The problems and opportunities presented by the use of mass media are explored, and the relative merits of mass media and personal selling techniques are briefly examined.

THE FUNDAMENTALS OF COMMUNICATION

Communication can be said to happen whenever the individual attributes significance to message-related behavior.[1] It is important to note that according to this definition communication is dependent upon neither a proper understanding of the message nor the intent of the source to send one. If the targeted receiver fails to attend to an intended message, communication has not taken place.

The task of the sender then is twofold: first, to communicate only at the time and in the way he wishes, and second, to communicate only the

---

[1] C. David Mortensen, *Communication; the Study of Human Interaction* (New York: McGraw-Hill Book Co., 1972), p. 14.

20

conteńt he intends clearly and persuasively. The nature of communication is best illustrated by an analysis of the communication process between two persons. Mass communication, which is not different in its essential nature, is discussed in the next section.

Interpersonal Communication

Assume that two persons, Mr. A and Mr. B, are engaging in a conversation. The nature of the communication between them is represented in Figure 2–1.

FIGURE 2–1

Interpersonal Communication

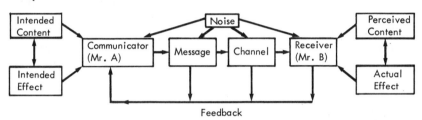

Feedback

Mr. A has something in mind he wants to present to Mr. B. He selects certain words which he arranges in a pattern or sequence to be communicated. This is referred to as encoding. The encoded message, which may or may not be an accurate representation of the intended content, is transmitted through some form of channel, probably the spoken word. Mr. B may or may not attend to the message. If he does and searches for meaning, he thereby attempts to decode the message. The actual effect of the message is determined by his perception of the message, not its intended content.

Mr. B's perception is dependent not only upon the message Mr. A intended to convey but also upon the other verbal and nonverbal behavior of Mr. A, the influence of the total environment in which the interaction takes place, and his own internal mental and physical state at the time. These stimuli extraneous to Mr. A's intended content are called noise because they inhibit the clear reproduction of Mr. A's intended content in Mr. B's perception. The responses that Mr. B initiates in reaction to his perception of Mr. A's message are called feedback. Mr. A's perception of the feedback, however, is subject to interference by noise, just as was Mr. B's original perception of Mr. A's message.

The model in Figure 2–1 is a composite of many models and theories which have appeared in the vast literature on communication. Although writers may differ on details, most now agree on the essence of the process.[2]

The Communicator.   Mr. A begins with both an intended content for his message and an intended effect. In order to encode this intent into a message which will be meaningful, he must attempt to understand the internal and external stimuli affecting Mr. B. The ability to place one-self "in another's shoes," which is called empathy, is absolutely necessary to effective communication.

Empathy begins early in life, through learning to take the role of an-other. The child imitating his father or mother in play is an example. As the child matures he becomes acquainted with his social heritage and is introduced to the expectations of those around him. Sooner or later he acquires a common set of meanings and definitions by which men regulate their lives. Taking the role of others becomes commonplace at this point, and effective communication is facilitated.

The Message.   Mr. A next encodes his message into a form that can be transmitted to Mr. B. Although the message can be transmitted in either verbal or nonverbal form, spoken or written language is most fre-quently used.

All languages are composed of *signs* and *symbols*. As one authority points out:

Signs may be divided into two major types, natural and conventional. A natural sign is an event in our experience which refers to some other event because our experience has taught us that the two events are associated or connected in some fashion. Thus, a Kansan sees a dark cloud on the horizon, and he interprets what he sees as the sign of an approaching tornado. The cloud is a natural sign of the tornado. A conventional sign, which we shall call a "symbol," is an arti-ficial construct made by human beings for the purpose of referring to something. A symbol is a sign which is deliberately employed in order to convey a meaning.

---

[2] Among the standard sources are H. D. Lasswell, "The Structure and Function of Communication in Society," in L. Bryson (ed.), *The Communication of Ideas* (New York: Harper & Bros., 1948); G. Gerbner, "Toward a General Model of Com-munication," *Audio-Visual Communication Review*, Vol. 4 (1956), p. 173; C. Shan-non, "A Mathematic Theory of Communication," *Bell System Technical Journal*, Vol. 27 (1948), pp. 379–432 and 623–56; N. Wiener, *The Human Use of Human Beings* (Garden City, N.Y.: Doubleday Anchor Books, 1954); B. Westley and M. MacLean, "A Conceptual Model for Communications Research," *Journalism Quarterly*, Vol. 34 (1957), pp. 31–38; L. Thayer, *Communication and Communica-tion Systems* (Homewood, Ill.: Richard D. Irwin, Inc., 1968), pp. 122–23; W. Johnson, *People in Quandaries: The Semantics of Personal Adjustment* (New York: Harper & Bros., 1946); Colin Cherry, *On Human Communication*, 2d ed. (Cambridge, Mass.: MIT Press, 1966); M. L. DeFleur, *Theories of Mass Communi-cation* (New York: David McKay Co., Inc., 1966); D. K. Berlo, *The Process of Communication* (New York: Holt, Rinehart & Winston, 1960); and Wilbur Schramm (ed.), *The Process and Effects of Mass Communication* (Urbana, Ill.: University of Illinois Press, 1954), pp. 3–26.

Symbols become a part of a language when human beings agree that they shall "stand for" given referents. Symbols are signs, but not all signs are symbols.[3]

A symbol thus acquires a more or less unique meaning through social consensus. Hopefully, it will call for the same response from both Mr. A and Mr. B.

The unique functioning of symbols in human communication is further clarified by the authors of a text on social psychology as follows:

1. They constitute systems, so that the meaning of any single symbol cannot be grasped in isolation, but must be understood within the system. For example: "wife," which is intelligible only in terms of a wider linkage of symbols like "husband," "marriage," and the like.
2. Language symbols . . . are inherently social in character and meaning. They evoke from the person who produces or uses them the same or similar responses as those elicited from the persons to whom they are directed. If communication is faulty, if the speaker talks past the listener, then the words do not function as symbols.
3. They can be produced voluntarily even when the external events or objects to which they refer are absent or nonexistent.[4]

THE LEARNING OF LANGUAGE. Learning a language means far more than just developing proficiency in grammar and vocabulary.[5] Language introduces the child to the rules that regulate social relations and morality. In addition, he learns the roles he must play in later life through becoming aware of his own identity as a person and as a member of groups in which he seeks status. In fact, thinking cannot take place without use of the symbols learned as part of a language system.[6]

The newborn child is initially incapable of symbolic communication. Although he notices people and phenomena of various types, his only interaction with them is nonverbal, consisting of a motley collection of sounds. These sounds, which may serve as signs of his physical state, can be roughly understood only in terms of intensity, pitch, and duration. Soon he begins to imitate some of the sounds he hears and repeats them, with the result that he starts to associate words with objects. After a time he can use the word "ball," for example, without the physical object being present. The object and the word have become associated, so that he behaves toward the word in much the same manner as he behaves toward its referent.

---

[3] Lionel Ruby, *An Introduction to Logic* (Philadelphia: J. B. Lippincott Co., 1950), p. 18.

[4] Alfred R. Lindesmith and Anselm L. Strauss, *Social Psychology,* rev. ed. (New York: Holt, Rinehart & Winston, 1956), p. 56.

[5] For a more extensive discussion see Erwin P. Bettinghaus, *Persuasive Communication* (New York: Holt, Rinehart & Winston, 1968), ch. 6.

[6] See Lindesmith and Strauss, *Social Psychology,* ch. 5.

When the point is reached that a word calls forth the same responses as the original stimulus, the word is said to have attained *denotative meaning*. The words now stands for or denotes the object. The individual's own unique feelings and psychological predispositions also affect the meaning of words, however. The meaning that is unique to him is referred to as *connotative meaning*.[7] The child who is frightened by a dog, for example, will have a very different connotative meaning when he hears the term "dog" than will a child who has a friendly pet, even though the denotative meanings attributed by the two children to this term may be identical.

The distinction between denotative and connotative meaning is of real significance in persuasive communication. Consider these advertising appeals:

> You will be greeted warmly at the door by one of our youthful staff members.
> You will be greeted warmly at the door by one of our juvenile staff members.

The denotative meaning of each appeal is identical, but the connotative meanings are quite different. The second message substitutes the word "juvenile" for "youthful." The advertiser would probably receive a more favorable response to the first message.[8]

USING LANGUAGE IN THE MESSAGE.   For Mr. B to receive and grasp the point of Mr. A's message, two requirements should be met: (1) the message should be designed to gain attention, and (2) it should employ symbols referring to common meaning. This means, in essence, that the message should be oriented as closely as possible to Mr. B's background, interest, needs, and psychological predispositions.

Communication is facilitated when Mr. A and Mr. B are as much alike as possible in terms of background, stored information and experience, needs, social influences, and so on. In other words, they should experience an *overlap in psychological fields*—that is, an overlap in the sum total of influences on their behavior. Imagine the confusion that might result if there were no overlap whatsoever. Anyone who has visited a foreign country is well aware of the difficulties two individuals face when they attempt to communicate in entirely different languages. The consequence is likely to be noise rather than communication.

Social norms (expected uniformities in behavior) at least partially come to the communicator's rescue. Norms provide approximate uniformities in behavior and ways of thinking which result from the pressures of others. In most situations Mr. B and Mr. A are probably subject to certain common social influences. Assume, for example, that they both

---

[7] Berlo, *Process of Communication,* p. 209.

[8] See Bettinghaus, *Persuasive Communication,* p. 134.

are fathers, members of the same church, members of the same civic organizations, residents of the same suburban community, and accountants with the same company. Both are expected to behave in a similar manner in the groups to which they belong, and they also are exposed to similar environmental influences. Thus they should be able to anticipate each others' reactions and communicate with relative ease.

The Channel. The channel signifies the medium through which the message is sent. This usually consists of the spoken word, although various forms of writing can be used. The importance of nonverbal communication must not be overlooked, however. Such forms as body movement (kinesic behavior), paralanguage (voice qualities and nonlanguage sounds such as laughing or yawning), skin sensitivity to touch and temperature, and use of dress and cosmetics all enter into the communicative act.[9]

The fidelity or accuracy of communication is greatly influenced by noise which enters into both the message and the channel. Noise refers to any extraneous factors which can interfere with reception of the message.[10] One important source of noise can be internal to either Mr. A, or Mr. B in the form of illness, stress, and so on. In addition there can be a variety of competing stimuli which distract the recipient and prevent him from grasping the full impact of the message. This becomes especially crucial in mass communication, where (it is commonly accepted) the average individual is exposed to several hundred advertising stimuli in the course of a typical day. It is small wonder that any given advertisement can easily become "lost" and fail to register as intended.

The Receiver. For effective communication to occur, the content of the message as perceived by Mr. B must closely correspond to the actual content transmitted by Mr. A. It is undeniable, however, that this exchange frequently does not occur, because Mr. B must respond in terms of his own background and psychological processes. The words and other symbols in the message only serve to activate the learned responses which Mr. B has stored within his memory.[11]

It is known from the literature on the psychology of communication (to be reviewed later) that humans perceive selectively; communication undertaken without regard to Mr. B's motivational influences is doomed to failure unless the communicator has phenomenal luck. Mr. B retains full power to expose himself to message selectively, and he may chose to ignore the communication, especially if the content is seen as being

---

[9] See S. Duncan, "Nonverbal Communication," *Psychology Bulletin,* Vol. 72 (1969), pp. 118–37.

[10] For an excellent discussion of the barriers to communication, see John Parry, *The Psychology of Human Communication* (New York: American Elsevier Publishing Co., 1968), pp. 83–126.

[11] Berlo, *Process of Communication,* p. 175.

unwanted or threatening. In addition Mr. B may somehow "miss the point" of what is being communicated and thereby selectively distort the content of the message. Finally, he will retain in memory only those things he wants to retain.

This perceptual selectivity is perhaps the greatest obstacle faced by the communicator. One notable example is mentioned here to illustrate this point. From the propaganda studies undertaken during World War II, it was concluded that propaganda intended to induce Nazi surrenders became effective only after the Wehrmacht had disintegrated and the war cause appeared hopeless to the individual soldier.[12] Prior to that time group morale remained high, and powerful barriers stood in the way of effective propaganda.

Feedback. The model of the communication process in Figure 2–1 shows the significance of feedback from the receiver, the channel, and the message. Feedback from the receiver is, of course, of greatest significance. A smile, an affirmative reply, a frown, or some other response (such as no reaction at all) provides the basis to determine whether or not Mr. B is "getting the message." If the message appears to be off target, Mr. A can try again and modify the message to achieve successful communication.

Mr. A also receives feedback from the message and the channel. As he sees or hears the message he may detect that its form is not appropriate for the intended purpose, in which case modifications are introduced. Similarly, he may detect noise in the channel that provides undue distraction.

The factor of instantaneous feedback makes face-to-face communication highly efficient. Both sender and receiver are enabled to keep trying until effective contact is made. Such feedback is at best indirect in attempts to communicate to a large group, however. As is stressed later, this becomes a major problem for the advertiser.

Mass Communication

Mass communication requires a process in which the message is transmitted to a large group of individuals (mass) at roughly the same point in time. The basic model of mass communication is illustrated in Figure 2–2.

It will be noticed that the communicator now is designated as an organization, because the message is the output of many individuals. In addition, the audience consists of an interconnected group of receivers,

---

[12] Edward Shils and Morris Janowitz, "Cohesion and Disintegration in the Wehrmacht in World War II," in Schramm, *Process and Effects of Mass Communication,* pp. 501–16.

FIGURE 2–2

Mass Communication

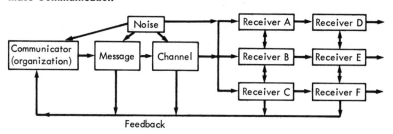

each of whom may interact with others and thereby directly affect the content which is communicated.

The process of mass communication also may be represented as a social system, in Figure 2–3. The communicator in Figure 2–3 is the production subsystems, which include the variety of groups involved in

FIGURE 2–3

The Mass Media as a Social System

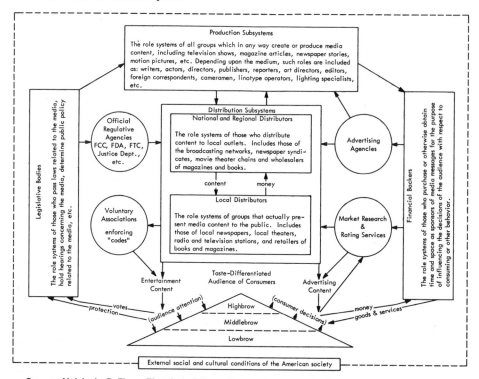

Source: Melvin L. DeFleur, *Theories of Mass Communication*, 2d ed. (New York: David McKay Co., 1970), p. 166. Used by special permission.

creation of message content. Each individual within the subsystem has his own role to play—hence the term "role system." The distribution subsystems comprise all who present and distribute media content to the public on a national, regional, or local level. The audience itself is designated as the taste-differentiated audience of consumers.

Each of the subsystems is profoundly affected by various legislative bodies which enact codes to regulate media content. The diagram also represents the inputs from such facilitating services as advertising agencies, research services and financial sponsors.

Arrows connect the individual subsystems, to indicate flow of influence or effect between them. The consumer audience affects the production subsystem, for example, through information collected by market research and rating services which, in turn, is disseminated to those who design and distribute the mass media message.

The Communicator. The communicator through mass media most frequently is a commercial, governmental, or educational agency. The purpose generally is to persuade members of the audience to accept a particular point of view or to inform and educate the audience with respect to a particular topic. Many individuals interact in a complex process to determine message content. As a result, speed of communication usually is drastically reduced by the necessity for collective decisions.

The Message. The message format does not differ greatly from that in interpersonal communication because it comprises both verbal and nonverbal symbols. The primary difference is that it generally must be more impersonal than the message transmitted through face-to-face channels because it is directed to a group rather than to an identified individual. As a result it is difficult to orient its content to achieve maximum impact on a given person. This inflexibility is one of the primary disadvantages faced when the mass media are used.

Determination of message content for a large group presents obvious problems in that one message must be suitable for many individuals, each of whom differs in certain ways. Direct role taking is impossible and the function of social norms becomes especially significant, as Berlo points out:

Knowledge of a social system can help us make accurate predictions about people, without the necessity of empathizing, without the necessity of interaction, without knowing anything about the people other than the roles that they have in the system. . . . For every role there is a set of behaviors and a position. If we know what the behaviors are that go with a role, we can predict that those behaviors will be performed by people who perform that role. Second, if we know what behaviors go with a given rank of position, we can make predictions about people who occupy that position.[13]

---

[13] Berlo, *Process of Communication,* p. 149. Copyright 1960 by Holt, Rinehart & Winston. Used by permission.

The Channel. The channel includes such media as radio, television, magazines, daily and weekly newspapers, films, books, and so on. These media generally are published, aired, or viewed at regular intervals, with the result that speed and flexibility of communication are further hindered. In addition, communication is indirect because of the fact that the communicator and the recipients are not simultaneously present in space or time. These disadvantages are counteracted, however, by the fact that many people can be reached relatively quickly at a much lower cost than would be possible through the face-to-face channel.

The Receivers. The audience is best conceived as a group, no member of which is directly known to the communicator. Each member perceives selectively in that he retains full powers to "screen out" unwanted communication through selective exposure, distortion, and retention. Selective screening is especially pronounced with mass media because of the necessity to design the message to be acceptable to many people. As a result it may be off target for many of the intended recipients and thus become ignored, distorted, or forgotten. This is perhaps the key problem encountered in advertising strategy.

It also must be recognized that communication through the mass media is a social process in the sense that individuals interact with others regarding the message content. Word-of-mouth communication can either enhance or hinder the communicator's objectives. Favorable word of mouth can be an asset, because the message is disseminated and reinforced to a much greater extent than usually is possible through the mass media. The opposite, of course, can also be true in that unfavorable word of mouth can almost totally counteract anything the mass communicator attempts to say.

Feedback. The fact that communicator and recipient are physically separated means that effective feedback is difficult. At the very least it is quite delayed, because resort usually must be made to some type of audience survey. Readership of a magazine article or the viewing audience of a television program can be determined by asking people what they have read or seen. Standardized techniques for this purpose are discussed in Chapter 14.

Audience surveys are expensive and time-consuming, and the results may not be known for weeks or months. Obviously, feedback is too late to permit altering the message during initial contact between communicator and audience. Feedback in the sense discussed here is used primarily to determine the messages to be transmitted in the future.

Interpersonal versus Mass Communication

The comparative advantages and disadvantages of interpersonal and mass communication are summarized in Figure 2–4. The mass media

FIGURE 2–4

Comparative Advantages and Limitations of Interpersonal and Mass Communication

	Interpersonal Communication	Mass Communication
Reaching a large audience		
Speed................................	Slow	Fast
Cost per individual reached...........	High	Low
Influence on the individual		
Ability to attract attention.............	High	Low
Accuracy of message communicated..	Low	High
Probability of selective screening......	Relatively low	High
Clarity of content.....................	High	Moderate to low
Feedback		
Direction of message flow.............Two-way		One-way
Speed of feedback....................	High	Low
Accuracy of feedback.................	High	Low

suffer from delayed feedback, inflexibility, and a greater likelihood of selective screening by audience members. These disadvantages are substantial and present real problems that must be dealt with in promotional strategy. The costs of reaching an individual through the mass media, however, are substantially lower. In addition the accuracy of the message communicated to a large audience is likely to be high because the message does not change, as it might if it were passed from one individual to the next through face-to-face channels.

Because individuals are so prone to screen out the content of mass media, it is quite difficult to achieve major changes in attitudes and predispositions. The result is more likely to be stimulation of interest or awareness and reinforcement of present views. The greater flexibility and feedback permitted in interpersonal communication allow the communicator to counter objections and comments and thereby achieve changes in attitudes and predispositions more readily.

In a practical situation, it is necessary to compare the communication advantages with the cost advantages of using a particular channel. When the audience is large it usually is necessary to accept the inefficiencies of mass communication because of the distinctly lower cost per individual contacted.

COMMUNICATION IN MARKETING

At one time all promotion was undertaken on a face-to-face basis through personal selling, and in terms of total expenditures personal selling still is of greater importance than the mass media. From a communications point of view, personal selling involves Mr. B interacting directly with Mr. A. The advantage is that bargaining can take place as the salesman "feels out" his prospect and thereby determines the proper communication content in view of the customer's background and psychological influences.[14] He then can phrase his message so that effective communication results, and if the message somehow misses its mark the availability of direct and immediate feedback permits him to try again. The customer, in turn, can readily express his needs and thereby procure necessary information in a direct and expeditious fashion. Both parties therefore engage in mutual role taking, and the communication difficulties, while they are never to be minimized, are less than those presented when the mass media are used. The communication process in personal selling is discussed in greater detail in Chapter 15.

Because managers of promotion in most firms, especially those in the consumer goods market, must contend with large groups of buyers, the mass media also must be utilized. The resulting problems in communication are significant. Those of special importance are: (1) the need to isolate market segments, (2) the selection of appropriate communication media to reach target segments, (3) the design of persuasive messages for groups rather than one individual, and (4) the delay in response feedback.

Isolation of Market Segments

Because mass media messages must be aimed at many individual recipients, direct mutual role taking cannot occur. Fortunately, however, it is possible to isolate relatively homogeneous *segments* of a total audience who have enough in common through shared social roles that communication can take place. An advertising campaign, for example, might be directed to young, midwestern mothers in the middle social classes whose husbands are junior executives with college degrees. Each of these demographic factors (young, midwestern, mother, middle class, college educated, junior executive) implies certain modes of behavior, and messages framed in these terms can reach desired targets and communicate without any direct interaction between source and recipient.

The way to adapt to this communication situation is to define the target market and to study the backgrounds and motivational influences of its members *before* communication is undertaken. Such an analysis is advisable also when reliance is placed on personal selling, but it is a necessity when the mass media are used.

How should segmentation be undertaken? This subject is discussed in

---

[14] For a more thorough discussion see Frederick E. Webster, Jr., "Interpersonal Communication and Salesman Effectiveness," *Journal of Marketing*, Vol. 32 (July 1968), pp. 7–13, and Allen L. Pennington, "Customer-Salesman Bargaining Behavior in Retail Transactions," *Journal of Marketing Research*, Vol. 5 (August 1968), pp. 255–63.

detail in Chapter 9, but for now it is sufficient to point out that the most obvious and least troublesome classification is along such demographic dimensions as geographical location, age, income, social class, occupation or education. These data usually can be obtained rather easily and inexpensively with the tools of marketing research.

It also is necessary to segment buyers in terms of the influences that motivate them to buy or not to buy. For instance, skillful use of research will permit classification of consumers as heavy, moderate, light, or nonusers of a product or brand. In addition the reasons for placement into each of these classifications should be determined, such as differences in underlying motives, styles of life, pressures from friends or relatives, and so on.

By no means, however, are demographic and usage classifications the only distinctions that are valuable in segmentation. The growing tendency in the United States to greater human diversity and rapid changes in attitudes and values make it necessary to be alert to segments which are distinguished by commonly held attitudes and interests but which may include a cross section of demographic classifications. In any case, the objective is to isolate homogeneous groups and to determine the factors that members have in common with respect to the product being promoted. Efforts then are directed at segments where the probability of successful communication and persuasion appears to be greatest. Without segmentation analysis it is unlikely that a successful promotional campaign can be undertaken on a mass scale.

Selection of Communication Media

A mass market can be reached through a variety of media, including the usual mass media (such as television, magazines, or newspapers), direct mail, display of a product on a shelf, and point-of-sale advertising. These media all share the common characteristic that one message or appeal is used to reach more than one prospect.

As will become apparent later, selection of appropriate media is a difficult task. Fortunately, there now are many sources of data which document the characteristics of the audience reached by a given medium, say a women's magazine. If market segments are properly defined and classified, it is possible to select media which reach the desired target audience. The objective is to minimize waste coverage insofar as possible.

Design of the Persuasive Message

Promotion through mass media requires that the story be told in such a way that it will communicate to groups of prospects, an inflexibility that may cause the message to miss the mark with some individuals. The salesman, on the other hand, is free to vary the message to meet each situation; this is the powerful advantage of personal selling.

If the market has been properly segmented the probability of successful communication is increased. From the point of view of promotion, the goal of segmentation is to achieve homogeneity so that one message will be suitable for many individuals. Success is further enhanced by pretesting the message so that the probability of effective communication can be gauged before funds are invested in the campaign and modifications can be introduced when they are found to be appropriate or necessary.

Feedback of Response

Feedback is delayed when the mass media are used, whereas the salesman has the advantage of instantaneous feedback through gestures or verbal reactions. The advertiser must use measures to analyze readership, message comprehension, attitude change, or other forms of response. Feedback of these types is useful, however, only to measure effectiveness and to permit postmortem analysis of the reasons for success or failure. Management can gauge the performance of its advertising department or agency as such, but feedback comes too late to save a sale if the message has been off target.

The Paradox

It is obvious that the mass media present some significant communication problems. Advertising and publicity through the mass media always will represent inefficient communication, even with precise definition of market target, motivation research, and feedback of results through various media. This is because of the very nature of the communication process. Nevertheless, a mass market generally can be reached economically *only* with mass media. This leads to the seeming paradox that advertising provides *efficient promotion through inefficient communication.*

SUMMARY

This chapter has explored the fundamentals of the communication process. A model of interpersonal communication was presented which comprised the communicator, the message, the channel, the receiver, noise, and feedback. The model was modified slightly for mass communication to show that the communicator is an organization, the message is sent through mass channels, and the audience consists of many receivers who are connected by interpersonal channels.

The mass media, of course, are of greatest significance in modern marketing. Stress was placed on the problems presented by the inflexibility of the message sent through mass channels, delayed feedback, and difficulties of audience identification. These disadvantages generally are offset by the low cost per person reached. Thus the marketer usually cannot avoid use of the mass media, although a distinct role remains for interpersonal communication in the form of personal selling.

REVIEW AND DISCUSSION QUESTIONS

1. What is meant by the term "empathy"? What role does it play in the communication process?

2. Describe how a child might have learned meaning for the following terms: "cow," "mother," "ugly," "Republican," and "snow."

3. Describe what kinds of connotative meaning most people have for the following terms: "affection," "love," "fondness," "tenderness," "attachment," "endearment," "liking," "devotion." How might the connotative meanings differ from the denotative meanings?

4. What are the requirements which should be met if Mr. A is to communicate effectively with Mr. B? What is the function of social norms?

5. What is meant by noise in communication? What types of noise can enter when a salesman talks with a customer? What types of noise can enter when a commercial for a brand of deodorant is aired during an afternoon soap opera on television? What, if anything, can be done to reduce noise in marketing communication?

6. It is frequently said that "human beings see and hear what they want to see and hear." What is the effect of this perceptual selectivity when Mr. A attempts to communicate with Mr. B? Do the effects differ when Mr. B is a member of the audience exposed to a television commercial?

7. What types of feedback are received by the salesman when he attempts to sell his company's product, aluminum cookwear, to a new bride? How does feedback change when the same company communicates to its market through use of television commercials?

8. Is advertising more efficient or less efficient than personal selling?

9. Given the problems of communication with a mass market, how can advertisers still experience success through use of the mass media?

10. Explain the importance of market segmentation in promotional strategy.

3

Promotional Strategy:
An Overview

THE FACT that mass marketing generally requires predominate use of mass communication (that is, communication that is not on a face-to-face basis and includes more than one individual) gives rise to major difficulties in communication efforts. These difficulties result from the necessity to use one message for many recipients, inability to modify the message instantaneously if it misses the mark, and considerable delay in feedback of response.

Given these problems, what procedures should be used to approach promotional strategy in the business firm? This is, of course, the basic issue to which this book is addressed. It is useful at the outset to gain an overview of the stages in promotional strategy. This chapter begins with an outline of a systematic approach to promotional decision making which provides the format for the content and ordering of the topics introduced in the chapters to follow. To provide a picture of the promotional process in its entirety, a case history of the introduction of a new product comprises the remainder of the chapter.

THE STAGES IN PROMOTIONAL PLANNING AND STRATEGY

Figure 3–1 provides a summary of a systematic approach to promotional planning and strategy. The approach encompasses the following stages: (1) situation analysis, (2) establishment of objectives, (3) determination of budget, (4) management of program elements, (5) measurement of effectiveness, and (6) evaluation and follow-up.

Figure 3–2 presents the same sequence graphically. Note, however, that it is depicted as an "adaptive" process in that it specifically en-

FIGURE 3-1

Stages in Promotional Planning and Strategy

I. Situation Analysis
   A. Demand
      1. Cultural and social influences
      2. Attitudes
      3. Individual differences
      4. Decision processes
   B. Competition
   C. Legal considerations
   D. Internal organizational considerations
      1. Personnel
      2. Monetary
      3. Established policies and procedures
      4. Operational distinctives
II. Establishment of Objectives
   A. Definition of market targets
   B. Communication message
III. Determination of Budget
IV. Management of Program Elements
   A. Advertising
      1. Analysis of media resources
      2. Selection of advertising media
      3. Message determination
      Personal selling
   B. 1. Analysis of resources
      2. Selection, motivation, and deployment
   C. Stimulation of reseller support
      1. Analysis of reseller resources
      2. Stimulation of performance
      3. Improvement and augmentation of performance
   D. Supplemental communications (public relations, sales promotion)
      1. Assessment of relevant publics
      2. Determination of media and message
V. Coordination and Integration
   A. Achievement of proper balance between program elements
   B. Scheduling of execution
   C. Utilization of personnel and outside services
VI. Measurement of Effectiveness
VII. Evaluation and Follow-up

compasses systematic procedures for gathering information which then can lead to needed program adaptations. For example, advertising message and media decisions are interrelated. The decisions in one area can lead to modifications in another, as the two-way arrows indicate. Furthermore, a feedback loop represents the fact that the initial budget may have to be modified as planning proceeds. Evaluation and follow-up are shown as providing vital new input to the situation analysis for suceeding planning periods. Thus the continual and ongoing nature of planning is graphically portrayed.

FIGURE 3–2

A Decision Sequence Analysis of Promotional Planning and Strategy

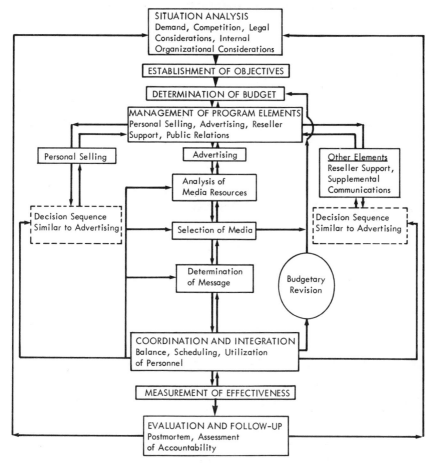

Note: This is similar in certain respects to the diagram utilized by Michael Ray which in turn was adapted from the sequence suggested in earlier editions of this text. See Michael L. Ray, "A Decision Sequence Analysis of Developments in Marketing," *Journal of Marketing,* Vol. 37 (January 1973), p. 31.

Situation Analysis

The starting point is analysis of the environment, with special focus on demand. Specifically, it is necessary to evaluate cultural and social influences, attitudes, individual differences, and decision processes. This provides needed input for determination of both market targets and message strategy.

It also is important to analyze the reactions of prospective customers to product, price, the mix of distributive outlets, selling appeals, and other ways in which the organization adapts to demand. Obviously this focuses on what competitors are doing as well. The objective is to uncover areas of opportunity not presently being exploited by others.

Marketing law is another of the components of the environment for marketing efforts, and it seldom can be disregarded in the process of planning. Prohibition of false and misleading claims is only one example of pertinent legislation which must be heeded. In addition there often are trade regulations and other rulings which are specific to a given industry or firm and which serve as a definite constraint on decision making.

Finally, the internal environment of the business firm also is an important factor. As was pointed out in Chapter 1, careful consideration must be given to available financial resources, managerial capabilities, production facilities, established policies, and various profit inhibitors.

Establishment of Promotional Objectives

The decision as to establishment of market targets is pivotal in promotional success. The next step is to identify the objectives. As the communication function of marketing, promotion makes a unique contribution to the overall marketing program, which implies that promotional objectives should be stated in terms of concrete, measurable communication results. The situation analysis should indicate, for example, whether it is necessary to increase awareness, stimulate trial, change attitudes, and so on. Whatever the form of the objective, the statement should be in specific quantitative terms so that success or failure can be measured.

Determination of Budget

Once objectives have been established it is necessary to determine a preliminary promotional budget. This is a difficult task, as later chapters indicate. The initial estimate usually can only be tentative, and modifications become necessary as the planning process proceeds.

Management of Program Elements

Among the various communication resources available to the firm are personal selling, advertising, resellers (wholesalers and retailers), and supplemental communication activity such as public relations and sales promotion (packaging, price offers, etc.). Decisions must be made with respect to the overall promotional mix using these elements.

Personal Selling. Although the mass media have assumed a dominant position in many industries, the personal selling function is still important. Frequently it is the salesman's responsibility to call on wholesalers and retailers to achieve product distribution and to stimulate their support in promotion of goods and services. At times the salesman is the sole means of reaching the customer, especially in the industrial market. Among the important management decision areas are analysis of present resources, selection of new salesmen, motivation and compensation, and deployment and use of the sales force.

Advertising. There are two primary decision areas in advertising: (1) media selection and (2) message determination. Media selection has become an especially demanding task because of the vast number of available options.

Reseller Support. Wholesalers and retailers frequently are in a position to provide meaningful promotional assistance. Although personal selling long has been a major form of communication in the retail store, its importance has diminished as manufacturers have placed increased reliance on preselling through advertising. Therefore, the retailer now is called upon to provide display, ample shelf space, and so on. Often it is difficult to achieve this type of cooperation, since the objectives of resellers and manufacturers can conflict. As a result it is necessary to use various means to stimulate and to supplement the performance of both wholesalers and retailers.

Supplemental Communications. Two additional activities often are needed in the promotion mix: (1) public relations and (2) sales promotion. Public relations is the function which "evaluates public attitudes, identifies the policies and procedures of an individual or an organization with the public interest, and executes a program of action to earn public understanding and acceptance."[1] The publics include employees, shareholders, resellers, suppliers, the educational community, government, consumer groups, and the public at large.

Sales promotion has been variously defined over the past two decades. In a general sense it is "the supplementary selling activity which coordinates personal selling and advertising into an effective persuasive force."[2] The usual media are packaging, trade fairs and exhibitions, sampling, premiums and trading stamps, and price incentives.

Coordination and Integration of Efforts

Coordinated management of various components of the promotion mix obviously is essential. Advertising, for example, cannot be overemphasized relative to other types of communication unless the problem calls for dominant use of mass media. Too often one phase is allowed to get out of balance, with the result that profit opportunities are lost.

---

[1] Bertrand R. Canfield and H. Frazier Moore, *Public Relations Principles, Cases, and Problems* (Homewood, Ill.: Richard D. Irwin, 1973), p. 4.

[2] *Studies in Sales Promotion* (Chicago: Advertising & Sales Promotion, 1964), p. 1.

Coordination also requires skillful use of managerial talent. Decisions must be made regarding the necessity of using outside services such as advertising agencies, research suppliers, and media buying services. Because the advertising agency is in such widespread use, the decision may focus on division of responsibilities between management within the firm and agency personnel.

Measurement of Effectiveness

Another area for managerial decision lies in providing for feedback of results to assess the effectiveness of promotional strategy. At times sales can be used for this purpose, although sales usually result from the coordinated impact of the *entire* marketing program. Therefore reliance more frequently is placed on measures of communication performance such as recall of selling points, advertising readership, attitude change, and so on. Other measures are used to determine the results of personal selling and reseller support. This complex subject is discussed in depth in Part Five.

Evaluation and Follow-Up

Every effort should be made to assess the strengths and weaknesses of the promotional plan with the objective of cataloging experience for use in future planning. Given that management turnover is a way of life in many organizations, it is not surprising that past mistakes are repeated continually. Part of the problem lies in the fact that records are not kept, perhaps for the reason that managers are avoiding accountability for performance. Whatever the reason, failure to use the results of experience in future planning is inexcusable, and a formal postmortem analysis should be a routine part of the management process.

MAX-PAX GROUND COFFEE FILTER RINGS: A CASE HISTORY

A more concrete indication of the steps in promotional strategy in an actual market situation can be provided by a case history of the introduction of a new product. The product is Max-Pax[3] ground coffee filter rings, an innovative product in the food industry marketed by General Foods.

---

[3] Max-Pax, Maxwell House, Yuban, Maxim, and Sanka are registered trademarks of General Foods Corporation.

BACKGROUND

The General Foods Corporation, through its Maxwell House Division, has long been a leader in both ground and soluble (instant) coffee. Before the introduction of Max-Pax, its product line included regular (ground) and instant Maxwell House, Sanka brand decaffeinated coffee, Yuban, and Maxim freeze-dried coffee.

Each of the coffees in the line was positioned differently for a particular market. Yuban (ground and soluble) and Maxim freeze-dried are both premium coffees costing more than ground and instant Maxwell House. Maxim is further differentiated in that it uses the process of freeze-drying and was the first to do so. Sanka (ground and soluble) is a low-caffein brand clearly different from the other products.

The Product

Marketing research had indicated to General Foods that there might well be a market for a more convenient form of ground coffee. Many people still regarded the taste of ground, percolated coffee as superior to that of instant, but there remained the problem of consistently making a good cup of coffee free from oil and bitterness, as well as the messiness of the grounds.

To help answer this problem, Max-Pax was developed. The product itself consists of 34 grams of coffee enclosed in a nonwoven, rayon base, white fabric filter. The tablets are designed to fit in 90–95 percent of existing percolators, and each one yields 4–6 cups of coffee.

Tests indicated that the coffee thus percolated was clearer and less bitter, with less coffee oil and sediments than the major ground-coffee competitors. Consequently, the taste was most often described as more "mild" than the "stronger" flavor of coffees brewed without the filter. There were, of course, no messy grounds, since the filter was easily emptied into the trash.

SITUATION ANALYSIS

Experimentation had suggested a market for a product such as Max-Pax. The product had been developed and was feasible to mass produce. Before commitment to such a project, however, a closer look at the prevailing situation was mandatory.

Demand

The total coffee market had been declining steadily during recent years, due primarily to the lower incidence of coffee drinking by the younger age segments. During this same period, the instant-coffee market had been riding strong growth trends, due primarily to the innovation of freeze-dried coffees. The decaffeinated market had also been growing steadily on the heels of increased consumer concern over caffein. The growth of the instant and decaffeinated coffees had been at the expense of ground coffee. With the one major exception of electric-perk blends, introduced in 1968, this market had been characterized by ever-increasing price competition and limited product innovation.

The consumer emphasis on convenience has a profound effect on the marketing of coffee and virtually all other consumer products. Successful new products in most major categories have been those that have combined added convenience with quality and consistency of performance. This combination has justified in the consumers' mind the normally higher prices required to cover costs of technological development. This has been the case with product innovations such as freeze-dried coffees, instant breakfast foods, shaving cream in foam dispensers, oven cooking bags, and one-pan family dinners.

The Max-Pax concept was derived specifically from these basic attitudes regarding coffee consumption and the growing demand for convenience in preparation. More specific research into the concept, especially in relationship to actual decisions to purchase, provided additional support for the project. In a national study conducted by Babette Kass, "Consumer Wants and Needs with Respect to Coffee" (August 1964) several *major* consumer problems were identified in the preparation and handling of ground coffee:

1. *Measurement*—spilling of grounds, losing count, etc.
2. *Grounds disposal*—messy, time-consuming.
3. *Cleaning the pot*—oils and sediment, untidy.
4. *General simplicity and speed of preparation.*

Prior to a June 1967 home-use test, a concept described both in flavor and in convenience terms attained extremely high ratings on purchase intention. Of the respondents, a majority indicated that they would definitely or probably purchase a new coffee with the following characteristics: "Here is a totally new ground coffee which offers you the easiest, fastest way ever to prepare coffee in your percolator. It's premeasured and packed in a disposable filter. No measuring, no mess in preparation or disposal. The filtered coffee keeps your percolator clean. And, it tastes good."

Based on results of concept testing, the filter bag product was assigned top priority. It offered, for the first time, the opportunity to market a preemptive ground-coffee product innovation with an advertisable and highly visible point of difference.

Competition

There definitely appeared to be a demand for Max-Pax, but the competition also had to be taken into account. The first concern was with the competition Max-Pax might provide to the other coffees marketed by General Foods.

It was hoped that the taste difference between Max-Pax and Maxwell House would prevent cannibalization to some extent since, if the tastes were identical, a large number might leave Maxwell House simply for the convenience of Max-Pax.

The concern over cannibalization also played a major factor in the naming of Max-Pax. There were two major considerations involved in the choice of the name:

1. The name should identify the distinctive convenience feature of the product (Pax).
2. The name should maintain some quality association with Maxwell House but yet remain a separate and distinctive product (Max).

This name was also the leading candidate as ranked by consumers in a name reaction study.

The second concern was with the competing brands of coffee produced by other companies. To a large extent the actual brands against which Max-Pax would be competing were determined by the positioning of the product. While, viewed in the broadest possible terms, Max-Pax was competing with all other brands, the decision was made to position it specifically against the other ground coffees.

The promotional spending, then, would be against ground-coffee rather than instant-coffee consumption. Even though the ground-coffee market had been declining, it was hoped that the introduction of this first true innovation in many years would stabilize and then reverse the decline as far as General Foods involvement was concerned.

In addition, it was believed that taste/flavor should be included in the positioning. The rationale for this decision included these considerations:

1. Max-Pax is an entirely new concept in the ground-coffee category. Its convenience benefits are easily communicated to consumers.
2. The housewife can more easily justify the higher cost of Max-Pax if she believes that it offers a superior taste.
3. The Max-Pax filter presents a unique opportunity to support taste claims visibly.

The packaging of the product was also basically a decision largely determined by the competition. The standard metal cans with plastic lids were selected for packaging the product because:

1. Many of the product protection needs for filter rings are similar to those of loose ground coffee (ease of opening and closing, maintenance of freshness, etc.)
2. Metal provides excellent antibreakage protection.
3. The use of a conventional coffee can would enhance consumer perceptions of the product as ground coffee.

The importance of having multiple sizes was demonstrated in later research done in the test markets. The graphics for the introductory period included "New from General Foods" to emphasize the newness of the product, and a brown lid with a yellow embossed logo (New Max-Pax, Ground Coffee Filter Rings) to reinforce brand identification.

The final consideration involved the pricing of the product. Traditionally, the consumer had been willing to pay a premium for added convenience, and a premium price would be necessary, as Max-Pax would cost more to produce.

Legal Considerations

The company was, of course, subject to the general regulations enforced by the federal Food and Drug Administration. No unusual legal questions were raised concerning either the product or its designation. "Ground coffee filter rings" provided an adequate and accurate description of the product.

Internal Organization

A brand manager was put in charge of the project, and the existing departments of General Foods were used to provide for the necessary internal procedures. Ogilvy & Mather, Inc., a New York–based advertising firm which had long handled various coffees marketed by General Foods, was chosen to develop the advertising campaign.

ESTABLISHMENT OF OBJECTIVES

In order to properly evaluate the effect of Max-Pax upon the marketplace, certain goals and objectives were set for each phase of its introduction. A schedule was developed for its marketing so that the success or failure of the product could be tested and evaluated before General Foods was committed to nationwide distribution.

The product was to be first test marketed in several cities. Expansion was to take place first in the western regions of the country, being introduced in Chicago in January 1971, the far western regions in March 1971, and the Minneapolis–Kansas City–St. Louis region in May 1971.

If sales went well in these markets, national expansion was scheduled for March 1972 and completed by fiscal year 1973.

The goals for the western expansion markets during fiscal year 1973 were to:

1. Achieve specific share and volume goals.
2. Obtain a high incidence of regular usage through repeat purchasers, that is, to develop a strong franchise of those using primarily Max-Pax.

The promotional campaign was directed primarily toward ground-coffee users, especially those using both ground and instant coffees, since they seemed likely purchasers of a convenient ground coffee.

PROGRAM ELEMENTS

In order to accomplish these objectives, a two-year promotional program was designed. The program was to be conducted in two phases and involve three basic areas: (1) pricing, (2) advertising through the use of the mass media, and (3) promotional incentives for purchase.

Year I

The goal of the first phase, or Year 1, was to build awareness of the product and to gain regular users.

Pricing. The promotional campaign first involved the pricing of the product. Despite the increased production costs of Max-Pax, it was decided that during Year 1, Max-Pax would have to have the same wholesale price as regular Maxwell House. The reasons for this procedure involved both the consumer and the reseller:

1. In the market for ground coffee, price is an extremely important criterion for selection. The consumer would simply not pay a premium price for ground coffee until a brand loyalty had developed.
2. With wholesale price parity, a specialty image of Max-Pax would not be likely to develop among resellers. A specialty image would likely mean failure, since it would lead to low merchandising support and poor shelf display.

Advertising. The advertising for Year 1 in the expansion markets made primary use of blanket television coverage in all expansion areas, with heavy supplemental print advertising in the first quarter and sustaining supplementary print throughout the rest of Year 1. Finally, heavy use was made of outdoor billboard spending during Year 1.

The actual advertising message and media had been examined extensively in test markets before widespread regional distribution.

FIGURE 3–3

First Introductory Commercial

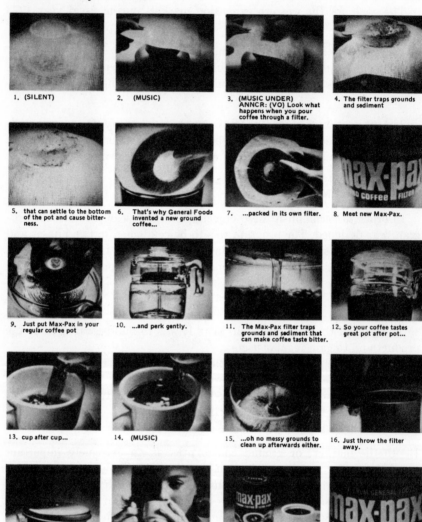

1. (SILENT)

2. (MUSIC)

3. (MUSIC UNDER) ANNCR: (VO) Look what happens when you pour coffee through a filter.

4. The filter traps grounds and sediment

5. that can settle to the bottom of the pot and cause bitterness.

6. That's why General Foods invented a new ground coffee...

7. ...packed in its own filter.

8. Meet new Max-Pax.

9. Just put Max-Pax in your regular coffee pot

10. ...and perk gently.

11. The Max-Pax filter traps grounds and sediment that can make coffee taste bitter.

12. So your coffee tastes great pot after pot...

13. cup after cup...

14. (MUSIC)

15. ...oh no messy grounds to clean up afterwards either.

16. Just throw the filter away.

17. (MUSIC)

18. The new Max-Pax ground coffee filter ring.

19. It's the difference between good coffee and great coffee.

20. (MUSIC)

Through the recall tests of the television commercials, specific guidelines were developed for the creation of the introductory commercial and supportive follow-up commercials.

The most effective selling proposition was discovered to be that Max-Pax is a new, good-tasting ground coffee which is more convenient than other ground coffees. The unique filter ring provided support for the claim in that good taste is achieved by filtering out grounds and sediment which can cause coffee bitterness, and the convenience factor could be easily demonstrated through ease of preparation and disposal. The use of the General Foods name was designed to assure consumers of quality.

The tone of the initial advertising was to be a news atmosphere basically designed to be informative, modern, and memorable. This tone in the first introductory commercial (Figure 3–3) was obtained through the use of a voice-over announcer and a demonstration to make the point of the filter's use in giving a consistently good cup of coffee by preventing grounds and sediment. The better taste is certainly the emphasis of the commercial, since the convenience factor is so obviously illustrated.

The second commercial (Figure 3–4), used as a follow-up in the west and east introductions, illustrates coffee as a social drink and, while the basic message is certainly that Max-Pax tastes good, that message is linked to the status of being able to make excellent coffee. It offers security. In addition, research showed it to be an effective communicator of the lack of bitterness and consistency.

Original spending for advertising was equal across all geographical areas.

FIGURE 3–4

Second Introductory Commercial

1. WOMAN: I had the girls over for lunch and
2. everything tasted fantastic! Everything ... but the coffee.
3. Maybe I used too much... too little...
4. It never tastes the same way twice.

  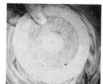 

5. But now I've got a sure thing.
6. Max-Pax. Pre-measured so you can't make a mistake.
7. And this filter — traps grounds and sediment that can cause bitterness.
8. What joy —

9. great coffee every time.
10. Max-Pax. It's a sure thing!
11. (SILENT)

Promotional Incentives. The promotional incentives for Year 1 involved the provision of low cost–low risk purchase opportunities during the first quarter, followed by low-level price-oriented promotion for the remainder of the year to strengthen repurchase. For the first quarter, a 25-cent prepriced four-ring can was sold, and 25-cent coupons were distributed by direct mail. For the rest of the year, 7-cent mail coupons, 7-cent and 10-cent Sunday supplement coupons, and 7-cent and 15-cent packed-in coupons were employed.

Year II

The general goals for Year II involved building consumer brand loyalty and maintaining awareness.

Pricing. After Year I, pricing was based on an independent system of production costs and profit margins. In most markets this procedure resulted in a price disparity between Max-Pax and the other major brands. It was believed that price disparity could then be sustained on the basis that:

1. It was a coffee innovation, and emphasis in advertising was to be put on the product's benefits rather than on price.
2. Consumers will have broken their previous coffee buying habits and be willing to pay a premium price.
3. Max-Pax had retail price premiums as high as 40 percent in its test markets for over a year, without adverse effects on share.

Advertising. During Year II advertising was to maintain awareness of Max-Pax and reinforce its unique benefits. Advertising was again to proceed with follow-up spot TV commercials until national distribution was attained and then by network coverage.

Promotional Incentives. All trade promotional incentives ended, and low-value promotional incentives were directed toward the consumer.

MEASUREMENT OF EFFECTIVENESS: POSTMORTEM

Campaign Effectiveness

Six months after the expansion of Max-Pax into the Western market, it became quite clear that the market-share goal was not going to be fully met. With negative indicators very much in evidence, there was a question as to whether or not Max-Pax could achieve its objectives without overspending its budget.

Inquiry into the cause of the problems was along three lines:

1. Had the test market performance actually been a valid indicator of product success?

2. Had the introductory marketing plan made best use of its resources in exploiting the product's potential?
3. Were there new consumer concerns which had not been taken into account in the original marketing plan?

Discovery of the Problems

Marketing research into the expansion areas overturned several problem areas which had not been taken into account previously.

First, Max-Pax sold much better in urban areas than in rural areas, despite the fact that promotional efforts had been equal regardless of geographical area. The test markets had provided very little information on the performance of Max-Pax in rural areas.

Secondly, since supermarkets in some areas had priced Max-Pax higher despite wholesale price parity, the product was able to be evaluated under various pricing conditions. It was discovered that while a reasonable price disparity had been no deterrent to the initial purchase of Max-Pax, which was often made on the basis of convenience, it nonetheless prevented many consumers from making a repeat purchase. These two factors had resulted in a restricted development of brand loyalty.

The implications of these findings upon the marketing strategy were twofold. First, the growth of a loyal group of repeat purchasers would seem to be highly dependent upon building awareness of product benefits beyond convenience, since that factor alone did not give the consumer adequate justification for a premium price. Also, spending efficiency and leverage would be optimized by concentrating efforts in the high-potential urban markets.

Solving the Problems

The initial step taken in providing a solution to these problems was to develop a Brand Opportunity Index based on county-size population skew, total population concentration within the market area, and subjective judgments as to trade receptiveness, competitive climate, and past consumer response to a new product. Using this index as a guide, areas were rated as high (Group I) and low (Group II) potential, and separate marketing plans were developed for both areas. The revised marketing plans involved the following changes:

Objectives. The market-share goal was moved downward to reflect judgment made from western expansion experience, primarily urbanization and pricing.

Pricing. Instead of an absolute parity for the duration of Year I a pragmatic parity based on favorable pricing relationships against major brands was the objective for six months.

This procedure was followed since absolute price parity had made little difference on initial purchase and other promotional devices were used to bring about repeat purchases.

Advertising. Network and spot TV advertising along with heavy print support was allowed for all of Year I in Group I markets. In Group II markets, the spot TV and print support was used only in the first quarter. Emphasis was placed consistently upon good taste instead of convenience.

Promotional Incentives

In Group I markets, the prepriced can was used in conjunction with the high-value direct mail coupon, while in Group II markets the value of the coupon was dependent upon the market potential. In addition, two strong trade features were offered during the introductory six months in Group I markets, but only one in Group II markets. Finally, instead of following the original plan of using low-value packed-in coupons during the third quarter, high-value coupons were used during the first two quarters to bring about repeat purchases.

During Year II, support was continued for the product through network television, with additional spot TV support in Group I markets and promotional incentives dependent upon Year I performance and growth potential. With this revised marketing planning, nationwide expansion was undertaken, and Max-Pax firmly established its niche in the ground-coffee market.

A LOOK AHEAD

The remainder of the book roughly follows the outline in Figures 3–1 and 3–2. Part Two is devoted to the first topic, situation analysis, with most of the part centering on analysis of demand. A sophisticated understanding of buyer motivation and behavior is perhaps the greatest key to promotional success. Some emphasis also is given to legal constraints.

Part Three covers basic considerations in planning, including the second and third topics, determination of objectives and establishment of the budget. The fourth topic, management of program elements, forms the core of the book. In Part Four, "Management of Advertising Efforts," the topics discussed are analysis of media resources, selection of media, design of the advertising message, and measurement of advertising effectiveness.

Part Five continues the discussion of management of program efforts by considering the management of personal selling, reseller support programs, and public relations. The detailed topics include use of personal selling resources, sales force management, stimulation of reseller support through various policies, improving and supplementing reseller performance, and management of supplemental communications.

Part Six is devoted to the fifth topic, coordinating and integrating the complete promotional program. The discussion centers first on problems of organization, followed by an analysis of ways to improve coordination and integration in planning and strategy. The final chapter also discusses the final topic of the framework promotional planning: Evaluation and follow-up.

Quite a different perspective is assumed in the concluding part, as the broader questions of social responsibility discussed at various points throughout the book are raised once again and analyzed in greater depth. Given the increasingly critical problems of a strifetorn world, the concluding chapter may well raise the most important questions considered in the book.

It should be stressed that the issues faced in the management of promotion are too complex to allow pat answers. Certain decision routines are developed later, but they are intended only to discipline thinking and to guarantee systematic and rigorous analysis. It is human nature to give way to a "quest for certainty" (a search for concrete and definite answers where none exist). The proper attitude of inquiry, however, calls for an awareness of the state of knowledge and an appreciation of the need for research in areas where knowledge is scanty or missing. A keen appreciation for research and a certain sophistication in its use are central to promotional success.

REVIEW AND DISCUSSION QUESTIONS

1. In what ways can the internal environment of the business firm affect promotional planning and strategy?

2. What reasons can you give for the fact that "preselling" through advertising has largely precluded the role of personal selling at the retail level? Will this trend continue? In what areas does a role for personal selling remain? Why?

3. Given the decline in the need for retail personal selling, what forms of promotional support can the retailer be expected to offer?

4. Analyze the Max-Pax case history in terms of the outline given in Figure 3–1 and answer the following questions:
    a. Was the situation analysis sufficiently complete to permit realistic planning?
    b. Were the objectives for the campaign reasonable? Did they adequately meet the criteria of specificity and measurability?
    c. Were the television commercials properly oriented to the findings discovered in the analysis of demand?

    d. Would it be reasonable to make extensive use of spot television rather than local newspapers, radio, Sunday supplements, or other forms of local media?

    e. Were proper questions asked in the analysis of effectiveness? In other words, did management have a sufficient basis to proceed with campaign planning in succeeding years?

5. What is the "quest for certainty?" Why is it such an ever-present danger? How can it be avoided?

part two

Situation Analysis

The first stage in the model of the stages in promotional planning and strategy presented in Chapter 3 is the situation analysis, which covers demand, competitive response, legal constraints, and considerations within the firm. These determinants of promotional strategy are discussed in this section, with the exception of competition and internal considerations. Competition is referred to at various points in later chapters where it is appropriate to do so, and internal factors were discussed in Chapter 1.

In the analysis of the promotional problem, the inquiry of necessity focuses first on demand. Four chapters are devoted to this important subject. The first (Chapter 4) centers on audience response to persuasion and thus defines both the opportunities for and the limitations on persuasion. Chapter 5 clarifies social influences on behavior from the points of view of culture, social class, and reference groups, and Chapter 6 discusses the significance of attitudes and individual differences in promotional strategy. Chapter 7, which concludes the discussion of demand, is intended to clarify the function of promotion in consumer decision making.

The remaining factor in the situation analysis, legal constraints, is discussed in Chapter 8. Legal issues are growing in importance, so the review of pertinent legislation and judicial rulings is of considerable significance in promotional strategy.

4

Demand: Audience Response
to Persuasion

EVERY DAY, American men, women and children are bombarded with myriad attempts to persuade them about one thing or another. As defenses against these stimuli are naturally developed, they function in quite an effective manner, much to the dismay of the advertiser and seller.

How do people respond to persuasion? What kinds of defenses do they erect? Can people be manipulated to act in a nonrational manner, with the result that marketing communication leads to socially undesirable ends? These are the questions addressed in this chapter, and the answers provided are fundamental in arriving at a clear understanding of both the opportunities for persuasive communication to influence consumer behavior and the limitations on its ability to do so.

CONSUMER INFORMATION PROCESSING

A housewife ironing in front of her television set while watching her favorite afternoon show, "As the Stomach Turns," watched 12 commercials (including station breaks) without leaving the room at any point. Yet when questioned she could not recall the content of a single commercial, including the 30-second spot she had just finished watching seconds before. She freely related the story of the program, however, which routinely dealt with such issues as murder, divorce, drug addiction, and perversion in the life of a "typical" American family. Later in the afternoon she browsed through her favorite movie magazine and was able to recall only two of the 50 or more advertisements with which she was confronted while turning the pages.

FIGURE 4–1

Registration of Featured Idea—Recall after 24 Hours

	Magazines		Television	
	Number of Ads	Recall Range (%)	Number of Ads	Recall Range (%)
Tires				
	13	0– 3.9	13	0– 3.9
	21	4– 7.9	5	4– 7.9
	11	8–11.9	5	8–11.9
	2	12–15.9	4	12–15.9
	3	16–19.9		
	2	24–27.9		
	2	28–31.9		
Automobiles				
	20	0– 1.9	49	0– 1.9
	33	2– 3.9	29	2– 3.9
	47	4– 5.9	19	4– 5.9
	27	6– 7.9	6	6– 7.9
	12	8– 9.9	4	8– 9.9
	7	10–11.9	2	10–11.9
	7	12–13.9	2	12–13.9
	1	14–15.9	4	14–15.9
	1	16–17.9	1	16
	1	18–19.9		
	3	20–21.9		
	3	22–23.9		
	1	24		
Life insurance				
	24	0– 1.9	8	0– 1.9
	23	2– 3.9	13	2– 3.9
	10	4– 5.9	7	4– 5.9
	2	6– 7.9	5	6– 7.9
	1	8– 9.9	3	8– 9.9
			1	10–11.9
			1	14–15.9
			1	18–19.9
			1	20–21.9
TV sets				
	5	0– 1.9	6	0– 1.9
	6	2– 3.9	9	2– 3.9
	4	4– 5.9	4	4– 5.9
	4	6– 7.9	3	6– 7.9
	3	8– 9.9	1	8– 9.9
	1	10–11.9	3	10–11.9
	2	12–13.9	2	12–13.9
	1	14–15.9	1	14–15.9
	1	18–19.9	3	16–17.9
Aftershaves, colognes				
	2	0– 3.9	7	0– 3.9
	10	4– 7.9	4	4– 7.9
	3	8–11.9	3	8–11.9
	1	12–15.9	2	12–15.9
	1	16–19.9	1	16–19.9
	1	20–23.9	3	24–27

Source; *Advertising Age,* April 12, 1971, p. 52. Reprinted with permission of *Advertising Age.* Copyright 1971 by Crain Communications, Inc.

The situation described above is not as atypical as it might seem, as the data in Figure 4–1 indicate. The typical advertisement makes only a minimal impact on its audience, as is shown by the fact most people recall less than 5 percent of the content after 24 hours. Furthermore, data from many sources indicate that advertising impact, on the whole, is diminishing.

The reason why these patterns are occurring is, in part, the fact that advertising exposure is taking place under *involuntary* conditions. The consumer attends to the medium for such purposes as entertainment and information, and the advertising message intrudes on this primary purpose. This is in sharp contrast to *motivated exposure,* in which case the consumer is actively seeking information to aid in the buying process. The results of exposure then will be quite different, as the discussion in Chapter 7 indicates.

Whatever the reason, those responsible for promotional strategy must contend with the fact that selective attention, comprehension, retention, and response to commercial persuasion are a fact of life. It is the purpose of this section to analyze consumer information processing and to assess its implications for promotional strategy.

The Filtering Process

It is apparent from a psychological point of view, that the consumer actively filters persuasive communications and responds to them selectively. This means, of course, that successful communication requires more than mere exposure. Full account must be taken of the way in which the consumer behaviorally and psychologically processes incoming stimuli. This requires an understanding of the individual's psychological makeup.

The Psychological Makeup.[1] The individual has a command center, so to speak, which includes both memory and basic facilities for thinking and for directing behavior. Figure 4–2 designates this as the *central control unit,* of which the primary components are information and experience, evaluative criteria, attitudes, and personality. These factors together comprise a filter through which all incoming stimuli are processed. The diagram of the central control unit presented in Figure 4–2 is the basis for illustration of all the various aspects of demand considered in Chapters 4–7.

STORED INFORMATION AND EXPERIENCE. The individual learns from experience and retains information in either conscious or unconscious memory. Buying action obviously is affected by the extent to which the consumer is aware of available alternatives and their attributes.

---

[1] The discussion in this section closely follows James F. Engel, David T. Kollat, and Roger D. Blackwell, *Consumer Behavior,* 2d ed. (New York: Holt, Rinehart & Winston, 1973).

FIGURE 4–2

The Central Control Unit

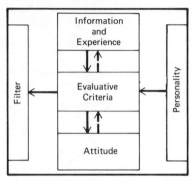

Source: James F. Engel, David T. Kollat, and Roger D. Blackwell, *Consumer Behavior*, 2d ed. (New York: Holt, Rinehart & Winston, 1973).

EVALUATIVE CRITERIA. The individual uses evaluative criteria as specifications to compare alternatives. Examples are durability, performance, and price. These criteria, which are manifestations of the individual's basic motives, personality patterns, stored information, and social influences, tend to resist change and function as standards against which alternatives are evaluated.

ATTITUDES. An attitude is a mental and neural state of readiness to respond that is organized through experience and exerts a directive or dynamic influence on behavior.[2] In terms of consumer behavior, attitudes reflect an evaluation of a product, brand, or store in terms of criteria which are pertinent in the evaluation and choice process. Figure 4–2 shows a direct functional relationship between information and experience, evaluative criteria, and attitudes, which indicates that an attitude is formed from the interaction of these first two factors. There also is a reverse feedback relationship, however, as depicted by broken arrows, which results from the fact that there are restrictions on changes in evaluative criteria and stored information once attitudes are formed.

PERSONALITY. Each individual is unique in many ways. The sum total of these factors is referred to here as personality. It is reflected, in part, by differences in such *demographic* factors as age, income, occupation, and education. There also are significant variations in lifestyle patterns which are referred to as *psychographic* differences. Personality has

[2] Gordon Allport, "Attitudes," in C. Murchison (ed.), *Handbook of Social Psychology* (Worcester, Mass.: Clark University Press, 1935), pp. 798–884.

an especially direct role in the formation of evaluative criteria which are product-specific manifestations of underlying values, traits, and motives.

FILTER. All of these variables in the central control unit form a filter through which all incoming stimuli must pass. Some are discarded and others are attenuated. The active functioning of consumer filters is reflected in the data of Figure 4–1.

The Functioning of the Filter. A stimulus, say an advertisement, reaches one or more of the five senses. This is referred to as exposure in Figure 4–3, which shows how the central control unit operates in

FIGURE 4–3

Information Processing

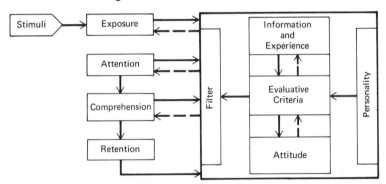

Source: James F. Engel, David T. Kollat, and Roger D. Blackwell, *Consumer Behavior,* 2d ed. (New York: Holt Rinehart & Winston, Inc., 1973).

information processing. The filter functions to regulate those stimuli that receive further analysis and storage within long-term or permanent memory.

A stimulus will not attract attention, be comprehended, or retained unless it survives preliminary processing, which is referred to as *preattentive processing.*[3] At this point it enters short-term storage and is analyzed, mostly along such physical dimensions as pitch, volume, and shape. Far more stimuli receive preattentive processing than ever enter into long-term memory. Attention might be attracted, for example, by a colorful advertisement. What the individual does with the message, how-

---

[3] See U. Neisser, *Cognitive Psychology* (New York: Appleton, 1966); and D. A. Norman, "Toward a Theory of Memory and Attention," *Psychological Review,* Vol. 75 (1968), pp. 522–36, and *Memory and Attention* (New York: John Wiley & Sons, 1969).

ever, is determined by a second stage of processing, referred to as *analysis of pertinence*.[4]

All of the dispositions stored within the central control unit filter interact during the analysis of pertinence. The findings of a number of recent experiments verify that the recipient of a communication message is involved actively in accepting or rejecting its content.[5] This seems to take the form of subvocal responses, referred to as rehearsal[6] or counter-argumentation.[7] The message is accepted and attended to if the recipient rehearses cognitions (thoughts) which are consistent with its theme and conclusions. It is rejected if he counterargues by rehearsing cognitions opposing the position which is advocated or rejects the source of the communication as being biased or untrustworthy.[8]

The filter also works at all successive stages of information processing: comprehension, retention, and response (the last named is not depicted in Figure 4–3). Thus a consumer might attend to an advertisement while not comprehending or retaining its content, and so on. Attention does not guarantee comprehension, and comprehension does not guarantee retention or response.

The implications of information processing for promotional strategy are discussed at length in the following sections, but it is worth noting at this point that exposure is strictly a function of careful media selection and does not involve the message itself. In other words, the message is gotten to the recipient where he is at the appropriate time, but the greater difficulty lies in designing the message so that the filter is not activated to prevent further processing of the input. As a general rule, this requires the message to be compatible with the recipient's psychological makeup.

PROCESSING THE PROMOTIONAL MESSAGE

What happens in the "real world" when the consumer is exposed to an advertisement or other type of promotional message? What are the implications of selective information processing for promotional strategy?

---

[4] Ibid.

[5] A. G. Greenwald, "Cognitive Learning: Cognitive Response to Persuasion and Attitude Change," in A. G. Greenwald, T. C. Brock, and T. M. Ostrom (eds.), *Psychological Foundations of Attitudes* (New York: Academic Press, 1968).

[6] Ibid.

[7] T. C. Brock, "Communication Discrepancy and Intent to Persuade as Determinants of Counterargument Production," *Journal of Experimental Social Psychology*, Vol. 3 (1967), pp. 296–309.

[8] For a useful discussion in a marketing context, see Peter L. Wright, "The Cognitive Processes Mediating Acceptance of Advertising," *Journal of Marketing Research*, Vol. 10 (1973), pp. 53–62.

Exposure

Exposure occurs when one or more of the five senses is activated and transforms stimulus energy into the sensations of sight, smell, touch, taste, and hearing.[9] As was mentioned above, exposure is achieved through careful media selection. The media planner, however, must contend with a large amount of evidence documenting the fact that people *selectively* expose themselves to persuasive stimuli. In particular, there appears to be a tendency to avoid attitude-discrepant messages.

An individual holding a strongly imbedded attitude may avoid a message which attempts to bring about change. The phenomenon of selective exposure was first called to the attention of communication theorists convincingly in a report on the 1940 presidential election campaign.[10] It was found that "exposure to political communications during the presidential campaign is concentrated in the same group of people, not spread among people at large."[11] Furthermore, interest in the election appeared to be the motivation for high exposure to campaign appeals. More recently a 20-hour telethon by the late Senator William Knowland, intended for non-Republicans, attracted mostly Republicans to its audience.[12]

Selective exposure also has been documented extensively outside the field of politics. Some of the most convincing data come from a study undertaken to determine exposure to and acceptance of articles alleging a relationship between smoking and cancer. Data showed that 67 percent of nonsmokers interviewed claimed high readership of such articles, versus 44 percent of smokers.[13] Similarly the overwhelming majority of the audience for a film critical to American involvement in Vietnam knew the orientation of the film before entering the theater and shared its point of view.[14]

From these and other data it appears that only a subset of all possible prospects will be exposed to a given message. Does the consumer simply avoid those messages he considers to be irrelevant? There are some who

---

[9] For a good review of current research see H. W. Leibowitz and L. O. Harvey, Jr., "Perception" in *Annual Review of Psychology*, Vol. 24 (Palo Alto, Cal.: Annual Review Press, 1972), pp. 200–240.

[10] Paul F. Lazarsfeld, Bernard B. Berelson, and Hazel Gaudet, "Radio and the Printed Page as Factors in Political Opinion and Voting," in Wilbur Schramm (ed.), *Mass Communications* (Urbana: University of Illinois Press, 1949), pp. 481–95.

[11] Ibid., p. 484.

[12] Wilbur Schramm and R. F. Carter, "Effectiveness of a Political Telethon," *Public Opinion Quarterly*, Vol. 23 (1960), pp. 121–26.

[13] C. F. Cannell and J. C. MacDonald, "The Impact of Health News on Attitudes and Behavior," *Journalism Quarterly*, Vol. 33 (1956), pp. 121–26.

[14] D. L. Paletz, J. Koon, E. Whitehead, and R. B. Hegens, "Selective Exposure: The Potential Boomerang Effect," *Journal of Communication*, Vol. 22 (1972), pp. 48–53.

argue affirmatively that input is censored to avoid disturbance of existing beliefs. For example, Elihu Katz argues that:

> . . . (a) an individual self-censors his intake of communications so as to shield his beliefs and practices from attack; (b) that an individual seeks out communications which support his beliefs and practices; and (c) that the latter is particularly true when the beliefs or practices in question have undergone attack or the individual has otherwise been made less confident of them.[15]

Not all agree, however, that selective exposure is a motivated act. A common attitudinal bias in the audience may be shaped by other factors, such as education, background, or lifestyle.[16] Selective information processing then occurs *after* exposure, not *before*.

Probably both of the above points of view are valid and explain instances of selective exposure. In any event, this phenomenon is a problem that any communicator must contend with because the actual audience almost always is less than the desired audience.

Attention

After exposure, preattentive processing occurs, followed by analysis for pertinence. Selective attention is the end result of this step in the processing of the promotional message.

Preattentive Processing.   The first stage in preattentive processing is triggering of the *orientation reaction*. This may take the form of a turning in direction, a sense of alertness, and so on.[17] Its function is to prepare the organism to contend with novel stimuli, and it serves to arouse the central nervous system.[18] Certain stimulus patterns are particularly effective in stimulating the orientation reaction: (1) surprise and novelty, (2) intensity, (3) color, and (4) conditioned stimuli (those for which a previously learned pattern of response is called forth).[19]

Analysis for Pertinence.   Preattentive processes are almost automatic, whereas analysis for pertinence requires an internally directed scan. At this time the filter operates to admit only those stimuli that have pertinence in terms of the individual's needs and dispositions.[20]

---

[15] Elihu Katz, "On Reopening the Question of Selectivity in Exposure to Mass Communications," in R. P. Abelson et al. (eds.), *Theories of Cognitive Consistency: A Sourcebook* (Chicago: Rand McNally & Co., 1968), p. 789.

[16] D. O. Sears, "The Paradox of De Facto Selective Exposure without Preferences for Supportive Information," in Abelson et al., *Theories of Cognitive Consistency*, pp. 777–87.

[17] R. Lynn, *Attention Arousal and the Orientation Reaction* (Oxford: Pergamon Press, 1966).

[18] This process is discussed thoroughly in Engel, Kollat, and Blackwell, *Consumer Behavior*, pp. 213–17.

[19] D. E. Berlyne, *Conflict, Arousal and Curiosity* (New York: McGraw-Hill Book Co., 1960).

[20] Neisser, *Cognitive Psychology*, pp. 102–4.

THE INFLUENCE OF NEED STATES. It is reasonable to expect that an aroused bodily need will affect attention. It has been shown, for example, that hungry people are more likely to give food-related responses when ambiguous stimuli are seen or heard.[21] In addition, psychological motives can have the same effect, as was demonstrated in one experiment in which those with a strong affiliation motive identified a greater number of pictures of persons as standing out most clearly in a larger grouping of pictures than did those with a weaker affiliation motive.[22]

There are some obvious implications for promotional strategy. The hungry consumer, for example, will more readily notice food advertisements. An appeal to greater social acceptance through avoidance of body odor will in all probability be more effective with those who fear social rejection. Many other examples could be given.

PERCEPTUAL DEFENSE AND VIGILANCE. Further documentation of the fact that "people see and hear what they want to see and hear" has been provided, initially through a series of experiments undertaken to analyze the influence of personal values on the speed of perception for value-related words. It has been found rather consistently that words connoting important values to the individual are perceived more readily. This selective influence of values has come to be called *perceptual vigilance*.[23] Although this area of research has been plagued with methodological problems, it is now generally accepted that vigilance can occur under properly controlled conditions.

It seems reasonable that perceptual vigilance might be manifested through enhanced speed of perception for preferred brand names. This hypothesis was confirmed in one study where it was found that consumers recognize preferred brand names significantly more readily than they do nonpreferred brand names.[24]

The opposite of perceptual vigilance is *perceptual defense,* a process in which perception of threatening or low-valued stimuli is delayed or avoided. The evidence is extensive that barriers can be raised which

---

[21] See, for example, R. N. Sanford, "The Effects of Abstinence from Food upon Imaginal Processes: A Further Experiment," *Journal of Psychology,* Vol. 3 (1937), pp. 145–59; J. W. Atkinson and D. C. McClelland, "The Projective Expression of Needs: II, The Effect of Different Intensities of the Hunger Drive on Thematic Apperception," *Journal of Experimental Psychology,* Vol. 38 (1948), pp. 643–58; and R. Levine, I. Chein, and G. Murphy, "The Relation of the Intensity of a Need to the Amount of Perceptual Distortion," *Journal of Psychology,* Vol. 13 (1942), pp. 283–93.

[22] J. W. Atkinson and E. L. Walker, "The Affiliation Motive and Perceptual Sensitivity to Faces," *Journal of Abnormal and Social Psychology,* Vol. 53 (1956), pp. 38–41.

[23] See, for example, L. Postman and B. Schneider, "Personal Values, Visual Recognition, and Recall," *Psychological Review,* Vol. 58 (1951), pp. 271–84.

[24] Homer E. Spence and James F. Engel, "The Impact of Brand Preference on the Perception of Brand Names: A Laboratory Analysis," in P. R. McDonald (ed.), *Marketing Involvement in Society and the Economy* (Chicago: American Marketing Association, 1970), pp. 267–71.

prevent or inhibit perception.[25] Undoubtedly consumers at times avoid perception of promotion for nonpreferred brands in this manner, although there is no direct evidence that perceptual defense is operative in a marketing context.

MAINTENANCE OF COGNITIVE CONSISTENCY. The elements within the central control unit interact to provide a "map of the world," and attitudes are particularly important in this context. A demonstrated human tendency to resist changes in this map is referred to as maintenance of cognitive consistency.[26] It is now known, for example, that attitudes are change resistant to the extent that:

1. They are strongly held.
2. They are embedded in a set of related and supportive values and beliefs.
3. They are related to a person's conception of himself relative to others.
4. The system of which they are a part is not complex and differentiated, thereby causing one to respond in terms of "all black or all white."
5. They are associated with important needs or personality traits.

Selective Attention to Promotional Messages. As was pointed out at the beginning of this chapter, data from a variety of sources indicate that the typical advertising message is attended to by only a fraction of the potential audience. On the average, for example, the 30-second television message will be attended to by fewer than 30 percent of those who are exposed. As Leo Bogart points out, "Advertising research data accurately reflect the fact that many messages register negative impressions or no impressions at all on many of the people who are exposed to the sight or sound of them."[27]

Probably the most significant reason why so many filter out unwanted messages is that advertisements in particular are frequently avoided just because of sheer disinterest and boredom. People are often quite unconcerned about what is said. This is further complicated by a high level of *noise* resulting from vast numbers of competing stimuli. Estimates of the average volume of commercial messages confronting us during an average day range from 300 to 400. Is it any wonder that

[25] See, for example, F. H. Nothman, "The Influence of Response Conditions on Recognition Thresholds for Taboo Words," *Journal of Abnormal and Social Psychology*, Vol. 65 (1962), pp. 154–61, and E. Zigler and L. Yospe, "Perceptual Defense and the Problem of Response Suppression," *Journal of Personality*, Vol. 28 (1960), pp. 220–39.

[26] See Shel Feldman (ed.), *Cognitive Consistency* (New York: Academic Press, 1966); and Abelson et al., *Theories of Cognitive Consistency*.

[27] Leo Bogart, "Where Does Advertising Research Go From Here?" *Journal of Advertising Research*, Vol. 9 (March 1969), p. 6.

many of them are just lost in the noise? Bogart's analysis of these points is highly pertinent:

. . . a cornerstone of communications research has long been the notion of selective perception, the idea that people tend to pay attention to messages that support their predispositions and to block out incongruent messages. Recently this theory has been questioned, but the experimental evidence that contradicts it is largely in the domain of highly charged subject matter, on which there are indeed opposing viewpoints. The problem must be posed quite differently in the case of messages that arouse no contradictory prior judgments, simply because they arouse no reactions at all. Perhaps the main contribution that advertising research can make to this study of communications is in the domain of in-attention to low-key stimuli, as exemplified by the ever-increasing flow of un-solicited and unwanted messages to which people are subjected in our over-communicative civilization.[28]

Given a high level of noise, what can be done to capture attention? This subject is discussed at much greater length in Chapter 13, but it is worth pointing out here that something must be done to break through the noise. Recourse is frequently made to novelty, unusual graphics, color, and other such means of attracting attention. The advertisements in Figures 4–4 and 4–5 are highly unusual and would probably capture attention simply because they stand out from surrounding text material and utilize visual "gimmicks." Attraction of attention, however, does not necessarily mean that these are good advertisements. That judgment must be reserved pending evidence on comprehension, retention, and response. Furthermore, the American Tourister ad has been cited by the Federal Trade Commission as false and misleading.

The other principal reason for selective attention to marketing communication is maintenance of cognitive consistency. Assume, for example, that a strongly committed opponent of fluoridation of the water supply is exposed to the advertisement in Figure 4–6. This stimulus probably would never survive the analysis for pertinence because it advocates use of a chemical additive which the consumer considers to be un-acceptable. Furthermore, there may be no way to bring a shift in this attitude through persuasive communication. This leads to the obvious strategy that appeal should be made to the "waverer" (i.e., those whose views are changing) as contrasted with a frontal attack on those with opposing points of view. The latter strategy is destined to failure.

In reality the existence of boredom and noise is the most significant reason for selective attention. Few consumption alternatives are likely to arouse such strong feelings that maintenance of cognitive consistency becomes much of a factor.

---

[28] Bogart, "Where Does Advertising Research Go?" p. 6. Reprinted from the *Journal of Advertising Research,* copyright 1969, Advertising Research Foundation.

FIGURE 4–4

Use of Unusual Layout to Attract Attention

"We were flying along at 70 mph when suddenly it flew off the car..."

"We saw our suitcase hit the highway, bounce, and fall all over."

We think that when a suitcase goes traveling, you shouldn't have to kiss it goodbye.

So we take sixteen different strong materials and mold them into every American Tourister.

We tie the whole thing together with a tough stainless steel frame.

We reinforce it with fiber glass. All over.

And we give American Touristers nonspring locks that won't spring open on impact.

"My wife thought our clothes would be all over the place, but the suitcase didn't even open. Everything inside was fine."

If you're traveling around with an ordinary suitcase, maybe it'll never fall from a car going 70 miles an hour.

Or smash into a concrete overpass.

Maybe, if you're lucky, things like that will happen only to other people.

"I just thought you'd like to know how pleased we were."

Mr. R. E. Benson
Palos Verdes Estates, Calif.

American Tourister

Used with the permission of the American Tourister Company.

FIGURE 4–5

Use of Contemporary Art Forms to Attract Attention

Reproduced with permission of the American Telephone and Telegraph Company.

FIGURE 4–6

Appeal to Strongly Held Attitudes

An idea for every mother whose child had too many cavities last year

If your child gets more than his share of cavities, he needs extra help.

You can give him extra help by making sure he brushes more often, and by making sure he uses Crest—proved effective against cavities in 12 years of tests.

One way to encourage your child to brush more often—try packing a tube of Crest and a toothbrush in his lunch box.

When your youngster has his next checkup, ask your dentist what he thinks of brushing with Crest after lunch at school. And ask him about the value of avoiding between-meal treats and of having regular checkups, in order to prevent trouble before it starts. This is the program most dentists recommend for good dental health.

To make such a program more effective, make sure your child uses Crest —the toothpaste that gives extra help.

"Crest has been shown to be an effective decay-preventive dentifrice that can be of significant value when used in a conscientiously applied program of oral hygiene and regular professional care."

Accepted **Council on Dental Therapeutics**
AMERICAN DENTAL ASSOCIATION   *American Dental Association*

Source: Reproduced with permission of the Procter & Gamble Company.

Comprehension

It must be stressed that attraction of attention does not guarantee comprehension, because the filter within the central control unit can function to categorize the meaning of the stimulus in a way which deviates from objective reality.

Voting studies indicate that recipients of communications interpret them largely in accord with their attitudes. Consider this comment:

Voters cannot have contact with the whole world of people and ideas; they must *sample* them. And the sampling is biased. People pick the people and the ideas to suit their personal equilibrium and then project that sample upon the universe. First, selective perception, then misperception, then strengthening of opinion, and then, in turn, more selective perception.[29]

Two other recent studies confirm these observations. The main result of the telethon conducted by the late Senator Knowland was reinforcement of existing dispositions to vote for Knowland.[30] Similarly, the John Kennedy–Richard Nixon debates, as measured by political leanings before and after exposure to the telecasts, failed to change voting intentions to a great extent.[31] Although Kennedy's image apparently was improved somewhat in the eyes of most voters, the primary effect was adjustment of the images of the candidates to suit viewers' political preferences.

Some of the most convincing evidence can be found in studies of persuasion designed to counteract cigarette smoking. In C. F. Cannell and J. C. MacDonald's research, for example, articles claiming a relationship between smoking and cancer were reacted to favorably by 54 percent of nonsmokers as compared with only 28 percent of smokers,[32] and similar results were found in a more recent study.[33] It may be that the alleged relationship between smoking and cancer is threatening to some smokers, with the result that acceptance of the evidence is resisted. Others, however, are able to live with the inconsistency generated by this knowledge, as well as with continued smoking.[34]

Selective comprehension has been found to take the form of:

1. Distortion and misinterpretation of appeals to make them consistent with attitudes.

---

[29] B. R. Berelson, P. F. Lazarsfeld, and W. N. McPhee, *Voting* (Chicago: University of Chicago Press, 1954), p. 232.

[30] Schramm and Carter, "Effectiveness of a Political Telethon."

[31] K. Lang and Gladys E. Lang, "Ordeal by Debate: Viewer Reactions," *Public Opinion Quarterly,* Vol. 25 (1961), pp. 277–88.

[32] Cannell and MacDonald, "Impact of Health News."

[33] M. T. O'Keefe, "The Anti-Smoking Commercials: A Study of Television's Impact on Behavior," *Public Opinion Quarterly,* Vol. 35 (1971), pp. 242–48.

[34] Ibid.

2. Rejection of the source and message as being biased.
3. Communication of factual information but short-circuiting of the persuasive appeal.[35]

A reader opposed to fluoride may read the advertisement in Figure 4–6, for example, and completely distort the message. He might overlook any reference to fluoride and simply notice that brushing more often reduces cavities in children. Or it is possible that he will reject the message as being incorrect because of his mistaken belief that fluoride is harmful. Finally, he may retain such factual information as a need for a regular checkup while overlooking the appeal to use Crest regularly.

Thus *exposure* to an advertisement by no means infers that the message will be perceived as the advertiser intends. Those with contradictory attitudes can completely short-circuit the appeal. This short-circuiting process would be far less likely with those who already favor the use of fluoride and, more specifically, the use of the brand in the example above.

Retention

It is generally recognized that individuals retain in memory that which is relevant for their needs, values, and other predispositions. Much advertising is forgotten, therefore, because it is largely irrelevant to those who are exposed.

One frequently quoted experiment conducted in 1941 pertained to an attempt to change attitudes toward the Soviet Union.[36] Small Communist and anti-Communist groups, each with strong feelings, served as subjects. First the memory ability of each person was tested. Then all subjects were exposed to anti-Communist and pro-Communist passages. A period of 15 minutes intervened, and each subject was asked to recall what he had read. This procedure was repeated at weekly intervals for four consecutive weeks, as part of a secondary objective to measure learning ability. Then memory was tested at five weekly intervals without the paragraph present. The results indicated that remembering was more accurate when the material learned was consistent with initial biases.

If selective recall is a commonplace phenomenon, it would be reasonable to expect that the nonbeliever in therapeutic value of fluoride would probably forget that he ever read the advertisement in Figure 4–6. The message would probably be retained longer by those whose attitudes favor the use of fluoridated toothpaste. Nevertheless, recall drops rapidly among all who are exposed. In one study it was found that only 24 per-

---

[35] The basic evidence is reviewed in Engel, Kollat, and Blackwell, *Consumer Behavior,* pp. 218–20.

[36] J. M. Levine and G. Murphy, "The Learning and Forgetting of Controversial Material," in T. M. Newcomb and E. L. Hartley (eds.), *Readings in Social Psychology* (New York: Henry Holt & Co., 1947), pp. 108–15.

cent could name at least one advertised product on the television show they were watching. Only one third could identify a commercial which had appeared within less than two minutes prior to an interview. Residual recall after a longer period of time leveled off at 12 percent.[37] See also the data in Figure 4–1.

One plausible explanation why this rapid fading of memory occurs was pointed out above—attitude-discrepant material is more readily forgotten. Others have been unable to find the same results.[38] J. C. Brigham and S. W. Cook, for example, have concluded that the attitude-memory relationship, if it exists at all, applies only under certain circumstances which are not as yet understood.[39]

The boredom barrier hypothesis may be a more reasonable explanation for why so much advertising is forgotten. Most of the appeals are for familiar products which are of only minor psychological relevance to the consumer. If the message is more novel or if it features a product more closely related to the consumer's ego, different results may be found.

Subliminal Perception

Because the issue arises so frequently, it is necessary to comment briefly on whether or not people can be influenced without their awareness. The more technical term for this type of influence is subliminal perception. Subliminal perception is said to occur if stimuli are correctly perceived or categorized when they are presented at a speed which is below threshold (i.e., faster than the point at which correct stimulus identification occurs 50 percent of the time).[40]

A controversy arose a number of years ago when James Vicary presumably flashed the words "Drink Coke" and "Eat Popcorn" on a movie screen at speeds below the thresholds of audience members.[41] Supposedly sales of Coca-Cola increased 18.1 percent, while sales of popcorn increased 57.7 percent. Vicary's findings have been unanimously dismissed as methodologically invalid by his peers, and nearly all attempts at

---

[37] Leo Bogart, *Strategy in Advertising* (New York: Harcourt, Brace, & World, 1967), ch. 5.

[38] See A. G. Greenwald and J. S. Sakumura, "Attitude in Selective Learning: Where Are the Phenomena of Yesteryear?" *Journal of Personality and Social Psychology,* Vol. 7 (1967), pp. 387–97, and P. Waly and S. W. Cook, "Attitude as a Determinant of Learning and Memory: A Failure to Confirm," *Journal of Personality and Social Psychology,* Vol. 4 (1966), pp. 280–88.

[39] J. C. Brigham and S. W. Cook, "The Influence of Attitude on the Recall of Controversial Material: A Failure to Confirm," *Journal of Experimental Social Psychology,* Vol. 5 (1969), pp. 240–43.

[40] See W. N. Dember, *The Psychology of Perception* (New York: Holt, Rinehart & Winston, 1961), ch. 2.

[41] J. J. Bachrach, "The Ethics of Tachistoscopy," *Bulletin of the Atomic Scientists,* Vol. 15 (1959), pp. 212–15.

replication have failed. Only one replication in a marketing context reportedly shows that levels of drive can be affected by subliminal presentation, while behavior remains unchanged.[42] Nevertheless, the popular press sounded the alarm that it is now possible to influence the consumer without his awareness. If this is true, a serious ethical question is raised.

The critics' fears are without foundation, however, because it is now known that consumers continue to perceive selectively even when stimuli are presented at subliminal levels. One study revealed that GSR scores (electroconductivity of the skin) respond before individuals can give verbal responses when they are exposed to such taboo stimuli as swear words.[43] This indicates that perceptual defense can function at below-threshold levels. Other studies have found the same effect; one of the most definitive reports demonstrates that GSR does not register at all when speed of exposure is so fast that no perception is possible.[44] Hence the power to screen out unwanted stimuli apparently is retained until that point is reached at which perception is impossible.

Given these findings, it is clear that subliminal advertising will not circumvent the consumer's natural defenses. Thus there is little merit in using a fragmentary stimulus and thereby increasing the probability that the message will not be seen.

SUMMARY

This chapter has examined the manner in which the consumer processes persuasive messages. It was noted that there are a number of phases: exposure, attention, comprehension, retention, and response. Following exposure, preattentive processing classifies the stimulus, largely on physical properties. Further processing then takes place to determine the pertinence of the stimulus for the individual in terms of dispositions and needs. Both phases must be completed before the stimulus can be said to have attracted attention. The individual thus filters incoming messages, and many messages will fail to attract attention. Moreover, filtering continues in that not all stimuli that capture attention are correctly comprehended, retained, or responded to. Selective information processing was shown to be a pivotal concern in marketing communications, and the reasons for its importance as well as some of the social implications of its use were explored.

---

[42] Dell Hawkins, "The Effects of Subliminal Stimulation on Drive Level and Brand Preference," *Journal of Marketing Research*, Vol. 7 (1970), pp. 322–36.

[43] E. McGinnies, "Emotionality and Perceptual Defense," *Psychological Review*, Vol. 56 (1949), pp. 244–51.

[44] J. H. Voor, "Subliminal Perception and Subception," *Journal of Psychology*, Vol. 41 (1956), pp. 437–58.

REVIEW AND DISCUSSION QUESTIONS

1. A reader's attention is attracted by a back-cover advertisement in a popular magazine. The advertisement is in four colors and features a new model of color television. What does it mean to say that attention is attracted? How does it happen? What can artists and writers do to influence preattentive processing? To influence analysis for pertinence?

2. Assume that a teen-ager cannot remember seeing advertisements for any other brand of deodorant than her preferred brand, even though she has just finished paging through a consumer magazine featuring advertisements for five competing brands, one of which was a two-page, four-color spread. What explanations can be given?

3. Most of the examples given of selective information processing come from the literature of the behavioral sciences and do not refer directly to consumer buying situations. Can the generalizations advanced be applied to consumer response to promotion? Why, or why not?

4. Under what circumstances might you expect perceptual defense to affect the perception of brand names?

5. A leading critic of advertising contends that advertising has the power to influence people to buy unwisely—to act in a way which they would not otherwise. What would your response be?

6. Assume that you have been given the assignment to investigate the possibility of subliminal presentation of advertisements on television for a brand of hair spray. What problems could occur? What would happen if similar attempts were to be made in women's magazines?

7. Under what circumstances, if any, would you expect to encounter consumer avoidance of attitude-discrepant advertisements?

8. What is the "boredom barrier"? How does it affect response to advertising?

5

Demand: The Social Environment

MAN COULD SURVIVE only with great difficulty if he were forced to cope with his environment without the help and support of those around him. The goods and services most people take for granted would not exist. The human being cannot develop in a nonsocial environment, a fact underscored by the animalistic behavior exhibited by children forced to survive in noncivilized surroundings. People in close contact for extended periods of time have remarkably related preferences and behavior. Their actions are correlated, and this has real significance for planning promotional strategy.

The discussion in this chapter proceeds from the broadest level of social influence, culture, to the most intimate face-to-face interaction between the individual and those who serve as reference groups. Attention is focused on those aspects which make Western culture unique, the function of smaller cultural subgroups such as race and social class, and the impact of reference groups on decision making. Family influences on consumer decision making are discussed in greater detail in Chapter 7.

THE CULTURAL CONTEXT

The term "culture" is used here to refer to that complex of ideas, values, attitudes, and other meaningful symbols created by man to shape human behavior, and the artifacts of that culture as they are transmitted from one generation to another.[1] An understanding of culture provides meaningful clues to *why* certain decision processes and consumption acts

---

[1] Alfred L. Kroeber and Talcott Parsons, "The Concepts of Culture and of Social System," *American Sociological Review,* Vol. 23 (October 1958), p. 583.

are preferred over others. In the most fundamental sense, man's ways of perceiving his world are molded by his cultural background.[2]

The Significance of a Cross-Cultural Perspective

Some maintain that consumer behavior is influenced by factors which are universal and largely beyond cultural influences,[3] but many organizations have discovered to their peril that assumptions based on Western experience can lead to disastrous results. For example:

The managers of a joint-venture tobacco company in an Asian country were warned that their proposed new locally named (a token adaptation) and manufactured filtered cigarettes would fail. Filters had not yet been introduced there. Nevertheless, the resident Western managers, along with their local executives whose SRC (self-reference criterion) was dominantly Western because of their social class and education, puffed smugly on their own U.S. filtered cigarettes while the product flopped, leaving the company with idle equipment and uncovered setup and launch costs.

The basic reason for the prediction of failure was a difference in fear of death—especially from cancer of the lungs. A life expectancy of 29 years in that Asian country does not place many people in the lung cancer age bracket. Moreover, for those in this age bracket, there is not the general cultural value of sanitation, the literacy rate, or a *Reader's Digest* type of magazine to motivate them to give up unfiltered cigarettes.[4]

Numerous other illustrations are available of what is known as *ethnocentrism*—the tendency to evaluate all other cultures against a unique frame of reference such as the Western one.[5] Such an attitude is completely untenable. The foundation of marketing strategy must, without exception, be an adequate understanding of cultural foundations.[6]

Cross-Cultural Marketing Research

Cross-cultural marketing research is only in its infancy, but its importance is being increasingly recognized.[7] While a detailed review of

---

[2] R. P. Cuzzort, *Humanity and Modern Sociological Thought* (New York: Holt, Rinehart & Winston, 1969), p. 256.

[3] Erik Elinder, "How International Can European Advertising BE?" *Journal of Marketing,* Vol. 29 (1965), pp. 7–11.

[4] J. A. Lee, "Cultural Analysis in Overseas Operations," *Harvard Business Review,* Vol. 44 (March–April 1966), p. 107. Copyright 1966 by the fellows of Harvard College; reproduced by special permission.

[5] See, for example, J. H. Donnelly, Jr., and J. K. Ryans, Jr., "The Role of Culture in Organizing Overseas Operations: The Advertising Experience," *University of Washington Business Review,* Vol. 30 (1969), pp. 35–41.

[6] For an analysis of the relationship between culture and marketing strategy see M. S. Sommers and J. B. Kernan, "Why Products Flourish Here, Fizzle There," *Columbia Journal of World Business,* Vol. 2 (1967), pp. 89–97.

[7] See J. N. Sheth and S. Prakash Sethi, "Theory of Cross-Cultural Buyer Behavior," Faculty Working Paper No. 115, University of Illinois, May 31, 1973.

FIGURE 5–1
Outline of Cross-Cultural Analysis of Consumer Behavior

---

1. *Determine relevant motivations in the culture:*

    What needs are fulfilled with this product in the minds of members of the culture? How are these needs presently fulfilled? Do members of this culture readily recognize these needs?

2. *Determine characteristic behavior patterns:*

    What patterns are characteristic of purchasing behavior? What forms of division of labor exist within the family structure? How frequently are products of this type purchased? What size packages are normally purchased? Do any of these characteristic behaviors conflict with behavior expected for this product? How strongly ingrained are the behavior patterns that conflict with those needed for distribution of this product?

3. *Determine what broad cultural values are relevant to this product:*

    Are there strong values about work, morality, religion, family relations, and so on, that relate to this product? Does this product connote attributès that are in conflict with these cultural values? Can conflicts with values be avoided by changing the product? Are there positive values in this culture with which the product might be identified?

4. *Determine characteristic forms of decision making:*

    Do members of the culture display a studied approach to decisions concerning innovations, or an inpulsive approach? What is the form of the decision process? Upon what information sources do members of the culture rely? Do members of the culture tend to be rigid or flexible in the acceptance of new ideas? What criteria do they use in evaluating alternatives?

5. *Evaluate promotion methods appropriate to the culture:*

    What role does advertising occupy in the culture? What themes, words, and illustrations are taboo? What language problems exist in present markets that cannot be translated into this culture? What types of salesmen are accepted by members of the culture? Are such salesmen available?

6. *Determine appropriate institutions for this product in the minds of consumers:*

    What types of retailers and intermediary institutions are available? What services do these institutions offer that are expected by the consumer? What alternatives are available for obtaining services needed for the product but not offered by existing institutions? How are various types of retailers regarded by consumers? Will changes in the distribution structure be readily accepted?

From *Consumer Behavior*, Second Edition, by James F. Engel, David T. Kollatt and Roger D. Blackwell. Copyright © 1968, 1973 by Holt, Rinehart and Winston, Inc. Reprinted by permission of Holt, Rinehart & Winston, Inc.

---

appropriate methods is beyond the scope of this text,[8] Figure 5–1 provides an outline for use in cross-cultural analysis.[9] Answers to the questions proposed will provide the necessary information for the development of an appropriate promotional strategy in a specific culture.

---

[8] For a thorough review, see James F. Engel, David T. Kollat, and Roger D. Blackwell, *Consumer Behavior,* rev. ed. (New York: Holt, Rinehart & Winston, 1973), ch. 4.

[9] For a different perspective, see Sheth and Sethi, "Theory of Cross-Cultural Behavior."

The American Culture

Though America as a whole is composed of many subcultures, there are certain pervasive factors in all of them. Change, of course, is continuous, and many values have undergone substantial modification, especially in the younger segments. The forecasting of these changes and their impact on buying decisions has become an important part of the skills of consumer research.[10]

Institutional Influences on Values. Three institutions are primarily responsible for the transfusion of values from one generation to another: (1) the family, (2) the school, and (3) religion. If these institutions were stable, values would be stable. However, these institutions are changing rapidly, and there have been some significant results.

THE FAMILY. In many societies the basic family unit consists of members of the *extended family*—i.e., grandparents, uncles and aunts, and so on. The net effect is that values tend to be stable and resistant to change. In Western society, however, the extended family becomes separated, and thus one source of value stability disappears.

The influence of the family also is affected by such factors as rapidly rising divorce rates, the growing incidence of working wives, and the relative absence of fathers from the home because of occupational pressures (often referred to as the phenomenon of the "weekend father"). Collectively, these changes have resulted in less parent-child involvement and reduced opportunity for parents to instill their values in children. It is small wonder that the values of today's consumers differ from those of their parents.

THE SCHOOL. Schools have increased their contacts with people through rising preschool and college enrollments. Of greater significance, however, are profound changes within the school itself. First, the teacher of today is no longer necessarily a product of the upper middle class, with the result that a wider spectrum of perspectives and values is communicated. Second, there is a decreased emphasis on description and memorization in favor of analytical approaches questioning old solutions and formulating new ones. Often there are no correct answers to problems, and rigid definitions of "right and wrong" are rejected. Thus the consumer mind of today does not operate in a framework of black or white.

RELIGION. Annual Gallup polls ask people to reflect on the influence of religion on American life. In 1959 only 14 percent felt religion was losing its influence, but current reactions indicate approximately 70 percent believe this to be the case. There is considerable evidence, in particular, that younger people reject traditional religious values to a greater degree than their counterparts did in earlier generations. Thus values are being established in more personal and more diversified ways.

---

[10] Alvin Toffler, *Future Shock* (New York: Random House, 1970).

It should be noted, however, that rejection of the traditional religious institution does not imply diminished interest in the divine or the supernatural. Quite the opposite is true, as indicated by the influence of the Jesus movement, the occult, eastern religions, and so on.

IMPLICATIONS OF INSTITUTIONAL INFLUENCES. Of the three institutional determinants of value transfusion, two are losing their influence—the family and religion. The educational institution thus assumes a more profound role in this setting. Traditional value stabilizers are not so functional, and change must be accepted as a way of life.

The Rising Influence of Youth. Significant population growth in the 1970s in the United States (as in other countries) has been concentrated among segments under age 35, especially those in the 25–34 bracket.[11] By 1980 this will be the most important age category in terms of purchasing power. Not surprisingly, marketers are placing increased emphasis upon the so-called "youth market."[12]

The great majority of under–35 consumers had not been born during the depression of the 1930s, and only a minority were alive during World War II. These two events were pivotal in shaping the values of the older generations; the relative economic deprivation of the depression and the war led to emphasis on values such as job security, patriotism, and material achievement. Such achievements help fill the void of what they were deprived of as children.

The critical lifetime experience of the younger consumer, on the other hand, has been shaped by such factors as the nuclear age, the civil rights movement, the paradox of continued poverty in an economy of affluence, ecological concern, and a revolution in communication technology. The influence of these factors has been accentuated by the declining influence of the family and a concern about the absence of love and meaningful relationships. Thus for many the basic life motivation centers on love, community, and understanding, as opposed to material achievement. An appeal to American patriotism based on a high and rising gross national product and standard of living will be rejected as hypocritical by this generation because of the by-products of pollution such production entails, together with the effects of the factors mentioned above. In short, their perceptual filters are closed to appeals which remain meaningful to people who grew up in other eras.

Emerging American Values. American values are being affected by emerging cultural traits, many of which represent modifications of more long-standing traditions. The emerging values described here include

---

[11] See D. T. Kollat, R. D. Blackwell, and J. F. Robeson, *Strategic Marketing* (New York: Holt, Rinehart & Winston, 1972), ch. 6.

[12] See, for example, "Identity Crisis in Consumer Markets," *Fortune,* Vol. 83 (March 1971), pp. 92–95 ff., and Lee Adler, "Cashing in on the Cop-Out," *Business Horizons,* Vol. 13 (1970), pp. 19–30.

(1) creative eroticism, (2) the leisure life, (3) the theology of pleasure, (4) youthfulness, and (5) security.

CREATIVE EROTICISM. Contemporary society is characterized by a lifting of constraints, especially concerning sex. While this does not necessarily signal great change in behavior, there undeniably is a much greater willingness to talk openly about previously taboo issues.

In a very real sense, contemporary advertising can be characterized as in the midst of a sexual revolution. The advertisement for the Rice Council in Figure 5–2 represents an unusually direct use of this appeal. Not surprisingly, the appeal to sex has generated considerable controversy. Some assert that it can only contribute to declining standards of morality.[13] Others justify the emphasis as long as it sells the product. Unfortunately, many who take this latter position never stop to question whether sex is a *relevant* appeal for the product in question. Is it relevant, for example, to sell rice on the basis of a sexual suggestion as opposed to featuring such product benefits as flavor and uses? There is no doubt that attention will be attracted, but it is an open question whether or not sales will be affected. Unfortunately, sex can become a misused creative gimmick.

It is incorrect, however, to claim that the use of sex in advertising, in itself, is contributing greatly to moral decline. It must not be overlooked that this appeal was almost totally unused in earlier decades for the reason that social values were greatly different. The Rice Council advertisements probably would have met with selective attention, comprehension, and retention. On the other hand, there is no question that uninhibited sexuality is given endorsement when it is so widely seen in the mass media, and this may serve to accentuate what many view as a socially deleterious decline in morals. Thus it should be used only where it is appropriate to the product in question, and then with discretion.

THE LEISURE LIFE. One major change is less emphasis on the values of hard work and long hours and a correspondingly greater emphasis upon leisure. Justin Voss offers this insightful comment: *"Leisure* is a period of time referred to as *discretionary time*. It is that period of time when an individual feels no sense of economic, legal, moral, or social compulsion or obligation nor of physiological necessity. The choice of how to utilize this time period is solely his."[14]

Thus the budget of time available for leisure may be a more significant factor in buying and consumption than the budget of available money. Time-saving appliances, for example, assume a new importance, and

---

[13] See for example Kathy McNeel, "You Dirty Old Ad Men Make Me Sick," *Detroit News,* November 25, 1969.

[14] Justin Voss, "The Definition of Leisure," *Journal of Economic Issues,"* Vol. 1 (1967), pp. 91–106.

FIGURE 5–2
An Appeal to Sex

Used with the permission of
the Rice Council of America.

consumers are prepared to pay the monetary cost in return for increased leisure. Longer vacations, earlier retirement, more holidays are becoming more common, as is the four-day work week. Henry Ford said in 1926 that "It is the influence of leisure on consumption which makes the short day and the short week so necessary."[15]

THE THEOLOGY OF PLEASURE. Traditionally, the American religious heritage has emphasized the worth of an individual, and values have developed which condone consumption of products for reasons of self-interest and fulfillment of reasonable physical needs. It has been stressed that the ways to achieve these goal objects are hard work and the accumulation of wealth. It is this set of values, often identified as the Puritan ethic, which is under increasing challenge in today's culture.

The Puritan ethic is being replaced with a theology of pleasure, which releases prohibitions on pleasure and challenges the legitimacy of "delayed gratification." The demand for leisure, of course, is just one expression of this new theology. It also is manifested in such things as the general acceptance of bright and sensual colors, cosmetics which emphasize bodily pleasure (Figure 5–3 is an example), and products for personal use which previously would not even be hinted at in intimate conversation, let alone the mass media (Figure 5–4).

YOUTHFULNESS. At one time, the aged were objects of veneration and prestige. Experience with life brought respect and considerable social influence. Today the primacy of experience has been usurped by education and creativity, so that the educated college graduate may receive greater prestige and influence than the seasoned senior executive. The result is that the young are increasingly being given responsibility for running society in general, as well as its institutions.

The social rewards for youthfulness generate powerful motivations to appear as youthful, regardless of chronological age. Figure 5–5 shows an advertisement which capitalizes on this desire. Another illustration is provided by the market acceptance of a sporty compact car with an image of racing and sensuality. Although this car was introduced as a direct appeal to youth, the age of the typical buyer turned out to be 46!

SECURITY. Americans, on the whole, used to believe that they controlled their own destinies, or at least that they should do so. That probably is still true as a verbal value for the majority, but behavior today indicates increasing reliance on institutions to cope with the basic problems of life and survival. And, increasingly, the institution relied upon to meet these needs is government—local, state, and federal.

The change from self-reliance to reliance on outside agencies is traceable to the desire for security in the provision of the basic amenities of life. Governmental transcendence is only for selected aspects of life,

---

[15] As quoted in Engel, Kollat, and Blackwell, *Consumer Behavior,* p. 106.

FIGURE 5–3

Emphasis on the Pleasure of Bodily Concern

The blushing generation wears

'Blush-On'

the first and only (can't-be-copied)
totally transparent blusher

Nothing turns on that 'real thing' glow like 'Blush-On'. The
sheerest breath of color you fluff on all over your face. Other
blushers are obvious put-ons. Only 'Blush-On' looks sincere.
Because the color is transparent. Like the real thing. It's made
a whole generation of beauties blush. As if they meant it.

'Blush-On' invented by Revlon

Reproduced with the permission of the Revlon Company.

FIGURE 5–4

Advertisement for a Previously Taboo Product

Ten very personal questions

(With answers to match)

1. Does a woman need more than an underarm deodorant?

Yes.

2. Is there another kind of deodorant made especially to complete feminine confidence?

Yes. There's FDS*... feminine hygiene deodorant spray.

3. What is FDS?

FDS is the accepted feminine hygiene deodorant spray for the most personal part of you, the external vaginal area. The spray is gentle, lightly scented, almost warm. Best of all, it is a spray, applied externally.

4. How safe is FDS?

FDS is so gentle, you can use it as often as you wish. FDS has been tested by doctors and proven to be most gentle in a clinical study.

5. Does FDS stop odor or mask it or does it have an odor of its own? What should I expect?

FDS is formulated to help eliminate offensive odor, and also the fear of odor. FDS contains the best known odor-fighting ingredients available to modern science. FDS has a very faint, delicate scent (not strong enough to clash with your favorite perfume . . . not strong enough so people will know you are wearing it).

6. How often should FDS be used?

For a feeling of total confidence—use FDS daily.

7. What kind of woman uses FDS?

The modern woman surrounded by people. Active and actively feminine. The woman who wants to feel fresher. The nice-to-be-near woman uses FDS.

8. Can FDS be used during the menstrual period?

Yes. FDS keeps you fresh and feminine every day . . . even during "that time of the month."

9. Does FDS come in any other form?

Yes. New FDS towelettes are the same FDS formula in handy take-along form. Lint-free, premoistened cloths in purse-size, foil-wrapped packets go everywhere you go.

10. Where can FDS be purchased?

You'll find FDS Spray and FDS Towelettes wherever personal products are sold.

The first feminine hygiene deodorant spray.

Reproduced with the permission of the Alberto-Culver Company.

FIGURE 5–5

An Appeal to Youthfulness

Hands off that bridal bouquet, Mrs. Massnick!

Even though your hands have that creamy, young, un-married look, we know you're sixteen years older than those other bridesmaids. You're thirty-eight—and married and wash dishes for your husband and four gorgeous children. Of course, creamy-looking mild Ivory Liquid helps leave any married lady's hands with that creamy, young, un-married look. But that doesn't mean you Ivory Liquid ladies can go around catching bridal bouquets. Just be real proud of your young-looking hands.

Source: Used with permission of the Procter & Gamble Company.

however, not for all of it. Few are willing to accept infringement on their personal rights, but there is strong acceptance of such actions as regulation of waste, conservation, rent control, and protection of consumer interests.

There are several effects of rising dependence on the government. First, the increasing interest in consumerism probably indicates that consumers expect products to be safe for consumption and not to be fraudulently sold. Increasingly, government is relied upon to ensure that this is true. Additionally, government is expected to *provide* a wider range of products and services than ever before, such as medical services, low-priced housing, retirement, and transportation.

At a more fundamental level of analysis, it can be expected that increasing dependence upon government will change the basic orientation of buying decisions. As consumers come to expect that provision will be made for the basic needs of food, shelter, medical care, and education, they will be freed from these concerns as the focus of much of their activity. Thus it is likely that pleasure, fashion, and other accouterments of gracious living will dominate consumption. Nonsecurity themes will be the rule in marketing strategies, even for products that fulfill basic needs. The home-buying decision, for example, shifts from evaluation of the shelter provided to an emphasis on the character of life facilitated by a residential environment.

Marketing and the Question of Values.   Since our discussion has only been suggestive of the basic values of American culture and their influence on buyer behavior, the reader is encouraged to explore this subject more deeply.[16] Up to this point it has been assumed that the business firm must adapt to culture and that an individual organization is powerless to bring about much change. This assumption is sharply challenged by some critics, however. Some allege that marketing is largely responsible for certain adverse aspects of the world as we know it today. Advertising, in particular, is identified as the villain that has brought undue emphasis on materialism, youthfulness, and so on. It cannot be denied that the sheer volume of marketing stimuli will have some influence in this manner, but it is quite another matter to argue, for example, that marketing *causes* materialism.

It must be remembered that consumers retain the powers to screen out unwanted appeals through selective perception. Given this pervasive human response to unwanted stimuli, it is fallacious to claim that advertising and other forms of promotion have caused materialism. Striving for a high and rising standard of living is a basic motivation, and promotional efforts are only a reflection of the fact that this is basic to our way of life. In the most basic sense, *marketing reflects the values of a society.*

---

[16] For a thorough review see Ibid., ch. 4.

If present consumption patterns and emphases may lead to long-run adverse effects (this may well be the case, as is argued in Chapter 23), the primary blame lies in the area of human values, not in the practices of business firms.

SUBCULTURES

Within society as a whole there are many subcultures or groups organized around such attributes as nationality, religion, geographical areas, or race. Often these form important markets in their own right. Geographic segmentation is discussed in Chapter 9, but it is useful here to describe briefly the differences in motivation and consumption which characterize one important subculture—the "black market."

The black subculture is a rapidly growing segment which shows some distinct differences from its counterparts in other marketing segments: (1) buying patterns, (2) communication behavior, and (3) purchasing patterns.

Buying Patterns[17]

Significant buying patterns among black people include:

1. Blacks save more out of a given income than do whites,[18] but they use fewer savings services and hence do not attain the relative well-being of the white household.[19]
2. They spend more for clothing and nonautomobile transportation; less for food, housing, medical care, and automobiles; and roughly equal proportions for recreation and leisure and home-centered items with comparable levels of whites.[20]
3. There is a tendency to own higher price class automobiles than comparable-income white families.[21]
4. Blacks seem to be more brand loyal than equivalent whites.[22]

---

[17] For a more thorough review see R. A. Bauer and S. M. Cunningham, *Studies in the Negro Market* (Cambridge, Mass.: Marketing Science Institute, 1970).

[18] Marcus Alexis, "Some Negro-White Differences in Consumption," *American Journal of Economics and Sociology,* Vol. 21 (January 1962).

[19] S. Roxanne Hiltz, "Black and White in the Consumer Financial System," *American Journal of Sociology,* Vol. 76 (1971), pp. 987–99.

[20] Alexis, "Some Negro-White Differences"; also James Stafford, Keith Cox and James Higginbottom, "Some Consumption Pattern Differences between Urban Whites and Negroes," *Social Science Quarterly,* (1968), pp. 619–30.

[21] F. C. Akers, "Negro and White Automobile-Buying Behavior: New Evidence," *Journal of Marketing Research,* Vol. 5 (1968), pp. 283–90.

[22] F. G. Davis, *Differential Factors in the Negro Market,* (Chicago: National Association of Market Developers, 1959), p. 6; privately published report based upon data collected by *Ebony* magazine.

5. The black family purchases more milk and soft drinks, less tea and coffee, and more liquor than its white counterpart.[23]

Communication Behavior

The communication behavior of blacks is likely to be characterized by the following:

1. The black can apparently be reached more effectively by general media for those products that have a nonracial appeal, whereas black-oriented media are more appropriate for products specifically directed to this segment.[24]
2. The black reacts more favorably to advertisements with all-black models or to integrated models,[25] although those under age 30 are negative to advertisements with integrated settings.[26]
3. Black consumers appear to show greater recall and attitude shift in response to advertisements than do whites.[27]
4. Black television viewers dislike programs emphasizing white-oriented subjects and watch more on the weekend than do whites.[28]

Purchasing Patterns

Tendencies in the purchasing patterns characteristic of blacks include:

1. The black appears to have greater awareness of brands and to be better informed about prices than the white consumer.[29]
2. Black consumers are less likely to shop by phone or mail order.[30]

---

[23] R. O. Oladipupo, *How Distinct Is the Negro Market?* (New York: Ogilvy & Mather, Inc., 1970), pp. 30–34. Data from Bernard Howard & Co. and *Ebony*.

[24] J. V. Petrof, "Reaching the Negro Market: A Segregated vs. a General Newspaper," *Journal of Advertising Research*, Vol. 8 (1968), pp. 40–43.

[25] B. S. Tolley and J. J. Goett, "Reactions to Blacks in Newspapers," *Journal of Advertising Research*, Vol. 11 (1971), pp. 107–9.

[26] J. W. Gould, N. B. Sigband, and C. E. Zoerner, Jr., "Black Consumer Reactions to 'Integrated' Advertising: An Exploratory Study," *Journal of Marketing*, Vol. 34 (1970), pp. 20-26.

[27] Tolley and Goett, "Reactions to Blacks in Newspapers," pp. 13–14; Petrof, "Reaching the Negro Market," p. 42.

[28] J. W. Carey, "Variations in Negro-White Television Preference," *Journal of Broadcasting*, Vol. 10 (1966), pp. 199–211.

[29] R. L. King and E. R. DeManche, "Comparative Acceptance of Selected Private-Branded Food Products by Low-Income Negro and White Families," in P. R. McDonald (ed.), *Marketing Involvement in Society and the Economy* (Chicago: American Marketing Association, 1969), pp. 63–69; L. P. Feldman and A. D. Star, "Racial Factors in Shopping Behavior," in Keith Cox and Ben Enis (eds.), *A New Measure of Responsibility for Marketing* (Chicago: American Marketing Association, 1968), pp. 216–26.

[30] Feldman and Star, "Racial Factors in Shopping Behavior."

3. Blacks tend to shop more at discount stores as compared to the department store than comparable white consumers.[31]
4. Black consumers tend to be unhappier with supermarket facilities and functions than do whites (poor prices, service, etc.).[32]

From a broader point of view, it is useful to probe the frequently heard criticism that the poor (both white and nonwhite) pay more.[33] There is an extensive literature on this subject, in which the findings are contradictory.[34] At this point it appears safe to generalize that retailers usually do not discriminate between buyers on the basis of ethnic characteristics. The poor still may pay more, however, because of fewer supermarkets and discount outlets in their immediate neighborhoods, differences in quality and service, and a greater tendency to purchase in small quantities and small package sizes.[35]

SOCIAL CLASS

One of the most useful ways to stratify a society is in terms of social class. Social classes are large and relatively permanent homogeneous groupings within society which have the function of transmitting cultural patterns to families in such a way that family members have more or less clearly defined expectations about life. People within a class, in other words, *tend* to behave in a like manner. Although America is often thought of as being classless, quite the opposite is true, and the differences between classes are of significance in promotional planning.

Measurement of Social Class

An individual's social position is determined by (1) the prestige of his occupation, (2) performance within his occupational class as evaluated by others, (3) social interactions and acceptance by others, (4) possessions, (5) value orientations, and (6) class consciousness. Any of these criteria could be used to measure social position, but the most commonly used measures in survey research are multiple-item indexes.

[31] Ibid.

[32] J. V. Petrof, "Attitudes of the Urban Poor toward Their Neighborhood Supermarkets," *Journal of Retailing*, Vol. 47 (1971), pp. 3–17.

[33] David Caplovitz, *The Poor Pay More* (New York: Free Press, 1973).

[34] See particularly R. G. Mogull, "Where Do We Stand on Inner City Prices?" *Journal of Retailing*, Vol. 47 (1971), pp. 32–40, and D. E. Sexton, Jr., "Do Blacks Pay More?" *Journal of Marketing Research*, Vol. 8 (1971), pp. 420–26.

[35] Sexton, "Do Blacks Pay More?"; B. W. Marion, L. A. Simonds, and D. E. Moore, "Food Marketing in Low-Income Areas: A Case Study of Columbus, Ohio," *Bulletin of Business Research*, Vol. 45 (August 1970), pp. 1–8; and Richard Teach, "Supermarket Pricing Practices in Various Areas of a Large City," in McDonald (ed.), *Marketing Involvement in Society*, pp. 57–62.

The multiple-item index which has received the greatest use to date is Warner's Index of Status Characteristics (ISC), which utilizes a weighted summation of occupation, source of income, housing type, and dwelling areas. Hollingshead's Index of Social Position (ISP) is similar,[36] and there are a number of other approaches as well.[37]

Social Classes in America

While researchers have utilized different methods of measurement and hence have not exactly agreed on the proportions within each class, the following estimates give a rough indication of the social class structure in America:

1. *Upper-upper*—roughly 1 percent. This is the social elite characterized by inherited wealth.
2. *Lower-upper*—1 to 2 percent. Often called the *nouveaux riches*, members of this class have earned their wealth and position and hence do not have the prestige of those in the upper-upper stratum.
3. *Upper-middle*—10–21 percent. Comprised largely of successful professionals and businessmen earning from $15,000 to $30,000, members of this class have a way of life centered around career, education, and consumption of quality items.
4. *Lower-middle*—28–30 percent. This group is most often described as the "typical Americans." The home is very important; occupation is usually white collar.
5. *Upper-lower*—35–45 percent. This is the largest segment; it is characterized by blue-collar occupations and lack of change in life. This group is discussed in more detail below.
6. *Lower-lower*—10–25 percent. These are the true "forgotten Americans"—the slum dwellers with poor educations.

The Marketing Significance of Social Class

An extensive literature has developed on social class and buying decisions, with the result that some useful generalizations are possible. In addition to market segmentation, these generalizations concern consumer lifestyle and behavior.

---

[36] See W. Lloyd Warner, Marchia Meeker, and Kenneth Eels, *Social Class in America: A Manual of Procedure for the Measurement of Social Status* (Chicago: Science Research Associates, Inc., 1949), and Jerome K. Myers and Bertram H. Roberts, *Family and Class Dynamics in Mental Illness* (New York: John Wiley & Sons, 1959), pp. 24 and 25.

[37] For a thorough review, see Engel, Kollat, and Blackwell, *Consumer Behavior,* pp. 121–30.

Market Segmentation. Social class has proven to be a useful way to differentiate consumer behavior with some product categories,[38] although there is skepticism about its universal value in marketing strategy.[39] In particular, income often is found to be a better predictor of buyer behavior than is social class.[40] The obvious conclusion is that the social-class perspective does not apply in every situation, but it remains, nonetheless, as a useful variable for segmenting markets.

Consumer Lifestyle and Behavior. There are a number of demonstrated differences between social classes in consumer decision making and behavior.[41] Since space does not permit a thorough review of all classes, the blue-collar (upper-lower) class is used as an illustration.[42]

The blue-collar-class housewife traditionally was characterized as centering her values and social life on the home. A feeling of uncertainty and reluctance to think for herself often was manifested in reliance on national brands and other buying patterns which gave her a sense of certainty. The home orientation, in turn, was reflected in the high value placed on the latest in labor-saving appliances and ways to make otherwise dull surroundings as attractive as possible.

1973 findings reflect some dramatic changes in this pattern which are of significance to the marketer. First, the blue-collar wife shows a new confidence in her ability as a consumer and will not accept advertising she feels is trying to derogate her. Second, the emphasis is on a much smaller family, which reflects a modification in the traditional orientation toward the home. Women of the upper-lower class appear to have been influenced by women's liberation to the extent that they do not want to be enslaved by the home. This does not, however, indicate that children and home are unimportant; rather it is a sign that their horizons have broadened.

The market for convenience foods and labor-saving appliances is even greater now in this class than it was in the past decade, but the basic reason is that these products facilitate the expanded role of the wife both inside and outside the home. Furthermore, today's women are more con-

---

[38] See Ibid. and J. A. Howard and J. N. Sheth, *The Theory of Buyer Behavior* (New York: John A. Wiley & Sons, 1969), pp. 87–89.

[39] R. E. Frank, W. F. Massy, and Yoram Wind, *Market Segmentation* (Englewood Cliffs, N.J.: Prentice-Hall, 1972), pp. 47–49.

[40] J. H. Myers, R. R. Stanton, and A. F. Haug, "Correlates of Buying Behavior: Social Class vs. Income," *Journal of Marketing,* Vol. 35 (1971), pp. 8–15.

[41] See Engel, Kollat, and Blackwell, *Consumer Behavior,* pp. 151–57.

[42] Adapted from Lee Rainwater, Richard P. Coleman, and Gerald Handel, *Workingman's Wife* (Dobbs Ferry, N.Y.: Oceana Publications, 1959) and updated by a 1973 study undertaken by Social Research, Inc. for the Macfadden Women's Group, as reported in *Advertising Age,* October 8, 1973, p. 33.

cerned with personal care and grooming and hence offer an expanded market for cosmetics and other personal care products.

The working-class wife is critical of big business as an institution and distrusts its practices. Yet there is little support for consumerism, for the suggested reason that "they are in the midst of a full-blown romance with acquiring new products and services they never had before."[43]

Careful attention must be paid to media choice. *Cosmopolitan* or the *New Yorker* reaches a market segment totally different from this class, whereas *True Story* is an appropriate medium to use. Obviously, data must be available on the audience reach of various media, a subject discussed in depth later.

This short example should make it abundantly clear that buyers differ in ways which are important for promotion. An appeal to the upper-lower class without awareness of motivation and behavior could result in advertisements which do little more than activate the buyer's abilities to screen out the message through selective perception. A well-designed appeal can build effectively on such known motivating influences as strong family involvement by showing how and why the product is an important alternative for need satisfaction.

REFERENCE GROUPS

A reference group is "any interacting aggregation of people *that influences an individual's attitudes or behavior.*"[44] The use of the term "group" may be misleading, because a single individual can perform this same function,[45] but it has become the conventional term and is utilized for that reason.

Sensitivity to the reactions of others takes several forms. First, the individual may be motivated to conform when others are in a position to exert rewards or punishments. Some church groups, for example, prohibit certain forms of behavior, and conformity pressures are strong indeed. The group then serves as a *normative reference* group. Others, however, may also be used simply as evidence about reality. The buyer of a new suit may observe what others are wearing in order to discover the latest styles, while feeling perfectly free to buy what he likes. In this example, others serve as a *comparative reference group*. Finally, a desire may exist to avoid behaving in certain ways which are similar to the ways of those who are unacceptable. The young business executive will consciously avoid wearing the extreme styles of certain youth groups.

---

[43] Quoted from the *Advertising Age* report cited above.

[44] Engel, Kollat, and Blackwell, *Consumer Behavior,* p. 161.

[45] Herbert Hyman, "Reflections on Reference Groups," *Public Opinion Quarterly,* Vol. 24 (1960), pp. 383–96.

Reference Groups and Attitude Change

Some of the most significant studies of the effects of reference group influence on attitude change have been based on analysis of political campaigns. Consider this comment:

It is voters with homogeneous and agreeable associates who believe strongly in the rightness of their candidate and party. . . . Those with friends in both camps are less sure of their vote. Thus, the political conviction of the individual is closely bound to the political character of his personal relations—or at least his perception of their political complexion. A sense of security about one's judgment seems to be a function of the congeniality of the personal environment; here, as elsewhere in the realm of political attitudes and behavior, the private political conscience of the citizen rests upon a near-by group norm represented by the people around him. Without their full support it is not easy to hold strong political attitudes, and relatively few people do.[46]

A myriad of reported studies confirms the importance of group influence on attitudes; unwillingness to recognize this significant relationship no doubt has led to the downfall of many promotional campaigns. The example was presented in an earlier chapter of the failure of propaganda campaigns designed to induce Nazi surrenders early in World War II.[47] Devotion to Hitler and a firm belief in the invincibility of the German army caused propaganda to fall on deaf ears. The onset of unmistakable defeat, however, led to a disintegration of the will to fight and a sharp decline in group morale and solidarity in the army. Only then did appeals to surrender begin to produce results. It was concluded that earlier propaganda contradicted strong group influence, and success followed the crumbling of group support and morale.

Kurt Lewin, on the other hand, effectively contended with group influence on attitude change.[48] It was his assignment to assist the Red Cross during World War II to change attitudes toward the consumption of visceral meats (sweetbreads, hearts, and other internal organs) versus the more scarce cuts. Group discussions were substituted when lectures to housewives produced no visible effects. Interaction between group members seemed to provide the needed support for individual action, and 32 percent responded in a favorable manner.

It seems safe to conclude that persuasion is destined to fall short of its full potential if it contradicts important reference group norms. Strong

---

[46] B. R. Berelson, P. F. Lazarsfeld, and W. N. McPhee, *Voting* (Chicago: University of Chicago Press, 1954), p. 232.

[47] Edward A. Shils and Morris Janowitz, "Cohesion and Disintegration in the Wehrmacht in World War II," in Wilbur Schramm (ed.), *Mass Communications* (Urbana: University of Illinois Press, 1949), pp. 501–16.

[48] Kurt Lewin, "Group Decision and Social Change," in Theodore M. Newcomb and Eugene L. Hartley (eds.), *Readings in Social Psychology* (New York: Henry Holt & Co., 1947), pp. 330–44.

reference group involvement is difficult to overcome, and successful persuasion builds upon this influence, enhances it, and directs it to desired ends by showing how and why the desired action is consistent with this important motivating factor. Undoubtedly, weak group influence can be overcome by appeals to more basic motivational determinants, but the important point is to assess the priority of motivating determinants and to build upon those that are found to be central.

Adapting to Reference Group Influence

Unfortunately, empirical studies on the importance of group influences on consumer behavior are few. In one study it was found that informal groups have a definite influence on brands of bread preferred by their members,[49] although replications of this study at The Ohio State University failed to confirm this finding. In another experiment, group influence was found to influence the type of suit selected by college students,[50] but another researcher found little group influence with certain other products.[51]

The absence of published research inhibits generalizations at this point, but it does appear that group or social influence will vary from one consumption or buying situation to the next. A monograph published many years ago provides some useful insights, and there is no reason to doubt that many of the conclusions advanced are still valid today.[52]

First, certain individuals differ in the extent to which they are sensitive to reference group influence. As might be expected, those who have high group status feel more secure relative to those around them and are most free to deviate when necessary. With such individuals it seems logical to base the promotional appeal on the merits of the case. Those with less status will be more sensitive to group involvement, and powerful appeals may be based on group norms and demands.

Second, social influence is known to be strongest in an informational vacuum. When the consumer has considerable information to guide his actions, others will be less likely to dominate his decisions. In other words, group influence may not be potent if it contradicts other criteria used by the buyer in his decision making.

Third, product visibility seems to be the most important aspect under-

---

[49] J. E. Stafford, "Effects of Group Influence on Consumer Brand Preferences," *Journal of Marketing Research,* Vol. 3 (1966), pp. 68–75.

[50] M. Venkatesan, "Experimental Study of Consumer Behavior Conformity and Independence," *Journal of Marketing Research,* Vol. 3 (1966), pp. 384–87.

[51] Fleming Hansen, "Primary Group Influence and Consumer Conformity," in McDonald (ed.), *Marketing Involvement in Society,* pp. 300–5.

[52] *Group Influence in Marketing and Public Relations* (Ann Arbor, Mich.: Foundation for Research on Human Behavior. 1956).

lying the susceptibility of a product purchase to group influence. If the product stands out and says something to others about the individual, it no doubt will become highly involved with his self-esteem. If everyone uses the product, of course, it is less likely to stand out in this sense. Also it will not stand out if it is consumed in private.

It is instructive for the reader to attempt to apply the criterion of visibility to determine which products and services will show sensitivity to group influence. Notice that this influence can extend to both the product class and the brand. It may be that automobiles, cigarettes, and beer pass the tests of visibility. The ownership of an automobile may be a necessity today, but the brand which is purchased no doubt is determined at least in part by its acceptability in one's social group. Beer is group sensitive in two ways: (1) the group dictates whether or not beer is served and (2) certain brands of beer are more acceptable than others in various social settings. Group involvement in the purchase of cigarettes, however, is less clear cut. Perhaps the product image of certain brands introduces significant variations in acceptability. The reader no doubt can provide many similar examples based on his own observations and experience.

Effective appeals may be made to social influence when the buyer is a follower and not a group leader, when he is in an informational vacuum, and when the product or service is visible and says something to others about the user. This may be accomplished by featuring those who buy and use the product, thereby reinforcing the stereotypes of users. This method was employed successfully in the advertisement reproduced in Figure 5–6. Similarly, important group values or attitudes may be stressed and reinforced in the selling appeal itself. Many more suggestions are given elsewhere in the text.

One caution should be observed, however. It should not be assumed without solid evidence that all buyers are subject to the same type of reference groups. An appeal to one type may alienate key groups of users. A policy of market segmentation (to be discussed later) should be followed in which the appeals and media used are closely tuned to consumer market targets, and variations should be employed to avoid market overlap and the resulting alienation. It can never be assumed that one appeal is appropriate for all.

SUMMARY

This chapter has analyzed the nature and effects on social influence which evolve from culture, social class, and reference groups. A promotional program cannot disregard these factors, because social influence often is of major importance in the purchasing decision.

This chapter could, of course, only highlight some of the major

FIGURE 5–6

An Appeal Reinforcing the Social Stereotypes of Users

Source: Reproduced with the permission of the Taylor Wine Company, Inc.

generalizations from a wealth of research findings. The serious student of consumer behavior will find a vast literature on this subject. Moreover, no direct attention has been paid to the methodological problems which plague research in this area. These difficulties, however, are not sufficient to prevent collection and use of information on social influences. The major strategic implications discussed here should provide the framework for part of the research inquiry underlying every program of promotional strategy.

REVIEW AND DISCUSSION QUESTIONS

1. A well-known business executive made the following statement: "Oh the youth of today are no different from when I was a kid. They will take their place in the business world, and things will carry on. All this stuff about a youth market is just a bunch of bunk." Evaluate.

2. Assume that you are in the position of explaining the traditional Judeo-Christian view of creation to a group of high school seniors today. This viewpoint stresses that God created the world and that evolution is, as yet, an unproved hypothesis. Would you approach the youth of today in a manner different from the approach used for the youth of another generation? If so, how and why?

3. The manufacturer of a new brand of soft drink wishes to gain a high degree of acceptance among Negro consumers in large cities. An advertising strategy is contemplated which will be directed specifically at this group. Is this advisable? What policy recommendations would you make?

4. What variables determine social class? How should they be ranked in importance?

5. The manufacturer of a nationally distributed washday detergent has asked you, as his director of marketing research, to evaluate possible social class influences on use of the product. Would product preferences and consumption patterns vary between social classes? Why, or why not?

6. The operator of a large discount chain is contemplating opening a store in the inner-city area. What precautions would you recommend he take?

7. The manufacturer of a well-known make of electric range is introducing a new model. This model is improved by the addition of a new automatic timing system and a dual oven which allows the housewife to bake at two different temperatures at the same time. Unfortunately, the price is $200 higher than existing models. It is believed, therefore, that promotion should be aimed toward upper-middle-class families. Do you concur? Why, or why not?

8. For which of the following products is reference group influence most likely? (a) canned peaches; (b) diet cola; (c) color television; (d) men's suits; and (e) dining room furniture.

9. Assume that a manufacturer is interested in assessing the influence of reference groups in evaluating why a new automotive diagnostic center has been unsuccessful. The center features a process whereby an automobile is diagnosed mechanically and an objective indication is given of necessary repairs. The price for diagnosis is $9.95. What would your hypothesis be regarding the probable influence of reference groups on consumer choice?

6

Demand: Attitudes and Personality

As THIS CHAPTER continues the discussion of demand analysis, the focus is first on attitudes—basic orientations for or against alternatives for choice and consumption. Because attitudes form a system of evaluative orientations, they comprise the central component of the individual's "map of the world." Behavior also is shaped by personality, which is defined here as enduring traits or characteristics which make a person unique. Of particular significance are demographic and psychographic (lifestyle) characteristics which reflect behavioral differences. This chapter considers the nature and function of attitudes and personality and their implications for promotional strategy.

ATTITUDES

In the context of this book, an attitude refers to "a consumer's assessment of the ability of an alternative to satisfy his purchasing and consumption requirements as expressed in evaluative criteria."[1] As Figure 6–1 indicates, attitudes are formed in the central control unit (see Figure 4–2) from (1) stored information and experience and (2) evaluative criteria, or those specifications used by the individual to compare and evaluate alternatives for choice and consumption.

Attitudes become formed throughout life as individuals learn to cope with day-to-day problems. Certain feelings, beliefs, and responses are repeatedly evoked and thus become stored in memory. The individual

---

[1] James F. Engel, David T. Kollat, and Roger D. Blackwell, *Consumer Behavior,* 2d ed. (New York: Holt, Rinehart & Winston, 1973), p. 267.

FIGURE 6–1

Attitudes in the Central Control Unit

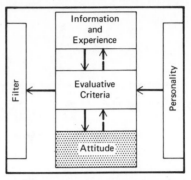

Source: James F. Engel, David T. Kollat, and Roger D. Blackwell, *Consumer Behavior*, 2d ed. (New York: Holt, Rinehart & Winston, 1973).

becomes programmed to think and behave in predictable ways and thus can avoid the difficulties of coping with strange phenomena.[2] More precisely,

1. Attitudes promote an adjustive economy by providing the individual with the ready basis for making decisions. They are dispositions toward objects belonging to certain cognitive categories.
2. Attitudes confer greater stability and social predictability on an individual, making possible the precise and intricate interactions that characterize human beings in contrast to lower organisms.[3]

Attitude Organization

Attitudes exist within a complex structure that seems to impart a consistent tendency to resist change and maintain balance. Therefore it is necessary to understand why resistance to change takes place and the ways in which this process is manifested.

Internal Consistency. The components of attitude exist in balance, and introduction of inconsistency is resisted.[4] Each individual seems to have a tolerance limit for inconsistency. When this point is reached changes take place to restore balance through (1) screening out the stimulus input that induced inconsistency, (2) a fragmentation of the

---

[2] Edward E. Jones and Harold B. Gerard, *Foundations of Social Psychology* (New York: John Wiley & Sons, 1967), ch. 7.

[3] Ibid., p. 433.

[4] M. J. Rosenberg, "Inconsistency Arousal and Reduction in Attitude Change," in I. D. Steiner and Martin Fishbein (eds.), *Current Studies in Social Psychology* (New York: Holt, Rinehart & Winston, 1965), pp. 123–24.

attitude so as to isolate an inconsistent component, or ,(3) some sort of accommodation so that internal stability is once again achieved.[5]

Interattitude Structure.   Attitudes that are closely related to an individual's self-concept (his conception of himself relative to others) are said to have *centrality*. In other words, attitudes are formed about subjects which have high personal goal relevance and thus are firmly *anchored* at these strategic points. Attitudes which are so anchored, in turn, tend to become organized, so that change in one affects the others.

Those attitudes that are only tangentially related to one's self-concept and hence are not central can be more readily changed. Attitudes toward most products and brands undoubtedly are of this nature. Even under these circumstances, however, maintenance of *cognitive consistency* is a pervasive tendency.

Determinants of Attitude Strength.   The probability of attitude change varies inversely with its strength. In addition to centrality, strength is determined by the quantity of stored information and experience which is relevant for the object or act under consideration. When extent of centrality or amount of stored information and experience are high, attempts to bring about change may well activate the filter in the central control unit and prevent information processing. Conversely, change is most probable when one or both of these determinants is less operative.

Evaluative Criteria

Evaluative criteria are of considerable significance in understanding the nature and functioning of attitudes. In a very real sense, these specifications are the foundation of attitude. Moreover, they can be highly resistant to change, in that they are formed from stored information and experience and personality. Personality seems to be the dominant determinant, and it is not an overstatement to point out that evaluative criteria often are a specific manifestation of underlying traits and motives. Some of the more common types are appearance, price, and durability.

There are, of course, some distinct limitations on the number of criteria that a consumer can utilize simultaneously. As a general rule, usually no more than six enter into the decision in any major way. Also it is to be expected that one or two will dominate the others in importance; these must be satisfied before an alternative will be evaluated favorably.

Measurement.   Evaluative criteria are an integral component of the leading models of buyer behavior.[6] Hence the question of measurement has assumed considerable importance. There are a number of com-

---

[5] Ibid.

[6] J. A. Howard and J. N. Sneth, *The Theory of Buyer Behavior* (New York: John Wiley & Sons, 1969); and Engel, Kollat, and Blackwell, *Consumer Behavior*.

plexities which are beyond the scope of this book,[7] but measurement usually includes the following general approach:

1. *Assessment of the Relevant Categories of Criteria.* Often this will be done through unstructured interviews focusing on those aspects that are most important in evaluation and decision. The most common approach is some type of direct questioning.

2. *Measurement of Importance.* As was mentioned above, criteria will vary in importance. Hence it is usually felt to be necessary to rank the relative importance of each, either through some type of scaling procedure or through statistical procedures which infer the relative weights.

3. *Reduction of Redundancy in the Data.* Because certain criteria can be highly correlated and hence measure essentially the same thing, various statistical routines are often utilized to arrive at nonrelated categories.

Figure 6–2 provides an illustration of criteria for an ideal retail store that were uncovered through this procedure. These statements then were utilized as the basis for rating competing retail chains.

Implications. As was pointed out earlier, evaluative criteria tend to be deeply rooted and hence resistant to change. This tendency results in the following implications: (1) the importance of appeal to relevant criteria, (2) the difficulty of bringing about change, (3) the emerging importance of a strategy of "benefit segmentation," and (4) the social significance of consumer education.

APPEALING TO RELEVANT CRITERIA. Men's hair styles today are characterized by greater length and an easy, natural look. Thus few men want their hair to look greasy or plastered down, but how can long hair be controlled without this effect? One of the answers was the campaign saying, "The wethead is dead. Long live the Dry Look from Gillette." In two years this product jumped from a 12.2 percent share of the market to 20 percent, and the product did not even exist prior to 1968.[8] The marketing program of the Gillette Company has been geared to meeting the most salient evaluative criteria of its prospective users, and success has been the result.

On the other hand, the Mennen Company introduced Mennen E deodorant containing vitamin E. The appeal was that use of this vitamin eliminated harsh germicides in the deodorant. Yet the product failed during its national introduction, even though $12,000,000 was budgeted for advertising. The apparent reason was that the advertising stressed a product attribute which was not relevant to the consumer.[9] In other

---

[7] See Engel, Kollat, and Blackwell, *Consumer Behavior,* pp. 254–60.

[8] T. G. N. Chin, "New Product Successes and Failures—How to Detect Them in Advance," *Advertising Age,* September 24, 1973, p. 61.

[9] Ibid.

FIGURE 6–2

Characteristics of an Ideal Retail Store

Salespeople

One can trust the salespeople.
The salespeople are friendly; they don't act as if they're doing you a favor.

Value

The store always gives you value for your money.
It takes returns any time you're unsatisfied. No fuss.
It represents its merchandise values honestly.

Quality

It carries good-quality merchandise.

Advertising

One can believe what it tells you in its advertising.

Style

One can find every color and size in stock.
Its merchandise styling is well accepted.

Price

It has a number of different price lines for each item of merchandise.
It will always match competition on a price.

Shopping Convenience

It is easy to get around the store, and it is a convenient place to shop in.

Feeling of Belonging

One gets a feeling of belonging when shopping there.

Children's Wear

It is a good store to buy teen-age clothing.
It is a good store to buy children's and infants' clothing, such as coats.

Women's Articles

It is a good store to buy women's dresses and coats.
It is a good place to buy articles such as bras and foundation garments.
It is a good store to buy inexpensive cosmetics and beauty aids.

Men's Wear

It is a good store to buy men's slacks and jackets.
It is a good place to buy men's clothes.
It is a good place to buy men's apparel, such as underwear and socks.

Hardlines

It is a good store to buy small electrical appliances, such as toasters.

Family Store

You can find just about everything you want for every member of the family.

Source: W. T. Grant Case in Roger Blackwell, James F. Engel, and David T. Kollat, *Cases In Consumer Behavior* (New York: Holt, Rinehart, and Winston, 1969), pp. 86 and 87.

words, the consumer will try a new product only if it solves one of his problems and hence meets the specifications of important evaluative criteria.

THE DIFFICULTY IN CHANGING EVALUATIVE CRITERIA. Undoubtedly it is obvious to all that the ideal situation is to have a product such as Gillette Dry Look which is squarely on target with the desires of prospects in a large market segment. But did Mennen E have to be a failure? Could not advertising have changed the criteria of deodorant users to convince them that the absence of germicides is significant?

If Mennen were selling only door to door with personal communication, it is quite possible that this strategy might have paid off. It will be recalled that the salesman has the benefit of instantaneous feedback and ability to counter the prospect's objections. Such a strategy, of course, is prohibitively expensive for a convenience item, with the result that the mass media are the only practical recourse. But the mass media provide full opportunity for the consumer to filter out the message, and this can be very difficult, if not impossible, to overcome.

A manufacturer of ceiling tiles was in a similar situation. A new product had just been introduced which had no holes or other disfigurement on the surface. In addition, it offered superior sound-deadening properties. It did not sell, however, for the reason that buyers felt that holes must be present for full sound-absorption capability, and no amount of promotion was able to reverse this belief. While it would be incorrect to assume that criteria *never* change, many other examples could be cited in which manufacturers failed in the attempt.

The best conclusion is that no amount of advertising or promotion can save a product which is improperly positioned with respect to salient evaluative criteria.

BENEFIT SEGMENTATION. The argument to this point has been that the consumer retains full sovereignty and accepts or rejects alternatives to the extent to which they either meet or fail to meet his salient evaluative criteria. In this situation the best marketing strategy is to accept strongly held evaluative criteria as a given and modify the marketing program to meet these specifications. The only exceptions are when these criteria are fluid or are not strongly held.

A strategy of benefit segmentation builds upon an analysis which matches the evaluative criteria of prospective buyers against the attributes of competitive offerings. The objective is to find segments where competitors have failed to capitalize on buyer desires, and design a marketing program to gain a foothold. The Vega and Pinto were introduced after such an analysis. In each instance, the automobile was a *result* of unmet specifications of a large segment of buyers, especially those under the age of 30.

THE SOCIAL SIGNIFICANCE OF CONSUMER EDUCATION. Do consumers buy wisely? This, of course, is the subject of endless debate that can be answered ultimately only from the perspective of the individual. Yet it seems apparent that the presence of such a vast variety of alternatives coupled with the rapidity of product change can only serve to compound the consumer's problem. At times it is probably true that subjective evaluative criteria such as reputation of manufacturer are substituted by necessity for more objective and potentially more valid considerations. For example, many have come to realize that the chemical formulation of all aspirin is essentially the same, by government regulation. While there may be some minor differences in the manner in which the pill is made, thus permitting faster action, the basic properties of all aspirin are identical. Unfortunately many, if not most, buy it on the basis of manufacturer reputation and hence pay a substantial price premium. In situations such as this, consumer education in the schools and elsewhere meets a valid need.

Some manufacturers unfortunately are fighting consumer education, or at least are hoping it will go away. What possible objection, for example, can there be to posting of octane ratings on gasoline pumps? The manufacturer will be hurt if the consumer uses this objective criterion as a determinant of choice *only* if he has failed to meet usual industry standards by hiding under the guise of his brand name. It is a poorly kept trade secret that one major company, in the past at least, has done just exactly this, even though its advertising trumpets "quality." Is it any wonder the pressures for consumerism continue to grow? Hopefully, consumer education will expand and industry will recognize and support this significant function in a world of future shock.

Attitude Measurement

There are a number of ways in which attitude can be measured, but space does not permit a general methodological review here.[10] Attitude has been defined specifically as a measure of the perceived utility of alternatives for choice on the basis of appropriate evaluative criteria. The most popular approach to measurement has come to be known as the "expectancy" model, which is described here. The reader also is referred to an alternative approach which utilizes a combination of non-metric multidimensional scaling and multidimensional unfolding analysis.[11]

The expectancy model approach was initially developed independently

---

[10] See N. Cliff, "Scaling," in P. H. Mussen and M. R. Rosenzweig (eds.), *Annual Review of Psychology,* Vol. 24 (Palo Alto, Cal.: Annual Reviews, Inc., 1973), pp. 473–506, and G. S. Day, "Evaluating Models for Attitude Structure," *Journal of Marketing Research,* Vol. 9 (1972), pp. 279–86.

[11] See for example W. W. Talarzyk and Reza Moinpour. "Comparison of an Attitude Model and Coombsian Unfolding Analysis for the Prediction of Individual Brand Preference," paper presented at the Workshop on Attitude Research and Consumer Behavior, University of Illinois, Champaign, December 1970.

by Milton J. Rosenberg[12] and Martin Fishbein.[13] Their methods are similar conceptually, but they have certain important differences when applied to marketing problems.[14] Marketing applications, however, usually involve a modification and adaptation of the basic underlying models to encompass the following steps:

1. *Isolation of Salient Categories of Evaluative Criteria.*

2. *Rating of the Importance of Each Criterion.* There is some disagreement on the necessity of this step but, at the very least, the analyst must guarantee that the criteria utilized are those that are relevant to the consumer.

3. *Rating of the Alternative and/or Proposed Action.* This rating is done along each pertinent evaluative criterion, using some type of scale of satisfaction. The criteria, for example, might be "low price relative to other brands," "quick relief," and "pleasant taste." The product or brand then would be rated on each criterion using some type of scale which ranges from satisfactory to unsatisfactory.

4. *Computation of the Attitude Score.* At times it is useful to compute a single attitude score. This usually is done with a formula similar to the following:

$$A_b = \sum_{i=1}^{n} W_i B_{ib},$$

where

A_b = Attitude toward a particular alternative, b
W_i = Weight or importance of evaluative criterion i
B_{ib} = Evaluative aspect or belief with respect to the utility of alternative b to satisfy evaluative criterion i
n = The number of evaluative criteria utilized

In other words, numerical weights are assigned to the attitude ratings, and one total score is computed which takes explicit account of the rating and the importance of each evaluative criterion. The attitude score thus is the total numerical value. In many instances, however, this type of single score has little practical marketing significance, as is pointed out later. Others are of the opinion that nothing is gained by this type of

---

[12] Milton J. Rosenberg, "Cognitive Structure and Attitudinal Affect," *Journal of Abnormal and Social Psychology,* Vol. 53 (1956), pp. 367–72.

[13] Martin Fishbein, "The Relationships between Beliefs, Attitudes and Behavior," in Sidney P. Feldman (ed.), *Cognitive Consistency* (New York: Academic Press, 1966), pp. 199–223.

[14] J. N. Sheth and C. W. Park, "Equivalence of Fishbein and Rosenberg Theories of Attitudes," Faculty Working Paper No. 108, College of Commerce and Business Administration, University of Illinois, April 1973.

summated score and propose alternative ways at arriving at the attitudinal value.[15]

Assessment of Attitude Strength

Because attitude change is a common marketing objective, it is necessary to focus on the strength of the resulting attitude. As has been
stressed repeatedly, a direct frontal attack on a strongly held attitude
is likely to result in selective screening of the message. The two major
determinants of attitude strength are (1) personality centrality and (2)
the extent of underlying information and experience.

Analysis of Centrality. If a prospect's attitude toward an organization
and its offerings is anchored in his self-concept, his attitude is said to
have centrality. In such a case he is likely to screen out any communications designed to induce attitude change. In other words, he may be
brand loyal for some psychologically significant reasons.[16]

Centrality can be measured by giving the individual the choice between alternatives that are considered to be acceptable and those that
are considered to be unacceptable. The former category is termed the
latitude of acceptance, and its counterpart is the *latitude of rejection.*[17]
The greater the latitude of rejection (i.e. the number of unacceptable
alternatives) in comparison with the latitude of acceptance, the greater
the personal commitment to the preferred alternative. In other words,
the latitude of acceptance under conditions of high centrality will contain only the preferred brand, and the latitude of rejection will contain
all others. It has been found that brand loyalty varies inversely with
the proportion of alternative brands in the latitude of acceptance.[18] Obviously consumers with this profile represent an unresponsive promotional target.

Given a measure of attitude and a measure of centrality, it is possible
to relate the two, as in Figure 6–3. Those prospective consumers who fall
into cell A represent poor targets, because an unfavorable attitude toward the organization's offerings is anchored in personality. Those in
cell B, on the other hand, are loyal users who are unlikely to be switched
by competitors' efforts. Users in cell D are more vulnerable to com-

---

[15] See, for example, J. N. Sheth, "Measurement of Attitude Scores from Beliefs
and Importances," Faculty Working Paper No. 50, College of Commerce and
Business Administration, University of Illinois, May 1972.

[16] See Jacob Jacoby and D. B. Kyner, "Brand Loyalty versus Repeat Purchasing
Behavior," *Journal of Marketing Research,* Vol. 10 (1973), pp. 1–9.

[17] C. W. Sherif, Muzafer Sherif, and R. E. Nebergall, *Attitude and Attitude
Change* (New Haven, Conn.: Yale University Press, 1961).

[18] H. E. Brown, "The Role of Personality and Perceived Risk in the Purchase
of Branded Headache and Pain and Cold Remedies," unpublished doctoral dissertation, The Ohio State University, 1969.

FIGURE 6–3

Analysis of Evaluative Ratings of Products or Services in Terms of the Rater's Personality Relationship to Them

Attitude	Centrality of Attitude					
	High		Medium		Low	
	User	Nonuser	User	Nonuser	User	Nonuser
Favorable	B				D	
Neutral						C
Unfavorable		A				

Cell A: Very poor prospect
Cell B: A user who is likely to be highly brand loyal
Cell C: May be possible to change this prospect's attitude, depending upon his knowledge, etc.
Cell D: This user may well be a brand switcher. If many fall into this cell, there can be high competitive vulnerability

petitive efforts because their loyalty is not buttressed by high involvement with the product. The brand purchased probably is of relatively little concern, and brand switching could readily occur. Finally, those in cell C are essentially indifferent and have no strong personality reason for not using the brand. This means that they probably can be induced to switch through sampling, price offers, and other direct means of demand stimulation.

Analysis of Knowledge and Experience.   Classification of people in terms of their knowledge and experience frequently results in better prediction of actual behavior.[19] A general method of analysis is presented in Figure 6–4.

In this simplified illustration three categories of knowledge are used, ranging from high to low, as well as three categories of attitude. When these are cross classified together, nine basic cells result, which are then further subdivided by user and nonuser. The purpose of the analysis is to determine the proportions that fall into each cell.

Each cell represents different strategy implications. Three are identified in the figure for purposes of illustration. Cell A represents nonusers

---

[19] R. S. Halpern, "Some Observations about Attitudes, Attitude Measurement and Behavior," in Lee Adler and Irving Crespi (eds.), *Attitude Research on the Rocks* (Chicago: American Marketing Association, 1968), p. 41.

FIGURE 6–4

Analysis of Evaluative Ratings of Products or Services in Terms of Raters' Knowledge and Experience

Attitude	Knowledge and Experience					
	High		Medium		Low	
	User	Nonuser	User	Nonuser	User	Nonuser
Favorable					C	
Neutral						B
Unfavorable		A				

Examples of questions:
  Have you ever shopped at Grant's?
  What is the price of the Westinghouse 5,000-BTU air conditioner?
Cell A: Very poor prospect
Cell B: May be a good opportunity to stimulate greater awareness of specific features
Cell C: Company may be lacking an opportunity to increase sales among users

with an unfavorable attitude based on extensive knowledge. It is unlikely that members of this group can be induced to change their attitudes through promotional efforts; selective perception of the message is a more probable result.

Users in cell B represent more promising prospects. A neutral attitude is based on low information and experience, and it is probable that attitudes will change as a result of exposure to advertising which imparts relevant information.

Consumers in cell C also may represent good prospects. Their favorable attitude is anchored in low information, which implies that they may be unaware of other ways in which the product can be used. New uses might be the theme of promotion directed toward this group, and it is possible that sales within the segment would increase as a result.

A Composite Analysis. Extensive analyses of the types discussed above should isolate some segments which offer greater probability of demand stimulation than others. The best prospects are those who hold no worse than a mildly negative attitude but who also demonstrate low knowledge and centrality. A promotional campaign designed to stimulate greater awareness could have substantial payoff. Centrality is a less important determinant than information at this point, because high centrality could be an asset in the respect that favorable results might ensue when the prospect is shown how the product fits into an overall style of life. Centrality is of greatest significance when it provides the anchoring for a negative attitude, because that is an indication of a segment where the probability of favorable response is not good.

Focus also should extend to the attitudes of current users. How many have a strongly favorable attitude based on information and centrality? These are the most secure customers the firm has, and relatively little need be done to ensure their loyalty. Others may be waivering in loyalty, with the result that remedial efforts are needed in the form of suggested new uses and so on.

It should be possible to array segments so that the most responsive as well as the least responsive markets become identified. In so doing vital clues are provided as to the most appropriate strategy.

Using Attitude Analysis in Promotional Strategy

The question of whether attitude change is a valid promotional goal must be assessed before any indication of the implications for strategy can be made. Given an affirmative answer, attention can be directed to the ways in which attitudes can be changed.

Is Attitude Change a Valid Promotional Goal? It has long been assumed that a change in attitude will lead to a change in behavior. This has given rise to what is known as the hierarchy of effects hypothesis, that advertising and promotion work to stimulate awareness, which leads to attitude change, which leads to behavior change. This assumed relationship has been severely challenged in recent years, however, and both positive and negative evidence has been produced.

NEGATIVE EVIDENCE. As early as 1934 a study showed that behavior could not be predicted from written statements which presumably measure attitudes.[20] More recently, Leon Festinger was able to find virtually no published evidence that attitudes and behavior are related, although in all fairness it should be pointed out that his review neglected much of the evidence which is discussed later.[21] I. Deutscher agrees with Festinger and states that "disparities between thought and action are the central methodological problem of the social sciences.[22] The argument is that it is not possible to identify whether or not people will act on

---

[20] R. T. LaPiere, "Attitudes vs. Actions," *Social Forces,* Vol. 13 (1934), pp. 230–37.

[21] Leon Festinger, "Behavioral Support for Opinion Change," *Public Opinion Quarterly,* Vol. 28 (1964), pp. 404–17.

[22] I. Deutscher, "Words and Deeds: Social Science and Social Policy," *Social Problems,* Vol. 3 (1966), p. 235.

stated intentions. Other negative results have been reported in a number of published studies.[23]

POSITIVE EVIDENCE. Many contend that a positive relationship does exist between behavior and attitude and that part of the problem mentioned by others may lie in faulty measuring instruments. It has been reported, for example, that good commercials lead to an effect on both attitude and behavior,[24] that attitudes predict behavior when the artificiality of measurement is reduced,[25] that attitudes toward financial outlook are related to spending behavior,[26] that attitudes toward trading stamps reflect trading stamp usage,[27] and that first-brand awareness (a type of attitude scale) predicts short-term purchase behavior.[28]

Several researchers in advertising and marketing feel that attitude change should be a primary goal of promotional strategy. Cornelius DuBois, for example, showed that the better the attitude level, the more users are held, and the more nonusers are attracted.[29] A series of studies at Grey Advertising, Inc., pointed up the importance of attitude change as follows: "More and more psychologists are coming to the conclusion that to result in a sale an advertisement must bring about a positive change in the *attitude* of the reader or viewer . . . That there is a definite relationship between *change of attitude* toward a brand and buying action is not only a logical conclusion but is supported by a preponderance of *evidence*.[30]

IS THERE A CENTRAL GROUND? Such a conflicting mass of evidence is discouraging indeed, but some rather definite conclusions do emerge. First, it is naive to expect that attitudes and behavior will always be related in a one-to-one manner. There are a number of other variables which intervene to affect behavior, especially environmental circum-

---

[23] See Engel, Kollat, and Blackwell, *Consumer Behavior,* pp. 270–71.

[24] J. K. Lair, "Splitsville: A Split-Half Study of Television Commercial Pretesting," *Dissertation Abstracts,* Vol. 27 (1965), pp. 2894–95.

[25] J. M. Fendrich, "A Study of the Association among Verbal Attitudes, Commitment, and Overt Behavior in Different Experimental Conditions," *Social Forces,* Vol. 45 (1967), pp. 347–55.

[26] George Katona, *The Powerful Consumer* (New York: McGraw-Hill Book Co., 1960), part II.

[27] Jon G. Udel, "Can Attitude Measurement Predict Consumer Behavior?" *Journal of Marketing,* Vol. 29 (1965), pp. 46–50.

[28] Joel N. Axelrod, "Attitude Measurements That Predict Purchases," *Journal of Advertising Research,* Vol. 8 (March 1968), p. 3.

[29] Cornelius DuBois, "Twelve Brands on a Seesaw," in *Proceedings of the Thirteenth Annual Conference* (New York: Advertising Research Foundation, Inc., 1968).

[30] *Grey Matter,* Vol. 39 (November 1968), p. 1. Also see A. A. Achenbaum, "Advertising Doesn't Manipulate Consumers," *Journal of Advertising Research,* Vol. 12 (1972), pp. 3–14.

stances.[31] In addition, there is growing evidence that attitudes toward the situation must be taken account of, as well as attitudes toward the object or brand, if accurate behavioral predictions are to result.[32]

Next, careful consideration must be given to the measuring instruments. Minor wording changes can make a great difference in predictive accuracy.[33] Indeed, the basic problem may lie in the very definition of attitude, and there is by no means full agreement on this starting point. It can be said, however, that the expectancy model discussed in this chapter is finding widespread marketing use, and it has been subjected to extensive validation study in recent years.

Much of the dilemma is dissipated when an additional variable is taken into consideration—*behavioral intention.* There is growing evidence that intention to act is a better predictor of behavior than attitude.[34] Attitude and intention are highly related, however, as Figure 6–5 suggests.[35]

Notice that intention is hypothesized to be a function of attitude (which, in turn, is formed from stored information and experience and evaluative criteria, as discussed earlier), anticipated situation, and the social environment. The anticipated situation includes all other activities that are likely to be operative at the time of anticipated future behavior. For example, an expected shortage of spending power can inhibit an intention to buy a new automobile. The social environment, on the other hand, includes the whole set of influences discussed in the preceding chapter. There is, in other words, a relationship between attitude and intention, but it is not necessarily one to one if these other factors are operative.

---

[31] L. W. Doob, "The Behavior of Attitudes," *Psychological Review,* Vol. 54 (1947), pp. 135–56.

[32] M. Rokeach and P. Kieljunmas, "Behavior as a Function of Attitude-Toward-Situation," *Journal of Personality and Social Psychology,* Vol. 22 (1972), pp. 194–201 and Rolf Sandel, "Effects of Attitudinal and Situational Factors on Reported Choice Behavior," *Journal of Marketing Research,* Vol. 5 (1968), pp. 405–8.

[33] C. R. Little and R. J. Hill, "Attitude Conditions and Measurement Techniques," *Sociometry,* Vol. 39 (1967), p. 203.

[34] For representative evidence see V. Kothandapani, "Validation of Feelings, Belief, and Intention to Act as Three Components of Attitude and Their Contribution to Prediction of Contraceptive Behavior," *Journal of Personality and Social Psychology,* Vol. 19 (1971), pp. 321–33; Martin Fishbein and I. Ajzen, "Attitudes and Opinions," in P. H. Mussen and M. R. Rosenzweig (eds.), *Annual Review of Psychology,* Vol. 23 (Palo Alto, Cal.: Annual Reviews, Inc., 1972), pp. 188–244; and I. Ajzen and Martin Fishbein, "Attitudes and Normative Beliefs as Factors Influencing Behavioral Intentions," *Journal of Personality and Social Psychology,* Vol. 21 (1972), pp. 1–9.

[35] J. N. Sheth, "A Field Study of Attitude Structure and Attitude-Behavior Relationship," Faculty Working Paper No. 116, College of Commerce and Business Administration, University of Illinois, July 1973.

FiGURE 6–5

Relationship between Attitude, Intention and Behavior

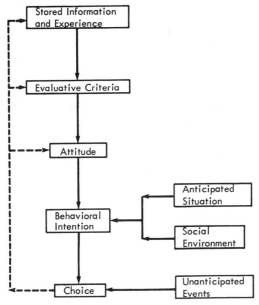

Source: Adapted from J. N. Sheth, "A Field Study of Attitude Structure and Attitude-Behavior Relationship," Faculty Working Paper No. 116, College of Commerce and Business Administration, University of Illinois, July 1973.

Choice is conceived of as a function of intention as well as unanticipated events. This latter factor comprehends a whole set of influences which cannot be forecast.

Now, what happens if attitude is changed? It will, all other things being equal, change intentions which, in turn, will change behavior. The relationship will, of course, be modified by the anticipated situation, social environment, and unanticipated events. Therefore, in answer to the question posed earlier, attitude change *is* a valid goal, because a change in attitude can lead to changed behavior through modified intentions.

Strategies for Attitude Change. At least three strategies are appropriate in securing attitude change: (1) provision of new information, (2) induced change in behavior, and (3) induced change in evaluative criteria.

PROVISION OF NEW INFORMATION. A major manufacturer of industrial electronic relays, Sigma Instruments Company, was not finding the de-

FIGURE 6–6

Ratings of Relays Manufactured by Sigma Instruments Company and Competitors

Industrial-Commercial Use (83 returns):	Allied	Clare	Potter & Brum- field	Sigma
a. Its reputation as a manufacturer of relays for industrial applications (0–very poor, 10–excellent)	6.01	7.84	7.64	7.92
b. The usefulness of the catalog information it provides (0–not useful, 10–very useful)	5.74	7.61	6.58	6.98
c. The broadness of its line of industrial relays (0–not broad, 10–extremely broad)	5.95	6.36	8.05	5.72
d. The long service life of its relays (0–short, 10–very long)	6.03	8.28	7.26	8.03
e. Cooperation of company (0–poor, 10–good)	6.81	7.27	7.24	7.30
f. Helpfulness of sales representatives (0–not helpful, 10–very helpful)	5.88	6.88	6.17	6.64
g. Competitive pricing of its industrial relays consistent with quality (0–not competitive, 10–very competitive)	7.71	6.51	8.23	6.60

Conclusion:
Awareness of Sigma's competitiveness in prices and in breadth and length of line was low, and it has inhibited sales. Strengthened awareness is a valid goal for promotion.

Source: Used with special permission of the Sigma Instruments Company.

sired measure of acceptance in certain market segments.[36] In particular, it seemed to be lagging behind a leading competitor, Potter & Brumfield, to an increasing extent. A decision was made to step up promotional efforts. The basis for strategy was provided by a survey of electronic engineers subscribing to *Electrical Design News* who were asked to rate Sigma and three of its competitors on seven evaluative criteria.

A portion of the data compiled is reproduced in Figure 6–6. The data consist of the average attitude scores given to each of the major competitors (the higher the score the better). Sigma rated high on all but two: broadness of line and competitive pricing consistent with quality. These are known to be important considerations in choice.

The first question to be asked is whether or not the company is competitive in these respects. If not, product and pricing changes may be

---

[36] "Sigma Instruments," in James F. Engel, W. Wayne Talarzyk, and Carl M. Larson, *Cases in Promotional Strategy* (Homewood, Ill.: Richard D. Irwin, 1971), pp. 271–79.

called for. Because the company was in fact fully competitive, it appeared that the problem was one of buyer awareness. The promotional strategy featured broadness of line and competitive pricing, along with other factors (for details see Chapter 9). After one year a follow-up survey showed dramatic increases in awareness, accompanied by a 26 percent sales increase. This is a clear example of how research data can pinpoint strategy for conveying new information to the consumer.

As is pointed out in other chapters, awareness stimulation is a common promotional objective. Fragrance manufacturers, for example, found that few consumers know the difference between perfume, cologne, eau de cologne, and toilet water.[37] These and other significant information gaps led to the conclusion that the industry is faced with the need to build consumer awareness and understanding if sales are to be increased. Many other illustrations could be given.

INDUCED CHANGE IN BEHAVIOR. The model in Figure 6–5 shows a feedback relationship (depicted by broken lines) which indicates that a change in behavior (choice) can lead to changes in stored information, evaluative criteria, and attitude. Thus attitude change can be generated by inducing a person to engage in attitude-discrepant behavior. For example, there was for years a long-standing belief that high fidelity sound reproduction required large-size speakers. Yet attitudes often changed substantially once the consumer listened to the smaller units which now are common. Dissonance thus was generated between established beliefs and the content of the new information, with attitude change as the result.

INDUCED CHANGE IN EVALUATIVE CRITERIA. As was pointed out earlier, evaluative criteria usually are highly resistant to change and should be accepted as a given. Yet there are examples where change in evaluative criteria has been induced by manufacturer efforts. The relatively quick acceptance of the smaller high fidelity speaker units is one good illustration. This can be done on occasion, but it usually will require the concentrated, cooperative promotional effort of many organizations.

PERSONALITY

Personality refers to a set of consistent responses to environmental stimuli.[38] It thus can be considered for marketing purposes as those factors and characteristics that make one individual different from another. These, of course, are the general underlying characteristics (as

---

[37] Lorraine Baltera, "Fragrance Seminar Reveals Consumer Info Gap," *Advertising Age,* September 24, 1973, p. 90.

[38] H. H. Kassarjian, "Personality and Consumer Behavior: A Review," *Journal of Marketing Research,* Vol. 8 (1971), p. 409.

FIGURE 6–7

Personality in the Central Control Unit

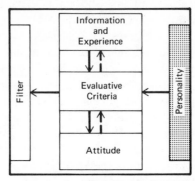

Source: James F. Engel, David T. Kollat, and Roger D. Blackwell, *Consumer Behavior*, 2d ed. (New York: Holt, Rinehart & Winston, 1973).

Figure 6–7 indicates) which exert a strong influence on evaluative criteria and attitudes.

For many years attempts have been made to relate general personality characteristics measured by clinical instruments to various aspects of buying behavior. Literally hundreds of studies have been undertaken, most of which have proved to be unfruitful.[39] There are many possible explanations for the relative barrenness of this line of inquiry, but one of the most logical is that the measurement instruments used were designed for the psychological clinic and not for the marketplace. In addition, some questionable statistical analysis procedures have been utilized.[40]

More recently, personality has been conceived as those activities, interests, and opinions which comprise general *lifestyle*. Tailormade research inventories utilized to determine lifestyle in market research have proved to be highly fruitful, and real insights have been gained for promotional strategy.[41] Two different types of data normally are collected: (1) demographic and (2) psychographic.

Demographic Characteristics

The most useful dimensions of demographic classification are: (1) age, (2) income, (3) geographic location, (4) life cycle, (5) social class,

---

[39] For a thorough review see ibid. and Engel, Kollat, and Blackwell, *Consumer Behavior*, ch. 12.

[40] F. M. Bass, D. J. Tigert, and R. T. Lonsdale, "Market Segmentation: Group versus Individual Behavior," *Journal of Marketing Research*, Vol. 5 (1968), pp. 264–70.

[41] See Engel, Kollat, and Blackwell, *Consumer Behavior*, pp. 297–303.

(6) occupation, (7) home ownership, and (8) education. These variables are of major significance, first of all, in defining market targets. As is emphasized in Chapters 11 and 12, it is possible to collect data on the demographic characteristics of the audiences of most advertising media in considerable detail. In this way the basis is provided for a media strategy which reaches a desired market segment with relatively great precision.

It is often overlooked, however, that these same data can provide insight into important differences in lifestyles *between* segments. For example, the heavy buyer of Kentucky Fried Chicken has the following demographic profile:

Working wife.
More children than average.
Significantly higher family income than average.
Average educational attainment.
Middle-class occupational status.[42]

It is not difficult to conclude that time is at a premium for this working wife. Undoubtedly she is willing to incur the extra cost of purchasing prepared food (compared with home food preparation) in return for the gains in leisure time. Given the relatively high income status, it also is probable that she would be responsive to buying with a credit card, and so on.

Psychographic Characteristics

Obviously demographic measurements alone are an incomplete indicator of lifestyle. It is necessary to focus also on the consumer's activities, interests, and opinions using what are now known as AIO measures. What does the Kentucky Fried Chicken user think of her housekeeping tasks? Is she interested in fashion? Does her life revolve around her children? Is she a homebody or a swinger? These types of data provide a *psychographic* profile of market segments.[43]

Consider the heavy users of eye makeup. It has been found demographically that they are younger and better educated than average, more likely to be employed outside the home, and located in metropolitan

---

[42] D. J. Tigert, R. T. Lathrope, and M. J. Bleeg, "The Fast Food Franchise: Psychographic and Demographic Segmentation Analysis," *Journal of Retailing,* Vol. 47 (1971), pp. 86–7.

[43] See T. P. Hustad and E. A. Pessemier, "Segmenting Consumer Markets with Activity and Attitude Measures," Research paper No. 298, Institute for Research in the Behavioral, Economic, and Management Sciences, Herman C. Krannert Graduate School of Industrial Administration, Purdue University, March 1971, and W. D. Wells and D. J. Tigert, "Activities, Interests, and Opinions," *Journal of Advertising Research,* Vol. 11 (1971), pp. 27–35.

areas.[44] Notice, however, how much is added in understanding when it is pointed out that users differ from nonusers in the following psychographic terms:

Highly fashion conscious.
Desirous of being attractive to men.
Oriented to the future.
Interested in art and culture.
Interested in world travel.
Not home centered.
Relative rejection of the traditional.

These data, of course, say nothing about awareness or attitudes toward specific brands or types of eye makeup. The usefulness in promotional strategy enters in providing clues about the type of person the prospect is and the way she should be depicted in the message.

One could use this psychographic profile in a mechanical way and depict an overdressed "chick" with a man worshipping at her feet as they sit in an art institute in Paris with a letter from mother crumpled on the floor. Needless to say this is absurd, but an appeal to the wrong type of person in contradictory settings will have the effect of activating selective screening of the message by the prospect. Therefore, the key is to utilize people and settings in such a manner that they are consistent with and not contradictory to the psychographic profile.

The two advertisements in Figure 6–8 should be examined to determine whether these models and settings are psychographically appropriate. Are these girls likely to be the types that are cosmopolitan in tastes, oriented toward fashion, and interested in men? Probably most will give an affirmative answer. If so, it can be concluded that proper use has been made of psychographic data.

SUMMARY

This chapter has examined the nature, significance, and measurement of two significant consumer attributes—attitudes and personality. Attitude was defined as a rating of the utility of an alternative for choice according to pertinent evaluative criteria. It was shown that attitude change is a valid marketing goal in that attributes are related to behavioral intentions and intentions are related to behavior. Hence, a change in attitude will, all things being equal, change both intentions and behavior. Various strategies for attitude change were discussed.

Personality was discussed here as being those traits and characteristics that make an individual unique. Two types of data were shown to have

---

[44] Wells and Tigert, "Activities, Interests, Opinions."

FIGURE 6–8

Two Appeals to the Heavy User of Eye Makeup

Helena Rubinstein creates Long Lash.

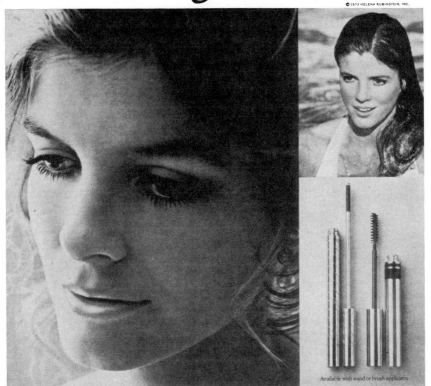

Now... mascara that conditions as it waterproofs.

Long Lash is more than just a mascara. It's a whole beauty treatment for your delicate, hard-working lashes.

Now you can darken them, lengthen them, thicken them, waterproof them, with no fear of drying them out.

For it has an oil base that softens. Proteins that condition. And emollients that make lashes a snare of silk.

Dermatologist tested and approved.

Helena Rubinstein

FIGURE 6–8 (continued)

Reproduced with permission of the Almay Company.

particular usefulness in promotional strategy: demographic and psychographic (lifestyle) profiles.

REVIEW AND DISCUSSION QUESTIONS

1. An evaluative criteria mentioned by many college girls in the purchase of an underarm deodorant is that "it makes me feel more confident in the presence of others." What are the probable underlying determinants of this criterion?

2. Before World War II, the Customer Research Department of General Motors Corporation asked consumers to appraise the relative importance of various product attributes. Dependability and safety usually come out on top, followed by price and styling. What uses, if any, can be made of these data?

3. What are the causes of the so-called consumer movement which is leading to today's emphasis on consumer education? What role does the business firm have in helping the individual to "buy wisely"?

4. What functions are performed by attitudes?

5. Is it likely that attitudes toward brands of toilet paper will assume centrality? Canned peaches? Color television? Women's coats? What factors did you use in making these judgments?

6. What explanations can be given for contradictory evidence regarding the relationship of attitudinal change to behavioral change? Is attitude change a valid goal?

7. A product which used a synthetic substance as a substitute for leather failed in test market. Consumers said it could not possibly have the same properties as leather. Is it likely that this attitude could be changed through revamped advertising?

8. What is the difference between demographics and psychographics?

9. List and describe the most common dimensions of demographic classification. What can analysis along these dimensions reveal?

10. Survey data reveal that the market for a line of name brand stereo units selling for a minimum of $200 is concentrated among males under 35, bachelors, located on the east and west coasts, college graduates, earning $12,000 and over. How can these findings be used in promotional strategy?

11. What is the probable psychographic profile of the market segment described in question 10? How would psychographic data be useful in planning this campaign?

7

Demand: Audience Decision Processes

THE PROCESSES by which individuals make purchasing decisions, with special emphasis on the use of information sources, are considered in this chapter. The discussion focuses on an analysis of extended decision behavior, a process accompanied by information search and alternative evaluation. This is in contrast with habitual decision making, which omits the activities of search and evaluation. An understanding of extended decision making, however, provides essential background for analysis of decision processes of all types.

PROBLEM RECOGNITION

The first stage in any type of decision activity is problem recognition, which occurs when "a consumer recognizes a difference of sufficient magnitude between what is perceived as the desired state of affairs and what is perceived as the actual state of affairs."[1] Problem recognition as it is used here differs from the concepts of *awareness* and *interest*, which are often conceived of as the first stage in a decision. This is because a problem can be recognized without awareness of available alternatives for choice. Similarly, awareness of or even initial interest in any given alternative does not necessarily precipitate problem recognition.

Figure 7–1, which includes environmental influences as well as the central control unit and information processing format, illustrates problem recognition as the first step in the decision process. As Figure 7–1 indicates, a problem can be recognized without action being taken because it

---

[1] James F. Engel, David T. Kollat, and Roger D. Blackwell, *Consumer Behavior,* 2d ed. (New York: Holt, Rinehart & Winston, 1973), p. 352.

FIGURE 7–1

Problem Recognition in the Decision Process

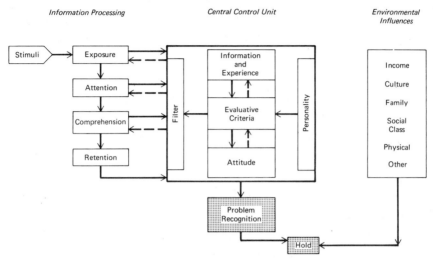

Source: James F. Engel, David T. Kollat, and Roger D. Blackwell, *Consumer Behavior,* 2d ed. (New York: Holt, Rinehart & Winston, 1973).

is perceived that it would not be appropriate at that time. In particular, constraints can enter from the external environment, such as conflict with group norms, family disagreement, absence of necessary financial means, and so on.

Determinants of Problem Recognition

Many factors can activate problem recognition. One of the most common is need activation, which causes the individual to become alert, responsive, and vigilant as a result of the feelings of discomfort which are generated.[2] The outcome is arousal of *drive,* which energizes need-satisfying action.

Another common cause is depletion of an existing stock of goods. The housewife, for example, perceives that the coffee can is empty and makes a note on her shopping list to purchase coffee. In other situations problem recognition is precipitated by dissatisfaction with present alternatives. Perhaps the washing machine has failed to complete its full cycle and it is found that the costs of repair are excessive.

Changes within the family also can trigger problem recognition. Perhaps the birth of children gives rise to a perceived need for new furniture. Changes of this type are observed throughout the family life

---

[2] D. O. Hebb, *The Organization of Behavior* (New York: John Wiley & Sons, 1949).

cycle.[3] At times an increase in income can lead to a change in desired circumstances, and the same effect can result from changes in the consumer's perceptions of future financial status.[4]

Another possibility is that problem recognition results from a change in reference groups. The family might move to a different community and associate with a group whose demands vary considerably from those of previous associates. Also, the demands of existing reference groups often change over time, with the same effect.

Finally, it is possible that marketing efforts can stimulate problem recognition. As the discussion in the next section indicates, however, the sources discussed above are usually of greater significance.

Not surprisingly, some types of people tend to recognize a problem earlier than others do. In particular, early problem recognition with respect to a new product is most probable among those with higher education and incomes, positive attitudes toward change, strong achievement motivation, high exposure to mass media, willingness to participate in groups and to deviate from group norms where desired, exposure to interpersonal communication, and predispositions which favor innovation.

The Implications for Promotional Strategy

It would appear to be logical that stimulation of problem recognition should be an important goal for promotional strategy. Such is usually not the case, however, for a variety of reasons.

First, as was stressed earlier, problem recognition most frequently occurs as a result of factors beyond the control of the business firm. The purchaser of a new home, for example, may recognize a problem because of change in community or awareness that existing quarters are too small. Also, stimulation of problem recognition often requires changing some strongly held attitudes regarding the desired state. The difficulties of attitude change were discussed in Chapter 4; the results generated by promotional activities undertaken for this purpose will not justify the costs.

Consider the obstacles faced by a firm selling swimming pools for home installation. Installation of a pool may indeed appeal to such basic motives as status and prestige, but an initial desire to buy can be opposed by many factors, with the result that a problem will not be recognized and acted upon. Cost and safety are just two of the many possible constraining influences. If opposing forces dominate, no amount of adver-

---

[3] See Wiliam D. Wells and George Gubar, "The Life Cycle Concept in Marketing Research," *Journal of Marketing Research*, Vol. 3 (November 1966), pp. 355–63.

[4] Eva Mueller, "The Desire for Innovations in Household Goods," in Lincoln H. Clark (ed.), *Consumer Behavior: Research on Consumer Reactions* (New York: Harper & Row, Publishers, 1958), p. 37.

tising and selling is likely to change matters. Family members must decide whether or not to purchase and, for the most part, promotion will only be a minor influence.

Promotion, of course, can serve to bring a product to the buyer's attention, thereby triggering some initial interest prior to problem recognition. It can also stress how and why product features are consistent with basic motives, attitudes, group norms, and so on. It can, in addition, help the buyer to cope with barriers which might constrain decision making, for example by suggesting the availability of financing plans to minimize cash outlay, by showing the compatibility of the product with group norms, or by countering other perceived opposing factors.

What we have stated, in essence, is the long-accepted viewpoint that the greater opportunity exists for promotion when primary demand (favorable attitude toward product class) is at a high level. Strong primary demand usually presumes that the buyer has come to recognize the product as a feasible alternative. Prior to that point, the message will not have much effect. Much so-called primary demand advertising tends to have a low return for this reason. The sporadic campaigns of the milk producers are a case in point. Certainly the costs required to change basic attitudes and stimulate interest are in excess of the funds usually available to an individual producer, thus giving rise to the fact that primary demand campaigns generally are cooperative industry efforts.

It should not be assumed that promotion serves no purpose when a large proportion of prospects have not, as yet, recognized a problem. Stimulating awareness and initial interest may, in effect, "qualify the product for the finals." Product awareness is thus stored in memory and becomes relevant when a problem is recognized. For this reason, stimulation of awareness is often the most important single goal for promotion.

Most authorities now agree that efforts designed to stimulate problem recognition are destined for low payout, because some degree of problem recognition usually must exist before marketing efforts are even perceived by consumers. Thus it usually is more profitable to orient efforts to stimulate awareness so that the product or brand is in the feasible set of alternatives once a problem is recognized by the prospective buyer.

SEARCH PROCESSES

After problem recognition the individual may or may not search for additional information. At times *internal search* (i.e., recall from memory) will be insufficient to define available alternatives, to say nothing of determining the appropriateness of each, and the consumer will therefore consult various external sources of information. This type of search is largely the subject of this section.

As the expanded diagram of the decision process in Figure 7–2 desig-

FIGURE 7–2

Internal and External Search in the Decision Process

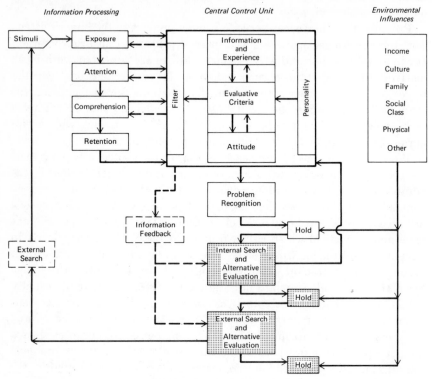

Source: James F. Engel, David T. Kollat, and Roger D. Blackwell, *Consumer Behavior*, 2d ed. (New York: Holt, Rinehart & Winston, 1973).

nates, internal search takes place upon problem recognition. This internally directed scan then results in information feedback. If information is sufficient to permit a decision, external search will be omitted, and the decision will be characterized as routinized or habitual. If it is insufficient, external search is activated and leads to the collection of necessary information which is processed as discussed earlier. This will continue until the information base is perceived to be sufficient to permit an optimal choice.

As before, the external environment can influence the decision process, and various constraining factors could serve to introduce a "holding stage" until they are resolved or are seen to be nonoperative.

Determinants of External Search

Whether or not search occurs is based on a comparison between the *value* perceived to result from this effort and the perceived *costs* of information collection.[5] Value is, of course, determined by the utility of the information, whereas costs may include psychological frustrations and expenditures of time and travel.[6]

Determinants of Perceived Value. Perceived rewards from search are affected by (1) the amount of presently stored information, (2) the utility of stored information, (3) ability to recall and use stored information, and (4) the degree of perceived decision risk.

The individual learns from his behavior and becomes more proficient over time. Therefore, the longer alternative products and brands have been purchased and used, the lower the tendency to search.[7] Stored information, however, is not always appropriate for a given purpose, especially when satisfaction from previous purchases has not been optimum, a long period of time has elapsed since previous experience, and the mix of alternatives has changed in important characteristics.[8] Thus propensity to search also is a function of perceived utility of the stored information.

Ability to recall relevant information is another determinant of search, because memory fades over time. Recall is enhanced when a current problem is similar to one faced previously. It also is strengthened if relevant previous behavior has been undertaken in the recent past.[9]

The extent of perceived financial, social, or physical risk is the final major determinant of external search.[10] As a generalization, the propensity to search increases with the degree of perceived risk.[11] More specifically, search increases with (1) the perceived importance of the action,[12] (2) the price of the product,[13] (3) the length of time the consumer is committed to use the product,[14] (4) the degree to which the product is socially

[5] R. H. Whiteley, Jr., and W. A. Watts, "Information Cost, Decision Consequence, and Selected Personality Variables as Factors in Predecision Information Seeking," *Journal of Personality,* Vol. 37 (1969), pp. 325–41.

[6] Wesley C. Bender, "Consumer Purchase Costs—Do Retailers Recognize Them?" *Journal of Retailing* (Spring 1964), pp. 1–8.

[7] George Katona, *The Mass Consumption Society* (New York: McGraw-Hill Book Co., 1964), pp. 289–90.

[8] George Katona, *Psychological Analysis of Economic Behavior* (New York: McGraw-Hill Book Co., 1961), pp. 67 and 68.

[9] Katona, *Mass Consumption Society.*

[10] Raymond A. Bauer, "Consumer Behavior as Risk Taking," in Robert S. Hancock (ed.), *Dynamic Marketing for a Changing World* (Chicago: American Marketing Association, 1960), pp. 389–98.

[11] See Donald F. Cox (ed.), *Risk Taking and Information Handling in Consumer Behavior* (Boston: Harvard University Graduate School of Business, 1967).

[12] J. T. Lanzetta and J. M. Driscoll, "Effects of Uncertainty and Importance on Information Search in Decision Making," *Journal of Personality and Social Psychology,* Vol. 10 (1968), pp. 479–86.

[13] William P. Dommermuth, "The Shopping Matrix and Marketing Strategy," *Journal of Marketing Research,* Vol. 2 (1965), pp. 128–32.

[14] George Katona and Eva Mueller, "A Study of Purchasing Decisions," in Clark (ed.), *Consumer Behavior,* p. 46.

visible,[15] (5) the extent to which some physiological risk is present, such as side effects in drug usage,[16] and (6) the number of separate decisions required within the purchase, such as choice of style, color, and brand.[17]

Determinants of Perceived Cost. It is often overlooked that information gathering has both psychological and monetary costs. In the first place, search delays the purchase, and pressures to culminate the act can become extreme, especially as the alterantives become increasingly defined and clear.[18] Moreover, visits to dealers are associated with the frustrations of finding parking places, interacting with indifferent or incompetent sales personnel, and so on. Finally, frequently financial outlays are required, in the form of dealer visits, purchase of magazines, and travel to see friends and relatives, to mention only several. The result is that consumers often minimize search first by limiting their attention to a familiar brand and secondly by choosing to pay an average price.[19] This also seems to be the common practice among those with the least educational attainment.[20]

Search from the Perspective of Consumer Welfare. Some who are concerned with consumer welfare feel that "rational" decision making requires exhaustive search. The frequently cited remedy to the pressures of consumerism thus is to provide better quality information in greater quantity.

There are undeniable consumer benefits resulting from such actions as improved nutritional labels on canned foods,[21] but there are also some important unanswered questions. First, how much information is enough? Is it possible to overload the information-processing ability of the consumer? Tentative pilot studies in consumer psychology at Purdue University have demonstrated the possibility that information overload can occur and that there may be limits on the quantity of information

---

[15] *Group Influence in Marketing and Public Relations* (Ann Arbor, Mich.: Foundation for Research on Human Behavior, 1956).

[16] James F. Engel, David A. Knapp, and Deanne E. Knapp, "Sources of Influence in the Acceptance of New Products for Self-Medication: Preliminary Findings," in Raymond M. Haas (ed.), *Science, Technology and Marketing* (Chicago: American Marketing Association, 1966), pp. 776–82.

[17] Donald F. Cox and Stewart Rich, "Perceived Risk and Consumer Decision-Making," *Journal of Marketing Research,* Vol. 1 (1964), pp. 32–39.

[18] John T. Lanzetta and Vera Kanareff, "Information Cost, Amount of Payoff and Level of Aspiration as Determinants of Information Seeking in Decision Making," *Behavioral Science,* Vol. 7 (1962), pp. 359–73.

[19] J. W. Newman and R. Staelin, "Prepurchase Information Seeking for New Cars and Major Household Appliances," *Journal of Marketing Research,* Vol. 9 (1972), pp. 249–57.

[20] Ibid.

[21] E. H. Asam and L. P. Bucklin, "Nutritional Labeling for Canned Goods: A Study of Consumer Response," *Journal of Marketing,* Vol. 37 (1973), pp. 32–37.

that can be absorbed.[22] In fact, one leader of the food industry maintains that consumers now have too much information, and the undereducated and the poor are unable to utilize the facts such as open dating and nutritional labels which were designed for their benefit.[23] Others, including the authors, are dubious of this allegation. In any case, it is debatable public policy to force information on the public unless it can be proved to be functional and useful.

The second question pertains to the quality of information. It seems likely that advertising and other forms of commercial persuasion are viable only if they provide information pertinent to salient evaluative criteria. In other words, it is not how much information is given but the pertinence of it from the consumer's point of view.

Related to this point is the very real danger of implied deception. For example, an experiment was undertaken comparing misleading versions with "straight" versions of the same commercials.[24] In one people were told that a make-believe product, Pro-Gro plant food, is protein enriched. Even if this were literally true, protein is of no value to plants. Yet it was believed by consumers that Pro-Gro is scientifically formulated as a result. Similarly, it was believed that sweaters from Heather Mills, a fictitious U.S. organization, were imported. The point is that even literal truth in the message can lead to a *comprehended message* which deviates from the truth and thereby is deceptive. Again, *more* information is not necessarily a benefit to the consumer.

In the final analysis this whole question is resolved on the basis of the information the consumer both *needs* in decision making and is *willing* to use. Industry is obligated to meet these legitimate needs.

Information Sources

What are the sources consumers use when they engage in external search? The variety of alternatives seems to be endless, but there are several basic categories: (1) the mass media, (2) personal sources, and (3) marketer-dominated sources. At the outset it should be stressed that these are complementary, and rarely is one used to the exclusion of others.

---

[22] Jacob Jacoby, D. E. Speller, and H. Kohn, "Brand Choice Behavior as a Function of Information Load: Study One," Purdue University Papers in Consumer Psychology No. 125, 1972, and Jacob Jacoby, "Consumer Reaction to Information Displays: Packaging and Advertising," paper delivered at Advertising and Public Interest Workshop, American Marketing Association, May 1973.

[23] Address delivered by Ray Stokes, director of the Consumer Research Institute to the American Marketing Association, Chicago chapter, October 10 1973.

[24] See "Research Shows Impact of Implied Deception," *Advertising Age,* April 2, 1973, p. 2.

Mass Media. In a world characterized by rapid communication through the mass media, it is to be expected that information from this source will be consulted frequently. The expert status reached by certain newspaper columnists and the phenomenal selling success of Johnny Carson attest to the power of certain well-known figures who have achieved reputations of impartiality and knowledge.

The mass media are also a source of information on new trends. *Better Homes and Gardens* and other magazines in the "shelter group" are widely used sources on furnishings and decorating trends. Similarly, *Mademoiselle, Playboy,* and other magazines relay information on fashions. Even a general magazine can perform this function, as is illustrated by the fact that the majority of the people patronizing a new automotive diagnostic center first became interested in this concept of car care through an article in *Reader's Digest.*[25]

Of considerable importance also is the rapid rise of independent organizations devoted to the testing and analysis of products and dissemination of this information. Consumers Union, publisher of the widely used *Consumer Reports,* is an outstanding example. *Consumer Reports* seems to be followed faithfully by its subscribers, with the result that published ratings can either greatly help or hinder the success of a product. It is said that the market success of the Accoustical Research (AR) high fidelity speakers is almost directly attributable to a favorable rating in this publication.

Personal Sources. Personal influence is a major information source in consumer decision making. Those who serve the important role of information dissemination through this channel are referred to as *opinion leaders,* although this term can be misleading, for reasons to be discussed later.

To illustrate the importance of personal influence, it has been found that nearly two-thirds of Indianapolis housewives told someone else about new products they purchased or tried.[26] Exposure to favorable word-of-mouth communication markedly increased the probability of purchase of a new food product.[27] Advertising stimulated initial interest in purchase of Contac, an over-the-counter cold remedy, but word-of-mouth communication was most significant in product trial.[28] Finally,

[25] James F. Engel, Robert J. Kegerreis, and Roger D. Blackwell, "Consumer Use of Information in the Adoption of an Innovation," *Journal of Advertising Research,* Vol. 9 (1969), pp. 3–8.

[26] C. W. King and J. O. Summers, "Technology, Innovation and Consumer Decision Making," in Reed Moyer (ed.), *Consumer, Corporate and Government Interfaces* (Chicago: American Marketing Association, 1967), pp. 63–68.

[27] Jon Arndt, "Role of Product-Related Conversations in the Diffusion of a New Product," *Journal of Marketing Research,* Vol. 4 (1967), pp. 291–95.

[28] Unpublished findings, Ohio State Studies in Self-Medication, 1970.

those who were the first users of an automotive diagnostic center were heavily prone to search for information through word of mouth.[29] Of the sources used to become aware of the center in the local market, 34 percent were reported to be word of mouth; when additional information was sought prior to use of the center, 85 percent of the information passed through this channel. Similar results have been found in such diverse areas as general fashions,[30] dental products and services,[31] and food products.[32]

THE OPINION LEADER. It should not be assumed that the source of the word-of-mouth influence, usually referred to as the opinion leader, is greatly different in characteristics from the recipient of this information. In this sense, the word "leader" is a misnomer, but it has become conventional.

There has been considerable research in recent years regarding opinion leader motivation and characteristics. The following generalizations are emerging:

1. _Motivation._ Motivations to talk about products or services fall into one or more of these categories:
   a. Product involvement—the more interested an individual is in product or service, the more likely he is to initiate conversations about it.[33]
   b. Self-involvement—sharing with others often performs the functions of gaining attention, showing connoisseurship, suggesting status, giving the impression that "inside information" is possessed, and asserting superiority.[34]
   c. Concern for others.
   d. Message involvement—some people find it entertaining to talk about certain advertisements, especially those that are unusual or humorous.[35]
   e. Dissonance reduction—sharing with others, on occasion, can

---

[29] Engel, Kegerreis, and Blackwell, "Consumer Use of Information."

[30] Charles W. King, "Fashion Adoption: A Rebuttal to the Trickle Down Theory," in S. A. Greyser (ed.), _Toward Scientific Marketing_ (Chicago: American Marketing Association, 1964), pp. 108–25.

[31] Alvin J. Silk, "Overlap among Self-Designated Opinion Leaders: A Study of Selected Dental Products and Services," _Journal of Marketing Research,_ Vol. 3 (August 1966), pp. 255–59.

[32] "Rare Research Opportunity in Word of Mouth Advertising" _Proceedings of the Advertising Research Foundation_ (New York, 1967), p. 10.

[33] Elihu Katz and Paul F. Lazarsfeld, _Personal Influence_ (Glencoe, Ill.: Free Press, 1955), pp. 249–52; 274–75; 239–42.

[34] Ernest Dichter, "How Word-of-Mouth Advertising Works," _Harvard Business Review,_ Vol. 44 (November–December, 1966), pp. 147–66.

[35] Ibid.

serve the functions of reducing doubt that the right alternative for purchase was chosen.[36]

2. *Scope of influence.* Contrary to earlier findings,[37] opinion leaders overlap across various product areas and are not product specific.[38]

3. *Demographic characteristics.* There is a tendency for leaders and followers to be homogeneous but there can be differences, as illustrated by the fact that women with large families tend to be neighborhood opinion leaders in treatment of children's ailments.[39]

4. *Social characteristics.* Gregariousness is often the most important distinguishing characteristic of the opinion leader.[40]

5. *Psychographic characteristics.* The findings are highly mixed, but a number of studies do identify such differences as greater willingness to innovate,[41] greater self-confidence,[42] and emotional stability.[43]

6. *Product-related characteristics.* The opinion leader is usually more interested in the topic such as fashion than the non-leader.[44]

7. *Media exposure.* The opinion leader is active in receiving interpersonal communications about products within their area of influence.[45] Also there is a tendency to be more exposed to the mass media, especially those that are relevant to the sphere of influence.[46]

EXPRESSION OF INTERPERSONAL INFLUENCE. For many years, it was felt that there was a "two-step flow" of communication. Specifically, this hypothesis stated that influences and ideas "flow from [the mass media]

---

[36] See the comprehensive literature review in Jon Arndt, "Word-of-Mouth Advertising," in D. F. Cox (ed.), *Risk Taking and Information Handling in Consumer Behavior* (Boston: Division of Research, Graduate School of Business, Harvard University, 1967), pp. 188–239.

[37] See for example Elihu Katz, "The Two Step Flow of Communication: An Up to Date Report on an Hypothesis," *Public Opinion Quarterly,* Vol. 21 (Spring 1957), pp. 61–78.

[38] This literature is reviewed in Engel, Kollat, and Blackwell, *Consumer Behavior,* pp. 399–400.

[39] Ohio State Studies in Self-Medication, 1970.

[40] F. D. Reynolds and W. R. Darden, "Mutually Adaptive Effects of Interpersonal Communication," *Journal of Marketing Research,* Vol. 8 (1971), pp. 449–54; J. O. Summers, "The Identity of Women's Clothing Fashion Opinion Leaders," *Journal of Marketing Research,* Vol. 7 (1970), pp. 178–85.

[41] J. O. Summers and C. W. King, "Interpersonal Communication and New Product Attitudes," in P. R. McDonald (ed.), *Marketing Involvement in Society and the Economy* (Chicago: American Marketing Association, 1969), pp. 292–99.

[42] See for example Reynolds and Darden, "Mutually Adaptive Effects," p. 450.

[43] Summers, "Women's Fashion Opinion Leaders."

[44] Ibid.

[45] Summers and King, "Interpersonal Communication."

[46] See for example Katz and Lazarsfeld, *Personal Influence,* pp. 309–20; Summers, "Women's Fashion Opinion Leaders," and Reynolds and Darden, *Mutually Adaptive Effects.*

to opinion leaders and from them to the less active sections of the population."[47] In other words, as Figure 7–3 illustrates, the mass media exert their greatest influence on the opinion leader, who then influences others.

FIGURE 7–3

The Two-Step Flow Hypothesis of Communication Processes

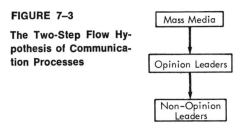

The two-step flow hypothesis no longer is felt to be accurate. The greatest error is that the audience is viewed as passive recipients of influence, whereas it has been found that up to 50 percent of word-of-mouth communications are initiated by consumers seeking information.[48] Indeed, the mass media can perform the important function of stimulating word-of-mouth communicating from both leaders and nonleaders, as Figure 7–4 shows.

FIGURE 7–4

Multistep interaction Model of Personal Influence

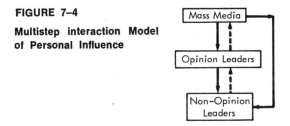

IMPLICATION FOR PROMOTIONAL STRATEGY. The importance of word-of-mouth communication should be obvious. The problem with this method of communication lies in developing reasonable strategies to capitalize upon it.

The greatest problem lies in identifying the opinion leader. Often they do not form a discrete segment which can be isolated and thus reached through appropriate media. Where they can be identified (and

[47] Paul F. Lazarsfeld, Bernard R. Berelson, and Hazel Gaudet, *The Peoples Choice* (New York: Columbia University Press, 1948), p. 151.

[48] D. F. Cox, "The Audience as Communicators," in Cox, *Risk Taking and Information Handling*, pp. 172–87.

this is possible on occasion,[49] several strategies are possible. First, advertisements can be directed to them in the hopes that they will use the product and talk to others. Second, the opinion leader tends to be an innovator, so monitoring of their behavior can be an advance notice of consumption trends. Third, products can be given or loaned to these individuals with the objective of stimulating interest among the non-leaders.

An alternative strategy is to stimulate interest among the public at large and hopefully encourage them to talk with others who might be leaders or influentials. Such campaigns as Alka-Seltzer's "Try it, you'll like it" are said to have stimulated considerable word of mouth.[50] The example was given earlier of the influence exerted by the initial advertisements for Contac in stimulating conversations from users to non-users and vice versa.

Whatever the strategy, the importance of word of mouth must not be ignored. The interpersonal channels are often most influential, in that most buyers assume that their friends have no commercial ax to grind. On the other hand, friends and neighbors may be perceived as lacking the competence to provide detailed information, and advertisements are consulted for this purpose. At the moment, it is not clear what type of information is likely to pass through one channel relative to another, and it becomes necessary continually to monitor the informal word-of-mouth channels.

Marketer-Dominated Channels. The major sources which are designated marketer dominated because of their commercial motivation are (1) advertisements, (2) visits to retail outlets, and (3) publicity.

ADVERTISEMENTS. Once a problem has been recognized, the buyer as a rule becomes more receptive to advertising.[51]

The objectives for advertising shift from stress on the generic product to brand superiority. A final purchase action may be stimulated by featuring special inducements such as price offers or coupons. The chances of advertising success are relatively high, because basic motivational determinants are more likely to be consistent with the suggested action. It must be stressed again, however, that accurate information must be

---

[49] See J. O. Summers, "Media Exposure Patterns of Consumer Innovators," *Journal of Marketing*, Vol. 36 (1972), pp. 43–49; R. C. Brooks, Jr., "Word of Mouth Advertising in Selling New Products," *Journal of Marketing*, Vol. 22 (1957), pp. 154–61; and T. Robertson, "The Process of Innovation and the Diffusion of Innovation," *Journal of Marketing*, Vol. 31 (1967), pp. 14–19.

[50] See for example J. R. Mancuso, "Why Not Create Opinion Leaders for New Product Introductions?" *Journal of Marketing*, Vol. 33 (1969), pp. 20–25.

[51] Robert W. Pratt, Jr., "Understanding the Decision Process for Consumer Durable Goods: An Example of the Application of Longitudinal Analysis," in Peter D. Bennett (ed.), *Marketing and Economic Development* (Chicago: American Marketing Association, 1965), pp. 244–60.

available on attitudes, needs, and other variables to avoid engaging the buyer's powers of selective attention, comprehension, and retention.

RETAIL VISITS. Personal selling can have a major part in those purchases in which perceived risk is likely to be greatest. It also is of significance in those situations where it is necessary to "fine tune" items at point of sale. Cases in point are the purchase of automobiles, expensive clothing involving fashion, major appliances, and furniture. In other instances, products are largely presold through advertising, and shelf availability and point-of-purchase promotional displays serve to bring the product to the buyer's awareness. Personal selling in these instances is less important than package design or displays.

All good salesmen know that brand preferences are least stable immediately prior to a purchase. Most readers can recall examples of impatience to buy once they have made a decision to do so. Many people are willing to accept more expensive items with many extras or even to buy substitutes rather than return home empty handed. The buyer, therefore, is probably most susceptible to suggestion at this point, and the opportunity is indeed bright for the salesman who correctly sizes up his prospects and directs their desires skillfully.

Retail salesmanship often seems to be a forgotten art today. Frequently an opportunity for profitable promotion is not capitalized upon effectively, and the reader should view personal selling as a remarkably effective tool to be used whenever the buyer requires adjustment of his demands to available products at point of sale. Salesmanship is discussed at greater length later.

PUBLICITY. Publicity is "information designed to advance the interests of a place, person, organization, or cause and submitted to the mass media to be used without charge because of its *general interest* to readers or listeners."[52] The usual objectives of business publicity are to help influence sales, to gain an acceptance of company policies, and to enhance the understanding between public and a business. In a very real sense, these objectives are long run and are designed to enhance continued survival and profitability. Through provision of press releases and other means information appears on product discoveries, scientific advances, company news, participation in community affairs, and so on. On occasion the information thus provided will be used by the consumer in decision making, especially when the news centers around new or improved products.

The Relative Importance of Information Sources. Since the prospect will often use multiple information sources, which is most important? Effectiveness of a given source can be evaluated using the following

[52] "Public Relations and Public Publicity," in A. W. Frey (ed.) *Marketing Handbook,* 2d ed. (New York: Ronald Press Co., 1965), pp. 19–21.

typology suggested by James F. Engel, David T. Kollat, and Roger D. Blackwell:

1. *Decisive effectiveness*—This category could be used when an information source played a specific role and was the most important source.
2. *Contributory effectiveness*—This category could be used when an information source played some specific role but was *not* the most important source.
3. *Ineffective*—This category could be used to describe an information source that did not play an role in a purchase situation, although the consumer was exposed to it.[53]

Based on research to date, the following generalizations[54] can be advanced regarding the relative effectiveness of the sources discussed above:

1. *Exposure.*—Marketing-dominated sources are usually most important in bringing about exposure, and this tends to prevail regardless of the type of choice or decision.
2. *Effectiveness.*—In terms of effectiveness, however, personal sources usually are superior to all others, largely for the reasons mentioned earlier.

It should be pointed out, however, that these generalizations are based on research done in the United States, and there can be substantial variations in overseas markets. For example, it has been a longstanding generalization that religious conversion is best stimulated through word-of-mouth influence. Yet, recent research in Thailand indicates that Muslims are most receptive to the Christian message if audio casettes are utilized, and other examples could be cited.[55]

In general it appears that the mass media perform an *informing* function, whereas personal sources assume a *legitimizing* role. Greater confidence in word of mouth seems to underlie this distinction.

PURCHASE PROCESSES

An extensive discussion of purchase or choice processes is beyond the scope of this book.[56] Since the subject is raised in later chapters with special reference to retail salesmanship and promotional policies, it is

---

[53] Engel, Kollat, and Blackwell, *Consumer Behavior*, p. 413.

[54] This research is reviewed in Ibid. pp. 415–16.

[55] J. F. Engel and H. W. Norton, *What's Gone Wrong With the Harvest: God and Man in the Mission of the Church* (Grand Rapids, Mich.: Zondervan Publishing, in press).

[56] See Engel, Kollat, and Blackwell, *Consumer Behavior*, ch. 19–21.

FIGURE 7–5

Purchasing Processes in the Decision Process

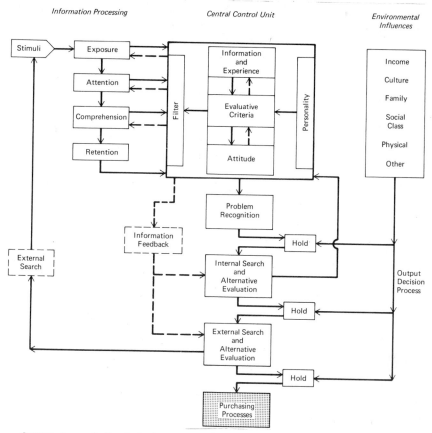

Source: James F. Engel, David T. Kollat, and Roger D. Blackwell, *Consumer Behavior*, 2d ed. (New York: Holt, Rinehart & Winston, 1973).

discussed only briefly here. The addition of purchasing processes to the decision process format is illustrated in Figure 7–5.

First it should be obvious that consumers often engage in an extended decision process in retail store selection. Determination of retail image is thus an important consideration, and the evaluative criteria used by consumers for this purpose can be complex.[57]

The consumer also may engage in further search while in the store. Stock on the shelves provides information for this purpose, as does

---

[57] For a good illustration see the "W. T. Grant (A)" case in R. D. Blackwell, J. F. Engel, and D. T. Kollat, *Cases in Consumer Behavior* (New York: Holt, Rinehart & Winston, 1969), pp. 82–88.

various point-of-purchase promotional material such as banners and "shelf talkers."

In-store promotion can do much to stimulate a sale. Advertisements and other attempts to stimulate purchase of a brand are stored in the buyer's memory and may remain latent until some stimulus in the store brings the earlier promotion to mind. The value of memory triggers of this type cannot be overestimated, especially in view of the fact that the typical self-service retail outlet carries thousands of products and brands.

In this context it is worth noting that what often appears to be an impulse purchase occurs because the housewife uses the shelves as a kind of shopping list. Her general purchase intentions may have been formed, but the presence of the items serves as a reminder of specific needs. Seeing the item, then, can trigger problem recognition which results in an immediate purchase decision. The consumer seldom is a victim of blind impulse during shopping trips.

Postpurchase Evaluation

As is indicated in the model in Figure 7–6, there can be two outcomes of purchasing choice: (1) triggering of new behavior and (2) postpurchase evaluation. The first outcome is obvious and requires no further discussion, but the possible implications of postpurchase evaluation are not so apparent.

There has been a series of studies raising the possibility that the consumer may experience doubts following a purchase.[58] This is referred to as post decision dissonance, and it is more probable when both the chosen and unchosen alternatives have desirable and (or) undesirable attributes, especially when the consumer has made a substantial outlay in the purchase.[59] It has been suggested that the consumer may search for information to buttress his decision, as the search arrow in Figure 7–6 designates. If this is so, then the manufacturer may stand to benefit by providing advertisements or other forms of promotion to the new purchaser to guarantee that he will arrive at a state of satisfaction with the product. A failure to do so, according to some, may lead to negative word of mouth.

It may well be that consumers do read advertisements following purchase, but it should not be assumed that this is done to reduce doubts. They may simply have a greater interest in the product category at this

---

[58] Sadaomi Oshikawa, "Can Cognitive Dissonance Theory Explain Consumer Behavior?" *Journal of Marketing,* Vol. 33 (October 1969), pp. 44–49.

[59] See J. W. Brehm and A. R. Cohen, *Explorations in Cognitive Dissonance* (New York: John Wiley & Sons, 1962).

FIGURE 7–6

Postpurchase Evaluation in the Decision Process

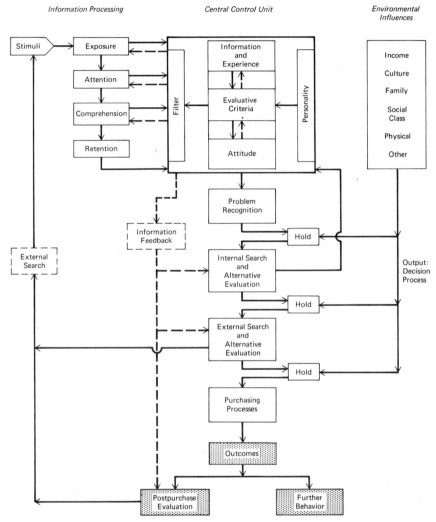

Source: James F. Engel, David T. Kollat, and Roger D. Blackwell, *Consumer Behavior*, 2d ed. (New York: Holt, Rinehart & Winston, 1973).

point than they did before purchase, and it is not at all evident that they avoid advertising by competitors.

Even if the consumer does use advertisements to reduce dissonance, this does not mean that specific appeals should be designed for that purpose. The dissonant consumer wants evidence of brand superiority, and that is exactly what most promotional appeals emphasize. Thus, in most situations postdecision evaluation need not be a concern in promotional strategy.

Habitual Decision Process Behavior

Thus far the discussion has centered only on extended decision-process behavior, which is most likely to occur when the consumer perceives some type of risk in the choice process. Risk may be financial, physical, social, or some combination of these three.[60] Extended decision making, especially external search, then occurs in order to reduce perceived risk to a tolerable level.

At the opposite end of a continuum is the habitual decision behavior depicted in Figure 7–7. Problem recognition occurs, but internal search provides adequate information to permit choice. External constraints may operate to inhibit the decision process, but their effect is usually less. There will be no external search, and postdecision evaluation is not likely.

To illustrate the differences, consider the purchase of a tank of gasoline. In most instances, the purchase will be largely on the basis of habit, and extended problem-solving behavior arises only when the driver is faced with unusual circumstances.[61]

Problem recognition usually will occur when the gauge is seen to be approaching empty (although some seem to disregard this signal and let the tank run out before acting). The usual act is to drive to the nearest familiar service station and refill the tank. No search process or alternative evaluation ensues, and it is unlikely that there is any type of complex purchase process or any post purchase evaluation.

Brand loyalty in the gasoline industry is a common phenomenon. Rather than preference for only one brand, however, it seems several brands are about equally preferred. If one brand receives a larger percentage of sales than the others, it will be determined by station preference. The products themselves tend to be quite similar, but there are very real perceived differences in station quality. Therefore a good marketing job at point of sale assumes major importance.

The use of credit cards also has served to promote company loyalty. Until recently, the companies considered the presence of a credit card in a buyer's hand to be a great asset, but multiple card usage and the almost universal acceptance of general bank cards such as Mastercharge

---

[60] R. A. Bauer, "Consumer Behavior as Risk Taking," in R. S. Hancock (ed.), *Dynamic Marketing for a Changing World* (Chicago: American Marketing Association, 1960), pp. 389–98.

[61] This discussion is based on unpublished studies undertaken by a leading firm in the gasoline industry.

FIGURE 7–7

Habitual Decision-Process Behavior

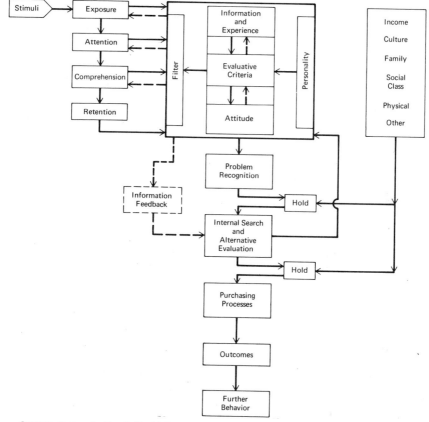

Source: James F. Engel, David T. Kollat, and Roger D. Blackwell, *Consumer Behavior,* 2d ed. (New York: Holt, Rinehart & Winston, 1973).

and BankAmericard have diluted this source of brand loyalty. In other countries such as Canada, however, the credit card is still important as a source of loyalty.

Why does any brand loyalty occur in this type of purchase? One obvious reason is the consumer's desire to avoid making decisions in the interest of greater buying efficiency. He establishes buying routines for this purpose. In other situations, he might be personally committed to the brand in that it somehow is an extension of his conception of himself. Although this may be a bit farfetched in this situation, the buyer might feel that the heavy emphasis on racing by his preferred company contributes to his own desire for power. It is more probable that trust in the local station overrides any such commitment to the brand itself.

Company and station loyalty, for many people, is quite small, and some genuine switching was promoted by the emphasis on competing games and promotional appeals that various companies featured in the late 1960s until widespread abuses and public apathy led to a change of emphasis. In other instances, however, the buyer would switch for one or two purchases but would return to his preferred brand sooner or later, to preserve his usual buying routine. Promoting brand switching through marketing efforts can be a formidable and costly task.

FAMILY INFLUENCES ON THE DECISION PROCESS

The family, in contrast to the larger social systems discussed in Chapter 5, is a *primary group*, characterized by face-to-face association and cooperation. This means that the family is uniquely important in determining individual personality and attitudes. The family also differs in that it is both an earning and a consuming unit. Finally, it serves to filter the norms and values of larger social systems so that these influences upon the individual often are altered.

In this section, the significance of the family in the decision process is the primary consideration. Two aspects in particular are relevant: (1) effects on individual predisposition and (2) family role structures in household decision making.

Effects on the Individual

The family is a primary group with continuous person-to-person interaction. As a unit it shares financial resources and has common consumption needs. Thus motives of family members become more homogeneous than do those of members of other groups. At times, however, there will be conflict in motives of individual members, with the result that purchase decisions will generate conflict. For promotional planning it is necessary to know which motives are operative and the degree to which they are unique to the individual or common to family members. When they are unique to the individual, of course, appeal will be made only to that person. Where motives are shared without conflict, appeal is made to all members in common. The problem arises when conflict exists, as it might, for example, when the wife prefers cultural activities for recreation and the husband prefers sports. The best promotional strategy might be to legitimize the motive of each member (for example, the husband needs golf to relax) and communicate this to the family as a whole.

A considerable degree of attitude convergence exists in most families as individuals interact with each other. Moreover, attitudes may exist in harmony or in conflict. In some situations the attitudes of other family members will not be taken into account; in others, they will be highly relevant. It appears that the extent to which one individual considers others' attitudes in a given purchase is a function of: (1) the individual's decision-making competence, (2) cultural norms clarifying which members should dominate, (3) the individual's needs for power and affiliation, and (4) the extent to which others contribute economic and social resources to the family.[62]

Unfortunately, the process of family decision making has not been extensively investigated, and it is difficult to generalize how conflict situations become resolved. There are a number of purchases, however, in which the family functions as a unit, in which case promotional strategy must be based on evidence concerning the interaction process.[63]

Family Role Structures

Role structure refers to the behavior of family members at each stage in the decision process. There are the following possibilities: (1) autonomic—equal number of decisions made by each spouse; (2) husband dominant; (3) wife dominant; and (4) syncratic—most decisions made by both partners.[64] Of course, these will vary from product to product.

Bases of Role Structure Variations. All societies have different roles for men and women, and it is common for the male to take leadership in task fulfillment, whereas the wife more often functions to bring about family cohesion and morale.[65] But these general role specifications differ in such subcultures as the black market, where the mother often must serve as family leader. Moreover, the role of each member changes throughout the family life cycle. As the length of marriage increases, for example, the degree of joint decision making decreases as each member gains competence.[66] Other factors also intervene, such as social class and geographical location.[67]

Variations by Product and Stage in Decision. Figure 7–8 contains material in summary form documenting how role structures vary by product and by stage in the decision process.

---

[62] See James N. Morgan, "Household Decision Making," in Nelson Foote (ed.), *Household Decision Making* (New York: New York University Press, 1961), p. 91.

[63] Most of the published literature to date and the marketing implications are reviewed in Engel, Kollat, and Blackwell, *Consumer Behavior,* ch. 7.

[64] See P. G. Herbst, "Conceptual Framework for Studying the Family," in O. A. Oeser and S. B. Hammond (eds.), *Social Structure and Personality in a City* (London: Routledge and Kegan Paul, 1954).

[65] See Bernard A. Berelson and Gary A. Steiner, *Human Behavior* (New York: Harcourt, Brace & World, 1964), p. 314.

[66] Elizabeth H. Wolgast, "Do Husbands or Wives Make Purchasing Decisions?" *Journal of Marketing,* Vol. 23 (October 1958), pp. 151–58.

[67] See Engel, Kollat, and Blackwell, *Consumer Behavior.*

FIGURE 7–8

The Roles of Husbands and Wives at Various Stages of Household Decision-Making Behavior* (in percent)

Product	Initial Recognition of Problem by		Information Seeking				Alternative Evaluation (Brand)		Purchase	
			Personal Sources		Nonpersonal Sources					
	Husband	Wife	Husband	Wife	Husband	Wife	Husband	Wife	Husband	Wife
Refrigerators	71.4	89.0	91.8	84.9	59.2	54.8	32.7	45.2	71.4	79.4
Vacuum cleaners	35.7	83.1	76.2	87.0	26.2	42.9	35.7	62.3	54.8	81.8
Automobiles	92.8	38.7	79.8	80.7	56.7	43.3	75.3	20.7	93.8	52.0
Frozen orange juice	31.4	82.0	20.0	44.1	41.4	48.6	—	—	38.6	93.7
Rugs, carpets	49.3	93.5	68.1	81.3	55.1	65.4	14.5	53.3	58.0	91.6
Paint	60.0	74.2	70.9	63.5	21.8	28.7	74.5	53.4	70.0	47.2

* Percentages are based on each spouse's self-appraisal. The percentages indicate whether or not the spouse in question was involved. Categories such as "both husband and wife" or "children" were not used, so the percentages can total more or less than 100 percent.

Source: "A Pilot Study of the Roles of Husbands and Wives in Purchasing Decisions," conducted for *Life* magazine by L. Jaffe Associates, Inc., New York, 1965, parts I–X. Interviews were held with 301 middle-income and upper-income households in Hartford, Cleveland, and Seattle.

Notice, for example, that the greater the price of the item, the greater the tendency for the husband to be involved in problem recognition; automobiles and refrigerators are examples. Also, the extent of involvement seems to vary according to cultural norms of specialization, such as the obvious interest of the husband when the product is technically or mechanically complex.

It is apparent that both husbands and wives have a greater tendency to seek information from personal sources such as friends or relatives than from advertisements. Also, wives appear to be involved to a greater extent than husbands in information seeking, except in those products having mechanical or technical complexity or high price. Finally, wives' participation seems to vary less across products than does the participation of husbands.

Not surprisingly, husbands are more involved in evaluation of alternatives when the product attains some complexity. Yet in absolute terms wives are more involved in this stage of the decision process than are husbands.

Finally, the wife is most frequently involved in the actual purchase, and it is not uncommon for her to be designated as the *household purchasing agent*. This designation does vary substantially from product to product, however, as is indicated by the data in Figure 7–8. For example, the husband is more involved in purchasing refrigerators, paint, and automobiles.

It should be stressed that the percentages in Figure 7–8 are only rough indicators, and it is probable that there is wide interfamily variation. Stage in life cycle, for example, is a variable which will account for a number of differences.

Implications of Family Role Structures. Family role structures are of importance in determining, first, who should be the primary recipient of promotional messages. Second, the type of information featured will vary depending upon the role each member assumes. The wife may be more interested in the color and appearance of the automobile, and advertisements with this type of emphasis should be designed with female influence in mind. The husband, on the other hand, will generally be more concerned with performance and should be appealed to in these terms. Many other examples could be given.

SUMMARY

A wealth of material has been covered in this chapter and a number of implications for promotional strategy have been suggested. Discussion centered mostly on extended decision-process behavior, although the contrasts with habitual decision-process behavior were clarified. Regardless of the type of decision situation, it was pointed out that promotion usually plays only a small role in triggering problem recognition, its real impact is felt as the consumer undergoes search and alternative evaluation, later stages in the process. Many information sources are used, including the mass media, word of mouth, and various forms of marketer-dominated communication (advertising, retail visits, and publicity). The manufacturer must be aware of these information sources so that media selection and the promotional message itself are properly oriented.

It should be stressed that extended decision-process behavior is probably the exception rather than the rule with most products. For various reasons it is necessary to develop buyer routines. As a result, limited decision behavior or habitual purchasing are more common. The marketing implications differ in each situation, so it is necessary to understand the decision process before promotional strategy can be formulated.

REVIEW AND DISCUSSION QUESTIONS

1. Compare and contrast the decision processes that might be involved if the purchase of a pair of mens' slacks is represented as: (a) extended decision-process behavior, or (b) habitual decision-process behavior. Which type of behavior is most likely?

2. How does problem recognition differ from product or brand awareness and initial interest?

3. Assume that you are the director of marketing planning for a large cosmetic manufacturer that recently has become the leader in the market for womens' electric hair-setting machines. Your product consists of a number of electrically heated curlers which allow the woman to set her hair in 30 minutes or less. Management has suggested that it is necessary to stimulate problem recognition in a larger proportion of the market. What are your recommendations concerning (a) the desirability of stimulating problem recognition, (b) the techniques that should be used for this purpose, and (c) the probability of success?

4. The majority of purchases are not preceded by external search. Why?

5. What is the two-step hypothesis? Is it an adequate model for the word-of-mouth process? Why, or why not?

6. Studies show that consumers usually visit only one store before making a purchase. Does this mean that store visits are not an important source of information? Discuss.

7. What is an opinion leader? Do they differ from those they seek to influence?

8. Prepare a statement which gives generalizations on the relative roles of mass media, personal sources, and marketer-dominated sources in the consumer's processes.

9. What are evaluative criteria? Can they be changed through promotion?

10. You are a consultant for a major manufacturer of refrigerators. Your research shows that wives are more actively involved in alternative evaluation but that husbands play an important role in determining how much to

spend and in evaluating mechanical features. What are your recommendations for the firm's promotional strategy?

11. What is meant by company or brand image? How is it measured? Can images be changed? Is the concept of image also useful for the retailer?

12. What is meant by impulse purchase?

13. The brand manager for a brand of soft drink sees an article on cognitive dissonance and goes to his advertising agency with the question of whether or not users of this product experience postdecision dissonance. What do you think the answer would be? Why?

14. Would postdecision dissonance be more probable if the product in question 13 was radial tires? What are the implications for advertising?

15. As a consultant for a large firm which manufactures stereo equipment you find from group interviews with families that brand preferences are very unstable during the alternative evaluation and purchase-process stages of decision making. Based on this information, what are your recommendations for promotional strategy?

8

The Legal Environment
for Promotion

THE CREATIVE PROCESS which is the basis of effective promotional strategy by definition requires discipline. One of the areas of discipline is to see that there are no violations, intentional or unintentional, of laws and regulations controlling the content or mode of delivery of promotional communication.

The legal constraints on marketing in general and promotion in particular have multiplied rapidly over the years. Congress has been especially busy over the past decade and a half. Although it is necessary to review the major restrictions on promotion in this text, this review cannot be exhaustive. Enough detail is provided, however, to enable the reader to sense the current direction of governmental regulatory policy and to establish whether or not a proposed promotional campaign meets the legal requirements set by Congress and the various regulatory agencies.[1]

PERTINENT LEGISLATION

Federal Legislation

Prior to the 20th century the doctrine of *caveat emptor* prevailed, with little or no buyer protection against false and deceptive methods of

---

[1] For a more detailed background on legislation see S. Watson Dunn, *Advertising: Its Role in Modern Marketing,* 2d ed. (New York: Holt, Rinehart & Winston, 1969), pp. 119–24.; Earl Kintner, "How Advertising Has Policed Itself," in *Advertising Today, Yesterday and Tomorrow* (New London, Conn.: Printers' Ink Publishing Co., 1962), pp. 408–11.; "How Government Regulates Advertising," *Advertising Age,*

sale. Post Office fraud laws were adopted in 1872 to provide remedies against the use of the mails to defraud, but effective legal curbs awaited passage of the Pure Food and Drug Act in 1906 and, most significantly, the Federal Trade Commission Act of 1914.

The Pure Food and Drug Act. A series of articles was published by Samuel Adams in 1906 to expose quackery and unfair practices in the sale of patent medicines. Shortly after this exposé, the Pure Food and Drug Act was passed by Congress. This act was intended from its inception to have limited applicability; it served only to require correct description of contents on the package of drug items. It was superseded in 1938 by the Federal Food, Drug, and Cosmetic Act, to be discussed later.

The Federal Trade Commission Act. The Pure Food and Drug Act did little to prevent advertising and selling abuses, and the first truly effective legislation passed was the Federal Trade Commission Act of 1914. While the prevention of deceptive advertising was only a secondary purpose, Section Five prohibited unfair methods of competition in interstate commerce where the effect is to injure competition. The Federal Trade Commission (FTC), strengthened by key Supreme Court decisions, began to move against false and misleading advertising, and 70 percent of the cases processed by the Commission fell into this category by 1925.[2] Enforcement efforts, however, were severely limited by the Raladam case of 1931, in which the Supreme Court held that the Commission lacked jurisdiction over false and misleading advertising in the absence of proof of substantial competitive injury.[3]

In 1936 Congress passed the Robinson-Patman Act, a law designed to give the FTC broad powers to control discriminatory pricing practices. Sections 2d and 2e of the act prohibit the offering by sellers or the seeking by buyers of advertising allowances and promotional services which are not available on a proportionately equal basis to all firms selling the same product or service in competition with one another.

The Wheeler-Lea Amendment to the Federal Trade Commission Act in 1938 added significantly to the Commission's powers.[4] Congress provided that intent to defraud no longer needed to be proved before action could legally be taken, thereby giving the Commission broader jurisdiction. Other fundamental changes were as follows: (1) "unfair methods of competition" was expanded to encompass deceptive acts or practices,

---

November 21, 1973, pp. 144–55.; "How the U.S. Regulates Advertising," *The World of Advertising* (Chicago: Advertising Publications, 1962), p. 182 ff.; and the monthly publication *Washington Report* (Washington, D.C.: American Advertising Federation).

[2] See Kintner, "How Advertising Has Policed Itself," p. 409.

[3] Ibid.

[4] Public Law 447, approved March 21, 1938, 75th Cong., 3d sess., U.S. Stat. L., Vol. 52.

(2) the Commission was empowered to issue cease and desist orders which become binding after 60 days, (3) the Commission was given jurisdiction over false advertising of foods, drugs, and cosmetics, and (4) the Commission was permitted to issue injunctions to halt improper food, drug, or cosmetic advertising when it appeared the public might be harmed.

The years following the Wheeler-Lea Amendment have been marked by a series of congressional actions aimed at requiring certain industries to provide special disclosures of information through their labeling and advertising activities, to prevent consumer deception and to facilitate consumer comparison of alternate product or service offerings. The specific laws which have given the FTC greatly increased powers over the promotional activities of firms in these industries include the following six laws, the names of which indicate the nature of their applicability: the Wool Products Act (1939), the Fur Products Labeling Act (1951), the Textile Fiber Products Act (1958), the Fair Packaging and Labeling Act (1966), the Truth in Lending Act (1969) and the Fair Credit Reporting Act (1970).

The Commission staff continually monitors all forms of interstate advertising.[5] For example, television networks are required to submit typed scripts covering one broadcasting week each month. Also a substantial number of complaints from individual citizens are processed and acted upon yearly.

A preliminary investigation is held if it appears that action is required. Minor complaints may be turned over to the Division of Stipulation for an informal nonpublicized settlement, but more serious cases result in a formal complaint issued by the Bureau of Litigation upon the approval of the full Commission. A respondent has 30 days to answer a formal complaint, after which a hearing is held before an examiner. The examiner's decision may be appealed to the Commission by either side, and, in turn, Commission decisions may be appealed through the federal courts. A consent order may be issued by the Commission whereby actions are enjoined but no guilt is admitted by the respondent. A finding of guilty after formal proceedings, however, culminates in a cease and desist order. Both consent orders and cease and desist orders are binding.

The Commission on its own volition or at the request of an industry group occasionally will call a trade conference to establish a code of fair practice. The codes thus established may cover activities deemed to be illegal by the Commission, such as the use of fictitious list prices, or unethical practices which technically are within the law.

In late 1973, the FTC was further strengthened by passage of legisla-

---

[5] See Advertising Alert No. 2, February 12, 1962, published by the Federal Trade Commission.

tion appended to the Alaska Pipeline Bill. The law authorizes the FTC
to institute its own court actions if the Justice Department does not act
within ten days on an FTC request; increases penalties for violation of
cease and desist orders from $5,000 to $10,000; and permits the FTC to
obtain preliminary injunctions against unfair or deceptive advertising.
In addition, the bill grants all federal regulatory agencies, including the
FTC, far-reaching information-gathering powers.

   The Federal Food, Drug, and Cosmetic Act.   The earlier act of 1906
was supplanted in 1938 by the Federal Food, Drug, and Cosmetic Act.
The Food and Drug Administration (FDA) is empowered to investigate
and litigate advertising claims appearing on the label or package of food,
drug, and cosmetic items. The FTC monitors all other forms of advertising for these products.

   As a result of increasing pressures for more effective efforts to protect
the consumer, the Hazardous Substance Labeling Act was passed in
1960. This law requires special disclosure on the label for household
products that have toxic, corrosive, irritant, or similar characteristics.[6]
In 1962 still more regulatory power was granted the FDA with the
amendment of the 1938 act to give the FDA authority to establish
"comprehensive procedures providing for pre-marketing approval of
claims and labels for prescription drugs, as well as provisions which
assure that advertising is consistent with permissible labeling claims."[7]
This legislation was especially aimed at gaining the full disclosure of
side effects and complications that might be associated with prescription
drugs.

   The Truth in Packaging Act (1966) granted the FDA additional
powers to require disclosure of information on labels of food, drug, and
cosmetic products and to regulate packaging procedures which might
tend to confuse consumers or make product comparisons difficult.[8]

   The FDA has the power to seize shipments of goods upon receipt of
evidence that its regulations have been violated. Notable examples of
seizure in recent years include shipments of frozen orange juice allegedly
containing misrepresentation of contents and shipments of coffee containing false price information.[9] Of course, in the situations where consumer health is endangered the FDA has recalled entire batches of
canned tuna, mushrooms, and soups where the threat of botulism appeared to exist.

   For many years the FDA and the FTC were antagonists because of
the overlapping nature of their jurisdictions. It is important to note that

---

[6] The 1972 law which created the Consumer Product Safety Commission transferred to it from the FDA the responsibility for enforcing the 1960 law.

[7] "How Government Regulates Advertising," p. 148.

[8] Ibid.

[9] See "How the U.S. Regulates Advertising," p. 182.

in recent years the two agencies have become close collaborationists rather than rivals. The FDA with its vast scientific resources does the testing of product efficacy. Although the FDA is limited to what goes on the label (with the exception of prescription drugs where it also controls advertised claims), the results of its experimentation are used by the FTC as the basis of its charges of misrepresentation or fraud.

In 1962, with the advent of the new legislation, the FDA undertook a study of the effectiveness of all prescription drugs then on the market. Findings announced ten years later resulted in the removal from the market of several products which were deemed to be ineffective. At that time the FDA began a similar study of over-the-counter products such as analgesics and antacids.

With a markedly increased budget in recent years, with vast scientific resources, and with a new era of cooperation with the FTC, the FDA is a potent force in the regulation of product development and promotion by members of the food, drug, and cosmetics industries. Insofar as firms in these industries are among the largest spenders for promotion, the influence of the FDA on American marketing practices is formidable.

State and Local Regulation

The inadequacies of the Pure Food and Drug Act passed in 1906 led to demands for regulation within the advertising industry itself, and *Printers' Ink* responded by proposing its "model statute" in 1911. This has since been adopted in whole or in modified form by the great majority of states. The provisions of the model statute specify clearly what practices constitute deceptive advertising, and it undergoes occasional modification to reflect changing standards of practice.

The variety of local laws pertaining to advertising truly defies description. Some legislation strongly parallels the *Printers' Ink* model statute. Other laws regulate house-to-house selling, advertising appeals, and the use of such media as billboards and signs.

IMPORTANT AREAS OF REGULATION

The vigor of regulatory activity by the federal government with respect to the promotional activities of business has increased steadily over the past decade and a half. The special message sent to Congress by President John F. Kennedy in 1962 entitled "Strengthening of Programs for Protection of Consumer Interests"[10] can be said to have marked the beginning of an era. Certainly the years since the early sixties have been marked with legislation and administrative actions

---

[10] *Congressional Record,* March 15, 1962, 108, 3813–3817

aimed at promoting a fuller realization of the rights of consumers. In his special message Kennedy enumerated the following four basic rights:

1. *The right to safety*—to be protected against the marketing of goods which are hazardous to health or life.
2. *The right to be informed*—to be protected against fraudulent, deceitful, or grossly misleading information, advertising, labeling, or other practices and to be given the facts he needs to make an informed choice.
3. *The right to choose*—to be assured, wherever possible, access to a variety of products and services at competitive prices, and in those industries in which competition is not workable and government regulation is substituted, an assurance of satisfactory quality and service at fair prices.
4. *The right to be heard*—to be assured that consumer interests will receive full and sympathetic consideration in the formulation of government policy, and fair and expeditious treatment in its administrative tribunals.

As noted in the preceding sections, the Federal Trade Commission and the Food and Drug Administration are the major but by no means the only recipients of power to regulate promotional activity by business. We will discuss briefly some of the regulatory efforts of these two agencies and the philosophy underlying their actions.

Content of Advertisements

A large proportion of present and proposed regulation involves restriction or control of the content of the advertisement.[11] These questions of content include whether or not the advertisement is truthful, in bad taste, invades the reader's right of privacy, and so forth. The FTC has been especially concerned with cases of deception, while the legislative branch of the federal government has passed laws which actually forbid the advertising of certain products in selected media.

Misleading Representation. Many of the complaints issued by the FTC were aimed at stopping such overt deceptions as the misrepresentation of foreign merchandise as having domestic origin or claiming in the absence of proof that a wheat germ oil improves heart action.[12] A more important issue from the viewpoint of the mass communicator, however, has arisen from a series of complaints issued by the FTC pertaining to the representation of products in television commercials.

The so-called sandpaper case stands as a landmark. The Ted Bates

---

[11] See Dunn, *Advertising,* pp. 107–10.
[12] Advertising Alert No. 8, August 30, 1963.

Advertising Agency claimed in a series of television commercials that Palmolive Rapid Shave would soften sandpaper sufficiently to permit shaving the sand grains from the paper.[13] To illustrate this claim on television a sheet of plexiglass covered with sand was substituted for sandpaper. The Commission held that such a representation was false and misleading, but the respondents answered that the technical requirements of television present such difficulties that substitutes often must be made for materials used in commercials. They went on to point out that there was no intent to deceive and that such substitution in no way misrepresented product qualities. The FTC ruled as follows, however:

The argument . . . would seem to be based on the wholly untenable assumption that the primary or dominant function of television is to sell goods, and that the Commission should not make any ruling which would impair the ability of sponsors and agencies to use television with maximum effectiveness as a sales or advertising medium. . . . Stripped of polite verbiage, the argument boils down to this: "Where truth and television salesmanship collide, the former must give way to the latter." This is obviously an indefensible proposition. . . .[14]

As a result of this decision, *both the client and the agency were prohibited from making any type of deceptive claim in the future.* Notice that the order issued was so broad as to prohibit future deception, although criteria defining deception were not in existence. The courts held that such a broad order was improper and remanded the FTC to reconsider the case. A revised order was later issued.[15] The Commission was upheld by the federal courts, and it was a final decision that the sandpaper mock-up used was deceptive. This finding does not mean that mock-ups and other artificial devices are prohibited; rather, it constrains the advertiser from using demonstrations which are likely to mislead.

The courts have traditionally held that advertising must be written so as not to deceive "the trusting as well as the suspicious, the casual as well as the vigilant, the naive as well as the sophisticated."[16] In the sandpaper case the product did not remove grains from sandpaper in the manner claimed in the television commercial. Doubts have been expressed, however, as to whether such a presentation really misrepresents product features in such a manner as to be harmful to the consumer. The problem is, of course, one of defining where puffing stops and misrepresentation begins.

Since the sandpaper case the FTC has handled several similar situations. In one case the FTC accepted an assurance of voluntary compliance from Lever Brothers Company, Inc., to discontinue certain TV commer-

---

[13] Advertising Alert No. 1, January 12, 1962.

[14] Ibid.

[15] Advertising Alert No. 6, June 28, 1963.

[16] "How the U.S. Regulates Advertising," p. 184.

cials advertising its laundry detergent, All. The TV spots in question showed an actor wearing a stained shirt being immersed in water up to his chin. As the water rose the actor added the detergent and expounded on its efficacy. As the water receded the actor showed off his stainfree shirt. The FTC ascertained that the shirt had been washed in the interim by means of a standard washing machine and had not been cleaned by the immersion process.

Voluntary compliance rather than more formal means of procedure was accepted in this use by the FTC because it was held that the commercial in question was of a "fanciful or spoofing" variety. The FTC held, however, that even these types of commercials can be misleading and suggested that any advertiser in doubt as to whether his commercial had the capacity to deceive should make application to the FTC for an advisory ruling prior to the dissemination of the commercial for broadcast.[17]

A recent action against misleading advertising occurred in March 1970 when the FTC issued a consent order prohibiting the Colgate-Palmolive Company and its advertising agency from using "deceptive tests, experiments or demonstrations to sell its products." The FTC specifically challenged the truthfulness of a water demonstration TV commercial for Baggies, the company's brand of plastic bag wrap.[18]

It should be noted that "consent orders differ from orders in litigated cases only in that they do not constitute a finding or an admission that respondents have violated the law."[19] They are fully as binding in forbidding respondents to engage in the practices prohibited by the order. Consent orders cannot be appealed to the courts. Sixty days after their issuance they become enforcable by fines up to $10,000 per violation.

The Fairness Doctrine.   The cases discussed above are illustrative of the FTC in its classic role: directing its efforts to the elimination of fraud and deception. With the increased public interest in consumerism and the additional powers granted the FTC by Congress during the decade of the sixties, a subtle but important change took place in the regulatory philosophy of the FTC. No longer would the main concern of the agency be the elimination of fraud and deception. The new goal was to make certain that promotional efforts of businessmen, and especially advertising efforts, would be "fair" to the consumer. Thus the birth of what the FTC has termed the "fairness doctrine."

Given the concept of fairness in advertising, several important new questions are raised. For example, should product shortcomings as well as product advantages be publicized? Should the availability of com-

---

[17] Advertising Alert No. 3, March 31, 1969.
[18] Ibid.
[19] Ibid.

peting products of equal price and quality be communicated? Should children be shielded from promotional messages which might induce them to pressure their parents to buy a product? In attempting to answer these questions many advertisers reached the conclusion that regulation had moved to a higher and perhaps more dangerous level.

As a corollary to the fairness doctrine, in 1971 the FTC developed a program of "advertising substantiation" under which advertisers would be required to submit proof of claims made in their current advertisements. In that same year companies in over a dozen industries, including manufacturers of automobiles, health and beauty aids, and electrical appliances, were ordered by the FTC to submit proof of advertised claims.[20]

As yet another outgrowth of the "fairness doctrine" the FTC developed the concept of "corrective advertising." This called for an advertiser found guilty of misrepresentation to devote a certain portion of his future advertising to "correct" his past errors. In 1971, for example, the Sun Oil Company and its advertising agency were charged by the FTC with falsely advertising that cars will operate at maximum power and performance only with Sunoco gasoline. The company was also charged with creating the false impression that its gasoline had unique properties not found in other brands. In addition to taking action to stop the alleged misrepresentations, the FTC sought to require that 25 percent of all Sunoco ads for the next 12 months be devoted to "a clear disclosure that contrary to prior representations . . . automobiles do not perform better with Sunoco than with other gasolines of equal octane."[21]

Sugar Information Inc. and Sugar Association Inc. were also cited for their ads which suggested that weight watchers could control their appetites with premeal snacks containing sugar. Because the FTC believed that the sugar groups would not advertise for a year if the same remedy were applied to them as to Sun Oil Company, a new "corrective" was sought. This would be the mandatory placement of a corrective ad in every magazine in which a challenged ad had previously appeared.[22]

As of this writing there has been no resolution of the Sunoco case, but in 1972 the sugar group agreed to the FTC consent order. In that same year Profile bread and Ocean Spray cranberry juice also agreed to run corrective advertising.

Inasmuch as the fairness doctrine espoused by the FTC had its origination in the Federal Communication Commission's equal-time requirements for political candidates, it is not surprising to find yet an-

---

20 "How Government Regulates Advertising," p. 147.

21 *Washington Report*, December 9, 1971, p. 7.

22 *Washington Report*, August 29, 1972, p. 4.

other idea brewing at the FTC—"counteradvertising." Under this concept the FCC would apply its equal-time rules to product advertising on the airwaves. For example, if the manufacturer of a large-sized automobile advertised on radio and television that his product offered a smoother and safer ride than small cars did, equal time would be offered to groups that might wish to point out that larger cars use more fuel and are more likely to pollute the atmosphere than are small cars. Ironically, the manufacturer of small cars who advertises the fuel economy and low pollution attributes of his product may face counteradvertising from safety groups who wish to point out that small cars are inherently less safe than larger ones.

The FTC has filed comments with the FCC strongly supporting counteradvertising as applied to products. The FCC is studying the problem but seems reluctant to endorse an across-the-board application of its fairness doctrine to product commercials.[23]

Health Claims. The FTC is also using its regulatory powers to control advertised health claims. In March 1969 the FTC made public its "Proposed Guides for Advertising Over-the-Counter Drugs." Although advisory, these guides were aimed at assuring that: (1) the benefits, efficacy, or safety of these drugs are not misrepresented, (2) advertising is consistent with labeling, and (3) untruthful claims of superiority of one product over another are not made.[24] These guidelines follow a long series of complaints such as those the FTC has lodged against the J. B. Williams Company because of certain advertised health claims made for the company's product, Geritol. In 1965 the FTC issued a cease and desist order requiring that Williams and its advertising agency stop misrepresenting the effectiveness of Geritol. The company appealed the order to the federal courts, and in August 1967 the U.S. Court of Appeals for the Sixth Circuit upheld the Commission's order with minor modifications. In 1968 the FTC claimed that its modified order was being violated again and threatened Williams with punitive action unless the offending commercials were promptly withdrawn.[25]

Obscenity and Bad Taste. It is difficult to define what is obscene or what is in bad taste. Generally, advertisers and the media have policed themselves to avoid advertising which might prove to be illegal or offensive, given present-day community standards. Because of many complaints about receipt of "sexually provocative" direct mail advertisements, a law was passed by Congress in 1967 entitled "Prohibition of Pandering Advertisements in the Mails."[26] This act allows a householder

---

[23] *Washington Report,* January 24, 1973, p. 12.

[24] Advertising Alert No. 3, March 31, 1969.

[25] Advertising Alert No. 8, December 31, 1968.

[26] Title III of the 1967 Postal Revenue and Federal Salary Act.

to file a notice with his postmaster requesting that certain advertisements not be delivered to his address. When notified by the postal authorities, the advertiser must remove the householder's name from the mailing list and make certain that no future mailings are sent to him. A U.S. Supreme Court decision of May 1970 upheld the 1967 law and interpreted it so broadly that a citizen of the United States has the right to prevent a direct mail advertiser from sending him anything at all he does not wish to receive.

Lottery. Several major oil companies and retail grocery chains have utilized the lottery approach to sales promotion, with considerable success in recent years. The FTC has been very concerned about such promotions because lotteries which involve the three elements of (1) a prize, (2) a consideration, and (3) chance are illegal in interstate commerce. States define what constitutes these elements differently, and in some states the requirement that a person go to a particular retail outlet to play a game would be construed as a consideration.

The FTC initiated proceedings in January 1969 to promulgate a Trade Regulation Rule relating to games of chance in the gasoline and food retailing industries. By August 1969 the FTC had announced that such a rule relating to possible deception by the use of games in both industries would be ready in 60 days.[27] As subsequently published, the rule defines as an unfair or deceptive act or practice any attempt by game sponsors to "engage in advertising or other promotions which misrepresent by any means, directly or indirectly, participants' chances of winning any prize." In addition, the rule spelled out in considerable detail how such games will be managed and promoted.[28]

By December 1969 the FTC had issued a complaint against Shell Oil Company and Glendinning Companies, Inc. (a sales promotion organization) for violating the new rule on several counts.[29]

Type of Product Advertised

There are social conventions which prevent certain types of products from being advertised. For example, hard liquor is not as yet advertised on television, and only in recent years have women been seen in printed media advertisements for liquor. Social objection to advertising is diminishing, with the result that more freedom is being exercised not only with respect to what is being advertised but also with respect to how it is presented.

The most important restriction upon the promotion of a product in

---

[27] Advertising Alert No. 8, August 29, 1969.

[28] Ibid.

[29] Advertising Alert No. 12, December 31, 1969.

the history of advertising occurred on January 1, 1971. After that date the FTC was empowered to ban the advertising of cigarettes on radio and television. The amount of revenue lost by the broadcast industry has been enormous, and although some of the funds used for broadcast advertising have been shifted to other media, in total the cigarette industry has drastically cut back on advertising expenditures. In addition to the ban on broadcast advertising, the legislation also required that the cigarette label contain the statement, "Warning, The Surgeon General has determined that cigarette smoking is dangerous to your health."

The FTC also acquired the authority to monitor the cigarette industry's other advertising activities to see if a large buildup of promotion in nonbroadcast media would occur. As noted above, there was no such buildup, and this part of the law has remained inoperative.

Vertical Cooperative Advertising

Advertising in which the manufacturer shares the cost with his resellers is called vertical cooperative advertising. This type of promotion is big business; estimates have been made that over $1 billion is spent annually in this country on co-op advertising.[30] Because payments for co-op advertising may be used as disguised price discrimination, a practice which is illegal under the Robinson-Patman Act, the FTC is quite vigilant in monitoring co-op programs to ensure their legality. On June 1, 1969 the latest revised guidelines for the use of co-op advertising were issued by the FTC. These guidelines are reviewed in some detail in Chapter 19. At this point it is sufficient to recognize that the use of cooperative advertising programs is subject to considerable legal constraint.

Advertising and Competition

An opinion held by an increasing number of governmental officials is that the excessive use of advertising can have a harmful effect on competition. This opinion received a great deal of impetus from the U.S. Supreme Court's decision in 1967 to uphold the FTC's order that Procter & Gamble divest itself of the Clorox Company which it had acquired ten years earlier.[31] "One of the principal considerations involved in this decision was the fact that the huge advertising outlay of Procter & Gamble and the advertising expertise it has at its disposal substantially reduced competition in the liquid bleach industry."[32]

---

[30] Dunn, *Advertising,* p. 110.

[31] A High Court Backs FTC; Orders P & G to Drop Clorox," *Advertising Age,* April 17, 1967, p. 1.

[32] Dunn, *Advertising,* p. 110.

In February of 1971, the FTC accused four major cereal manufacturers of having a joint market monopoly. Kellogg, General Mills,
General Foods, and Quaker Oats were alleged to have engaged in "actions or inactions" over a period of 35 years that have resulted in a highly
concentrated, noncompetitive market for ready-to-eat cereals. The FTC
stated that this had been accomplished by "proliferation of brands and
trademark promotion, artificial differentiation of products, unfair methods of competition in advertising and promotion, and acquisition of
competitors."[33]

In attempting to set new legal precedents through the application of
antitrust law to oligopolies as well as monopolies, the FTC is facing
years of litigation. The four companies cited filed formal denials of the
charges stating that competition in their industry is "vigorous, substantial
and effective."[34]

Although strong arguments have been made to support the view that
advertising adds to the competitive nature of our economy rather than
subtracting from it,[35] it seems clear that for the foreseeable future
governmental antitrust actions will be a constraining influence on larger
users of advertising. This issue is discussed further in Chapter 23.

THE HOWARD REPORT

In the fall of 1971, the FTC held a series of exploratory hearings on
a wide range of marketing techniques, with special emphasis on advertising. Over 90 representatives of industry, consumer groups, and
academia met to discuss new developments in the field of promotion and
to inform the FTC of changes in the field relevant to the agency's
regulatory responsibility.

Although the hearings covered a broad range of topics, four areas
received special attention:

First, what was the impact of various kinds of advertising on children; *second,*
whether certain kinds of advertising may unfairly exploit desires, fears and
anxieties of consumers; *third,* what kinds of physical, emotional and psychological responses did various kinds of advertising elicit from consumers; and
fourth, whether modern techniques of design and production—for example,
sound effects, cutting, splicing and color—might facilitate unfair or deceptive
effects.[36]

---

[33] *Washington Report,* May 12, 1972, pp. 5–6.

[34] *Washington Report,* July 26, 1972, p. 8.

[35] See Jules Backman, *Advertising and Competition* (New York: New York
University Press, 1967).

[36] Robert Pitofsky in the Foreword to John A. Howard and James Hulbert,
Advertising and the Public Interest (Chicago: Crain Communications Inc. 1973),
p. iii.

As consultants to the FTC, John A. Howard and James Hulbert of Columbia University prepared a summary and analysis of the hearings which is usually referred to as the "Howard Report." Although essentially a recapitulation of the voluminous testimony of the many witnesses, the last two chapters of the report contain a set of criteria for the evaluation of advertising by a regulatory agency such as the FTC, as well as other recommendations for future action.

The Howard Report is important because it is an attempt to propose a regulatory rationale for advertising which would evaluate the effects of advertising techniques and strategies on consumers and relate these efforts to one of American society's most basic values—consumer freedom of choice. Six criteria are presented as the basis of evaluating advertising in terms of its contribution to providing optimal conditions of choice. These criteria are: (1) timeliness, (2) intelligibility, (3) relevancy, (4) completeness, (5) truthfulness, and (6) the accuracy of the target audience.[37]

Each of the above criteria is related in some way to the consumer's ability to process information, and the legitimacy of the criteria is based on a theory of consumer behavior developed in the report.[38] This theory is an extension of the theory of buyer motivation and behavior originally published by Howard in 1963.[39] It is also similar to the comprehensive model of consumer behavior developed by James T. Engel, David T. Kollat and Roger D. Blackwell in 1968, which has been used as the basic model in this text.[40]

The Howard Report defined each criterion and made recommendations to the FTC. Following is a brief review of these definitions and recommendations:

1. *Timeliness.* Defined as whether or not the advertisement catches the attention of the consumer in time for him to purchase the brand when he needs it, timeliness appeared to be in no need of regulatory action.[41]

2. *Intelligibility.* Defined as the capacity of an ad to transmit clearly its meaning to the consumer, intelligibility also was an area in which the Howard Report concluded that there was no need to regulate "per se." "Where ommissions in incomplete comparatives (i.e., better, bigger —without saying better or bigger than what) result in an incomprehensible message, however, the problem can be considered as an aspect of

---

[37] Howard and Hulbert, *Advertising and the Public Interest,* pp. 80–81.

[38] Ibid., ch. 4.

[39] John A. Howard, *Marketing Management, Analysis and Planning,* rev. ed. (Homewood, Ill.: Richard D. Irwin, 1963), ch. 3–4.

[40] James F. Engel, David T. Kollat, and Roger D. Blackwell, *Consumer Behavior* (New York: Holt, Rinehart & Winston, 1968).

[41] Howard and Hulbert, *Advertising and the Public Interest,* p. 86.

truthfulness,"[42] and hence would fall under the purview of regulatory agencies.

3. *Relevancy*. Defined as the extent to which an ad informs the consumer of his desired benefits (as specified by his attitudes towards the brand) to be derived from a particular brand, relevancy was an area in which the Howard Report saw a need for more "relevant information in product ads, especially in the form of affirmative disclosures."[43]

4. *Completeness*. The capacity of an ad to provide enough information for the consumer to choose a brand, completeness was another area in which it was concluded that "In many cases, advertising does not provide as much information as it should."[44]

5. *Truthfulness*. As connoted by the report, truthfulness asks, "Does the performance [of the product] equal promise?"[45] It was concluded that "substantial progress" has been made in recent years in this area, although some ads are untruthful and deceptive.[46]

6. *Accuracy of Target Audience.* "Does the advertiser accurately identify his target audience, and is he able to beam his message to only the desired audience?" is an area in which the report admitted efforts have not been "very precise," especially with respect to children.[47]

Other important recommendations of the Howard Report included:

1. The continuation and review of the FTC advertising-claim substantiation program, with "cases to be selected at random in order to keep the offenders 'off guard.' "[48]
2. The development by the FTC of a formal organization to keep alive the contacts developed among the representatives of industry, academia, and the consumer groups.
3. The formulation by the FTC of a consumer education program, the establishment of a behavioral research department, and increased coordination among the FTC, FCC, and the FDA.

Response to the recommendations of the Howard Report was quite prompt. In the spring of 1973, Mary Gardner Jones, a member of the FTC, presented "A Critical Analysis of the Howard Report."[49] While accepting the rationale of consumer freedom of choice as a worthy goal of regulation, she questioned the role of advertising as a provider of the

---

[42] Ibid., p. 86.
[43] Ibid., p. 86.
[44] Ibid., p. 87.
[45] Ibid., p. 84.
[46] Ibid., p. 87.
[47] Ibid., p. 88.
[48] Ibid., p. 89.
[49] Mary Gardner Jones, "A Critical Analysis of the Howard Report," press release, U.S. Federal Trade Commission, May 9, 1973.

information needed by consumers to make a free choice in the market-place. She stated:

The informational role of advertising is now more typically articulated as relating solely to the dispensing of only such information as is consistent with the *advertiser's* basic objective of promoting sales and persuading consumers about the advantages of his products. There is no doubt that this latter rationale comes much closer to the actual role which advertising performs today. This does not mean that advertising may not or cannot be informative. Rather, it means that whether advertising is or is not informative and to what extent it does in fact inform is entirely a matter of the advertiser's discretion in terms of where he sees his self-interest rather than in terms of the consumer needs or interests. The two interests may coalesce but need not. The advertiser would have it that they always coalesce. Consumer groups see most of today's advertising as an expression of the advertiser's self-interest alone.[50]

Commissioner Jones further took exception to the suggested application of the "relevancy" criterion to the appraisal of advertising. She stated that, in her opinion, the Howard-Hulbert model would validate as "informational" only advertising appealing to a consumer's self-concept attitudes. Granting that such attitudes are important and that consumers should have the freedom to make choices on an irrational as well as on a rational basis, she maintained that enforcement of the "relevancy" criterion as suggested in the Howard Report would not guarantee that consumers would receive the facts which would inform their rational attitudes as well as their irrational ones, thus not ensuring consumers free choice in the marketplace.[51]

Finally, Jones criticized the suggestion that the relevancy criterion be applied to the advertiser's total promotional mix. Howard and Hulbert had suggested, for example, that if all of the product information was not presented in one advertisement or in one medium the regulatory agency should look to see if additional information was provided in other ads or other media.[52] Jones stated that television "has a special potential in penetrating consumer consciousness whether or not consumers are actively seeking information,"[53] and that "any rationale which validates the 'relevancy' of an advertisement appearing in some other media or in some other part of an advertiser's marketing mix is wholly unrealistic."[54] She continued,

. . . the Federal Trade Commission's jurisdiction is to evaluate the truth and fairness of individual advertisements. It surely could never be a defense to a

---

[50] Ibid., pp. 4–5.

[51] Ibid., p. 13.

[52] Howard and Hulbert, *Advertising and the Public Interest*, p. 83.

[53] Jones, "Critical Analysis of the Howard Report," p. 14.

[54] Ibid., p. 17.

charge of deceptive or unfair advertising that the information which might obviate or correct the challenged ad was contained in some other facet of the advertiser marketing strategy. It is difficult enough to know whether disclaimers within a single advertising message are sufficient to cure defects in that message, much less to evaluate the effect on an ad's truthfulness or fairness of information communicated to consumers through other channels or in other formats.[55]

It appears that the Howard Report will remain a subject of interest and controversy for some time. Whether or not its recommendations will influence FTC thinking cannot be discerned at present. What is important, however, is that for the first time the FTC has been confronted with proposals to consider how consumers receive and utilize information in the purchase decision process when it is formulating regulatory policy.

SUMMARY

This chapter provided a brief review of some of the more pressing legal problems that are likely to face the marketing executive in the design of a promotional strategy. The focus was on advertising because it is the communication tool most often singled out for control by state and federal government. Content of advertising, type of product being advertised, and the impact of advertising on competition are all areas that require special attention by management if legal problems are to be avoided. Considerable attention was given to the Howard Report because it is the most recent and most laudable attempt to suggest a framework for regulation of advertising based on concepts of buyer behavior and aimed at providing consumer freedom of choice in the marketplace.

REVIEW AND DISCUSSION QUESTIONS

1. What have been the major turning points in the historical development of state and federal laws to protect the consumer against false and deceptive methods of sale in the United States since the turn of the century?

2. Explain briefly the original role of the Federal Trade Commission in preventing advertising and selling abuses. How has this role expanded since the early 1960s?

3. What is the *Printers' Ink* model statute?

4. What is meant by the term "misleading representation"? What happened in the famous "sandpaper" case?

5. What is meant by the term "voluntary compliance"? What is a consent order?

---

[55] Ibid., p. 18.

6. What is the fairness doctrine, and where did it originate? What would be the implications of the application of the fairness doctrine to the broadcast advertising of consumer goods?

7. What is meant by the FTC concept of claim substantiation, and how does this concept differ from counteradvertising?

8. How do the FDA and the FTC work together to regulate the marketing of food, drug, and cosmetic products?

9. What are the elements of a lottery? Why do some states allow "games" while other states do not find similar games legal?

10. What has been the impact of the ban on radio and TV advertising of cigarettes?

11. What are the implications of the FTC complaint against the "big four" of the breakfast cereal industry?

12. What is the Howard Report, and why is it important?

13. In your opinion, is it still possible to develop viable and effective promotional programs, given the extent of governmental regulations?

part three

Determination of Objectives and Budget

Determination of objectives and utilization of the organization's basic financial resources comprise the second and third stages in the framework for promotional planning introduced in Chapter 3. These considerations are discussed jointly in this part because many of the issues overlap and are relevant to both areas.

Three types of objectives are required in promotional strategy: (1) definition of market targets, (2) determination of message content, and (3) selection of bases for geographic allocation of effort. The program ultimately stands or falls on the accuracy and validity of these objectives, so Chapter 9 is one of the most important in the book. Chapter 10 considers procedures to be followed in arriving at a financial budget.

At this stage the promotional program is viewed in its broadest terms; the topics covered are those that can precede detailed consideration of each element of the promotion mix. Subsequent parts pertain specifically to the management of advertising (Part Four) and personal selling, reseller support, and other elements (Part Five). Part Six summarizes the remaining stages of the promotional planning framework with a discussion of how the program is coordinated and evaluated.

9

Promotional Objectives

FOLLOWING situation analysis, the first main stage of a promotional strategy, the next stage is determination of objectives, or clearly stated desired end results. There are three principal concerns: (1) definition of market target, (2) determination of message content, and (3) geographical allocation of efforts.

The chapter begins with a suggested procedure for focusing the situation analysis to arrive at workable objectives. The emphasis lies mostly on the use of the mass media; specific considerations appropriate to reseller support and personal selling programs are elaborated on in Part Five.

USING THE SITUATION ANALYSIS TO DETERMINE OBJECTIVES

Preceding chapters have provided essential background on consumer motivation and behavior and other considerations in the situation analysis. It is now necessary to pinpoint this inquiry in a structured way so that the opportunities for promotional strategy emerge in sharp focus. Figure 9–1 provides an outline procedure for this purpose.

The basic classification is in terms of product and brand usage, ranging from the nonuser segment to the various segments who are users of the alternative brands. Demographic characteristics and media exposure patterns provide the basis for proper media selection and geographic allocation. Data on individual dispositions, social influences, and other environmental influences are most useful in establishing objectives for the message. The analysis will disclose, for example, whether or not there are deficiencies in awareness, the evaluative criteria that

FIGURE 9–1

Analysis Procedure for Determination of Objectives

Necessary Information	Nonusers of Product Category	Users of Product Category and Company Brand	Users of Brands A . . .n
Demographic Characteristics			
Individual Dispositons			
Stored information and experience			
Past product usage			
Awareness of alternatives			
Pertinent evaluative criteria			
Attitudes toward product and alternative brands			
Psychographic characteristics			
Media exposure and usage			
Purchase patterns and preferences			
Social Influences			
Cultural			
Reference group			
Family			
Other Environmental Influences			

underlie choice, images of both the product and alternative brands, the lifestyle or psychographic characteristics related to product or brand usage, and purchase patterns and preferences.

Nonusers of Product Category

It is important to determine whether or not nonusers offer a potential market. Frequently the problem is only lack of awareness. If this is the case, an opportunity may exist to build familiarity through promotion and thereby lay the groundwork for later sales.

In other instances, a basically favorable attitude may exist but may be constrained by opposing forces from the environment. For example, if the problem is concern over financing, advertising or personal selling possibly could stimulate sales by promoting availability of easy credit.

Most likely the analysis of nonusers will document segments that will not respond, regardless of the strategy. There may be basic conflict between the company offer and evaluative criteria, lifestyles, and so on. Every attempt should be made to avoid such segments if possible, because the probable return from the effort is not likely to be worth the expense.

Users of Product but Not the Company Brand

The purpose of this inquiry is to assess the probability of making inroads into competitors' markets. If their offerings or images are weak in certain respects or fail to satisfy important evaluation criteria, it may be possible to increase market share. On the other hand, competitors may be found to be invulnerable in certain segments, especially if there is brand loyalty based on psychological commitment or centrality. The best strategy always is to *appeal to the waverers* (those whose commitment is diminishing) rather than to attack an entrenched competitor head-on.

Regardless of competitive market shares, many feel that the best strategy is to appeal to heavy users of the product class, often referred to as the *heavy half*. For example, the so-called heavy half of the beer drinkers' market (in actuality this is 17 percent of the total market) consumes 88 percent of all beer; the heavy half in the market for canned soup (16 percent of the total) consumes 86 percent of the product sold.[1] The assumption is that the heavy half is the most productive segment, and there probably is some merit for this viewpoint. Certainly the propensity to respond will be higher. Concentration on this segment has been made more feasible through use of data provided by syndicated research services which show the extent of product consumption by audiences of various advertising media.

Efforts should not be concentrated on the heavy half, however, unless there is evidence documenting that it is not feasible to turn nonusers into users and light users into heavy users. There should be an inquiry into why they buy or do not buy, what the product means to them, and other related questions. It may be found that sales increases are a possibility.

---

[1] Dik W. Twedt, "How Important to Marketing Strategy Is the 'Heavy User'?" *Journal of Marketing,* Vol. 28 (1964), p. 72.

Users of Product and Company Brand

The greatest asset possessed by any organization is its core of satisfied users, and the present user cannot be overlooked in promotional strategy. It is of particular importance to monitor brand image and to clarify that the company offerings are still satisfying salient evaluative criteria better than the perceived offerings of a competitor. Any deficiencies should, of course, be remedied.

In addition, it is useful to monitor awareness of the company brand and competitive brands. In a highly volatile market, eroding awareness can be followed by a sales decline. A frequent advertising objective is just to maintain "share of mind"—that is, relative awareness vis-à-vis competitors.

It also may be possible to assess the potential for increasing brand loyalty among light to moderate users, stimulating new product uses, encouraging switching from competitive brands, and preventing inroads by competitors, to mention only a few of the many possibilities.

Application of the Analysis Procedure

The Flavorfest Company (the company name is fictitious) manufactures and distributes a well-known bottled seasoning product. The firm long has dominated the market, and its share is approximately 85 percent. Thus for all intents and purposes, sales of the product class and the brand are synonymous.

Management could base its promotional program on the assumption that everyone is an equally valuable prospect, but it is more likely that there are substantial differences among segments. An analysis by product use disclosed three distinct segments, each of which offered very different prospects for strategy. A summary of these findings appears in Figure 9–2.

The three market segments analyzed were heavy users (at least twice a week), light to moderate users (once a week or less), and nonusers. The heavy-use segment is large, and the product is well regarded. Important evaluative criteria are distinctive taste and value in creative cookery. The user shows the psychographic profile of avoidance of tradition and a desire to express individuality. Attitudes toward the product are favorable in that it is seen as enhancing these aspects of the user's lifestyle. Thus a good opportunity would appear to exist to stimulate even greater product use. Media exposure patterns would suggest the use, in particular, of the "shelter group" of magazines, which includes *Better Homes and Gardens* and others.

The nonuser segment presents a different situation. While it tends to be large at present, it is comprised mostly of those with minimum pur-

FIGURE 9–2

Application of Analysis Procedure: The Market for Flavorfest

Necessary Information	Nonusers of Product (41% of total)	Light–Moderate Users (20% of total)	Heavy Users (41% of total)
Demographic Characteristics	Older, large families, low income, eastern and southern states and farm areas	35–54; large families; children under 12; middle income; Southeast, Pacific, and Southwest, suburban and farm	20–45; well educated; high income; small families; children under 5; suburban areas in Northeast and Midwest
Individual Dispositions			
Awareness and usage	Limited past usage	Usage less than once a week on average; concentration at holiday periods	Frequent (twice a week or more) use, year around
Evaluative criteria	No interest in creative cookery; exotic tastes not desired	Interest in creative cookery; interest in products which give minimum performance risk	Desire exciting and exotic taste; interest in experimental cookery
Attitudes toward product	Flavorfest viewed as connoting exotic taste and modernity, neither of which is desirable.	Favorable image toward product but desire to use it only with one type of food category.	Image highly favorable; Flavorfest suggests exciting taste, appearance, and food value; viewed as asset in creative cookery.
Media exposure and usage	Daytime television, movie magazines	Women's magazines, daytime television, women's section of daily paper	Shelter group of magazines, news magazines, daily paper, FM radio
Psychographic characteristics	Maintenance of tradition, home oriented, identification with mother, nonventuresome and conservative	Desire for self expression constrained by maintenance of tradition; home oriented	Contemporary; desire to express individuality; view role of housewife with displeasure; not family oriented
Social Influences	Desire to please family	Desire to please family	Desire to please family is not a factor

chasing power living in stagnant population-growth areas. In addition, Flavorfest appears to contradict the evaluative criteria for this type of potential user, as well as lifestyle. Not surprisingly, product image is poor. The existence of these negative dispositions raises the probability that promotion would be screened out.

The light to moderate user segment represents the greatest opportunity. The desire for creative cookery is there but is constrained by a need to maintain tradition and a lack of confidence in results of experimental efforts. Yet, the product is liked in nearly all respects. Lack of confidence perhaps could be minimized by stressing "nonfail" recipes. The interest in pleasing the family can be shown as compatible with creative cookery by stressing favorable family reaction to new tastes and recipes. Finally, Flavorfest can be featured as an ideal accompaniment for a variety of foods. Obviously there is no certainty that greater inroads can be made into this market, yet there appears to be no reason why some experimental promotion should not be tried.

SETTING THE OBJECTIVES

The most important topics in this section pertain to (1) definition of market targets and (2) objectives for the communication message. The discussion here centers mostly on advertising objectives, but most of the considerations are common for all areas of the promotional mix.

Current Business Practice

A major industry study by the National Industrial Conference Board (NICB) indicated that only a minority of business firms regularly specify objectives.[2] The primary reasons seem to be: (1) advertising often is only a minor element in the marketing mix, especially when the firm produces industrial products; (2) some companies are not oriented toward marketing planning; and (3) erroneous assumptions exist regarding the role of advertising versus other marketing efforts. Therefore, there is no real way to know what advertising weight or expenditure is needed.

Another review of current business practice disclosed that less than 1 percent of so-called successful advertising campaigns were based on a statement specifying (1) the basic message to be delivered, (2) the target audience, (3) the intended effect, and (4) measurement methods and criteria.[3] Sixty-four percent met the first three criteria, but nearly

---

[2] National Industrial Conference Board, *Setting Advertising Objectives* (New York, 1966).

[3] Steuart H. Britt, "Are So-Called Successful Advertising Campaigns Really Successful?" *Journal of Advertising Research,* Vol. 9 (1969), p. 8.

all failed to specify measurement procedures. In addition, 99 percent did not state objectives in quantifiable terms, and 16 percent did not specify the audience to be reached.

These studies provide a disturbing indication that there is a wide gap between theory and practice. Moreover, this gap cannot be justified, because management today is increasingly insisting upon goal orientation and accountability for performance.

Communication versus Sales Objectives

It is interesting to ask executives to indicate what the objectives for their advertising actually encompass. The answer is likely to be, "to increase sales 10 percent," "to make a greater penetration in the Midwest," or "to increase buyer preference," to mention several typical responses. On careful analysis it is apparent that these statements encompass an entire marketing program rather than advertising. It is unreasonable to ask advertising to carry the whole burden *unless* advertising is the only variable in the marketing mix.

A debate has arisen over the appropriate form for advertising objectives. Some maintain that success can only be measured in terms of sales. Others contend that each element in the marketing mix has a more specific role and that a change in sales is the result of each component working together with the others. According to this view, advertising performs the function of persuasive communication through use of mass media, with the result that objectives should be stated in *communication* terms.

The Case for Communication Objectives. The Association of National Advertisers focused industry attention on the case for communication objectives in 1961 through its influential position paper authored by Russell Colley.[4] Colley's thesis was that advertising should be managed to attain clearly stated communication goals so that success and failure can be measured. This philosophy has since become known as DAGMAR (Defining Advertising Goals, Measuring Advertising Results). It is argued that sales cannot serve as the objective because *all* marketing efforts blend imperceptibly to increase volume and profits. In Colley's words: *"Advertising's job purely and simply is to communicate, to a defined audience, information and a frame-of-mind that stimulates action. Advertising succeeds or fails depending on how well it communicates the desired information and attitudes to the right people at the right time and at the right cost."*[5]

The NICB study on setting advertising objectives referred to above disclosed that the minority of companies that do set advertising ob-

[4] Russell H. Colley (ed.), *Defining Advertising Goals* (New York: Association of National Advertisers, Inc., 1961).

[5] Ibid., p. 21.

jectives for the most part state them in communication terms. Many embrace this approach for the reasons mentioned by Colley and for the additional reason that communication objectives are more workable. The argument is that communication response can be measured using existing tools, whereas advertising efforts usually cannot be related to sales short of full-scale market experiments in which all other marketing variables are held constant, while advertising varies. Few firms can afford this type of research on a continuing basis.

The Case for Sales Objectives.   There have been some vigorous attacks on the DAGMAR concept. One leading critic maintains that it is a philosophy of despair:

. . . as a goal for advertising, communication is not superior to sales because it is no longer exclusively caused by advertising. Both communication *and* sales are caused by many factors. In either case, it would be very pessimistic to believe that weather or competition or other uncontrollable factors bias the future one way today and another way tomorrow. As Einstein once put it: "Nature may be obscure, but she is not devious." We assume, in other words, the basic stability of enough of the phenomena we *cannot* control or measure to permit the successful prediction of an effect from a few causes we *can* measure and control. Since both sales and communication studies require this assumption, why not measure sales?[6]

Thus, according to this view, it is erroneous to assume that communication is a more precise measure than sales.

Other critics have maintained that promotion can indeed accomplish communication goals yet have no influence whatsoever on sales. It will be recalled that communication is effective only to the extent that it predisposes a prospect to buy at some future point or reinforces his existing preference. But if communication fails in this sense, it is not the fault of the *type* of objective used but the *determination* of the objective.

Assume, for example, that research discloses 60 percent of potential customers who are not aware of a new soap product. Assume further that an advertising campaign then intervenes and communicates product benefits to 50 percent of this group. Does this mean that advertising has been successful? The answer may be no, because communication can implant facts without having any influence in terms of persuasion.[7] In fact, recipients can even be made *less likely to buy* after awareness is stimulated. The point is that the message which is communicated can be irrelevant and totally ineffective in stimulating the necessary predisposition to buy. This danger can be avoided through proper problem analysis, as discussed in Part Two.

---

[6] A. J. Vogl (quoting Charles A. Ramond), "Advertising Research—Everybody's Looking for the Holy Grail," *Sales Management,* November 1, 1963, p. 43.

[7] Jack B. Haskins, "Factual Recall as a Measure of Advertising Effectiveness," *Journal of Advertising Research,* Vol. 4 (1964), pp. 2–8.

On the other hand, the case for sales objectives advanced by the critics of DAGMAR is not especially convincing. They have not refuted the fact that *all* marketing efforts influence sales in most situations. How, then, can advertising be related to sales in such a way that concrete objectives can be established and performance measured at reasonable cost? The fact that needed answers have not been forthcoming virtually necessitates the establishment of communication goals except in those situations where sales is more appropriate as a measure, as is discussed in the section below.

A Recommended Approach. It is apparent that there is a division of opinion on the question of communication versus sales. However, this is not an irreconcilable issue, because there are situations where communication objectives are required and others where specified sales response is more appropriate.

It will be recalled that some buying situations can be classified as extended decision making in which the buyer proceeds through various stages until the purchase is made. The process begins with problem recognition and extends through such other stages as alternative evaluation and search. It is clear that an individual in the early stages of problem recognition most likely will not be stimulated to make a purchase by being exposed to an advertisement, especially when the planning period for purchase is relatively long, as it might be with such products as major appliances. All that advertising can legitimately be expected to do is to affect his *propensity to buy* through stimulation of awareness or initial interest. Exposure to communication hopefully should have some effect, therefore, in moving him closer to a purchase at some future point. Stimulation of an immediate sale, on the other hand, is not an appropriate aim.

However, what if the potential buyer has already decided to purchase and is engaging in search. At this point an advertisement or other promotional stimulus may succeed in triggering a sale. Various forcing methods such as price reductions may well be advised for this purpose. In this situation, a sales objective is quite appropriate.

Sales objectives also are acceptable when the planning period for purchase is relatively short—perhaps even a matter of seconds. Relatively little thought, for example, will precede trial of a new soft drink. Similarly, a sales objective was chosen for the Goodyear Christmas Album campaign in which the objective was to present the album at its $1 price so forcefully that consumers would make a special visit to their Goodyear tire dealers to obtain it.[8] It is reasonable to expect that advertising exposure would have this effect.

From these three different situations, it is clear that *the form of the*

---

[8] "The Goodyear Christmas Album Campaign," in *Outstanding Advertising Case Histories* (Southport, Conn.: Thomas E. Maytham, 1967), p. 46.

objective depends on the stages of consumer decision making found in the target market segments. Stimulation of a purchase is, on occasion, proper, but it must not be overlooked that this is accomplished through communication of a persuasive message. Therefore, all promotion goals, in the final analysis, are communicative goals; the only real difference lies in the nature of the expected response.

Criteria of Workable Objectives

A statement of objectives for the promotional mix should meet four basic criteria: (1) proper definition of market target, (2) clear statement of message content, (3) quantitative statement of benchmarks, and (4) specification of appropriate measurement methods and criteria.

Definition of Market Target. As has been noted, it is necessary to know both the demographic characteristics of target segments and their media exposure patterns. Fortunately, it now is possible to utilize syndicated research services which provide extensive demographic data on audiences of various media. Thus, the objective of media strategy is to select media which reach the desired audience with a minimum of overlap and waste.

Proper media strategy obviously requires that the target market be defined *specifically.* Examples where sufficient specificity was attained include the following:

1. Research showed that purchasers of Hamilton watches are 35 and older and are in the upper income and education brackets.[9] Media were then selected to reach this segment.
2. The media objectives for the Shell Oil "racing" campaign for premium motor oil were (1) to reach a mass male audience and (2) to emphasize the 18–49 age group in which racing interest is highest.[10]
3. Bostonian shoes range in price from $19.95 to $40.00, with the result that greatest appeal is to higher-income segments. Thus the objective of a recent campaign was to direct emphasis to adult males, 18 years of age and over, in middle- and upper-middle-income groups.[11]

In each of these instances, research was undertaken to isolate the demographic characteristics of the target market so that media could be selected to reach the target segment with a minimum of waste.

Consider this statement, however. In a recent year, Arrow shirts were advertised with the objective of reaching both men and women, with

---

[9] "The Hamilton Watch 'Excitement' Campaign," in *Outstanding Advertising Case Histories,* p. 18.

[10] "The Shell Oil Company Campaign," in *Outstanding Advertising Case Histories,* p. 20.

[11] "The Bostonian Shoe Campaign," in *Outstanding Advertising Case Histories,* p. 23.

special emphasis on "younger readers."[12] Who are "younger readers"? And what is meant by "special emphasis"? This fuzzy objective gives the media analyst no real guidance.

Fortunately, the growing use of the computer in media selection has forced management to be more precise in its thinking, because the computer permits storage of vast amounts of information about media audiences. Therefore there is no excuse for failure to match target audience and media in precise demographic terms.

Clear Statement of Message Content. At some point it is necessary to specify the basic substance of the communication message. This usually is stated in fairly general terms, with specific details of execution left to artists and writers. As such, this statement is often referred to as the creative platform or purchase proposition. An acceptable creative platform must first of all be based on consumer research which documents the fact that the product features emphasized are an important motivating influence. In addition, it must be stated with sufficient clarity to provide meaningful guidance to those who must execute the concept in a finished advertising campaign.

A good example of a well-stated creative platform is provided by a campaign for Westinghouse electric ranges. The objective was to establish Westinghouse as the "best buy." Market surveys disclosed that advertising should feature the new "No-Turn Speed Broil," an exclusive product feature that was well received by those surveyed. The following creative platform was specified: "Only Westinghouse has the new "No-Turn Speed Broil" for superior broiling. It seals in juices for finest flavor. It broils in half the time and is cleaner, safer, and easier—no smoke—no spatter—no flame up—no turn." Notice that judicious use was made of information on consumer motivation (a desire for a clean and smokeless broiler) and information on product characteristics.

On the other hand, consider the difference in this statement of objective: Diet-Rite will be promoted for ". . . its real old-time Cola taste and refreshment."[13] This is little more than a general creative philosophy which lacks the specificity necessary to be of any operational value.

Quantitative Benchmark Statement. Effectiveness cannot be measured unless there is a quantitative indication of present status concerning awareness, market share, attitude, or other response criteria which form the basis for a statement of objectives. Measurement of effectiveness requires a thorough before-and-after study which documents present status before the campaign and then isolates changes which have taken place. For example, consumers might be asked "Which brand first comes

---

[12] "The Arrow Shirt Campaign," in *Outstanding Advertising Case Histories,* p. 7.

[13] "The Diet-Rite Cola Campaign," in *Outstanding Advertising Case Histories,* p. 4.

to mind when you think of typewriters?" Assume that brand A receives an awareness level of 35 percent and that the objective for advertising is to raise this figure to 55 percent. An identical study after the campaign has ceased will indicate whether or not the increase in awareness was achieved.

The Shell Oil campaign mentioned earlier fell short of this criterion because its advertising was undertaken to (1) increase awareness of Shell Oil among the total male audience and (2) obtain greater awareness of product benefits among present customers.[14] Benchmarks are lacking as well as specified percentages of change, with the result that it would be impossible to measure advertising effectiveness. Similarly, the Humble Oil & Refining Company set out to (1) win new customers, (2) increase station sales volume, and (3) increase the sales ratio of premium gasoline compared with regular.[15] Once again there are no benchmarks or projected percentages of change.

Contrast the following objectives listed in the NICB study on objectives to those mentioned above:

1. Increase the percentage of heavy family flour users from 20 percent of the total market to 25 percent.
2. Increase the number mentioning brand A when asked "What brand of all-purpose flour claims it gives you a feeling of confidence when you use it?" from 35 percent to 45 percent.
3. Increase the number mentioning brand A when asked "What brands of all-purpose flour have you seen or heard advertised recently?" from 60 percent to 90 percent.[16]

Assuming that the responses specified are valid for purposes of the campaign, this statement of objectives is an ideal illustration of the proper use of benchmarks and expected percentages of change.

Statement of Measurement Methods and Criteria.   In advertising campaigns studied by Stewart Britt, proofs of success were unrelated to campaign objectives in 69 percent of the cases.[17] For example, the goal of a campaign for Welch's grape juice was to convince mothers that this product is the best drink for their children because of its nutritious value and good taste. Although increased awareness and conviction comprised the objective, success was measured in terms of a sales increase for which many other factors may have been responsible.[18] There was no measurement whatsoever in terms of awareness or conviction. Similarly,

---

[14] "The Shell Oil Company Campaign," in *Outstanding Advertising Case Histories,* p. 20.

[15] "Humble Oil & Refining Gasoline Campaign," in *Outstanding Advertising Case Histories,* p. 34.

[16] National Industrial Conference Board, *Setting Advertising Objectives.*

[17] Britt, "Are Campaigns Really Successful?" p. 5.

[18] Ibid., p. 67.

a sales increase was cited as proof of advertising success for Betty Crocker potato products, even though the stated objective was to show how these products can make meals more varied and interesting.[19] While a sales increase is gratifying, it is an irrelevant measure of advertising effectiveness, because a change in sales was not the objective.

A better approach is illustrated by the advertising undertaken for the Aero Commander Division of the Rockwell-Standard Corporation.[20] An objective of increasing awareness was measured by the number of inquiries to the company resulting from the campaign. It was specified initially that the number of inquiries received would be presumed to reflect the awareness that was generated.

In summary, if an increase in sales is desired, then changes should be measured in sales. If an increase in awareness is the objective, changes in awareness *and only awareness* are the proof of success or failure.

The Process of Setting Objectives

As mentioned previously, promotional objectives must be consistent with overall marketing objectives, and the task is to define the role for communication within this broader framework. Unfortunately, there is no simple way to translate the marketing goal into communication terms. Suppose it has been determined that the marketing program for an airline is to increase customer traffic 20 percent within the next year. What is the role for communication?

The logical approach, of course, is to begin with the problem analysis. The answer might lie in stimulating traffic among present customers, among light users, or perhaps among nonusers. Is there any area where buyers feel that the company is failing to meet their needs? It is possible, for example, that scheduling problems in the past have discouraged some potential travelers, or perhaps previous delays in arrival are at fault. Whatever the case, valuable clues should emerge from the problem analysis, and, if so, the role for communication should be clarified.

Assume that the difficulty indeed lies in buyer dissatisfaction with delays in arrival and resulting inconveniences. It may be that this situation can be remedied; if so, communication of this fact to prospective travelers may be a key to increasing sales. Obviously, however, an increase in sales will be the result of a properly tuned marketing program consisting of product, services, price, and so on.

The key, therefore, lies in a careful situation analysis, especially in the area of consumer demand. The following aspects are of particular importance: (1) the rating received by the product according to evalua-

---

[19] Ibid., p. 7.
[20] Ibid., p. 7.

tive criteria; (2) the information base of those in the target market—i.e., awareness of the product and its features; (3) the nature of the search process, if any, and the sources of information which are used; and (4) strength of preference and attitude.

In the survey of engineers' attitudes toward relay brands conducted by the Sigma Instruments Company (see Chapter 6), the company received a good overall rating along evaluative criteria with the exception of two aspects: (1) breadth of line and (2) competitive prices. Apparently prospective buyers were unaware that the company was quite competitive in these respects. To build awareness an advertising campaign was undertaken which featured a four-page insert in a limited number of publications. Advertisements featured both competitive prices and breadth of line; and a free relay was offered for trial. The results were higher ratings along the dimensions of price and breadth of line as well as a strong pattern of increase in sales. The campaign thus featured relevant information which, when communicated effectively, resulted in increases in both awareness and sales.

Obviously it is impossible to provide a general formula to be followed in setting objectives. It is useful to describe one example in detail because it offers a good illustration of effective use of background analysis, to say nothing of highly analytical promotional planning.[21]

General Motors Corporation: A Case History. The General Motors Corporation has modified the DAGMAR approach to fit the unique needs of its various divisions. The basic research instrument used is a relatively standardized questionnaire which covers many of the points previously discussed in Part Two. A prospective buyer is first asked to indicate brands he considers to be competitive for his business, regardless of whether or not they are regarded favorably or unfavorably. Then those brands that receive favorable consideration are determined, and the respondent is run through a product-image battery of questions consisting of 35 different image items for each brand included in the buying class. The general format of the questionnaire is indicated in Figure 9–3.

The heart of the GM approach is measurement of advertising goal accomplishment through a series of matched independent surveys. The benchmark wave of interviews leading to objectives for the campaign is followed by five subsequent waves throughout the year. If the campaign is not progressing as planned, changes are made in objectives and plans.

Using this procedure, it is possible to place a value on each of the preference levels isolated through consumer interviews. In one example, given the fictitious name "Watusi," the data in Figure 9–4 resulted.

Five percent of those studied considered Watusi their first choice.

---

[21] "How G.M. Measures Ad Effectiveness," *Printers' Ink,* May 14, 1965, pp. 19–29. Facts and figures are reproduced with special permission.

FIGURE 9–3

Content of Questionnaire to Establish Advertising Goals for GM Products

I. Preference levels by brand by series of brand
   1. Awareness
   2. "Buying class"
   3. "Consideration class"
   4. First choice
II. Product image
III. Message registration
   1. Specific product attributes
   2. Pricing structure of the market
   3. Familiarity with the market
   4. Slogans
IV. Market behavior
   1. Shopping behavior, dealer visits
   2. Intentions
   3. Purchases
V. Product inentory
   1. Content and condition
VI. Demographics
VII. Media consumption (hours per week)
   1. Television by selected programs
   2. Magazines by selected magazines
   3. Radio by time slot
   4. Newspapers by type

Subsequent interviews indicated that 84 percent will actually visit a dealership, and 56 percent will purchase the automobile. Thus it is possible to relate preference and awareness to later buying action and to *assess the economic worth of moving a prospect from one preference level to another.*

Assume that a decision is made to aim promotional efforts to people in the "buying class" with the objective of moving them to include

FIGURE 9–4

Value of Preference Levels for Watusi in Terms of Probability of Purchase and Dealer Visitation

	Preference Level (Pèrcent) March 1965	Probability Will Visit Watusi Dealer	Probability Will Buy Watusi
Watusi first choice..................	5%	.840	.560
Watusi in consideration class........	7	.620	.220
Watusi in buying class..............	8	.400	.090
Aware of Watusi.....................	14	.240	.050
Not aware of Watusi.................	66	.015	.004
Total........................	100%		

Watusi in their "consideration class." To move a person from one preference level to another it is necessary to modify his attitude toward the product so that he regards it favorably. At this point the research data on various components of the product image become useful. In the Watusi example, the findings in Figure 9–5 were reported.

FIGURE 9–5

Item Ratings of Watusi by Those Considering It to Be in Their Buying Class (on scale of 1–100)

	Will Not Give It Favorable Consideration	Will Give It Favorable Consideration	Difference
Smooth riding	88	91	3
Styling	76	89	13
Overall comfort	81	87	6
Handling	83	86	3
Spacious interior	85	85	0
Luxurious interior	79	85	6
Quality of workmanship	80	83	3
Advanced engineering	77	83	6
Prestige	73	82	9
Value for the money	76	79	3
Trade-in value	59	77	18
Cost of upkeep and maintenance	63	67	4
Gas economy	58	58	0

Thus the image of Watusi was available for two target groups. If no difference is detected in opinion regarding a feature, it has little significance at this level of preference. While Watusi had a poor reputation for gas economy, there was no difference between the two preference levels on this issue, and this factor was of little relevance. The feature where the difference was greatest is trade-in value. While this make, in fact, did offer the highest trade-in value, this point had not registered with a certain market segment. So the advertising goal was to improve the Watusi reputation for trade-in value, and the statement of objectives outlined in Figure 9–6 was used.

The strategy used to attain these goals was not specified, but a measurement of results showed a change from 59 to 75 in evaluation of trade-in value of the Watusi by those who previously would not give it favorable consideration, a sharply favorable increase.

The method used here, of course, is by no means suggested for every

FIGURE 9–6
Advertising Goal Statement for Watusi

Division	Series or Product—Watusi
Advertising objective.............	To increase rating of Watusi regarding trade-in value
Target market...................	All male heads of new car-owning households
Size of target market.............	19,100,000
Dates goal is to be in effect.......	October to following September

problem. But it illustrates how one company grappled with the issues and established concrete and measurable research-based objectives.

Problems in Determination of Objectives

It should by no means be inferred that determination of objectives is an easy process. Several difficulties can assume major importance: (1) determining a realistic expected result stated in quantitative terms, (2) relating communication results to profit, and (3) setting up before-and-after studies to measure effectiveness.

Determining a Realistic Expected Result. A realistic expected result can be discussed in the context of an actual problem—promotion of sales in the tea industry.[22] An association of importers and producers recognized that tea consumption was lagging behind the growth of population and total food sales. The 10 percent who were steady tea drinkers consumed over 50 percent of the total; those who drank it occasionally totaled another 40 percent. A large remaining segment regarded it as a "sissy" drink. The industry agreed to attempt to change the image and make tea a more popular drink, and the marketing goal was to increase tea consumption an average of 5 percent per year.

How does one move from this overall marketing goal to a realistic promotion objective? In this situation, it was obvious that consumers regarded tea as something for the "sick, weak, or elderly" and did not view it as a preferred mealtime drink. Therefore, the role for communication was to change this basically unfavorable image through stressing regular home consumption and associating the product with such positive terms as "cheery," "friendly conversation," and so on.

Assuming that $2 million is available to spend and that only 20 percent now view tea favorably, the question is how much change can be accomplished through this expenditure. This is an extremely difficult question. In this example the goal was to raise the image to a rating

---

[22] Colley, *Defining Advertising Goals,* pp. 74–76.

of 40 percent after five years, and there is every indication that it was achieved. How the specified 20 percent increase was determined is not known.

Determination of a realistic expected result usually must begin with past experience, and this can be an invaluable guide. Ideally, records have been kept over time so that the response from past campaigns has been logged. Postmortems are particularly valuable in determining what works and what does not work. Unfortunately, records of this type are seldom kept in usable form.[23] No doubt the growing insistence by management on more precise objectives and accountability for performance will do much to remedy this deficiency in the future.

Another possibility is to undertake experimentation to ascertain the amount of change that can reasonably be expected. Sometimes this can be done in a laboratory, although expensive test market experiments may also be required. The artificiality of the former approach and the costs of the latter make experimentation the distinct exception rather than the rule. This may change as computer simulation becomes more commonplace, because it is possible to simulate the behavior of a market segment and thus gain some rough insight into possible response to promotional efforts.[24]

Relating Communication Results to Profit. On occasion it is possible to attain a communication result which has no effect in stimulating a sale at some point in time. Although sales and resultant profit are not the usual objective for promotion, all efforts must nevertheless contribute to this end.

Too often communication objectives are based on mere conjecture. A leading refrigerator manufacturer, for example, was faced with the unfortunate situation of having no competitive advantage; "unexposed cooling coils" was the only feature unique to this line. An advertising program could have been undertaken to communicate this feature, but the result would have been disastrous, because a survey of prospective buyers disclosed that this feature was totally irrelevant in their decision to buy a refrigerator.

This is a good example of a communication result which would not stimulate buying action. While the message may be successfully communicated, *it is devoid of persuasive power.* This conclusion cannot be stressed too heavily, because the danger of irrelevant objectives is always present and can be minimized only through research centering on the evaluative criteria used by consumers in the target market.

---

[23] See Patrick Robinson and David Luck, *Promotional Decision Making Practice and Theory* (New York: McGraw-Hill Book Co., 1964).

[24] For a discussion of simulation see David B. Montgomery and Glen L. Urban, *Management Science in Marketing* (Englewood Cliffs, N.J.: Prentice-Hall, 1969), ch. 2.

Setting Up Before-and-After Studies. While measurement of effectiveness is the subject of later chapters, it is worth pointing out here that measurement methods can present some real obstacles. One problem is to select matched samples on a before-and-after basis. Even more critical is the need to isolate what would have happened in any event had no advertising been undertaken.

Implications of Objective Setting

The many issues in the setting of objectives for advertising make it clear that objectives cannot be established through automatic use of checklists or rules of thumb. There is no substitute for research into the problem, with proper market segmentation at the heart of the inquiry.

Selection of the best or optimum strategy probably is an illusive goal. It is more realistic to anticipate that careful attention to objectives will, at the very least, help management to avoid gross misallocation of resources. In addition, establishment of a research tradition within a business firm which insists upon postmortems of campaigns and collection of records documenting success or failure should lead to an accumulation of invaluable experience. The base is then provided for growing precision in promotional strategy.

GEOGRAPHIC ALLOCATION

Geographic variables often provide a useful basis for determination of promotional strategy. It is necessary to determine the *relative sales possibilities* from one geographic area to the next. For example, if a product is sold nationwide, should twice as much effort be placed in the Chicago market as in Columbus, Ohio? Or should Columbus receive an equivalent allocation of promotional funds? Such questions can be answered only when *market potentials* are computed, for as a general rule efforts are allocated in proportion to potential, all other things being equal.

Several different potentials might be computed for a given product:

1. Volume attainable under ideal conditions, i.e., if all efforts were perfectly adapted to the environment.
2. The relative capacity of a market to absorb the products of an entire industry, such as the major appliance industry.
3. The relative size of market for a company's type of product, i.e., sales of color television sets versus stereo sets.
4. The actual sales a company can expect.

The last category, of course, is the equivalent of the sales forecast for a firm, or the sales volume which can be expected if the firm continues

on its present course. Potential, on the other hand, refers to sales possibilities rather than expected sales, and it is of greater significance for
purposes of demand analysis. Although forecasting is necessary in determining allocations and budgets, it is beyond the scope of this book.[25]

The measure of potential which is generally found to be most useful
comprehends either category 2 or category 3—market strength (capacity)
for industry products or types of products rather than the specific
products of a firm. This is not to say, however, that potential is the sole
basis for allocation of resources, because potentials for industry sales do
not reveal the competitive structure of a market or the firm's ability to
make inroads. Columbus, for example, might appear to offer high potential, whereas in reality competitors are so entrenched that inroads would
be impossible. Ideally, then, potentials must be augmented with information about the competitive structure as well as the firm's previous
experience in the market. The goal, of course, is to make an optimum
allocation of resources to alternative markets, and this never can be
done with great precision without a reliable estimate of the impact of a
given level of promotional expenditure on market share. Nevertheless,
an array of markets in terms of potential provides a workable estimate
of the probability of response to sales efforts.

The methods used to compute potentials include: (1) a corollary
products index, (2) market surveys, (3) test markets, (4) industry sales,
(5) general buying power indexes, and (6) custom-made indexes.

Corollary Products Index

At times it is possible to use the sales of another product as an indication of potential. Presumably the corollary product and the product in
question are related in some way. If such a product can be found and
its sales are available, these data may be used as clues of expected
variations in sales patterns of one's own product from one market to
the next.

Residential building permits, for example, should be a realistic indication of the sales potential for bathroom fixtures. The danger, of course, is
that association between one product and another does not mean that the
two sell in direct proportion in different areas. As a result this method
should be used with caution, and in many instances it will be found to
be inapplicable.

Market Surveys

When the problem is to introduce a new product to the market, there
may be no alternative to a direct survey of the intentions of prospec-

---

[25] See *Forecasting Sales,* Business Policy Study No. 106 (New York: National
Industrial Conference Board, 1963).

tive buyers. Prospective buyers are asked what their purchasing plans are relative to the product, and the stated intentions of the sample are projected to the entire market as the measure of potential. Obviously there can be a divergence between stated intentions and actual purchasing behavior, with the result that this method should not be depended upon to produce a highly reliable index of potential. Yet it is better than no measure at all.

Test Markets

The test market is an important step past the market survey in that it measures actual buyer behavior in one or more specially chosen areas. The test market consists of an experiment where every attempt is made to study behavior without the expense of marketing efforts in all areas. The shortcoming, of course, is that test marketing can be time-consuming (six months or more) and expensive. In fact, where considerable investment is required in fixed assets of various types before a test can be made, it may not be feasible at all.

Industry Sales

In this method use is made of sales of the industry or a major portion of it as the measure of potential. It is thus possible to clarify areas where the industry has made maximum penetration. The advantage is that it takes the experience of all competitors into consideration and avoids the error of considering only the circumstances peculiar to an individual firm. From the industry sales it is relatively easy to compute the share of market possessed by the firm and thereby arrive at a measure of sales possibilities.

Assume, for example, that industry sales are available and that a firm is discovered to derive 1.3 percent of its sales revenue from Connecticut versus 3.4 percent for the total industry. It is clear that remedial steps are needed, and it is probable that a larger share of promotional dollars should be allocated to this state, all other things being equal. It is thus possible to capitalize on areas where industry products sell strongly and to avoid excessive promotion in the weak markets.

One limitation of this method is the frequent unavailability of industry sales data. In some circumstances (automobiles and motorboats are examples) license or tax records are a good source. Trade associations such as the National Electrical Manufacturers Association also make such statistics available to their members.

Sales data, however, reflect only *what is*, not what *might be*. In other words, there is no certainty that resulting data measure untapped market opportunity for both the industry and the firm. Moreover, it is assumed that past experience is a good measure of the future. In some industries

producing staple commodities, this may be true. It is doubtful, for example, that total sales of men's shirts vary drastically from year to year.
In dynamic markets, however, the probable existence of untapped demand makes this an unsafe assumption. As a result, other types of indexes may be preferable.

General Buying Power Indexes

The index of relative buying power in various localities is a good
indication of potential for many products. A number of data sources
are used for this purpose, among them magazine circulation. This index
is based on the assumption that those reading magazines have money
to spend. No doubt this is often true, especially among subscribers to
special-purpose periodicals. A manufacturer of fishing reels, for example, might find the circulation of *Sports Afield* to be a reliable criterion; similarly, manufacturers of photographic equipment selling to
skilled amateurs could use *Popular Photography* for this purpose.

Total retail sales in various markets also are used for a buying power
index. Census of Business data are issued periodically and are updated
annually by *Sales Management* and other publications for this purpose.
This measure should not be used, however, unless it is clear that there is
a high correlation between variations in total retail sales and variations
in sales of the product under analysis.

Usually the most accurate indexes are those which are constructed
using several factors in combination. The best-known combination index
is the *Sales Management Survey of Buying Power* published annually.
This index is derived by weighting population by two; effective buying
income by five; and total retail sales by three. If the state of Illinois, for
instance, were found to have 5 percent of effective buying power, a
manufacturer using this index would allocate 5 percent of his promotional dollars to that state. Regardless of absolute sales volume, this
state should generate about 5 percent of the total. Data also are provided by counties and cities so that a more precise allocation can be
made.

A buying power index offers several advantages: (1) it is available in
published form and can be used directly without additional computations, (2) the indexes are issued frequently and in considerable geographic detail, and (3) they may be used when other data which might
be of greater use cannot be procured. A general index of this type, however, is not always appropriate. It is assumed that demand varies directly with this index, but this is likely to be correct only for those products whose demand rises or falls with purchasing power, regardless of
other considerations. The demand for milk should not vary with buying
power, and the use of snow tires is more associated with climatic conditions than anything else.

Custom-Made Indexes

It may be necessary to construct an index unique to a given product. In order to do so, it is necessary to isolate the important factors affecting demand, obtain data on these factors, and combine them into one index, with appropriate weights assigned to those with greatest influence. These factors may include any of the data mentioned previously. Buyer studies may be helpful, but the method usually depends more on informed guess than on scientific procedure.

To take an example, a large manufacturer of high-style belts, braces, garters, and jewelry found that the *Sales Management* buying power index did not reflect the urban concentration of demand for his product.[26] As a result, he used urban population (with a weight of three), retail sales (weight of three), and disposable income (weight of four). The result was a more precise indication of potential. Similarly, a brewery used the *Sales Management* index to compute new-product potentials and found that sales in metropolitan areas did not meet expectations based on the index.[27] It was discovered that total retail sales have little relation to the sales of beer, and the important determinants instead were found to be the number of people over age 18, social class, and per capita consumption of malt beverages.

Such an index is often constructed in somewhat arbitrary fashion by selecting and trying those factors that seem to be relevant. A more sophisticated procedure is to experiment with a greater variety of factors and choose those that are found to have the greatest relationship to sales through use of multiple correlation analysis. Correlation analysis measures the extent to which two or more variables are related by assessing the variation in one variable (say industry sales) which is accounted for by the association between this variable and others (say disposable income and housing starts).

The task of computing measures of multiple correlation once was formidable, but electronic computers have greatly simplified the procedure. Once various combinations have been tried, they may be readily compared. Assume that five series are tested and found to have coefficients of correlation with sales of .66, .81, .91, .84, and .87. The third (.91) obviously is the best of the five, since a correlation of 1.0 is ideal. In reality, however, it is doubtful that a correlation of .91 will be found because this in an exceptionally high degree of relationship.

Probably this procedure is the most acceptable of all of those discussed in this section, but it also has its disadvantages. First, the correlation may be spurious—a coincidence rather than a cause and effect relationship. Moreover, it is assumed that past industry sales success will

---

[26] *Sales Management,* May 10, 1959, p. 49.

[27] John A. Howard, *Marketing Management Analysis and Planning,* rev. ed.; (Homewood, Ill.: Richard D. Irwin, 1963), p. 214.

hold in the future, and it is obvious that this might not be so in a volatile industry in early stages of its growth. Finally, the data needed may not be attainable or may be of questionable accuracy. Regardless of the problems, it does focus on finding the combination of factors which offers the best relationship to sales, and as such it is likely to be superior to a more general index under most circumstances.

SUMMARY

While all would agree that promotional strategy should be based on objectives, determination of objectives is a demanding task. Only a minority of firms actually take this step, with the result that it often is impossible to measure success or failure in meaningful terms. This can lead to perpetuation of ineffective promotional strategy.

All of the elements of the promotional mix, in essence, are communication functions. As such they should be managed to attain communication goals which have been discovered by a research-based situation analysis.

It was stressed in this chapter that communication objectives should encompass the target market, message content, the desired effect, and measurement methods and criteria. Many examples were given to illustrate varying degrees of success or failure in meeting these criteria. Enough is now known, however, to refute any justification for management not being goal oriented, and it is anticipated that the growing insistence by management on accountability will lead to a sharp increase in goal orientation.

REVIEW AND DISCUSSION QUESTIONS

1. What is the current status of business practice concerning determination of specific objectives for the promotional mix? Why is this? What can be done?
2. In one sense it can be said that stimulation of a sales increase is a communication objective. Elaborate.
3. Under what circumstances is a sales objective appropriate? Under what circumstances would it be more appropriate to attempt to stimulate changes in awareness, attitude, or other so-called communication responses?
4. A leading manufacturer of camping trailers based its advertising campaign on this statement of objectives: "Our goal is to tell as many people as possible that camping is fun for the whole family as well as inexpensive and easy." Evaluate.
5. Why must benchmarks be stated? How can they be derived?
6. Evaluate the procedure used by General Motors in determining advertising strategy for the Watusi.
7. The advertising manager for a firm manufacturing a new type of home laundry presoaking agent has $6 million to spend. Present levels of aware-

ness for this new product are approximately 11 percent in most markets. He is faced with the problem of ascertaining how much of an increase in awareness can be generated with expenditure of his budget. How can this problem be solved?

8. What can be done to ensure that attainment of a communication objective will, at some point, also have a positive influence on sales and profit?

9. A leading public relations practitioner made the following statement: "You boys in advertising just don't understand the problems we face. We have to do your dirty work. Whenever you blow it, we have to mop up and make the customer happy again. We have to try to make the company look good in the community. We have to tell them that we are concerned about product quality, water pollution, abatement of slums, etc. Your job is easier. Don't tell me I can set goals for what I do. There just isn't any way we can measure performance." Evaluate.

10

The Promotional Budget

THE QUESTION of how much should be spent for promotion represents one of the most perplexing problems facing management today. Unfortunately, the answer is not easily found. At best, available methods of budgeting are only rough approximations of an ideal expenditure level.

In approaching this subject, it is important first to understand something of the economist's notion of the "optimum" expenditure. With this background it is possible to analyze existing budgeting procedures, to grasp the extent to which these methods approximate the ideal, and to analyze the potential of newer methods. Because advertising gives rise to the most perplexing problems in the promotional budget, most of the chapter focuses on problems inherent in advertising budgeting.

THEORETICAL FOUNDATIONS OF THE BUDGETING PROBLEM

In his pioneering treatise on managerial economics,[1] Joel Dean devoted considerable space to advertising. He suggested that the outlay for advertising or any demand stimulation effort ideally is approached in the manner shown in Figure 10-1, using the fundamentals of marginal analysis.

The horizontal axis in Figure 10-1 refers to the number of units produced, and the vertical axis represents dollars per unit allocated for particular purposes, in this case advertising. Notice that price remains constant over the entire range of production; this assumption correctly

---

[1] Joel Dean, *Managerial Economics* (Englewood Cliffs, N.J.: Prentice-Hall, Inc., 1951).

designates that price is seldom changed during any short-run planning period. Moreover, per unit production costs (marginal costs) are assumed to be constant at .20 over nearly the entire range of output. The per unit production cost sharply rises, however, at the point where certain limits on plant capacity are reached. Costs of physical distribution of products are included in production cost per unit.

It may be somewhat difficult at first glance to determine which line represents advertising cost per unit. These costs are shown by line *AB*, and the amount per unit at any given level of output can be read off

FIGURE 10-1

Short-Run Determination of Advertising Outlay by Marginal Analysis

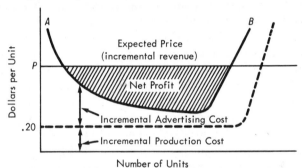

Number of Units

Source: Reproduced by permission of Prentice-Hall, Inc., from Joel Dean, *Managerial Economics* (Englewood Cliffs, N.J.: Prentice-Hall, Inc., 1951), p. 356.

the vertical axis by extending a horizontal line from *AB*, reading the dollar figure at that point, and subtracting the .20 allocated for production costs.

It also may be puzzling why line *AB* is represented as a curve which first declines, then is constant, and later rises at an increasing rate. On careful analysis it is apparent that a promotional campaign will usually involve a substantial expenditure, and if only a small number of units is produced, the costs per unit will be high. In Figure 10-1 these costs are even represented as exceeding the price per unit at low levels of output. This cost line soon drops, however, as top prospects are won as customers and the values of repeated messages and resulting learning strengthen consumer response. At a later point returns diminish because fewer prospects are being attracted, and the cost per "conquest" necessarily rises. Costs also may rise after a certain point because quantity discounts from media become less and the efficiency of invested dollars declines.

The important question now becomes how much should be spent on advertising and other forms of promotion. Notice that net profit is represented in Figure 10–1 as a diagonally striped area. Whenever promotion costs per unit drop below the price per unit, a profit results. In other words, when the total of production and advertising costs per unit is less than the price per unit, a profit results. Profit continues to be earned until cost line *AB* once again exceeds the price per unit. *Therefore, the firm should continue to advertise until the costs of new business exceed the sales revenue per unit.* This point is reached when line *AB* equals the price line *P*. At this point, the marginal return from advertising equals marginal revenue, and it does not pay to invest more dollars. Thus the advertising and selling costs needed to reach this point would be totaled, and this sum would represent the promotion budget.

The value of marginal analysis is to detect when inefficiencies set in and to direct the investment of dollars to that point where gains are offset by costs. Unfortunately, marginal analysis is little more than a textbook exercise at this time. Consider the problem of determining the advertising response per unit sold. Does it drop in the manner depicted by line *AB*, or does it assume some other shape? Moreover, sales response is not the only relevant factor, for much advertising is directed toward attitude change, changes in awareness, and other strictly communication objectives. What will be the shape of response curves for these factors? Marginal analysis assumes full knowledge of the shape of the response function, but in reality only educated guesses can be made.

The short-run marginal analysis also overlooks the fact that promotion dollars continue to work for a period in the future. The result of this continued effect is that past efforts affect the response in the future and the dollars spent today will continue to pay off for an undetermined future period. This "lead and lag" effect is not represented in the short-run response curve.

Granted the validity of these problems, marginal analysis truly is the ideal approach to budgeting. It focuses on profit, which is the ultimate measure of a business activity. Nevertheless, it can only be crudely approximated by existing budgeting methods. Some newer operations research techniques have been used which appear to offer some promise. As yet, however, the most practical procedure is to use existing methods in combination. This chapter focuses on a procedure to approximate marginal analysis with existing tools.

TRADITIONAL APPROACHES TO BUDGETING

There never has been complete agreement on the components that should make up the promotion budget, but it is fairly well accepted that the *Printers' Ink* chart of budgetary items reproduced as Figure 10–2 represents a realistic standard for advertising efforts, at least. There

FIGURE 10–2

Advertising Charges

Space and time costs in regular media
Advertising consultants
Ad-pretesting services
Institutional advertising
Industry directory listings
Readership or audience research
Media costs for consumer contests, premium and sampling promotions
Ad department travel and entertainment expenses
Ad department salaries
Advertising association dues
Local cooperative advertising
Direct mail to consumers
Subscriptions to periodicals and services for ad department
Storage of advertising materials
Catalogs for consumers
Classified telephone directories
Space in irregular publications
Advertising aids for salesmen
Financial advertising
Dealer help literature
Contributions to industry ad funds
Direct mail to dealers and jobbers
Office supplies
Point-of-sale materials
Window display installation costs
Charges for services performed by other departments
Catalogs for dealers
Test-marketing programs
Sample requests generated by advertising
Costs of exhibits except personnel
Ad department share of overhead
House organs for customers and dealers
Cost of cash value or sampling coupons
Cost of contest entry blanks
Cross-advertising enclosures
Contest judging and handling fees
Depreciation of ad department equipment
Mobile exhibits
Employee fringe benefits
Catalogs for salesmen
Packaging consultants
Consumer contest awards

Premium handling charges
House-to-house sample distribution
Packaging charges for premium promotions
Cost of merchandise for tie-in promotions
Product tags
Showrooms
Testing new labels and packages
Package design and artwork
Cost of non-self-liquidating premiums
Consumer education programs
Product publicity
Factory signs
House organs for salesmen
Signs on company-owned vehicles
Instruction enclosures
Press clipping services
Market research (outside produced)
Samples of middlemen
Recruitment advertising
Price sheets
Public relations consultants
Coupon redemption costs
Corporate publicity
Market research (company produced)
Exhibit personnel
Gifts of company products
Cost of deal merchandise
Share of corporate salaries
Cost of guarantee refunds
Share of legal expenses
Cost of detail or missionary men
Sponsoring recreational activities
Product research
House organs for employees
Entertaining customers and prospects
Scholarships
Plant tours
Annual reports
Outright charity donations

This chart, which appeared in *Printers' Ink*, December 16, 1960, shows proper, improper, and borderline charges against the advertising account. Items in the white area were considered chargeable to the advertising budget by two thirds of a sample group of advertisers. Items in the gray area, split at 50 percent, fell within the advertising budgets of from one third to two thirds of the companies. Items in the black area were considered to be in the realm of advertising by one-third or less of the advertisers.

Source: Reproduced with special permission from *Printers' Ink*, December 16, 1960.

is little question that space and time costs, cooperative advertising charges, advertising production costs (costs of plates and talent), salaries, and other clearly essential costs are legitimate budgetary charges. The advertising budget often is the catchall for nonadvertising items, however, such as those in the black area of Figure 10–2. The only addition to this chart which many firms make is to include a reserve fund of from 10 to 15 percent to cover unanticipated expenditures.

The standard budgetary methods are: (1) arbitrary allocation, (2) percentage of sales, (3) return on investment, (4) competitive parity, (5) all you can afford, and (6) objective and task. In reality no method is used to the exclusion of others. Each is examined below, prior to suggestion of a composite approach.

Arbitrary Allocation

It goes without saying that allocation by arbitrary methods without careful analysis has always been common. The shortcomings of such an approach are numerous. For example, advertising frequently seems to serve as a vent for executive emotion and personality traits. One authority puts it this way:

Noneconomic, or psychological, criteria by which management evaluates advertising also need to be understood . . . the function of advertising is highly cathartic, it is the focus of many strong emotional needs and drives relating to "self-expression" or aggressiveness . . . executive decisions on advertising philosophy and budget often may reflect as much the executive's psychological profile as they do the familiar economic criteria. The advertising philosophy and budget may be determined as much by personality as by profit maximization . . . each type of executive personality has a characteristic mode of feeling toward advertising in the light of this association of advertising with self-assertiveness or aggressive tendencies. Those who have either naturally or compensatorily induced strong self-expressive tendencies clearly tended to budget more for advertising. The latter tended to have wider swings in "intuition" or feelings of satisfaction or dissatisfaction.[2]

Moreover, the budget may in no way be relevant for promotion tasks. Proper management obviously focuses on profit maximization to the fullest extent possible.

Percentage of Sales

A commonly used method is the percentage of sales approach. This technique involves nothing more than calculation of the proportion of

---

[2] Melvin E. Salveson, "Management's Criteria for Advertising Effectiveness," *Proceedings, 5th Annual Conference* (New York: Advertising Research Foundation, Inc., 1959), p. 25. Quoted with special permission of the Advertising Research Foundation.

the sales dollar allocated to promotion in the past and application of this percentage to either past or forecasted sales to arrive at the budget. A fairly common variation is to allocate a fixed amount per unit for promotion, and then accumulating the budget is by forecasting unit sales. The percentage of sales invested by advertisers in a great many industries is reproduced in Figure 10–3. It should not be inferred, however, that these firms determine budgets through use of the percentage of sales approach.

One survey of company practices disclosed that many firms use the sales ratio as a fixed guideline for their budgeting.[3] The base figure is the sales volume projected or forecasted for the period that the budget will cover. Many reported that the percentage used remains constant from year to year, and in some cases industry averages are taken as the point of reference. Variable ratios find favor with some companies, especially when new products are to be introduced.

The percentage of sales approach is in wide use for several basic reasons. It is simple to calculate, and it is almost second nature for management to think of costs in percentage terms. Because it gives an illusion of definiteness, it also is easy to defend to management, to stockholders, and to other interests. In addition, it is a financially safe method because expenditures are keyed to sales revenues, thereby minimizing the risk of nonavailability of funds. Finally, when it is widespread throughout the industry, advertising is proportional to market shares, and competitive warfare is made less probable. This competitive aspect is especially appealing to those who give strong credence to the human inclination to resist change.

It should be clear to the preceptive reader that the advantages of the percentage of sales approach are illusory. Most important is the inherent fallacy that budgeting for promotion as a percentage of past sales views advertising as the *result and not a cause* of sales. This logical deficiency is widely recognized, and forecasted sales rather than past sales are more widely used. The use of forecasted sales, however, is fraught with circular reasoning, because how can sales be forecasted without knowing how much is to be invested in sales-generating efforts? Basically, the fundamental and perhaps fatal weakness is that the focus is not on the promotional job to be done; deceptively simple and arbitrary means are substituted for the comprehensive analysis which must, of necessity, be undertaken to approximate the goals of marginal analysis.

The percentage of sales method, then, is seldom an adequate tool unless the environment is almost totally static and the role for promo-

---

[3] David L. Hurwood, "How Companies Set Advertising Budgets," *The Conference Board Record,* March 1968, pp. 34–41.

FIGURE 10–3

100 Leaders' Advertising as percent of Sales (covering total 1973 ad expenditures, including measured and unmeasured media)

AD RANK	COMPANY	ADVERTISING	SALES	ADV. AS % OF SALES
	Cars			
4	General Motors Corp.	$158,400,000	$35,798,289,281	0.4
8	Ford Motor Co.	127,200,000	23,015,100,000	0.6
11	Chrysler Corp.	95,800,000	8,300,000,000	1.2
52	Volkswagen of America	43,003,000	6,343,000,000	0.7
86	American Motors Corp.	24,600,000	1,739,025,000	1.4
87	Toyota Motor Co. Ltd.	23,800,000	5,366,045,000	0.4
98	Mazda Motors of America	18,784,000	1,700,000,000	1.1
100	Nissan Motor Co. Ltd.	17,000,000	4,640,000,000	0.4
	Food			
3	General Foods Corp.	180,000,000	2,209,500,000	8.1
22	General Mills	74,200,000	2,000,103,000	3.7
23	Kraftco Corp.	74,000,000	3,030,079,000	2.4
27	Nabisco	69,050,000	1,015,000,000	6.8
33	Norton Simon Inc.	61,700,000	1,201,333,000	5.1
43	Pillsbury Co.	50,000,000	1,004,231,000	5.0
43	Standard Brands Inc.	50,000,000	1,102,155,000	4.5
48	McDonald's Corp.	46,500,000	1,507,000,000	3.1
49	Kellogg Co.	45,000,000	828,408,328	5.4
53	Campbell Soup Co.	40,000,000	1,089,116,000	3.7
56	Ralston Purina Co.	38,500,000	2,433,599,000	1.6
65	CPC International	34,200,000	856,556,014	4.0
73	Thomas J. Lipton Inc.	28,000,000	403,287,000	6.9
76	Nestle Co.	27,000,000	590,000,000	4.5
79	H. J. Heinz Co.	26,000,000	1,438,251,000	1.8
79	Quaker Oats Co.	26,000,000	990,767,000	2.6
94	Carnation Co.	21,000,000	1,472,198,191	1.4
	Soaps, cleansers (and allied)			
1	Procter & Gamble	310,000,000	4,912,279,000	6.3
9	Colgate-Palmolive Co.	120,000,000	982,281,000	12.2
25	Lever Bros.	70,000,000	566,000,000	12.4
45	S. C. Johnson & Son Inc.	49,600,000	270,000,000*	18.4
78	Clorox Co.	26,385,000	402,500,000	6.6
	Tobacco			
16	R. J. Reynolds Industries	85,000,000	3,294,913,600	2.6
26	Philip Morris Inc.	69,300,000	2,602,498,000	2.7
35	American Brands	58,500,000	3,096,369,000	1.9
41	Brown & Williamson Tobacco Co.	53,000,000	934,975,000*	5.7
60	Liggett & Myers Tobacco Corp.	35,880,000	728,922,627	4.9

FIGURE 10–3 (continued)

Drugs and cosmetics

5	Warner-Lambert Pharmaceutical	141,723,000	973,777,000	14.6
6	American Home Products Corp.	133,000,000	1,348,037,000	9.9
7	Bristol-Myers Co.	132,000,000	1,036,995,000	12.7
13	Sterling Drug Inc.	95,000,000	534,246,000	17.8
20	Gillette Co.	75,000,000	1,064,427,000	7.0
21	Richardson-Merrell Inc.	74,816,000	505,384,000	14.8
30	Alberto-Culver Co.	63,000,000	184,420,140	34.2
34	Rapid-American Corp.	59,134,000	2,696,724,000	2.2
42	Schering-Plough Inc.	52,000,000	357,577,000	14.5
47	Miles Laboratories Inc.	47,000,000	245,092,000	19.2
51	Johnson & Johnson	43,800,000	975,685,000	4.5
53	Chesebrough-Pond's Inc.	40,000,000	317,632,000	12.6
58	SmithKline Corp.	37,800,000	444,133,000	8.5
62	Revlon Inc.	35,000,000	506,085,000	6.9
64	Pfizer Inc.	34,300,000	617,900,000	5.6
66	Carter-Wallace Inc.	33,800,000	148,694,000	22.7
67	Morton-Norwich Products	30,171,000	406,950,000	7.4
70	Merck & Co.	28,500,000	613,250,000	4.6
76	Block Drug Co.	27,000,000	97,106,000	27.8
91	Noxell Corp.	22,700,000	91,850,000	24.7
92	Squibb Corp.	22,344,000	880,625,000	2.5

Gum & candy

72	Wm. Wrigley Jr. Co.	28,100,000	231,868,000	12.1
97	Mars Inc.	19,000,000	155,000,000	12.3

Liquor

18	Heublein Inc.	$77,800,000	$1,310,810,000	5.9
29	Distillers Corp.-Seagrams Ltd.	65,192,000	1,688,487,000	3.9
88	National Distillers & Chemical Corp.	23,500,000	1,245,792,000	1.9
89	Hiram Walker-Gooderham & Worts	23,000,000	839,269,809	2.7

Beer

59	Anheuser-Busch Inc.	36,520,000	1,442,720,000	2.5
63	Jos. Schlitz Brewing Co.	34,500,000	892,745,000	3.9

Oil

71	Exxon Corp.	28,230,000	28,022,442,000	0.1
89	Standard Oil Co. (Indiana)	23,000,000	6,467,639,000	0.4
95	Shell Oil Corp.	19,500,000	5,749,566,000	0.3

Tires

24	Goodyear Tire & Rubber Co.	72,600,000	4,675,265,000	1.6
40	Firestone Tire & Rubber Co.	54,500,000	3,154,919,000	1.7

Airlines

69	UAL Inc.	28,868,000	2,060,268,000	1.4
85	Trans World Airlines	24,738,300	1,810,990,000	1.4
93	American Airlines	22,195,000	1,481,987,000	1.5
96	Eastern Air Lines	19,400,000	1,259,808,000	1.5

FIGURE 10–3 (concluded)

───────Soft drinks───────

19	Coca-Cola Co.	76,000,000	2,144,988,601	3.5
37	PepsiCo	58,000,000	1,324,380,720	4.4
75	Seven-Up Co.	27,358,000	**	18.6

───────Appliances, tv, radio───────

15	General Electric Co.	88,500,000	11,575,300,000	0.8
17	RCA Corp.	80,500,000	4,280,700,000	1.9
30	Westinghouse Electric Corp.	63,000,000	5,702,310,000	1.1
83	Zenith Radio Corp.	25,150,000	1,007,000,000	2.5

───────Retail chains───────

2	Sears, Roebuck & Co.†	215,000,000	12,306,229,000	1.7
30	Marcor Inc.	63,000,000	4,077,415,000	1.5
38	J. C. Penney Co.	57,000,000	6,423,700,000	0.9
82	Great Atlantic & Pacific Tea Co.	25,350,000	6,747,689,000	0.4

───────Chemicals───────

| 28 | American Cyanamid Co. .... | 68,000,000 | 996,227,000 | 6.8 |
| 39 | Du Pont .... | 55,013,000 | 3,700,000,000 | 1.5 |

───────Photographic equipment───────

| 36 | Eastman Kodak Co. .... | 58,428,500 | 4,035,520,000 | 1.4 |
| 84 | Polaroid Corp. .... | 24,800,000 | 700,637,000 | 3.5 |

───────Telephone service, equipment───────

| 12 | American Telephone & Telegraph Co. | 95,200,000 | 23,527,320,000 | 0.4 |
| 14 | International Telephone & Telegraph | 90,968,260 | 4,900,000,000 | 1.9 |

───────Miscellaneous───────

10	U.S. Government	99,200,000	———	—
46	Columbia Broadcasting System	47,267,000	1,555,200,000	3.0
50	Loews Corp.	44,592,000	766,436,000	5.8
53	Hanes Corp.	40,000,000	275,883,000	14.5
57	Greyhound Corp.	38,000,000	3,421,400,000	1.1
61	Sperry Rand Corp.	35,200,000	1,541,756,740	2.3
68	Time Inc.	29,124,000	728,266,000	4.0
74	American Express Co.	27,700,000	1,904,920,000	1.5
79	Kimberly-Clark Corp.	26,000,000	1,178,000,000	2.2
99	Mattel Inc.	17,900,000	280,829,000	6.4

Note: All ad totals are domestic. Wherever possible, AA has reported the company's domestic sales figure in this table, although for some companies only a worldwide sales total was available.

* Domestic sales estimated by AA.

** No % of sales figure is listed because the ad total is for Seven-Up, whereas the sales figure is for sales of the basic extract only, which is all the company sells.

† Percentage shown would be two and a half times more if Sears's $250,000,000 in local advertising were added to the $215,000,000 national total. The other retail chains' ad totals also do not include local advertising.

Source: Reproduced with special permission from **Advertising Age,** August 26, 1974, pp 28, 30. Copyright 1974 by Crain Communications, Inc.

tion is unchanging from period to period—a highly unusual situation. This method should be used only as a starting point to calculate how many dollars would be allocated if conditions remain the same. Then the promotional objectives must be examined to fine tune the budget to the job to be done. More is said later about this use of percentage of sales.

Return on Investment

Joel Dean suggests that advertising should be viewed as an investment, in much the same manner as additions to plant or other uses of funds.[4] His contention is that dollar flows are not unlimited, and advertising should compete for its share in the same fashion as alternative investments. This method seems to be especially logical for institutional advertising, which frequently is considered as an investment.

This type of analysis obviously is only an appealing exercise in logic, because, as Dean recognizes, management can do little more than guess at the probable return from dollars invested. Nevertheless, it is true that payout analysis for other forms of investment is frequently as inexact, so his purpose no doubt is to admonish management to think of promotion in terms of larger organizational objectives. It is probable, however, that estimates of the return on dollars spent for promotion relative to other investments will be an impregnable barrier for some time to come.

Competitive Parity

Dollars are sometimes allocated through emulating competition and spending approximately the same amount. The data in Figure 10–3 could easily be used for this purpose, and similar data are available from many sources, including advertising periodicals, the U.S. Internal Revenue Service, and various trade associations.

Competitive parity offers the advantage that competition, a major component of the environment, is specifically recognized and adaptation to it is sought. In this sense, at least, it represents a small step past the percentage of sales method. It also offers the advantage that competitive relationships are stabilized and aggressive market warfare minimized.

Aside from coping with the variable of competition, however, this technique in no way recognizes other components of the promotion task, and the most gross oversight is total lack of emphasis on the buyer. It also is assumed that all competitors have similar objectives and face the same tasks—a most dubious assumption. It is further assumed that the competitor or competitors matched spend dollars with equal effectiveness; however, identical expenditures seldom imply identical effective-

---

[4] Dean, *Managerial Economics,* pp. 368–69.

ness. Finally, the only data available to management, short of outright collusion or competitive espionage, are past expenditures. These data become useless, however, if the competitor changes his promotional mix. Future spending plans are seldom known, so the ability to match competitor expenditures will always be limited by available information.

In all fairness it must be stated that few companies rely on competitive parity as the sole means of budgeting. It should not be rejected totally as a budget approach, because competitive efforts can be the dominant variable to be met in the promotional environment. The firm's objectives may by necessity be largely defensive in nature. While it seldom is practical to match the competitor to the degree implied in competitive parity, this consideration often will weigh heavily in promotional strategy.

All You Can Afford

Occasionally it is reported that some firms budget largely on the basis of available funds.[5] It is not unusual for the need for satisfactory

FIGURE 10–4

Computation of Promotion Cost per Unit

Selling price	$1.00
Retailer margin 30%	−.30
Wholesalers' selling price	$ .70
Wholesalers' margin	−.11
Manufacturer's price	$ .59
Manufacturer's production cost	−.40
Revenue minus costs	$ .19
Specified 6% profit (on retail price)	−.06
Residual for selling and other costs	$ .13

profits in a given year to limit advertising expenditures. Also, upper limits are sometimes based on customary ratios between total advertising expenditure and forecasted sales revenue. When these are exceeded, the budget will be pared. In other words, management spends as much as it is felt that company can afford without unduly interfering with financial liquidity.

It cannot be denied that liquidity is an important consideration. Assume the situation shown in Figure 10–4. With successive deduction of margins and other costs and a planned profit of 5 cents per unit, a residual of 13 cents remains for advertising, taxes, and other expenses. Assume further that it is determined that 10 cents will be allocated to

---

[5] Hurwood, "How Companies Set Advertising Budgets."

advertising and that forecasted unit sales are 100,000. Then the advertising budget cannot exceed $10,000, unless funds are available from other sources. Management may be hard put to counteract financial necessity unless compelling reasons exist for expansion of the budget by borrowing or other means, although management may, with considerable justification, propose "payout planning," a procedure to be discussed later in connection with new-product budgeting.

It is apparent that the $10,000 budget may in no way be related to objectives in that it may lead to either underspending or overspending. For this reason it is seldom relied upon exclusively except possibly in the case of new products or in situations where it is grossly apparent that the firm has underspent in the past and that any amount of funds within reason will still generate a positive marginal return. Regardless of the situation, however, liquidity will always be an important factor, and management must be prepared with convincing arguments to justify requested increases.

Objective and Task

No method discussed thus far stands up under close scrutiny, either because of failure to focus on the job to be done or because of the assumed availability of virtually unobtainable data. This leads to the last major method of budgeting, objective and task. Of all those discussed, it clearly has the most merit.

The objective and task approach is simple to describe. All that is necessary is to spell out objectives realistically and in detail and then calculate the costs necessary to accomplish the objectives. Often financial liquidity will enter as a constraint on the upper limit of the budget. It is assumed that research has been done to specify the tasks necessary to attain the objectives, and all that remains is to put dollar estimates on these efforts.

On the face of it, one cannot argue with this approach. Truly it epitomizes the thinking of marginal analysis in that it forces a striving for the intersection of marginal cost and marginal return. It avoids the arbitrary thinking and the illusory certainty of other approaches and generates research-oriented analysis consistent with a modern philosophy of promotional strategy.

No matter how compelling the advantages, it must be stated that management frequently has no conclusive idea of how much it will cost to attain the objective or even whether or not the objective is *worth* attaining. What is the best way, for example, to increase awareness by 20 percent next year? Should a combination of network television, spot radio, and newspapers be used with hard-sell copy, or should these variables be changed? Obviously all possible combinations of efforts cannot be evaluated, and it is perhaps impossible to isolate the *best* promotion mix. Nevertheless, what other alternative exists for profit-oriented management? There is no shortcut to experimentation and other forms of research, if scientific management is to be implemented.

A realistic goal is to find an approach that seems to work well on the basis of research, estimate the costs, and then accumulate a budget by this means. It may not be the best mix of efforts, but it no doubt will excel that arrived at by percentage of sales or other arbitrary means. Measurement of results then will permit the accumulation of data which, over time, should provide an invaluable source of information for future budgeting with the objective and task method. The difficulty of the method cannot continue to be a barrier to its practice. More suggestions for implementation will be given later in the chapter.

Conclusions on Approaches to Budgeting

Of the budgeting methods discussed, the objective and task approach most nearly approaches the ideal as provided by marginal analysis. Yet implementation of this approach is fraught with the difficulty of estimating the tasks necessary to accomplish objectives, to say nothing of costs. As a result, existing tools are exceedingly blunt.

The concept here has been that objective and task, properly utilized, encompasses the attitude of inquiry inherent in marginal analysis. This attitude is essential, for as Dean points out:

The difficult problem in applying economic analysis to advertising is to find the empirical equivalents of the theoretical curves. The deep uncertainty surrounding the productivity of advertising is perhaps the origin of such methods as percentage of sales and objective and task. But whatever rationale these methods once have had, their basic weakness is that they hide rather than highlight the economic issues in the advertising problem. Despite its limitations economic analysis can be helpful in reaching a better decision on the amount of advertising by focusing attention on the relevant (even though unmeasurable) relationships as opposed to the irrelevant (but measurable) ones. Though the complete theoretical solution to the advertising problem is too complex for practical use, manageable approximations may sometimes be feasible.[6]

David Hurwood, reporting on budgeting practices of firms during the middle 1960s, indicated that only 1 in 10 companies used research in any way.[7] This would include market surveys, corporate image studies, media and readership studies, advertising testing, effectiveness measurement, and determination of sales results. More recent surveys have dis-

---

[6] Dean, *Managerial Economics,* p. 375.

[7] Hurwood, "How Companies Set Advertising Budgets."

closed, however, that top management is increasingly insisting on rigorous implementation of the task method. Of the 1969 advertising budgets in the consumer goods field, for example, 29 percent were prepared using the task method, compared with 43 percent of industrial products advertisers.[8] By 1972, 27 percent used a relatively pure form of the task method in that objectives were set and the cost of reaching them was determined.[9] Another 27 percent, however, utilized the task method in combination with the percentage of anticipated 1973 sales. Less than 15 percent employed a straight percentage of sales approach.

It is apparent that the rigor of budgetary procedures is increasing. The primary objective is to guarantee promotional accountability. Many companies have introduced semiannual, quarterly, or monthly reports for the purpose of reviewing decisions and introducing modifications where necessary. Procter & Gamble, Quaker Oats, Bristol-Myers, and North American Philips are all reported to have instituted this type of system.

IMPLEMENTING THE TASK AND OBJECTIVE APPROACH

The ideal approach to budgeting builds upon the concepts inherent in marginal analysis. The logical procedure would be to establish objectives and then to experiment until that level of expenditure is found which most closely approximates the optimum. It is not uncommon for larger firms to follow this procedure, although it can be time-consuming and expensive.

In one three-year test experiment the Missouri Valley Petroleum Company divided a large number of cities into three test groups and one control group.[10] One test group received half as much advertising as normal; expenditures were twice the normal rate in another group, and three times the rate in the third. It was found that a 50 percent reduction had no great effect, whereas the greatest sales increases were in the double-expenditure markets. A tripling of the budget led to only minimal further increases. Similarly, a six-year research program at the Anheuser-Busch Company comprising advertising variations in 200 geographical areas showed that it was possible to reduce advertising expenditures and still increase sales.[11] Many feel, as a result, that experimentation is the

---

[8] *The Gallagher Report,* May 6, 1969, p. 3.

[9] *The Gallagher Report,* December 4, 1972.

[10] Leo Bogart, *Strategy in Advertising* (New York: Harcourt, Brace & World, 1967), p. 29.

[11] Thomas M. Newell, "What Is the Right Amount to Spend for Advertising?" talk delivered at the A.A.A.A. Western Region Annual Meeting, October 6–9, 1968.

only feasible approach, given management pressures for greater promotional efficiency and accountability.[12]

Experimentation obviously is not feasible for most firms because of time and cost constraints. Therefore, some combination of the procedures mentioned above usually must be employed. A logical approach encompasses the following steps:

1. Isolation of objectives.
2. Determination of expenditures through a "build-up" analysis.
3. Comparison against industry percentage of sales guidelines.
4. Comparison against a projected cost figure based on percentage of future sales.
5. Reconciliation of divergences between built-up costs and percentage of sales figures.
6. Establishment of a payout plan where appropriate.
7. Modification of estimates in terms of company policies.
8. Specification of when expenditures will be made.
9. Establishment of built-in flexibility.

Isolation of Objectives

The first step in building a budgetary plan is to estimate the total market for the product category. These figures may be available from governmental sources, trade publications, or from market research firms such as A. C. Nielsen or the Market Research Corporation of America. Then it is necessary to estimate the share of the total market that the firm most likely can attain. Factors underlying this estimate are:

1. Product uniqueness—the advantages relative to competition and the ease with which they can be duplicated.
2. Number of competitors—it is difficult to obtain a large share in a highly fragmented market.
3. The spending pattern of competition—a large share is more feasible where competition has not been aggressive and is unwilling and (or) unable to become so in the future.

Estimated market share becomes significant in that it is possible to approximate necessary spending levels based on past industry performance, as is discussed later.

In addition, of course, communication objectives must be specified. These objectives should be combined into a comprehensive and specific

---

[12] Malcolm A. McNiven, "Introduction," in McNiven (ed.), *How Much to Spend for Advertising* (New York: Association of National Advertisers, 1969), pp. 1–10.

statement upon which a detailed plan of efforts producing measurable results can be built.

Expenditure Estimation through Built-Up Analysis

Once objectives have been specified, the next question concerns what is required to accomplish these tasks. This analysis, in turn, should encompass mass media expenditures (advertising and public relations), direct selling costs, and costs of stimulating reseller support.

Advertising and Public Relations. If the objective, for example, is to saturate the teen-age market through repetitive advertising, it is clear that a large budget will be required for continued advertising in media which reach this market segment. In more technical terms, media strategy would be established to achieve *frequency*. On the other hand, the task may call for reaching as large a market as possible, in which case a wide variety of media would be utilized to attain *reach*. Reach and frequency requirements, therefore, are instrumental in determination of the required budget.[13] The basic approach is to "build up" or select the necessary media.

The analysis underlying media selection, which is complex, is the subject of Chapter 12. It is recognized that media analysis lies at the heart of the task and objective approach; in fact, Roger Barton, a widely quoted authority, does not even mention percentage of sales and other approaches in his discussion of budgeting.[14] It is his contention that the final budgetary figure is based upon: (1) definition of the types of media to be used, (2) the costs of individual media, (3) frequency of insertions, (4) the media mix, and (5) other related considerations. This analysis, in turn, is common to both advertising and public relations, although much publicity is achieved at no cost to the firm.

Direct Selling Costs. Next it is necessary to determine the required selling activities and resulting costs to reach wholesalers and retailers and stimulate their promotional support. Computations are usually made by territory or other subunits of the firm where environmental situations are known to differ. Judgment armed with research data is the only tool available. Recourse must be made to historical records detailing efforts under similar sets of alternatives in the past and the costs which were incurred. In the absence of appropriate records, experimental research may be required.

The costing of efforts raises problems which require some discussion. A first step always will be to determine the total of fixed selling costs,

[13] See Paul M. Roth, *How to Plan Media* (Skokie, Ill.: Standard Rate & Data Service, 1968), ch. 10.

[14] Roger Barton, *Media in Advertising* (New York: McGraw-Hill Book Co., 1964), pp. 15–19.

because, in all probability, they will change only slightly from period to period. A similar relationship may be found for semivariable costs which, for all intents and purposes, are fixed over large ranges of output. The problem comes in estimating variable costs, and detailed historical records are required for the estimates to have any meaning.

The problem of variable costs is clarified considerably if standard costs can be constructed for each activity. A cost standard is a predetermined norm for an operation intended to represent the costs under usual operating conditions. Standard costs frequently are based on time and duty analysis whereby time intervals required to perform an activity are translated into monetary terms. The availability of standard costs then permits the computation of a sales budget on the basis of estimates of the functions to be performed, multiplied by the appropriate cost standard for each function. It might be discovered, for example, that the standard cost per sales call in territories 1, 7, and 9 is $10 and the best estimate of calls required during the coming year is 1,000, 1,200, and 870 respectively. The budgeted costs then would be $10,000 in territory 1 (1,000 × $10), $12,000 in territory 2, and $8,700 in territory 3.

The two most widely used cost standards are cost per sales call and cost per dollar of net sales. Standards also are established frequently for the salaries and expenses of home office sales administration, the expenses of field supervision, costs of home office and field office clerical efforts, and other related functions.

Even though standard costs are a significant aid, the applicability of standards is highly dependent on the nature of the tasks performed. Clerical activities, of course, are routine, and it is not difficult to establish standards such as cost per invoice line posted. Creative selling, on the other hand, may be far from routine in that a sale may not be made until many preliminary customer contacts are completed. In such instances, it may be impossible to establish reasonable standards.

The tasks of calling upon wholesalers and retailers, however, are frequently more routine than they may appear at first glance. A regular schedule of calls is typical, and the selling job itself may be little more than order taking. In such instances cost standards can be set and followed for both budgeting and cost control.

Cost standards, then, should be used whenever possible. In addition, conferences should be held at all management levels with those directly involved in the execution of planned efforts, to utilize combined judgment. The result hopefully will be a realistic estimate of marginal returns from sales efforts.

Stimulating Reseller Support. The departure point of analysis is the history of trade efforts in the product category. What is the ratio of trade expenditures to advertising of major competitors? In most product categories it is necessary to be competitive, or support will be lost. Costs will be incurred in the form of product sampling, couponing, margin manipulation, cooperative advertising, provision of displays, and so on.

Comparison against Industry Percentage of Sales Guidelines

It is frequently found that *share of industry advertising* is a primary criterion of success, especially in marketing a new product.[15] The advertising share of most successful products, for example, generally exceeds sales share by 1.5 or 1.6 to 1 in such product categories as household needs, food products, and proprietory medicines. It would of course vary somewhat from one product area to another. This would indicate that the firm should advertise, on the average, at a 45 percent rate to attain a 30 percent sales share.[16] A strong brand might reduce this ratio somewhat, whereas a brand in second or third position may have to advertise in the range of 2 or 3 or 1. Also the quality of advertising will make a difference. Therefore, this type of ratio can only be a rough guideline.

Comparison against Projected Percentage of Future Sales

It was suggested earlier that the percentage of sales devoted to promotion in the past is a useful starting point in budgeting. These figures are readily available in conventional accounting statements, and breakdowns can be provided for sales territories and products.

The application of percentages to forecasted sales involves circular reasoning to the extent that it is difficult to forecast sales without knowing the investment in promotion. As a result this is not a sufficient basis for budgeting, but it does provide an estimate, all things being equal, of what would be spent if proportions were not altered to meet changed objectives. Thus it serves as a benchmark against which to compare the built-up budgetary sum.

Reconciliation of Divergences between Built-Up Costs and Percentage of Sales Figures

Once the projected percentage figure for both the industry and company and built-up expenditure figures are available, the focus can be

---

[15] James O. Peckham, "Can We Relate Advertising Dollars to Market-Share Objectives?" in McNiven (ed.), *How Much to Spend for Advertising*, pp. 23 and 24.

[16] Ibid., p. 24.

on reconciling differences. If a 1.6 to 1 ratio is reasonable given past industry experience in the product category and projected spending is far in excess of the ratio, it may be necessary to revise premises, assumptions, and other factors in order to ascertain whether the projected figure is reasonable. The budgetary analysis is a continuing process of this type, because only by accident will a sum be arrived at which clearly is the optimum appropriation.

Payout Planning

It frequently is desirable to extend the budgetary period, especially when new products are introduced, because one calendar year may not be sufficient to accomplish objectives. Strategy may encompass three to five years, and the appropriation must be viewed in that time perspective. Moreover, profitability may not be realized until the end of the period. In other words, the payout from the expenditures is expected to occur at a later point in time, and this extension of the planning period is frequently referred to as payout planning. Because this is most frequently used in introducing new products, further discussion is reserved for the next section of the chapter.

Modification of Estimates in Terms of Company Policies

It is also pertinent to fine tune the appropriation figures to make the sums consistent with the overall framework of company policy and dollars invested in other functions. Financial liquidity must always be considered, for there are bound to be financial constraints which cannot be exceeded, even in payout planning, regardless of logic or compelling necessity. Moreover, *too much can be spent* for promotion in view of the entire company situation. There is the possibility that advertising and selling can easily disturb orderly flows of manpower, inventory, and cash by borrowing sales from the future and introducing unwarranted fluctuation in other flows. It must never be overlooked that the company is a system of related flows, and dollars must be invested to maximize the response of the *system* and not the *function* itself. The danger to be avoided is suboptimization, which results when management loses sight of the system in which it lives.

Specification of When Expenditures Will Be Made

Another requirement for a good budget is designation of when dollars will be expended during the budgetary period. This is to permit forecasting of cash flow requirements by the company comptroller to ensure that funds are available when needed.

Building in Flexibility

The budget should never be viewed as a perfect map to be followed without variation. The dangers of inflexibility are analyzed at length in the management literature, and there is compelling logic for building in sufficient flexibility to allow for changing conditions.[17] Markets are becoming more volatile, product planning deadlines are shortened, and there are many possibilities of tactical shifts by competition. This flexibility may be provided by a 10 to 15 percent reserve sum which is not allocated until needed.

Adaptation to change, of course, requires maintenance of detailed records of results. More and more companies are now establishing a new management post—the advertising controller.[18] He is appointed to be a watchdog over spending, with the result that there may be a more or less continual review of performance. Records also are useful as guides to future strategy decisions. Unfortunately, this type of record frequently is not kept on any systematic basis, and this lack can serve as a real impediment to the application of the philosophy of marginal analysis.

Comments on the Suggested Approach

This section has not been presented with the objective of providing a formula which can be automatically followed. Rather, a step-by-step procedure has been suggested to approximate marginal analysis through the task and objective approach, and it must be adapted creatively and analytically to each situation. The final result should never be construed as being ideal, because there always may be good reasons for major changes throughout the planning period. Also, the tendency to use the budget as a screen to hide inefficiencies must be guarded against. Consider this argument:

One of the latent dangers sometimes found in budgetary controls is the tendency for budgets to hide inefficiencies. Budgets have a way of growing from precedent, and the fact that a certain expenditure was made in a prior period becomes prima facie evidence of its reasonableness in a current period. . . . Also, some managers soon learn that budget requests are likely to be pared down in the course of their final approval and therefore ask for much more than they actually need. The somewhat deceptive definiteness of reducing plans to budget figures should never be allowed to overshadow the basic purposes of planning and control. Unless budget making is accompanied with constant re-examination of standards and the other bases by which planning policies are translated into

---

[17] See Harold Koontz and Cyril O'Donnell, *Principles of Management* (New York: McGraw-Hill Book Co., 1955), ch. 25, for an excellent statement.

[18] *The Gallagher Report,* February 18, 1969, p. 1.

metric terms, there is a danger that the budget may become an umbrella under which slovenly and inefficient management can hide.[19]

These dangers can be avoided if top management insists on measurement of results and evaluates the competence of personnel in performance terms.

BUDGETING FOR NEW PRODUCTS

There are some special considerations which enter into the budgeting process for new products, in addition to those that have been mentioned. Payout planning assumes particular importance, and experimentation with quantitative methods is providing some interesting new insights.

Payout Planning[20]

A payout plan is a procedure which extends the planning period for longer than one year, and it has proved especially useful in evaluation of the proper course of action in introducing new products. Most often it covers three years, but in the case of slow-maturing products such as proprietary medicines or where large initial expenditures are necessary, the payout plan may be extended to cover four or five years. The stages in payout planning are: (1) estimation of market share objectives, (2) assessment of needed trade inventories, (3) determination of needed expenditures, (4) determination of the payout period, and (5) evalaution.

Estimation of Share Objectives. It was previously mentioned that the first step in budgeting is to estimate the total market for the product category and then to assess the probable share to be captured by the firm. It should be noted that most new products reach their peak share and then decline to a lower level. Share builds slowly as distribution is achieved, promotion pressure is applied, and consumer trial is generated. Usually a brand will hit its peak share approximately 6 to 12 months after introduction in a new area, and then level off or decline. It is then necessary to recycle the brand through product improvement.

This short life cycle for most consumer products makes it important to accelerate trial through heavy advertising expenditures in the first few months. Products are only new once, and this is the most important period in the life of a brand. The higher the peak share, the greater the probability that the brand will be a success.

Assessment of Needed Trade Inventories. The company also makes money on what is sold to the trade, so the goods necessary to "fill the

---

[19] Ibid., p. 559. Copyright 1955, McGraw-Hill Book Co. Used by permission of McGraw-Hill Book Co.

[20] This section was contributed by Robert Sowers, formerly senior vice president, Ogilvy & Mather, Inc.

pipeline" must be added to consumer sales to get the total volume for the manufacturer. There are two general guidelines to follow.

1. The larger the projected volume, the shorter the number of weeks supply necessary in trade inventories.
2. Most products lose inventory in the second year through resellers' cutbacks unless share is climbing; this exerts a negative force on sales in that year.

Determination of Needed Expenditures. There are several guidelines to be followed in arriving at the proper budget level based on experience:

1. The first-year budget should permit a heavy introductory schedule (13–26 weeks) followed by a sustaining schedule at least equal to the second year advertising budget.
2. A good rule of thumb is that expenditures for the introductory schedule should be about twice the rate currently spent by competitors who have shares equal to the company objective.
3. Carefully check expenditures on a per unit basis against competitors. The brand with the highest shares usually has a lower cost per unit, and vice versa.

Determination of the Payout Period. In today's competitive marketplace, the trend is toward shorter payout plans. Most product development can be duplicated by competition in a short time. There is also reason to believe that brand loyalty is not as great as it once was. Finally, there is a high rate of new-product failures. Long payouts are justified only when the projected life cycle of the product is very long and the potential rewards are very big.

Two payout plans are shown in Figures 10–5 and 10–6. Notice that

FIGURE 10–5

Payout Plan for a New Food Product (000 omitted)

	Theoretical Marketing Years		
	First	Second	Third
Total market (units)	50,000	52,000	54,000
Market share (percentage)	5.0	5.2	5.0
Volume (units)	2,500	2,704	2,700
Pipeline (units)	400	(50)	—
Total volume (units)	2,900	2,654	2,700
Total sales (@ $9.00)	26,100	23,886	24,300
Gross profit (@ $4.00)	11,600	10,616	10,800
Advertising ($)	6,500	4,000	4,000
Promotion to the trade ($)	8,000	2,000	2,000
Total advertising & promotion ($)	14,500	6,000	6,000
Gross trading profit ($)	(2,900)	4,616	4,800
Profit (percentage of sales)		19.3	19.8
Cumulative gross trading profit ($)	(2,900)	1,716	6,516

the new food product considered in Figure 10–5 was projected to return a loss in the first year and pay out in the second year. The drug product considered in Figure 10–6, on the other hand, was not expected to pay out until the fourth year. In the former example, the total promotional budget was highest in the first year so that maximum impact could be made, whereas the opposite is the case with the drug product, which matures more slowly.

FIGURE 10–6

Payout Plan for a New Drug Product (000 omitted)

	Theoretical Marketing Years				
	First	*Second*	*Third*	*Fourth*	*Fifth*
Total market (units) ....:...200,000	211,000	223,500	235,500	246,000
Market share (percentage) 2.0	3.3	4.4	5.6	6.7
Volume (units) 4,000	6,963	9,834	13,188	16,482
Pipeline (units) 700	750	780	800	800
Gross sales ($) 4,700	7,013	9,864	13,208	16,482
Gross margin (percentage) 7	7	7	7	7
Gross profit ($) 3,290	4,909	6,905	9,246	11,537
Advertising ($) 4,400	4,200	5,000	5,760	6,000
Promotion to the trade ($) 1,500	700	800	900	1,000
Total adv. & prom. ($) 5,900	4,900	5,800	6,660	7,000
Gross trading profit ($) .... (2,610)	9	1,105	2,586	4,537
Profit (percentage of sales) .... —	—	16.0	27.9	39.3
Cumulative gross trading profit ($)	(2,601)	(1,496)	1,090	5,627

Evaluation. In evaluating the soundness of a payout plan, management usually directs attention to the first year (the year of heavy investment) and to the first year after payout is achieved. This latter year gives management an opportunity to assess the long-term rewards of the investments they have made in the other years. By comparison with other opportunities and other competitive products, it is possible to make an experienced judgment on the wisdom of the investment. Of particular importance are examination of profit margins and the financial implications of an investment of this size.

Adaptation. It must be emphasized that a payout plan is a theoretical financial plan calling for a national introduction at one specific point in time. Management has the option of making the plan fit overall company fiscal goals more closely by, first of all, picking the most propitious time to introduce a product. For example, introducing at the end of a fiscal year could fatten company profit for that year by accumulating the profits from heavy initial trade sales, while deferring the heavy introductory advertising expenses until the next fiscal year.

Companies frequently choose to introduce in waves. They might introduce in 20 percent of the market to start, and then 20 percent in the next two months, and so on. This has the effect of lowering the deficit position at any one point in time. There are other advantages, such as leveling production schedules and correcting errors found in the first regions. The disadvantages are that it may result in shortening lead time over competition and that it might be necessary to pay a premium to do regional advertising instead of national advertising.

Evaluation of Payout Planning.   Payout planning is being followed by an increasing number of firms. An assumption is made, of course, that environmental conditions existing during the first year will not change greatly during the planning period. Competition might enter and drastically change the competitive environment, to mention only one possibility. Also, it is assumed that the effect of promotional expenditures on sales can be estimated with some accuracy. Nevertheless, payout planning encompasses a managerial philosophy which has merit, for a realistic attempt is made to implement the task and objective method without imposing arbitrary restrictions on funds in any given year.

New-Product Models

The new-product decision may be conceived of as consisting of four stages: (1) search for new product ideas, (2) screening of ideas to eliminate those that obviously are unsuitable, (3) analysis of remaining alternatives, and (4) implementation of the marketing plan. A number of quantitative models have been proposed for use at the various stages, and considerable experimentation has been undertaken to relate a product's marketing variables in such a way that quantitative expressions can be derived to predict the sales effects of marketing strategies.[21] Models of this type are most useful in the analysis stage of the new-product decision.

The starting point for a demand analysis will be estimates of sales, given a forecast of the market and competitive environment and certain assumed levels of expenditure for various areas of the marketing mix. Then the quantitative demand model describes how sales change if the marketing mix changes. It may be felt, for example, that advertising affects awareness and that awareness, along with reseller efforts, determines trial rate for the product. Then trial rate, competition, and price would determine sales. One new-product model, DEMON, assumes that advertising dollars affect media weight, which in turn specifies advertising

---

[21] See David B. Montgomery and Glen L. Urban, *Management Science in Marketing* (Englewood Cliffs, N.J.: Prentice-Hall, 1969), ch. 7; also Edgar A. Pessemier, "Models for New-Product Decisions," Working Paper No. 247, Herman C. Krannert Graduate School of Industrial Administration, Purdue University, May 1969.

awareness. Then promotion, distribution, and awareness determine trial rate, which, in turn, determines usage rate.[22] Once these linkages are specified it is possible to predict the effects, given a certain level of expenditure on advertising and other efforts. The advantage in budgeting is obvious in that the probable effects can be predicted.

Awareness is often assumed to be the contribution of advertising to overall demand stimulation. As part of the new-products model used at Batten, Barton, Dusstine & Osborn (BBD&O), Albert J. Martin, Jr., predicted the following relationship between awareness and advertising level:[23]

$$A_j = KA_{j-1} + (A_m - A_{j-1})(1 - e^{-\Sigma n_j}),$$

where

j = Time period determined by the timing of data collection
A_j = Level of awareness at the end of time period j
A_m = Maximum expected level of awareness
e = Base of the natural logarithm
Σn_j = Cumulative average number of exposures delivered by the media schedule from $j = 0$ to the end of time period j
A_{j-1} = Level of awareness at the end of the previous time period $(j - 1)$
K = The fraction of A_{j-1} remembered at the end of time period j

An empirical test of the model proved that it gave an accurate prediction of actual levels of awareness for a new convenience item. Assuming that the necessary input data can be collected and that a level of desired awareness has been specified, it then is possible to solve the equation to determine the level of advertising exposures needed to attain the desired awareness. This basic approach has been expanded by Larry Light and Lewis Pringle, and even better results have been generated.[24]

New-product models, for the most part, are only in the early stages of development. Much work remains before enough is known to permit widespread use. It seems certain, however, that quantitative statements of the relationship between advertising and expected response will be used increasingly, because much of the guesswork previously necessary in new-product planning can be avoided. Thus, it is to be expected that the computer will be increasingly used in making the budgeting decision.

---

[22] See David B. Learner, "DEMON New Product Planning: A Case History," in Frederick E. Webster, Jr. (ed.), *New Directions in Marketing* (Chicago: American Marketing Association, 1965).

[23] Albert J. Martin, Jr., "An Exponential Model for Predicting Trial of a New Consumer Product," doctoral dissertation, The Ohio State University, 1969.

[24] Larry Light and Lewis Pringle, "New Product Forecasting Using Recursive Regression," in David T. Kollat, Richard D. Blackwell, and James F. Engel (eds.), *Research in Consumer Behavior* (New York: Holt, Rinehart & Winston, Inc., 1970), pp. 702–9.

SUMMARY

This chapter began with a brief review of the theoretical model underlying the budgeting decision. It was then pointed out that the idealized marginal approach to budgeting can only be crudely approximated by the existing methods. The task and objective procedure is most suitable, and a nine-step process was suggested whereby a realistic budget estimate can be made, given a statement of objectives.

It is no doubt apparent that the ideal of marginal analysis never will be attained with the precision specified by economists. Nevertheless, utilization of the systematic approach suggested here will in time provide a reasonable approximation, especially as a backlog of documented results becomes available. Even with the use of quantitative methods, however, judgment will never be eliminated—it will only be sharpened.

APPENDIX TO CHAPTER 10:
APPLICATION OF QUANTITATIVE METHODS

The limitations of existing budgetary procedures have caused increasing interest in quantitative techniques. Much has been said regarding the potential of these methods, but many claims are commercially motivated. Therefore it is necessary to examine several of the most widely publicized approaches with the objective of ascertaining whether existing methodology has been augmented in a meaningful way. Obviously it is only possible to give a brief introduction in these few pages. The reader interested in further details must turn elsewhere.[25]

The General Approach

Nearly all models include a mechanism for relating the effects of expenditures on sales. This mechanism usually is referred to as the *sales response function*. Then data are collected on promotional decision variables of the firm and its competitors. It is the purpose of the sales response function to relate these variables in a meaningful way. Finally, a decision model is developed to generate optimal promotional expenditures.

The quality of the model, of course, is dependent initially upon the sales response function. In turn, its usefulness is determined at least in part by the way in which decision variables are related to sales, especially with respect to underlying assumptions which must be satisfied.

---

[25] An especially useful source is L. J. Parsons and R. L. Schultz, "Setting Advertising Appropriations: Decision Models and Econometric Research" Working Paper No. 328, Krannert Graduate School of Industrial Administration, Purdue University, January 1973.

Many of the models reviewed in these pages cannot be considered as especially useful from a practical point of view, yet progress is being made.

The Sales Model

In the simplest case, advertising is the only variable affecting sales in the current period. Profit therefore is expressed by David B. Montgomery and Glen L. Urban[26] as:

$$Pr = pq - A - C(q)$$
$$= pf(A) - A - C[f(A)],$$

where

p = Unit price
Pr = Total profit
A = Advertising
q = Quantity sold
$C(q)$ = Cost of producing and marketing

If there are decreasing returns to advertising at some level of A, then optimization procedures may be used to determine the profit-maximizing budgetary level. It is obvious, however, that this equation generally is an oversimplification of reality in that it fails to comprehend all factors which affect the budgeting decision. Its primary value is in specifying one possible relationship between advertising and profit.

Dynamic Models

In reality, advertising undertaken in previous periods will affect the current period; in the same sense current advertising will have future effects. To take this carry-over effect into consideration, dynamic models are required. There have been several published dynamic models; one is presented here to illustrate something of its variables and potential usefulness.[27]

M. L. Vidale and H. B. Wolfe[28] have combined the following factors into a mathematical model describing sales response to advertising.

1. *The sales response rate*—the relative ease of moving people toward purchase.

---

[26] Montgomery and Urban, *Management Science in Marketing*, p. 116.

[27] See for example Julian Simon, "A Simple Model for Determining Advertising Appropriations," *Journal of Marketing Research* (1965), pp. 285–92; and M. Nerlove and K. J. Arrow, "Optimal Advertising Policy under Dynamic Conditions," *Economica*, Vol. 29 (May 1962), pp. 129–42.

[28] M. L. Vidale and H. B. Wolfe, "An Operations-Research Study of Sales Response to Advertising," *Operations Research*, Vol. 5 (June 1957), pp. 370–81.

2. *The saturation level*—the maximum sales that can be achieved in a given campaign period.
3. *The response constant*—the sales generated by advertising.
4. *The sales decay rate*—the extent to which countervailing forces erode brand preference in the absence of advertising.

The basic equation is:

$$\frac{dS}{dt} = rA\,\frac{M - S}{M} - \lambda S,$$

where

S = Sales rate at time t
r = Response constant (sales generated per dollar of advertising when $S = 0$)
A = Rate of advertising expenditure at time t
M = Saturation level (the maximum sales for a given campaign)
λ = Sales decay constant (sales lost per time interval when $A = 0$)

In words, this equation states:

The instantaneous rate of increase of sales at any time, $t =$

$$\underset{\text{constant}}{\text{Response}} \times \underset{\substack{\text{advertising} \\ \text{at time } t}}{\text{Rate of}} \times \frac{\text{Saturation level} - \text{Sales rate at time } t}{\text{Saturation level}}$$

$$- \text{ Sales decay constant} \times \text{sales rate at time } t$$

Vidale and Wolfe have tested this equation in the real world through estimating the various parameters in test market experiments. If it is an accurate statement, it says, in effect, that the sales response per advertising dollar times the number of dollars spent, reduced by the percentage of unsaturated sales plus sales lost through decay, are the factors which result in the increase in the rate of sales.

This equation still needs much testing before it can be accepted as valid, and the necessary confirmatory evidence has not appeared in the literature. Also, it is apparent that it may be difficult, if not impossible, to estimate such factors as response constant, saturation level, and sales decay constant without almost prohibitively expensive test market experimentation. In other words, it is often easy to assume that such variables are known and then specify an equation which relates them in a functional way. Nevertheless, this model does relate some important factors in sales response to advertising and hence should be viewed as a meaningful step forward in the search for new analytical methods.

Competitive Models

None of the models discussed thus far explicitly take competitive factors into consideration. Game theoretic models, building on the classic work of John von Neumann and Oskar Morgenstern,[29] explicitly focus on this vitally important factor. The basic assumption is that all players are interdependent and that uncertainty results from not knowing what the others will do. Strategy then is devised to reduce and control uncertainty. This requires use of the principle of minimax, in which each competitor acts as the "cautious pessimist," fully expecting the worst to happen and trying to minimize competitive inroads. In the game it would be, by assumption, irrational to try to maximize and produce the largest reward, because the competitor following the minimax strategy theoretically will always win.

It has been suggested that the theory of games is potentially applicable to the problem of budgeting for promotion. While the mathematics of complex solutions is beyond the scope of this book, it is possible to convey the basic nature and strategies of game theory through a comparatively simple example.[30]

Assume that four possible advertising strategies are available to the two dominant competitors in an oligopolistic industry:

1. An expenditure of $250,000 on hard-sell copy using network and spot television.
2. An expenditure of $300,000 on soft-sell "image" type advertising using consumer magazines in four colors.
3. An expenditure of $500,000 on mixed hard- and soft-sell copy using local spot television and newspapers.
4. An expenditure of $500,000 on a mixture of network television and three consumer magazines using hard-sell copy.

Assume further that the revenue produced by competitor A following these strategies in light of expected retaliation by competitor B is that appearing in Figure 10–7. This payoff matrix indicates, for example, that if A follows strategy 1 and B does so also (cell A_1–B_1), the return to A would be $2,000,000. However, if it follows strategy 1 and B uses strategy 4 (cell A_1–B_4), $500,000 would be lost. The problem, then, is to arrive at the proper minimax strategy for both competitors, simultaneously behaving as cautious pessimists.

In the above example A will reason that he wants to make the maximum gain *assuming the strongest retaliation from B*. Hence, he will follow the strategy which gives him the *best of the minimum returns*. This strategy is determined by listing the minimum return under each strategy and following the strategy with the maximum minimum return, or the

[29] John von Neumann and Oskar Morgenstern, *Theory of Games and Economic Behavior* (Princeton, N.J.: Princeton University Press, 1944).

[30] This example is adapted from Harold Bierman, Jr., Lawrence E. Fouraker, and Robert K. Jaedicke, *Quantitative Analysis for Business Decisions* (Homewood, Ill.: Richard D. Irwin, 1961), pp. 94–98.

minimax solution. A would thus list the minimum value in each row in Figure 10–7 and designate the maximum minimum value. This value is $800,000, which is achieved by following strategy A_3.

In turn, B would follow the same reasoning, and his best decision is arrived at by consulting the payout matrix, determining the *maximum* return in each column, and choosing the minimum value. The maximum value in each column, of course, represents the worst that can happen to him (in that A makes his greatest gain), so naturally he will play the strategy which minimizes his losses. This solution will be optimum for him. The best B can do is to play strategy B_4, which gives A his smallest maximum return.

FIGURE 10–7

Conditional Returns to Competitor A, Given Retaliation by Competitor B (000 omitted)

	B's Strategies			
A's Strategies	B_1	B_2	B_3	B_4
A_1................	$2,000	$2,500	$4,000	−$500
A_2................	1,500	1,400	200	400
A_3................	1,200	1,000	1,000	800
A_4................	3,500	1,000	500	0

The minimax solutions for the payoff matrix in Figure 10–7 are computed in Figure 10–8. A return of $800,000 is the maximum A can expect, assuming competitive retaliation, and this return is produced by strategy 3. In turn, B can clearly see that it minimizes A's inroads by playing strategy 4, which gives A the smallest return of $800,000 and enables B to maintain his position.

Notice that the solution is the intersection of A_3 and B_4. This unique intersection is called the "saddle point," and neither competitor gains at the expense of the other, as would easily happen if this intersection had not been produced. Because no competitive gain results, this is called a "zero-sum" game. Not all games have a unique saddle point or a zero-sum solution, in which case mixed strategies are used to arrive at the actions which give the greatest *probability* of a minimax solution. Space precludes discussion of these complexities.

Lawrence Friedman[31] has elaborated on simple game theory models and suggested a number of ways in which advertising strategy can be arrived at. He admits, however, that his models have not been sub-

---

[31] Lawrence Friedman, "Game Theory Models in the Allocation of Advertising Expenditures," in Frank M. Bass et al. (eds.), *Mathematical Models and Methods in Marketing* (Homewood, Ill.: Richard D. Irwin, 1961), pp. 230–41.

jected to empirical verification. Such verification may be difficult, for game theory is based on several troublesome assumptions:

1. Competitors will always allocate funds to take maximum advantage of each other's mistakes in budgeting.
2. The relative effectiveness of dollars spent is identical for each competitor.
3. Each competitor knows the rules of the game and follows them—i.e., each player thoroughly understands the available strategies and follows the minimax philosophy.
4. All players have complete information on the payouts from following various strategies, in view of competitive retaliation.

The first assumption is noncontroversial, but is it realistic to assume that payouts are fully known, that all players comprehend and follow

FIGURE 10–8
Computation of the Minimax Solutions (000 omitted)

A's Strategies	B's Strategies				Row Minimums
	B_1	B_2	B_3	B_4	
A_1........................	$2,000	$2,500	$4,000	−$500	−$500
A_2........................	1,500	1,400	200	400	200
A_3........................	1,200	1,000	1,000	800	800
A_4........................	3,500	1,000	500	0	0
Column maximums.......	3,500	2,500	4,000	800	

the rules, and that the relative effectiveness of expenditures is equivalent for each? The answer obviously is no, and it is debatable that any kind of realistic solution can be arrived at with such assumptions.

Game theory has some intuitive appeal in that competitors must, of necessity, second-guess each other in oligopolistic markets. Perhaps modification might be introduced to permit practical applications. At the present time, commercially motivated claims that game theory has practical payoff should be rejected, because this has not been demonstrated. Nevertheless, all new techniques should be analyzed carefully, because any gain in the precision of budgeting is well worth the effort.

Stochastic Models

Several attempts have been made, using the laws of probability, to attack the budgeting process, the most notable being Markov chain analysis and the Stochastic learning model.

Markov Chain Analysis. A. Markov, a Russian mathematician, first developed an extension of probability to analyze the movement and distribution of gas particles in a container. Using this approach, now called Markov chain analysis, it is possible to predict the concentration of particles at one point in time through knowledge of the concentration in the preceding time period. The data required are the location of particles at one point, called state 1, and the probabilities (called transitional probabilities) that the particles will either remain stationary or move at later states.

It became apparent that Markov analysis might be used to advantage to predict the movement of buyers from one brand to another; brand loyalty is an important consideration in promotional strategy. The required data are estimates of the probability that buyers will stay loyal to a given brand or move to another brand. These data can be estimated through survey research or, more often, educated guesses by management.

FIGURE 10–9

Transitional Probabilities of Brand Loyalty and Brand Switching

	Switch to Brand		
From Brand	A	B	C
A.................	.55	.30	.15
B.................	.20	.70	.10
C.................	.10	.10	.80

The Markov model potentially can be utilized to advantage to predict the movement of market shares a product may have, given an empirical estimate of the probabilities that buyers will either stay with a given brand or switch to another. Assume that the transitional probabilities of brand switching shown in Figure 10–9 have been discovered from survey research. Notice that the rows all add to one, indicating that all possible actions have been itemized. Of A's customers, for example, the probabilities are that he will retain 55 percent, B will gain 30 percent, and C will take the remainder (reading across the rows). In turn (reading down the columns), A will capture 20 percent of B's customers and 10 percent of C's.

Let it be assumed further that the current market shares are: A—20 percent, B—50 percent, and C—30 percent. This provides sufficient data to calculate market shares in the future, *assuming that the transitional probabilities remain constant.* Through use of matrix multiplication it is apparent that A's share of the market in the next period will be 24 percent ($.55 \times 20\% + .20 \times 50\% + .10 \times 30\%$). That is, he will retain 55 percent of his present market share, gain 20 percent of B's, and gain 10 percent of C's. These computations may be carried on for as many periods as is desired. The resulting market shares are listed in Figure 10–10.

Notice that market shares ultimately stabilize at 25 percent, 37.5 percent, and 37.5 percent, respectively. The shares in period n, or the "steady state," are calculated using the Markov formulation with the tools of either matrix algebra or difference equations. The mathematics required is not difficult, and computer programs are available.[32]

The concern here is not with the computation of solutions but with the uses to which this type of analysis might be put. Comparatively little of substance has appeared in the published literature, but Markov analysis has been found useful in two related ways: (1) projection of

FIGURE 10–10

Market Shares in Ensuing Periods Given Transitional Probabilities

Period	Market Shares		
	A	B	C
1.....	20%	50%	30%
2.....	24	44	32
3.....	25.2	41.2	33.6
4.....	25.46	39.76	34.78
5.....	25.4333	38.948	35.619
.	.	.	.
.	.	.	.
.	.	.	.
n.....	25%	37.5%	37.5%

market shares period by period into the future and (2) analysis of the steady-state solutions resulting from experimental manipulation of promotion variables.[33]

Analysis of probable market shares in coming periods may give useful information for strategy. A high probability of movement from one brand to another may indicate, for example, that advertising claims are exaggerated and have led to disillusionment. A change in strategy is clearly called for. Moreover, exceptionally high probabilities of brand loyalty are a good sign of promotional invulnerability, and strategy may then turn to means of strengthening loyalty of existing consumers

---

[32] See Samuel Goldberg, *Introduction to Difference Equations* (New York: John Wiley & Sons, 1958), pp. 221–43.

[33] See Benjamin Lipstein, "The Dynamics of Brand Loyalty and Brand Switching," *Proceedings, 5th Annual Conference* (New York: Advertising Research Foundation, Inc., 1959), pp. 101–8; and Michael H. Halbert, "A Practical and Proven Measure of Advertising Effectiveness," *Proceedings, 6th Annual Conference* (New York: Advertising Research Foundation, Inc., 1960), pp. 77–82.

instead of emphasis upon making inroads on competitors' shares. The reader no doubt could easily provide many similar examples.

Of more importance for budgeting is analysis of a family of steady-state solutions resulting from experimental studies of variations in the promotion mix. By steady-state solutions are meant the outcome of market shares at period n—the theoretical ending point of change, often referred to by mathematicians as infinity. DuPont has used this approach successfully.[34] Assuming that brand loyalty is a function of promotion and price, variations are introduced in promotion in various matched test and control markets. Consumer interviews are conducted to detect resulting changes in brand usage, and the changed probabilities of purchasing one brand versus another are projected to predict market shares at the steady state. The various resulting steady-state solutions are then compared to detect the effectiveness of changes in the advertising mix. The strategy resulting in the largest market share at period n would then be utilized more extensively by the firm. This approach clearly isolates the monetary values of changes in brand loyalty through promotion, and valuable information is provided to implement the objective and task budgeting approach.

There are several difficulties, however, which will impede the widespread application of Markov experimentation:

1. It is assumed that the purchase of a brand in a coming period is correctly mirrored by the purchase in the last period, but empirical analysis has challenged this assumption. Alfred L. Kuehn found that prior purchases earlier in the purchasing history tend to strengthen a buying response in the future, as one might expect, and much switching occurs from one period to another without permanent changes in brand loyalty.[35] Therefore, the probabilities based only on the last purchase may be inaccurate.
2. It is also assumed that the transitional probabilities remain constant. Such an assumption, of course, is unrealistic in a volatile competitive world, and this becomes especially crucial if much reliance is placed on projections of shares for a few periods into the future. In analysis of steady-state solutions, however, this assumption is not crucial. No one expects the steady state to result. The intent is only to isolate what *would* happen, given changed transitional probabilities.
3. It can be exceedingly expensive to procure necessary data. Continuing studies are required to generate the probabilities, and experimentation with changed probabilities resulting from promotional

---

[34] Michael Halbert, class presentation, University of Michigan, May 12, 1962.

[35] Alfred L. Kuehn, "A Model for Budgeting Advertising," in Bass et al., *Mathematical Models,* pp. 315–48.

expenditure requires elaborate experimental designs (the difficulties of experimentation are analyzed further in another chapter).

4. The analysis becomes virtually impossible with products other than certain convenience goods with fairly regular purchase rates. A durable good purchased infrequently tends to defy analysis of this type.

These problems are indeed barriers, and sufficient experimentation has not yet been reported to permit a full assessment of the potential of Markov analysis. Yet on the basis of preliminary results, it seems to be promising where the promotional objective is to manipulate transitional probabilities of brand loyalty, and the future in all likelihood will bring modifications which will permit its use as a tool in the task and objective approach.

The Learning Model.   Alfred Kuehn has specifically attacked the assumption of Markov analysis that repurchase is dependent only on the last purchase.[36] The effect of prior purchases appears to carry over into the future in the form of an exponential curve, with the result that considerable residual influence from past buying action tends to remain. This conclusion is very similar to that found in psychological learning experiments. Kuehn modified a stochastic learning model of the Bush-Mosteller type for computational purposes, basing his model on household brand shifts in grocery product purchases. Price, changes in product, and distribution factors are specifically introduced, as well as advertising policy.

The sales revenue earned by a company in a given period is assumed to be generated by a combination of brand shifts by buyers and the functions of advertising, price, product characteristics, and distribution. Assuming that advertising effectiveness is independent of dollars spent, the model introduces advertising costs in terms of both present and discounted future return for dollars spent, and the result is an optimal solution maximizing a brand's market position. The unique contribution is that the profitability of an advertising expenditure is related to future sales, and, as such, it provides a rich basis for experimentation and empirical investigation.

While the Kuehn model will generate an optimum advertising expenditure, it requires a considerable body of data, including the following:

1. The rates of decay of brand loyalty (which are assumed to be constant over time).
2. The percentage of purchasers staying with a brand due to loyalty.
3. Net growth of industry sales per time period.
4. An estimate of the lag between placement of advertising dollars and sales results.

---

[36] Ibid.

5. The percentage of consumers who are impervious to marketing effort.
6. The share of brand shifters attracted by price, product, distribution, and advertising.
7. An index of advertising effectiveness.

This list could be extended, and it is clear that such data are usually unattainable except by the most tenuous of estimates. The difficulties are magnified greatly when many brands are compared.

While the difficulties of application are enormous, the importance of Kuehn's contribution should not be minimized. He has systematically implemented economic analysis by relating marketing-mix variables to empirical brand shift data to derive a mathematical model which yields an optimum promotional expenditure. The model obviously needs considerable refinement and extension as it now stands, to say nothing of sharpening the means of deriving the necessary input data. But the growth in the practical utility of computer models has been phenomenal, and it may be that the problem of budgeting is at last yielding to practical and significant new approaches.

Simulation

Various attempts to simulate the behavior of a market on a computer have appeared in the literature in recent years.[37] All have in common the representation of the behavior of a sample of consumers stored in the computer so that the probability of consumer response in a certain way, given the input of marketing efforts, can be assessed. One of the most interesting simulation models has been designed to permit evaluation of advertising budgeting strategies.[38]

This model, referred to by the acronym NOMAD, is a combination monte carlo and analytic demand model designed to forecast purchase behavior of 500 consumers in a well-defined market containing up to ten major brands. The model can be used to predict awareness, initial trial, peak purchase rates, sales for a new product, and demand for existing products. The individual consumer is described statistically. Three types of data are needed: (1) consumer panel purchase histories, (2) records of advertising by all leading brands in a product category, and (3) survey and market test data. There are then three principal initial values related to choice behavior for each consumer, based on records of past purchase behavior: (1) revealed brand preferences, (2) revealed store preferences, and (3) satisfaction level.

---

[37] See Montgomery and Urban, *Management Science in Marketing,* pp. 29–53.

[38] Jerome Herniter, Victor Cook, and Bernard Norek, "Micro Simulation Evaluation of Advertising Budget Strategies," working paper published by the Marketing Science Institute, Boston, Mass., 1969.

Inputs are then introduced to modify brand choice behavior. NOMAD has been validated in two product categories, and there was a close fit between actual and simulated purchases for each brand in these situations. Given this fit, attempts were then made to experiment with different advertising budget levels. Some statistically significant effects on market shares and purchase sequences were found, thus giving rise to the prediction that this type of simulation can prove useful in arriving at the optimum expenditure level.

Obviously, this type of model is new and largely untested. It does, however, offer the realism of assessing the effects of advertising under competitive circumstances. It offers the advantages of providing essential information quickly and at low cost. As a result, simulation may in the future find widespread use as management strives to implement the marginal approach to promotional budgeting.

Conclusions on Quantitative Methods

This has by no means exhausted the literature on potentially applicable quantitative models. Others which might have been described if space allowed use simultaneous equations[39] or adaptive models which are continually updated with inputs of new information.[40]

Have quantitative methods remedied the deficiencies of traditional budgeting tools? The answer at the present time unfortunately is not clear, because there are some problems which have not been resolved. In the first place, the information required often is virtually unobtainable at a reasonable cost. Second, and perhaps more crucial, is the limitation that most of the models described here make budgetary recommendations based on the assumption that advertising is the only variable. Interdependencies within the marketing mix are ignored, and this causes the models to be highly unrealistic under most circumstances. Finally, many of the assumptions of the models themselves tend to be arbitrary, although it cannot be denied that the traditional tools of budgeting, such as percentage of sales, are also built on assumptions which frequently are even more unrealistic.

There are some who deny the utility of quantitative methods. As K. H. Schaffir and E. W. Orr, Jr., put it:

Efforts in this area have unfortunately often involved complex mathematical formulations which are difficult to interpret and impossible to verify. Urging

---

[39] Leonard J. Persons and Frank M. Bass, "Optimal Advertising Expenditure Implications of a Simultaneous-Equation Regression Analysis," Working Paper No. 234, Herman C. Krannert Graduate School of Industrial Administration, Purdue University, February 1969.

[40] J. D. C. Little, "A Model of Adaptive Control of Promotional Spending," *Operations Research,* Vol. 14 (1966), pp. 175–97.

the adoption, on the basis of their logical merits alone, of complex and time-consuming methods which are inadequately supported by evidence is unreasonable, and has caused many practitioners to reject these methods altogether. A better approach would be to identify the basic elements of scientific method which can be useful, and to apply them, with judgment, to the degree supportable by such limited evidence as we possess.[41]

A survey of the top 100 national advertisers found that fewer than 40 percent make any use of mathematical models for budgeting purposes.[42] Most of these, in turn, found a model useful merely as a starting point, and only 5 percent found them to be of real value. Some have had bad past experiences, and others complain that models are either too complicated or oversimplified.

Granted the present difficulties, it must not be overlooked that many tend to reject the new in favor of the familiar. To do so in this promising area, however, may lead to overlooking potentially useful tools and thereby failing to square constructively with budgeting problems. It appears to be a safe prediction that it will not be long before quantitative methods find their position as a standard management technique.

REVIEW AND DISCUSSION QUESTIONS

1. What is the basic idea of the theoretical approach to determining the advertising appropriation as presented by Joel Dean? Can this approach be used in the business firm? Why, or why not?

2. What are the cost or expense items which should be included in the advertising budget? Why does it often become a catchall for irrelevant items?

3. Sears, Roebuck & Company spent $215,000,000 on national (as opposed to local store) advertising in 1972, making it the second largest advertiser. This figure amounted to 2.2 percent of sales. Assume that you are assigned the responsibility of determining the next advertising budget. What role would you assign to the percentage of sales figure? What other factors would enter into your decision?

4. The Kellogg Company spent 6.5 percent of its total sales of advertising in 1972, whereas the International Telephone & Telegraph Company spent only 1.8 percent of its sales for advertising. Why is there such a difference?

5. It is said that the 1970s will be characterized by vigorous emphasis on advertising accountability on the part of top management. How will this influence budgetary practice?

6. What is meant by a built-up analysis? How does it fit into the task and objective approach?

---

[41] K. H. Schaffir and E. W. Orr, Jr., "The Determination of Advertising Budgets for Brands," *Journal of Advertising Research,* Vol. 3 (1963), p. 8.

[42] S. Banks, "Trends Affecting the Implementation of Advertising and Promotion," *Journal of Marketing,* Vol. 37 (1973), pp. 19–28.

7. Assume that the advertising share of successful products in the soft drink industry exceeds sales share by about 2.1 to 1. You are the advertising manager of Twink, a new dietary soft drink. Would you abide by this customary ratio? What size budget would result if first-year sales were estimated at $8 million? What factors might lead you to depart from the customary ratio?

8. The president of a large advertising agency, a man who has long been considered by many to be a leader in the industry, made the following statement: "Our experience has shown that the operations research boys have just sold us a bunch of hogwash. It sounds good but they cannot deliver the goods when it gets down to the final analysis. As far as I'm concerned, leave the computers for the eggheads in the universities." Evaluate.

9. Some feel that simulation is the quantitative method which offers the most promise in advertising budgeting. What might this be? Do you agree? Why, or why not?

10. What is payout planning? How can you explain its widespread use in new-product introductions? What possible dangers must be faced?

part four

Management of Advertising Efforts

The topic of management of program elements will be approached first with consideration of the issues involved in using advertising as one of the most significant parts of the promotional program. Chapter 11 surveys the array of available advertising media, and Chapter 12 considers the basic aspects of media strategy.

Media selection, however, is only part of advertising. Design of the message perhaps offers the greatest challenge to the decision maker. Chapter 13 reviews what is referred to in the trade as "creative strategy." No attempt is made to present rules or practices in message design; rather the focus is on more fundamental considerations and trends. Such detailed issues as design of headlines and television commercials are discussed in the Appendix to this book.

The tools of survey research find considerable use in advertising strategy. Chapter 14 analyzes procedures used to pretest the message before it is run in the media, as well as the methods utilized to analyze the actual sales and communication effectiveness of the campaign.

Analysis of Mass Media Resources

THE INVESTMENT OF dollars in the mass media to reach the desired audience with a minimum of waste and a maximum of efficiency requires careful analysis and selection of media vehicles. Selection and use of the mass media is the subject of the next several chapters. In this chapter the concern is with media resources—types of available media and their characteristics. Sources of information and media strategy are covered in the following chapters.

EXPENDITURE TRENDS

In 1972 the total volume of advertising exceeded the $23 billion mark for the first time in history. As the data in Figure 11–1 comparing U.S. advertising volume in 1971, 1972, and 1973 show, most of the media gained in overall revenue, with the exception of weekly magazines and network and spot radio. There are important differences in the rate of growth, however. In line with the trend in recent years, in 1973 local advertisers increased their expenditures at a faster rate than national advertisers did, especially in the newspapers and local television. Television and newspapers also showed the most rapid overall growth.[1]

The trend toward increased spending is expected to continue. Total yearly advertising expenditures are expected to reach between $37 and $45 billion by 1980, depending on the rate of inflation.[2]

---

[1] "U.S. Advertising Hits $23.1 Billion; Expect Rise to $37 Billion by 1980," *Advertising Age,* November 21, 1973, pp. 6–7.

[2] Ibid.

FIGURE 11-1

Advertising Volume in the United States, 1971-1973

Medium	1971 Millions	1971 Percent of total	1972 Millions	1972 Percent of total	1973 Millions	1973 Percent of total	Percent Change 1973 versus 1972
Newspapers							
Total..........	6,198	29.9	7,008	30.1	7,595	30.2	+ 8.4
National.......	991	4.8	1,103	4.7	1,111	4.4	+ 0.7
Local..........	5,207	25.1	5,905	25.4	6,484	25.8	+ 9.8
Magazines							
Total..........	1,370	6.6	1,440	6.2	1,448	5.8	+ 0.6
Weeklies.......	626	3.0	610	2.6	583	2.3	− 4.5
Women's.......	340	1.6	368	1.6	362	1.5	− 1.6
Monthlies......	404	2.0	462	2.0	503	2.0	+ 8.9
Farm publications	57	0.3	59	0.3	65	0.3	+11.0
Television							
Total..........	3,534	17.0	4,091	17.6	4,493	17.9	+ 9.8
Network.......	1,593	7.7	1,804	7.7	1,968	7.8	+ 9.1
Spot..........	1,145	5.5	1,318	5.7	1,450	5.8	+10.0
Local..........	796	3.8	969	4.2	1,075	4.3	+11.0
Radio							
Total..........	1,445	7.0	1,612	6.9	1,690	6.7	+ 5.0
Network.......	63	0.3	74	0.3	70	0.3	− 5.0
Spot..........	395	1.9	402	1.7	380	1.5	− 5.0
Local..........	987	4.8	1,136	4.9	1,240	4.9	+ 9.0
Direct mail.......	3,067	14.8	3,420	14.7	3,698	14.7	+ 8.1
Business papers.	720	3.5	781	3.3	865	3.4	+10.8
Outdoor							
Total..........	261	1.2	292	1.2	308	1.2	+ 5.5
National.......	172	0.8	192	0.8	200	0.8	+ 4.0
Local..........	89	0.4	100	0.4	108	0.4	+ 8.0
Miscellaneous							
Total..........	4,088	19.7	4,597	19.7	4,958	19.7	+ 7.9
National.......	2,202	10.6	2,437	10.4	2,590	10.3	+ 6.3
Local..........	1,886	9.1	2,160	9.3	2,368	9.4	+ 9.6
Total							
National.......	11,775	56.8	13,030	55.9	13,845	55.1	+ 6.3
Local..........	8,965	43.2	10,270	44.1	11,275	44.9	+ 9.8
Grand Total.	20,740	100.0	23,300	100.0	25,120	100.0	+ 7.8

Note: This table contains latest revisions of all previously published figures for 1971, 1972 and 1973.
Source: *Advertising Age*, August 12, 1974, p. 53. Reproduced with special permission.

NEWSPAPERS

Newspapers have long maintained first place among all media in terms of combined national and local advertising revenues. Newspapers are for the most part a local medium with daily circulation confined to the city of publication and immediately surrounding areas. The circulation of Sunday newspapers, however, frequently is much greater, often extending beyond state boundaries.

The syndicated Sunday supplement is a distinct exception of the local flavor of newspaper editorial content. *Parade* and *Family Weekly* in effect are national sections inserted in more than 400 Sunday papers. Other supplements are local in editorial content and advertising. Some offer regional editions to permit insertion of advertising in a group of cities rather than purchase of the entire circulation.

Characteristics of Newspapers

Advantages. The use of newspapers as an advertising medium has the following advantages:

1. *Broad Consumer Acceptance and Use.* Newspapers are truly a unique way of life to most Americans, according to a study conducted by Audits & Surveys under supervision of the Bureau of Advertising, American Newspaper Publishers Association. Some highlights of the results are:

a. Daily newspaper readership is high. Newspapers are read in 77 percent of all U.S. households, and within the top 300 markets, newspaper coverage includes 87 percent of households. Over one week's time, the daily newspaper has a cumulative reach of 89 percent of all U.S. adults.

b. Readership is 88 percent for college graduates, 70 percent for grammar school graduates.

c. Newspaper reading increases with income. Of those making over $10,000, 87 percent read newspapers daily, compared to 67 percent of those earning $5,000 or less.

d. Of the readers, 67 percent claim thorough readership, 25 percent say they only scan the paper, and 4 percent just look at specific sections. Those who have set aside a specific time of day to read the paper represent 73 percent of readers. Almost all read their newspapers at home.

e. Because so many readers go through newspapers on a page-to-page basis, the average page has a 84 percent chance of being opened, ranging from lows of 75 percent for men's pages and 76 percent for classified advertising to a high of 88 percent for general news.

f. The newspaper reader is involved in his daily paper. At one time or other, 93 percent evidenced some newspaper-related behavior other than reading or responding to advertisements. In the three months prior to the survey, 56 percent of the adult population had clipped one or more editorial items. Over 70 percent had at least once mentioned, shown, or read an article to someone else.

g. Weekend readership is also high, with 67 percent for Sunday papers (many papers do not publish Sunday editions) and 58 percent for

Saturday readership. Within a given month, however, Saturday papers will reach about 80 percent of all U.S. adults.[3]

2. *Short Closing Times.* Closing times refer to the deadline prior to publication by which advertising copy must be submitted. For daily newspapers, this period seldom exceeds 24 hours, thus giving the advertiser the opportunity to make last-minute changes. Closing dates for Sunday supplements, however, generally are much longer, usually ranging from four to six weeks.

3. *Improvements in Color Reproduction.* Standard newspaper color printing (ROP or run-of-paper color) has become widely available. In mid-1972, about 86 percent of all daily newspapers offered black and white plus one ROP color; 66 percent offered black and white and three ROP colors.[4] Fine shadings and pastels are now possible but, because of the porosity of newspaper stock, truly fine color reproduction is difficult. The average costs for a full-page ad with black and three colors run about 31 percent above those for black and white.[5]

Since high-quality color is so hard to achieve with ROP, increasing use is made of preprinted color advertisements on a heavier stock of paper. This procedure, called Hi-Fi color, is available in 87 percent of the markets and usually runs about $19 per 1,000 circulation above the cost of black and white.[6] The chief disadvantage is that Hi-Fi methods require preprinting on a continuous roll of paper, and it is impossible to have the cuts coincide with the end of the copy. This problem may be eliminated, however, by the use of still another process called Spectacolor, available in approximately 25 percent of the papers and costing little more than Hi-Fi.[7]

4. *Increased Geographic and Market Flexibility.* Newspapers are increasingly recognizing that one edition for a large market is not adequate to provide full local coverage. As a result many papers now offer zone editions. The *Chicago Tribune,* for example, offers several zone variations and supplements corresponding to suburban areas. In addition, special-interest newspapers are becoming more established. While many underground newspapers started during the latter part of the past decade have folded as U.S. society has changed, others have continued to flourish and become more commercialized, for example.

Perhaps the most significant trend, however, is the growth of community and suburban newspapers and the further segmentation of large

---

[3] *A National Survey of the Content and Readership of the American Newspaper,* (New York: American Newspaper Publishers Association, December 1973).

[4] *Editor & Publisher,* March 1973, Newspaper Preprint Corporation.

[5] *Circulation and Rates,* November 1973.

[6] Ibid.

[7] Ibid.

central-city newspapers. In a survey done among publishers, general managers, and presidents of newspapers, 77 percent predicted growth in the number of community newspapers.[8]

5. *Communication Advantages.* The printed page is often believed to offer greater prestige and believability, perhaps based on the adage that "seeing is believing." There is no convincing research to verify this claim, but it is known that print induces superior retention of complex factual material when compared with oral presentation. Also it is thought that print forces the reader to become more involved in the subject matter through groping to understand and to evaluate. Such involvement is less evident when material is presented in spoken form.[9]

6. *Reseller Support.* Of all media, newspapers are most used for the following purposes: (*a*) cooperative plans whereby dealers share costs, (*b*) identification and promotion of the local dealer, (*c*) promotion of quick action through coupons, and (*d*) other means to enlist dealer support. Dealer enthusiasm for this use of advertising dollars often runs high.

Disadvantages. Newspapers also have disadvantages as an advertising medium, including the following:

1. *Rate Differentials.* National advertising linage in newspapers has not realized as rapid gains as local advertising has. This lag is due in part to wide differentials between local and national (nonlocal) rates. As might be expected, rate differentials have been under fire. Defenders of the differentials in rates claim several justifications:

a. National volume is not as dependable as local retail volume and therefore costs more to handle.

b. The national competitor will have a large edge over his local counterpart and hence should be penalized.

c. National advertisers are requesting more merchandising assistance in the form of special promotion to dealers, assistance in advertising plans, and other services.

d. It costs more to handle national advertising. Newspapers claim that these costs are from 20–25 percent higher because the 15 percent discount is granted to agencies (this is the standard method of agency compensation), a cash discount is given, and representatives must be paid to solicit nonlocal advertising.[10]

The first three claimed justifications have little basis in fact. The widespread use of newspapers by many national advertisers on a continuing

---

[8] *The Gallagher Report,* November 6, 1972, p. 1.

[9] For an excellent review of relevant research, see Joseph T. Klapper, *The Effects of Mass Communication* (Glencoe, Ill.: Free Press, 1960), pp. 110–12.

[10] "Newspapers Are Nation's Biggest Medium," *Advertising Age,* November 21, 1973, p. 66.

basis largely removes the charge of lack of dependability; the national and local firms seldom are competitors, and, in fact, it is more common for the national advertiser to work in partnership with his local dealers; and, finally, local advertisers seldom use an agency and therefore are prone to request more in the way of special services than the national firm. The payment of agency commissions, however, and the other costs are valid reasons for a nominal differential. The problem is that the usual differential is far in excess of this justifiable amount, and most newspapers at this point seem to be unwilling to change the status quo.

2. *Costs of National Coverage.* The costs of reaching a national market through newspapers can quickly become excessive. National coverage through this medium often requires an additional expenditure of 80 percent or more in comparison with network television and magazines.

3. *Short Life.* Newspapers usually are not retained in the home for extensive periods of time. As a result, little opportunity exists for repeat exposure to advertisements. This disadvantage is shared by all media, however, with the exception of magazines.

4. *Reproduction Problems.* Newspapers, of course, are printed on an absorbent paper stock resulting in an inability to offer fine reproduction. In addition, the speed necessary to compose a daily newspaper prevents the detailed preparation and care in production which is possible when time pressures are not so great.

5. *Small "Pass-Along" Audience.* Generally speaking, newspapers do not generate larger audiences through sharing of issues by purchasers, often referred to as pass-along readership. The pass-along audience of magazines may be substantial.

Buying Newspaper Space

Newspaper rates are quoted in detail in volumes published periodically by the Standard Rate and Data Service (SRDS). The basic space unit for strictly local advertising is usually the column inch. The national rate, however, is quoted in terms of agate lines (14 lines represent a column inch). The standard newspaper page consists of eight columns, approximately 300 lines deep. The total number of lines is approximately 2,400. The tabloid page consists of about 1,000 lines with five or six columns.

Published rates vary if special treatment is specified. Color, of course, always carries a premium, as does location in a specific part of the paper. Unless otherwise specified, copy will be inserted on an ROP (run-of-paper) basis.

Gross space rates are usually converted to a common basis for purposes of comparison. The milline rate, widely used for this purpose, is calculated as follows:

$$\frac{\text{Line rate} \times 1,000,000}{\text{Circulation}}$$

Rates are compared, then, in terms of costs of the circulation which is achieved. Otherwise an extremely low line rate might be deceptive if it fails to generate adequate circulation and advertising exposure.

The Future of Newspapers

There can be little doubt that newspapers will continue to be vitally important as a local advertising medium. Two major trends will probably continue.

First, and most vital to the survival of the newspaper, is the development of increased technological sophistication. Almost one half of the total newspaper copy in the United States is now printed on offset presses.[11] The use of electronic technology is also increasing. Among the new systems is one which basically consists of a typesetting computer linked to a visual display. It can be used for classified and display advertising as well as news copy because previously entered copy can be recalled directly from memory files.[12]

The second major trend is the segmentation and diversification of the newspaper industry with the growth of suburban and community newspapers and the publication of different sections of large central-city newspapers.

Family newspapers are also expected to grow in importance unless the federal government decides otherwise. Other newspapers are expected to expand into national distribution, like the *Christian Science Monitor*.

Of special concern are newsprint shortages and rapidly increasing costs. One solution of that problem which has been foreseen by many is broadcast of the local newspaper over two-way cable television. Hard copies could be made of items of particular interest through the use of a facsimile printer linked to the set.

TELEVISION

Television, a marvel of the electronic age, grew into a dynamic marketing force in less than 20 years. The type of television under consideration makes a difference in any discussion; network program advertising differs substantially from advertising on local television stations. We will center first on the characteristics of television in general and then on the use of network program advertising versus spot announcements.

---

[11] *INA President's Bulletin,* edited by A. L. Schrader, Washington, D.C., March 1973, p. 1.

[12] "Newspapers Are Nation's Biggest Medium," *Advertising Age,* p. 72.

General Characteristics of Television

Advantages. The advantages of television as an advertising medium include:

1. *The Combination of Sight and Sound.* Television, through its combination of sight and sound, provides audiences with a unique sense of participation and reality approximating face-to-face contact. As such it commands full attention from viewers. While it is not clear that information is retained better following television exposure than through the use of other media, it is reasonable to expect a high degree of emotional involvement and impact.[13]

The combination of sight and sound also is advantageous because of the creative flexibility offered to the advertiser. Full opportunity exists for product demonstration and the amplification of selling points with audio presentation. In addition, color telecasting is growing rapidly, with the result that the advantages of greater emotional impact and appetite appeal of color can now be transmitted to over 39 million homes. Of the more than 68 million U.S. households now equipped with television, 60 percent have color sets. Color television is owned by 80 percent of those making over $15,000 annually and by 71 percent of those with a year or more of college. The affluent and educated are most likely to be reached with the benefits of color television.[14] Of all television households, 39 percent have more than one set.[15] The total number of sets in the United States exceeds 109 million.[16]

2. *Mass Audience Coverage.* Television is now in 97.0 percent of all U.S. households.[17] During an average day, 92 percent of these households will be exposed to television programming, and in the space of a week, this percentage reaches 98 percent.[18] During 1972, the average viewing time per day per television household reached a new high of six hours, 12 minutes, up 10 minutes from 1971. During an average week the average television viewing time per television household is 43 hours, 24 minutes.[19] Television is truly a *mass* medium.

3. *The Psychology of Attention.* The television viewer is in a sense a captive before his set. Most viewers give way to inertia and watch commercials rather than exert the effort to change the set to other program material. From this it can be inferred that they will be consciously exposed to a majority of advertising messages, with the result

---

[13] Klapper, *Effects of Mass Communication.*

[14] A. C. Nielsen Co., February 1973.

[15] Ibid.

[16] National Broadcasting Company, 1973.

[17] A. C. Nielsen Co., February 1973.

[18] Ibid.

[19] Ibid.

that at least one hurdle to promotional response is cleared. It must not be overlooked, however, that exposure by no means infers favorable response, because of the mechanisms of selective perception and retention discussed earlier.

4. *Favorable Consumer Reaction.* Television appears to have lost very little of its tremendous popularity that was evident in the extensive nationwide survey by Gary Steiner in 1960, when 60 percent considered it to be the greatest invention in 25 years to make life more enjoyable.[20] Another nationwide survey done one decade later by the Roper organization, under the direction of Robert T. Bower, substantiates the still high popularity of television.[21] Some of the major findings of these surveys are:

a. People seem to be growing more dependent upon television as a source of news and opinion, as well as entertainment. In both 1960 and 1970 television ranked above all major media in terms of entertainment value and also in such categories as "most educational" and "creates the most interest in new things going on." In 1970 it also replaced newspapers in "giving the most complete news coverage," "presenting things most intelligently," "doing the most for the public," and "presenting the most unbiased news," and it replaced radio in "bringing the latest news most quickly."

b. In both 1960 and 1970, the better educated viewers reported less enthusiasm for television programming and different motivations for watching than others did, but these feelings actually made surprisingly little difference in actual television-watching behavior. The only exception was Educational Television (ETV) stations, which have a larger percentage of those with some college training in their audiences than do regularly programmed commercial stations.

c. Commercials still are widely accepted as necessary. In 1970, 70 percent indicated that they were a "fair price to pay for the entertainment." A larger percentage (54 percent in 1970 compared to 43 percent in 1960) stated that the commercials are "so good that they are more entertaining than the program." (This statement, of course, is open to a double interpretation.)

d. Though the viewers in 1970 found television a bit less "satisfying," "relaxing," "exciting," "important," and "wonderful" than viewers did in 1960, they nevertheless watched it longer.

e. The pervasiveness and importance of television in the United States at this point can be illustrated by the finding that of all the major

---

[20] Gary A. Steiner, *The People Look at Television* (New York: Alfred A. Knopf, 1963).

[21] Robert T. Bower, *Television and the Public* (New York: Holt, Rinehart & Winston, 1973).

media, television is considered both as the one that is "getting better all the time" and as the one that is "getting worse all the time."

Disadvantages.   Television also has certain disadvantages which affect its choice as an advertising medium:

1. *Negative Evaluations.*   Although the Bower 1970 report revealed very few strong objections to what was being programmed for television, it must be remembered that the survey was taken in 1970. Since that time there has been a growing tendency for programs to include more explicit sexual behavior and dialog, more realistic violence and free use of curses and vulgarity. While some have praised this trend as greater freedom in realistic programming, others have condemned it as the product of a morally degenerate society. The result has been a greater tendency to produce specialized programs and consequently more selective viewing, especially on the part of children.[22]

The question of bias in television news coverage becomes more acute as the proportion of Americans dependent chiefly upon television as their source of news becomes greater. Former Vice-President Spiro Agnew served as spokesman for a time, but his feelings have been echoed by others. The news coverage of the events surrounding the Watergate bugging incident has again posed the question of how media coverage could affect the judicial process. Were the principals in the case tried and convicted or acquitted by the news media? Did this coverage affect the likelihood of their having fair trials? These are obviously issues which go beyond a particular communications medium, but they do have great significance in terms of television, and they are likely to be hotly contested for some time to come.

The reaction of advertisers has largely been to seek a middle course, avoiding either extreme. Television still represents the least selective of the electronic and print media, and programs on the extremes are likely to offend a number of watchers. This could well bring negative as well as positive results to the advertisers on a particular program. The result is that truly unique programs winning critical acclaim may not survive because of failure to draw a large audience.

2. *Nonselectivity.*   Though there may be growing selectivity among television watchers, it is still difficult to reach precisely a small market segment using television as the medium. Variations in program content and broadcast time will obviously achieve some selectivity, especially through children's programs, soap operas with feminine appeal, or late-night talk shows, but more precise segmentation in terms of age, income, and interest is practically impossible on broadcast television. Cable television (CATV) may eventually allow for such segmentation if it

---

[22] Ibid., pp. 152–75.

continues to develop, as many expect it will. This is discussed further in the section on the future of television.

3. *Fleeting Impression.* The television message crosses the viewer's consciousness only momentarily and then is lost. If for some reason the message did not register, the promotional opportunity has been lost. The opportunity does exist for reexposure, however, through multiple commercials over a period of time.

4. *Commercial Clutter.* Once a problem chiefly in spot television, the growing use of 30-second commercials and participatory buying by advertisers have resulted in a greater number of different commercial messages in each program. The competition in each commercial break combined with the shorter time used in developing and communicating the message has many advertisers worried about the persuasive effectiveness of the commercial—the fear of being lost in the crowd.

The Network Television Program

Networks are dominant in television for the reason that they originate most of the popular programs. The networks are confederations of stations in which each one is compensated at the rate of 30 percent of the gross commercial rate for programs carried in its area. While it is assumed that each station will air most network shows, the station is free to originate local programming if a greater profit can be made.

Several smaller networks also offer shows on a regional or selective programming basis. The Hughes Sports Network makes available to subscribing stations coverage of sports events not covered by the major networks. The Christian Broadcasting Network, with headquarters in Portsmouth, Virginia, includes several stations nationwide which operate on a nonprofit basis to broadcast a wide variety of religious programming.[23] Metromedia owns six television stations which compete with the major networks in New York and several other large metropolitan areas.

Advantages of Purchasing Network Time. The advantages of network television programming as a medium for advertising include:

1. *Excellent Time Availabilities.* The networks have virtual control over the prime-time programming (7–11 P.M. New York time). FCC rulings regarding access to prime time put some limitations on network programming during that period, but the advertiser who wishes to reach a truly vast, nationwide audience at one time must necessarily buy time from the networks during prime-time hours.

2. *Simplicity of Arrangements.* The time purchase is greatly simplified when network television is used. The mechanics of purchasing spot time can become exceedingly cumbersome and costly.

---

[23] Pat Robertson, *Shout It from the Housetops* (Plainfield, N.J.: Logos International, 1972).

Disadvantages of Purchasing Network Time. The disadvantages of network time also must be considered:

1. *Costs.* Network television advertising is precluded for many because of the costs involved, although local spot announcements often can be purchased in network service times. In addition, commitments must be made well in advance, and modifications can be made only with great difficulty.

2. *Availabilities.* Even if smaller companies could come up with the money to buy prime time on network television, they might find it quite difficult to find time available, especially on high-rated programs. The virtual end of sole sponsorship of any program by a single advertiser may have eased this situation to some extent, but competition for the best programs still exists.

3. *Program Mortality.* The rate of program mortality is traditionally high each season. Even though the evening mortality rate for the 1973–74 season was the lowest in seven years, 27 of 75 shows in 1972–73 failed to return. An additional 12 shows were canceled in January 1974, including two originally held over from 1972–73.[24] There is no good way of determining in advance the probable success of a program, and time buys too often must be made on the basis of educated guesses. This represents another reason why sponsorship of a single program has been largely replaced by time buying on a participating basis.

4. *Variations in Program Popularity.* A program with a rating of 36 in one market (36 percent viewership) may produce a rating of only 10 in another. The advertiser's market potential would match variations in program popularity only by accident, with the result that dollars can become allocated in such a way that market potentials are not paralleled. A similar situation can result when program popularity does not parallel distribution. Occasionally it is possible to purchase only part of the national coverage of a program, but this flexibility is the exception rather than the rule.

Buying Network Time

Network time is quoted at varying rates, depending upon the time of the day and season of the year. Prime-time rates are most expensive, of course. Approximately 65 percent of all stations are members of the National Association of Broadcasters (NAB), which permits its members to air commercials within the following guidelines:

1. *Commercials*—9½–12 minutes per hour in prime time and 16 minutes per hour in nonprime time. 12 minutes per hour on children's weekend programs.

---

[24] "Compton Media Review," Compton Advertising, January 1974, p. 10.

2. *Number of interruptions:*
   a. Prime time—two per 30-minute program; four per 60-minute program; and five per 60-minute variety show.
   b. Nonprime time—four per 30-minute period; one per 5-minute period; two per 10-minute program; and two per 15-minute program.
   c. Number of consecutive announcements—four for program interruptions and three per station break.
3. *Multiple-product announcements.* There is a 60-second minimum on multiple-product announcements unless they are so well integrated as to appear to the viewer as a single announcement. Local retailers are excluded from this rule. The NAB guidelines are usually followed, although NBC announced in early 1970 that it would add three minutes of commercial time to the "Tonight" show and 20 additional commercial seconds between ten of its prime-time shows, to allow 62-second station breaks.[25]

Because of the escalating costs of advertising, most television time is purchased on a participating plan by which program costs are shared by other advertisers. The 30-second commercial dominates, comprising 71 percent of all network advertising (up from 20 percent in 1970 and only 7 percent in 1967).[26] Average costs per commercial minute on the participation plan range between $50,000–$75,000 in prime time and between $5,000–$15,000 in daytime.[27] A widely used method of cost comparison is cost per 1,000 homes, which is based on the cost of the commercial time and the program ratings.

Spot Announcements

Many of the disadvantages of network television can be overcome through use of spot announcements purchased on a market-by-market (nonnetwork) basis. Time availabilities generally range from 10-second ID's (station identification breaks) to a full 60 seconds.

Spot television was given its greatest impetus by the well-known success story of Lestoil. This product was introduced in Springfield-Holyoke, Massachusetts, in 1954 using spot announcements, and the investment was extended market by market. Four years later a $60 million sales volume was generated by an investment of $9,500,000 in spot time on 114 stations with 2,472 spots per week.[28]

---

[25] The Code Authority of the National Association of Broadcasters.

[26] BAR, March 1973.

[27] "Ogilvy and Mather Pocket Guide to Media," Ogilvy & Mather, Inc., 1973, p. 27.

[28] "Short and Sweet, with the Accent on Sweet," *Printers' Ink,* June 14, 1963, p. 262.

Advantages of Spot Television. The use of spot announcements on television has some advantages for the advertiser:

1. *Geographic and Time Flexibility.* A key problem of purchasing network program time is the commitment to appear in nearly all markets where the program is aired, even though market potentials may differ. Spot announcements are an effective alternative when the creative advantages of television are desired. Total costs are usually reduced through minimization of waste coverage.

2. *Reseller Support.* Spot television also offers one of the advantages of newspapers in that it can be used effectively in cooperative advertising programs, for identification of local dealers, and in other ways to achieve dealer support.

Disadvantages of Spot Television. The disadvantages of spot announcements include:

1. *Chaotic Buying Procedures.* When local time is purchased, the buying situation can become chaotic. There is little uniformity in rates or in quantity discount plans. In addition, favored advertisers receive desirable time periods, and a personal relationship and difficult negotiations may be necessary to achieve the best time purchase. Firms representing many stations, such as the well-known Katz Agency, simplify these problems, but the difficulties remain so great that there is no short-cut to long experience in time buying.

2. *Commercial Clutter.* An excess of commercials seems to be a problem for television in general, but the volume of nonprogram material appearing in station breaks is a real headache for the industry. Talent credits and announcements appear as trailers on network programs, several commercials are aired in the station break, and time still must be left for station identification and introduction of the next program. Not surprisingly, the Schwerin Research Corp. and others have reported lower recall of brand advertising when station-break commercials are used.

3. *Viewing at Station-Break Periods.* It is well known that the number of viewers declines during station breaks. Some leave the room, and the attention of those who remain is frequently attracted elsewhere. The total audience and viewer attention at station breaks may not be optimum.

Buying Spot Time

The purchase of network time involves only one contact; arrangements are considerably more difficult when local stations are used. The buyer either writes, teletypes, or telephones the station or its representative to request information on available time slots. These availabilities then are checked and communicated to the buyer, usually within 24 hours. The local station formerly guaranteed protection, in that advertisements for competing products normally will not be aired within 15 minutes of each other, but this practice is rapidly disappearing.

The listing of availabilities is always in writing, and a guarantee is given that the first buyer to make a request gets the time slot. Once the decision is made the order is usually submitted by telephone and later verified in writing.

Costs are always quoted in terms of time of day. Prime evening time carries the highest price and runs from 7:30 to 11:00 P.M. in all areas except the central time zone, where all classifications are one hour earlier. Stations affiliated with the network also quote fringe evening time from 6:00 to 7.30 P.M. and from 11:00 P.M. to 1:00 A.M. Daytime runs from sign-on to 5 P.M., Monday through Friday. In addition, it is common to quote a lower rate if the buyer is willing to run the risk that a competing buyer may later preempt the time spot. If he pays the full price, however, the buyer is guaranteed the time, and it is becoming increasingly common to reserve and hold desirable times over long periods by this means.

Most stations later verify, based on the program log, that the commercial actually was run. Following submission of this affidavit, the time bills become due.

It is obvious that spot-time buying can be complex, and most agencies have specialists in this field. In addition, these complexities have been instrumental in the formation of specialized media-buying services.

The Future of Television

Several specific issues promise to bring about changes in television programming and advertising: (1) the growth of cable television (CATV), (2) new governmental regulations, (3) video cassettes and discs, (4) changes in network programming, (5) overcommercialization, (6) domestic communication satellites. These issues are discussed below.

CATV. The continued growth and sophistication of cable television may well have a dramatic effect upon the television industry, dependent upon the rulings and guidelines created by the FCC. The major function of CATV at this point is to bring the regularly scheduled programs of commercial stations to areas beyond the range of their broadcast signals. Subscribers who formerly had poor reception and limited channel selection can, with cable hookups, receive clear pictures and a wide variety of channel selections.

As of January 1973, there were 2,883 operating systems reaching over seven million subscribers, or 11.1 percent of television households.[29] It is

---

[29] "TV Basics," Television Bureau of Advertising, Inc., New York (undated).

obvious that unless CATV can expand its services beyond the improved reception of signals from other stations, expansion in major metropolitan areas is limited. CATV's attempts to penetrate the major metropolitan markets has not at this point been extremely successful. The key to the success of CATV appears to lie in its tremendous potential in providing services, pay television, and programming not offered by network affiliates or independent stations.

Further expansion of the services of CATV seems to be assured by the ruling handed down by the Supreme Court in March 1974. This decision overturned a lower court ruling which, in effect, prevented the importation of distant television signals by a cable system. In overturning this decision, the Supreme Court held that importation of these signals was not in violation of the copyright law when the program also served as a carrier of commercial messages. Briefly stated, since consumers in all areas of the United States paid the costs of advertising through the purchase of advertised products, the extension of television coverage by CATV to those who would not otherwise see a "free" broadcast does not constitute a violation of the law.[30]

The FCC, however, will not allow CATV to import all its programming. Consequently, CATV will have to become more competitive in creating original programming. The FCC has ruled that new CATV systems in the 100 major markets must have a minimum capacity of 20 channels, one of which must be devoted to original programming. There must also be at least three public service channels, one of public access, one of educational TV, and one for local government.[31] Efforts at original programming in most cases have provided poor alternatives to the programs of broadcast stations. If any original programming of high quality is to be provided, much greater efforts to this end must be made by CATV.

A more attractive proposal to CATV operators is pay television, which involves a mechanism attached to the subscriber's set which makes certain broadcasts impossible to view without the payment of a separate fee beyond the monthly subscription charge. This system would make possible truly specialized programming, since only those subscribers who specifically decide to watch a particular program and are willing to pay a fee to do so will be in the viewing audience. If commercial time is made available, the segmentation potential could be at least equal to that of the magazine. Even without pay television, more precise segmentation should be possible once CATV begins to produce its own programs.

Theater owners and broadcasters have been most opposed to the growth

---

[30] "Cable TV Ruling Says Ads Hike Prices," *Advertising Age,* March 11, 1974, p. 1.

[31] "Ogilvy and Mather Guide," p. 30.

of pay television. Broadcasters fear that the additional options open to their audience would result in more selective viewing, lower ratings, and therefore lower revenues. Theater owners fear that if first-run movies are made available on pay television their business may just collapse altogether. The film makers, on the other hand, are excited about the possibilities of pay television because of the increased revenue it would bring. As of January 1974, pay-cable was in 15 cities serving between 30,000 and 40,000 homes. Subscribers who participate pay $8–$10 for all monthly programming, and others pay $2–$3 per film.[32]

Unlike broadcast television, CATV has the potential of two-way communication. Since the set is attached to a central point by cable rather than broadcast signals, impulses can travel in both directions, much like the telephone. The FCC has ruled that CATV systems operating in the 100 largest markets must have a technical capacity for at least nonverbal communication between the subscriber and the system.[33] This capacity offers many new services. Among those which have been suggested are:

1. Shopping via television using a televised catalog and a keyboard attached to the set so that orders can be entered.
2. Programs allowing dialog between the sender and receiver.
3. Protection against fire and housebreaking by attaching an alarm system to the set.
4. The broadcast of the local newspaper rather than home delivery. The set would serve much as a microfilm reader.

Just how soon CATV will offer these services, and the eventual effect on the industry of "free" television is still largely dependent upon court rulings and FCC decisions which will define the limitations and possibilities of this relatively young medium.

Governmental Regulations. The Federal Communications Commission is the regulatory body for television and radio broadcasts in the United States. Each broadcaster must be licensed with the FCC. Periodically each station is reviewed by the FCC to determine whether or not the license should be reissued. The license renewal procedure once used to be only a formality, but recently the FCC has become more serious about examination and review of the stations.

The House Communications Subcommittee completed work in February 1974 on a revision of the license renewal bill, but at the time of this writing the bill has not yet been scheduled for debate in the House of Representatives. The renewal bill basically concerns itself with two issues, the responsibility of the medium to the community it serves and

---

[32] "Compton Media Review," p. 4.
[33] "Ogilvy and Mather Guide," p. 30.

the ownership of two or more media in one market area by the same corporation.

As it is now, the bill extends the term of the license from three to four years, allowing broadcasters a longer period between examinations. It also requires the FCC to establish procedures which must be followed by the licensed broadcasters in discovering needs and interests within their broadcast area. At the time of license renewal, the FCC must be provided with evidence that the broadcaster has been "substantially responsive" to the needs of his market, probably by judging how closely the broadcaster followed a quota system stipulating that certain percentages of broadcasting time be devoted to news, local programming, and public affairs.[34]

The bill also prohibits the FCC from taking into consideration the other media holdings of the licensee, as long as it conforms to rulings already established. The bill would also require, however, that the FCC settle Docket 18110 within six months after the bill is enacted. Docket 18110 was issued by the FCC in March 1968 and proposed the limitation of media holdings within a single market by a single owner to one or more daily newspapers, or one television station, or one AM–FM radio combination. The docket was greeted with less than enthusiastic support by those with multimedia holdings and has not yet been enacted.[35]

Whether or not the license renewal bill is passed and Docket 18110 is settled, holders of more than one medium in a single market will have other challenges. The Justice Department promises to attempt to break up multiple ownership through antitrust suits brought against owners. The U.S. government shows definite concern over the concentration of media ownership within a single market. Consequently, the owners of multiple media are going to have a rather stormy time over the next few years.

The FCC also issued and upheld in March 1974 a revision of the prime-time access rule which originally went into effect October 1971 to limit network programming in prime time to three hours in the top 50 markets. The revision of the ruling relaxes the limitations on the networks to a large extent and restores three and one half hours of prime-time programming to the networks, Monday through Saturday, except that the networks may use one of these half-hour periods a week for a children's special or public affairs programming. The networks seem to welcome this new ruling. The National Association of Independent Television Producers and Distributors, which was largely responsible for filling the one hour of nonnetwork programmed prime time under the former ruling, was upset by the ruling but failed to convince the FCC

---

[34] "Subcommittee Clears Renewal Bill," *Broadcasting*, February 25, 1974.
[35] Ibid.

that it should postpone enactment for a year. It was scheduled to take effect September 1, 1974.[36]

As of December 1973, another ruling was being drafted by the FCC which would have a definite bearing on network programming. If enacted this ruling would bar the three major networks from producing their own entertainment programs, including movies made specifically for television. This ruling would come in the wake of a civil antitrust suit filed recently charging the networks with monopolizing prime-time entertainment programming. Although the networks presently produce very little of their own entertainment programs, they oppose the ruling because they feel the restrictions would reduce their flexibility. The FCC maintains that the network's production capabilities are a threat which helps control prices and increases their control over program production.[37]

Finally, the application of the "fairness doctrine" (both sides of controversial issues must be aired) is still being explored through FCC rulings and court tests. The question of whether the guidelines of the "fairness doctrine can be applied to commercial and paid political messages has not fully been decided. The answer to this question and the energy with which the FCC applies the guidelines could cause some real changes in programming content. The networks fear that liberal interpretation of this doctrine coupled with vigorous enforcement could seriously affect the quality of programming, in that stands of any serious issues and sound investigative reporting would be discouraged for lack of sponsors.

Rulings of other governmental groups can directly affect television as well. Total television billings declined 2 percent in 1971 when Congress passed legislation on the recommendation of the surgeon general and the Federal Trade Commission (FTC) forbidding the advertising of cigarettes on television.[38] The FTC has now turned its attention to items other than cigarettes, such as over-the-counter drugs, children's toys, and foods. With the case against cigarettes as a precedent, other manufacturers may be eventually forced to alter their products or stop advertising over television.

Video Cassettes and Discs. The use of video cassettes and discs, based on the same operating principles as cassette tape players and phonographs, may soon be common. Several companies are now marketing video cassette players, though the price is still out of the range of most buyers. As with the electronic calculator, however, prices will probably decline until outfits are within the price range for home use. The video

---

[36] *Broadcasting,* March 4, 1973, p. 26.

[37] "Compton Media Guide," pp. 11–12.

[38] "Television Changes a World," *Advertising Age,* November 21, 1973.

cassette player is a television set equipped to receive broadcast or CATV and also to play video cassettes which may be purchased (at high prices) and played in much the same manner as audio cassettes. The major difficulties to be worked out, besides the high cost of the unit, are the standardization of cassette sizes among companies producing the units and the development of units which can be attached to present television receivers. An alternative to the high purchase price is to provide for cassette rental, with the rental price being partially borne by advertisers who would purchase time on the cassettes for their messages.[39]

Of less potential to the advertiser but perhaps of greater acceptability to the consumer is a video disc system developed by MCA Inc. The basic playing unit would be similar to a record player and could be attached to present television equipment. The discs themselves would be packaged much like long-playing phonograph records. If massed-produced, they could be roughly competitive in price.[40]

If either of these systems reaches widespread use, broadcasters might well be forced to provide more specialized entertainment and to concentrate on live coverage which, of course, would not be available on discs or tapes.

Changes in Network Programming.   All of the developments discussed above would have a bearing on network programming. The major trend created by the pressures of CATV and disc or tape systems would be toward more specialized programming, which would be necessary to fit into more selective viewing patterns. It has been predicted that the time spent watching television will continue to grow with increases in the number of television sets within each household. Since virtually each member of the family will have his own set, however, each will seek to watch a program conforming to his own interests. The decision will no longer have to be a compromise of family interests. Television ratings on individual programs will drop as the audience becomes segmented, and eventually television programming may well become similar to that for radio. Due to a more highly segmented audience, the cost per thousand individuals will probably increase, but the cost per thousand *prospects* should remain about the same or decline. There will be movement in this direction for the remainder of this decade, but broadcasting as it is today will probably persist for quite some time.[41] Eventually, however, broadcasting may come to be referred to as "narrowcasting" to a highly segmented audience.[42]

[39] E. B. Weiss, "Advertising Nears a Big Speed-Up in Communications Innovation," *Advertising Age,* March 19, 1973, p. 56.

[40] Ibid.

[41] "Media in the '70's," Ogilvy & Mather, Inc., New York.

[42] Weiss, "Advertising Nears a Big Speed-Up."

Overcommercialization. Many individuals feel that overcommercialization is already a very serious problem, especially during station breaks and local programming. With the growing use of 30-second commercials, participating sponsorship, and multiple-product announcements, the situation on network television has also rapidly grown more cluttered. Clutter will probably be reduced through a growth of new stations and multiset ownership which fosters expansion of local programming to segment target audiences, commercials customized to local market needs, and local service programming. For a while, though, the advertiser is going to have to compete with a clutter of other commercials to gain viewers' attention.

Domestic Communication Satellites. The domestic use of communications satellites has exciting implications for the television industry. Communications Satellite Corporation (COMSAT), with partial support of Atlantic Telephone and Telegraph (AT&T), has proposed a $250 million communications satellite system consisting of three satellites, each with the capacity of handling 14,000 phone circuits, or 24 color television channels, or a combination of the two. Several other companies, including Western Union, Hughes Aircraft, RCA Global Communications, Fairchild, MCI Lockheed, and Western TeleCommunications have made specific proposals or are potential competitors. Western Union expects to have its system (Westar) in operation by mid-1974.[43]

The implications for television are basically in the two areas of programming and costs. The use of government-sponsored communications satellites has never been at the access of the networks, as these privately sponsored satellites would be. If an increased percentage of programming possibilities comes from overseas, it will tend to further splinter and segment the audience.

The chief benefit would be in terms of cost. Dependence on telephone lines as the basic means of transmitting television signals would be ended. The fact that the cost of transmitting from any one point on the globe to another would not vary regardless of distance would provide tremendous gains in economy and flexibility.

RADIO

Radio, once considered to be a dying medium following the rise of television, has come back to exert a dynamic and vigorous competitive challenge. To underscore the extent of change, it has become almost totally a local medium, whereas it was dominated by networks prior to the onset of television. Moreover, there are four times more stations on the air today than in 1945. Radio networks now exist primarily to feed

---

[43] Ibid.

newscasts and a limited variety of additional programs. In addition, FM, an unknown in 1945, has risen to an 80 percent penetration of U.S. homes and offers a new resource to the advertiser.[44]

Characteristics of Radio

Advantages. Radio as an advertising medium has a number of advantages, including the following:

1. *The Mass Use of Radio.* In 1972, consumers purchased 63.5 million radio sets at an approximate cost of over $3 billion. Almost 99 percent of U.S. households have at least one set, and the average household has an average of 5.5 sets, mostly in bedrooms, kitchens, and living rooms. In addition, about 98 percent of cars have radios. Of the over 368 million sets in use, 93 million are car radios, 33 million are transistors, and the remainder are of the plug-in variety. At least 100 million are FM or FM–AM.[45] As of January 31, 1974, there were 4,898 commercial AM stations, 2,507 commercial FM stations, and 644 educational FM stations in operation.[46]

The availability of transistorized portable sets has enabled radio to become a medium which can be used anywhere. Within one week's time, radio will reach 96.6 percent of all the people in the United States over 12 years old. In fact, during a single week, radio will reach well over 90 percent of all sex and age demographic segments of the United States. The exception is 6–11-year-olds, where reach is 68.8 percent.[47]

2. *Selectivity.* Radio has become a selective medium because local stations have differentiated the program formats to appeal to various consumer segments. As a result it is possible to reach nearly any class of consumers in most markets. Of course geographic flexibility has long been a strength of radio, as is true of all local media.

While many still consider FM radio as reaching a somewhat richer and better educated segment than AM, the distinction is much less clear now that it was five to eight years ago. The rapid growth of FM radio (26 percent more stations now than in 1969, while there are actually fewer AM stations) has resulted in a change from the widely used classical and symphonic formats to almost as much diversity as AM radio. Music, however, still appears to play a greater part in programming FM broadcasts than it does for AM.[48] Many FM stations have also been

---

[44] Estimates provided by Ogilvy & Mather, Inc.

[45] "Radio Reach Is Everywhere—Homes, Autos, Outdoors," *Advertising Age,* November 21, 1973, p. 100.

[46] "Summary of Broadcasting," *Broadcasting,* March 4, 1974.

[47] "Radio Reach Is Everywhere," p. 102.

[48] Ibid.

more guarded than AM stations in the percentages of time given to commercial messages.

3. *Speed and Flexibility.* Of all media, radio has the shortest closing period in that copy can be submitted up to air time. This flexibility has been capitalized upon by many advertisers. For example, quite a few travel-related companies have found the radio to be of help in keeping their potential customers aware of the effects of the fuel shortage and encouraging them to still use their services.

4. *Low Costs.* For an expenditure of under $100 in most markets, any advertiser can purchase air time. Of all media, its cost per time unit rank among the lowest.

5. *Favorable Psychological Effect.* While the evidence is not unequivocal, there is some basis to the claim that there may be less resistance to persuasion over radio because many activities are directed by spoken word.[49] Radio has also been found to produce greater retention of simple material than print, especially among the least educated.[50] Finally, radio is easily attended to with little psychological resistance, but this casual attention can be a disadvantage when radio serves as musical background for other activities.

6. *Reseller Support.* Radio, along with newspapers and spot television, is also used on occasion with effective results to stimulate dealer cooperation and selling support.

Disadvantages. Counteracting the advantages of radio as an advertising medium are these disadvantages:

1. *The Nature of the Message.* Of course, radio permits only audio presentation, a disadvantage for products requiring demonstration, the impact of color, or the other features of visual media. Furthermore, the impression made is momentary, and, as with television, it is impossible to reexpose the prospect except through multiple commercials over a period of time.

2. *Chaotic Buying.* Spot radio and television share the disadvantage of chaotic and nonstandardized rate structures and the bookkeeping problems connected with the purchase of time. Once again, however, large-station representatives have simplified arrangements.

3. *Costs for National Coverage.* As with all local media, the costs of national coverage can become substantial. Some use still is made, of course, of network radio, and mass coverage is hereby achieved much more economically.

4. *Station Fragmentation.* Unless substantial investments are made,

---

[49] For a summary of relevant research, see Darrell B. Lucas and Steuart H. Britt, *Advertising Psychology and Research* (New York: McGraw-Hill Book Co., 1950), p. 209.

[50] Klapper, *Effects of Mass Communication.*

it is difficult to achieve high levels of reach among mass audiences because of multiple-station fragmentation.

Spot and network radio rates are published by Standard Rate and Data Service. For stations subscribing to the code of the National Association of Broadcasters, 14 minutes of commercial time are permitted for each hour computed on a weekly basis, and the number of commercials is never to exceed 18 per hour or five per 15-minute segment. Many stations do not subscribe to the code, however, and offer a greater frequency of commercial time, much to the dismay of the advertising critics. This may be limited in the future by the FCC, which is now taking the position that licenses will not be renewed when stations broadcast commercials more than 18 minutes per hour for more than 10 percent of the broadcast day.

As in television, radio rates are differentiated into prime and secondary time. In radio, however, prime time covers the morning wake-up period and late afternoon drive-home time, when the most sets, especially car radios, are in use. The units of time available range from a few seconds to 60 seconds, thus affording great flexibility.

The cost per thousand homes reached is computed in a manner similar to that described for television. Although the accurate computation of program ratings used to be difficult, RADAR (Radio All-Dimension Audience Research) was established in 1967 to help alleviate this problem, and the information available regarding radio available through RADAR is not too much different from the Nielsen television ratings.

The Future of Radio

Radio may be characterized in the future by increasing network participation, more specialization, and further growth of AM and FM stereo. Network radio appears to be making somewhat of a comeback. CBS has recently started the CBS Mystery Theater, and others of the old programs are growing increasingly popular when aired over local stations. Though this particular trend may be part of the overall mood of nostaliga, network radio is again exerting a greater influence through news and public affairs programming and giving advertisers more of a chance at national coverage.

Radio is one of the most segmented of the media. The ABC radio network is actually a combination of four basic networks: contemporary, information, entertainment, and FM. Almost every major market has an all-news station such as WBBM, Chicago, and some advertisers expect that eventually there will be nationally recognized frequencies where anyone in the major market areas of the country could turn for news, weather, or public affairs.[51]

---

[51] "Media in the 70's," Ogilvy & Mather, Inc.

The growth and specialization of FM is expected to continue. AM–FM radios are already standard equipment on some automobiles, and the commercial production of radio sets which will only handle one band is expected to decrease rapidly. FM stereo is expected to achieve a much better penetration than its present 30 percent, providing the economy remains in relatively good health.[52]

MAGAZINES

.Magazines have long been a significant medium and continue to show vitality, in spite of problems with paper shortages and postage rates. Magazines today reach nearly all market segments and cover a variety of special interests such as boating and photography. Some mass circulation periodicals continue to exhibit health despite the problems they face.

Characteristics of Magazines

Advantages. The advantages of magazines as an advertising medium include:

1. *High Geographic and Demographic Selectivity.* Once a non-selective mass medium, consumer magazines have attained a high degree of geographic selectivity. It is now possible to purchase one or more of 145 regional or demographic editions of *Better Homes and Gardens,* 129 editions of *Time,* 81 editions of *TV Guide,* and 70 editions of *Reader's Digest.* Twelve different consumer magazines with circulations ranging from 1.8 to 18.8 million offer 50 or more regional and demographic editions. Out of 76 of the most well-known consumer magazines in the United States, only 24 do not have any regional or demographic editions.[53] Small premiums are usually charged for regional or demographic advertising, but the increased efficiency of the advertisement in reaching prospects usually is worthwhile. The magazine also becomes more of an option for advertisers such as banking institutions which serve only a limited regional market.

Demographic flexibilty has long been a major virtue of consumer magazines. Appeal can be made to distinct groups of buyers with special interests, and virtually any segment of the market in terms of age, income, or other demographic variables can be reached with a minimum of waste circulation. The editorial content of the publication also is tailored to the interests of the audience being reached so that the advertising is usually received by the consumer in a receptive mood.

---

[52] Ibid.
[53] "Media Pocket Piece," Compton Advertising, Inc., New York, 1974.

2. *The Receptivity of Magazine Audiences.* Magazine readers appear more receptive to advertising than do television viewers. Younger segments of the audience also find magazine advertising more believable than what they see on television. Data from a survey of magazine readers revealed the following points:

a. Of 1,053 men and 1,156 women interviewed, 52 percent of the men and 58 percent of the women indicated that they preferred magazines to carry advertising. Only 37 percent of the men and 38 percent of the women preferred that television carry advertising.

b. While only 30 percent of the sample felt that magazines carried too much advertising, 66 percent felt that television had too many commercials. Advertising in magazines increased interest in the editorial copy to 37 percent, but 17 percent felt that television commercials increased interest in the programs.[54]

In answering questions regarding advertising in the media, young people between the ages of 14 and 25 responded in the following way:

a. 13 percent said that magazine advertising was annoying, compared to 35 percent for radio and 51 percent for television,

b. 25 percent indicated that magazine advertising was deceptive, compared to 19 percent for radio and 40 percent for television,

c. 23 percent indicated that magazine advertising was believable, compared to 13 percent for radio and 10 percent for television,

d. 47 percent said that magazine advertising was helpful as a buying guide, compared to 19 percent for television and 14 percent for radio.[55]

Findings of the type described above must be interpreted with caution, since they are quoted by the magazine industry to demonstrate the value of its offerings. Nevertheless, the findings do give some indications that the consumer is more receptive to magazine advertising and that magazines offer more prestige and authoritativeness.

Greater credence can be placed in the research undertaken by a respected syndicated research service, which presented these relevant findings:

a. There are 3.6 adult readers of the average magazine issue.

b. The average number of reading days per reader is 3.3.

c. The average reader devotes 83 minutes to this purpose.

---

[54] Data from survey commissioned by the Magazine Publishers Association quoted in "Magazines Hike Revenue 40% in Ten Years," *Advertising Age,* November 21, 1973, p. 78.

[55] Data from 1969 Gilbert Youth Survey reported in *Credibility: The Medium and the Message* (New York: Magazine Publishers Association, 1969).

d. The total adult reading days per issue is 11.9, for a total time of 299 minutes.[56]

Additional data from reliable sources reveal the following findings:

a. While heavy television watching, both daytime and prime time, peaks at just under $8,000 income and then declines, the proportion of heavy magazine readers increases steadily with income.
b. While daytime and prime-time television watching peaks among those who failed to finish high school and then declines, magazine reading grows increasingly heavier as educational level increases.[57]

The increased reading of magazines by those on upper income and educational levels is well established in survey findings and widely accepted as fact. The reach to prime prospects can be maximized by using the right publication for the purpose or, in some cases, a demographically selective edition of a popular magazine reaching many different groups of people.

The Future of Magazines

The immediate future should see the continued growth of special-interest and special-audience magazines and continued difficulties on the part of magazines for general readership. The growth of the special-interest magazine is reflected in the number of new magazines initiated in the decade from January 1964 to December 1973. During this time no fewer than 928 magazines were introduced in the United States, while 233 stopped publication.[58] During 1973 alone 160 new magazines were introduced, while 70 folded. Trade and professional journals comprised 57 of the 160 new magazines, while hobby and leisure magazines added another 37.[59]

The list of magazines ending publication during the past few years, however, includes such former giants as the *Saturday Evening Post, Look,* and *Life.* Recent advertising figures also show the decline of the general-interest magazine and the rise of special interest and audience magazines. In 1963, general-interest magazines claimed 42 percent of magazine advertising dollars, while special interest and audience magazines received the remaining 58 percent. By 1972, however, the general-interest magazine's share had decreased to only 14 percent.[60]

---

[56] W. R. Simmons and Associates Research, Inc., 1971.

[57] From the Brand Rating Index reported in "The 1970's New Demographics" published by the Magazine Publisher's Association.

[58] "Magazines," *Advertising Age,* November 21, 1973, p. 77.

[59] "Compton Media Review," p. 25.

[60] *The Gallagher Report,* April 16, 1973, p. 4.

The result of this trend for the advertiser will be a higher cost per thousand readers, because of decreasing circulation. This will be offset by the ability to isolate a narrow marketing segment for whom the commercial message would have relevance.

The magazine industry is not without its problems, basically in the form of rising postage, production, and labor costs and paper shortages. The paper shortage shows no promise of being only temporary. Some magazines, such as *McCall's,* have found it necessary to trim their page size, and others will probably follow. Another result of the paper shortage will probably be a higher advertising to editorial copy ratio as content is sacrificed to cost and supply pressures.[61]

Partly as a result of the shortage and partly due to inflation, production costs have risen steeply. During 1973 the cost of paper rose 20 percent and the cost of ink 45 percent. Labor costs has also risen significantly. Magazines will eventually have to pass these increases to their readers and advertisers.[62]

Finally, postal rates continue to climb, with the latest increase in effect in March 1974. A growing number of new magazines such as Time-Life's *People,* their new general interest magazine, may be designed chiefly for distribution through newsstands and retail outlets. Not only are postal costs thus avoided, but the cost of maintaining a subscription department also can be avoided. The main problem is building and maintaining a consistent circulation. Most magazines, however, have no real alternative to the U.S. Postal Service at this time, and it appears that higher postal rates will just have to be survived.

OUTDOOR ADVERTISING

Outdoor advertising is the oldest of all the media; outdoor signs were found in Pompeii and elsewhere in ancient times. It still is an important medium for certain specific purposes, and outdoor service is offered in most cities and towns. Approximately 270,000 standardized signs are available for use.

Characteristics of Outdoor Advertising

Advantages.   Several unique advantages are enjoyed by outdoor advertising.

1. *Flexibility.*   Outdoor may be readily tailored to create a truly national saturation campaign or to highspot in selected markets. The

---

[61] "Compton Media Review," p. 22.

[62] Ibid, p. 23.

frequency of exposure also can be varied from market to market to adapt precisely to variations in potentials.

2. *A Mobile Audience.* The buyer views outdoor advertising while on the move, and many of those exposed will be purchasers of the product within a short time after viewing. This last-minute promotion thus may serve as a link between previous advertising messages and a probable purchase, as a reminder of a need, or as the required trigger for a pending sale.

3. *Relative Absence of Competing Advertisements.* For the most part, outdoor signs stand alone and are not subject to the competition of other messages. Thus one source of distraction is removed, although it is apparent that outdoor surroundings substitute yet another and potentially more important source of distraction.

4. *Repeat Exposure.* The opportunity for repeat exposure is great. It was found that at the minimum level of exposure, referred to as a 100 showing, over 80 percent of all adults in the market are reached in the first week. At the end of the month 89.2 percent of the adults will have seen the message an average of 31 times.[63] These reach and frequency figures rise as income rises, in that exposure to adults in high-income households is higher than average, and the average recall of message content is approximately 40 percent.[64] Thus the advantages of repetition are clearly achieved.

Disadvantages. There are also certain disadvantages to the use of outdoor advertising:

1. *Creative Limitations.* The fleeting expression permitted by exposure to a mobile audience limits copy to a few words. Thus little more can be accomplished than a remainder or repetition of a brand name. When longer copy is required, outdoor cannot be used effectively.

2. *Mood of the Viewer.* The consumer on the move is subject to many distractions, and his prime attention is usually directed elsewhere. Furthermore, he may be faced with the inescapable irritations of heavy traffic, heat, and dirt, and the opportunity for a successful advertising impact is therefore diluted.

3. *Public Attack.* Outdoor advertising is under attack from many sources. The terms of the Highway Beautification Act, passed in 1965, authorize the federal government to require states to provide control of outdoor advertising and junkyards on interstate and primary highway systems.[65] Title I of this act requires effective control of signs, displays,

---

[63] "Reach and Frequency of Exposure of Outdoor Posters," study conducted by W. R. Simmons and Associates Research, Inc., for the Institute of Outdoor Advertising, Inc.

[64] "This Is Outdoor Advertising" Institute of Outdoor Advertising, New York.

[65] Phillip Tucker, "State Implementation of Highway Beautification Act," Outdoor Advertising Association of America, 1968.

and devices within 660 feet of the right of way on interstate and primary systems. Other provisions restrict outdoor advertising in commercial areas and check proliferation of signs.

The major effect of this act on the outdoor advertising industry, which actually supported its passage, has been the elimination of posters in small towns and the forced merger of small plants into larger ones to assure financial survival.[66] The clutter of business signs which is a major concern of environmentalists is not an aspect of outdoor advertising, since the owners of the respective business establishments have these signs constructed on their own property.

The industry is not guiltless in the unwise placement of signs, but it maintains that violations of good taste and of a strict professional code are the actions of an irresponsible minority, and the majority is in agreement with the need to prevent abuse.[67] To the credit of the industry, some positive action has been taken. A fairly extensive study was undertaken to assess the effects of the presence of billboards on people's reaction to the environment they see.[68] It was found that the majority of those who were viciferous about outlawing billboards were unaware when billboards were removed from a stretch of highway viewed in a laboratory. In addition, the presence or absence of billboards on the routes used did not prove to be critical in achieving "environmental quality"; the effect of removing utility poles was double the effect of removing billboards. However, it would be unwise to conclude on the basis of these limited results that consumers are indifferent to the presence or absence of billboards.

Purchasing Outdoor Space

Outdoor space is purchased through the National Outdoor Advertising Bureau (NOAB), a service organization owned cooperatively by over 200 advertising agencies and their branches. It gathers cost data and prepares estimates for any combination of markets, performs field inspections, and does the contracting.

Not all advertising agencies belong to NOAB, and some have complete departments equipped to handle outdoor contracts and billings. Space may be purchased also from any of the 700 individual outdoor companies, of course.

Space rates are published by the NOAB. Quotations have always been made on the basis of the desired showing. A 100 showing, for example, provides enough signs to reach 93 percent of the population an average

---

[66] "Compton Media Guide," p. 33.

[67] "This is Outdoor Advertising."

[68] "Measuring Human Response to the Urban Roadside," summary of a study conducted by Arthur D. Little, Inc., published by the Outdoor Advertising Association of America.

of 21–22 times in a 30-day period; a 50 showing provides sufficient signs to reach 85 percent an average of 10–11 times in this same period.[69] A 100 showing may require only one or two signs in smaller areas, but costs for some of these signs can run as high as $20,000 per month in larger localities.

Though the quotation based on showings is still used most often, the Outdoor Advertising Association of America (OAAA) has been promoting among its members a new rating system based on gross rating points. The OAAA maintains that this new system will give advertisers a more accurate basis for comparing outdoor advertising with the other media. Gross rating points are calculated by considering the number of "impression-opportunities" on the average weekday, regardless of repeat exposures, as a percentage of the entire market. Therefore, if the locations of signs during a campaign allowed for 400,000 impression-opportunities (calculated through the use of government traffic reports) daily in a market of 500,000, the plan would deliver 80 gross rating points daily.[70]

Standardized outdoor poster panels are approximately 12 ft. high and 25 ft. long, with a copy area of roughly 10 x 23 ft. Copy is printed in 10 to 14 sections. Painted signs represent about 10 percent of all outdoor structures, although they account for more than 30 percent of total space billings.

The Traffic Audit Bureau (TAB) is the research arm of the industry and is responsible for traffic counts underlying the published rates. Effective circulation is computed as the average daily gross traffic having a reasonable physical opportunity to see the panels. Total gross traffic is therefore reduced as follows to arrive at effective circulation: 50 percent of all pedestrains, 50 percent of all automobile passengers, and 25 percent of passengers on buses or other forms of mass transit. Thus the 100 showing is based on *effective* circulation.

Several other organizations with the industry provide services to its members and to advertisers. The OAAA is the primary trade association; its members operate more than 90 percent of outdoor facilities in the country. One of the services of the OAAA is the Institute of Outdoor Advertising, a central source of information which also develops research, creative ideas, and methods for using the medium more effectively.

The Future of Outdoor Advertising

At least temporarily, outdoor advertising appears to have successfully withstood the attacks of the environmentalists. Its major problem is one

---

[69] Estimates provided by Ogilvy & Mather, Inc.

[70] "Outdoor," *Advertising Age,* November 21, 1973, p. 112.

it shares with most U.S. citizens—the probable extent of the energy crisis. If auto traffic is significantly decreased in favor of public transportation, especially on trains and airplanes, outdoor advertising will be weakened. Continued growth is uncertain in the light of such developments.

TRANSIT ADVERTISING

Transit advertising has more than doubled its billings since 1969 and anticipates an annual volume of at least $70 million.[71] Though it is still seen basically as a supplement to large advertising expenditures elsewhere, it is becoming an attractive option to many advertisers that have not used it previously.

Characteristics of Transit Advertising

Advantages. Among the advantages of transit advertising are the following:

1. *Opportune Exposure.* Of those riding buses and subways, about half reported that their last use of transit was for purposes of shopping.[72] Moreover, 52 percent indicated some recall of inside vehicle advertising, and more than 80 percent of those named specific products.[73] Thus this type of advertising can serve as an effective last-minute stimulus to a purchase.

2. *Geographic Selectivity.* As a strictly local medium, transit offers the advantage of placing dollars in proportion to local market potentials. It also is used to provide extra advertising weight when required.

3. *High Consumer Exposure.* Exposure figures vary, of course, from transit system to transit system. It is believed that at least 40 million Americans ride transit vehicles every month. The New York Transit Authority alone claims over 152 million rides monthly.[74] A recent study of the Toronto transit system revealed that during one week the unduplicated audience represents 52.4 percent of the total market and that, in the space of a month, the reach encompasses 67.5 percent of the market. The individuals comprising this 67.5 percent coverage average 11 rides monthly.[75]

4. *Economy.* Transit advertising claims to be the least costly of all media. The cost per thousand inside-car exposures in the markets served

---

[71] "Transit Advertising Prospers," *Advertising Age*, November 21, 1973, p. 126.

[72] "The Transit Millions," New York Transit Advertising Association, and "Toronto Transit Rider Study, May–June 1971," Daniel Starch Ltd.

[73] "The Transit Millions."

[74] "Transit Advertising Prospers."

[75] "Toronto Transit Rider Study," p. 4.

averages between 15 and 20 cents, and for exterior exposure as little as 7 cents costs per thousand.

Disadvantages. Transit advertising also has some disadvantages:

1. *Weak Coverage of Portions of the Population.* Although advertising is now available on the outside of vehicles, it is apparent that nonriders will not be exposed to the transit advertising on the inside of vehicles.

2. *Creative Limitations.* The basic inside poster sizes are 11 × 28, 11 × 42, and 11 × 56 inches. With such small areas little opportunity is provided for creative presentation other than short, reminder-type messages. Greater opportunities are presented by the use of outside displays, where it is possible to purchase the king-size poster, $2\frac{1}{2}$ × 12 feet in size. Creative opportunities are being expanded through the placement of exterior displays and such innovations as "Moods in Motion," in which an advertiser will purchase all the space in the interior of the vehicle and place his advertising in a setting he hopes will motivate the rider. Displays placed in transportation depots and terminals are also a part of transit advertising.

3. *Mood of the Rider.* The usual bus or subway is frequently crowded, riders are uncomfortable, and attention often is directed toward reaching the destination as quickly as possible. It is doubtful that such an environment is ideal for advertising exposure, but little has been published to verify or refute this possibility.

4. *Availabilities.* Transit space is decidedly limited in quantity, and some satisfied advertisers use long-term contracts for space. The availability of space, then, may be unsatisfactory at times for the potential user.

Purchasing Transit Space

Published space rates are available in the appropriate SRDS listing. Costs are based on a system of showings similar to that used in outdoor advertising, though transit authorities are also monitoring closely the success of gross rating points as an alternative. The New York Subways Advertising Co. will place an 11″ × 28″ card in all its 6,600 vehicles for a month for $20,498, though discounts are available for contracts of longer periods. Exterior displays (30″ × 144″) are available on 400 New York City buses for $21,200 monthly. Purchases may be made from either the individual companies or from centralized sources such as Metro Transit Advertising, a division of Metromedia.

The Future of Transit

The future of transit advertising is indeed bright. The energy crisis which may prove hazardous to outdoor advertising can only add to the already healthy billings of transit advertising. The United States is growing increasingly conscious of its need for effective mass transit. Present systems are being enlarged, new ones such as the Bay Area Rapid Transit System (BART) of San Francisco are being completed, and use of mass transit is growing rapidly. As mass transit grows, so will transit advertising.

THE NONCOMMISSIONABLE MEDIA

All of the media discussed thus far offer a 15 percent commission to advertising agencies, the standard means of agency compensation. Certain media do not provide this discount, however. These include direct mail, point of purchase advertisements, and advertising specialities.

Direct Mail

Direct mail is the third largest medium, ranking behind only newspapers and television and grossing $3.4 billion annually, although this figure includes both direct mail *selling* and *advertising*.[76] The most widely used forms are personal letters, booklets, brochures, catalogs, circulars and fliers, and mail cards.

Direct mail offers several distinct advantages to the advertiser: (1) preconditioning prospects in advance of a personal sales call, (2) stimulation of selective local store patronage, (3) extreme flexibility in pinpointing prospects with desired timing, (4) no limitations on space or format, (5) little competition from other advertising messages, and (6) personal nature of the appeal, among others. A 1972 Postal Service survey revealed that 63 percent of all pieces of direct mail are opened and read and 14 percent are set aside to read later. With direct mail that is expected by the consumer, immediate readership jumps to 70 percent and eventual readership to 85 percent.[77] Another recent USPS survey showed that 63 percent of the population purchased a product or service as a result of direct mail advertising.[78]

These disadvantages also must be considered, however: (1) high cost per thousand, (2) the difficulty of obtaining and maintaining a list of names, (3) the poor reputation of so-called junk mail, and (4) the creative skill required to create high readership. The high cost per thousand can be partially offset by the great selectivity offered, but in any event average production and mailing costs of 12 to 21 cents per unit (higher

---

[76] "Direct Mail—'Quiet Medium'," *Advertising Age,* November 21, 1973, pp. 116–17.

[77] "The Direct Mailstream," *Advertising Age,* November 21, 1973, p. 119.

[78] "USPS Studies Ad Mail, Finds 63% Have Bought," *Advertising Age,* May 7, 1973, p. 2.

for first-class mail) cannot be avoided. The problems with mailing lists can be minimized by renting lists from brokers, publishers, and various advertising media.

Direct mail is used widely by small businessmen, retailers, book and record clubs, catalog houses, magazine publishers, and the pharmaceutical industry.[79] Insurance companies also use it to identify prospects and serve as sales leads, and it is a common medium for coupons, product samples, and other forms of "direct action" advertising.

Point-of-Purchase Advertisements

Most advertising reaches the consumer when he is not near a store and in no mood to buy. Point-of-purchase stimuli reinstate earlier advertising and serve as final links in a purchase sequence. For this reason, point of purchase is an important medium. The largest users are manufacturers of soaps, packaged drugs, gasoline, beer, and liquors.

A study by the Louis Harris organization disclosed some interesting facts about the role of point-of-purchase advertising:

1. It can trigger latent or postponed purchases.
2. It persuades shoppers to indulge in a treat.
3. It can trigger a desire to buy something special for family members.
4. It can break a pattern of shopping intent and release a flood of unplanned purchases.
5. It can evoke a feeling that items are on sale.[80]

Other research has shown that a typical shopping tour takes 29 minutes, and at best the housewife can see only about 10 percent of the 12,000 or more items handled in a typical supermarket. In fact, she may have no more than one fifth of a second to see and decide to buy an item,[81] Studies show that eight out of ten shoppers are aware of point-of-purchase advertising, and 30 percent claim that exposure triggered a purchase.[82] On the average, a special display was found to boost sales 536 percent in the Dillion study sponsored by *Progressive Grocer*.

One especially effective way of stimulating consumer purchases is to offer shelves which are fully stocked; the Dillion study in *Progressive Grocer* reported sales increases of as much as 33 percent by this means.

---

[79] "Direct Mail—Quiet Medium."

[80] William W. Mee, "How Point-of-Purchase Is More Efficient as an Advertising and Sales Medium," *Media/scope*, September, 1963, p. 56.

[81] The role of point-of-purchase advertising is well documented in the Colonial Stores and Dillon studies published in booklet form by *Progressive Grocer*. These data come from the Colonial Stores study.

[82] "Point of Purchase Medium—Final Push to Help Close the Sale," *Advertising* January 15, 1963, p. 142.

Moreover, special signs on shelves, called product spotters, increased sales on the average of 152 percent, and positioning stock at eye level on the shelf was a powerful sales stimulus for some products.[83]

Some innovative point-of-purchase efforts have included recorded advertisements played over a store's public address system, special sales of 5 to 30 minutes announced over the public address system which are identified by such devices as flashing lights mounted on dollies so they can be moved from place to place, video cassettes to aid in making the sale of major purchases such as automobiles, and even motorized signs mounted on wires which travel around the store above the heads of the shoppers.

The importance of good point-of-purchase advertising can hardly be questioned. The difficulty, however, is stimulating retailers to use the many displays and banners they receive each month. Since this is a problem in working with resellers, it is discussed in depth in Part Five.

Advertising Specialties

Advertising specialties are a unique form of advertising which has been defined as employing "useful articles imprinted with the advertiser's name and address and frequently with a sales message. The advertising specialty is used to reach a preselected audience and is given without cost or obligation, real or implied, and with no preceding contest of any kind."[84]

Knives, bottle caps, pens, pencils, and rain hats are representative specialty items which are imprinted with the advertiser's name and perhaps a brief sales message. These items are inexpensive but may prove to be of real use to the recipient. Perhaps the greatest advantage is that the advertiser's name usually is seen many times. Moreover, specialty advertising can be made highly selective with little or no waste coverage.

Specialty advertising, of course, usually is used as a supplement to other media. As the *only* medium, it seldom will be sufficient. Its use seems to be expanding, however, and future growth as a supplementary medium seems likely.

SUMMARY

The purpose of this chapter has been to condense a wealth of material on media characteristics, advantages, disadvantages, possible uses, and

---

[83] See the Dillon study.

[84] Walter A. Gaw, *Specialty Advertising* (Chicago: Specialty Advertising Association, 1964), p. 10.

other factors which must be understood before discussing the media selection process itself. Of greatest importance is the way in which each of the media discussed is adapting to the current environment, because the changes have been great. Understanding of these changes makes it possible to discuss meaningfully the methods by which media should be analyzed and selected.

REVIEW AND DISCUSSION QUESTIONS

1. The nationally distributed Sunday supplement seems to be losing ground in comparison with other media. What reasons can you see for this trend? Can it be reversed? Why?

2. The differential between local and national line rates is said by many to be triggering an exodus of national advertisers from local newspapers. Given this fact, what reasons can be advanced for continuation of the differentials? Why, in your opinion, has there been so little change?

3. Contrast the milline rate and cost per thousand formula. What advantage is gained by their use? What possible dangers could you see?

4. One of the distinct trends in the television medium is the rapid rise of CATV. What effects will this have on both local and national advertising in the future?

5. The fairness doctrine of the FCC may soon be applied to both television programming and television advertising. What effects might this have on advertising? On the future of television as a medium?

6. Advertisers are showing a growing concern with commercial clutter in television and radio broadcasts. If clutter is allowed to continue, what might be the effects in terms of the consumer, as well as on the advertising copy and format?

7. The FCC is authorized to refuse to renew local station licenses if they fail to operate within broad guidelines of public interest. What are the advantages and dangers of this policy? What factors should the FCC consider in deciding license renewal?

8. Under what conditions might a 60-second television commercial be worth twice the cost of a 30-second version?

9. Radio continues its growth in advertising dollars. Do you think this steady upward trend will continue? Why?

10. What steps might be taken to save *Reader's Digest* from the same fate as *The Saturday Evening Post, Look,* and *Life?*

11. In what sense can it be said that magazines are a highly flexible medium?

12. With a 100 showing, over 80 percent of all adults are reached with an average frequency of 31. What do these terms mean? Does this mean that outdoor advertising has unique advantages in terms of reach and frequency when compared with other media? What are the advantages of gross rating points as a substitute system of measurement?

13. There are frequent outcries that billboards should be removed entirely

from the public roads. What arguments could you advance to refute this position?

14. For what types of products is transit advertising most suitable? Can it be used as a substitute medium for television or magazines?

15. Critics of direct mail advertising claim that the junk mail received in homes today is so excessive that government should step in to outlaw unwanted use of the mails. Would this be in the consumer's interest? Why, or why not?

16. It is sometimes said that point of purchase is the untouched "promised land" of advertising, the presumption being that it frequently is neglected. What roles can point of purchase play?

12

Media Strategy

THE TWO MAIN PROBLEMS faced in media strategy are selection of media vehicles and preparation of a media schedule. Factors which are fundamental in media selection are discussed in the following pages: (1) the requirements of creative strategy, (2) reaching the proper audience, (3) the requirements for reach versus frequency, (4) competitive factors, (5) cost efficiency, (6) qualitative factors, and (7) distribution requirements. Also discussed are media scheduling, with emphasis upon geographical and seasonal scheduling, and the use of the computer in media decisions.

THE REQUIREMENTS OF CREATIVE STRATEGY

As Warren Bahr, Director of Media at Young & Rubicam Advertising Agency, points out: "When you separate media buying from media planning, and the media function from the creative function, advertising becomes just a bits-and-pieces operation, separated from the marketing totality."[1] The advertising requirements for the product often can easily favor or eliminate certain media candidates. For example, it has been a long-standing agreement among broadcasters subscribing to the Code of the National Association of Broadcasters that liquor will not be advertised on radio or television. Moreover, the product may be so sensitive that good taste calls for its exclusion from certain media. A good example is the virtual absence of hemorrhoid remedy promotion on television, both as a result of the NAB code and a keen awareness that

[1] "Media Buying Services—The Shook-Up Agencies Now Strive for Respectability," *Advertising Age*, June 16, 1969, p. 85.

271

such products should be advertised with discretion in printed media only, so as not to offend prospects or nonprospects.

The product personality also will dictate media choice. The promotion of expensive French perfumes in *Mad* would clearly be inappropriate. The match between product prospects and media audiences would be poor, of course, but of even greater importance, association of the product with these media could affect its image adversely.

Finally, the requirements of the message may dominate the media decision. An automobile advertisement featuring acceleration and passing power will require a medium which dramatizes action for maximum creative impact, and where movement is required television or sales films are the only possible choices. Color might be specified to provide a more realistic representation of an automobile and to strengthen emotional impact. The finest color reproduction is available in magazines, although acceptable color can be purchased in both television and newspapers. Finally, the required use of sound eliminates substantially all media except radio and television (although some direct mail promotions contain small recorded discs). There are many other similar examples.

REACHING THE PROPER AUDIENCE

The pivotal consideration in media strategy is to select media vehicles which reach the target audience with a minimum of waste coverage. This is often referred to as selectivity. Computers make it possible to undertake selectivity analysis with considerable precision. This means, of course, that the analyst must have a grasp of the nature, scope, and uses of available sources of audience data. Audience data is discussed in some detail here, before focusing on the use of these data in media planning.

Media Audience Data

All practical considerations aside, most agree that it would be useful to have at least six categories of data for media planning and evaluation. The essential categories are: (1) media distribution—copies or sets carrying the advertising; (2) media audiences—people actually exposed to a medium; and (3) advertising exposure—people exposed to advertising units. In addition, data are also useful on (4) advertising perception—people aware of the message; (5) advertising communication—people affected by advertising; and (6) consumer response—people who make additional purchases.[2]

---

[2] See Paul E. J. Gerhold, "Better Media Planning: What Can We Do Now?" *Proceedings 5th Annual Conference* (New York: Advertising Research Foundation, Inc., 1959), pp. 43–48.

The difficulty is that the roles of the medium and the message itself intermix in categories 4–6. In these categories it is difficult to determine whether people's awareness of the message is more attributable to layout, design, and wording than to the medium itself. Thus only the first three stages focus on the medium itself, and media audience data are largely confined to these levels, as our discussion also will be.

Media Distribution.   Data in this category have long been available from such organiaztions as the Audit Bureau of Circulation (ABC). This organization is sponsored by national and local advertisers, advertising agencies, and publishers. It makes available sworn and audited statements of newspaper and magazine audiences. A publication must have at least 70 percent paid circulation (copies purchased at not less than one half the established prices) to be eligible for membership and listing. Most publishers meeting this qualification are members of ABC.

Publications which distribute to special groups, perhaps on a free basis, are audited by the Business Publications Audit of Circulation (BPA). The functions performed by BPA closely parallel those of ABC.

The notion of total physical distribution of media vehicles quickly loses its significance when one moves out of the publications field. While the Advertising Research Foundation has published a *National Survey of Television Sets in U.S. Households,* the most useful data on television and other media are confined largely to categories 2 and 3.[3]

These data are useful primarily in providing a verified audit of circulation claims. The figures sometimes are used as a guarantee for the rates established in magazine space contracts, but the data are of little additional use because there usually is a wide difference between physical distribution and audience exposure.

Media Audiences.   Media audiences refer to the actual number of people exposed to a medium on both one-time and repeat bases. The methods of audience measurement are complex, as the discussion below indicates.

MAGAZINE AUDIENCES.   The accepted definition of the audience of a given magazine is the number of people claiming to recall looking into an average issue. This definition is supported by evidence which indicates that those looking into a magazine tend to be exposed to most of its contents.[4] It should be apparent, however, that the problems of response distortion in survey research are often encountered. For example, it is not unusual for a respondent to deny reading a magazine which would appear to place him in a bad light in an interviewer's eyes or to claim readership of a prestigious publication. To underscore these dangers, we mention the report that the number of those who claim

[3] Published periodically by the Advertising Research Foundation, Inc.

[4] Darrell B. Lucas and Steuart H. Britt, *Measuring Advertising Effectiveness* (New York: McGraw-Hill Book Co., 1963), p. 225.

to be readers of a well-known prestige magazine can be more than 15 times the number of copies printed.[5]

It is obvious that methods used to measure actual readership must be designed to minimize response distortion. The most commonly used approach, the editorial interest technique, encompasses an attempt to make respondents feel that they are helping editors to evaluate the appeal of various editorial features. No attempt is made at the outset to determine whether or not the respondent actually read the issue. This question is usually reserved until the end and is often worded as follows: "Just for the record, now that we have been through this issue, would you say you definitely happened to read it before, or didn't read it, or aren't you sure?"[6] Questioning at the end of the interview and this careful wording are effective devices to guarantee a minimum of overclaimed or underclaimed readership.

Another approach used to assess magazine readership is to interview different samples of respondents every day for a period of time regarding "yesterday's reading." Confining the interview to yesterday's reading is intended to prevent memory loss. Extension of the interviewing period also permits useful estimation of the total readership of a given magazine over time. It is well known, for example, that issue life (the time in which it continues to be read) may run into months.

It is difficult to say which method gives the more accurate estimate of readership. In one study it was found that the readership generated by the editorial interest technique was 2.5 percent lower than that produced by an unaided recall procedure.[7] It also has been reported that claimed readership overestimates the audience for monthly magazines and underestimates the audience for weeklies and biweeklies.[8] Another expert feels that the best approach is use of simple direct questions such as "Which magazines do you read?" The first step is to determine the probability that claimed readership is accurate, through benchmark studies using several techniques. From then on it would be possible simply to ask respondents, "Do you read this magazine usually, regularly, quite often, seldom, or never?" and to modify the answers given by the probabilities of accuracy found from previous surveys.[9] This approach offers an ad-

---

[5] Ibid., p. 225.

[6] Ibid., p. 228.

[7] "An Experimental Study Comparing Magazine Audiences as Determined by Two Questioning Procedures," study conducted by Alfred Politz Media Studies for *Life* magazine.

[8] Donald G. McGlathery, "Claimed Frequency versus Editorial-Interest Method of Repeat Magazine Audiences," *Journal of Advertising Research,* Vol. 7 (1967), pp. 7–15. See also W. R. Simmons, "A New Look at Reach and Frequency," *Proceedings, 15th Annual Conference* (New York: Advertising Research Foundation, 1969), pp. 13–23.

[9] Jean M. Agostini, "The Case for Direct Questions on Reading Habits," *Journal of Advertising Research,* Vol. 4 (1964), pp. 28–33.

mirable degree of simplicity and definitely is worthy of further investigation.

Audiences can be measured also in terms of primary readers only (the person or household purchasing the magazine) or primary readers plus pass-along readers. Once there was a tendency to look with favor upon magazines with high percentages of pass-along readers, no doubt on the assumption that this premium is gained without extra cost, but survey evidence is disputing this assumption. The Advertising Research Foundation Printed Advertising Research Methods study (PARM) showed higher advertising recall in primary households.[10] Moreover, a Roper study for *Woman's Day* indicated that the average pass-along reader may be 35 to 40 percent less responsive to advertising than primary readers.[11] The 1964 *Reader's Digest* study by Alfred Politz, based on 5,062 interviews, disclosed that pass-along audiences are of less value to advertisers than primary readers because:

1. They spend less time reading.
2. They read on fewer occasions.
3. Readership often takes place outside of homes, in waiting rooms and elsewhere.
4. Less satisfaction is reported from reading.
5. These readers are in lower brackets of income and education.
6. Pass-along readers would be less disappointed if magazines suddenly ceased publication.[12]

NEWSPAPER AUDIENCES. The measurement of newspaper audiences involves essentially the same procedures as those reported for magazines. For example, a reader is defined as someone who has read a part of the medium being analyzed, and the time period covered generally does not exceed one day.

TELEVISION AUDIENCES. Television audience data are most frequently collected by means of a diary in which viewers record shows they have watched over a period of time. Several syndicated research services are widely used for this purpose, including A. C. Nielsen and American Research Bureau (ARB). Use also is made of the audimeter which automatically records the number of television sets tuned to a particular channel. Finally, there is some use of coincidental telephone recall in which a sample of people is contacted by telephone during programs to establish listening or viewing patterns.

There is some controversy surrounding the accuracy of reports gen-

---

[10] Darrell B. Lucas, "The ABC's of ARF'S PARM," *Journal of Marketing*, Vol. 25 (July 1960), p. 14.

[11] Paul M. Roth, "What Is the Value of Pass-along Magazine Audience?" *Media/scope*, November, 1963, pp. 84–87.

[12] "Digest Finds 'Total Audience' Idea Fallacious," *Advertising Age*, April 13, 1964, p. 3 ff.

erated by panels of viewers using either the diary or the audimeter. It is possible that the act of recording what is listened to or viewed will lead to atypical patterns of behavior. The extent of this conditioning of panels is not known, but attempts are made to minimize it through panel turnover.

The ratings firms have been attacked also for the adequacy of samples used.[13] It is well known that A. C. Nielsen and the other rating services faced serious criticism in the early 1960s by members of the Harris Investigation Committee in Congress and by the Federal Trade Commission. A number of irregularities were found, but this matter is now history in view of the substantial changes that have been made. Most now agree that advertisers can use program ratings with relatively great confidence that sample data can be projected, within known error limits, to the entire population.[14]

RADIO AUDIENCES. A unique problem is presented by the fact that radios are used everywhere; hence, diaries and audimeters have not proved to be adequate radio audience measures. Until recently this problem appeared the defy solution, but considerable promise is shown by RADAR (Radio's All Dimension Audience Research).[15]

In this measurement technique, two telephone panels are established, one in the spring and one in the fall. Each household is telephoned eight different times on consecutive days during the survey period and is questioned about radio listening habits for each quarter hour for the preceding 24 hours. Respondents also complete a standard questionnaire which gives such characteristics as age and sex. This permits a reporting of all radio listening and weekly cumulative audiences by subgroup within the population.

AUDIENCES OF OTHER MEDIA. Other media such as outdoor and transit advertising provide no information regarding this dimension of audience evaluation, since the total audience of the medium and advertising exposure coincide. Research measures for these media are discussed in the next section.

AUDIENCE PROFILES. Up to this point discussion has been confined to total audiences. Such data, however, are a poor indication of the characteristics of the individuals reached. Today most media data are also classified in such terms as age, income, occupation, sex, geographical location, and product purchases. It is commonplace for the media planner to receive many such reports. In fact, the volume of information has

---

[13] See "Broadcast Ratings Lose Spell," *Business Week,* April 13, 1963, p. 30.

[14] See Gale D. Metzger, Gerald J. Glasser, and Jay Eliasberg, "An Experiment in Ratings Research Methodology—the CONTAM Committee," *Proceedings, 15th Annual Conference* (New York: Advertising Research Foundation, 1969), pp. 24–31.

[15] "RADAR: Network Radio's Newest Yardstick," *Media/scope,* January 1969, pp. 67–68.

grown to the point that computer storage facilities are a virtual necessity.

Formerly it was necessary to consult research reports published by individual media when profile data were needed. This is no longer necessary because of the widespread use of the syndicated research services which report audience profiles for television and magazines, the two leading national media.

As yet there is no continuing source which provides multimedia data on the psychological characteristics of readers or viewers. Isolated reports of this type have been disseminated by individual media,[16] but attempts to compare audiences in such terms as sociability and family centeredness are quite recent and as yet fragmentary.[17] The published studies which have appeared are most noteworthy for pioneering use of factor analysis and other computer algorithms which permit the utilization of vast amounts of data. Undoubtedly the syndicated research services will expand their coverage in the future, because there are no remaining methodological barriers.

Advertising Exposure. In the third category of media evaluation, attention shifts to information on exposure to advertising units in a given vehicle. Comparatively few studies are available to report, and discussion must be somewhat tentative.

ADVERTISING EXPOSURE IN MAGAZINES. The purchaser of space cannot reserve a particular location in a publication without extra payment. He usually must run the risk of appearing anywhere in the issue, and it is important to determine the extent of advertising exposure throughout the medium. There is no necessary relationship between media exposure and advertising exposure.

In one early study, *Look* magazine surveyed a sample of subscribers by sending issues containing on each page an inconspicuous spot of glue which would not readhere after pages were separated.[18] Subsequent examination took into account the extent of accidental separation in handling through the mail. It was discovered that the exposure to advertising

---

[16] In one pioneering report, for example, readers of *Better Homes and Gardens* were compared along such dimensions as venturesomeness. See "A Twelve Months' Study of *Better Homes and Gardens* Readers," Meredith Publishing Co., Des Moines, Iowa, 1956.

[17] See Douglas Tigert, "A Psychographic Profile of Magazine Audiences: An Investigation of Media's Climate," paper given at the Consumer Research workshop, The Ohio State University, August 22, 1969; Charles W. King and John O. Summers, "Social Activity Patterns and Media Exposure," Working Paper No. 248, Herman C. Krannert Graduate School of Industrial Administration, Purdue University, July 1969; Frank M. Bass, Edgar A. Pessemier, and Douglas Tigert, "A Taxonomy of Magazine Readership Applied to Problems in Marketing Strategy and Media Selection," *Journal of Business,* Vol. 42 (July 1969), pp. 337–63.

[18] "A Study of Advertising Penetration in *Look* Households," Cowles Publishing Co., New York, 1959.

was surprisingly uniform throughout the issue, the average exposure being 85 percent. Similarly, advertising exposure for four different periodicals was compared by reader claims of exposure, using data collected by the yesterday's reading method.[19]

As was mentioned earlier, the syndicated services confine data collection to media exposure. A statistical method has been reported which claims to give accurate estimates of advertising exposure from media exposure data.[20] This has been offered on a syndicated basis, but its acceptance is uncertain as of this writing.

ADVERTISING EXPOSURE IN NEWSPAPERS. There is only one study of advertising exposure in newspapers to report. In this study it was found that 82 percent of all readers open the average advertising page which features a nationally distributed product.[21] It seems that exposure does not vary by demographic segments. This would mean that there are no important differences in exposure in various part of the newspaper.

ADVERTISING EXPOSURE IN TELEVISION. To some extent the measures of television audiences discussed earlier can be used to assess advertising exposure. It is reasonable to expect that most individuals will be exposed to commercials if their sets are turned on, and this observation has generally been confirmed by measurements taken during commercial minutes. Estimates of station-break exposure are less precise, however, because they generally are based on the average of program audiences immediately before and after the break.

Obviously there is some risk in assuming that diary or audimeter scores accurately indicate advertising exposure. In one study, for example, about one third of the homes tuned to network television programs were found to have no housewives viewing; one half had no exposure to the commercials; and less than one fifth of the housewives could recall advertising content 24 hours later.[22] The need for more accurate data on commercial exposure is apparent.

ADVERTISING EXPOSURE IN OTHER MEDIA. The measures of audiences reached by most other media, in effect, also focus on exposure to the advertising message. The Traffic Audit Bureau publishes reports on the number of people passing an outdoor poster and attempts to estimate the number having a reasonable probability of exposure. Obviously, posters can be passed without awareness by the individual, but no better

---

[19] "Advertising Exposure—Audiences, Issues, and Advertising Pages," Vol. 1, *Reader's Digest* Association, Inc., 1960.

[20] "Now a Way to Figure Reach & Frequency of Multi-Media Campaigns," *Media/scope*, August 1967, pp. 125–30.

[21] "A Study of the Opportunity for Exposure to National Newspaper Advertising," Bureau of Advertising, American Newspaper Publishers Association.

[22] Edward M. Stern, "Measure Ad Communication, Effects on Attitudes, Not Just Media Exposure," *Advertising Age*, June 29, 1964, p. 72.

research method has yet been proposed, even though attempts have been made to estimate advertising recognition and recall.

Exposure to transit advertisements typically is analyzed through counting vehicle traffic. The difficulties in this procedure should be apparent, in that it is next to impossible to determine whether or not a given person has perceived the message at the time of exposure. Furthermore, the relationship between traffic and advertising exposure is by no means clear.[23] One possible variation in the research procedure is to expose consumers to reproduced car cards in their homes and ask if they recall seeing the messages. The message on the car card would, of course, have to be unique to that medium in order to avoid confusion with exposure elsewhere.

Comments on Media Data. Ideally, it would be possible to estimate the fourth category of data on *advertising exposure* (not simply media audiences) for all possible media. One researcher underscores the gap in audience information in this way:

Our problem lies in the sad truth that we are stuck with a great mass of media statistics that relate (at best) only to superficial media vehicle exposure and really tell us nothing about the ability of the medium to help communicate what we are trying to say. It is in this area that we need all the help that research can provide. Past and current inter-media studies only hint at differences that may exist between individual media.[24]

In addition, as was pointed out in Chapter 9, market targets can be defined in terms that go far beyond the usual demographic classifications. However, media profiles have not expanded to this same extent. There is an obvious need to enrich the data base through provision of data on the activities, interests, and opinions (AIO scores) of media audiences. Fortunately, there is every reason to anticipate that this will be done in the near future.

Finally, data must be provided which go beyond numbers to consider the fifth and sixth categories of data, on advertising perception and consumer response. Leo Bogart's conclusions in this respect are worthy of note:

Audience research in the future must go further in the task of examining the *quality* of media experience rather than the numbers who experience it, and distinguish among different kinds of communications experiences which are now included together under the heading of Total-Audience Figures. A serious attempt along these lines will lead inevitably to an emphasis on analysis rather than measurement as the proper preoccupation of advertising research.[25]

---

[23] Lucas and Britt, *Measuring Advertising Effectiveness,* p. 280.

[24] Stern, "Ad Communication Effects," p. 72.

[25] Leo Bogart, *Strategy in Advertising* (New York: Harcourt, Brace & World, 1967), pp. 245–46.

Using Media Audiences Data.   The central task of media selection is to *achieve a media mix which reaches the target audience with a minimum of waste coverage and delivers exposure to the advertising unit in a proper frame of mind, apart from media content, so that the advertisement can perform its role.* The most demanding task is to match the target market with media audience, and this obviously requires a good data base.[26]

With available data and computer technology it is possible to utilize a number of characteristics of both the market target and media audiences in media selection. Thus there is little excuse for failure to make use of audience reached in building a media schedule, all other things being equal.

REACH AND FREQUENCY

Once determination is made of the extent to which a media schedule reaches the desired target market, it is important to determine both *reach* and *frequency.* Reach is defined as the number (or percentage) of *different* homes exposed to the advertising schedule during a given period of time (usually four weeks). Frequency is the number of times that the *average home reached* was exposed during that same period. A very useful summary measure referred to as *gross rating points* (GRP) combines both of these considerations; GRP is the product of reach times frequency. It is widely used as an indication of advertising weight or tonnage generated by the media schedule.

FIGURE 12–1

Reach and Frequency Patterns for Ten Television Homes over a Four-Week Period

Week	Message	A	B	C	D	E	F	G	H	I	J	Total Exposures
	1	x				x		x				3
1	2	x	x									2
	3			x	x		x	x				4
	4			x							x	2
2	5					x						1
	6					x						1
	7	x					x	x				3
3	8				x							1
	9		x		x							2
	10				x	x			x			3
4	11					x					x	2
	12		x								x	2
Total exposures		3	3	2	4	5	2	3	1	0	3	26

Source: Media Department, Ogilvy & Mather, Inc.

[26] See Paul M. Roth, *How to Plan Media* (Skokie, Ill.: Standard Rate & Data Service, Inc., 1968), ch. 4.

An example will promote understanding of these concepts. Figure 12–1 represents the television viewing record over four weeks in ten homes. Notice that all homes but home I were reached during the four weeks. This gives a reach figure of 90 percent. There were 26 total exposures. If 26 is divided by the nine homes reached, this gives a frequency of 2.9 percent. GRP (reach times frequency) then is 261.

The Problem of Audience Duplication

Reach was defined above as the number of different homes exposed. A given media schedule could fail to achieve reach by delivering multiple exposures of the same audience. If intensive coverage of the same group is the objective, it is desirable to select media that reach essentially the same people; an opposite strategy is required to maximize reach. Therefore, *duplication* of audiences is an important factor.

In Figure 12–2 the audiences of media A, B, and C are depicted. The circle for each represents its audience, and the area within the boundaries of all three (the union) is the total audience reach of these media used in combination. The area within the intersection of each circle represents the overlap between each media pair. Area AB, for instance, is the overlap or duplication between media A and B. Area ABC represents duplication among all three media.

In practice, the problem lies in estimating the extent of duplication present within a media schedule. Data for this purpose are far from ideal, although some estimates are provided by the various syndicated

FIGURE 12–2
Audience Duplication in Three Media, A, B, and C

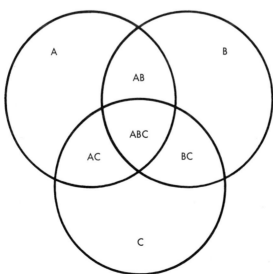

audience data services. The difficulty arises when a number of media are utilized, because available data sources then are inadequate. A partial answer has been provided by various mathematical formulas which are providing useful estimates without the vast data inputs that otherwise would be required.

Using Reach, Frequency, and GRP Measures

The starting point is to establish a media objective, usually in terms of desired GRP levels. For example, 100 gross rating points a week is a relatively heavy advertising schedule. In a highly competitive market, it is not unusual to invest at this level or even higher levels. The media planner must specify the media GRP levels desired. Then the media buyer can fit together an appropriate schedule.

For example, the media plan for a good product called for at least 200 gross rating points and maximum reach using prime-time television commercials. The media plan depicted in Figure 12–3 delivered 205 GRP with a reach of 78.6 percent of all television homes. Hence it was entirely satisfactory, all other things being equal. Notice, by the way,

FIGURE 12–3

Reach, Frequency, and GRP Levels Produced by a Media Plan for a Food Item

	Total Announcements	Average Rating per Announcement
Four-week schedule:		
1 announcement per week on the "Lucy Show"	4	20.0%
1 announcement every other week on "My Three Sons"	2	18.8
1 announcement every other week on "Mission: Impossible"	2	25.0
1 announcement every other week on "Beverly Hillbillies"	2	18.7
	10	

Reach—78.6 percent of all TV homes
Frequency—2.6
GRP—205.0

Frequency distribution: Number of Announcements	Percent of Homes	Cumulated Percent
0	21.4	—
1	21.6	21.6%
2	22.4	44.0
3	15.4	59.4
4	10.0	69.4
5	4.8	74.2
6	2.9	77.1
7	1.2	78.3
8	0.2	78.5
9	0.1	78.6
10+	0.0	78.6

Source: Media Department, Ogilvy & Mather, Inc.

that an equivalent GRP level could also be generated with much lower reach and higher frequency. Therefore it is necessary to specify both desired reach and GRP.

Guidance also is provided on which of several alternative plans would be most effective. Consider the data in Figure 12–4, which show

FIGURE 12–4

Reach and Frequency Analysis for a Luxury Product

Plan 1	Plan 2	Plan 3
Spot Life newsweeklies no monthlies Schedule (2x)	Spot Life newsweeklies monthlies (1x)	No Spot Life newsweeklies monthlies
1 Spot Life	1 Spot Life	2 Time
		1 Newsweek
2 Time	1 Time	1 U.S. News
2 Newsweek	1 Newsweek	1 New Yorker
2 U.S. News	1 U.S. News	1 Sports Illus.
2 New Yorker	1 New Yorker	1 Business Week
2 Sports Illus.	1 Sports Illus.	1 Sunset
2 Business Week	1 Business Week	1 Esquire
		1 Fortune
	1 Sunset	1 Nat'l. Geo.
	1 Esquire	1 Holiday
	1 Fortune	1 Harper's
	·1 Nat'l. Geo.	1 Atlantic
	1 Holiday	1 Reporter*
	1 Harper's	1 Town & Cntry.*
	1 Atlantic	1 Status/Diplo.*
	1 Reporter*	1 Commentary*
	1 Town & Cntry.*	1 Venture*
	1 Status Diplo.*	1 Réalités*
	1 Commentary*	2 Wall St. Journal
	1 Venture*	
	1 Réalités*	
	2 Wall St. Journal	

User Groups	Reach	Frequency	GRP
Plan 1			
Total men	37	2.9	107
Own luxury, intend to buy	46	3.2	149
Income of $15,000+	65	3.5	229
Plan 2			
Total men	53	2.0	103
Own luxury, intend to buy	61	2.3	142
Income of $15,000+	77	2.9	225
Plan 3			
Total men	53	2.2	115
Own luxury, intend to buy	60	2.5	154
Income of $15,000+	77	3.3	249

* Tabulated by Business Week.

Source: Paul M. Roth, How to Plan Media (Skokie, Ill.: Standard Rate & Data Service, Inc., 1968), p. 9–4. Used by special permission.

the reach and frequency analysis for a luxury item. The best media plan includes monthly magazines; this is especially evident when plans 1 and 2 are compared. Also, plans 2 and 3 show that spot television is probably optional, since the effects on reach and frequency are not great.

Finally, reach, frequency, and GRP measures can be an excellent guide to estimation of budget levels through the built-up analysis discussed in Chapter 10. The data in Figure 12–5, for example, give a

FIGURE 12–5

Reach (R) and Frequency (F) Estimates and Costs at Various GRP Levels

	Target Weekly GRP Levels							
	25		50		75		100	
	R	F	R	F	R	F	R	F
Daytime spots.............	34	2.9	53	3.8	63	4.8	69	5.8
Prime spots...............	50	2.0	70	2.9	80	3.7	87	4.6
Early-late evening spots....	43	2.3	65	3.1	77	3.9	83	4.8
Day network*..............	43	2.3	55	3.6	58	5.1	60	6.7
Night network*............	61	1.6	81	2.5	88	3.4	90	4.4

	TV Homes		Cost per Rating Point (30 seconds)			
(Women) DMA Group	(MM)	(%)	Day	Early Evening	Late Evening	Prime
Top 5...............	16.1	24.72	$ 288	$ 392	$ 444	$ 747
Top 10..............	22.6	34.81	413	600	658	1,112
Top 20..............	30.5	46.84	573	829	904	1,531
Top 30..............	36.3	55.78	708	1,030	1,097	1,883
Top 40..............	40.8	62.65	804	1,158	1,216	2,103
Top 50..............	44.6	68.62	887	1,263	1,326	2,298
Top 60..............	48.0	73.73	962	1,366	1,434	2,483
Top 70..............	50.8	78.05	1,012	1,444	1,520	2,614
Top 80..............	53.2	81.71	1,059	1,522	1,605	2,742
Top 90..............	55.1	84.69	1,091	1,576	1,658	2,828
Top 100.............	56.8	87.26	1,131	1,637	1,714	2,902

* Research is dependent to a large extent on scheduling patterns. Above estimates for day and night reflect common practices.
Source: Estimates provided by Media Department, Ogilvy & Mather, Inc., 1973.

general indication of the reach and frequency levels achieved by expenditure levels which produce from 25 to 100 GRP per week with a television schedule. To take just one illustration, 25 GRP in daytime spot television will reach, on the average, 34 percent of all television homes with a frequency of 2.9 times in a four-week period. The objective for a media plan for a convenience food item calls for 36 percent reach with a 2.8 frequency in the top 100 spot television markets using daytime placement. The 25 GRP level thus would be adequate. Figure 12–5 also indicates that the gross rating for one point in the top 100 markets on daytime television is $1,131. This would then yield a needed budget level of $28,275 (25 × $1,131).

Historically, reach and frequency are measures confined only to television and magazine audiences. Now data sources and computer technology, however, permit estimates *across media* and between various market segments. Therefore, these measures are finding widespread use in media planning.

COMPETITIVE CONSIDERATIONS

Competition can assume major significance in media decisions. At times the advertising objective will call, for example, for maintenance of "share of mind." This is especially likely in a situation where the boundaries of a total market are more or less static and a number of competitors are offering essentially similar products.

The rationale underlying a share-of-mind objective is that market share will roughly parallel advertising share. In such situations it is necessary, therefore, to analyze market share, share of total advertising expenditures, and share of advertising messages actually reaching prospects. Consider the data in Figure 12–6. The first column depicts share of market for competing brands, and the next column reveals the best estimate of share of advertising spending for television. Brands A and B are spending in proportion to market share, whereas the management of brand C apparently feels that a dominant position can be maintained with a smaller proportional investment. Brand D apparently is a new product and is spending to attain an anticipated share.

The third column in Figure 12–6 may be somewhat more puzzling. It provides an estimate of the *efficiency* of spending and is not necessarily equivalent to total dollar levels. With available data sources providing information on media audience, program ratings, and so on, it is possible to estimate the probable advertising exposure delivered by each firm's media schedule. Here brand A is highly efficient in that an 8 percent share of spending delivers 11 percent of total messages. Brand C on the other hand apparently is choosing media which do not reach its prospects in that it has attained only a 19 percent share as compared with a 25 percent dollar share. These figures become especially significant when they are related to the key segment, messages delivered to women, appearing in the fourth column.

Obviously the quality of the advertising and other factors will affect the figures, but the data are quite revealing. It would appear, for example, that the brand A schedule will lead to an increase in share of mind as well as a probable gain in market share. Brand B probably will remain stable, but brand C may be in trouble. All other things being equal, it will be difficult to maintain market share with spending levels which lag

FIGURE 12–6

Competitive Marketing and TV Advertising Shares of Nine Leading Brands

Brand	Share of Market (percent)	Share of TV Advertised Dollars (percent)	Share of TV Household Advertised Messages (percent)	Share of TV Messages Delivered to Women (18–39) (percent)
A	8	8	11	12
B	26	25	25	28
C	35	25	19	19
D	NA	14	9	8
E	17	16	17	16
F	3	2	4	4
G	7	4	6	6
H	NA	3	2	1
I	4	3	7	6

Source: Paul M. Roth, *How to Plan Media* (Skokie, Ill.: Standard Rate & Data Service, Inc., 1968), p. 6–2. Used by special permission.

competition to this extent. Finally, brand D should be watched closely, because it should achieve significant market inroads.

It should be stressed that this example represents a situation in which competition is a major factor, and this is not always the case. Nonetheless, competition is relevant in the majority of instances.

COST CONSIDERATIONS

Space and time costs are always important factors in media selection. These data usually will appear in the volumes published by the Standard Rate & Data Service (SRDS). It will be recalled from Chapter 11 that there are formulas (cost per thousand readers or homes and the milline rate) which permit comparisons of the cost efficiency of various media. The logic of these formulas is that gross space costs must be refined by the audience reached per dollar spent before useful comparisons can be made across media.

The data in Figure 12–7 provide an indication of the way in which cost per thousand (CPM) measures are used. This shows the average CPM ratings for network TV spot announcements. For example, a prime-

FIGURE 12–7

Average Network TV CPM's at Various Cost and Rating Levels

How to read: A prime time network 30 costing $45,000 and estimated to deliver a 25 rating will have a CPM (homes) of $2.78.

Nighttime

:30 Cost	CPM at Average Audience Rating Levels					
($000)	25	22	20	18	15	12
45...............	$2.78	$3.16	$3.47	$3.86	$4.63	$5.79
40...............	2.47	2.81	3.09	3.43	4.12	5.14
35...............	2.16	2.46	2.70	3.00	3.60	4.50
30...............	1.85	2.10	2.31	2.57	3.09	3.86
25...............	1.54	1.75	1.93	2.14	2.57	3.22
20...............	1.23	1.40	1.54	1.71	2.06	2.57
15...............	.93	1.05	1.16	1.29	1.54	1.93
10...............	.62	.70	.77	.86	1.03	1.29

Daytime

:30 Cost	CPM at Average Audience Rating Levels				
($000)	11	9	7	5	3
9..........................	$1.26	$1.54	$1.98	$2.78	$4.63
8..........................	1.12	1.37	1.76	2.47	4.11
7..........................	.98	1.20	1.54	2.16	3.60
6..........................	.84	1.03	1.32	1.85	3.08
5..........................	.70	.86	1.10	1.54	2.57
4..........................	.56	.69	.88	1.23	2.06
3..........................	.42	.51	.66	.93	1.54
2..........................	.28	.34	.44	.62	1.03

Source: Prepared by the Media Department of Ogilvy & Mather, Inc., 1973.

time network 30-second spot costing $45,000 with an estimated rating of 25 will result in a CPM of $2.78.

As useful as the CPM formula can be, it is often abused. First, it may be assumed that costs are the dominant consideration in media selection, whereas any of the other considerations mentioned thus far could be of great importance, especially selectivity in reaching target markets. Furthermore, notice that the denominator of these formulas is circulation, readership, or viewership, none of which is modified to ascertain the number of prospects reached. A CPM of $2.83 could easily be a CPM for prospects of $20 because of inefficient coverage of the target market. Thus formulas of this type should be used only when the denominator is refined to generate *cost per thousand prospects reached.*

Finally, it can be difficult to interpret CPM figures under certain circumstances, as Bogart points out:

As it is conventionally calculated, cost per thousand represents an average which treats all impressions alike, regardless of whether they are delivered to different people or repeated to the same people. So long as the value of a repeated message is assumed to be equal to that of a message which is delivered for the first time, cost per thousand automatically gives an apparent advantage to a medium which reaches a concentrated audience over and over again.[27]

It is possible, for example, to arrive at the same CPM with 10 percent of the people reached 10 times, 100 percent reached once, or 1 percent reached 100 times.

It can be concluded, therefore, that CPM must be used with caution. Cost efficiency is a useful criterion *only* when the other considerations mentioned in this chapter have also entered into the analysis. Even then it is only one criterion of an adequate media schedule, not the ultimate criterion, as many falsely assume.

QUALITATIVE MEDIA CHARACTERISTICS

The term "qualitative characteristics" has come to assume several possible meanings.[28] It is confined here to "the role played by the medium or vehicle in the lives of the audience; with the audience member needs fulfilled by the medium or vehicle; and with the positive or negative attitudes toward it and its advertising created by the medium or vehicle in its audience."[29] This definition stresses the meaning of the medium to its readers, viewers, or listeners.

Qualitative values defy precise measurement and analysis, and existing data are sparse. Yet it should be clear that these characteristics form the mood in which advertising is received, and the resulting significance can exceed that of other factors which enter into media strategy. For instance, favorable attitudes toward a television personality can increase the effectiveness of advertising on that program by as much as 21 percent.[30]

As of this writing there are no continuing data sources which can be used to assess the qualitative media characteristics across media classes. Rather, the analyst must rely on isolated research reports[31] and his own judgment. One especially useful study was undertaken by Douglas Tigert in which he assessed differences in lifestyle profiles of the audiences of

---

[27] Bogart, *Strategy in Advertising,* p. 257.

[28] William M. Weilbacher, "The Qualitative Values of Advertising Media," *Journal of Advertising Research,* Vol. 1 (1960), pp. 12–17.

[29] Ibid., p. 13.

[30] Roger Barton, *Media in Advertising* (New York: McGraw-Hill Book Co., 1964), p. 254.

[31] See for example "A Twelve Months' Study of *Better Homes and Gardens* Readers."

53 magazines falling into 13 related groupings.[32] *Reader's Digest,* for example, is the magazine of the establishment—people very interested in their community with little understanding of the problems of today's youth. The readers of *Newsweek* differ substantially from the readers of *Time* in that they look more for security, worry more about government and union power, read the Bible more, have somewhat old-fashioned tastes and habits, are very concerned about health, and have a strong negative attitude towards advertising. Through imaginative use of factor analysis, Tigert has demonstrated that qualitative data can be collected across media and that clear-cut differences exist.

 Other studies have appeared from time to time, but most are suspect in that biases in methodology too frequently appear to guarantee results that are favorable to the sponsor. In reality, few constructive steps have been taken to provide the necessary qualitative media information. The only recourse usually must be to unaided judgment. Judgment, moreover, frequently will suffice. It is intuitively obvious, for instance, that the editorial environment and subjective values of the reader of the *Atlantic Monthly* are such as to be incompatible with the advertising of washday detergents. In other situations, however, the qualitative considerations will not be obvious, and the need exists for more and better data. Fortunately, in this situation also, there is no serious methodological barrier to needed research.

DISTRIBUTION REQUIREMENTS

Distribution geography and stimulation of reseller support are considerations which easily can become dominant in certain situations.

Distribution geography refers to the density of distribution. Strictly national media would not be utilized if distribution were spotty across the country; local newspapers, radio, or television would represent a more economical media array. Promotional strategy also may call for heavy emphasis upon dealer cooperative advertising whereby the dealer places local advertising paid for in part by the manufacturer. Media choices in these cases are confined to local media by necessity, for the market reached by national media usually would substantially exceed that of the dealer. An identical situation is present when the manufacturer places advertising over the dealer's name without reliance on co-operative sharing of costs.

Promotional strategy will at times dictate heavy reliance on personal selling to gain retail distribution, and advertising may be used as a door opener. It often is very effective for the company salesman to point out to the retailer that his product has been nationally advertised

---

[32] Tigert, "Psychographic Profile."

in a prestigious medium; the pulling power of the advertisement thus becomes secondary to its role as a selling point to dealers. The sponsorship of network television programs and placement of advertisements in large-circulation magazines are popular strategies for this purpose.

Finally, it frequently is appropriate to advertise in consumer media for the sole purpose of stimulating dealer efforts. The Pepsi-Cola Company, for instance, sponsors such television spectaculars as the Miss America Pageant solely to serve as a rallying point for bottlers and a stimulus for greater efforts on their part.[33] Network television otherwise is of relatively minor importance in Pepsi-Cola's national media strategy.

SCHEDULING

Once the media to be used have been selected, it is necessary to determine the timing and allocation of advertising insertions. Of special importance are (1) scheduling by geographical region, (2) seasonal scheduling, (3) flighting (concentration of efforts in restricted time periods), and (4) scheduling within a chosen medium (size and location of insertions).

Geographical Scheduling

When the determination of geographical market potential was discussed in Chapter 9, it was indicated that it is necessary to determine an *index of relative sales possibilities* on a market-by-market basis. This index in turn serves as the foundation for geographical allocation of advertising dollars. The general principle is to allocate in proportion to market potential, all other things being equal.

Figure 12–8 presents the geographical selectivity of the media plan for a convenience food item. Notice that allocations were made so that the schedule closely paralleled the index of brand use by county size.

The data in Figure 12–8 provide only a very general indication of geographical selectivity. In addition, the agency utilized a computer program which permits media selection in proportion to market potential for each major metropolitan market. In this case the projected percentage of sales in a given area became the target figure for total advertising impressions as well. Estimates were made of the necessary impressions for the entire fiscal year. These figures then were converted into gross rating points per week, from which required dollar expenditure levels were estimated. In some cases judgmental modifications were made

---

[33] Nugent Wedding and Richard S. Lessler, *Advertising Management* (New York: Ronald Press Co., 1962), p. 370.

FIGURE 12–8

**Geographical Selectivity of the Media Plan for
a Convenience Food Item**

Country Size	Percentage in Sample Studied	Percentage of Users	Index of Brand Use (base 100)	Geographi- cal Selec- tivity of Media Plan*
A.......... 39.5%	52.0%	132	130
B.......... 26.1	28.0	107	100
C.......... 18.0	15.0	83	100
D.......... 16.4	5.0	30	40

* Combination daytime television and three women's magazines.

when it was deemed advisable to ensure that certain markets should receive greater media weight than others. Finally, a computer printout
compared original objectives for advertising impressions with actual
media delivery. Some of the results were as follows:

Market	Target Impressions	Media Weight
Portland, Maine	1.7	1.5
Albany, New York	2.2	1.9
Milwaukee, Wisconsin	2.5	1.8
Los Angeles, California	11.2	11.9
Toledo, Ohio	.9	1.1

Notice, first of all, that there was not an exact correspondence between
target objectives and actual media weight, but the differences were so
small as to be negligible. Also, the media schedule was evaluated in terms
of GRP delivered, not the number of dollars spent. The dollar figure is
not necessarily a good measure of *advertising message weight*, which can
only be estimated from audience ratings.

Seasonal Scheduling

Because many products show seasonal variations in demand, the advertiser is compelled to introduce appropriate modifications in the timing
of advertising throughout the year. In some instances media weight is
placed immediately prior to a seasonal upsurge so that maximum sales
are generated at the beginning of the season. The promotion of air-
conditioning or heating equipment is a good illustration. In other instances funds are allocated so that increases or reductions coincide closely
with sales patterns.

In the convenience food example, there were some slight seasonal variations in sales of the product. As the following data show, the media plan coincided closely with seasonal patterns:

Quarter	Percentage of Sales		Percentage of Media Weight	
June......................	26%	} 55%	34%	} 57%
September................	29%		23%	
December.................	24%	} 44%	22%	} 43%
March....................	21%		21%	

Flighting

At times media planners are forced to concentrate dollar allocations in certain time periods while cutting back at other times. This is referred to as flighting, and it is done to avoid spending at an inadequate level throughout the year. The objective is to achieve higher reach and frequency levels in a more limited period with the hope that the impact generated will carry over in the remaining periods.

Consider, for example, the data in Figure 12–9. Substantially higher

FIGURE 12–9

Effect of Flighting on Reach and Frequency Levels

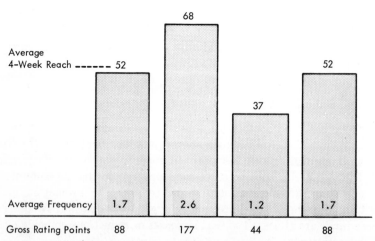

Source: Paul M. Roth, *How to Plan Media* (Skokie, Ill.: Standard Rate & Data Service, Inc., 1968), p. 10–4. Used by special permission.

reach and frequency levels are generated when the advertising is concentrated in 26 weeks rather than spread over 52 weeks.

Paul M. Roth claims that flighting offers the following advantages:

1. There are media rate and purchasing values such as better prices or discounts to be gained by concentrating ad dollars rather than spreading them.
2. There are communications values in concentrating advertising impact. A consumer awareness threshold may be crossed which is impenetrable at light advertising levels.
3. The availability of greater funds in shorter periods of time opens up new media strategy possibilities.[34]

The first claimed advantage is rather apparent in that discounts increase in proportion to the concentration of dollars within a medium in a limited time period. Similarly, the third advantage can be a significant consideration in that a greater variety of media opportunities often can be presented. The second point, however, is more debatable. Obviously a greater short-run impact can be made, but this may be at the sacrifice of continuing reinforcement during the interim periods. The net effect, therefore, can be the opposite of what is intended, especially if competitive efforts are strong.

Flighting is probably most useful when available funds are inadequate to sustain a continued effort at adequate levels. Indeed, at times it may be the only feasible strategy when it is considered that spending at an unduly low level may result in little or no impact in view of competitors' efforts.

Scheduling within Media

In media scheduling it is necessary to specify both the size of the space or time unit to be purchased and the location within the medium. These issues have been extensively researched, and it is now possible to advance a number of generalizations.

Size of the Advertisement.   The numerous studies of size of the advertisement on the printed page have made it clear that doubling size will not double results. In fact, readership increases roughly in proportion to the square root of space increase.[35] This does not mean, of course, that a half page should necessarily be preferred over a full page. Size offers real advantages in greater power of attraction, more flexibility in layout arrangement, and greater opportunity for dramatic use of space

---

[34] Roth, *How to Plan Media*, pp. 10–16.
[35] Barton, *Media in Advertising*, p. 109.

elements. Moreover, the impact of larger space units on *attitude* may be greater, although existing evidence is not clear on this point.

It is interesting to raise the question of relative impact of the small pages used in *Reader's Digest* versus other periodicals with greater page areas. A Gallup-Robinson study undertaken for *Reader's Digest* determined that size is important only in relation to other pages in the medium.[36] The absolute difference in page size between media was found to be of no significance.

The relative advantages of variations in the length of television or radio commercials defy generalization, although it is well known that longer commercials are often preferred for the reason that creative presentation is simplified when time pressures are not acute. The shorter commercial is usually more demanding to produce, but the rising costs of television time in particular have forced many advertisers to abandon the longer advertisement. Harry McMahan and others have stated that the shorter commercial can be equally effective if proper care is taken to prepare a direct and convincing appeal.[37] In fact, 30 seconds can be *too much* time for some messages, and the shorter 10-second commercial can be more effective.

Position of the Advertisement.   From the numerous studies documenting the role of position on the page in printed media, the following generalizations have emerged:

1. It makes little difference whether the advertisement appears on the left- or right-hand page in either newspapers or magazines. The analysis of readership of the Million Market Newspapers, for example, presents this conclusion unmistakably.[38] In fact, Starch has concluded from 40 years of research that the primary factor in readership is the advertisement itself—what it says and how it says it.[39]
2. In magazines, the greatest readership is usually attracted by covers and the first 10 percent of the pages, but beyond this the location of the advertisement is a minor issue.[40]
3. Page traffic is high in nearly *all* parts of a newspaper, and position within the paper is of little significance.[41]

[36] Lawrence G. Ulin, "Does Page Size Influence Advertising Effectiveness?" *Media/scope,* July 1962.

[37] Harry W. McMahan, "Advertising in the Television Age," seminar sponsored by the Columbus, Ohio, Advertising Club, December 5, 1963.

[38] See "Position in Newspaper Advertising: 2," *Media/scope,* March 1963, pp. 76–82.

[39] "How Important Is Position in Consumer Magazine Advertising?" *Media/scope,* June 1964, pp. 52–57.

[40] "Position in Newspaper Advertising: 2."

[41] "Position in Newspaper Advertising: 1," *Media/scope,* February 1963, p. 57.

4. Although position does not appear to be a crucial factor, some advantage accrues to the advertiser if the copy is located adjacent to compatible editorial features. Most newspapers and magazines attempt to ensure compatibility, and it can be specified by the advertiser for extra cost.

5. Thickness of the magazine has been found to exert only a slight effect on coupon returns and advertising recognition and recall.[42]

6. A number of other generalizations result from a series of analyses of newspaper readership:

   a. Position in the gutter (the inside fold) is no different from position on the outer half of the page.

   b. Position on the page has little effect except when competing advertisements become especially numerous.

   c. Some advantage accrues if the upper right-hand position is purchased.[43]

   d. There are known differences in readership by sex and age of different editorial features such as general news and sports.

It thus appears that position on the newspaper or magazine page and location within the issue are minor considerations. There can, of course, be significant exceptions to these generalizations, but the advertisement itself appears to be the determining factor in high readership or coupon return.

Position in broadcast advertising has been researched to a lesser degree, at least insofar as published literature shows. It is known from the meager published evidence, however, that commercials frequently perform better when inserted as part of a regular program rather than at the station break, which often becomes cluttered.[44] Location within a program seems to be especially advantageous for longer commercials, although the Schwerin Research Corporation has documented many examples of successful spot commercials. It also is felt by many that commercials at the beginning and end of a program are placed at a disadvantage because of the clutter of program announcements, production and talent credits, and other distracting nonprogram material.[45] If this disadvantage appears to be important, the sponsor purchasing time on a participating basis would do well to specify insertion within the program. Others feel that program commercial position is of no consequence,[46] and this issue is yet to be resolved.

---

[42] "Position in Newspaper Advertising: 2."

[43] "Position in Newspaper Advertising: 1."

[44] Barton, *Media in Advertising,* p. 255.

[45] "End-of-Show Ads Lose Viewers: Eaton to ANA: Not so, Say Vedder, Gromer," *Advertising Age,* June 22, 1964, p. 1 ff.

[46] Ibid.

COMPUTER MODELS IN MEDIA SELECTION

Since the early 1960s increasing attention has been directed toward the potential uses of computer models in selection of advertising media. Unfortunately the overly optimistic claims of certain early proponents of the computer have introduced a marked note of skepticism within the industry that persists as of this writing. It is fair to state that the payout from use of the computer has not lived up to initial expectations. Nonetheless, considerable progress has been made, and it is the purpose of this section to cover the nature and application of three types of computer models which have seen the greatest use: (1) linear programming, (2) iteration, and (3) simulation. Others such as dynamic programming,[47] nonlinear programming,[48] and heuristic programming[49] also have been utilized experimentally but appear to offer less promise insofar as application to media strategy.

Linear Programming

In 1963 Batten, Barton, Durstine & Osborn placed full-page advertisements stating that "Linear Programming showed one BBD&O client how to get $1.67 worth of effective advertising for every dollar in his budget." At the very least this was a gross overstatement, but considerable interest has been generated in the linear programming (LP) model, and it is examined here in greater depth than iteration and simulation.

The LP Model. Linear programming is intended to derive maximum values for a linear (straight-line) function, given certain constraints on the decision space. When applied to media selection, the model[50] takes the following general form:

Maximize:

$$\text{Total exposure} = \sum_{i=1}^{I} R_i X_i$$

Subject to:

$$\sum_{i=1}^{I} C_i X_i \leq B$$

---

[47] For an illustration see Richard B. Maffei, "Planning Advertising Expenditures by Dynamic Programming Methods," *Industrial Management Review*, Vol. 1 (December 1960), pp. 94–100.

[48] See Dennis H. Gensch, "Computer Models in Advertising Media Selection," *Journal of Marketing Research*, Vol. 5 (November 1968), pp. 414–24.

[49] See A. M. Lee and A. J. Burkhart, "Some Optimization Problems in Advertising Media," *Operational Research Quarterly*, Vol. 11 (September 1960), pp. 113–22.

[50] David B. Montgomery and Glen L. Urban, *Management Science in Marketing* (Englewood Cliffs, N.J.: Prentice-Hall, 1969), p. 144.

Where:

$X_i \leq L_i$

$X_i \geq 0$ for $i = 1, 2, \ldots, I$

X_i = Number of insertions in medium i

C_i = Cost per insertion in medium i

B = Total advertising budget available

L_i = Physical limit on insertions in medium i

R_i = Rated exposure value of a single insertion in medium i

The computation routine consists first of dividing each R_i by C_i to derive the rated exposure value per dollar. Then the objective is to select the medium which returns the highest rated exposure value per dollar (R_i/C_i) and purchase as much as is possible, given the limits imposed by B (advertising budget) and L_i (the total number of possible insertions, say, 12 issues of a monthly magazine). Then the solution proceeds to the medium with the next-highest rating and continues until a media schedule is chosen which maximizes the objective function, subject to the constraints imposed.

The steps in a well-conceived LP media allocation procedure are as follows:

1. Establishment of a target market objective.
2. Procurement of data on the audience profiles of various candidate media.
3. Application of an effectiveness rating procedure encompassing at least two phases: (a) audience profile match and (b) analysis of qualitative considerations.
4. Determination of the objective function in terms of rated exposure values per dollar.
5. Quantification of all constraint conditions, including budgetary limits, limits on media availability, and judgment, with respect to the maximum number of insertions desired in certain media.
6. Application of an LP computational routine.
7. Analysis of the resulting media plan to determine its sensitivity to changes in the constraint condition which are applied as well as changes in the rated exposure values of various candidate media. This will require a series of LP computations so that resulting changes can be isolated.
8. Selection of the final media plan on the basis of judgment as to which solution seems most appropriate in terms of stated objectives.

Advantages of Linear Programming.   The LP approach described above is valuable because it:

1. *Forces Definitions of Markets to be Reached.* Instead of guesses or hunches, data must be developed which characterize markets along

several dimensions. The computer, in other words, forces a precise definition of markets, which should be done in any event.

2. *Requires Quantification of Qualitative Factors.* Editorial climate and related considerations are subjective factors, yet they cannot usually be disregarded in media selection. The LP approach specifically requires management to cope with these considerations.

3. *Establishes a Clear Need for Audience Data.* It was previously mentioned that media audience data were only fragmentary, prior to the use of computers in media selection. Once LP came into use, however, the need for good data became painfully evident, and today's sophisticated media data services are a manifestation of that need.

4. *Can Be Applied to Problems with a Variety of Media.* There is no reason why LP cannot be applied to all media, assuming the availability of data. This makes it possible to consider a greater number of candidate media at any given time than would be the case without use of a computer.

5. *Allows the Blending of Many Factors.* As one authority points out:

In the past we have worked at it with stubby pencils and people, many people. However, no matter how much time and how many people, we have had too many factors to contend with. The real advantage of an electronic computer to us then—its principal purpose—is to give us an opportunity to change these relationships, to juggle with them, to work with them while at the same time keeping all of them in the forefront of the operation and to end up with an effort that examines the whole, not individual pieces of media . . . the way, incidentally, our customers view the campaign that we're putting together.[51]

Limitations of Linear Programming. The following limitations of linear programming should be recognized:

1. *The Assumption of Equal Effects for Repeat Exposures.* It is assumed that successive purchases in various media all contribute the same response value. Is it reasonable, however, to expect that the response to the 19th exposure is equivalent to the 1st? In all likelihood the response by the prospect will diminish after many exposures, thus introducing nonlinearity into the response function. Strictly speaking, LP is no longer applicable unless it is reasonable to assume that the response function is linear. It is possible to make the objective function nonlinear through a procedure called piece-wise approximation, but this has not found widespread use.[52]

---

[51] Herbert Maneloveg, "Linear Programming," paper from the 1962 Regional Conventions, American Association of Advertising Agencies, 1962.

[52] Douglas B. Brown and Martin R. Warshaw, "Media Selection by Linear Programming," *Journal of Marketing Research,* Vol. 2 (February 1965), pp. 83–88.

2. *The Assumption of Constant Media Costs.* At the present time LP must be used on the assumption that media costs are constant and that no discounts are granted for multiple space or time purchases. This is unreasonable, in that earned discounts can be considerable. Introduction of discounts, however, would make the cost function nonlinear, and LP then would not be applicable.

3. *The Danger of Fractional Time or Space Purchases.* The Simplex method, the basic LP computer algorithm, will not guarantee the purchase, for example, of full pages in magazines. What is the advertiser to do when the answer calls for 5.31 pages in *Ladies' Home Journal?* Is he safe in rounding the figure to 5.00 or 6.00? What will this do to the media schedule insofar as maximizing the objective function is concerned? Probably it is reasonably safe to round the answer to the nearest integer. The only feasible way to guarantee nonfractional purchases, however, is through use of integer programming, which, to the authors' knowledge, has yet to be successfully applied in media strategy.

4. *Solutions Determined without Consideration of Audience Duplication.* Obviously one cannot be certain that the solution given by the computer is optimal in terms of unduplicated audience. There is no way in which the problem of audience overlap can be handled with present computer algorithms.

5. *The Illusion of Definiteness.* The resulting solutions can give a misleading illusion of definiteness. It must never be overlooked that the solution is only as good as the data and the assumptions on which it is built. The computer will only compound any inherent weaknesses.

Evaluation of Linear Programming. In a thorough analysis of the practical problems associated with the use of LP in media selection, Frank M. Bass and Ronald T. Lonsdale concluded that "Linear models are crude devices to attempt to apply to the media selection problem. The linearity assumption itself is the source of much difficulty. Justifying an assumption of linear response to advertising exposures on theoretical grounds would be difficult."[53]

The linearity assumption thus introduces a distinct note of artificiality into the media selection generated. Some have felt that the resulting solution still is superior to any that can be chosen strictly on the basis of human judgment without the aid of a computer. Others have abandoned LP in the hope of finding more fruitful approaches. There have also been some modifications which have reduced the disadvantages cited here.

---

[53] Frank M. Bass and Ronald T. Lonsdale, "An Exploration of Linear Programming in Media Selection," *Journal of Marketing Research,* Vol. 3 (May 1966), p. 179.

Iteration Models

Media scheduling has made limited use of iteration models, in which the approach is to bring one medium at a time into the solution, depicted in the flow diagram in Figure 12–10.

Notice that the medium with the lowest cost per thousand prospects is selected first. Then remaining media vehicles are adjusted to show net unduplicated audience from the vehicle or vehicles already selected.

FIGURE 12–10

Flow Diagram for the Iteration Model

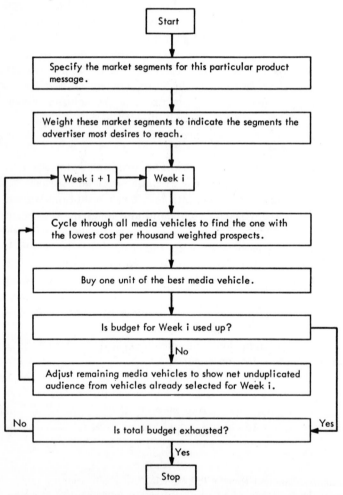

Source: Used by special permission from Dennis H. Gensch, "Computer Models in Advertising Media Selection," *Journal of Marketing Research,* Vol. 5 (November 1968), p. 416.

The process continues until the budget is exhausted. Among the models embodying this approach are the high assay model of Young & Rubicam,[54] the media schedule iteration model of the Standard Rate & Data Service,[55] and the Mather model.[56]

While the iteration model is not hampered with the linearity assumption of LP it has the disadvantage that it cannot guarantee an optimum or "best" solution, given stated constraints. This is because the computer algorithm is progressively limited as each medium is chosen. It cannot compute the value of different combinations of media because of the necessity of starting with the highest rated medium and proceeding to the next accordingly. While the first vehicle in the solution might be optimum, there is no guarantee that an optimum solution will result with two or more media candidates.

There are certain other limitations which also should be noted: (1) the model does not specify the timing of advertising, (2) the criterion function is too limited for a general model, (3) the model does not make use of integrated television and magazine audience data, and (4) there is no way in which advertising in past periods can be taken into account.[57]

Simulation

Simulation models are designed to assess how a given media schedule or group of schedules will affect a target market. The approach in effect consists of storing the characteristics of a number of individuals in the computer and then evaluating their probable response to the media input. Three different approaches to simulation are in fairly widespread use: (1) the CAM model, (2) the Simulmatics model, and (3) COMPASS.

The CAM Model. In 1964 the London Press Exchange began operational use of its Computer Assessment of Media (CAM) model.[58] It simulates the process by which individuals are exposed to both magazine and television advertisements. Viewing data are provided in four-week segments by Television Audience Measurement Ltd., and the data are converted into probabilities of viewing over the period of a year. Similar

---

[54] William T. Moran, "Practical Media Models: What Must They Look Like?" speech given at the Advertising Research Foundation Midwest Conference, Chicago, November 1962.

[55] P. W. Wenig, "Media Schedule Operations," *Data,* Vol. 1 (December 1964–April 1965), pp. 16–24.

[56] P. I. Jones, *The Thompson Medals and Awards for Media Research, 1965* (Kent: Tonbridge Printers, 1966), pp. 106–7.

[57] Gensch, "Computer Models in Media Selection," p. 418.

[58] Simon R. Broadbent, "A Year's Experience of the LPE Media Model," in *Proceedings, 8th Annual Conference* (New York: Advertising Research Foundation, 1962).

steps are taken on magazine data supplied by the National Readership Survey. Then the individuals in the two samples are carefully paired off so that television viewing and magazine reading patterns are assigned to each individual. These data are then stored in a computer.

Next a target audience for a campaign is selected and weighted. A perception value is assigned to each media vehicle, which attempts to assess the impact an advertisement will have on the viewer or reader in terms of exposure. This is further weighted by variations in prestige and influence from one publication to another. A final series of weights called impact weights is then assigned to assess the impact of the message on the person who sees or views it.

The model makes use of a single score which describes how much advertising an individual will receive. The probability of receiving an impression (PRI) is computed as follows:

PRI = Adjusted probability of seeing or viewing the media vehicle × perception × selectivity × impact.

Media schedules then are run, and a single score is produced from the simulated response of the sample of individuals which serves as the criterion for choosing between media schedules.

The Simulmatics Model. The Simulmatics Corporation stores information on nearly 3,000 imaginary individuals representing a cross section of the U.S. population four years of age and over. Data are included on socioeconomic characteristics as well as media exposure habits. As with the CAM model, the simulated audience is exposed to an actual media schedule. Modifications are introduced to account for habit formation, saturation with too many of one type of medium, and so on. The summary statistics depict the probable viewing or listening audience and the extent of their exposure.[59]

COMPASS. Ten large advertising agencies have retained a consulting firm to develop a simulation model referred to as COMPASS (Computer Optimal Media Planning and Scheduling System). No details have been made public.

Evaluation of Simulation. Simulation offers the unique advantage of realism in that an attempt is made to depict the actual behavior of an audience when exposed to a media schedule. It is possible to include data on forgetting, duplication, discounts, nonlinear responses, and so on. Thus, at least conceptually, simulation is a meaningful forward step.

One of the main difficulties, however, is that knowledge of actual advertising response is so fragmentary that these models may be assuming

---

[59] See "Simulmatics Media-Mix: General Description and Technical Description," (Simulmatics Corp., New York, 1962).

an unrealistic degree of precision and exactness. In other words, actual media exposure habits may deviate substantially from those that are assumed to exist.

Another limitation is that results are confined only to exposure (i.e., reach and frequency). There is no way to measure the probable persuasive response. This, of course, is a disadvantage shared by all computer models. Finally, simulation models cannot generate an optimum solution. It is possible to evaluate a given set of schedules, but the number of trials necessary to generate an optimum would be excessive. Therefore, an assist is provided in determining only a satisfactory but not optimum media schedule.

The Role of the Computer in Media Strategy

Has the computer lived up to expectations? The limited use made of computer models to date is one indication that the potential is yet to be realized.[60] Nevertheless, few are prepared to dismiss the computer's role in media scheduling, because the experimentation over the past decade has led to some solid gains.

First, many agencies and advertisers are making effective use of the computer in storing and retrieving audience information. For the first time it is possible to make sophisticated use of data on reach, frequency, gross rating points, cost per thousand prospects and so on, for a wide variety of media. While this is largely a data processing function, the payoff in more precise media selection has been great indeed.

Another adventage has been the growing demand for more and better audience data. The media information services have in large part experienced greatest growth since the advent of the computer.

Finally, there is every reason to expect that the computer models discussed here and others yet to be devised will overcome many of the present limitations. As Leo Bogart points out:

There will inevitably be further growth in the application of mathematical models to the solution of marketing and advertising problems. The deficiencies of existing models are to be found not in the limitations of data on markets and audiences, but in the lack of clarity with regard to the basic processes of advertising communication. No doubt the demands of the model builders will stimulate experimental research by bluntly posing questions that have always been asked, but hitherto easily evaded.[61]

---

[60] For figures on the extent to which the computer is used see "Marketing Managers Prepare for an Era of Sophisticated Data Processing," *Sales Management* July 1, 1969, pp. 64–65.

[61] Leo Bogart, "Where Does Advertising Research Go from Here?" *Journal of Advertising Research,* Vol. 9 (March 1969), p. 6.

SUMMARY

This chapter has investigated a number of factors which enter into media strategy, including requirements of creative strategy, audience selectivity, reach and frequency, competitive considerations, cost efficiency, qualitative factors, and distribution requirements, and scheduling.

Clearly it is impossible to present a conclusive set of steps leading to successful media selection in every problem. To do so would be to oversimplify relevant issues to an unrealistic degree. Media selection requires *research thinking* in that information must be sought at many points in the analytical procedure and utilized creatively and imaginatively. The considerations outlined above represent most of the major variables shaping the selection problem. A myriad of solutions is possible, depending entirely on these situational requirements. Fortunately, computer methods can now come to the aid of the media planner.

REVIEW AND DISCUSSION QUESTIONS

1. In what ways, if any, can ABC and BPA data be used in the media selection process?

2. What are the advantages of having continuing data on advertising exposure across media? What are the difficulties faced in providing such data?

3. Here are the gross rating point levels delivered by three different media plans: 267; 192; and 400. What do these figures mean? All other things being equal, which of the three plans probably would represent the best media buy?

4. The advertising agency for the Crummy Candy Company has submitted a media plan with the statement that "this plan is designed to achieve maximum frequency; reach is of little importance." The campaign is aimed at the market under 25 years of age, and the product being advertised is a popular chocolate bar which now has second place in market share in most local markets. Is frequency a desirable strategy for this type of product?

5. How can the media plan mentioned in question 4 be designed so as to achieve maximum frequency? What changes might be necessary if greater reach were desired?

6. For what types of products is "share of mind" likely to be an important consideration?

7. Magazine A gives a cost per thousand of $4.91; magazine B, $7.12; and magazine C, $8.38. Which of these magazines is the best media buy for the Simmons Mattress Company?

8. Refer to the description of the differences between qualitative characteristics of *Newsweek* and *Time* readers. Assuming that these descriptions are accurate, what types of products would best be advertised in *Newsweek?*

9. For what types of products is geography of distribution likely to be a significant consideration in media choice?

10. Under what circumstances would it be appropriate to allocate media *not* in proportion to the index of relative geographic sales possibilities?

11. Flighting is often used when introducing new products. What advantages are offered? What are the disadvantages?

12. The problem of commercial clutter has caused many to leave television for other media. What can the television industry do to overcome this problem?

13. What is meant by the linearity assumption of linear programming? Describe in detail the effects this assumption has on the applicability of this technique in media strategy. Are there any ways in which it can be overcome?

14. How would you answer the claim that linear programming gives "$1.67 worth of value for each $1.00 invested in advertising"?

15. What is meant when it is said that iteration and simulation are not optimizing models? Is this an advantage or a disadvantage?

16. Evaluate the various computer models and state which, if any, you feel offers the greatest future promise. Why? What questions remain to be answered?

13

The Advertising Message

BECAUSE THIS TEXT is concerned with basic considerations in promotional strategy, relatively little attention has been focused on methods of *execution* of that strategy. This is because execution generally is based on decision rules which are unique to a given set of circumstances. In keeping with this philosophy, this chapter is not intended to instruct the reader on how to design advertisements and write copy. In the first place, there are few if any general rules to be advanced for this purpose. Second, those responsible for determination of strategy may not be writers or designers, who are specialists employed for their ability to execute the strategy in written and verbal form. Much of their skill is an intuitive creative ability that those responsible for basic marketing and promotional strategy usually do not possess to the same degree. For those who are interested in methods of execution, the appendix to this book provides a brief overview of approaches to copy and layout.

This chapter begins with a review of the basic considerations in what is generally referred to as creative strategy. Then the subject of creative execution is approached through consideration of trends in advertising appeals and the manner in which they are presented. Thus the reader should gain a basic appreciation of the factors which differentiate a good message from a poor one, a topic discussed under the heading of analysis of the message.

CREATIVE STRATEGY

Creative strategy is based on two of the objectives discussed in Chapter 9: (1) proper definition of market target, and (2) a statement of message content.

Definition of Market Target

Definition of market target is the key to media selection, as has been stressed in the preceding chapters. It also enters into creative strategy in a significant way, since it is necessary to inform writers and designers of the types of people who are expected to be exposed to the message. This is especially critical in that those who must execute the message are usually not a cross section of the consuming public they set out to persuade. A study made by the Psychological Corporation in 1965, for example, showed that the average television viewing time of advertising executives was one and one quarter hours per day, roughly half that of the average consumer.[1]

A statistical definition of the market, however, is not a sufficient guide for creative strategy. It is of relatively little value, for example, to tell the copywriter that the user of Salvo detergent makes over $10,000 a year, lives in a metropolitan area, has fewer children than average, and is a working wife. But it is necessary to document users' lifestyles. What are the interests which compete for the time of the working woman? How does she view the time spent in doing the family wash? It was an analysis of activities, interests, and opinions which led the Procter & Gamble Company to initiate the "active woman" campaign which stresses the convenience offered by Salvo.

Statement of Message Content

It also is necessary to specify the basic substance of the message to be communicated. This often is stated in fairly broad terms so that artists and writers can determine details. This type of statement is referred to as the creative platform or purchase proposition.

The creative platform generally is based on research which answers the following types of questions:

1. What are the features that are unique to the product or brand?
2. What criteria are used by consumers in evaluating alternative brands?
3. What is the brand image in comparison with competitors—i.e., what are the brand's strengths and weaknesses?

The platform itself should feature first the basic promise (the product benefits). It also must provide support for the product claims, making certain that the unique benefits of the brand are featured, as the following examples indicate.

Contac.[2] When introduced in the early 1960s, Contac was a remarkable sales success. Its introductory advertising featuring the "tiny time

---

[1] Leo Bogart, *Strategy in Advertising* (New York: Harcourt, Brace & World, 1967), ch. 3.

[2] Ken Roman and Jane Maas, "Creative Secrets for Advertisers" Ogilvy & Mather, Inc., New York, 1973, p. 7.

pills" served to stimulate substantial word of mouth and subsequent sales. Contac began to lose ground to other cold remedies, however, especially those with such special features as nighttime relief. It reversed that trend by returning to its unique introductory positioning, which stated the claim that "Contac is the only product which allows 24-hour continuous cold relief." Its position as the market leader was reestablished through the reinforcement of this product benefit.

Purina Dog Chow.[3]   Consumer research undertaken by the Purina Company disclosed that dog owners wanted a pet food to be palatable, nutritious, economical, and convenient to store. A new dry dog food was developed, and in taste tests it was found that dogs preferred it 6 to 1.

It was initially thought that creative strategy should emphasize nutrition as the primary benefit, with palatability stressed to a lesser extent. This was because nutrition had proved to be the biggest selling point of other feeds in the Ralston line, and it also was the main claim of competitive dog foods.

Sales seemed to be up to expectations, but management was not satisfied. Consequently, further research was undertaken which focused on how the owner felt about his dog as opposed to what he expected in a new food. It was found that his main concern was whether or not the dog would really eat a given food. If he would not do so, nutrition was irrelevant.

With these findings it was determined that the following creative platform should be established: "New Purina Dog Chow makes dogs eager eaters." Since other companies featured nutrition, Purina was able to capture a large market share, which it still maintains.

Clark's Teaberry Gum.[4]   When the Philip Morris Company acquired the Clark Gum Company in the early 1960s, the largest selling item in the line was Teaberry, but Clark had never attained national distribution. It was the objective of Philip Morris to institute a line of national brands, with Teaberry as the featured item.

Three leading companies dominated the gum industry, with Wrigley taking the lion's share. Most of the approaches to advertising in the past had featured flavor. It became apparent to management that these flavor claims had in effect been preempted by competitors and that Teaberry could not succeed with a "me too" emphasis.

The eventual creative strategy was based on the insight that there is no necessary reason to emphasize why one brand is better than another.

---

[3] Noel Digby, "Purina Dog Chow: All You Add Is Love," paper presented at Central Region Convention, American Association of Advertising Agencies, October 14, 1966.

[4] Jim Shymkus, "Moment of Truth for Clark's Teaberry Gum," paper presented at Central Region Convention, American Association of Advertising Agencies, November 11–12, 1968.

It was found that most consumers do not evaluate gum brands in this way and decided that the strategy should concentrate on establishing awareness for the Teaberry flavor in such a way that people were left with pleasant and memorable thoughts about the product.

At about this time Herb Alpert had captured public attention with the Mexican Shuffle. The creative group arrived at the insight that the creative objective possibly could be achieved by a shuffle or jig implying that something happens when you taste Teaberry gum. Eventually the "Teaberry Shuffle" was used along with the phrase: "Have a little fun . . . try Clark Teaberry Gum." Teaberry sales rose more than 300 percent between 1965 and 1968.

Evaluation of Cases.   Obviously no precise formula was followed to arrive at these successful but very different creative platforms. Rather, insight was gained from knowledge of how the product is used, the desires satisfied, unique product features, competitive claims, and so on. The result was a strategy which differentiated each product and supported its claim with clarity.

CREATIVE EXECUTION: TRENDS IN ADVERTISING

While a correct strategy is essential to advertising success, this research in itself will never prove to be sufficient. There comes a point at which the strategy must be executed into the message. It is here that the creative ability of the writer or designer comes to the fore.

What is creativity? According to Webster something is created when it is produced, formed, or brought into being. True creativity is *not* undisciplined imagination. Controls and discipline may be highly subjective, personal, perhaps subconscious, almost secret or covered up with a facade of "absolutely no control," but this does not mean that they do not operate powerfully in the creative personality. Creative work is largely conscious, deliberate, and *disciplined*. It is disciplined by the objective toward which it is directed and by the information and experience upon which it is based. First the creator hunts for new information and details and arranges them into a pattern through discipline of his thought processes. The creative process at each step is the same, whether the discovery is made as a contribution to science, music, technology, art, advertising or some other area of interest. Rules or syntax can be developed, thereby keeping imagination within its most productive bounds.

There are some who at least implicitly imply that the creative result is hampered if imagination is constrained or inhibited in any way. As a result, "anything goes." Not surprisingly, emphasis is placed on approaches which are different or novel, primarily for the sake of being different. Novelty can, of course, provide a unique quality which causes one advertisement to stand out from others, but it is easily carried to extremes. As Edward N. Cole, former President of General Motors, points out: "Too much advertising today tries to be cute instead of making sense."[5] Cole is saying, in effect, that the true role of advertising is being sacrificed for the sake of novelty.

Part of the reason for the regard for novelty lies in the reward system which focuses on *how the advertisement is executed* rather than on the *results* in terms of consumer response. Consider Afred Politz's argument:

Let us imagine that the copywriter proposes an entirely efficient piece of copy for his client. This copy consists of simple language and uncluttered, straight-forward sales presentations—without gimmicks, tricks, or intellectual surprises—copy equipped with the most ingenious and most invisible device of *letting the product impress the listener or reader* [italics provided]. The client reviews the copy and, before approving it, happens to think, "This copywriter does not seem to be using his imagination. He talks only about the product itself, and does not add anything of his own." So, the copywriter not only goes unrewarded for his efforts but is actually rebuked for failing to show "imagination."[6]

At the minimum, an advertisement must "break through the noise" level and attract attention. This obviously is not sufficient in itself, however. Politz points out that the headline "Your Father in the Cesspool" would almost certainly attract attention.[7] It is imaginative in one sense, yet it is the product of questionable reasoning and cannot be regarded as anything more than a creative gimmick. Hence it is not creative in the true sense of the word, because the headline also must contribute to the objectives set for the message.

Real communication does not occur until the message is correctly comprehended, retained, and acted upon by members of the target market in the manner specified in the statement of advertising objectives. Results which fall short of this signify that true creativity was not achieved in the execution process.

This is not to deny the significant role played by the intuition and skill of the writer and designer. Comprehensive objectives provide the boundaries for creative work; they do not guarantee advertising success any more than staying within the sidelines of a football field guarantees a winning performance. Indeed, intuition and imagination are required, and it is this subjective element which differentiates ordinary advertising from great advertising.

---

[5] "Car Ads are Off Beam, GM's Cole Advises Four A's," *Advertising Age,* November 10, 1969, p. 8.

[6] Alfred Politz, "The Dilemma of Creative Advertising," *Journal of Marketing,* Vol. 25 (October 1960), p. 4.

[7] Ibid.

The Quest for Decision Rules

What distinguishes between a well-conceived and executed advertisement and those that are ineffective? Are there decision rules which can be followed? This question is of fundamental importance, and the answer can best be provided by consideration of some of the trends of recent decades.[8]

As recently as the 1930s little attempt was made to measure advertising effectiveness, and there obviously were no decision rules. The Great Depression led to demands for research, however, and industry settled for methods which documented readership or listenership (attraction of attention and, to a lesser extent, comprehension and retention). This gave rise to the "readership-listenership era" (1940–1960).

One generalization which quickly loomed above all others was that highest readership is captured by advertisements which resemble the editorial matter of the publication in which they appear. Since *Life* magazine dominated the 1940s, this meant that highest readership resulted when messages paralleled its easy-to-read short copy and predominantly visual style. Other appeals found to be highly effective were emphasis on service (i.e., provision of recipes, information on health and disease, and so on), humor, emotional writing, before-and-after demonstrations, and cartoon strips.

From the vast body of findings on readership and listenership, a number of so-called creative rules have been developed. Some of these appear in Figure 13–1. Much was learned from the research into readership and listenership that still is finding use today, but nevertheless some problems remain. In the first place, some who misinterpreted the proper use of research guidelines produced advertising copy which was routine, stilted, and stereotyped. At the same time, a proliferation of competing brands began to hit the market, especially after World War II, with the result that competition through advertising became intensified. Finally, there were some who wrongly assumed that attracting and holding attention was a sufficient condition for persuasive success. For these reasons and others, concern was increasingly focused on the persuasive impact of the message itself.

The 1960s saw the onset of the currently widespread tendency to challenge any social rule or tradition. Openness to change and emphasis on "doing your own thing" began to be reflected in all phases of life, and advertising was no exception. To the surprise of many, it was discovered that many of the established rules could be violated with outstanding results.

---

[8] Many of the concepts suggested here were suggested by William D. Tyler. See "Tyler Views Trends in Magazine Advertising of the Past 30 Years," *Advertising Age,* October 20, 1969, p. 94 ff.

FIGURE 13–1

Representative Findings Based on Readership-Listenership Studies

Headlines
1. Headlines should appeal to reader's *self-interest,* by promising her [or him] a benefit. This benefit should be the basic product promise.
2. Don't worry about the *length* of the headline—12-word headlines get almost as much readership as 3-word headlines.
3. Inject the maximum *news* into your headlines.
4. Include the *brand name* in every headline.

Copy
1. Don't expect people to read leisurely essays.
2. Avoid analogies—"just as," "so to."
3. Make the captions under your photographs pregnant with brand name and sell.
4. Be personal, enthusiastic, memorable—as if the reader were sitting next to you at a dinner party.
5. Tell the truth—but make the truth fascinating.

Visualization
1. Put "story appeal" in your illustration.
2. To attract women, show babies and women; to attract men, show men.
3. Illustrations should portray reward.
4. Use photographs in preference to drawings. They sell more.

Television Commercials
1. Make your *pictures* tell the story. What you *show* is more important than what you say. If you can't *show* it, don't say it.
2. In the best commercials, the key idea is forcefully demonstrated.
3. Repeat the brand name as often as you can.
4. Make the product itself the hero of the commercial.
5. Start *selling in the first frame.*
6. Use close-up pictures instead of long shots.

Source: David Ogilvy, "Raise Your Sights! 97 Tips for Copywriters, Art Directors and TV Producers—Mostly Derived from Research" (internal publication, Ogilvy & Mather). Reproduced with special permission.

Rules can place undue constraints on creative imagination if they are followed in rigid fashion. Because this was recognized by many artists and writers, they were open to approaches which were suited to changing times.

The Rush to the Behavioral Sciences

Prior to and during the readership-listenership era, teachers and academic researchers in advertising turned to the behavioral sciences in the hopes of finding new insights. The propaganda studies during World War II and the intriguing communication research at Yale under C. I. Hovland and his students made the prospects seem indeed good. Evidence was rapidly accumulating, for example, on the effects of a one-sided versus two-sided presentation, fear appeals, primacy versus recency, rational versus emotional appeals, source credibility, persuasibility, and a host of other areas.[9]

Not surprisingly, nearly every marketing and advertising book from the late 1940s until the present has dutifully quoted this evidence. The presumption is that important clues are provided for advertising practice. The only problem is that few, if any, advertisers have come to the same conclusion. In fact, this body of evidence has, for the most part, been ignored. Does this imply a kind of naive provincialism on the part of the advertising industry? The authors do not think so. Instead, we feel that the naiveté is on the part of those academics who so glibly assessed the "implications" of this research without proper critical analysis.

An example may indicate the difficulty of borrowing from this type of research. In 1953 Irving L. Janis and Seymour Feshbach indicated that a communication stressing the unfavorable consequences of not following a suggested course of behavior (a "fear appeal") can have an adverse effect on attitude change if this fear appeal is too intense.[10] This early study stimulated well over 100 additional studies, most of which have produced a contradictory result, thus indicating that a fear appeal perhaps can be a good strategy.[11] This even led to a *Journal of Marketing* article chiding the advertiser for overlooking fear appeals.[12]

How should an advertiser of, say, fire insurance view this evidence? Should a fear appeal be utilized? The evidence cited scarcely would support such a conclusion, for a number of reasons:

1. Most of the underlying research has been undertaken in artificial laboratory circumstances in which exposure to the message is non-voluntary. Hence there is little or no correspondence of the findings to real-world situations.[13]
2. The purposes of these studies usually were significantly different from those of the advertiser. Often the goal was to find better ways of in-

---

[9] For a recent review see M. Fishbein and I. Ajzen, "Attitudes and Opinions," in P. H. Mussen and M. R. Rosenzweig (eds.), *Annual Review of Psychology*, Vol. 23 (Palo Alto, Cal.: Annual Reviews, Inc., 1972), pp. 188–244; also James F. Engel, David T. Kollat, and Roger D. Blackwell, *Consumer Behavior*, rev. ed. (New York: Holt, Rinehart & Winston, 1973), ch. 14.

[10] Irving L. Janis and Seymour Feshbach, "Effects of Fear-Arousing Communication," *Journal of Abnormal and Social Psychology*, Vol. 48 (1953), pp. 78–92.

[11] This literature is thoroughly reviewed in Brian Sternthal, "Persuasion and the Mass Communication Process," unpublished doctoral dissertation, The Ohio State University, 1972, ch. 4.

[12] M. Ray and W. Wilkie, "Fear: The Potential of an Appeal Neglected by Marketing," *Journal of Marketing*, Vol. 34 (1970), pp. 59–62.

[13] Carl I. Hovland, "Reconciling Conflicting Results Derived from Experimental and Survey Studies of Attitude Change," *American Psychologist*, Vol. 14 (1959). pp. 8–17.

doctrinating people using face-to-face procedures. Furthermore, the topics considered usually deviated substantially from those in the domain of the advertiser.

3. The citation of evidence and "implications" in the marketing literature often overlooks important limitations and qualifications. In the case of fear, for example, what differentiates a fear appeal from a nonfear appeal? This question seldom has been addressed, and it leaves the comparability of findings open to challenge. Furthermore, most marketing writers have overlooked the latest evidence that the effects of fear are moderated by source credibility. That is, fear has a positive effect on attitude only if the communication source is perceived as credible.[14] From earlier chapters it should be obvious that advertising rarely has the necessary degree of credibility. For these reasons alone it is unwise to claim that advertisers have an "overlooked opportunity."[15]

One could extend this type of analysis to the primacy versus recency issue or any of the other areas of investigation mentioned above. The basic conclusion is that the majority of this evidence is totally devoid of empirical support under realistic field conditions, and therefore it is unwise to generalize from such a shaky base. The most that can be gained is a tentative indication of a persuasive approach that *might* work under certain circumstances. This is not to suggest that the behavioral science literature is of no value. Rather, it makes a plea for proper interpretation and applications.

A Balanced Contemporary Approach

The readership-listenership era underscored the importance of attention attraction. Contemporary advertising makes legitimate use of the guidelines which resulted, in that attracting and holding attention is now viewed as a necessary but not sufficient criterion of success. In addition, there has been some heuristic value resulting from the search of the behavioral sciences, although the practical payout to date has been minimal.

The Changed Environment of the 1970s. Contemporary advertising, of necessity, centers more on the attainment of persuasive results. More than ever, the audience is the focus, and there are some good reasons for this, including: (1) the consumer revolt against advertising, (2) legal attacks, and (3) management insistence on accountability.

THE CONSUMER REVOLT. Recent studies conclusively document a growing public disdain toward advertising. S. A. Greyser has shown that

---

14 See Sternthal, "Persuasion and Mass Communication."
15 Ray and Wilkie, "Fear."

nearly 30 percent of all advertisements are disliked, and the greatest negative response is with people between 18 and 34.[16] The practices most frequently singled out are (1) undue repetition, especially of detergent and proprietary drug advertisements; (2) irrelevant product appeals; (3) provision of inadequate information to assist in buyer decision making; and (4) insulting or even degrading advertising scenarios.[17]

This revolt certainly has been accentuated by the growing noise level referred to in Chapter 4. Television is usually considered to be the worst offender. The 30-second commercial, for example, means that the viewer is now exposed to more than 15 commercials per hour, double the level of the middle 1960s. Harry W. McMahan points out that only 1 viewer in 6 can recall who sponsors commercials, and 1 in 12 credits the average commercial to a competitor.[18] The consumers' response ranges from apathy to outright disdain. The upshot is that television is not the salesman it once was, and there is no doubt that the successful case histories of 1965 do not apply today.

The consumerism movement also has added fuel to the fire. One company after another has been singled out for such offenses as the relatively minor charge of insulting the consumer to the much more serious offense of outright deception. Consumerism is discussed in depth later; nothing more need be said here other than to point out that consumer skepticism has legitimately grown by leaps and bounds, partly, at least, as a result of these disclosures.

LEGAL ATTACKS. Chapter 8 reviewed the nature of the current legal attack on advertising. It does not need to be restated here other than to note the obvious conclusion that creative execution is likely to receive detailed public scrutiny. No longer can it be said that "anything goes." Literal truth is increasingly demanded, and it is probable that the criterion of truth will become the comparison of message content *as perceived by the consumer* with objective product features. Great caution must be followed in creative execution, therefore,[19] and review by competent legal counsel is a wise procedure.

INSISTENCE ON ACCOUNTABILITY. For years certain members of the advertising community claimed that success or failure could not be measured. Times have changed, however, and management is now insisting on accountability for performance. Creative strategy and execution

---

[16] Slether A. Greyser, "Irritation in Advertising," *Journal of Advertising Research,* Vol. 13 (1973), pp. 3–10, and "Advertising: Attacks and Encounters," *Harvard Business Review,* Vol. 50 (1972), pp. 22–36.

[17] *Grey Matter,* Vol. 44 (March 1973).

[18] Harry W. McMahan, "Television, the Great Salesman, Isn't Working Like It Used to," *Advertising Age,* January 3, 1972, p. 24 ff.

[19] See Roman and Maas, "Creative Secrets," for a particularly meaningful discussion of legal requirements.

must be based on concrete, measurable objectives, and this fact, in itself, exerts valuable discipline on the creative process.

Adapting to the Changed Environment.   Contemporary advertising is characterized by some trends which are worthy of note. It is not possible to capture the entire contemporary scene in a few pages, but the following are especially prominent: (1) the consumer dialog; (2) greater use of likable, entertaining appeals; (3) provision of meaningful product information; and (4) avoidance of excessive repetition.

THE CONSUMER DIALOG.   In the past consumers were exposed to much advertising which was not really directed to them. This was because of the wide audience reached by the media, especially television. There is a distinct trend away from *broad*casting, however, to *narrow*casting. Cable television, for example, permits much greater segmentation. This will serve to reduce the noise level and to permit "fine tuning" of content to reach the consumer in a more meaningful fashion.

At the same time it has become apparent that advertising which creates rapport with the consumer is likely to produce much better results. There is no doubt that *"how* a company speaks to its customers in its advertising conveys its *feelings* towards them."[20] Consumer attitudes toward brands and companies are in turn affected by the advertising they see and hear. The company that employs irritating jingles, trite and contrived "slice of life" scenarios, and other forms of execution which are inappropriate for the lifestyles of members of the target market is a prime target for consumer disapproval.

In short, it is increasingly obvious that the advertising message must be carefully positioned with respect to the *psychographic* characteristics of its customers. This extends to situational portrayals, music, appearance of characters, and language used.

Greater response also is generated by advertising which talks *with* the consumer rather than *at* her.[21] Notice how frequently the word "you" appears in a sampling of headlines from advertisements which appeared in a recent month:

Two-table test proves New Enriched Formula Pledge gives you hand-rubbed wax beauty instantly

What they do with tomorrow depends on what you give them today

You have good reasons to apply for a Bank-Americard right now

May all your sours be Galliano sours

The nice little things you can have with an Olds wagon

Hotpoint suggests five things to look for before you buy a washer

Sweeten up your holidays

---

[20] *Grey Matter,* Vol. 44 (March 1973).

[21] Ibid.

Can you tell which is hamburger and which is Top Choice?

The KitchenAid Trash Compactor. Neatest way yet to unclutter your kitchen.

The dialog is further enhanced by emphasis on people's reactions to products. The early days of television featured what is often referred to as "brag and boast" commercials. Strong hard-sell claims were made, but this approach is becoming less effective for the reason that many consumers are legitimately wary of anything which connotes hypocrisy. The reaction is likely to be, "Why should I believe you?" One way to circumvent this skepticism is to highlight reactions to products and brands in the form of testimonials. Name personalities were used for this purpose in the 1920s and 1930s, but the current trend is toward greater use of ordinary people in the hope that the authenticity of the spokesperson will lend credibility to product claims.

LIKABLE AND ENTERTAINING APPEALS. An adage of an earlier era was that advertising does not have to be liked to be effective. Undoubtedly there is truth to this in that it is not the purpose of advertising to entertain. But it is equally erroneous to allege that what the consumer thinks of the message and its execution is irrelevant. Today's consumer is increasingly screening out advertising he deems to be obnoxious, irrelevant, or dull. Therefore, increasing attempts are being made to create likeable and entertaining appeals.

Some of the most entertaining messages appear in the form of a "cool" commercial. Cool commercials are unstructured; they tell the viewer a fragment of the story or invoke impressions so that the viewer must fill in from his own imagination. They are most appropriately used to build a long-range image; when a product has no demonstrable advantage; when competitors are running hot commercials; and, of greatest importance, when appeals are primarily emotional rather than logical (cosmetics are an example). The television storyboard in Figure 13–2 provides an illustration. The "hot" commercial, on the other hand, is more structured and tells the viewer a complete story logically and sequentially. The Robert Burns commercial in Figure 13–3 is built around a distinct product benefit that can be visually demonstrated, with the result that the more structured approach is effective.

It should be stressed, however, that a message does not have to be humorous to be entertaining. While there are some undeniable benefits to humor,[22] a great many casualties have been due to it as well. One of the most enjoyable campaigns, for example, was the prize-winning "Excedrin Headache" campaign. It soon was dropped and the company returned to a straight product benefit appeal for the reason that sales

---

[22] Brian Sternthal and C. S. Craig, "Humor in Advertising," *Journal of Marketing,* Vol. 37 (1973), pp. 12–18.

FIGURE 13–2

A Cool Commercial

OGILVY & MATHER INC.

2 EAST 48 STREET, NEW YORK 10017
MURRAY HILL 8-8100

Client:	GENERAL CIGAR
Product:	TIJUANA SMALLS
Title:	"CENTRAL PARK"
Commercial No.:	OM21-0219-60C
Date Approved:	11/21/69

1. (SILENT)

2. SINGER: (VO) Tijuana Smalls.

3. It's something new, baby,

4. for you, baby.

5. You know who you are.

6. It's a little cigar -

7. Tijuana Smalls.

8. Things that you do, baby,

9. that's you, baby.

10. You know who you are.

11. It's a little cigar -

12. slim and mild.

13. Tobacco that's aged like wine -

14. slim and mild.

15. And you know who you are.

16. Tijuana Smalls. It's something new, baby,

17. for you, baby. You know who you are...

18. ANNCR: (VO) Tijuana Smalls -

19. for you, baby. You know who you are.

20. (SILENT)

Used with the permission of the General Cigar Company.

FIGURE 13–3

Hot Commercial

OGILVY & MATHER INC.

2 EAST 48 STREET, NEW YORK 10017
MURRAY HILL 8-6100

Client: GENERAL CIGAR
Product: ROBERT BURNS
Title: "GRAND BANKS"
Commercial No.: OM21-0209-67-60C
Date Approved: 1/10/68

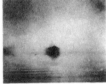

1. (MUSIC)

2. (MUSIC)

3. (MUSIC)

4. (MUSIC)

5. SCOTSMAN: Something's happened to Robt. Burns !

6. (SFX : DOGS)

7. (SFX)

8. Something's happened to Robt. Burns !

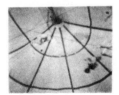

9. ANNCR: (VO) Everything's happened to Robt. Burns!

10. Outside, the new Golden Glove --

11. an airtight foil wrap

12. that keeps Robt. Burns cigars fresh as the day they were made.

13. Inside that Golden Glove,

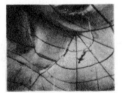

14. new cigars with a new mild flavor

15. that comes from a totally new blend

16. of rich tobaccos.

17. (SFX)

18. New cigars -- new air-tight wrap -- No wonder you'll hear ...

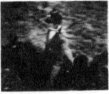

19. SCOTSMAN: Something's happened to Robt. Burns!

20. ANNCR: (VO) Isn't it time Robt. Burns happened to you? (MUSIC OUT)

Used with the permission of the General Cigar Company.

dropped severely. Humor can inhibit persuasion unless it is properly used. As a result, most authorities recommend against its use, except in unusual circumstances.[23]

MEANINGFUL PRODUCT INFORMATION.   The volume of competitive products on the market has led consumers to become outspoken in their demands that advertisements provide information which is useful in product buying decisions. Considerable use is made of all types of demonstrations and believable claims based on objective presentation of product benefits. The mere listing of product attributes is not enough, however. These attributes will be seen by the consumer as significant only when they demonstrably meet the demands of his or her evaluative criteria for that specific decision. Low-calorie beer, for example, died an early market death for the reason that product attributes were not perceived as offering consumer benefits.

AVOIDANCE OF EXCESSIVE REPETITION.   Repetition is a fundamental tenet of learning theory, and there is a large amount of evidence documenting the fact that repetition can enhance message reception (awareness and comprehension), retention, attitude change, and behavioral change.[24] Repetition, however, is one of the primary causes of consumer complaints, and there is no question that this strategy can be carried beyond the point of optimum response. When there has been undue repetition, the message is said to be satiated or worn out. Greater attention must now be paid to "wearout" to minimize the consumer revolt, and it is by no means easy to evaluate.

Each message performs in a unique manner, and no generalizations on the relationship between performance and wearout are possible. Some implications can be cited from the body of research findings, however, such as these:

1. Repetition aids consumer learning and hence can be effectively utilized at the start of a new campaign.
2. Repetition can help establish products or brands that are new to a particular medium.
3. A pool or group of commercials should not wear out as quickly as a single commercial, given the same frequency of exposure.
4. When it is not possible to produce a number of varied commercials, introduce several claims within the message to lengthen the learning process.
5. When several commercials are produced, introduce significant variations, or are they likely to be perceived as the same and hence wear out more quickly.
6. A commercial with humor or a single point wears out quickly.
7. Commercials for infrequently purchased products wear out more slowly

---

[23] Roman and Maas, "Creative Secrets."

[24] Much of this evidence is cited in Engel, Kollat, and Blackwell, *Consumer Behavior*, ch. 14.

for the reason that only a fraction of the audience are prospects at any given point of time.

8. The greater the time span between repetition, the longer a message can be run.
9. A message can be reintroduced after a period of absence from the air and hence be perceived as new.
10. Wearout is greatest among heavy television viewers.
11. If the budget is limited, a single commercial spread out over a period of time may produce greater learning than airing of a pool of commercials.
12. Commercials that involve the viewer wear out more slowly than those with a straightforward message.
13. Copy testing predicated on a single exposure can shed little light on wearout.
14. Performance must be tracked over time to assess wearout.
15. Only good commercials wear out—those that are ineffective to begin with will lose nothing.[25]

It is obvious that wearout must be monitored in the course of a campaign. This is easiest to do in terms of awareness. Once knowledge of, say, a brand name or product attribute peaks, serious consideration should be given to change. Changes in positive versus negative reactions can be monitored for the same purpose.

Implications of Trends in Advertising

This has not been an exhaustive listing of trends in advertising execution. Rather, an attempt has been made to illustrate some of the appeals, copy styles, and visual approaches which are becoming dominant. Notice how they embody adaptation to significant socialcultural trends. The creative person, therefore, must be an analyst of contemporary society if efforts are to be effective. An ability must be developed to translate observations and research findings into copy and layouts. Thus imagination is disciplined, but it is not straitjacketed by arbitrary guidelines.

ANALYSIS OF THE MESSAGE

From what has been said thus far the reader may conclude that it is impossible to differentiate a good advertisement from a poor one. Yet there comes a time when such a decision must be made so that time or space can be bought. In part this evaluation must be made on the basis of informed judgment, and some use also is usually made of copy tests (pretests).

---

[25] A. Greenberg and C. Suttoni, "Television Commercial Wearout," Reprinted from the *Journal of Advertising Research*, Vol. 13 (1973), p. 53. © Copyright (1973), by the Advertising Research Foundation.

Judgmental Analysis

This section will present some general criteria which can be used to evaluate both strategy and execution and then suggest some more detailed considerations which pertain strictly to execution.[26]

General Criteria. A new type of coffee, Maxim freeze-dried, was introduced by the General Foods Corporation in the middle 1960s. It proved to be a genuine success and was the trend setter in this product category. One commercial from the introductory campaign is reproduced in storyboard form in the three pages of Figure 13–4. A decision had to be made without extensive market evidence as to which of several alternative commercials should be aired. What criteria should be utilized for this purpose?

The most important factor to consider is whether or not the commercial is "on strategy," i.e., does it execute the creative strategy effectively in terms of appealing to the target audience and registering the message specified in the copy platform? The strategy here was to appeal to all coffee users (especially to users of ground coffee) and to promise perked coffee flavor in instant form. The regular coffee user is attracted in this commercial, first of all, by the frequent use of the percolator. The promise of perked coffee is stressed in nearly every frame with both pictures and words such as "It was discovered that freshly-brewed coffee could be frozen." The promise, in turn, is supported by stress on freeze-drying, a product feature which was unique to Maxim at the time of the introductory campaign. Therefore, in these general terms, it appears that this commercial is "on strategy."

Evaluation of Execution. An advertisement should be *memorable* in that it attracts and holds attention. It also must register its intended message and hence achieve its *persuasive* objective. The following types of questions are useful in assessing whether both memorability and persuasiveness have been achieved:

1. *Does the picture tell the story?* Given the large volume of competing advertising, no message has more than a fraction of a second to attract and hold the consumer's attention. Thus the visual portion of the message must register the message, without sole reliance on words.
2. *Are the words appropriate?* Do they communicate product benefits in terms that are meaningful to the target audience?
3. *Is one clear theme registered by the total advertisement?* Rarely will attention be held for a sufficient period to register more than one or two ideas, so the emphasis must be on a single-minded presentation of message theme.

---

[26] See Harry W. McMahan, "24 Questions to Help You Evaluate Your Commercials," *Advertising Age,* June 11, 1973, p. 49; also Roman and Haas, "Creative Secrets."

FIGURE 13–4

The Maxim Announcement Commercial

FIGURE 13–4 (continued)

FIGURE 13-4 (*concluded*)

Used with the permission of General Foods, Inc.

4. *Is the brand name registered?* Many times the brand name is not stressed, with the result that the reader or viewer fails to associate message and product.

5. *Is the tone appropriate?* In other words, is the style of message appropriate for the product? Demonstrations are best used with unique product attributes that can be illustrated. When this is not the case, the tone or impression left may interfere with the intended message. Humor is more appropriate when no unique product benefits are present; other times it may be entertaining but ineffective.

6. *Is the advertisement distinctive?* Does it stand out from the noise? The dangers of novelty have been stressed, but a message must have an element of distinctiveness in view of mass media clutter.

The Maxim commercial meets these guidelines rather well. Its visualization stands by itself because words are not required to register the message. The words, however, focus on product benefits, and the result is a single-minded registration of the "perked-flavor" theme. The viewer is also attracted by the promise of benefits in the very first frame, and the brand name is registered quickly and repetitively without carrying repetition to excess. The tone is serious and authoritative, as an announcement commercial ordinarily should be. Finally, there is distinctiveness in both the newness of the product itself and in the visualization of the freeze-drying process.

Thus not only is the Maxim commercial, generally speaking, "on strategy," but the execution appears to be effective. Obviously these conclusions are based on judgment, and there is considerable room for error. In the final analysis, the message cannot be fully evaluated apart from pretest research, and General Foods found that this was an effective commercial.

Copy Testing

It is obvious that a point is reached where reliance on judgment is insufficient. For this reason, use is made of pretests (or copy tests, as they are more frequently referred to in the trade). In a recent survey of leading advertisers, 61.6 percent indicated that advertisements are regularly pretested, and another 9.2 percent plan on instituting this type of research.[27]

Many approaches are used for copy testing, most of which are discussed in the next two chapters. The most frequently used procedure, however, is some type of recall test. Prospects are shown the message, usually under realistic reading or viewing conditions, *prior to* the invest-

---

[27] *The Gallagher Report,* Vol. 21 (November 26, 1973).

ment of funds in commercial production or purchase of time and space. Small samples of prospects generally are recruited, and sample size rarely exceeds 100.

Recall of content can mirror with reasonable accuracy the extent to which the message was correctly comprehended by the prospect. The following examples of successful pretesting point up the ability of research to:

1. *Catch omissions or misunderstandings.* A Johnson's Jubilee advertisement was worded "Wash Your Kitchen with Wax." Women were found to conclude that this wax could be used on floors, a definite misconception. Revised appeals specifically excluded reference to floors and avoided public relations problems.

2. *Determine the attention value of illustrations.* An appeal for Swift's baby foods featured a mother and baby, and an alternative version pictured only the baby. Mothers with babies out for a stroll in a park were shown each version, one in the right hand and one in the left. The version reached for first was deemed to attract the most attention, and the picture of the baby alone was preferred by three out of five mothers.

3. *Check comprehension of specific phrases.* A Swan liquid detergent commercial stated that "Dishwashing is for the Birds." Questions on the meaning of this phrase in several parts of the country disclosed a 76 percent miscomprehension.

4. *Prevent mistakes.* An All commercial was headlined "Wouldn't I be Dumb . . ." Ratings of liking versus dislike disclosed that the word "dumb" was inappropriate.

5. *Check the appropriateness of an illustration.* A picture of a man was presented to consumers and they were asked to indicate the mood he was in, using an attitude scale composed of such adjectives as "worried-unworried." The mood connoted was found to be ideal for its purposes.[28]

Use is also made of persuasion tests. Most procedures comprehend an assessment of changes in attitude or intention resulting from advertising exposure. In the final analysis, this type of measurement attains greatest significance, because it centers on response itself. Comprehension, on the other hand, is necessary but does not guarantee successful persuasion.

It would appear that the benefits from copy testing would be sufficient to justify its use by all advertisers. This is not the case, however, for several reasons:

---

[28] P. C. Nahl, "Speedy, Inexpensive Pretests of Ads—Capsule Case Histories," *Proceedings, Fourth Annual Conference* (New York: Advertising Research Foundation, Inc., 1958), pp. 49–58.

1. Recall and persuasion tests do not always succeed in discriminating good messages from poor messages. The reason may lie in the measuring instruments used, because others report high success in predicting successful copy from pretests.[29]
2. Small sample research often is suspect. In other words, some question the use of small judgmental samples. The justification, however, is that responses usually are found to converge in a fairly stable pattern after approximately 50 to 60 interviews. Thus little is gained from the extra expenses of large samples, assuming, of course, that the smaller sample is representative of the target market.
3. Some feel that creativity and copy testing are incompatible. This justification has little merit, because creative imagination can produce *ineffective* copy. In reality, many artists and copywriters do not want to be held accountable for the productivity of their output. Part of the difficulty is that some managements use copy tests as a "report card." A better approach is to give artists and writers possession of copy-testing results with the option to use them as they see fit and to reveal or not to reveal the results.

The authors feel, on balance, that the arguments for copy testing outweigh the arguments against it. The objective is not to find a definitive measure of communication success. The presently available methodology will not justify such a goal. Rather, all that can be provided is a good indication of whether or not copy will be comprehended and responded to as intended. While this does not guarantee production of a good advertisement, *it substantially lowers the risk of failure*. At the very least, copy tests will differentiate a poor message from a good one if properly used. What they cannot do definitively at the present time is to distinguish a *good* message from a *great* one. This type of fine discrimination awaits further methodological development.

SUMMARY

This chapter began with a distinction between strategy and execution. The fundamental issues concerned with creative strategy were reviewed in the first section, and the subject of creative execution then was approached through analysis of significant trends in types of appeals used and methods of presentation. It was stressed that there are no rules which can serve as conclusive guides to effective execution. Most of the so-called creative rules are based on ways to attract and hold attention, but this is only part of the task which must be accomplished by the message. It also

---

[29] J. S. Coulson, "You Have to Ask the Right Questions," *Advertising Age,* September 30, 1963.

must achieve its intended persuasive objective, and there is no way that rules can be established for this purpose.

It also was shown by a review of relevant literature that relatively few insights are available from the behavioral sciences that can be utilized in designing and executing creative strategy.

The chapter ended with a brief review of the types of questions which can be raised in a judgmental evaluation of strategy and execution. While these guidelines can be used in differentiating a poor message from a good one, there is no substitute for pretesting through survey research.

REVIEW AND DISCUSSION QUESTIONS

1. Is the description of market targets generally used in media selection also sufficient for use in determining creative strategy? Why, or why not?

2. What factors should be encompassed in the creative platform?

3. One authority states that the brand name should be stressed in every headline. Do you agree? Why?

4. Consult advertisements from past decades beginning in 1920. What changes do you observe? From these advertisements alone, what can be said about the social changes in these decades?

5. Assume that you have been selected as one of the judges who must select the 10 best from a group of 100 television commercials. What *two* criteria would you use for this purpose? Why?

6. Some contend that research hampers the creative person and constrains his imagination. Comment.

7. What can be done, if anything, to stimulate greater use of research by advertising writers and artists?

8. Many critics contend that too much advertising today is "gimmicky" and "cute." The argument is that creative people are carried away with attention-attracting devices and are forgetting that good advertising must sell. How would you analyze this criticism?

9. Studies show that recall is the most widely used copy-testing measure. Many refuse to measure other stages of the communication process, such as attitude change. Why does this occur? What arguments could you present in behalf of attitude and/or behavior measurement?

Measurement of Advertising Effectiveness

A PERSISTENT QUESTION is whether advertising effectiveness can be measured. The response in the past was mixed, but more than two thirds of leading advertisers now utilize some type of effectiveness measurement.[1] Research orientation is becoming increasingly commonplace, largely because management is demanding proof that funds invested pay off. Measurement tools are being used with greater sophistication as new techniques are developed, although there is still room for substantial progress in the area.[2]

Figure 14–1 is a classification of the most widely used measurement methods, classified first into those most useful in measuring response to the *advertisement* itself or its contents (awareness, comprehension, liking, and so on). The second classification differentiates actual impact of the message on product awareness, attitude, or usage. These data can be gathered under either laboratory conditions in which the respondents are aware they are being measured or "real world" conditions, in which there is no awareness of the measurement process. This chapter evaluates measures which are useful both in pretesting a message and in assessing its effectiveness following its placement in the media.

ADVERTISING-RELATED LABORATORY MEASURES

Under the category of advertising-related laboratory measures are those that yield data on attention, comprehension, retention or response

---

[1] *The Gallagher Report,* Vol. 21 (November 26, 1973).

[2] See Stewart H. Britt, "Are So-Called Successful Advertising Campaigns Really Successful?" *Journal of Advertising Research,* Vol. 9 (1969), p. 9.

FIGURE 14–1

Classification of Advertising Effectiveness Measures

	Advertising Related (reception or response to the message itself and its contents)	Product Related (impact of message on product awareness, liking, intention to buy, or use)
Laboratory Measures (respondent aware of testing and measurement process)	Readability tests HRB–Singer Eye Camera Tachistoscope Binocular Rivalry GSR/PDR Salivation Consumer jury Portfolio tests	Schwerin Trailer tests Laboratory stores
Real-World Measures (respondent unaware of testing and measurement process)	Dummy advertising vehicles Inquiry tests On-the-air tests Recognition tests Recall tests Association measures Combination measures	Pre-post tests Sales tests Mini-market tests

Source: Adapted from the classification schema utilized by Professor Ivan Ross at the University of Minnesota

to the message itself in a laboratory-type research situation, as opposed to measures under real-world conditions. Nonsurvey analysis of readability is discussed first, and then a variety of approaches which primarily measure the ability of a stimulus to attract and hold attention. The usefulness of these copy-testing procedures is greatest in pretesting advertisements, as was pointed out in the previous chapter.

Analysis of Readability

Procedures are available to permit analysis of the readability of copy without consumer interviewing. The foremost method was developed by Rudolph Flesch, whose formula is in wide use.[3] The Flesch formula focuses on the human interest appeal in the material, length of sentences, and familiarity of words. These factors are found to correlate with the ability of persons with varying educational backgrounds to comprehend written material.

Readability of advertising copy is assessed by determining the average number of syllables per 100 words. These factors are then substituted into the Flesch formula, and the results are compared with predetermined

---

[3] Rudolph Flesch, *How to Test Readability* (New York: Harper & Bros., 1951).

norms for the target audience. It is usually found that copy is understood most easily when sentences are short, words are concrete and familiar, and frequent personal references are made.

Mechanical rules should not be observed to the extent that copy becomes stilted or unoriginal. The Flesch method is only a means to check communication efficiency, and gross errors in understanding can be detected and avoided. It should always be used, however, in connection with other pretest procedures.

HRB–Singer: Measurement of Visual Efficiency

The HRB–Singer Corporation, in cooperation with the advertising research department of a large corporation, has designed a procedure to measure the visual efficiency of advertisements. The measures focus on ease of recognition of advertisements at a distance, under conditions of varying light, on short versus a longer time exposure, and in competition with other advertisements.[4] With the physical apparatus, which must be used in a laboratory, the subject is seated so that he views the stimuli through eyepieces. Stimuli are presented with variations in distance from the subject, illumination, time of exposure, and under conditions where a different stimulus reaches each eye (binocular rivalry).

In a typical study with 24 students, 36 advertisements were tested, and the results were compared with readership data gathered previously. The required response from each individual was a correct recognition of the stimulus through the equipment under conditions of experimental control. The stimulus was viewed, and the subject was then asked to identify it from among a group of 36 possible advertisements mounted at his side for easy reference. For purposes of analysis, the stimuli were broken down into 47 different components appearing to describe communication potential (such as low light reflection, considerable white space, and the headline message). Recognition scores under different conditions were then compared with variations in the 47 components to determine the characteristics that enable quick and certain recognition of the advertisement.

The results indicated that 22 dimensions correlated positively with one or more of the physical tests, and a weighted combination of these dimensions permitted an accurate prediction of the communication ability of a given advertising stimulus. Of the physical measures used, the distance and binocular rivalry tests were judged to be most useful.

The HRB–Singer procedure is elaborate, and results have not been sufficiently evaluated at this time. Yet it does appear that a large step

---

[4] See *The Measurement and Control of the Visual Efficiency of Advertisements* (New York: Advertising Research Foundation, 1962).

has been taken toward understanding certain factors which lead to the physical perception of advertisements. This type of procedure or variations of it should find an increasing place in pretesting methodology.

The Eye Camera

For many years it has been possible to track eye movements over advertising copy through use of the eye camera. The route that a person's eyes follow is then superimposed on the layout to determine which parts appear to capture and hold attention and whether or not various elements are perceived in the order intended by the creative man.

Eye camera results provide a guide to aid in designing the layout so that the eye follows the intended path, but the findings contain a large degree of ambiguity. In the first place, exposure is undertaken in highly unnatural conditions, and it is questionable that resulting eye movement patterns are similar to those expected when the consumer is not looking into a large apparatus. Furthermore, eye attraction does not necessarily reflect the person's thoughts or indicate success in capturing attention. Lingering at one point may also indicate difficulty in comprehension. For these reasons, the eye camera has never achieved wide usage.

The Tachistoscope

This laboratory device is basically a slide projector with attachments enabling the presentation of stimuli under varying conditions of speed and illumination. The tachistoscope has come to be a useful tool for many advertising researchers. The Leo Burnett agency, for example, uses it to assess the rate at which an advertisement conveys information.[5] The speed of response is recorded for various elements of an advertisement (illustration, product, and brand), and it has been found that high readership scores correlate with speed of recognition of the elements under analysis. Response to visualization seems to be especially important.

About 20,000 persons are tested with the tachistoscope each year at the Leo Burnett agency.[6] The typical sample size is from 10 to 20, and no person is tested more than four times during any one year. As an indication of success, tachistoscopic measurement verified quick recognition of the Allstate Insurance Company name in an advertisement, a basic promotional objective, and the campaign built upon this finding was

[5] Clark Leavitt, "Intrigue in Advertising—The Motivation Effects of Visual Organization," *Proceedings, 7th Annual Conference* (New York: Advertising Research Foundation, 1961), pp. 19–24.

[6] Emmett Curme, "Burnett Men Get Fast Test Results via Busy Creative Research Workshop," *Advertising Age,* September 10, 1962.

felt to be highly successful. All that Burnett researchers claim, however, is measurement of physical perception; response from this point on is solely a function of the copy.

Binocular Rivalry

Various types of advertising stimuli usually compete for the consumer's attention. Very convenient examples of these are found among advertisements appearing on several adjacent billboards, packages on the shelves of retailers, and advertisements on facing pages of newspapers and magazines which contain competing messages of rival or nonrival firms. The binocular rivalry technique has been employed to measure the effectiveness of a given visual device (such as an ad or package) in relationship to its competing visual device.

The equipment used (an arrangement of plane mirrors or prisms) is designed to present two different stimuli, one to each eye, at the same time. The stimuli are viewed through a stereoscopic device with an eyepiece; they can be in the form of ads, cards, or slides. Variations in the stimuli can be controlled by itensity of illumination and duration of exposure. The basic psychological theory upon which this technique is based is: when two stimuli are given an equal chance to dominate awareness, the one exerting the greater impact tends to predominate.

It is necessary to expose respondents to several nontest stimuli to eliminate the subject with low visual acuity and color-blindness, to determine eye dominance, and to permit the respondent to become familiar with the testing situation.

The usefulness of this technique for pretesting has been reported by John M. Caffyn, who suggests that it provides both a sensitive and a reliable measure.[7] It has been shown to be a valid predictor of visual dominance—one aspect of visual effectiveness.[8]

GSR/PDR

Recent research on galvanic skin response (GSR) and pupil dilation response (PDR) indicates that these measures isolate different aspects of attention attraction.[9] GSR measures first, the decline in electrical resistance of the skin to a passage of current and second, changes in the

---

[7] John M. Caffyn, "Psychological Laboratory Techniques in Copy Research," *Journal of Advertising Research,* Vol. 4 (1964), p. 48.

[8] Ibid.

[9] J. S. Hensel, "Physiological Measures of Advertising Effectiveness: A Theoretical and Empirical Investigation," unpublished doctoral dissertation, The Ohio State University, 1970.

potential difference between two areas of body surface.[10] When GSR elevates it is felt to be an accurate indicator of *arousal* in response to a stimulus.[11] PDR, on the other hand, measures minute differences in pupil size and appears to be a sensitive measure of the amount of information or load processed within the central nervous system in response to an incoming stimulus.[12] At one time it was widely claimed that PDR measured emotional response,[13] and several published studies purported to document that it could isolate attitudinal reaction to marketing stimuli.[14] The weight of current evidence, however, makes this interpretation highly questionable.

A series of studies was undertaken at The Ohio State University using both GSR and PDR with a variety of audio and print stimuli.[15] It was found fairly consistently that there is good short-term and long-term retention when both GSR and PDR are high in response to an advertisement. In addition, there is some tentative evidence that GSR also correlates with attitude change, but this finding needs further investigation.[16]

Salivation

The Schwerin Research Corporation has patented a device which allegedly measures the rate of salivation.[17] Saliva flow is reported to change markedly when the respondent views food stimuli. This type of measurement may have some promise in assessing the relative effectiveness of food advertisements.

The Consumer Jury

Consumers frequently are asked to analyze advertisements and rate the probable success on the assumption that "if the layman is superior to the advertising expert in his conscious opinion as to the effectiveness

---

[10] Roger D. Blackwell et al., *Laboratory Equipment for Marketing Research* (Dubuque, Iowa: Kendall Hunt Publishing Co., 1970), p. 42.

[11] This literature is reviewed in Hensel, "Physiological Measures."

[12] See Roger D. Blackwell, J. S. Hensel, and Brian Sternthal, "Pupil Dilation: What Does it Measure?" *Journal of Advertising Research,* Vol. 10 (1970), pp. 15–18.

[13] Eckhard H. Hess and James M. Polt, "Pupil Size as Related to Interest Value of Visual Stimuli," *Science,* Vol. 132 (1960), pp. 349–50.

[14] See for example H. E. Krugman, "Some Applications of Pupil Measurement," *Journal of Marketing Research,* Vol. 1 (1964), pp. 15–18.

[15] These are reviewed in Hensel, "Physiological Measures."

[16] Unpublished studies at The Ohio State University under the direction of James F. Engel.

[17] *Schwerin Research Corporation Technical and Analytical Review,* May 1963, entire issue.

of an advertisement, it is only because he is a better judge of what influences him than is an outsider."[18]

In one method referred to as the order-of-merit rating, a member of the jury (usually a sample of from 50 to 100 representative consumers) is asked to rank in order a group of layouts or copy blocks usually presented in rough, unfinished form and often mocked up on separate sheets. The questions might ask, for example:

1. Which of these advertisements would you most likely read if you saw it in a magazine?
2. Which of these headlines would interest you the most in reading further?
3. Which advertisement convinces you most of the quality of the product?
4. Which layout do you think would be most effective in causing you to buy?

The questioning progresses from the second best alternative to the worst. The verdict presumably indicates the relative effectiveness of each alternative presentation.

Order-of-merit rating is of decidedly questionable value, for several significant reasons:

1. It probably is asking too much of anyone to predict his behavior during and after communication exposure.
2. Ranking of many alternatives can be exceedingly difficult, with the result that the ratings have little validity.
3. Some people have a tendency to rate one or two preferred alternatives high on all characteristics, just as they emphasize the good traits of a close friend while overlooking bad attributes. This distortion in judgment, called the halo effect, cannot be eliminated.

These problems are sufficiently serious that order-of-merit ratings usually are abandoned for more precise approaches.

A better approach is to utilize some type of rating scale to elicit intensity of preference for each stimulus. No attempt is made to provide a ranking. In one reported example advertisements were developed to influence public attitudes toward the Prudential Insurance Company and to cause people to think better of the company than of the insurance industry in general.[19] Twenty-five attitude scale statements were developed, focusing on aspects of the company and its operation. Respondents were asked to rate on a 10-point scale the degree to which

---

[18] Charles H. Sandage and Vernon Fryburger, *Advertising: Theory and Practice,* 5th ed. (Homewood, Ill.: Richard D. Irwin, 1958), p. 537.

[19] Harry W. O'Neill, "Pretesting Advertising with the Differential Attitude Technique," *Journal of Marketing,* Vol. 27 (1963), pp. 20–24.

the statements applied to most life insurance companies and then to the company whose advertisements they were viewing in disguised form, with company identity blocked out. The effectiveness of the advertisement was judged on the basis of the extent to which it induced a change in the rating of the company to make it more favorable than that for the industry. Meaningful differences were produced, and it was possible to isolate the most effective creative treatment.

The advantages of the scale are that a basis is provided to isolate dimensions of opinion; the technique is standardized and susceptible to comparison over time; it is reliable and replicable; full allowance is made for individual frames of reference; and problems of question phrasing are eased. Furthermore, determination of degrees of intensity of feeling provides a basis for ranking of alternatives and assessment of how well each performs against predetermined norms. Finally, the wording of questions reduces the danger that the individual will "play expert" and distort his opinion.

At one time consumer jury measures were used more widely than is now the case. Many experts feel that the artificiality of the questioning procedure introduces such bias that the ratings can have little validity. For this reason, more use is now made of the other measures discussed in this section as well as the real-world measures to be discussed later.

Portfolio Tests

The portfolio test method requires the exposure of a group of respondents to a portfolio consisting of both test and control advertisements. The principal criterion of effectiveness is playback of the content following exposure. The test advertisement that induces the highest recall of content presumably will be most effective in capturing and holding attention.

Portfolio tests are widely used, but vigorous attacks have been directed at the pretest use of this device.[20] One critic's contention is that recall scores can vary from alternative to alternative for several reasons:

1. Variations can enter due to interviewing errors or memory defects, although this can be true of *any* research.
2. There may be legitimate differences between advertisements.
3. Differences may arise as a result of the consumer's interest in the products being promoted.

Variation from the second source, of course, is the fundamental premise of the portfolio test, but it is felt by some that interest in the product,

---

[20] John C. Maloney, "Portfolio Tests—Are They Here to Stay?" *Journal of Marketing,* Vol. 25 (1961), pp. 32–37.

the third source, may be the most important factor. If so, the portfolio method clearly is not differentiating between advertisements on the basis of variations in creative treatment.

For the portfolio method to perform as claimed, scores on recall of the control advertisements should vary less from test to test than scores on the stimuli under analysis. Yet data have been reported to indicate this relationship does not hold true, and it appears that product interest dominates all other factors. Apparently interest in the product seems to affect memory of the advertisements viewed and thereby obscures real differences between the stimuli.

These arguments against the portfolio test are plausible. Perhaps momentary reexposure to the alternatives viewed in the portfolio would sharpen memory and minimize distortions entering from product interest.

Regardless of the danger of memory distortion, this test serves its purpose well if recall data correlate with readership scores following investment of funds in the campaign. Each user must satisfy himself that the predictive power of this device is sufficient to warrant the costs of research. On this point, the sharing of information between users is long overdue.

PRODUCT-RELATED LABORATORY MEASURES

Some techniques can be utilized under laboratory conditions to determine the effects of the message on the product or service itself, such as awareness, attitude shift, changes in buying intentions, and so on. Included in this category are the Schwerin test, trailer tests, and laboratory stores.

The Schwerin Test

The Schwerin Research Corporation has devised a means whereby changes in consumer product preference after exposure to advertisements can be assessed. Tickets are mailed to 350 respondent households in New York, London, Montreal, and Toronto; in addition, testing sessions are often held at theaters in St. Louis, Chicago, San Francisco, Los Angeles, and New Orleans. The research format is essentially the same for all testing sessions:[21] inviting people to view new television shows with commercials inserted in the usual place. A drawing is held before the showing, and each consumer is offered his or her choice of various products as gifts. Product choices are noted, and then the show and

---

[21] Patrick J. Kelly, "The Schwerin Model: How You Can Use It to Build Your Share of Market," *Printers' Ink,* May 8, 1964, p. 31.

commercials are viewed. Another drawing and offer of gifts is held after exposure, and changes in stated brand preference are noted. Written comments are also solicited on the programs and the commercials.

At first glance, it would appear that changes in stated preferences for gift products would in no way be related meaningfully to advertising exposure. Some rather dramatic conclusions, however, have been derived from the Schwerin tests.[22] Those campaigns rated as superior on the basis of changing product preferences tended to produce increases in sales as more dollars were invested in advertising. On the other hand, increased investment in inferior campaigns allegedly was found at times to *decrease* sales.

A definitive evaluation of the Schwerin procedure must await disclosure of more details of research designed for purposes of validation. Many advertisers and agency executives have voiced dissatisfaction regarding its predictive ability, although it has been successfully used by a number of firms. On the other hand, a study reported by Robert D. Buzzell concluded that preference measurements were related to short-term changes in market share;[23] this would tend to substantiate the validity of the technique for this purpose.

The Schwerin test may tap a dimension of response which enables reasonably accurate prediction of advertising success, and for this reason it is in wide use. Respondents presumably are unaware that they are rating advertisements, and the tendency toward "buyer expertise" may thus be eliminated. There also are variations of this method in use.

Trailer Tests

Respondents may be brought to a central location, often a portable trailer or van set up in a shopping center, where they are shown several advertisements with or without surrounding editorial material or programming. Usually a comparative evaluation is made of two or more executions of the same theme. Respondents are told that the product can be made to different formulations and are shown copy describing each. Then they are asked to chose between the two formulations, and questioning reveals what the commercial communicates. While the technique is artificial, it is felt by many to be a useful way to measure comprehension of copy. Furthermore, it is quite inexpensive.

---

[22] H. Schachte, "Is There a Provable Relationship between Advertising and Sales?" speech given to the Grocery Manufacturers of America in 1963.

[23] Robert D. Buzzell, "Predicting Short-Term Changes in Market Share as a Function of Advertising Strategy," *Journal of Marketing Research,* August 1964, p. 31.

Laboratory Stores

The laboratory store is a variation on the Schwerin technique described above. Respondents are exposed to advertising under various types of conditions and then are permitted to shop in a small store. Usually coupons or chits are provided which can be redeemed for actual merchandise. In this way actual product movement in response to advertising can be monitored.

ADVERTISING-RELATED MEASUREMENT UNDER REAL-WORLD CONDITIONS

Procedures used in the second major category of technique depicted in Figure 14–1, real-world measures, usually involve exposure under real-world conditions such as would normally be encountered in the consumer's home. The greater realism provided is felt by most researchers to enhance the validity of the resulting data.

This section discusses the fairly extensive group of real-world measures of response to or liking for the message itself. They can be used for both pretesting of the message prior to investment in time or space and posttesting following airing or viewing.

Dummy Advertising Vehicles

Many testing organizations use a dummy magazine for purposes of pretesting, and accurate predictions of response are possible. Editorial features of lasting interest are permanent items in this magazine; the only variations in the five yearly editions are test advertisements. Each printing is distributed to a random sample of homes in various geographical areas. Readers are told that the publisher is interested in evaluations of editorial content and instructed to read the magazine in a normal fashion. A return interview focuses on both the editorial content and advertisements. Each advertisement is scored on recall, extent of copy readership, and whether or not the advertisement induces product interest.

Using a similar procedure, Batten, Barten, Durstine & Osborn and other agencies frequently air television programs using test commercials. Respondents are interviewed shortly after the show to assess the extent of commercial recall. Similar procedures are used by some commercial research firms.

The use of dummy vehicles is subject to the same criticisms as the portfolio test, but this procedure possesses the distinct advantage that advertisements are tested under completely natural surroundings—normal exposure in the home. Recall of content under such circumstances is likely to produce a more realistic indication of advertising success.

Inquiry Tests

Inquiry tests measure advertising effectiveness on the basis of return of coupons from advertisements run under normal conditions in printed media. Different creative treatments may be compared in several ways: (1) by running them in successive issues of the same medium, (2) by running them simultaneously in issues of different media, and (3) by taking advantage of "split-run" privileges offered by some media whereby alternate copies carry different versions of the message. The split-run procedure is mose widely used, because all variables other than creative differences between stimuli are held constant.

The inquiry test can focus on a number of creative variations: (1) one advertisement versus a completely different version, (2) variations in type or other elements of the same appeal, (3) summed inquiries compared over the total run of two or more campaigns, and (4) the effectiveness of different media when the same advertisement is run in each.

The advantages are apparent in that no interviews are required, and quantitative analysis of data usually presents no problems. As a result, the costs are not excessive. This approach, however, suffers from crucial limitations. First, the presence of a coupon attracts attention to the copy for this reason alone, and true differences in creative treatment can be obscured. Second, many people may read the copy and not return the coupon. Certain people are more prone to take this action than others, and "volunteer bias" can greatly overstate or understate the true effectiveness. One must constantly remember that the problem of pretesting copy is very different from the testing of individual elements. For example, the advertising manager of International Correspondence Schools has searched extensively for pretesting techniques that can accurately predict at least the relative inquiry pull of various ads. Just as there seems to be no relationship between scores and coupon returns, none of these methods, when tested, has yielded data that would indicate any useful predictive ability.[24] Finally, coupon return bears no special relationship to advertising effectiveness, for attitude change, changes in awareness, the communication of copy points, and a host of additional responses are not tested.

It must be concluded that the disadvantages far outweigh the ad-

---

[24] For an extensive discussion of the inquiry test as employed by International Correspondence Schools, see David J. Luck, Hugh G. Wales, and Donald A. Taylor, *Marketing Research,* 3d ed. (New York: Prentice-Hall, 1970), pp. 494–505.

vantages of the coupon-return method for most purposes. The inquiry test should be used only when coupon return is the objective of the advertisement. When this is so, it is a completely valid measure of response.

On-the-Air-Tests

Some research services measure response to advertisements which are inserted into actual television or radio programs in certain test markets. The "on-the-air" test is an example. The advantages and disadvantages are identical to those encountered in the use of dummy vehicles.

Recognition Tests

The readership of printed advertisements has long been assessed using a standard technique called "recognition measurement" which was developed by Daniel Starch.[25] The Starch method is described in detail because other related procedures are quite similar.

The Nature of the Starch Method. The Starch organization annually surveys approximately 30,000 advertisements in nearly 1,000 consumer and farm magazines, business publications, and newspapers. A national sample consisting of interviews in 20 to 30 geographical areas is chosen for each study. Although the sample is not a random selection, attempts are made to parallel the circulation makeup of each medium under analysis.

Interviewers are assigned a given number of readers over 18 years of age with certain demographic characteristics in terms of income and location. Studies usually include from 100 to 200 interviews per sex, and the quota for each interviewer is fairly small.

The interview is conducted in the respondent's home. The interviewer commences by asking whether or not the particular periodical has been read prior to the interview. If the answer is affirmative, the issue is opened at a page specified in advance to guarantee that the fatigue resulting from the interview will not unduly bias advertising appearing at the back of the issue. The respondent is then asked, for each advertisement, "Did you see or read any part of the advertisement?" If the answer is yes, he or she is asked to indicate exactly what parts of the layout and copy were seen or read.

Three principal readership scores are reported:

1. *Noted*—the percentage of readers who remember seeing the advertisement.

---

[25] See "Brief Description of the Scope, Method, and Technique of the Starch Advertisement Readership Service," Daniel Starch and staff, Mamaroneck, N.Y.

2. *Seen-associated*—the percentage of readers who recall seeing or reading any part of the advertisement identifying the product or brand.
3. *Read most*—the percentage of readers who reported reading at least one-half of the advertisement.

Several additional scores are also reported:

1. *Readers per dollar*—the number of readers attracted by the advertisement for each dollar invested in space.
2. *Cost ratios*—the relationship between readers per dollar and the median readers per dollar for all half-page or larger advertisements in the issue. A "noted cost ratio" of 121, for example, means that the copy exceeded the par for the issue by 21 percent.
3. *Ranks*—the numerical ordering of readers per dollar for all advertisements, from highest to lowest.

Data are available on the readership of component parts of each layout, such as secondary illustrations, the company signature, or various copy blocks.

The Starch method is a syndicated service, and other organizations offer similar features. In addition, individual advertisers and research consultants frequently conduct private specialized readership studies.

Analysis of the Recognition Method. The recognition method, especially the Starch approach, is by far the most widely used means of measuring advertising readership. However, a growing number of criticisms of the technique have been published in recent years. These criticisms for the most part are based on significant methodological questions. The potential research pitfalls which have been reported involve (1) the problem of false claiming, (2) the reproducibility of recognition scores, and (3) sensitivity to interviewer variations.

THE PROBLEM OF FALSE CLAIMING. The interview is conducted informally, with the respondent simply being asked to indicate whether or not he or she remembers seeing a given advertisement. It has been feared that the respondent could consciously or unconsciously give a completely false reply, because no means exists to check its accuracy. Research has brought this problem into sharper perspective.

In 1956 the Advertising Research Foundation undertook its famous Print Advertisement Research Methods study (PARM). The Starch method, among others, was subjected to intensive impartial analysis. The syndicated services studied an issue of *Life* and reported readership as usual, and the PARM staff duplicated this research using a large randomly chosen sample. The readership results were then compared, and additional analyses were undertaken to shed light on the meaning of readership data.

The analysis of recognition by the PARM staff showed a surprising tendency for scores to remain stable over time.[26] In other words, the scores showed little variation as the interval between the date of the claimed readership of the magazine and the date of the interview increased. If the recognition score truly measures memory, the scores should exhibit a reliable tendency to decline over time. In one study, for example, the recognition of meaningful data was 97 percent after 20 minutes, as compared with 75 percent after two days.[27] The failure of Starch scores to show this pattern indicates the possibility that factors other than memory are dictating research findings and distorting results.

Two researchers followed through on the PARM study and published findings which suggest that interest in the product leads to substantial overclaiming of readership.[28] In addition, the PARM study found that recognition of advertisements is significantly higher among owners of the advertised produced. These results taken together suggest the strong possibility that product interest markedly distorts memory and leads to false advertising readership claims.

It has also been discovered that some people seem to have a kind of generalized trait which leads them to overclaim readership.[29] In fact, for those claiming recognition of advertisements they could not possibly have seen, the average noted score for all advertisements was 75 percent! This is referred to by psychologists as a "noting set." It is related to multi-magazine readership in that the greater number of magazines read, the greater the incidence of false claiming. There are several reasons for this tendency:

1. The respondent may genuinely feel that he has seen the advertisement, whereas in reality he has seen a similar version elsewhere.
2. The respondent may be saying, in effect, that he would expect to have seen such an advertisement in the issue, so he inadvertently gives an incorrect report.
3. Readership may be either underreported or overreported to impress the interviewer, especially if the report is seen as indicating in some way social acceptability.
4. Interview fatigue can easily lead to underclaiming.

Morgen Neu of the Starch organization has issued a vigorous rebuttal of the research discussed above.[30] In the first place, he claims that there

---

[26] See Darrell B. Lucas, "The ABC's of ARF's PARM," *Journal of Marketing*, Vol. 25 (July 1960), pp. 9–29, and Seymour Banks "Analysis of ARF Study Shows How and Why Ad Scores Vary," *Printers' Ink*, September 6, 1957.

[27] As reported in Darrell B. Lucas and Steuart H. Britt, *Measuring Advertising Effectiveness* (New York: McGraw-Hill Book Co., 1963), p. 48.

[28] Valentine Appel and Milton L. Blum, "Ad Recognition and Response Set," *Journal of Advertising Research*, Vol. 1 (June 1961), pp. 13–21.

[29] Ibid.

[30] D. Morgan Neu, "Measuring Advertising Recognition," *Journal of Advertising Research*, Vol. 11 (1961), pp. 17–22.

is no reason to expect a dropoff in recognition scores over time. On this point his logic is not clear, and his argument is not completely convincing. He does present data, however, which indicate that false claiming declines markedly if the respondent is told that he may not have seen all of the advertisements presented to him; he may exercise greater discrimination if he is warned. Definitive research is obviously needed.

Perhaps all that can be done in the absence of further research is to utilize some type of controlled recognition procedure. One such measure has been published, and others have reported variations.[31] In one of the most promising approaches, false advertisements are used to detect overclaiming, and respondents indicate the certainty with which they remember seeing and reading an advertisement.[32] Overclaiming can be detected fairly reliably.

REPRODUCIBILITY OF RECOGNITION SCORES. The Starch organization, of course, uses a small national sample chosen by nonrandom means. Questions have arisen concerning the representativeness of this sample and the degree to which scores would differ if more rigorous sampling were used. The PARM study utilized a much larger randomly chosen sample so that these questions could be answered.

It was found that the average noted score in PARM interviews was 21.7 percent, as compared with the 26.4 percent average score reported by Starch. Although there is a small absolute difference, the coefficient of agreement was found to exceed .85 (1.00 is perfect).[33] As a result of this close agreement, concern over the sampling procedure has abated.

SENSITIVITY TO INTERVIEWER VARIATIONS. Starch interviewers are trained not to point or to direct the respondent's replies in any way. Presumably such gestures could introduce bias. The PARM study analyzed the sensitivity of data to interviewer variations through using both experienced and inexperienced interviewers. Separate tabulation of results showed no significant differences in the noted scores produced by each group.[34]

One might expect that the PARM results would be reassuring to the Starch organization, because a potential source of bias in recognition scores apparently is not present. Neu also challenges this finding, however, by noting that interviewers develop tendencies that produce either overly high or overly low claiming by respondents.[35] It is his opinion

---

[31] Darrell B. Lucas, "A Rigid Technique for Measuring the Impression Values of Specific Magazine Advertisements," *Journal of Applied Psychology*, Vol. 24 (1940), pp. 778–90.

[32] John S. Davenport, Edwin S. Parker, and Stewart A. Smith, "Measuring Readership of Newspaper Advertisements," *Journal of Advertising Research*, Vol. 2 (1962), pp. 2–9.

[33] Lucas, "Technique for Measuring Impression Values."

[34] Ibid.

[35] Neu, "Measuring Advertising Recognition."

that some of the studies criticizing the validity of Starch data have failed to control adequately for this factor.

Using Recognition Scores.   Given the many unanswered methodological issues, what uses can be made of recognition data? Certainly the approach can be helpful in three ways:

1. Readership scores are at least a rough indication of success in attracting and holding attention, because it goes without saying that an advertisement must be perceived before advertising objectives are realized.
2. The relative pulling power of variations in creative treatment can be assessed from one campaign to the next or within the same campaign by controlled experiments.
3. The pulling power of competitors' campaigns can be measured.

These data are most useful if an entire campaign is analyzed rather than each advertisement one at a time. It is possible, for example, that the individual score can be biased by an unrepresentative sample for a given issue or other random variations. These variations become neutralized when many stimuli are compared over time.

Perhaps the least effective use of recognition scores is to test the pulling power of minor components within an advertisement. It is asking far too much of any reader to remember his behavior in such minute detail.

Finally, these scores should not be projected to the entire market. The sample is not random, and for that reason no such projection can be made with measurable accuracy.

Recall Tests

Recall measures assess the impression of advertisements on the reader's memory through the extent and accuracy of answers given, without exposure to the stimulus.

Unaided Recall.   The purest measure of memory relies on no aids whatsoever. The respondent might be asked, for example, "What advertisements have you seen lately?" Such a question is obviously difficult to answer, because few respondents will retain such sharp recollections of advertising exposure that much detail will be recalled. Also, it is quite difficult to measure the impact of a specific campaign in this fashion, because answers will vary over a wide range of products. For these reasons, unaided recall is seldom relied upon as the only measure.

Aided Recall.   There is a practically limitless variety of means which can be used to jog the respondent's memory and thereby sharpen his recall. He might be asked, "What automobile advertisements do you remember seeing in yesterday's paper?" or "What brand of coffee do you remember hearing about recently?" The recall of a specific brand is a strong indication of the strength of the advertising impression.

THE GALLUP-ROBINSON IMPACT TEST. The Gallup-Robinson test, perhaps the best known of the aided recall measures, is offered as a syndicated service. Basically, the technique involves five steps:

1. The person interviewed must recall and describe correctly at least one editorial feature in the publication under analysis.
2. The respondent is then handed a group of cards on which are printed the names of advertised brands which appear in the issue, as well as some which do not. He is asked to indicate which of these products are advertised in the issue.
3. For each advertised brand the respondent recalls from the issue, he is interrogated in depth to assess the strength and accuracy of recall.
4. The issue is then opened to each advertisement the respondent recalls. He is asked whether this is the advertisement he has in mind and if it is the first time he has seen it. If he has seen it before, the data are discarded in order to arrive at a "proven name registration" figure.
5. Information is gathered on the age, sex, education, and other details of the background of each person interviewed.[36]

The interviewing usually commences on the day after the magazine appears. Responses are edited thoroughly to ascertain that the recall is genuine. The final score, *proven name registration* (PNR), is adjusted by size of the appeal, color, placement on the page, and the number of competing advertisements in the issue.

The PARM study referred to earlier also analyzed the Gallup-Robinson approach. The correlation between scores produced by the PARM staff and Gallup-Robinson was .82 for women and .61 for men.[37] Therefore, this technique was not found to be as fully reproducible as the Starch approach.

Gallup-Robinson scores were found to show the expected pattern of dropoff as time between reading the issue and the interview increased. For this reason if no other, it is quite likely that two different interviewing organizations would produce different results, for only by accident would all respondents be in exactly the same stages of memory decay.

The PARM study also detected that the Gallup-Robinson measure is highly sensitive to interviewer skill. The more inexperienced interviewer

---

[36] See Donald R. G. Cowan (ed.), *Annual Marketing Research Conference,* Michigan Business Papers No. 27 (Ann Arbor: University of Michigan, Bureau of Business Research, 1953), pp. 23 and 24.

[37] See Lucas, "Technique for Measuring Impression Values."

produced scores which differed significantly from those of the interviewer with greater experience, thus underscoring the need for rigorous training and tight field control.

It has been concluded that the PARM test in general verified that the Gallup-Robinson test truly measures memory, as its proponents claim, with a minimum of distortion from other factors (unlike the Starch measure).[38] However, unnecessary secrecy surrounds the procedures used to edit and adjust the proven name registration scores. It would be possible to interpret the data with more accuracy if these facts were available.

THE P-C-R-B METHOD. A modification of aided recall designed by Richard D. Crisp makes use of a playback technique.[39] Crisp calls this approach the P-C-R-B method—Penetration, Comprehension, Recall, and Believability. The respondent is permitted to examine a series of advertisements at his own pace and is interviewed upon completion. A series of aided and unaided recall questions determines the extent to which the advertisement has penetrated the respondent's consciousness, whether or not he believed the message, and the extent of details recalled. This measure is also applicable to broadcast media, where it appears to be a useful overall indicator of the impression made by the advertisement.

Evaluation of Recall Tests. It is apparent that unaided and aided recall both offer minimum cues to stimulate memory, and it may be that memory is *understimulated*. The triple-associates and identification tests, of course, minimize this difficulty.

Understimulation of memory may not seem to be a problem. Consider the situation, however, when the advertised product is a convenience good and the objective is merely to register the name repetitively over a long period. In all probability, the respondent will not recall seeing the advertisement, but the objective still could have been attained. The point is that recall favors the distinctive appeals, especially those that are highly entertaining. The danger arises when one assumes that a low score always implies failure to attract and hold attention.

One authority has suggested that understimulation might be overcome by taking the reader through a stripped-down version of the magazine, with only the editorial features left intact.[40] This could be done under the guise of asking for opinions on editorial features. After this additional exposure to the mazagine, the respondent may recall with more accuracy the advertisement communicated.

---

[38] Ibid.

[39] Richard D. Crisp, "A Case Study in Copy Research," *Journal of Marketing,* Vol. 17 (1953), p. 356.

[40] Lucas, "Technique for Measuring Impression Values."

Recall and Position in the Issue. It has frequently been felt that the position of the advertisement in the issue will affect recall. For instance, it seems reasonable to expect that the advertisement close to the editorial section will be favored. It has been found, however, that the environment and location of the stimulus was not a factor in recall scores.[41] The content of copy and the visualization seem to be the dominant factors.

Finally, it cannot be assumed that the true "impact" of the advertisement has been isolated. This observation is pertinent, because the Gallup-Robinson method is frequently referred to as "impact" measurement. If by impact is meant the stimulation of buying behavior or successful attainment of other advertising objectives, aided recall in no definitive way is an indication of success. All that can be said is that high recall scores (perhaps 5 percent or more) reflect that a strong conscious impression was made and that attention was successfully attracted and held.

Association Measures

A time-honored measure of message recall is the triple-associates test development by the late Henry C. Link. Respondents are asked the following type of question: "Which brand of gasoline is advertised as offering 'more miles per gallon'?" Two associates or factors are inherent in such a question: (1) the generic product (gasoline) and (2) the advertising theme ("more miles per gallon"). The third element, the brand name, is to be supplied by the respondent. The percentage of correct answers is thus a measure of the extent to which advertising has correctly registered a theme.

The triple-associates test can easily be modified to suit individual situations as long as it is confined to measurement of registration of a theme or a very abbreviated message. The communication of longer copy or advertising elements cannot be measured effectively with this technique. Also, registration of theme must not be taken as implying that advertising objectives have been achieved. All that can be said is that the advertisement communicated.

Combination Measures

It seems safe to observe that a recognition test *overstimulates* readers or viewers, while recall measurement *understimulates* them. It is possible, however, to combine these measures to capitalize upon the strengths of each.

---

[41] Lester R. Frankel and Bernard M. Solov, "Does Recall of an Advertisement Depend on Its Position in the Magazine?" *Journal of Advertising Research,* Vol. 2 (1962), pp. 28–32.

A Controlled Combination.   One of the authors combined the recognition and recall procedures by removing test advertisements from their editorial surroundings, exposing consumers to the copy for a controlled interval and asking for playback of copy and other features following exposures.[42] Respondents were first qualified as being readers of the issue in which the advertisements appeared, and they were then exposed to five advertisements, one by one, for a controlled short interval. The advertisement was then removed, and the respondent was asked to state whether or not he recalled seeing the advertisement. If his reply was affirmative, he was asked to state in detail his recall of major features, copy points, illustrations, and other components. Finally, one of the five stimuli was an advertisement scheduled for appearance one month following the date of the interview, and it was used to detect false recognition claims. The extent of false claiming was found to be minimal.

This procedure minimizes the overstimulation inherent in the Starch method. The interval of exposure appeared to be long enough to jog the memory but not long enough to permit further reading of the advertisement and false claiming. Furthermore, the recall phase verified the accuracy of recognition claims. Thus this type of measure seems to be a more accurate indication of readership than either recognition or recall measures used separately.

The Communiscope.   The communiscope overcomes a disadvantage in the technique just described by mechanically controlling the interval of exposure.[43] The communiscope is a portable tachistoscope which permits the presentation of stimuli at varying intervals of time. The advertisements are placed on slides and flashed at the correct interval. Playback of copy is then requested to verify the accuracy of readership claims.

The communiscope is sufficiently compact to permit use in a home under normal conditions. Because of the opportunity for precise stimulus presentation, its use should grow in the future.

The Controlled Ad Awareness Technique.   The Controlled Ad Awareness Technique (CAAT) consists of a set of mottled Zip-A-Tone opaque plastic screens placed over the stimuli to be analyzed.[44] As the screens are lifted, the stimulus becomes progressively sharper in its details.

---

[42] James F. Engel, "Are Automobile Purchasers Dissonant Consumers?" *Journal of Marketing,* Vol. 27 (April 1963), pp. 55–58.

[43] See Petterson Marzoni, Jr., "Some New Light on Advertising Recognition Measurement—Through a Field Test of the Communiscope," published report of the Advertising Research Workshop, January 15, 1958, Association of National Advertisers.

[44] Gordon M. Keswick and Lawrence G. Corey, "A Sensitive Measure of Ad Exposure," *Journal of Advertising Research,* Vol. 2 (1961), pp. 12–16.

Respondents are given four chances to identify the stimulus. Identification when all screens are intact indicates that recognition can correctly be made with minimum stimulus detail, presumably because of strength of recognition. Thus it possesses much the same advantage as the communiscope (precise stimulus presentation) but at much lower costs. Although this approach has not been used as a combination measure, it could easily be adapted to do so.

PRODUCT-RELATED MEASURES UNDER REAL WORLD CONDITIONS

The most sophisticated and demanding of the various measurement approaches is field measurement of the effects of advertising. Sales test techniques, in particular, generally require considerable time and expense and hence are utilized almost exclusively for purposes of posttesting the effects of an entire campaign. The pre-post test, however, is widely used in pretesting.

Pre-Post Tests

When it is not possible to establish a clear-cut sales objective for advertising, the objectives usually are stated in terms of stimulation of awareness, attitude shift, or changes in preference. Whether or not the advertising has been effective requires a measurement approach which encompasses assessment of changes in response from the initial position of the members of the market segment. Therefore, both a before (pre) and after (post) measurement will usually be required.

Case Studies of Pre-Post Measurement. To promote understanding of this type of analysis we will first analyze several case examples in which communication effectiveness was measured. Then issues and problems in the use of the technique will be examined.

An Association of Tea Importers and Producers. The problem was an unfavorable attitude toward tea among many consumers, and the advertising goal was to generate a favorable attitude toward tea from a positive rating of 20 percent to 40 percent over five years. An attitude scale was developed, and studies were conducted annually to assess progress toward the goal. In each periodic assessment the same attitude scale was used, apparently with a different sample of buyers.[45]

A Small Overseas Airline. The advertising objective of communicating the attributes of a luxury airline to an additional 20 percent

---

[45] Russell H. Colley, *Defining Advertising Goals* (New York: Association of National Advertisers, 1961).

in one year was established. Measurement consisted of mail question-
naires sent periodically to a representative sample of several hundred
persons who were overseas-traveling customers of travel services in
selected cities. The questions used were of the following type: "What
airlines can you name that offer all-jet service to _____?"
Survey costs were small (several hundred dollars), and a high return was
produced because a free booklet of interest to travelers was given as an
inducement. At the end of one year it was found that awareness of the
company had increased 14 percent; the image of a luxury all-jet overseas
airline was communicated to an additional 15 percent; and the proportion
of those indicating they would seriously consider this airline for their
next overseas trip increased 8 percent.[46]

A PAIN RELIEVER. The manufacturer of a leading brand of pain reliever previously had focused his advertising on the theme of "fast relief." Because leading competitors were also doing this, and it was decided that a new advertising objective should be to (1) hold the present
level of message penetration on the headache-relief theme (35 percent)
and (2) increase cold-relief message penetration from 15 percent to 25
percent in six months. This strategy was undertaken in test markets.
The results showed that the headache message registration actually declined 2 percent at the outset but overall penetration reached 28 percent
at the conclusion, thereby exceeding expectations.[47]

Analysis of the Cases. The case examples discussed above have
several aspects in common: (1) measurement of message penetration at
the beginning of a period, (2) a clear-cut communication goal, (3) another
measurement either during or at the end of the campaign period, and
(4) assessment of ensuing changes.

In general, these examples are representative illustrations of research-
oriented advertising management. There are problems, however, which
may not be apparent to the reader:

1. What is the nature of the sample studied at the beginning of the
   period? Is it representative? If it is intended to focus on prospects,
   where is such a list obtained? It may not be possible to draw a random
   sample because of these problems, and, of course, the price paid for
   nonrandomness is inability to project the results to the universe
   being studied.
2. Were the people studied either in the interim or at the end of the
   campaign period the same as those chosen in the beginning? If so,
   the distinct possibility exists that the process of measurement may
   seriously bias later replies. The fact that respondents are asked for

---

[46] Ibid., pp. 83–84.
[47] Ibid., p. 94.

their opinions frequently causes them to think more deeply and change their opinions at a later time.[48]

3. If the same people were not measured at a later point, were the samples studied clearly matched as to age, income, and other demographic variables? Even more to the point, is it known that the samples studied later possessed the same attitude at the beginning of the period as the sample used previously? Differences in any of these respects may vitiate the results.

4. Is it known what changes would have occurred in the interim without advertising? Even when there is no intervening advertising, up to 30 percent of respondents will change their attitudes or brand preferences.[49] In the same sense, it is essential to determine what non-viewers or nonreaders would do before concluding that any changes are a result of advertising.[50]

Until the above questions can be answered satisfactorily, conclusions cannot be drawn about the validity of the research. Basically, the only way in which these problems can be overcome is through utilization of an experimental design where attempts are made to control all the variables but one—in this case, the advertising used.

Experimental Designs. In a controlled experiment, the researcher intervenes, so to speak, to control for as many extraneous variables as possible. Usually it is necessary to use a test group and a control group. One group is exposed to the advertising and the other is not. The design is represented thus:

A Simplified Experimental Design

	Experimental Group	Control Group
Premeasurement	Yes	Yes
Exposure to advertising	Yes	No
Postmeasurement	Yes	Yes

Changes which would have occurred in any event, without the exposure to advertising, presumably will be detected as differences between the pre- and post-measurements in the control group. This change is subtracted from that noted in the experimental group, and the residual is the change attributable to advertising exposure.

---

[48] L. P. Crespi, "The Interview Effect in Polling," *Public Opinion Quarterly,* Vol. 18 (1948), pp. 99–111.

[49] Donald L. Kanter, "Research and the Creative Decision," *Proceedings, 6th Annual Conference* (New York: Advertising Research Foundation, 1960), p. 65.

[50] Jack B. Landis, "Methods of Evaluating Television Advertising Effectiveness," *Proceedings 7th Annual Conference* (New York: Advertising Research Foundation, 1961), pp. 49–54.

However, the simple design above, sometimes called the "before and after with control group" design, may be grossly inadequate for this type of problem. As was mentioned before, the simple fact of asking people for their opinions is known to change the opinions later, and a very real source of bias is thus introduced by using the same experimental subjects for before-and-after measurement. One way to control for this factor is to use a four-group, six-study design, as illustrated below:

A Four-Group, Six-Study Design

	Experimental Groups		Control Groups	
	1	2	1	2
Premeasurement...............	Yes	No	Yes	No
Exposure to advertising.........	Yes	Yes	No	No
Postmeasurement..............	Yes	Yes	Yes	Yes

Notice that four groups are used, and a means now exists to detect the possible biasing effect of premeasurement. If, for instance, the effect introduced by advertising in experimental group 1 is much greater than that in the second group receiving no premeasure, it is quite probable that the premeasurement biased later responses. In that case the premeasurement of the first group under each heading would be compared with the postmeasurement of the groups receiving no premeasure.

No doubt the four-group, six-study design would represent the ideal means of isolating the communication effectiveness of advertising. It would be a mistake, however, to fail to point out the difficulties arising when one attempts to use this "textbook ideal" research method:

1. Is it possible to establish equivalent test and control groups, especially when two or more are used under each to create the necessary four groups? Unless the answer here is yes, the research becomes questionable.
2. Is it possible to find equivalent groups, one of which is not exposed to the advertising? Where a saturation campaign is being used, this may be impossible. The individuals not exposed may be very different from those who are, and it may be exceedingly difficult to find typical groups of consumers who would qualify for this particular purpose.
3. Is the information gained worth the cost? The more elaborate the design, the greater the research costs. The basic issue, then, is the return for the investment relative to less ideal designs, and this question is exceptionally difficult to answer.

The problem of finding equivalent groups becomes somewhat less crucial when the numbers in each are large. Difference in various dimensions may then be offset by the force of large numbers. The second problem also may be overcome when the campaign is confined to a select group of media. For instance, assume that dollars are invested in one television program. It may then be possible to find equivalent exposed and unexposed groups, but it must never be forgotten that those who watch the program still may differ from nonviewers in psychological outlook and other characteristics. Finally, the last question is the most difficult of all. Little more than advance hunches regarding the return for an investment in research are possible until more is known about the strengths and weaknesses of various research methods.

Comments on Pre-Post Tests.   It should now be apparent that the examples above suffer from possible sources of bias, yet the application of experimental design also presents real problems. Probably it is safe to say that the kind of monitoring undertaken by the tea association and the airline is good practice if done on a routine basis. In other words, it is helpful to keep a running tally on the results of a campaign. This information, however, can never be a conclusive indication of success unless a control group of some kind is used.

The issue, then, once again revolves around the uses to which the research is put. Measurement without a control group provides a useful but rough indication of progress, and the strengths and weaknesses of the campaign can be pinpointed. If management uses these data with caution and fully recognizes that other factors in addition to advertising could be introducing change, the return of information for a minimum research expenditure can be worthwhile.

It is another matter, however, for management to take the results of uncontrolled research as a definitive indication of success or failure. The abandonment or continuation of a campaign theme involving millions of dollars should not rest on such a foundation. In this instance, experimental design procedures should be utilized. There are problems in methodology and possible sources of bias in experimental research, but the chances for error resulting from the research methods used or uncontrolled factors are substantially reduced.

Sales Tests

The question of whether the influence of advertising on sales can be measured has prompted much discussion in recent years, both pro and con. Consider, for example, the somewhat negative point of view expressed in the following quotation:

In essence, current sales figures are not the final yardstick of advertising performance unless one or more of these factors are present.

1. Advertising is the single variable.
2. Advertising is the dominant force in the marketing mix.
3. The proposition calls for immediate payout (such as in mail-order or retail advertising).
4. These conditions seldom prevail among so-called "nationally advertised" products.[51]

The point is that advertising is usually only one variable in the marketing mix, and it must pull together with the product, price, and distribution channel to produce sales. The contention is that the communication aspects of advertising are usually the only measurable results. As was noted in Chapter 9, this focus on communication has come to be referred to as DAGMAR (Defining Advertising Goals, Measuring Advertising Results).

DAGMAR, however, is referred to by some as a "philosophy of despair."[52] The argument is that communication goals are being substituted for the more relevant objectives of sales and profit and that communication comes from many sources other than advertising. Moreover, communication does not necessarily mean sales or profit, and examples are reported where one medium produced greater awareness or response but less sales or results than another. Therefore, there are some who advocate testing the influence of advertising on sales and attaining profit objectives rather than communication objectives.

The controversy over whether attainment of sales objectives is measurable has been briefly described. The authors do not take sides in the argument but feel it is pertinent to inquire into the possible ways in which the sales effectiveness of promotional dollars might be measured. These include the three discussed below: (1) direct questioning, (2) experimental designs, and (3) mini-market tests.

Direct Questioning of Buyers. On occasion it is fruitful to question buyers directly to define the factors that lead them to make a purchasing decision. For example, heavy television advertising for the *Living Bible* was undertaken in several test markets during the 1972 Christmas season. Direct questioning of buyers at point of purchase demonstrated high recall of television advertisements featuring Art Linkletter, although word of mouth was found to be the dominant influence on the decision.

The difficulties of direct questioning should be apparent. First, most people have great difficulty recalling the circumstances surrounding a decision. It is possible, of course, to minimize this difficulty by progressively taking the respondent back in time and asking him to restate the

[51] Colley, *Defining Advertising Goals,* pp. 10 and 12.

[52] A. J. Vogl, "Advertising Research—Everybody's Looking for the Holy Grail," *Sales Management,* November 1, 1963, p. 42.

situation as well as possible. For example, he may associate the purchase of a new automobile with a particular time of year, with particular family discussions, or with other events. Questioning can help him to recall the situation, so that the influences on his decision may come into sharper focus.

Even if the purchasing environment is clear in the respondent's memory, it still is doubtful that the role of advertising will be revealed. It seems to be natural for many to deny being influenced by advertising. Presumably this would be admitting in some way to being not rational in buying. Moreover, advertising often works in virtually undetectable ways. Awareness might have been stimulated years before, and it is impossible for the buyer to restate this influence by introspection.

These problems are potent barriers indeed. For this reason, introspection by the buyer is seldom relied upon to any great extent.

Experimental Designs. There is no satisfactory substitute for an experimental design to isolate the influence of advertising from the influence of other elements in the marketing mix. The application of experimental design to this problem, however, is complex, and the problems to be faced are many. They include (1) selecting the appropriate design, (2) selecting test and control markets, and (3) analysis of the results.

THE APPROPRIATE DESIGN FOR SALES TESTING. The before-and-after with control group experimental design is applicable for sales testing. This design uses several test cities and control cities. The procedure can be outlined as shown below:

A Before-and-After with Control Group Design for Testing the Sales Effectiveness of Advertising

	Test Markets	Control Markets
Before measure of sales	Yes	Yes
Introduction of advertising	Yes	No
Postmeasure of sales	Yes	Yes

Sales usually are measured by auditing the inventories of a sample of stores, perhaps using the A. C. Nielsen store audit or a similar service. There is no need in this case for the more complex four-group, six-study design, because no interviews are being made. As a result, there is little chance that premeasurement of sales will bias the results.

A sales test usually runs from six months to a year, to permit time for advertising influence to be exerted. Several test and control markets should be used to minimize the danger that the markets chosen are later found to differ in some important aspect.

SELECTING TEST AND CONTROL MARKETS. Every attempt must be made to assure that the markets chosen closely mirror the total market. In addition, the test and control areas must not differ in the following respects:

1. *Size*—Usually areas from 100,000 to 300,000 are used. The areas must be large enough to encompass a variety of economic activities, yet not be so great that measurement and analysis of results is unduly costly.

2. *Population factors*—Areas with distinct and unique ethnic characteristics usually should be avoided. Milwaukee, Wisconsin, with its German stock, would be an unlikely area to test advertising for French wines. The more representative the area, the less likely it is to be rendered atypical by local disturbances such as strikes or layoffs. A one-industry town would be severely shocked by such an occurrence.

3. *Distribution*—The product must be readily available in retail outlets. If possible, retailers and wholesalers should not be informed of the test, in order to prevent unusual sales activity on their part which would severely bias the results.

4. *Competitive considerations*—Competition in the test and control areas should not deviate from that usually faced in the entire market. The competitive climate during the test must be carefully monitored, because any changes may render the test invalid.

5. *Media*—Full advertising media facilities must be available for use, or comparable media must be available in the test and control areas.

ANALYSIS OF RESULTS. If the results of the experiment are those shown in Figure 14–2, the results in the test city must be adjusted by

FIGURE 14–2

Comparison of Test City and Control City Sales Returns

City	Sales before Test Advertising (Feb. 1– Mar. 31)	Sales during Test Advertising (April 1– May 31)	Percentage Increase or Decrease	Adjusted Percentage Increase or Decrease
Control City A:				
Dollars..........	$300	$270	−10.0	
Units...........	300	250	−16.7	—
Test City X:				
Dollars..........	$400	$480	+20.0	30.0
Units...........	400	460	+15.0	31.7

Note: For purposes of simplification, only one test city and one control city have been used in this example. In actual practice, at least three test cities and three control cities are used.

Source: Reproduced with special permission from David J. Luck, Hugh G. Wales, and Donald A. Taylor, *Marketing Research*, 2d ed. (Englewood Cliffs, N.J.: Prentice-Hall, Inc., 1961), p. 490.

the percentages for the control city to show the effect of advertising. Notice that the control city showed a definite decline in sales. If conditions were similar in both areas, it is necessary to calculate what would have happened in the test city without advertising. A 10 percent decline in the test city would give dollar sales of $360, whereas in reality the sales were $480. Therefore, $360 must be subtracted from $480 to give a net increase of $120. Thus the actual net increase is 30 percent in dollar sales and 31.7 percent in unit sales. The actual meaning of these changes must be assessed, using statistical tests such as the t test or chi square analysis.

Notice that the results are predicated on the assumption that all other things are equal. Again it must be emphasized that variation in any factor, such as competition or retailers' efforts, that is present in the test cities and not in the control cities (or vice versa) will vitiate the experiment. If it appears that factors have not varied, however, the data should give a reasonably accurate measure of the influence of advertising on sales.

A MULTIVARIABLE EXPERIMENTAL DESIGN. In the above example only one variable has been measured—the advertising campaign in the test areas. It is possible to study more than one variable at a time and in so doing to reduce the cost of repetitive individual experiments.

FIGURE 14-3

Media Combinations in a 16-Cell Design

Combination	Area No.	Combination	Area No.
No media	1	Outdoor-radio	10
TV only	2	Outdoor-newspaper	11
Radio only	3	TV-radio-newspaper	12
Newspaper only	4	Outdoor-radio-TV	13
Outdoor only	5	Outdoor-TV-newspaper	14
TV-radio	6	Outdoor-radio-	
TV-newspaper	7	newspaper	15
Newspaper-radio	8	Outdoor-TV-radio-	
Outdoor-TV	9	newspaper	16

Source: Reproduced with special permission from George H. Brown, "Measuring the Sales Effectiveness of Alternative Media," *Proceedings, 7th Annual Conference* (New York: Advertising Research Foundation, 1961), p. 46.

Assume that the research assignment is to analyze the relative pulling power of four different media used individually and in combination. This problem would call for a factorial design. While the mechanics of factorial design are clearly beyond the scope of this book, an indication of a possible structure for the experiment is given in Figure 14-3. This design has been used at Ford Motor Company, where it was reported that the data have revealed a definite relationship between advertising and sales but no significant advantage for any of the media tested.

Multivariable designs are elaborate, and the difficulties of controlling variables are compounded. The data must be analyzed by analysis of variance, a statistical technique which permits delineation of the significance of sales differences resulting from individual variables or from variables in combination. No doubt a computer would be required for the necessary computations. In addition, sales frequently are lost in areas where advertising is reduced; costs become high when test advertising proves to be ineffective; and it is costly to undertake the necessary rigorous analysis and interpretation of data. As a result, experimental designs, especially of such great complexity, are usually the province of the large advertiser. This is not to say, however, that such designs cannot be tailored to the means of the smaller advertiser.

COMMENTS ON EXPERIMENTAL DESIGN.   Even though the difficulties to be faced are great, there is no doubt that proper experimental procedures will permit measurement of the sales power of advertising. It is reported that duPont uses experiments regularly.[53] In one experiment, for instance, industrial advertising was undertaken in all but two states, which then served as the control, and changes in effectiveness were assessed in both sections. Similar examples are reported by others.[54]

Obviously, more elaborate experiments will not be undertaken by the smaller advertiser with a local or regional market. The costs simply are too great at the present time. However, the experimental design need be only as elaborate as the problem being tested. In future years advertisers of all sizes no doubt will begin to experiment, and the effectiveness of advertising should increase markedly.

Mini-Market Tests

There are ways of undertaking full-scale experiments without the time and expense necessary for the market tests discussed above. One way is use of the so-called "mini-market." The leading research service providing this type of procedure is AdTel, which utilizes a dual-cable CATV system and two balanced purchase diary panels of 1,000 households each. Because it is possible to control all variables except the one being tested over television, a precise measurement of effects is possible. This same service was formerly provided by the now defunct Milwaukee Ad Lab, which also permitted testing of media other than television.

---

[53] "Who Says Ad Impact Can't Be Measured?" *Sales Management,* April 19, 1963, pp. 37–43.

[54] James F. Merriman, "Evaluating Advertising Appeals through Sales Results," *Journal of Marketing,* Vol. 23 (1958), pp. 164–67.

SUMMARY

This chapter has examined the assumptions, strengths, and weaknesses of the various techniques for measuring advertising effectiveness. The use of some of these tools, however, does not shed light on the actual advertising response by the buyer. This may seem to be an obvious point, but it frequently is forgotten by users of research. A high Starch score, for instance, may be a favorable indication of success, but high readership does not necessarily imply a strong response, nor does it indicate a rising sales curve.

At the present time, no area of advertising research methodology is without important unknowns and doubts. As a result, no method can be used with complete certainty that it will always give desired results. The need for additional empirical research and improved methodology is apparent, yet this need is growing more rapidly than it is being met. It is strange that management is willing to devote funds to new-product development but is loathe to improve the tools with which advertising is measured.

Given the state of the art, it is essential to advance a strong warning against the quest for certainty. Everyone has a tendency to assume that a quantitative finding is absolute—something to be relied upon. The manager who relies upon research data religiously without a skeptical, questioning attitude is falling prey to the false god of certainty. He may be led into wrong conclusions that can be costly. Moreover, an unquestioning attitude implies intellectual inflexibility, which has no place in advertising today.

REVIEW AND DISCUSSION QUESTIONS

1. What is the essential distinction between laboratory and real-world measures?
2. Describe and discuss the usefulness of the various direct measures of opinion used in a consumer jury test.
3. Studies often show that recall is the most widely used measure of communication effectiveness. Many refuse to measure other stages of the communication process, such as attitude change or purchase. Why does this occur? What arguments could you present in behalf of attitude and/or behavior measurement?
4. Do you agree that laboratory measures, especially those focusing on the physiological aspect of attention, will see more use in the future? Why or why not?
5. Describe the recognition method.
6. The Starch method for measurement of readership is widely used, as are other approaches. What precautions would you suggest in using findings of this type?

7. Unaided recall is rarely considered to be a powerful method to isolate advertising impact. Why?

8. The Gallup-Robinson impact test is one example of an aided recall measure. Describe and evaluate this procedure.

9. Recall tests often are hampered by "understimulation." What does this mean, and in what way is it a problem for researchers?

10. How does position in an issue affect recall of printed advertising messages?

11. What are combination measures? Are they an improvement over other approaches? In what ways?

12. Are measures of attracting and holding attention necessary to evaluate advertising success? Are they a sufficient measure for this purpose?

13. It is often overlooked that actual responses to advertising are more important in the final analysis than the attraction of attention. Why, then, is so much reliance placed on measures of attention attraction as opposed to more clear-cut indications of advertising effectiveness?

14. What are the major types of advertising response which can be measured?

15. Attempts to measure communications effectiveness are plagued with problems in research design. What are these problems?

16. Describe the experimental design approach to communications measurement. What problems are encountered?

17. What is the basis of the argument which claims that advertising effectiveness should be measured in terms of communication of a message rather than in terms of sales?

18. Can direct questioning of buyers isolate the effect of advertising on sales? Why, or why not?

part five

Personal Selling, Reseller Support, and Supplemental Communications

Our consideration of the stages in promotional strategy outlined in Chapter 3 has given considerable attention to the management of mass communication efforts, particularly the management of advertising efforts. This part will continue the discussion of management of program elements by considering problems inherent in managing the personal selling resources available to the firm. These resources provide for face-to-face contact with potential customers with the purposes of informing them of new-product or service offerings and persuading them to buy.

Although personal selling is used at every level in business, from the manufacturer to the retailer, this section is primarily concerned with the use of a sales force by manufacturers to seek out new business by contacting end users or resellers. Many of the points discussed are applicable at all levels of the channel of distribution. Of special importance to all users of personal selling are the methods by which a sales force is developed and managed to attain maximum effectiveness.

This section also deals with the problem of gaining reseller support by examining the task resellers can be expected to perform, given their economic role and their objectives as independent businesses. Moreover, an attempt is made to suggest how manufacturers might stimulate reseller promotional activity or improve, supplement, or control reseller promotional efforts.

In conclusion, consideration is given to supplemental methods of communication, such as publicity and public relations, which serve to bridge the gap between the firm and its many publics.

363

15

Using Personal
Selling Resources

PERSONAL SELLING is a special form of interpersonal communication. Its goal is to "bring to the prospect's attention information that will satisfy a need and that will elicit a response, hopefully in the form of a purchase."[1] Although personal selling is only one of several communication tools used by marketing managers, it is unique in that it is a form of dyadic communication. In this it is opposed to advertising, sales promotion, and publicity, which are mass communication forms. Moreover, business firms spend more money on personal selling activities than on the other means of persuasive communication. It has been estimated by one source that industry spends twice as much on personal selling activity as it does on advertising.[2]

Although the use of personal selling is quite large in the aggregate, when compared with the use of other tools, not all firms favor personal selling over alternate means of communication. There are, however, many instances in which personal selling is vitally important to the attainment of the firm's marketing objectives. This chapter is concerned with those instances and especially with those firms that use salesmen to seek out buyers. These are typically manufacturing firms, although wholesaler salesmen also spend part of their time locating and developing new customers.

The first part of this chapter views personal selling as a communication process and considers how the nature of the firm's marketing strategy

---

[1] Kenneth R. Davis and Frederick E. Webster, Jr., *Sales Force Management* (New York: Ronald Press Co., 1968), p. 10.

[2] Ibid.

influences the role assigned to the salesman. The second part of the chapter discusses the managerial problems involved in building and administering a sales organization.

PERSONAL SELLING—A COMMUNICATION PROCESS

Modified Interpersonal Communication Model

A model of the interpersonal communication process was presented in Chapter 2 as Figure 2–1. A better understanding of personal selling as a communication process can be gained by examining a slightly modified version of this model. Figure 15–1 presents this modified model.

FIGURE 15–1

Personal Selling: A Communication Process

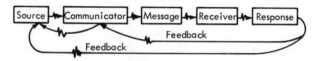

The Source.   Note that the element "source" has been added to the model presented in Chapter 2. This addition is necessary because in the personal selling process a distinction must be made between the firm, which is the true source of the message, and the salesman, who is the communicator of the message. This distinction is, of course, not needed in those instances where the source and the communicator are the same, as would be the case in casual nonbusiness-motivated conversation between two persons.

While the recognition that in personal selling activity there is a difference between source and communicator is self-evident, it is important nevertheless. Without such recognition one cannot fully comprehend the subtleties of the personal selling process. For example, when salesman X representing company Y calls on a prospect, the response which may be elicited is a function not only of the prospect's reaction to the salesman but also of the company he represents.

The Communicator.   The salesman himself is the communicator in the process; his message is the information that he transmits to his prospect. The channel in the case of a salesman-delivered message usually consists of the spoken word, although as noted in Chapter 2 the importance of nonverbal communication such as the appearance of the salesman or his personality must not be overlooked.

The Message.   In personal selling communication the message is the sales presentation or the series of attempts on the part of the salesman to provide information to the prospect. The purpose of the message is to persuade the prospect that he will find the salesman's offering useful. The ability of the salesman to custom design his sales presentation to the perceived needs of the prospect is one advantage that personal selling has over advertising. In addition, the sales presentation can be altered in light of feedback received by the communicator or the source. More is said about this in a later part of this section.

The Receiver. The receiver of the message is the prospective customer or prospect. This is usually an individual, thus preserving the dyadic relationship. There are exceptions, however, and in both the industrial and consumer markets the salesman may have to make his presentation to a buying group. In the former situation the salesman might prefer to see each member of the buying group on an individual basis, while in the consumer market the salesman of life insurance, a new home, or an automobile may prefer to have all the members of the group together when he makes his presentation.

In any event, the skill of the salesman will be demonstrated by his ability to identify those individuals to whom his sales message should be directed and to decide whether the recipients should be seen individually or in groups.

The Response. Another element that has been added to the communication model of Chapter 2 is response. For communication to have taken place some type of response must have been elicited from the receiver. This response may be in the form of overt behavior such as a refusal to buy or, more positively, a decision to buy. Or it may be psychological, in which case the receiver's awareness and (or) comprehension of the message may be increased, with a resulting change in the receiver's attitudes toward the product offering. While not all personal selling activity is aimed at evoking immediate buying action, a widely sought goal is a sufficiently favorable attitudinal change on the part of the receiver so that buying action is likely to occur in the future.

Feedback. The last of the elements to be considered in the communication process is feedback. This is a reverse flow of information. The receiver becomes the source and the response becomes the message, and either the salesman or the source is the receiver. Feedback allows message modification by the salesman during the period of his interaction with the prospect. It also enables the firm to alter the content of its suggested sales messages to conform better to customer information needs, or to meet competition more effectively.

In the portrayal of the expanded communication model the connections between adjacent elements as well as feedback loops have been illustrated by means of jagged lines. These lines indicate that interference or "noise" may be present in the system. Such interference is anything which can obstruct or alter the message as it moves from source to receiver.

Feedback also serves the purpose of monitoring the level of noise in the system and of indicating how clearly the message is coming through. It must be remembered, however, that feedback is just as susceptible as the original message to interference from system noise.

Implications of the Communication Process

If the sales strategy of a firm can be viewed as a communication process, the requirements of such a strategy become easier to define, as does the function of the salesman in carrying out the strategy. It has been suggested that the analysis of any communication process involves answering the question, *"Who says what to whom with what result?"*[3] It is further suggested that a sales strategy can be planned within the framework of the question, as is illustrated in Figure 15–2.

FIGURE 15–2

Sales Strategy as a Communication Process

	WHO says	WHAT to	WHOM with	what RESULT?
Elements of Communication	COMMUNICATOR	MESSAGE	RECEIVER	RESPONSE
Elements of Sales Strategy	SALESMAN	PRESENTATION	BUYER	OBJECTIVES
Information Needed— Inputs to Planning	Functions Selling Services Market Information Number of Accounts	Product Appeals Order of Presentation Handling Objections Length of Call Frequency of Calls	Needs Characteristics Location Buying Patterns Potential Decision Maker	Marketing Objectives Sales Forecast (Expected and Desired Results)

Source: Kenneth R. Davis and Frederick E. Webster, Jr. (eds.), *Readings in Sales Force Management* (New York: Ronald Press Co., 1968), p. 7.

THE NATURE OF THE PERSONAL SELLING TASK

Just what do salesmen do that makes their activity so important to a firm or to an economy? How is selling effort translated into completed transactions? A brief look into the nature of the selling task provides some answers to these questions. It must be recognized from the outset, however, that the selling job varies widely with respect to the product

---

[3] Kenneth R. Davis and Frederick E. Webster, Jr. (eds.) *Readings in Sales Force Management* (New York: Ronald Press Co., 1968), p. 7.

being sold, the level in the channel where the selling is taking place, and the strategy of the individual firm involved.

Functions of the Salesman

Regardless of variations in environmental or strategic factors, salesmen must seek out or meet prospective buyers, discover customer needs and attitudes, and help the prospective customer buy the product or service offering best suited to his requirements. In this process of helping the customer to buy, the salesman must be prepared to supply generous quantities of information about product or service characteristics. He must also persuade the buyer that a particular offering is best suited to his needs, and he must act decisively to overcome buyer uncertainty by sensing how and when to close the sale. Follow-up after the sale is also important to ensure that the buyer receives the fullest utility from his purchase and to prevent dissonance by assuring the customer that he has made the correct choice.

Thus the essential tasks of personal selling consist of: (1) locating and (or) meeting prospective customers, (2) discovering customer needs and attitudes, (3) recommending a product package to fill the needs of the customer, (4) developing a sales presentation aimed at informing the customer of product attributes and persuading him to buy the recommended package, (5) closing the sale, and (6) following up to ensure total satisfaction with the purchase.

Of course, all salesmen do not place equal emphasis on the various components of the selling task. This may be the result of inadequate performance or simply because the selling strategy requires a different pattern of behavior. It is essential that the selling task be clearly defined so that the salesman understands the nature of the job he is to perform. Without a clear definition of what is to be done, evaluation of selling performance is impossible.

Basic Sales Tasks

To illustrate the variety to be found in selling activities it is useful to consider three basic sales tasks: (1) order getting, (2) order taking, and (3) supporting.

The "order getter" engages in "creative selling" and aggressively undertakes a campaign to seek out potential buyers and to persuade them to buy a specific product or service. The "order taker," on the other hand, operates on a more relaxed basis. He makes routine calls on customers to maintain a continuing relationship. His approach is a low-pressure one designed to enable him to live well with his customer group for a long time. It is a mistake to compare an order taker unfavorably with an order getter, for the basic goals of the two men are different. However, if a salesman who is supposed to be an order getter performs as an order taker, management must step in to assure that the proper emphasis is placed on creative and aggressive selling activity.

In the supporting category are found selling activities which do not in themselves aim at getting or taking an order; missionary selling, technical support, and assistance in management or promotion fall into this grouping. These indirect selling activities build goodwill for the seller and increase the ability of the order-oriented salesmen to close the sale.

It is obvious that the role of the individual salesman in any of the three classifications will vary. Certainly the channel position of the seller has a profound effect on the nature of the selling job. Manufacturer salesmen selling to wholesalers or end users will play a role that differs from that of wholesaler salesmen selling to retailers or retail salesmen selling to people who enter their stores. Product characteristics as well as market characteristics are important influences on the nature of the basic selling task.

Determining the Proper Sales Tasks

To clarify the function of personal selling in promotional strategy, three case histories detailing the experience of a drug manufacturer, camera manufacturer, and a welding service are given below.

Proprietary Drug Manufacturer. Imagine a situation in which a manufacturer is desirous of launching a new patent medicine through retail drugstores. Market research has indicated that the market is geographically dispersed and that a large percentage of present proprietary drug users are potential buyers of the new product. Cost analysis has indicated that national advertising by means of newspapers and radio and TV spots will provide the most economical coverage of the market. Accordingly, $2,000,000 is appropriated for consumer advertising and $200,000 for personal selling effort. Why the disparity in budgeted amounts, and what is the role assigned to personal selling?

The answer to the first question is that the product type and the large and dispersed market present a situation in which advertising can stimulate demand more economically than can personal selling. The patent medicine has hidden qualities and appeals to emotions concerned with health and well-being. Moreover, the usage rate of the product promises revenues of sufficient size and continuity to sustain a costly advertising campaign. In brief, this situation is ideally suited to dominant emphasis on advertising.

Personal selling effort is utilized, however, at three different levels in the channel: manufacturer, wholesaler, and retailer. At the first of these levels the manufacturer uses his salesmen to call on large whole-salers and chain drug retailers. The advertising aimed at the household buyer is creating a "pull" effect, and the primary task of the salesman is to make certain that middlemen have ordered adequate stocks of the product. The selling task here is essentially order taking, with con-siderable time being allocated to supporting activities to ensure that wholesaler and retailer point-of-sales efforts are coordinated with the national advertising campaign.

The budget does not allow very much personal selling activity by the manufacturer, so whatever effort is available is directed to those cus-tomers that appear to offer the greatest potential. The great bulk of the orders are received by mail from interested wholesalers and retailers.

At the wholesale level a different type of personal selling activity is taking place. The wholesaler sales force is engaged in making routine calls on members of the wholesaler's customer group. These salesmen carry catalogs and price lists describing thousands of items. Their essential functions are of the order-taking variety. If, however, the de-mand for the new patent medicine is being felt at retail and the sales-men are aware of the promotional plans of the manufacturer, they may engage in some promotional selling aimed at getting the retailer to carry special stocks and to provide in-store promotional tie-ins.

Personal selling at the retail level is still another type of activity. In this case the retail clerk or the pharmacist may suggest the particular brand of product to those customers who ask for a remedy of the general type. If the situation is as highly advertisable as is assumed, it is more likely that the customer will ask for the remedy by name, thus reducing the personal selling task at retail to one of order filling. Retailer sup-port, in this instance, is largely confined to providing ample display and counter space for the product.

Camera Manufacturer. After many years of experimentation, a manu-facturer located in New England has developed a new type of camera which develops its own pictures in 60 seconds. Limitations of capacity and the requirements of channel compensation and overall promotion have dictated what is called a "skim" or high initial price strategy. Distribution is planned through 5,000 selected retailers. A modest ad-vertising campaign directed to the trade and to buyers is planned. The bulk of promotional effort, however, is to be in the form of personal selling at both the manufacturer and retailer levels.

The manufacturer has developed a highly skilled personal selling team whose prime objective is to get 5,000 of the best retailers in the country to stock, display, and sell the new type of camera. This is not an easy task because the product type is totally new, its cost is high, and the magnitude of demand is unknown. The personal selling task of the manufacturer salesman is one of order getting. Creativity and aggressiveness are necessary to get the most desirable retail outlets in each market to carry the line and engage in its promotion.

Selling effort at retail is also very important. A potential customer must be shown the new camera and given a demonstration of how it operates. Knowledge of the product and persuasive ability are required of the retail salesman if a sale is to be made. Thus the manufacturer's margin payment to the retailer must include payment for the first-class selling task required at retail.

The above, of course, is a description of some of the elements of the Polaroid Company's promotional program in the introductory stage of the product life cycle. This program today requires a different promotional strategy in which both the extent and type of personal selling activity have changed.

For example, a Polaroid Camera is no longer a totally new type of product. Buyers are aware of the capabilities of the camera and how it operates. Selective distribution required in the early days to get maximum dealer "push" has given way to more intensive market coverage through diverse outlet types. Although direct distribution is available to large customers, wholesalers play an important part in the distribution of the camera to retailers. Prices are down, and expenditures for advertising have increased greatly since the earlier period.

In brief, the Polaroid camera has matured as a product concept. It is not too difficult to conjecture what has happened to the personal selling task as market development has progressed.

From the manufacturer's standpoint the need is no longer to gain key outlets but rather to increase sales of the product through present outlets and to gain new outlets where market research indicates a need for greater coverage. The selling task thus has become more routinized, and there is greater emphasis on order taking and service than on order getting, compared with the earlier stages. Similarly, at retail the requirements for a creative selling job have lessened. At all levels in the channel personal selling has given way to the more economical methods of advertising and price promotion.

In 1972 Polaroid introduced a revolutionary new camera, the SX–70. This highly automated instrument sets its own exposure, electrically advances the film, and delivers a plastic-coated color photo which develops as the photographer watches. With a list price of $180, the SX–70 is backed by a large-scale promotional effort. Although the company is still placing considerable emphasis on advertising, the pendulum has swung back to greater reliance on personal selling efforts. Inasmuch as the best results are obtained when the subject is kept within 10 feet of the camera, demonstration and instruction at point of sale are important. The company's personal selling strategy is aimed at getting dealer support in terms of stocking, service, and, especially, proper demonstration.[4]

Electron Beam Welding Service. As a third illustration of the determination of proper sales tasks, consider the promotional problems facing a small company offering an electron beam welding service to industry.[5] The electron beam technology, developed in the aircraft industry, had not gained widespread acceptance in the manufacture of industrial goods and consumer products, although it offered many advantages over conventional welding techniques.

The company hired a manufacturers' representative on an expenses-plus-commission basis to contact potential accounts within the market area. After two years the owners found, much to their dismay, that the sales rep was not producing enough business to cover his expenses. A reappraisal of promotional strategy was very much in order.

If the owners of this small company would have analyzed their present customers in terms of informational requirements, they would have found that some customers required much more information input than others did. For example, buyers who had previously used the process or who had a relatively small job to be welded did not require a great deal of selling effort. On the other hand, those who were unfamiliar with the nature of electron beam welding or who had large and expensive jobs to complete required a great deal of information about the technical capability of the supplier, the price, and the delivery date for the finished work. In one case it took six months of inquiry and negotiation to close a sale.

From this type of analysis it would appear that although a manufacturers' representative might handle some of the routine buying situations, he would have neither the expertise nor the time to apply himself to the more complex situations. Given such a set of circumstances, the owners would either have to hire another salesman of their own to engage in the complex selling task or, if such an addition were not economically feasible, the owners would have to assume the responsibility themselves for the specialized personal selling effort required to make a sale.

Implications of the Cases. The three situations discussed above illustrate briefly how product and market influences affect the role played by personal selling in the promotional strategy mix. In the consumer area, as products mature the role of personal selling is diminished and advertising becomes more important. In the industrial market, as the product moves through its life cycle personal selling is generally a more

---

[4] See "How Polaroid Bet Its Future on the SX–70," *Fortune,* January 1974, p. 82 ff.

[5] See the "Advanced Technologies, Inc." case in Stewart H. Rewoldt, James D. Scott, and Martin R. Warshaw, *Introduction to Marketing Management,* rev. ed. (Homewood, Ill.: Richard D. Irwin, 1973), p. 220 ff.

important element in the promotional mix than is advertising. But even in the industrial market, as the information requirements of customers vary so does the extent and nature of the personal selling task.

BUILDING THE SALES FORCE

The building of an effective selling organization must begin with a clear understanding of the nature of the selling task. If, for example, the selling job is one of calling on wholesalers to get stocking and promotion of a relatively homogeneous line of products, the recruitment, selection, and training processes are different from a situation where the salesman is faced with diversity in terms of types of customers to be contacted or products to be sold.

The important consideration is a clear grasp of overall promotional strategy by those in the company responsible for the recruitment, selection, and training of salesmen. The overall strategy determines the *kind* of selling that is required. The *kind* of selling, in turn, determines the personal qualifications needed by members of the sales force and the methods of training, compensation, and motivation.

Job Descriptions and Recruitment

Before recruiting activities for salesmen can take place, a clear exposition must be made with respect to the nature of the selling task. In writing, this exposition is the job description. It is necessary to have a carefully thought out and fully updated job description for every position on the sales force. Examples of job descriptions for different types of selling situations are shown in Figures 15–3, 15–4, and 15–5.

Once the specific kind of selling job to be filled has been determined, the search for a likely employment prospect can begin. The ranks of currently employed salesmen, college campuses, and persons in business currently holding nonselling jobs make up the prime areas from which

FIGURE 15–3

Example of a Sales Representative's Job Description, Power Tools Division, The Stanley Works

---

Function:
   To promote sales of the division's products, to attain the sales and profit objectives of an assigned territory for the division.
Responsibilities:
   1. Devises necessary plans to accomplish territory goals and account objectives.
   2. Analyzes sales potential of all customers and prospective customers in his territory so that he can place sales emphasis in the proper order of importance.

FIGURE 15–3 (continued)

3. Promotes and solicits sales by personal calls on assigned accounts and prospective accounts to obtain maximum profitable sales potential.
4. Develops a thorough understanding of the basic needs of our accounts and their customers. Establishes a sales call plan to include personal calls on industrial user of importance on a regularly scheduled basis.
5. Develops and implements an effective and well-planned call frequency schedule which includes accounts, prospects, and users that will yield the maximum "return on time invested."
6. Plans in advance his strategy for each call in order to increase effectiveness and maximize results.
7. Supports industrial accounts with sales meetings, dual sales calls with their men, and user calls in proportion to their importance.
8. Develops a thorough knowledge of the problems of his customers and prospects and provides prompt assistance in accomplishing their solution. When problems concern product service, he communicates with appropriate service station and Product Service Manager. Monitors and follows up (when required) specific credit and collection problems.
9. Communicates his actions and accomplishments by submitting weekly call and expense reports. Identifies market conditions and service problems by submitting biweekly market reports and quality complaint reports.
10. Maintains a thorough and current knowledge of Stanley Power Tools' product lines, policies, prices, promotions, and procedures, including product applications.
11. Maintains a thorough and current knowledge of competitors' products, prices, programs, and promotions and reports changes and variations to those concerned.
12. Controls travel and business expenses while representing Stanley Power Tools, in order to accomplish the division's budgetary requirements.
13. Maintains company property (automobile, samples, and records, etc.) assigned to him in such a way as to maximize their use within established procedures and policies.
14. Participates in and/or attends national or regional meetings, trade shows, conventions, etc., as requested by sales management.
15. Suggests new techniques, fixturing, tooling and/or other modifications to users to provide greater sales value.
16. Recommends changes in procedures, products, or services and other actions to reduce cost and/or to improve sales and profits.

Relationships:
1. *Regional Manager*
   Reports on progress towards total sales accomplishment as compared to objective and by specific account as requested. Consults regularly concerning policy and future planning.
2. *Customers*
   Promotes and maintains good relations with customers.
3. *Other Company Personnel*
   Represents the interests of his customers with other company personnel by reflecting customer requirements clearly and following closely their fulfillment.
4. *Corporate and Divisional Staff*
   Understands the functions of the various corporate staff organizations so their help can be solicited as determined by the Regional Manager.
5. *Public*
   Promotes and maintains good relations with the public in general and the local community.

Source: The Stanley Works, rev. March 1, 1973. Reproduced by permission

FIGURE 15–4

**Example of a Salesman's Job Description,
Grocery Products Division, General Mills, Inc.**

I. PURPOSE

To represent General Mills and to secure the maximum in profitable sales volume and product distribution through selling and merchandising the entire line of Grocery Products (within limits of established policy and expense programs) to all assigned accounts within a specific territory.

II. ACCOUNTABILITIES

1. Achieve programmed volume deliveries by product and product categories.
2. Maintain planned coverage against both direct and/or retail accounts to ensure:
   a. Delivery of programmed volume.
   b. Complete distribution.
   c. Correct shelf placement.
   d. Adequate inventories and placements.
   e. Proper stock rotation.
   f. Proper pricing.
   g. Good account relationships.
   h. Programmed calls per day.
3. Accomplish timely and productive execution of sales and marketing plans and promotions, in accord with established timetables.
   a. Secure trade support via adequate display, ad feature, and/or pricing promotions at direct and retail levels.
   b. Ensure compliance with the terms and intent of trade activation plans, exercising proper control over volume and payments.
4. Maintain and/or develop sound customer relations and goodwill with all accounts.
   a. Assure proper handling of all sales practices and Company policies including GMI legal responsibilities with and to all accounts.
   b. Ensure proper and prompt handling of all customer problems/complaints and prompt payment of any amounts owed to the customer.
   c. Achieve full acquaintance with the organization chart and people at all levels of responsibility in all accounts, i.e., Management, Financial, Buying, Sales, Warehousing, Delivery and Clerical.
   d. Firmly and diplomatically protect the company's interest in all credit and/or collection problems.
5. Secure and relate to management complete information on:
   a. Market and/or product problems with recommendation for solution.
   b. Competitive activities.
   c. Market and product opportunities.
   d. Needs for addition and deletion of stores in coverage pattern to achieve maximum retail volume and distribution.
6. Operate assigned territory within established limits of approved expense program.
7. Arrange communication to region office and all affected salesmen of details relative to assigned account's promotional activity, product distribution and other pertinent information.
8. Practice and follow through on concepts covered in the Selling-by-Objectives and Advanced Selling-by-Objectives training programs.

III. RELATIONSHIPS

This position reports and is responsible to the District Sales Manager and is a direct representative of General Mills in his territory.

Source: General Mills, Inc. Effective January 1, 1971. Reproduced by permission.

FIGURE 15-5

Example of a Salesman's Job Description, Household Products Manufacturer

Basic Function

To sell the budgeted quantities of the company's household and automotive products in his assigned territory and to maintain distribution and promotion of these company products marketed through retail outlets.

Product Knowledge

Knowledge of the company's household, automotive, and insecticide line to:

1. Demonstrate and sell these products in the assigned territory to direct retail outlets, chain outlets, and wholesale distributors in accordance with established sales objectives, policies, and programs.
2. Carry out specific assignments, as assigned.
3. Answer questions of a routine nature relative to uses and applications of household, automotive, and insecticide products and handle routine complaints.

Promotion

1. Develop in-store merchandising techniques that increase the turnover of the household, automotive, and insecticide products.
2. Conduct wholesale distributors' sales meetings as assigned to educate their salesmen and create enthusiasm and cooperation in the sale of household products.
3. Engage in field selling with wholesale distributors' salesmen to demonstrate successful selling techniques.
4. Arrange for advertising and promotion of household products by wholesale distributors, chain headquarters, and key direct retail accounts.
5. Erect consumer displays in stores of direct retailers and post all advertising material supplied by the advertising department as assigned.
6. Establish and maintain good will of the company with all its customers.
7. Inform the area, district, or zone manager of any potential customers for company products other than those for which he is responsible.
8. Maintain a constant rate of turnover of wholesale distributors' stock through work in retail outlets.

Contacts

1. Contact buyers and sales promotion personnel, advertising managers and sales managers of direct retail outlets, wholesalers, and chain outlets in the direct sale and promotion of household products.
2. Contact wholesale distributors' salesmen to assist them in selling and to demonstrate successful selling techniques.
3. Contact, as directed, local advertising media such as newspapers to arrange tie-in advertisements.

Planning

1. Plan own work schedule within limits assigned by area or zone manager.
2. Control expenses within the budget for the assigned territory.
3. Maintain accurate sales coverage records according to plan and make changes in count by class of outlet.

Direction

None

Personnel Relations

Assist the zone and area manager in the training of new salesmen according to Sales Training Plan.

Source: Kenneth R. Davis, *Marketing Management* (New York: Ronald Press Co., 1961), p. 480. Copyright © 1961, The Ronald Press Company.

candidates for sales jobs may be sought. The recruitment process, however, is a difficult one, for personal selling is not as attractive a career choice to many of the more talented or better educated people as are other alternatives. The career image is one of long hours, frequent travel, and constant discouragement. The growing recognition of the value of the sales force as a resource of the firm has resulted in attempts by management to improve salesmen's working conditions and financial remuneration and to provide them with security for the future. Unfortunately, it takes time to change career images, and personal selling is still handicapped by such stigmas as "hucksterism" and the "Death of a Salesman."

In addition to the image issue, recruitment is also made difficult by the problem of turnover. Undeniably, not all people who attempt a career in selling are successful. Those who are poor producers either become discouraged and drop out or are eventually terminated by their employers. Successful salesmen, on the other hand, may shift to other companies to improve their positions or rise to a position in sales management in the same company. Regardless of the cause of turnover, the net result is that openings on the selling staff are frequent. Attrition because of failure or success by salesmen means that the recruitment task must be continuous and closely attuned to the future needs of the selling organization. A simple illustration of the effect of turnover on recruitment needs is seen in terms of a company with a sales force having an average strength of 200 men. Its separation rate is 20 men per year, or 10 percent. Thus the entire sales force must be replaced every ten years![6]

Selecting Salesmen

Assuming that a continuing supply of applicants for selling positions is available, the next step in the process of building a sales force or adding to an existing organization is that of selection. This phase of the sales force building process is of great importance because success here can have a great impact on the effectiveness of the selling organization. Selection of qualified and motivated people means that more and higher quality selling activity may take place. It also reduces separation, either voluntary or involuntary. This in turn means less turnover and lower expense incurred by the firm.

Three tools are useful in the selection process: (1) the personal history statement, (2) psychological tests, and (3) the personal interview.

Personal History Statement. The personal history statement or application form is designed to elicit information about the prospect which

---

[6] Edward W. Cundiff and Richard R. Still, *Basic Marketing* (Englewood Cliffs, N.J.: Prentice-Hall, 1964), p. 527.

will be of use in initial screening. Conventional practice is to cover data such as:

1. *Personal data*—age, height, weight, marital status, and number of dependents.
2. *Education*—including a resumé of applicant's educational background with data on performance, extent of self-support, and extracurricular activities.
3. *Experience*—prior employers, types of jobs held, and reasons for leaving.
4. *References from several sources*—former teachers, employers, and current acquaintances who can provide information about specific traits or abilities.
5. *Personality and motivation*—general questions about interests in hobbies, organizations, sports, and so on. The applicant may also be asked to explain why he is interested in selling as a career and why he chose the specific company as a possible employer.[7]

It is evident that a great deal of information about the job prospect can be gathered by means of a well-designed personal history form. Not only the specific information but its mode of presentation can give insight as to the type of person involved. If used as a preliminary screening device, great care must be taken to have the questionnaire designed to get the type of information *relevant* to the nature of the job to be filled. In addition, analysis and interpretation of the application form must be carried out by persons skilled in psychology, aware of the nature of the job to be filled, and involved in the design of the application form.

Psychological Tests. Perhaps the most controversial of the tools used in selecting salesmen are psychological tests. These devices are used to supplement the information gained from personal history forms and from the interview. It would, however, be very unwise to view them as a substitute for the other approaches used in the selection process.

Tests are designed to provide insights about the applicant's intelligence, personality, and interests. The intelligence tests are perhaps the least criticized of all of the tests, in terms of reliability and validity. The problem is not with intelligence tests themselves but rather with the relations of a given level of intelligence to probable success in the sales position. It is clear that a minimum level of intelligence is required of salesmen and that perhaps higher levels are needed for the successful performance of more technically oriented selling tasks. However, it is also suggested that too high a level of intelligence for a given selling job may result in boredom and subsequent job dissatisfaction.

---

[7] Kenneth R. Davis, *Marketing Management* (New York: Ronald Press Co., 1961), p. 480.

It appears that the successful use of intelligence tests is predicated on screening out extremely low and high performers for further investigation. If some relationship can be found between a range of intelligence and success in a particular type of selling job, then of course the tests assume predictive value.

Tests of personality, interests, and aptitudes appear to have greater relevance than intelligence tests. These tests deal with human traits that are important in a sales situation. Unfortunately, they are not easily validated—that is, shown to be successful in predicting success in a given situation. As John A. Howard has noted, "Tests are designed to predict, but often it is not at all clear as to just what is being predicted."[8] What is required is that the user must analyze the nature of the selling job to be filled in terms of the personality traits most likely to lead to success. Then he must construct a test to measure the existence of such traits or use a standardized test of some sort and engage in sufficient experimentation to validate the test or, more likely, the battery of tests. The goal is to be able to predict which persons from a group of applicants are most likely to succeed in a given selling situation. It is quite clear that this goal requires personnel skilled in psychological testing procedures, time, money, and a sales force of sufficient size and turnover rate to provide opportunities for validation experiments. Smaller firms may utilize the services of testing consultants. It must be reemphasized, however, that without validation in terms of the particular selling task, testing should be considered only a small part of the selection procedure.

The Personal Interview.   Another approach to selection is the personal interview. It is a flexible device and may be used for such diverse purposes as initial screening, as in college campus recruitment, or for final investigation prior to hiring.

The purposes of the interview include the discovery of traits not uncovered by the application or by testing, probing to find out more about interest and motivation, and evaluation of such characteristics as personal appearance and oral expression. The interview may either be structured through a questionnaire or unstructured, depending upon the preference of management. Regardless of the type of interview used, management must provide well-defined criteria which can be used to evaluate the person taking the interview as well as to validate the interviewing process. This provision of criteria is especially important when selecting salesmen because of the many ill-founded preconceptions about the personality attributes of a good salesman which are held by interviewers.

In order to prevent interviewer biases or preconceptions from lessen-

---

[8] John A. Howard, *Marketing Management: Operating, Strategic, and Administrative,* 3d ed. (Homewood, Ill.: Richard D. Irwin, 1973), p. 289.

ing the effectiveness of the interview as a selection device, many firms have the applicants appraised personally by several interviewers. Regardless of the method, the personal interview can be a useful tool if it can be validated against later sales success. Such validation, in turn, requires a standardized approach.[9] Traits that are important to the selling task at hand must be identified, and all the interviewers must agree on how the existence of these traits is to be discovered and measured.

Training Salesmen

The third component in building a successful sales force is training. After recruitment and selection of new additions to the sales staff, effort must be expended to prepare these people to assume their selling responsibilities. However, training must not be limited merely to new personnel, because it is a continuing process encompassing all members of the sales force—old as well as new.

Training programs vary widely from firm to firm, and the type and extent of training required is a function of several factors, including:

1. The complexity of the product line and product applications.
2. The nature of the market in terms of buyer sophistication.
3. The pressure of competition and the resulting need for nonsales service.
4. The level of knowledge and the degree of the sales experience of the trainee.

Goals of Training. Regardless of the type of program required in a specific situation, the objectives of a training program for newly selected salesmen are quite clear: To make the salesman more productive; to enable the salesman to reach his sales norm more rapidly; and to reduce the rate of sales force turnover.

In terms of increasing selling productivity, training can:

1. Provide the product knowledge necessary for all beginning salesmen.
2. Introduce new products and new applications of old products to regular members of the sales force.
3. Point out opportunities in which the existing line can be used to satisfy customer needs.
4. Emphasize nonselling activities aimed at improving customer relations or cultivating selected accounts.
5. Increase salesmen's productivity by showing them how to utilize

---

[9] Robert N. McMurry, "Validating the Patterned Interview," *Personnel,* Vol. 23 (1946–47), pp. 263–72.

their time more effectively and how to engage in personal expense control.

It takes considerable time for a new salesman to become broken in with respect to a territory. Not only is the learning process time-consuming, often it is several months before the new man has the feel of the territory and can develop sales volume consistent with sales potential. The training program must be viewed as a means of supplementing the role of experience in the learning process. Its goal is to shorten the time span required between introduction of a new salesman to a territory and his attainment of a satisfactory level of sales volume.

Because of the considerable expense involved in the process of building a sales force, each salesman represents a large investment of the firm's resources. When salesmen leave for one reason or another the investment is lost. In addition, the replacement of an old salesman by a new recruit results in a lag in sales volume until the new man becomes experienced. Thus turnover, although inevitable to some degree, is expensive.

Training, both initial and continuing, may be viewed as an additional investment made to reduce the rate of turnover and thus the related costs and losses of revenue. Proper training may help the individual salesman to be more successful by teaching him new techniques and approaches. Perhaps of even greater importance is the supportive role training plays by indicating to the salesman the concern of the company for his success. It thus has a motivational role which may be as important to the building of a successful selling organization as its informational role.

SALES FORCE MANAGEMENT—
COMPENSATION AND MOTIVATION

In the actual management of an ongoing sales organization, it is assumed that the sales force has an acceptable rate of turnover and that new men are being added to fill vacancies caused by terminations or territorial growth or a combination of both factors. It is further assumed that a training program is available for the new men as well as a continuing program of retraining for the more seasoned members of the sales force. Given this type of situation, the next aspect of sales force management to be considered is that of compensation.

Compensating Salesmen

Company policies which determine the level and type of payment received by salesmen have an important influence on the effectiveness of the sales force. Policies that are fair in terms of recognizing variations in territorial sales potentials and reward individuals for a job well done attract a better caliber of applicant and help keep the more productive salesman satisfied with his position. Thus well-designed and executed compensation plans can help to upgrade the quality of the selling force while reducing the turnover rate. This latter benefit means that the costs of recruitment and selection are lessened and the investment in training is utilized more effectively.

The goals of a good compensation plan have been stated in various terms, but most agree that the purpose is to gain the cooperation of the men and further the interests of the employer. This is not an easy objective to achieve because individual self-interest on the part of a salesman does not always coincide with the goals of the firm. Thus the most effective compensation plans are designed to provide an incentive for salesman performance of those activities the employer deems most profitable. These activities include making sales, of course, as well as provision of service, the cultivation of new accounts, and the gathering of market intelligence, not to mention many other tasks. The difficulty encountered in devising a good compensation plan is caused by the diverse nature of the typical selling job in terms of tasks to be performed as well as the breadth and heterogeneity of the typical product line or customer list. The complexity of the problem becomes especially evident when the dynamics of product line development, customer turnover, and competition are added to this situation.

The starting point for appraising or redesigning a compensation plan is again the all-important job analysis. The particular selling task at hand must be analyzed in terms of the components of the task which, when well performed, lead to salesman success. These are the components the compensation plan must spotlight to get more and better performance from the sales force. Second, an income analysis of the salesmen involved must be made. Will the compensation plan proposed provide competitive levels of income to members of the sales force? Will any members of the force receive a reduced income if the plan becomes operative?

It is desirable to avoid instituting a new compensation plan which will cause major changes in the income of participants in the short run. Instead, it is preferable to change the rewards for performance of certain activities or for the sale of certain products over a period of time so that changes are evolutionary rather than abrupt.

After a careful job analysis, including a definition of objectives for the compensation plan, a tentative approach can be developed and discussed with the salesmen. This step provides an opportunity for feedback—a chance to pick up new ideas from the salesmen as well as to hear their criticisms. It also allows management to explain the way in which the plan will operate and to anticipate and assuage fears the salesmen may have about the impact of the proposed plan upon their well-being. The plan proposed may be modified in view of suggestions and fears brought to light in the meeting with the salesmen.

After preliminary analyses the plan is ready to be tested. A test can be simulated by utilizing past sales records to see what earnings would have been if the new plan had been in force. Or the new plan can be put into effect in specific territories representing a range of competitive conditions and salesman skill and experience. The second approach is much preferred because it is impossible to tell how salesmen will react to a new plan until they actually work under it. Information from the test run can be used to improve the plan further and to indicate whether or not it should be fully implemented.

Components of Compensation. The methods of compensation are: (1) base salary, (2) commission, and (3) bonus.

BASE SALARY. The base salary is payment for certain routine activities performed by salesmen. It is a means of control by which management can require that a route be covered or that certain types of supporting activities be performed through guaranteed income. It also provides a cushion against too great fluctuations in salesmen's income caused by conditions beyond their control. Hence the greater the routinized selling activity or the larger the fluctuation in sales volume, the more the reliance is likely to be placed upon base salary in the compensation mix.

COMMISSION. A commission or percentage payment associated with the sale of certain items in the line is used by management to direct selling effort to specific items (or customers). Rates of commission may be periodically adjusted to reflect changes in product or customer profitability or the market environment. The role of the commission form of compensation is determined by the incentive requirements and the stability of sales volume. Customer needs for nonselling services place limits on the degree of sales incentive which management can blend into the compensation mix. With too much emphasis on incentive compensation the salesman becomes a high-spotter, spending his time with larger accounts and neglecting his smaller customers.

BONUS. Bonus compensation is a more diffused type of incentive payment. Generally bonuses are paid for exceeding a predetermined quota, although they may represent some allocation of profits based on performance and length of service. A bonus is a means of letting a salesman share in the progress of the firm without making the payment as directly related to performance as is the case with a commission. The bonus may assume considerable importance in the compensation of technical representatives who back up salesmen by solving customer problems but do not actually make sales.

An actual compensation plan may call for any combination of the three components. The nature of the selling task and the requirements of the market which determine the role of personal selling also suggest the emphasis to be placed on salary, commission, and bonus payments.

Objectives of a Good Compensation Plan. The following have been suggested as four general objectives of a compensation plan:

1. To attract and hold good salesmen.
2. To stimulate the sales organization to produce maximum attainable volume by profitable sales.
3. To control selling expense, especially where there are major fluctuations in sales volume.
4. To ensure full attention to customer needs through complete performance of the sales job.[10]

Although the general objectives are common to all compensation programs, the relative importance of each one may change with respect to different firms or to individual firms in different stages of development. For example, the small firm just starting out may find that expense control is the most important objective of its compensation plan. On the other hand, a more established firm might find that competition requires that the compensation plan motivate the firm's salesmen to the complete fulfillment of customer needs.

In addition to the general objectives there are more individualized goals "designed to achieve specific company marketing and sales objectives."[11] The following goals have been suggested:

1. To encourage solicitation of new accounts and development of new sources of revenue.
2. To encourage full-line selling.
3. To stimulate the sale of more profitable products.
4. To hold a salesman responsible for the profit contribution on sales where he can influence margins.[12]

The specific objectives listed above are by no means exhaustive. Neither are they common to all plans for compensating salesmen. A truly effective program will contain the means to reach goals common to all firms and, in addition, will be tailored to reach specific objectives which are an outgrowth of the resources, competitive environment, and particular promotional strategy of the individual firm.

Motivating Salesmen

The very nature of the selling job requires that special attention be paid to the proper motivation of personnel. The salesman who works

---

[10] Davis and Webster, *Sales Force Management,* p. 627.

[11] Ibid.

[12] Ibid., p. 628.

alone, often away from his home, faces considerable discouragement in his daily routine. The depressing effects of loneliness and rejection usually require some type of supportive action from management. For some personalities the selling task may be sufficiently intriguing to require little more in the way of motivation than a good incentive compensation plan and a new list of prospects. Such salesmen are rare, however, and the average member of the sales force requires some motivating efforts in addition to that provided by his regular monetary compensation. The human traits of laziness and procrastination are as present among salesmen as in any other group in society, and managers have learned from experience that effort expended to overcome human inertia pays off in increased sales productivity.

The types of motivating action which might be taken by management are varied. Essentially, they may be classified as: (1) additional incentive compensation, (2) career advancement, and (3) contests or other types of special sales stimulation promotions.

Additional Compensation. This attempt at providing added motivation for the salesman is predicated on the belief that monetary rewards are the most meaningful. The payment of special compensation in addition to the regular plan may be used to motivate salesmen to reach special short-run objectives in terms of sales volume, customer coverage, or product emphasis. Monetary rewards have the advantage of being direct, easily understood by salesmen, and readily administered. The question is simply this: Do they motivate men to sell as well as other alternatives do?

Career Advancement. In this approach the better sales performers are offered transfers to more lucrative territories or invited to join the ranks of sales management. Thus the income advantage of job betterment is combined with the prestige of a rise in the organizational hierarchy. The motivating appeal of job advancement is less immediate in its impact than a direct monetary payment. But the reward, if achieved, has longer lasting benefits to the salesman. The problem, of course, is the lack of immediacy of payoff.

Special Activities. Somewhere between the immediate and somewhat prosaic approach of direct monetary payoffs and the longer run approach involving job advancement lies a range of special activities including contests and other types of special sales promotions aimed at increasing salesman motivation. Contests are especially popular among sales managers for this purpose. They are viewed as a means of evoking extra effort to achieve short-run goals by means somewhat more dramatic than purely monetary payments. Contests may liven the competitive spirit of the salesmen, may involve wives and children, and may promise rewards such as travel or vacations with pay which may have more general appeal than mere money.

The dangers inherent in their use as motivators, however, are numerous. Contests, like any other form of stimulation aimed at getting extra effort in the short run, may lose their impact with continued use. The nature of some contests and other events may alienate the more serious and professionally oriented members of the sales force. Moreover, contests by their very nature engender rivalry among members of the sales organization and may thereby break down a close group relationship built over a long period of time. Thus they must be used with care and never as a substitute for effective activity in the other aspects of sales force management discussed earlier.

Methods of Communication

Because salesmen work at a distance from the home office and are usually on their own a great deal, management has a special problem in establishing lines of communication to them. Written messages going one way and reports from the field flowing in the other direction are found in almost all sales situations, but there is serious question as to the effect of this type of communication on salesman morale or motivation. Certainly, a note from a superior congratulating a salesman on a job well done will have a favorable influence on the salesman's feeling of being recognized and appreciated, but a routine written pep talk too often has little or no effect on salesman motivation.

Recognition of the shortcomings of written communication has led many sales managers to use the telephone instead of the memo. Of course, personal contact is the best method of communication between salesmen and their managers. Traditionally, the sales manager has attempted to build a personal relationship between himself and his individual salesmen. In fact, a psychiatrist, highly experienced in these matters, has indicated that salesmen often view their sales manager as a father figure and are quite disturbed emotionally when separated from this superior by transfer or promotion.[13]

New evidence has been reported to indicate that the traditional man-to-man pattern of organization common to so many sales management situations may not be the best approach in terms of salesman motivation and productivity. Because the problem of motivation is so closely related to the ways in which salesmen are paid, controlled, and supervised, some attention should be paid to the effects of management organization patterns on salesman performance.

Patterns of Organization for Sales

Research findings based on a large number of studies made during the past two decades have indicated that the pattern of management

[13] Leonard E. Himler, M.D., "Frustrations in Selling Activities," in Martin R. Warshaw (ed.), *Changing Perspectives in Marketing Management* (Ann Arbor: Bureau of Business Research, University of Michigan, 1962), pp. 81–82.

or organization may be an important factor in the motivation and productivity of sales organizations.[14] As indicated in Figure 15–6, given a manager with a well-organized plan of operation, high performance goals, and a high degree of technical competence, the method of supervision will affect (1) organizational morale and motivation and (2) organizational attainment. The findings as reported by Rensis Likert indicate that sales managers who supervise their salesmen in accordance with the principle of supportive relationships and by group methods will develop better adjusted and more productive sales organizations than will sales managers who use the traditional methods based on direct hierarchical pressure for results, including the usual contests and other practices of the traditional systems.[15]

The principle of supportive relationships means that the relationships between the sales manager and his salesmen should be such that they build the ego of the subordinate and maintain and support values, both economic and noneconomic, that are deemed important by *the subordinate*. The principle has been stated as follows:

The leadership and other processes of the organization must be such as to ensure a maximum probability that in all interactions and all relationships with the organization each member will, in the light of his background, values, and expectations, view the experience as supportive and one which builds and maintains his sense of personal worth and importance.[16]

In addition to utilization of the principle of supportive relationships, Likert believes highly productive sales organizations should consist of "overlapping, highly effective work groups with each group having high group loyalty and high performance goals."[17]

Thus in the newer approach to management the group pattern of organization replaces the man-to-man pattern. Figure 15–7 illustrates these two patterns. In the group type of organization (part b), the sales manager or sales supervisor would supervise a *group* of perhaps 6 to 12 salesmen by holding meetings once or twice a month. Likert describes a typical meeting as follows:

As a rule, the sales manager or one of his sales supervisors presides. Each salesman, in turn, presents to the group a report of his activity for the period since the last meeting of the group. He describes such things as the number and kinds of prospects he has obtained, the calls he has made, the nature of the sales presentations he has used, the closings he has attempted, the number of

---

[14] Rensis Likert, *New Patterns of Management* (New York: McGraw-Hill Book Co., 1961).

[15] Rensis Likert, "New Patterns of Sales Management," in Warshaw (ed.), *Changing Perspectives in Marketing Management*, pp. 1–25.

[16] Ibid., p. 6.

[17] Ibid., p. 6.

FIGURE 15–6

A Well-Organized Plan of Organization in Traditional and Newer Management Systems

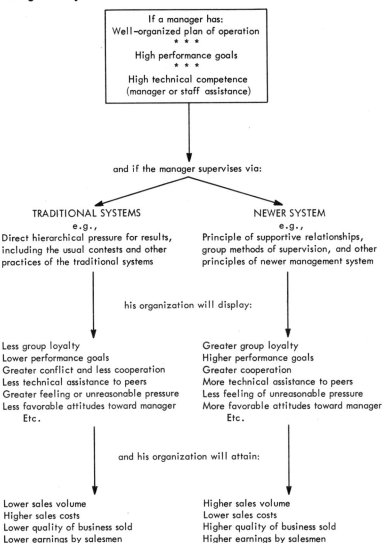

Source: Rensis Likert, "New Patterns in Sales Management" in Martin R. Warshaw (ed.), *Changing Perspectives in Marketing Management* (Ann Arbor: Bureau of Business Research, University of Michigan, 1962), p. 24.

FIGURE 15–7

Man-to-Man and Group Patterns of Organization

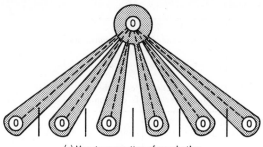

(a) Man-to-man pattern of organization

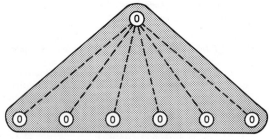

(b) Group pattern of organization

Source: From *New Patterns of Management* by Rensis Likert. Copyright 1961, McGraw-Hill Book Co. Used by permission.

sales achieved, and the volume and quality of his total sales. The other men in the group analyze the salesman's efforts, methods, and results. Suggestions from their experience and know-how are offered. The outcome is a valuable coaching session. For example, if sales results can be improved through better prospecting, this is made clear, and the steps and methods to achieve this improvement are spelled out.

After this analysis by the group, each man with the advice and assistance of the group sets goals for himself concerning the work he will do and the results he will achieve before the next meeting of the group.

The manager or supervisor acts as chairman of the group but the analyses and interactions are among the men. The chairman keeps the orientation of the group on a helpful, constructive, problem-solving basis. He sees that the tone is helpful and supportive, not ego-deflating as a result of negative criticisms and comments.[18]

The supporters of the newer pattern, which involves supportive management and group supervision, believe strongly that this approach is the key to motivation and thus to better sales productivity. Critics of

---

[18] Ibid., p. 16.

the new pattern claim that it is nothing more than would be expected of good management. They also point out that there are situations in which group supervision of the sales force is impractical, such as when salesmen are widely dispersed geographically.

Regardless of its applicability in all situations, the new pattern has placed attention on the role of sales supervision as an important motivating factor. There is little argument with the suggestion that noneconomic motives such as ego enhancement should reinforce the more direct economic motives in order to increase salesman motivation. Research findings indicate that the use of the principle of supportive relationships and group supervision does provide for this reinforcement and thus leads to higher morale, greater motivation, and higher productivity.

SUMMARY

This chapter has considered personal selling as a special form of interpersonal communication. Inasmuch as the salesman is the key element in the communication process, the nature of his task was examined in some detail. In addition, the process by which a sales force is built into an effective promotional resource was examined. Furthermore, attention was paid to the compensation and motivation of the individuals who make up the selling organization.

In this chapter the sales force was treated in a manner similar to that in which advertising was approached—as a "controllable." This implies that the type, amount, and direction of promotional effort are subject to variation in the short run by marketing management.

The view of personal selling as a promotional input subject to control in the short run is generally sustainable. However, a really effective selling organization cannot be built overnight. Thus, although short-run control is possible in terms of type of effort, extent of effort, or direction of effort, the truly qualitative aspect of the effort is dependent on a continuing process of recruitment, selection, training, supervision, and control. Good management is vital at each of these stages if the firm is to get the best payoff possible from its personal selling effort.

REVIEW AND DISCUSSION QUESTIONS

1. How does personal selling differ from consumer advertising as a communication process?

2. Why do firms vary in their dependence upon personal selling as opposed to other tools of persuasive communication?

3. Describe the elements of a personal selling communication process in terms of their roles in achieving the firm's communication goals.

4. How does viewing sales strategy as a communication process help to define the nature of the salesman's task?

5. What are the essential tasks of personal selling? Do all salesmen perform these tasks with the same emphasis?

6. Why must the particular selling task be clearly defined for each salesman? How might these tasks vary at different levels in the channel of distribution?

7. How do product and market characteristics influence the nature of the personal selling task?

8. Why may it be said that the written job description is the foundation upon which a sales force is built?

9. Discuss the reasons behind this statement: Recruitment for the sales force is both a difficult and a never-ending process.

10. Why is the selection process so important in building a sales force? What tools are available to aid in this process?

11. What are the dangers of too great reliance on psychological testing to select salesmen?

12. What are the purposes of the personal interview? What dangers must be avoided in conducting such interviews?

13. What are the goals of a training program for salesmen? Can sales force training ever cease?

14. What are the goals of a good compensation plan for salesmen? Why is it so difficult to devise such a plan?

15. What guidelines should be considered in attempting to change a plan of compensation of salesmen?

16. Under what circumstances would you recommend greater reliance on base salary in the compensation plan?

17. Compare and contrast commission and bonus methods of compensation in terms of their objectives.

18. Why must management be concerned about sales force morale and motivation?

19. What role do contests play in motivating salesmen? What dangers are involved in their use?

20. What is a pattern of organization, and how might it influence salesman performance?

16

Evaluation and Control of Sales Force Efforts

THE EVALUATION AND CONTROL of promotional effort which involves personal selling is a prime responsibility of marketing management. Promotional activities include those performed by the firm as well as those performed by members of its channel of distribution. This chapter pays special attention to the evaluation and control of the personal selling efforts of the firm. Evaluating and controlling reseller promotional efforts will be considered in Chapter 19.

The evaluation and control process encompasses four distinct steps: (1) the development of standards of performance, (2) the measurement of actual performance, (3) the comparison of actual performance with the norm or standard, and (4) the taking of corrective action to remedy substandard performance. The fourth step may involve a reallocation of effort and is discussed at some length.

PURPOSES OF EVALUATION

The general purpose of evaluation of sales force efforts is to ensure that the resources allocated by the firm to these efforts are being used efficiently and in such a way as to facilitate the achievement of the firm's profitability goals.

In the short run, evaluation can determine whether more specific objectives such as revenue goals and expense goals are being met. Without such evaluation management cannot take those steps necessary to improve sales force performance during the current period.

In the longer run, evaluation is necessary in order to make better decisions about such inputs as the number of persons to be employed at various levels in the sales force organization, the hiring and training requirements, and the development of the sales budget.

In addition to its evident impact on sales force productivity, such an evaluation program can improve the morale of individual salesmen by providing them with information as to what is expected of them and how well they are performing relative to expectations. Opportunities are thus presented to management to praise good performance and to provide help in improving substandard performance.

INFORMATION NEEDS

In developing a system of evaluation and control the manager is faced with the problem of what is to be measured. Of course, some information on individual performance is required in most situations. There are times, however, when information on group performance is also useful. This is especially true when the pattern of organization is such that a group participative approach is being used. In still other cases information about the performance of the entire sales organization will be required.

It is the responsibility of the manager to evaluate the relative costs and values of different types of information and to adjust his information collection procedures accordingly.

THE EVALUATION AND CONTROL PROCESS

Developing Performance Standards

Considerable information about the firm and its market is necessary for the development of standards for sales force performance. The firm must develop its sales forecast from data on market potential or aggregate demand for a specific good or service. This forecast is the best estimate of sales to be expected during a given period, assuming a given set of environmental conditions and a specific marketing plan or program. The sales forecast is thus the basis for the promotion budget. It can, however, also be used as a starting point from which to develop sales goals or quotas for specific products, territories, or classes of customers. As such it is vital to the development of criteria for performance evaluation.

Measurements of sales potential, however, should not be the sole basis of performance standards. Special territorial characteristics such as terrain or dispersion of customers must be considered, as well as special attributes of products, customers, and the salesmen if meaningful performance standards are to be developed.

With respect to characteristics of individual salesmen, some consideration must be given to the fact that not all salesmen perform in the same way. For example, the high-pressure type may do very well in the short run if results are measured in terms of sales volume in relation to potential. His methods may, however, lead to a decline in sales in the long run as customers tire of his approach. On the other hand, the low-pressure type may not score well on the basis of short-run performance but over the years may show a rising sales trend.

Because of the unique circumstances faced by each firm in terms of market potential, customer and product mix, competition, and qualitative characteristics of the sales force, the development of standards of sales performance must be closely related to the specific sales objectives previously planned. As stated by one source:

The standards of performance selected, therefore, should facilitate the measurement of progress made toward departmental objectives, both general and specific. Although the specific goals vary from time to time in accordance with changes in the firm's marketing situation, they should always be reconcilable with the general goals of volume, profit, and growth.[1]

Standards of Measurement of Performance

Quantitative Standards. The most commonly used standards are quantitative and are based on single ratios or combinations of ratios. Those expressed in quantitative form offer the advantages of ease of calculation and explanation to salesmen. This latter factor is most important, especially when the performance standard is being used for incentive purposes as well as for control. Some ratios or measures commonly used include:

1. Sales volume as a percentage of sales potential.
2. Selling expense as a percentage of sales volume.
3. Number of customers sold as a percentage of total number of potential customers.
4. Call frequency ratio, or total calls made divided by total number of accounts and prospects covered.

There are other measures in addition to those cited above, such as average cost per call and average order size, which can be used for this purpose. The correct choice of the combination of measures to use is best set by the sales manager to meet the needs of his specific situation.

Profit Contribution Standards. Most writers on the subject agree that the key measurement for setting standards is sales volume achieved in relation to sales potential. After all, the main objective of the sales

---

[1] Richard R. Still and Edward W. Cundiff, *Sales Management* (Englewood Cliffs, N.J.: Prentice-Hall, 1958), pp. 272–73.

force is to make sales, and without such sales considerations of profitability cannot begin. However, more and more the norms of sales performance are being combined with those of expense control so that profitability standards may be set. Perhaps the best way to control and appraise salesmen's performance is by the application of the techniques of distribution cost analysis. In this manner not only can relative profit contributions of individual salesmen be measured but standards can be set which reflect such diverse factors as gross profits, product mix sold, customer mix, direct selling expenses, and the amount of sales promotion assistance going into the territory.

In very simple terms a distribution cost analysis would be used to find out the gross margin contribution of each salesman. This computation based on sales volume less cost of goods sold would give some idea of the *initial* profitability of the product mix being sold. From gross margin would be subtracted those expenses that can be allocated to the salesman on a causal or benefit basis. This means that only those items that are *caused* by his activity or *benefit him* in terms of reaching his goals (direct mail advertising, for example) should be charged against his gross margin contribution. The residual is the contribution to general overhead (not allocated to the territory) and to profit. This amount, often termed the "contribution margin," is an excellent measure of the *relative* performance of individual salesmen. But, equally important, the technique allows the development of both revenue and cost standards based on actual as well as desired performance. Several sources are available which discuss cost standards in greater detail than can be done here.[2]

The contribution margin can also be used as part of a return on investment analysis. For example, if a certain territory produced a contribution margin of $80,000 on sales of $1,000,000 and if $500,000 of company assets had been employed in support of the territory, the following return on investment (ROI) calculations[3] could be made:

$$\frac{\text{Contribution: } \$80,000}{\text{Sales: } \$1,000,000} \times \frac{\text{Sales: } \$1,000,000}{\text{Investment: } \$500,000} = 16 \text{ percent ROI}$$

The use of two fractions rather than one (contribution over investment) is to illustrate that the ROI is a function of both the profitability of the sales volume and the turnover rate. Thus ROI can be improved in a given territory by increasing sales with investment held constant,

---

[2] See especially Charles H. Sevin, *Distribution Cost Analysis*, Economic Series No. 50 (Washington, D.C.: Government Printing Office, 1946), and Donald R. Longman and Michael Schiff, *Practical Distribution Cost Analysis* (Homewood, Ill.: Richard D. Irwin, 1955).

[3] See Michael Schiff, "The Uses of ROI in Sales Management," *Journal of Marketing*, Vol. 27 (July 1963), pp. 70–73.

by increasing profitability of sales, or by reducing the investment needed to sustain the present level of sales.

By indicating the relative ROI's of various territories, the analysis can be used to appraise how well the various salesmen are doing, given the assets at their disposal.

Qualitative Criteria. The setting of quantitative performance standards, whether based on revenue, cost, or other considerations, has as its major shortcoming the inability to measure activities and traits which may pay off for the salesman in the longer run. To make certain that these qualities are not overlooked in the appraisal process, many firms use a more subjective approach in order to develop norms of performance standards related to the qualitative aspect of the salesman's job. In some cases the sales manager or supervisor uses his judgment in appraising how well the salesman displays the desired traits. In other cases, a more formalized merit-rating checklist may be used.

Comparing Salesmen's Performance to Standards

It is inevitable that some attempts will be made to appraise salesmen's performance. Appraisals are needed to indicate where performance is substandard and to provide evidence to support salary adjustments or promotions. Appraisal also provides a good check on how well the sales force building process—selection and training—is being carried out. Last, but very important, is the beneficial effect that a well-administered appraisal program has on salesman morale and motivation.

The difficulties encountered are many. The selling task itself is quite complex, and short-run effort by salesmen may not have immediate results. In addition, some of the results may not be measurable or as a consequence of joint effort may not be separable.[4]

The appraisal process begins with a rather mechanical step. It is the comparison of the actual performances of salesmen or groups of salesmen with the performance standards previously developed. Data on actual performance may come from an analysis of company records or from special reports required of salesmen. Once the data are collected the evaluation process can begin.

A brief example may be helpful here.[5] Baker and Kent are two salesmen whose sales to date are $93,000 and $98,000 respectively. Their performances are to be measured primarily on the basis of sales in rela-

---

[4] Salesmen rarely work alone. They are aided by other salesmen, supervisors, managers, or product specialists. The question of who is responsible for the sale is very difficult to answer. See D. Maynard Phelps and J. Howard Westing, *Marketing Management,* rev. ed. (Homewood, Ill.: Richard D. Irwin, 1960), p. 741.

[5] Harold H. Maynard and James H. Davis, *Sales Management,* 3d ed. (New York: Ronald Press, 1957), pp. 476–77.

tion to sales potential, the latter being expressed as a quota figure, as follows:

	Sales in Thousands to Date		Increase or Decrease	Quota (thousand)	Percentage of Quota to Date	
	This Year	Last Year			This Year	Last Year
Baker..........	$93	$ 80	+16%	$170	55	47
Kent............	98	104	− 6%	200	49	52

If performance is measured on sales alone it might appear that Kent is outperforming Baker. In terms of quota, however, Baker is performing better. Indeed, if the trends from last year are considered, Kent appears to be slipping while Baker is improving his position.

Although the relatively sparse data presented above can provide for some important analysis, it cannot answer all of the questions required for a complete performance evaluation. For example, the appraiser would need to know the relative profitability in the short run of the sales volume recorded. An analysis of gross margins less allocable expenses would provide the answers needed in this area.

Salesmen's activities performed in the current period which may have payoffs in the future require the use of different standards of performance. Evaluation may take place on the basis of effort expended to gain new accounts or to cultivate old ones. Regardless of the approach, the objective is to gain some feel for the way in which the salesman is performing the non-order-seeking portion of his job.

In addition to the quantitative evaluation of the salesman's performance there is the appraisal of qualitative factors such as attitude, judgment, and appearance. Here the appraiser may use some sort of rating scale. It is good policy to have several people involved in subjective evaluation of salesmen to avoid bias on the part of those engaged in the rating process.

It cannot be stressed too strongly that the criteria, both quantitative and qualitative, used as the bases for appraisal must be consistent with the salesman's task as *communicated to him* by the written job description. The selling job differs widely from firm to firm, and the appraisal process must be custom-made to fit the specific needs and goals of the individual selling organization.

Corrective Action

If the preliminary stages of the control process have been handled correctly, the sales manager should have a good idea as to the relative performance of the salesmen under his supervision. The concept of relative performance is based on performance as compared with pre-determined standards. In those cases where individual performances are well below the norms, the sales manager or supervisor can take corrective action. The philosophy underlying his action is that a better utilization of the resources (salesmen) under his control will increase the contribution of the sales organization to the goals of the firm. This philosophy might also provide the basis for remedial action in the case of salesmen whose performances are substandard. Essentially, this approach would involve helping the salesman to utilize his most valuable resource—time—more effectively. After this type of remedial action has been undertaken, a second approach may be considered—the direction of activity to areas of greater opportunity.

Time and Duty Analysis. This approach to the better utilization of salesmen's time is an adaptation of the time-and-motion studies used by industrial engineers in the factory. A well-planned study by James H. Davis reported several pertinent conclusions about salesmen's time utilization.[6]

In brief, the findings show that there is a measurable relationship between selling time and sales volume. In addition, the actual amount of selling time available to a salesman in a typical day is very limited. In his study of wholesale drug salesmen Davis reported that city salesmen spent only 17 percent of their day in actually attempting to promote new merchandise, and 37 percent in all essential activities inside the retail store. Experiences of other companies in different industries have indicated about the same fraction of time available for promotional selling and essential activities.[7]

As a result of the recognition of the time-sales relationship and the limited time available to salesmen, two points become apparent:

First, through careful training and scheduling, management should do all it can to increase the amount of time available for essential activities at the expense of nonessential ones. Second, the essential activities that management wants performed should be scrutinized carefully to see if they are, in fact, essential. For example, many companies ask their salesmen to perform some or all of the task of collecting in their territories. If this task is really an essential one for the salesman, no further question need be raised. In many cases, however, it will be found to be more nearly desirable than essential. In this event, the value of time spent in collecting should be carefully weighed against the value of the same time available for more direct selling activities.[8]

---

[6] See James H. Davis, *Increasing the Wholesale Drug Salesman's Effectiveness* (Columbus: Bureau of Business Research, College of Commerce and Administration, The Ohio State University, 1948).

[7] Maynard and Davis, *Sales Management,* pp. 468–69.

[8] Ibid., p. 469.

In addition to the recognition of the value of selling time and the suggestion that management attempt to maximize the availability of such time by careful planning is the question of how time is used by individual salesmen. It does little good to increase selling time at the expense of other activities when selling time is poorly utilized.

In the Davis study activities of 70 wholesale drug salesmen were analyzed. It was found that when genuine sales arguments or reasons to buy were presented to prospects, sales resulted in 50 percent of the cases. A mere mention of an item resulted in a sale only 13 percent of the time.[9]

Of course, the selling argument or reason-to-buy approach is only one way in which the salesman may make his limited time available for selling more productive. The point is that management may be in a better position to correct substandard selling performance if it knows how much selling time is available and how well it is being used. Time and duty analysis is one way of getting this information.

Routing. If about one half of the salesman's time is spent in contact with the customer (perhaps with ⅙ of his time used for promotional selling and ⅓ of his time engaged in nonselling activity), the other half is spent in traveling. Such time is totally nonproductive and bears a very high hourly cost. If careful routing and travel plans are made by sales management in those selling situations where such control is feasible, the savings in time may well be substantial. Thus improving total time utilization is an important step toward correcting substandard sales performance.

REALLOCATION OF EFFORT

The process of changing the nature of the salesman's task or of reducing his travel time to allow more opportunity for creative selling is in a very real sense a reallocation of resources. In this case time is the scarce item and attempts are made to provide more of it for selling and to improve the utilization of that which is available. In a way the type of action described above may be viewed as an attempt to optimize the performance of each individual salesman in his territory.

From the standpoint of the sales manager viewing all of the territories under his control such efforts may be only one approach to improving overall performance of the sales force. Certainly, corrective action should begin at the level of the individual salesman, but time utilization is only a part of the story. Time must be used effectively, but the chances of success are conditioned strongly by the sales targets chosen. If individual salesmen are using their selling time effectively yet their performance is substandard, perhaps their effort should be

[9] Ibid., pp. 470–71.

reallocated to different products or to different customers. Further analysis of product types sold and customer classes covered may provide answers to the question of whether the product mix or customer mix can be changed to improve the performance of the subpar salesman.

However, the sales manager has one other alternative to consider. Briefly, that is whether or not to reallocate selling resources to the various territories which make up the market. Economic analysis provides the conceptual ideal for allocation of selling effort among territories. The

FIGURE 16–1

Optimum Allocation of Selling Expense

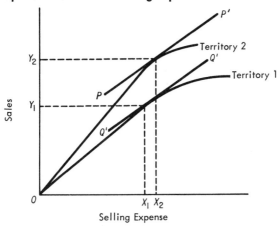

Note: The curved lines indicate the relations between sales and selling expenditures in two sales areas, territory 1 and territory 2. The optimum allocation of a given personal selling appropriation is to spend OX_1 in territory 1 and OX_2 in territory 2 because PP' and QQ', which are tangent to the respective territorial personal-selling-sales relations, are parallel.

Source: John A. Howard, *Marketing Management*, rev. ed. (Homewood, Ill.: Richard D. Irwin, 1963), p. 448.

rule for an optimum allocation is that the level of selling expenditures in each territory should be such that the incremental receipts per dollar of selling effort should be equal among all territories. Figure 16–1 illustrates this concept graphically.

Although the precise application of this approach probably **cannot be** made to the problem of reallocation of selling effort, a simplified version may be usable. This is the rule that for an optimum allocation the ratio of the variable cost of personal selling to sales in each territory should be equal.[10] This rule is illustrated in Figure 16–2, which shows a selling expense to sales relationship for two sales territories. The allocation of

[10] J. A. Norden, "Spatial Allocation of Selling Expense," *Journal of Marketing,* Vol. 7 (January 1943), pp. 210–19.

$2,000 to each territory results in total sales of $5,000 plus $20,000, or $25,000. If, however, expenditures are reduced by $1,000 in territory 1 and increased a like amount in territory 2, total sales will be $2,500 plus $30,000, or a net increase of $7,500 with no increase in total sales expense.

The marketing or sales manager must know *how much* of a shift in selling expenditures among the territories is necessary to achieve the optimum allocation. A mathematical method for answering the question can be constructed based on two assumptions: (1) relationships between

FIGURE 16–2

Comparison of Two Allocations of Selling Expense

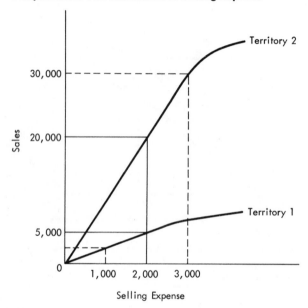

total variable selling costs and sales in each territory are known from past experience and (2) underlying factors which determined the relationship in the past have not changed significantly.[11]

In contrast to the methodology described above is the more pragmatic approach of the field sales manager. It is useful to look briefly at the way he might approach the problem of redeployment of sales effort.

A Case History

The director of sales of the Dow Chemical Company, has provided valuable insights into how one company views the problem of reallocation

---

[11] See John A. Howard, *Marketing Management: Operating, Strategic, and Administrative,* 3d ed. (Homewood, Ill.: Richard D. Irwin, 1973), pp. 175–80.

FIGURE 16–3

Relationship of Marketing Effort to Corporate Profitability

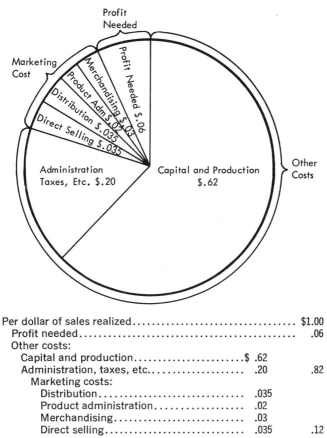

Per dollar of sales realized		$1.00
Profit needed		.06
Other costs:		
Capital and production	$ .62	
Administration, taxes, etc.	.20	.82
Marketing costs:		
Distribution	.035	
Product administration	.02	
Merchandising	.03	
Direct selling	.035	.12

or redeployment of the field sales force.[12] The corporate objective in this example was to achieve a 6 percent profit on total sales dollars. The planned distribution of costs was as indicated in Figure 16–3. Of special importance to the problem at hand was the budgeting of approximately 3.5 percent of sales revenue to direct selling effort. The major question is not whether the 3.5 percent figure is correct but how direct selling resources can best be deployed, given this cost-revenue constraint.

Figure 16–4 illustrates the territorial objectives, which are clarified in the following statement:

---

[12] William R. Dixon, "Redetermining the Size of the Sales Force: A Case Study," in Martin R. Warshaw (ed.), *Changing Perspectives in Marketing Management* (Ann Arbor: Bureau of Business Research, University of Michigan, 1962), p. 59.

FIGURE 16–4

Territorial Objectives

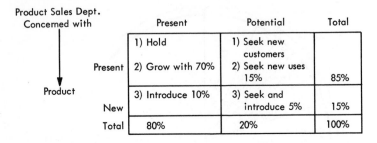

Territory Concerned with ⟶ Accounts

Product Sales Dept. Concerned with		Present	Potential	Total
Product	Present	1) Hold 2) Grow with 70%	1) Seek new customers 2) Seek new uses 15%	85%
	New	3) Introduce 10%	3) Seek and introduce 5%	15%
	Total	80%	20%	100%

In [Figure 16–4] we see that the field force is primarily concerned with the subject of accounts. The major efforts of a going field force are usually directed toward present accounts (column 1). The major job is to hold and grow with present accounts on present products of the company. We have indicated some approximations of the amount of effort going toward these objectives, with the field force which is under study. In a company with a complex product line like the Dow Chemical Company, we feel that the field force should spend a certain part of its time (10 percent for this group) introducing our new product lines to the present customers. Hence, we see about 80 percent of the field force's time spent with present customers. Likewise, we find that this particular field force should spend about 20 percent of its time with potential customers, seeking new customers for new products. As a by-product, we note that it is spending 85 percent of its time on present products and 15 percent of its time on new products. The mix of every organization is different, of course. In our other marketing groups we apply effort to these different objectives in varying magnitudes. Likewise, variation will be found from company to company. Yet we feel that any company which has a complex product mix and which is constantly creating new products will face some combination similar to this. My illustration shows a single territorial force of one marketing group in the Dow Chemical Company. We shall examine later some of the major methods that we use to arrive at this deployment of effort.[13]

Having recognized the constraints imposed by profit and cost criteria and having defined the territorial objectives, the next step was to ascertain the cost of keeping a man in the field. Compilation of salary, fringe benefit, automobile, supervision, and other expenses resulted in a figure of about $30,000 per year per man of direct selling cost (or variable cost). If this expense were to reflect the 3.5 percent of revenue average, then sales should be about $850,000 per man ($30,000/.035). The profit

---

[13] Ibid.

FIGURE 16–5

Analysis of Effort

Field Man	
Salary	
Fringe	
Automobile	
Travel and entertainment	
Supervision	
Stenographer	
Office and supplies	
Communication and other	
Total.............................	$30,000

Effort	÷	Effort/Results	=	Results
$30,000		.03		$1,000,000
		.035		850,000
		.05		600,000

picture does not allow a performance of much below $600,000 or a 5 percent expense to sales ratio. Performances of over $1 million (3 percent expense to sales) raise the question of what an additional salesman might do in the territory.

An analysis of effort and a review of current performance are shown in Figures 16–5 and 16–6. From the latter it appears that all is well. In ten territories 42 men sold $35.8 million, for an average of $850,000 per man. The cost-revenue relationship is 3.5 percent, or directly on target.

FIGURE 16–6

Present Performance

Territory	$ M Sales	Performance Field Men	($ M/Man)
1........................	10,000	9	(1,110)
2........................	6,000	5	(1,200)
3........................	4,500	5	(900)
4........................	3,500	4	(875)
5........................	2,500	3	(833)
6........................	2,400	4	(600)
7........................	2,300	4	(575)
8........................	2,000	4	(500)
9........................	1,800	3	(600)
10........................	800	1	(800)
	35,800	42	(850)

Closer inspection indicates that performance might be improved. Specifically, while in territories 1 and 2 sales exceed $1,000,000 per man, in territory 8 four men are selling $500,000 apiece—quite a bit below the minimum goal.

Figure 16–7 compares present performance against sales potential as developed by market research. Some answers become evident here. In those areas in which sales were high per salesman, market penetration in terms of potential was about 30 to 33 percent. In the areas where volume per man was low, sales were at 50 percent of potential.

Analysis indicated that, although Dow had started with a total penetration larger than the present 35.8 percent, sales lost to competitors were greatest in the territories with the largest potential.

The immediate reaction might be to attempt to regain company position in all territories. Such action might, however, be costly and might also invite retaliation which would disturb revenue and profit contributions. A crucial decision is, therefore, what *share* of market can Dow *profitably* attain?

Assuming that the decision to try for 40 percent of the market has been made, Figure 16–8 illustrates the plan to capture $40 million in revenues. The basic philosophy underlying the plan is to increase effort in those territories where (1) potential is large and (2) Dow participation is small. Conversely, ground will be given in those territories where performance is close to marginal.

A closer analysis of individual territories gives a clear indication of how many men might be profitably redeployed from one territory to another. In territory 1, for example, nine men were selling $10 million or 33 percent of the market. An analysis of customers summarized in

FIGURE 16–7

Present Performance versus Potential

Territory	$ M Sales	Performance Field Men	($ M/Man)	Potential $ M	Perf./Pot.
1.............	10,000	9	(1110)	30,000	33%
2.............	6,000	5	(1200)	20,000	30
3.............	4,500	5	(900)	13,000	35
4.............	3,500	4	(875)	10,000	35
5.............	2,500	3	(833)	7,000	36
6.............	2,400	4	(600)	6,000	40
7.............	2,300	4	(575)	5,000	46
8.............	2,000	4	(500)	4,000	50
9.............	1,800	3	(600)	3,000	60
10.............	800	1	(800)	2,000	40
	35,800	42	(850)	100,000	35.8%

FIGURE 16–8

Analysis of Market

Territory	Potential $ M	Our Sales $ M	% Mkt.	Our Plan % Mkt.	$ M
1...............	30,000	10,000	33	40	12,000
2...............	20,000	6,000	30	40	8,000
3...............	13,000	4,500	35	35	4,500
4...............	10,000	3,500	35	45	4,500
5...............	7,000	2,500	36	36	2,500
6...............	6,000	2,400	40	40	2,400
7...............	5,000	2,300	46	40	2,000
8...............	4,000	2,000	50	45	1,800
9...............	3,000	1,800	60	50	1,500
10...............	2,000	800	40	40	800
	100,000	35,800	35.8	40	40,000

Figure 16–9 showed that 20 percent or 200 accounts were providing 90 percent of the sales volume. It was decided to concentrate on those "target accounts" which brought in $9 million of business.

Figure 16–10 shows the call time needed to service each of the 200 target accounts in territory 1. Factors entering this analysis are the salesman's itinerary, the location of the account, the nature of the purchasing influence in the company and—very important—the *desire of the customer* concerning frequency of calls.

A careful appraisal of the total call requirements of the 200 target accounts indicates that 1,800 man-days should bring in $9 million in sales, while $1 million of noncall business is likely to be generated because of the presence of an efficiently run sales office in the territory. Judgment indicates that an additional 360 man-days would bring in $2 million in added volume. Thus the allocation of 2,160 man-hours of effort to territory 1 should attain the goal of $12 million as planned. Di-

FIGURE 16–9

Territorial Account Analyses (Territory 1)

Number of Accounts	Accounts Number	Percent	Dollar Sales $ Million	$ Million	Percent
	(Cumulative)			(Cumulative)	
20...............	20	2	4.0	4.0	40
80...............	100	5	3.5	7.5	75
100...............	200	20	1.5	9.0	90
800...............	1,000	100	1.0	10.0	100
1,000			10.0		

FIGURE 16–10

Call Time Needed for Each Target Account

Target Account	Planned Calls per Year	Travel and Call Time (days)	Man-Days per Year
	Majority 8–26	¼–½	
	Limits 6–52	⅛–1	
Acct. No. 1.....................	6	½	3.0
Acct. No. 2.....................	26	¼	6.5
Acct. No. 3.....................	18	⅛	2.2
Acct. No. 4.....................	20	⅓	6.7
Acct. No. 5.....................	8	¾	6.0
Acct. No. 6.....................	12	1	12.0
.	.	.	.
.	.	.	.
.	.	.	.
Acct. No. 200.................	52	⅛	6.5
Total 200..................			1,800

viding 2,160 by 180 (the average number of call days available to a salesman after deducting vacation, holidays, meetings, travel, illness, etc.) indicates a need for 12 men in the territory. This effort should provide $12 million, or 40 percent of market within acceptable cost limits.

The same procedure shows that by reducing input in territory 8 from four men to two men, penetration will slip from 50 percent to 45 percent. But in sales volume the drop will be only $200,000, or from $2 million to $1.8 million. The important point is that two men are freed to be redeployed to territory 1.

FIGURE 16–11

Results of Redeployment

	Present Performance			Potential Performance		
Territory	$ M Sales	Field Men	($ M/Man)	($ M/Man)		Field Men	$ M Sales
1..........10,000		9	(1,110)	(1,000)	+	12	12,000
2.......... 6,000		5	(1,200)	(1,000)	+	8	8,000
3.......... 4,500		5	(900)	(900)		5	4,500
4.......... 3,500		4	(875)	(750)	+	6	4,500
5.......... 2,500		3	(833)	(833)		3	2,500
6.......... 2,400		4	(600)	(600)		4	2,400
7.......... 2,300		4	(575)	(667)	−	3	2,000
8.......... 2,000		4	(500)	(900)	−	2	1,800
9.......... 1,800		3	(600)	(750)	−	2	1,500
10.......... 800		1	(800)	(800)		1	800
	35,800	42	(850)	(870)		46	40,000

The results of the total process are illustrated in Figure 16–11. The following conclusions resulted:

Let us now look at our general redeployment [Figure 16–11]. Here we see that by redeploying four men from offices in territories 7, 8, and 9, plus the expansion of our force from 42 to 46 men, we are able to increase our participation significantly in territories 1, 3, and 4. Despite the modest loss in territories 7, 8, and 9, our overall participation went up to $40 million.

Here is another very interesting point. You will note that in offices 1, 2, and 4, the new men who were added sold less than the men already there, as indicated in the middle two columns by the lower average sales per man. Despite the fact that these new men sold less than their predecessors, their performance in these particular territories, plus the moving of men from the marginal territories 7, 8, and 9, actually brought the sales per man in the entire sales force up from $850,000 to $870,000. It does not always work out this way. Nor is it always necessary to gain in sales per man in order to gain in profitability.

But this particular case illustrated a double effect of the fruits of redeployment. By concentrating on the areas of greatest potential *and* lesser Dow participation and by giving insignificant ground in marginal territories, we significantly improved our position and profitability. This improvement started from an original position which we thought in the beginning was pretty good.

We have covered a few aspects of decision making relevant to resizing a sales force. We have glossed over many. I certainly do not want to leave you with the impression that analysis is a substitute for that priceless possession of a successful sales marketing manager—judgment. However, I hope that I have left you with the impression that a philosophy of orderly planning and analysis is an essential prelude to the *best* judgment. If I may summarize the points which need to be considered in the redetermination of the size of your territorial sales force, they would be as follows:

1. Know quite clearly your territorial objectives.
2. Analyze your territorial market.
   a. Determine by market research the position of each territory.
   b. Determine the territories in which you are likely to gain the greatest return for the effort to be invested and, conversely, those territories which are marginal in respect to return on effort.
3. Analyze the sales effort needed.
   a. Man-days for target accounts.
   b. Man-days for potential accounts.
   c. The cost of this effort.
4. Relate the sales return expected to the cost of the effort.
5. Within your corporate profit objective determine the cost parameters within which you can profitably expand effort to gain a dollar's worth of sales.
6. Perform the above steps in a continuum. And remember that the constantly changing market environment as well as the changing environment within your own corporation require constant maintenance of this process.[14]

---

[14] Ibid.

SUMMARY

The evaluation and control of sales force efforts requires diverse types of information input dealing with individual, group, and organizational performance. Actual performance is then compared with predetermined standards and appraisals are made by management on the basis of how well actual performances met the norms. The final step in the process is the taking of corrective action to improve and (or) reallocate sales efforts.

The short-run goal of the evaluation and control process is to meet more effectively the firm's revenue and expense objectives for the current period. In addition, the process can improve the productivity and morale of individual members of the sales force. The longer run and more general objective of the evaluation and control process is to ensure that sales force strength, training, and mode of deployment are such that it is making an optimum contribution to the overall profitability of the enterprise.

REVIEW AND DISCUSSION QUESTIONS

1. What are the four basic steps in the process of evaluation and control of sales force efforts?

2. What are some of the purposes of the evaluation process in the short run? In the longer run?

3. What types of information input might be desirable in developing a system of evaluation and control of the sales force?

4. How does one go about setting sales force performance norms or standards? What are some quantitative standards?

5. What is a profitability standard? Why is its use superior to the mere application of sales volume standards?

6. What are qualitative performance standards, and why are they important in appraising salesman performance?

7. What type of remedial action is available to the sales manager who finds some of his salesmen with substandard performance records?

8. What is a time and duty analysis, and how might it be of use to sales management? Why is routing so important?

9. Of what aid, if any, is economic theory in solving the problem of allocation of resources to sales territories?

10. What are some of the lessons to be learned from the description of the Dow sales force redeployment analysis?

17

Resellers as Promotional Resources

IN CONSIDERING the various promotional resources available to the firm which make up the elements of the promotional program, we have emphasized communication with the consumer through the mass media. Except in cases where the manufacturer sells directly to the end user, however, the next owner of the good is not the ultimate consumer but a marketing middleman such as a wholesaler or retailer. These middlemen, often referred to as resellers, perform the vital functions of effecting exchange so that the goods produced by diverse manufacturers are available to buyers in usable assortments. The important implication for promotion, however, is that when the title to the goods passes from manufacturer to middleman, so does a large portion of the control a manufacturer can exert over how his goods are sold.

The situation is one in which the channel of communication to the ultimate consumer may be direct, but the path of ownership and control of the goods is exceedingly indirect in the sense that marketing middlemen are used. Thus the success of the entire program may depend on how skillful the manufacturer is in gaining the cooperation of his wholesalers and retailers and exploiting the tremendous selling potential inherent in the aggregate reseller organization.

To develop a promotional program which effectively utilizes reseller resources, an understanding of the concept of a channel of distribution and how certain channel attributes influence the overall promotional strategy of the manufacturer is necessary. Another necessity is knowledge of what resellers are and how *they* view their roles as channel intermediaries. With these insights, manufacturers can develop policies and programs which will be successful in gaining promotional support from their channel intermediaries.

THE CHANNEL OF DISTRIBUTION

The marketplace contains literally thousands of firms which can perform all or part of the functions required to move goods from producer to consumer. Be they wholesalers or retailers, agents or brokers, these marketing intermediaries make up what has been termed the distribution structure. The course through this structure that a manufacturer chooses for his product to follow on its way to the consumer is referred to as a channel of distribution.[1]

Channels of distribution may vary in many ways. In fact no two channels are alike because they are made up of independent middlemen. Channels can, however, be classified in terms of three dimensions which are especially important when considering the development and implementation of a promotional strategy. These are (1) channel length, (2) extent of market coverage afforded or intensity of distribution, and (3) locus of control. Although the implications of variations in these dimensions for the development of an overall promotional strategy are developed in greater detail in the following two chapters, a brief discussion of how these channel variations come about is in order here.

Channel Length

If the ownership of goods changes several times as different resellers take part in the distribution process, the channel of distribution is described as long or multistaged. An example of such a channel would be one used by a manufacturer of automotive parts who would sell to a large wholesale distributor who in turn would redistribute the parts to a number of smaller distributors or "jobbers." These jobbers would service an even larger number of retailers of diverse types who make the parts available to the end users. This three-stage channel (wholesaler, jobber, retailer) would be chosen by the manufacturer because it affords wide distribution at relatively low cost. To gain the market coverage and the economies of a long channel, the manufacturer has accepted the loss of control which occurs when title passes many times between the level of production and consumption. A short channel, in contrast, is one in which there are very few if any stages between producer and consumer. The Fuller Brush Company or the Avon Products Corporation are examples of firms which sell directly to consumers and thus use a zero-stage channel.[2] Other firms might sell directly to

---

[1] For a more definitive discussion of the distribution structure and channels of distribution see Stewart H. Rewoldt, James D. Scott, and Martin R. Warshaw, *Introduction to Marketing Management,* rev. ed. (Homewood, Ill.: Richard D. Irwin, 1973), ch. 8.

[2] See Philip Kotler, *Marketing Management: Analysis, Planning and Control,* 2d ed. (Englewood Cliffs, N.J.: Prentice-Hall, 1972), p. 522.

retailers for subsequent resale, thus using a single-stage channel strategy. Although distribution costs rise as the number of stages is reduced, the control over the mode of resale of the product is increased. Thus the promotional advantages gained from short channels might outweigh the cost and coverage considerations.

Intensity of Distribution

The number of resellers utilized at each stage in the channel also has important effects upon market coverage and promotional effort by resellers. The greater the number of wholesalers or retailers franchised to carry the product or product line, the greater will be the coverage of the market. Unfortunately, as coverage increases, the incentive for any one reseller to support the product promotionally diminishes. As will be discussed in the following chapters, it may be necessary for the manufacturer to engage in selective distribution, limiting the number of resellers at each level in the channel in order to gain reseller support at the sacrifice of coverage.

Channel Control

Every seller is seeking maximum control over resellers consonant with meeting the coverage requirements of his product type. This control extends to the setting of margins, the holding of basic stocks, the maintainance of resale prices, and the like. Such control is easier to exercise in a manufacturer-dominated channel where a unique product and effective advertising have created a strong selective demand. If such a demand cannot be created, the locus of channel control may shift to the wholesale or retail stages, where the power of large reseller institutions may overshadow that of the manufacturer. Because the marketing goals of a powerful reseller generally do not coincide with those of a manufacturer, an adjustment of marketing strategy would then be required. Thus, as the locus of power in a channel of distribution may vary, the manufacturer's promotional strategy must also vary. But before considering this aspect of the problem it is necessary to look more closely at the nature of reseller institutions and how they perform.

WHOLESALERS AS PROMOTIONAL RESOURCES

The efficient movement of goods from diverse producers to the market requires intermediate exchange or the performance of wholesaling functions. Regardless of whether or not these functions are performed by an organization owned by a producer or a retailer, the activities required for concentration and dispersion at a level between the producer and end user are wholesaling activities. The independent merchant middle-man who performs these functions for profit, and takes title to the goods he handles is known as a wholesaler.

Wholesalers as promotional resources can be classified in accordance with (1) the extent of their functional performance, (2) the breadth of assortments carried, and (3) the geographical areas covered.

Classification of Wholesalers

Functional Performance.   Merchant wholesalers may be divided into two groups: service wholesalers and limited-function wholesalers. In this text concern is primarily with service wholesalers, who comprise over 90 percent of the total and who perform the full array of whole-saling functions. The term wholesaler, distributor, or jobber refers here-after only to those full-service middlemen designated by the Bureau of the Census as wholesale merchants and distributors and defined as:

. . . merchant wholesale establishments primarily engaged in buying and selling in the domestic market who perform most of the principal wholesaling functions. They buy and sell merchandise on their own account; sell principally to retailers or to industrial, commercial, or professional users; usually carry stocks; assemble in large lots and generally redistribute in small quantities, usually through sales-men; extend credit to customers; make deliveries; service merchandise sold; and render advice to the trade.[3]

The limited-function wholesaler eliminates certain functions such as granting credit and delivery in the case of a cash-and-carry grocery wholesaler. By shifting these functions to the buyer he attempts to re-duce his operating expenses and thus be in a better position to compete on the basis of price.

Degrees of Specialization by Line.   Wholesalers who carry broad as-sortments of goods cutting across many merchandise lines are known as general-merchandise wholesalers. They are analogous to the general store at the retail level. The general-line wholesaler also carries a broad assortment of goods but is limited to a single line or a few closely associated lines of merchandise. Grocery wholesalers distributing health and beauty aids or drug wholesalers carrying liquors are examples of general-line wholesalers.

Those wholesalers that carry only a portion of a merchandise line are called specialty wholesalers. The wholesaler who concentrates on carrying only tea and coffee for distribution to retailers and restaurants,

---

[3] U.S. Bureau of the Census, *U.S. Census of Business: Wholesale Trade, Summary Statistics, 1954* (Washington, D.C.: U.S. Government Printing Office, 1957), Vol. III, App. 3.

for example, is specializing in a very small portion of the dry grocery line.

Territorial Coverage.   Some wholesale establishments operate on a national or regional basis; others are strictly local. Although national or regional organizations such as McKesson and Robbins or Greybar Electric are large-scale operations, the bulk of wholesaling activity is carried out on a local basis. This is because the advantages in terms of operating cost and market awareness are with those wholesalers who are located closest to their customers. The larger wholesaler organizations which cover the region or the nation have overcome the disadvantages which accrue with distance from customers by developing local branches. In addition, their volume makes specialized management feasible and contributes to effective performance.

Wholesaler Performance of the Selling Function[4]

The selling jobs that can be expected from a wholesaler involve a variety of selling tools, including personal selling, samples, and advertising. The success of the individual wholesale merchant, like that of any other business enterpriser, depends upon his ability to distribute sufficient quantities of goods at margins high enough to cover his costs and provide a profit. It is rare, indeed, for a wholesaler to reach a profitable volume level without exerting selling effort.

The general requirements of his business usually determine what volume sales must be reached, but he may also have to exercise considerable discretion in formulating a selling plan which will reach his secondary objectives. These objectives may include attaining quotas set by manufacturers of franchised lines, exerting special effort to gain preferential treatment from manufacturers of certain lines, and building goodwill for his own establishment so that future sales will be achieved with less effort.

Selling Tools.   The problem facing the wholesaler is rarely whether to sell or not to sell; it is rather to determine the type, direction, and amount of selling efforts that will enable him to reach his planned objectives. In planning selling effort wholesalers have access to most of the tools available to other marketing institutions. The emphasis of most wholesalers on local or regional markets, however, limits their utilization of media to those covering these market areas rather than those providing national coverage. The tools used include (1) personal selling, (2) samples, and (3) advertising.

---

[4] This section relies heavily on Martin R. Warshaw, *Effective Selling through Wholesalers* (Ann Arbor: University of Michigan, Bureau of Business Research, 1961), ch. 3.

PERSONAL SELLING. Among service wholesalers personal selling is the most widely used sales tool. It has been estimated that approximately one third of all operating expenses of wholesalers is directed toward the delivery of a continuous sales effort.[5] Further, the cost of engaging in personal selling has been judged to account for between 80 and 90 percent of the total wholesaler promotional expenditure. Personal selling, defined as an oral presentation of the sales message, is carried on mainly by the wholesaler's field salesmen, although counter salesmen are becoming increasingly important. The growing emphasis on inside selling is noted in such industries as auto parts and electronic parts, in which wholesale selling is exhibiting many retailer characteristics.

Personal selling encompasses a wide range of activities which may include some or all of the following: (1) checking the customer's inventory; (2) assisting in arrangements for advertising and merchandise displays; (3) helping to make adjustments on customer complaints; (4) providing advertising material, catalog information, and other dealer helps; (5) suggesting seasonal merchandise and advising the account on stock needs; and (6) providing technical assistance and advice.

Although the above activities are highly routinized, they account for an important portion of the personal selling effort expended by wholesalers. The remaining time is, of course, available for special activities or the kind of aggressive selling visualized by many manufacturer promotional programs.

SAMPLES. The sales tool which ranks next to the almost universal use of personal selling is the use of samples. Ranging all the way from models, photographs, or visual aids carried by the salesman to many trunks of merchandise displayed in hotel rooms, samples often constitute an important selling expense. They tend to increase the productivity of personal selling effort and are especially effective when the attributes of the product are difficult to describe and when the quality and workmanship of the product are decisive factors in its sale.

ADVERTISING. Generally used as an adjunct to personal selling, advertising expenditures by individual wholesale establishments are small compared to those made for personal selling activities. Advertising expenditures have been estimated to run between 10 and 20 percent of the amounts wholesalers allocate to their sales forces. Advertising is used by wholesalers to pave the way for their salesmen, to inform customers of new products, and to promote the patronage appeals of the wholesale establishment. One authority points out that

generally . . . the advertising programs of wholesalers are simple, limited to direct mail, trade paper advertising with institutional copy, and to miscellaneous

---

[5] Harry R. Tosdal, "Selling and Sales Promotion in Wholesale Field," *Journal of Marketing*, 14 (September 1949), p. 232.

media of varying but frequently doubtful value. The local wholesaler who wishes to promote the sale of his private brands may go much further in newspaper advertising, radio programs, or other local or regional media.[6]

The preparation and distribution of catalogs are also sizable items of promotional expense for the wholesaler. Because of the breadth of their product lines, salesmen depend heavily upon catalogs for information about the goods they sell. Although catalogs are prepared primarily for field and counter selling personnel, they may also be distributed to certain key accounts.

OTHER TOOLS. Promotional activities such as displays, shows and expositions, demonstrations, and nonrecurrent selling efforts which serve to coordinate personal selling and advertising are supplementary tools used by the wholesaler. Another tool is publicity or nonsponsored commercially significant news. Although it is probably never free, publicity is an effective way for the wholesaler to promote himself as a key part of the local business community.

Factors Influencing Wholesalers' Ability to Sell

Although wholesalers generally have access to the same array of selling tools, their individual selling programs may be quite diverse. Factors which account for the diversity and thus influence the type and amount of selling effort expended for the manufacturer include: (1) the product line at wholesale, (2) the character of the market served, (3) service requirements, and (4) the competitive environment.

The Product Line. The composition of the wholesaler's line in terms of whether it is made up of standardized or differentiated items, low unit-value or high unit-value items, and other factors determines to a large extent the selling support provided for the manufacturer. Lines composed of standardized, relatively low unit-value supply items lend themselves to cataloging and routine personal selling. There is little need for the wholesaler to advertise these products, for such patronage appeals as availability, delivery, and credit extension weigh more in customer's minds than the brand of any particular product.

In contrast, wholesaler lines composed of products which are more highly differentiated or which have unique appeal suggest different kinds and amounts of selling effort. The history of an electrical distributor illustrates a situation in which a wholesaler was able to engage in active selling and promotion because of the nature of his product line.[7] This particular wholesaler sold a line of industrial equipment which was less standardized and of higher unit value than the items sold by mill supply

---

[6] Ibid., p. 239.

[7] Ibid., p. 234.

houses. He recognized that personal selling effort must locate customers, must grant important presale services such as cost and engineering estimates, and must reach the many people who influence the final decision to purchase. Furthermore, this wholesaler utilized direct mail and advertising in trade publications in support of his personal selling activities. Not to be overlooked is the important fact that he sold a line with a margin and turnover sufficient to provide the funds needed to support an ambitious program of selling and promotion.

Wholesalers of consumer goods often take a different approach to promotion. In the drug and grocery industries, for example, it is common to deal with numerous and differentiated products of low unit value with high rates of turnover. Because of the intensity of distribution required to sell these convenience goods and because of the importance of the economies of physical distribution, the wholesalers in these industries concentrate on gaining coverage and on selling themselves as efficient distributors. To ensure continued demands for their services they devote much of their effort to cultivating their retail customers rather than to stimulating demand for specific products.

The most striking characteristic of wholesaler lines is their breadth, and certainly one generalization is reasonable: *the broader the line, the greater the limitation on aggressive selling or promotion of an individual line or product.* Although aggressive selling is a routine part of the manufacturer's program, the wholesaler uses such selling sparingly when his breadth of line is extensive. Aggressive selling may be used for special products or to open new accounts, but as Harry R. Tosdal notes, "the best type of salesmanship for an extensive array of product lines is that in which the confidence of the retailer is developed so that the salesman becomes a trusted buying advisor and his house becomes a trusted source of many products."[8]

Character of Market Served.   In addition to product types carried and breadth of product lines, the nature of the market in which the products are sold also influences the kind and amount of selling support provided for the manufacturer. Wholesaler markets consist of either final users or other resellers. Within each of these classifications the kind and quantity of firms may vary. A mill supply house selling industrial operating and maintenance supplies to manufacturers may have a rather uncomplicated market situation. Even though its customers probably produce a variety of end products, they all are manufacturers who are purchasing for final use. In the consumer goods area an analogous situation might be one in which drug or grocery wholesalers are serving a relatively homogeneous market composed of single types of retail outlets specializing in the sale of drugs or dry groceries.

---

[8] Ibid., p. 238.

In contrast, there might be other situations in which wholesalers face a considerably more complex market structure. A paper wholesaler, for example, may serve both the industrial and consumer goods markets by selling to retail stationers for resale and to industrial and institutional users for final consumption. An electrical wholesaler selling primarily to the industrial market may also supply public utilities and large electrical contractors. An electric appliance wholesaler may sell only durable goods for resale to household buyers, but even within the market he deals with many kinds of retailers—radio, radio and appliance, music, hardware, dry goods, and department stores.

Variations in not only markets served but also in kinds of customers within each market explain why selling programs are so diverse. With only a given amount of resources available to the wholesaler for selling and sales promotion, the complexity of the market structure he faces influences his ability to provide concentrated selling effort to any one particular segment. This ability to concentrate selling effort is also related to the number of customers to be covered and to their location.

Wholesale selling programs are also influenced by varying needs to divert effort from the creation of present sales to the cultivation of potential customers who may provide future sales.

Finally, but not the least important, the profitability of the average order received from specific customers or kinds of customers determines, in great part, the frequency with which personal calls can be made or the amount of selling help which can be offered.

Service Requirements. Traditionally the services provided by wholesalers for their customers are buying, selling, transportation, storage, financing, risk taking, and market information and advice. However, wholesalers do not provide the same array of services or perform the same functional mix for each type of customer. These differences in what is needed to keep old customers or to gain new customers explain much of the variation in ability to grant specific kinds and amounts of selling effort.

The change in functional mix performed by wholesalers is most pronounced in the grocery industry. In order to help their retailer customers survive the price competition from integrated chains, grocery wholesalers shifted the performance of the routine selling function (actually order taking) to the retailer and assumed some of the management function which should have been, but was not, performed by the retail merchant himself. Specifically, they provide weekly order forms for their retailer customers which suggest retail prices and show gross margins. They plan promotions and help prepare newspaper display advertising. Wholesalers also provide management advice on store design and layout, accounting, and personnel relations problems.

The need for wholesalers to provide management services to retailers is not confined to the grocery industry. The same pattern of functional shifting is to be found in the sale of drugs and hardware. In fact, the concept of the "voluntary chain" is that the wholesaler grants management services and buying economies in exchange for the retailer's commitment of continual patronage. This guarantee of demand eliminates for the wholesaler the expense of sales solicitation.

The traditional service patterns which preceded those discussed above still are dominant in many industries. Traditional services include frequent calls in which product and market information are provided and orders solicited, holding large stocks in wholesale warehouses, speedy delivery, credit extension, and after-sale service, among others. These are all parts of the service mix. But providing these "bundles" of services, although necessary in some instances, is very costly. Any pressures on margins, from either the cost or the revenue side, causes the wholesaler to reexamine the quantity and quality of his functional performance. It is the provision of selling support for the manufacturer—perhaps because of the relatively easy manner in which it can be diluted and curtailed—which is most likely to be reduced in the face of cost or competitive pressure.

Nature of Competition.   The kind of competition that wholesalers face has a major influence on their ability to provide specific kinds and amounts of selling effort. Competition bears down on the entire array of functions performed, but it is especially meaningful in terms of its impact upon ability to engage in promotional support. As discussed here, competition is defined as rivalry, of both the price and nonprice varieties, emanating from other resellers within the wholesale channel as well as from other channels.

The pressures of competition, no matter what their source or type, fall on wholesale margins. If the wholesaler protects his share of market against competitors by responding to price or nonprice moves of rivals, unit revenues go down as prices are shaved and unit costs go up as promotional effort is increased. Unless the end result of his action is greater volume, the wholesaler finds himself with a shrinking bundle of dollars to cover his costs of operation and to provide a return on his investment.

If he is caught in a margin squeeze, the wholesaler, like any other business firm, resists the change in his profit position, and he shows this resistance either by reducing expenditures for functional performance or by reducing investment in plant and inventory. The outward evidence of margin squeeze may, at first, be an attempt to shift the storage function back to the manufacturer. Thus greater dependence upon drop shipments and the practice of hand-to-mouth buying are indications that wholesalers are attempting to compensate for falling margins by increasing turnover. Selling support also may be reduced to compensate for increased price competition which must be met with increased discounts to his customers.

Economic Role of the Wholesaler

Although wholesaler promotional programs are quite diverse, they do share certain characteristics. These characteristics are an outgrowth of the wholesaler's economic role and have important influences on his ability to engage in promotional activity.

Wholesalers base their economic justification for being merchant middlemen largely upon their abilities to reduce the total costs of physical distribution. Because of their specialized function and because of their ability to reduce the number but increase the scale of transactions necessary to effect intermediate exchange, wholesalers are able to provide distributional economies to their many sources and customers. Since these economies are derived from serving many firms, however, the inherent nature of the wholesaler's role usually prevents him from serving any one source or any one customer on an exclusive basis.

The economies of wholesale distribution result largely from performing efficiently the functions of physical distribution such as breaking bulk, storage, making of assortments, and the delivery of these assortments to customers. There is, therefore, an understandable tendency on the part of wholesalers to concentrate their efforts in that area rather than on promotional functions. When the wholesaler does have an opportunity to engage in other than routine order-taking activities, he finds it to his advantage to build up his own patronage appeals rather than to stimulate demand for the branded products of his suppliers. From his vantage point in the distributive structure, the most effective promotional strategy he can use is to develop a loyal customer group which will continue to patronize him. He reasons that his success is closely related to his ability to satisfy the desires of his customer group rather than those of individual manufacturer sources. Fred E. and Carrie Patton Clark note that:

In considering the jobber's selling activities it is important to bear in mind that his marketing efforts are directed primarily toward providing retailers with satisfactory goods and services at satisfactory prices, and building up good will for his own services which will insure the continued patronage of his retail customers. He succeeds only to the extent that he can sell to retailers at a profit. It follows that he is more concerned with giving satisfactory service to them than in serving the manufacturer whose product he sells. Consequently, his efforts to create demand are directed primarily to this end, not to creating demand for any particular manufacturer's product.[9]

---

[9] Fred E. Clark and Carrie Patton Clark, *Principles of Marketing,* 3d ed. (New York: Macmillan Co., 1945), p. 252.

This orientation makes it difficult for the wholesaler to concern himself with the problems or requests of individual manufacturers whose promotional activities do not increase the size of the wholesaler's market but merely recut the pieces of the pie. The manufacturer, on the other hand, is necessarily concerned with selling his brand or product line. His promotional strategy is directed toward stimulating a selective demand, exercising control over the methods of sale of his line, and accruing whatever goodwill arises from the use of his products. His strategy, in essence, is oriented toward *brand*. This strategy is in marked contrast to that of the wholesaler, whose aim is to increase the sales of the *commodity* by building a loyal customer following.

The wholesaler finds that his profits lie in building a reputation for himself as a good house with which to do business. Prompt delivery, competitive prices, and convenient credit extension are but a few of the usual inducements the wholesaler uses in his sales message to his customers. When he does promote a specific product, it is generally the one that most benefits his customers in terms of ease of sale and subsequent profitability. Such promotion is consistent with the wholesaler's goal of increasing his patronage appeal. It is equally evident that if a wholesaler actively supports a product by applying extra effort to its sale, the manufacturing source will benefit. But if the wholesaler thinks that the expenditure of such effort is unwise or unprofitable in terms of his total program, he is quite likely to ignore the demands of any one manufacturer. This pattern of behavior is most characteristic of general-line, full-service wholesalers and is the cause of much disagreement and conflict between them and the manufacturers they represent.

It can be seen that the economics of wholesaling, as well as the divergence of promotional strategy common to firms occupying different positions in the distributive structure, explains several of the characteristics shared by wholesaler selling programs: (1) the inability of wholesalers to grant exclusive attention to any one of their suppliers, (2) the tendency among wholesalers to devote more attention to the performance of the functions of physical distribution than to those of a promotional nature, and (3) the wholesaler strategy of promoting their own patronage appeals rather than the products of specific manufacturers. Those characteristics are the common denominators in almost all wholesaler selling situations, and they account for the similarities in the promotional effort which wholesalers give their manufacturers.

Factors Influencing Wholesalers' Allocation of Selling Effort

The wholesaler's economic role, as well as the nature of his product line and market environment, influences his *ability* to put forth selling effort. There remains, however, the question of how the effort that can be expended is allocated to the individual products in the wholesaler's line. The answer to this question requires analysis of: (1) the objectives of wholesalers, (2) the division of the selling task, (3) the type and extent of manufacturer help, (4) the type and extent of competition, and (5) the adequacy of margin.

Objectives of Wholesalers. The long-run economic goal of any wholesale establishment is, essentially, to maximize profits. As such it does not differ markedly from those of any other business enterprise. Individual wholesalers, however, may seek a wide variety of shorter run objectives which they hope will maximize profits in the long run. How the wholesaler *defines* these shorter run market objectives may influence his willingness to allocate selling effort to particular manufacturers. For example, if a wholesaler believes that his success and that of his customer group are based upon the ability to compete on a price basis, the allocation of selling effort will be heavily biased toward the promotion of private brands or the brands of those manufacturers that provide products with price rather than nonprice appeals. On the other hand, if the demands of the market indicate a preference for advertised brands, with low price being a secondary appeal, the wholesaler may allocate his support in favor of the manufacturer selling branded, nationally advertised lines.

It would appear that, given a range of short-run objectives *based on the market requirements of his customer group,* the wholesaler will allocate his selling and promotional effort to those manufacturers whose products and programs best fit the needs of this group. Admittedly this is a broad generalization, but here is a case in point: In the grocery industry prior to World War II, private brands were a major means by which wholesalers could provide their independent customers with merchandise which could undersell national brands at retail, retain goodwill for the distributors, and provide wider margins at wholesale and retail than would national brands. With the rapid growth of self-service among independent as well as chain grocers during the postwar decade, however, the household buyer's influence became more clearly felt. The desire to trade up in food, supported by rising national income, negated much of the price appeal of private brands. In addition, the self-service process gave advantage to manufacturer brands, especially those whose distinctiveness made possible the stimulation of brand preference through national advertising. To meet this changing condition, wholesalers serving independents had to change their merchandising and promotional emphasis. Private brands often were consolidated or dropped, and renewed promotional support was given to those manufacturers that supplied well-advertised branded products. This is not to say that private brands are unimportant today, only to illustrate the influence of customer requirements on wholesalers' efforts.

Division of the Selling Task. Essentially, the wholesaler faces the problem of allocating limited promotional resources over a broad product line. At the same time he must anticipate the needs of his customer group and carry and promote those products they find easy and profitable to sell. Thus in apportioning selling effort to specific products or product lines the wholesaler is greatly concerned with how much of the total selling job has been done by the manufacturer and how much remains to be performed by him and his customers.

With established products wholesalers can estimate the existing level of demand and thus determine the extent of the demand-stimulation task they must undertake if the product is to be properly handled. It should be recognized, however, that wholesalers are wary of diverting large amounts of efforts to demand-stimulation activities that may be necessary for the sale of particular products. The reasons for this hesitation are purely economic, for the diversion of selling effort from the bulk of a wholesaler's line to the promotion of one product may result in a less favorable profit position. Such a situation will occur if the loss of sales and profits in the area from which effort has been withdrawn is greater than the gain in revenues and profits resulting from the newly directed effort. Therefore, in order for an established product to receive a larger portion of the wholesaler's selling effort, its promotion must promise a net revenue and profit gain. The manufacturer who divides the total selling task between the firm and its wholesalers so as to make such a gain possible generally receives the needed selling support.

New products pose an especially troublesome problem for the wholesaler. Whereas in the case of established products some evidence of the level of demand is available, such information is often lacking for new products. The problems arising from the lack of information about demand are further compounded by the continual introduction of a wide variety and large number of new products by manufacturers, especially in consumer goods. One wholesale grocer reported that he received an average of 100 "new" items per week for his consideration.[10] (Many of these, however, were actually variations of old products.) Unless new items result in increased *commodity* sales, the result for the wholesaler is usually an increased investment in inventory and a further dilution of selling effort over an expanded product line. Acting rationally, wholesalers do not like to allocate effort if the new result is a shifting of market shares between manufacturers without a concomitant gain at wholesale. Therefore, they divert effort to new products and lines *only* when they

---

[10] See "Abner A. Wolf, Inc. (A)," *Michigan Business Cases,* Marketing Series No. 41 (Ann Arbor: Graduate School of Business Administration, University of Michigan, 1958).

feel that such diversion will provide profits in excess of those lost by the reduced selling effort allocated to the remainder of the line.[11]

The preceding analysis assumes that the manufacturer pursues a "push" type of strategy, in which the active selling support of the wholesaler is needed to gain sales to industrial users or retailers. If the manufacturer's product is highly advertisable, however, he might elect to utilize a "pull" type of strategy, in which heavy advertising to the final user (the consumer) pulls the product through the channel.

Wholesalers like some degree of pull, because the product thereby becomes easier to sell. But if the manufacturer resorts to "forcing" by pulling the product through the wholesale channel at lower than average margins, the wholesaler's attitude changes, in many cases, to one of open hostility. Under these extreme circumstances he may refuse to engage in any promotional program suggested by the manufacturer.

Type and Extent of Manufacturer Help. Assuming that the manufacturer has decided on the general division of the selling task between himself and his wholesalers, he still must make adjustments to the needs of individual establishments. Recognition of this requirement by a manufacturer and his subsequent activities to give promotional assistance have great influence upon the willingness of the individual wholesaler to cooperate. Wholesalers are especially interested in the manufacturer providing such support as missionary salesmen (i.e., manufacturer salesmen who try to gain new customers for the line), training programs, cooperative advertising, and packaged promotions. These helps are discussed in greater detail in Chapter 19. At this point it is sufficient to note that the type and extent of assistance offered by manufacturers affects not only the wholesaler's promotional costs but his ability to perform his part of the distributive and selling task as well. Inevitably, therefore, the amount of help the manufacturer will give has a great deal to do with a wholesaler's decision as to where to allot his selling effort.

Type and Extent of Competition. When allocating promotional resources to specific manufacturers, wholesalers consider the type and ex-

---

[11] Ibid. An interesting example of a new-product policy is noted in the Abner Wolf, Inc., case. This company, the largest dry grocery wholesaler in Michigan and one of the largest in the nation, served 100 chain supermarkets and 900 independents. Using the order book method, it supplied over 4,400 items to its retail customers. A products committee consisting of wholesaler and retailer representatives every week sifted through an average of over 100 new items which were presented for their attention by various manufacturers. Those products that showed promise were in turn presented to a merchandising committee which continually evaluated the performance of each of the firm's many merchandise departments. If the product suggested had merit and if the merchandising committee felt that it could be a profitable addition to a line or a replacement for an existing product, the buyer in charge of the department was granted permission to negotiate for its purchase.

tent of competition they expect to face in selling a given product or
product line. They are concerned about the rivalry of other wholesalers handling the same product, as well as that emanating from the direct
channel. Another aspect of the problem is whether the rivalry encountered will be essentially of the price variety or whether it will assume
nonprice forms.

Wholesalers scrutinize that portion of manufacturer policy which determines selectivity of distribution within the wholesale channel for an
indication of the possible intensity of intrachannel conflict. And they
take a good look at the manufacturer's past channel policies for some indication of the interchannel competitive pressures they must be prepared
to face.

The one area most closely examined is the manufacturer's direct sale
policy. Although excessive rivalry from resellers in other channels is not
to a wholesaler's liking, competition from the manufacturer is a severe
irritant. Wholesalers do not like to give support to sources that compete with them for customers. The direct sale policy of a manufacturer,
therefore, is of vital concern to wholesalers who must determine their
allocation of selective selling effort.

Adequacy of Margin.   The adequacy of the spread between the price
at which they buy and the price at which they can sell specific products
is another major consideration influencing wholesalers in their allocation
of selling and promotional effort. The discussion of margin is placed last
in this section because margin is a meaningful criterion only in relation
to the extent of the total wholesaling job to be done. This job includes
the full range of functional performance in the areas of both physical
distribution and selling.

Inasmuch as a single margin payment must cover the cost of wholesaler performance and provide a profit, any factors that affect the price
at which wholesalers can sell or the costs of functional performance result in margin adjustments. (The extent of the selling job to be done at
wholesale and the amount of help provided by manufacturers, for example, influence costs. The intensity of the price competition he faces,
on the other hand, influences the price at which the wholesaler can sell.)
The truly unique nature of margin squeeze at wholesale, regardless of
whether the cause is from the cost or the revenue side, or both, is that
*the effects upon the wholesaler's willingness to perform fall unequally
on different functional areas.* The promotional functions appear to be
much more amenable to dilution or shifting than do the functions of
physical distribution. Of course, wholesalers attempt to shift the storage
function back to their sources by hand-to-mouth buying, relying more on
drop shipments, and by carrying narrower assortments. Such shifts, however, are more quickly recognized than are reductions in the quality of
wholesaler selling effort.

Wholesaler selling effort in general goes where it pays to go. It can go, however, where it is *paid* to go by manufacturers who desire more effort at wholesale than can be profitably provided by normal wholesale margins.

RETAILERS AS PROMOTIONAL RESOURCES

Retailers are those marketing intermediaries that resell commodities to final users, generally for household consumption. They compose the final link in the chain which begins with the manufacturer and ends with the household. Retailers perform those marketing functions that enable them to build assortments of goods which will appeal to their markets. In addition to making the goods available, they often must convince the target customers of the satisfaction to be obtained from them.[12]

Retailers are the most numerous of all types of business establishments. Recent census data indicate that there are about 1.8 million retailers in the United States, as compared with about 260,000 merchant wholesalers and 300,000 manufacturers.

The economic basis of retailing is the ability of these many, often small, widely dispersed business enterprises to act as the buyer's purchasing agent by anticipating and satisfying his wants.[13] In addition, retailers perform the typical mix of functions necessary to engage in intermediate exchange such as buying, selling, transporting, and storing.

Other than the generalization that retailers make most of their sales to the final buyer, there is not much else about them that falls in a very clear pattern. They vary enormously in terms of size of establishment, type of goods carried, functional mix performed, and ownership. Regardless of their size or type, they face intense competition because of ease of entry into retailing. Moreover, retailers have difficulty in building or maintaining a competitive advantage over other retailers of their own type or over newer forms of retailing organizations. Perhaps one other valid generalization is that retailing and retailers are in a constant state of change because of the competitive forces prevailing and because of the ever-changing tastes and desires of buyers. The implication of this dynamism for the marketing manager is quite clear. Continual careful monitoring of retail outlets in the pattern of distribution is essential to the success of a marketing program. Retail leaders of the not too distant past may be displaced very quickly by other entrants to the competitive scene.

---

[12] E. J. McCarthy, *Basic Marketing—A Managerial Approach,* 4th ed. (Homewood, Ill.: Richard D. Irwin, 1971), p. 401.

[13] William J. Stanton, *Fundamentals of Marketing,* 3d ed. (New York: McGraw-Hill Book Co., 1971), p. 279.

Classification of Retailers

A classification of retail establishments, for purposes of this text can be made in terms of (1) store types, (2) functional mix of marketing efforts, and (3) ownership.

Store Types. Retail stores might be classified into three types: (1) convenience, (2) shopping, and (3) specialty.[14] A convenience store is one which customers patronize because of its excellent location or other factors which add to customer convenience. A shopping store is one which attracts customers on the basis of width and depth of assortments carried and which might also be in close proximity to other shopping stores. A specialty store is one which has developed a strong selective demand because of its particular product, price, and service offering, as well as its

FIGURE 17–1

The Product-Patronage Matrix

1. *Convenience Store—Convenience Good:* The buyer, represented by this category, prefers to buy the most readily available brand of product at the most accessible store.
2. *Convenience Store—Shopping Good:* The buyer selects his purchase from the assortment carried by the most accessible store.
3. *Convenience Store—Specialty Good:* The buyer purchases his favored brand from the most accessible store which has the item in stock.
4. *Shopping Store—Convenience Good:* The buyer is indifferent to the brand of product he buys, but shops among different stores in order to secure better retail service and (or) lower retail price.
5. *Shopping Store—Shopping Good:* The buyer makes comparisons among both retail controlled factors and factors associated with the product (brand).
6. *Shopping Store—Specialty Good:* The buyer has a strong preference with respect to the brand of the product, but shops among a number of stores in order to secure the best retail service and (or) price for this brand.
7. *Specialty Store—Convenience Good:* The buyer prefers to trade at a specific store, but is indifferent to the brand of product purchased.
8. *Specialty Store—Shopping Good:* The buyer prefers to trade at a certain store, but is uncertain as to which product he wishes to buy and examines the store's assortment for the best purchase.
9. *Specialty Store—Specialty Good:* The buyer has both a preference for a particular store and a specific brand.

Source: Louis P. Bucklin, "Retail Strategy and the Classification of Consumer Goods," *Journal of Marketing*, Vol. 27, no. 1, January 1963, pp. 53–54.

location. Customers prefer to shop at this type of store for a variety of goods.

A really clear picture of how a consumer views his alternatives at

---

[14] See Louis T. Bucklin, "Retail Strategy and the Classification of Consumer Goods," *Journal of Marketing*, Vol. 27, no. 1 (January 1963), pp. 50–55. Also McCarthy, *Basic Marketing*, pp. 402–4.

retail is gained if the classification of products and stores types is made jointly. Figure 17-1 illustrates the range of combinations. The implication of this type of classification for promotional strategy is clear: In those situations where the convenience appeals of the outlet dominate the specialty or patronage appeals, promotion must seek to gain maximum coverage of the market for the manufacturer. In other situations, where patronage appeals of the individual outlets are stronger than selective demand for the product, the manufacturer's campaign must be aimed at getting distribution and promotional support from these key retailers.

Functional Mix of Marketing Efforts. The marketing functions performed at retail are quite similar to those performed by wholesalers. They include buying, selling, storage, transportation, and the granting of credit, among others. Retailers far exceed wholesalers, however, with respect to the variety of ways in which they alter the relative emphasis placed on specific areas of performance. To illustrate the range of variation possible it is useful to consider several types of retail establishments in terms of the functions performed and the services offered to the consumer.

The department store (epitomized by Macy's, Field's, or Hudson's) is an example of a full-service retailer that is analogous to the full-service wholesaler. It offers a wide variety of goods at different price-quality levels. In addition, such customer services as delivery, return privileges, credit, warranty, and service are offered. Of special significance to the promotion manager is the fact that department stores perform the selling function *in its entirety.* Local media advertising, personal selling, window and interior display, and special sales promotional events all are utilized to stimulate demand for the store and the products it carries.

In contrast to the full-service department store, is the discount department store, which emphasizes price in its product-price-service offering. In order to reduce their operating expenses from the 38 to 40 percent of sales typical of full-service department stores to the 20 to 25 percent level needed to make a profit, given their lower gross margins, the discount stores must cut back on functional performance. Areas of customer service such as credit, delivery, and service are not offered on a "free" basis. In addition, in-store personal selling activities are at a minimum, and the major burden of promotion is placed on display and advertising.

The supermarket is yet another type of retailer. Specializing in groceries, although carrying nonfood items to an increasing extent, supermarkets are a hybrid of the department store and the discount house. They emphasize price and convenience, and most are departmentalized. Personal selling by store employees is supplanted by self-service; the goods are left to sell themselves with the help of manufacturer and retailer advertising and retailer-allocated shelf space and position.

These are but three examples of literally thousands of combinations of ways in which retailers may perform their functions. The way in which selling is performed at retail is especially important for manufacturers that require retailer selling support for their products. More is said about this later.

Ownership. Type of ownership influences the way in which retail stores sell. Census data indicate that about 90 percent of all retail units in the nation are independently owned and operated. These independent units account for about two thirds of all retail sales. Although chain stores account for only 10 percent of the total number of stores, their sales make up one third of the retail total, with the trend being in favor of greater penetration. In certain trades the chain stores account for a very large percentage of total volume.

Thus two distinct types of retailers serve the consumer market. The independents are usually, but not always, smaller than the chains. They generally lack the specialization of management possible with larger organizations. On the other hand, independents can build a strong patronage appeal based on the personality of the store owner who is a local resident. From the standpoint of the manufacturer's promotional strategy, a program must be developed that is acceptable to both chains and independents if full coverage of the market is required. Cooperative advertising plans, demonstrators, and point-of-sale displays suitable for independents may not fit in with the scheduled programs of the chains. The problem for the manufacturer is to coordinate promotional programs with diverse types of retailers.

Selling Effort at Retail

While recognizing the tremendous variation in selling which takes place in individual retail stores, according to the type of merchandise carried, store type, or store ownership, selling activities at retail can nevertheless be considered in general. An understanding of the qualitative aspects of retail promotion can be as important to the manufacturer as an understanding of wholesaler selling activities.

Personal Selling. The activity of face-to-face selling in a retail store bears very little resemblance to the activity as performed at the manufacturer and wholesaler levels in the channel. The basis of retail selling consists of providing product information and taking orders. In many cases even these aspects of the selling task are poorly performed, for creative selling at retail is almost a lost art. The reasons for this decline in personal selling performance derive in part from the nature of the average retail salesman's job. In addition to meeting customers and attempting to fill their needs from the assortments carried, the salesperson is also responsible for housekeeping duties dealing with stock, displays, or the sales book. These duties serve to keep the salesperson occupied while waiting for customers, but they are not highly productive efforts in terms of sales. When customers do come in, the average sale is small for the time consumed in making the transaction. In addition, customers tend to arrive in bunches, so the retail selling staff is often unable to handle them efficiently.

The economics of a situation in which the retailer is usually either overstaffed or understaffed to gain sales of modest magnitude results in low productivity and low wage levels. These wages do not attract the most gifted sales types into retail trade because the opportunities are greater for them as wholesaler or manufacturer salesmen. Of course, the preceding statement may not be true when the type of product being sold has considerable profit potential and requires some technical knowledge for its sale, as is the case with automobiles. But even among these situations there are many examples of poor-quality personal selling effort.

Attempts to improve retailer selling performance and to gain in-store selling support are discussed in a later chapter. For now it is sufficient to recognize the tremendous potential offered by sales personnel in the many retail outlets in a typical pattern of distribution. The low qualitative level of performance of the personal selling function by many retailers also must be recognized, however.

Advertising.   The average retail merchant who engages in advertising utilizes the local newspaper, with perhaps some supplementary support from the local radio station. Newspaper display advertising is of the direct-action type and is aimed at informing the consumer of specific product and price offerings. Grocery retailers rely almost entirely on price promotion; their weekly advertisements are little more than published price lists. Stores of the shopping or specialty type generally limit their advertising efforts to the promotion of a small number of specific products or even to the patronage appeals of the stores themselves. In most cases where small independents are concerned, the advertising layout is planned with the help of the media representative or, in the case of groceries and drugs, with the assistance of the wholesaler salesman. In almost all industries manufacturers provide standardized advertisements and layouts in the form of mats which can be cast into type by the local newspaper.

Radio advertising by retailers is generally limited to spot announcements which are used to publicize special promotional events or to supplement newspaper display advertising.

Display.   One of the most potent tools available to the retailer is display—both window and point of sale. Display makes the buyer's searching task easier by indicating the type of merchandise carried by a store in terms of assortments and price-quality levels. It thus enables buyers to judge whether they are at a store where prices and assortments meet their requirements without the necessity of making an inquiry. In addition to its function as a locater and classifier, display also serves to trigger impulse buying. The housewife who enters a supermarket and leaves only with those items on her shopping list is a very rare case.

Because of its power to influence customers, display space at retail is valuable. The wise retailer uses his window and in-store display areas well by merchandising them carefully, keeping them neat and clean, and changing displays frequently to keep his store interesting to the consumer. Promotional programs of manufacturers often require retailer display cooperation. So great is the rivalry among manufacturers for limited window, shelf, or in-store display areas that often retailers sell space to the highest bidder. Even then there is little assurance that once display space is "purchased" by the manufacturer the retailer will cooperate for very long.

The allocation of display areas in supermarkets is being made on a more sophisticated basis. Progressive managers allocate space to products or groups of products in terms of their profitability. Such profitability is calculated by subtracting the costs associated with carrying the product in the line from the revenues brought in by the product. The relative size of the profit contribution made by various products or groups of products determines the size and location of shelf area assigned.

Other Sales Promotion.   Retailers may also engage in special promotional activities such as providing in-store demonstrations, special selling events, or participating in communitywide merchandising events such as bargain days or street fairs. The range of promotional activity is almost limitless. In fact, the variation in type, amount, and quality of activity available makes manufacturer development of a workable program a most difficult undertaking.

Factors Affecting Retailer Ability to Sell

The factors that influence the retailer's ability to engage in promotion are very similar to those affecting wholesalers. They include, among others, (1) the type of store, (2) the nature of the product line carried, and (3) the character of the market served. In considering these factors it is important to recognize the extreme variability among retailers. Even among retailers of the same type selling similar items to a common market, the qualitative and quantitative aspects of promotional efforts may be quite dissimilar.

Type of Store.   Given the classification of retail stores based on whether buyers view them as convenience stores, shopping stores, or specialty stores, a reasonable generalization is that those stores that are shopping or specialty types offer greater opportunity for promotional effort at retail than do the convenience stores. Location and broad assortments of competitively priced goods are the primary ways by which convenience stores attract patronage. In contrast, the shopping store carries fewer lines of more costly merchandise and usually engages in a full array of promotional effort. This is also the case with specialty type outlets which have even narrower lines but engage in advertising, display, and in-store personal selling.

Product Line. The product line carried by the retailer also influences his ability to engage in selling support. If items in the line are highly differentiated from others of a similar type, if they are profitable to sell, and if they add to the patronage appeal of the store, then they provide the opportunity for retailer promotion. On the other hand, lines composed of routine commodity-type items on which price competition is severe provide little opportunity for nonprice promotion at retail.

Segmentation of Market. Because of the wide diversity in buyer wants and tastes, most retailers aim their merchandising programs at a particular segment of the market. The choice of such a segment by the retailer influences his ability to engage in promotional support. For example, if a retailer is serving a market composed of buyers who are very price conscious, his ability to engage in nonprice promotion is limited. In contrast, if his target segment is made up of those who want quality and are willing to pay for it, then there will be more opportunity and margin to support nonprice activities such as personal selling, advertising, and display.

Factors Affecting Retailer Willingness to Sell

Although retailer ability to engage in promotional activity varies widely, all retailers can do some promotion of the goods they carry. The factors that influence how the retailer allocates available selling effort to products of specific manufacturers are similar to those that guide wholesaler allocations. They include: (1) the strategies and objectives of retailers, (2) the division of the selling task and the margin payment, (3) the type and extent of manufacturer's help provided, and (4) the nature of competition.

Strategies and Objectives of Retailers. Retailers are, of course, in business to make money. They are agreed on the point that in order to make money they must carry assortments and provide services that suit the needs of a sufficient number of customers. Retailers are also convinced of the necessity of selling their stores as convenient, economical, and interesting places to shop. The one promotional strategy common to all independent retailers, therefore, is that of developing patronage appeals and of communicating these appeals to prospective customers.

There are many variations of the common strategy of building and promoting patronage appeals. In many instances the retailer emphasizes his own name and carries a large assortment of private brand merchandise. Macy's in New York or the A & P grocery chain illustrates this type of strategy. Given this strategy it is very difficult for a manufacturer to get promotional support for his product from retailers unless it fills an important gap in their product lines. In contrast, a retailer may feel that, given his type of business, the brand names of the manufacturers who supply him with goods are more meaningful to his customers than are his patronage appeals. If this situation prevails the retailer may promote the goods of specific manufacturers and indicate that such items are to be found in his store.

The way in which the retailer seeks to reach his objectives of growth and profitability in terms of emphasizing his own appeals or those of the goods of specific manufacturers thus is an important determinant of how he will allocate the effort he can expend. Essentially, the manufacturer whose brand appeal is stronger than the appeal of the retailer himself will get retailer support. This support will, however, be tempered by the other considerations to be discussed below.

Division of the Selling Task and the Margin.   If the retailer feels that he must engage in selling support of the goods of a specific manufacturer to reach his business objectives, he still must choose from a large array of products. In attempting to maximize his return from expenditure of effort he could engage in rather detailed studies of product profitabilities to guide his allocation of effort. Many larger firms do just that. However, the bulk of retailers who, because of their size, lack specialized management use the margin payment as a criterion of profitability. Against this payment they weigh the extent of promotion undertaken by the manufacturer and the amount required of them. If the size of the task required seems reasonable in light of the manufacturer's efforts and margin payment, the retailer may allocate some of his limited resources to the promotion of a specific brand or product line.

Extent of Manufacturer Help Provided.   In addition to the margin payment, the retailer also considers the type and extent of support he might receive from the manufacturer. Cooperative advertising allowances, display material, advertising layouts, and demonstrators are some of the supporting services or payments which might be provided. These, of course, have a monetary impact because they reduce the cost of selling for the retailer. The inherent danger is that the retailer may be persuaded to engage in promotion for a particular manufacturer, even though the product promoted has little appeal to the members of his customer group.

Nature of Competition.   Promotion by retailers is expensive even if monetary support is provided by manufacturers. Retailers are therefore hesitant to invest their money unless they have a chance to recoup it with a profit. The type and extent of competition they face is a very important determinant of profitability and thus is a consideration retailers examine when deciding on allocations of promotional effort.

Retailers cannot hold manufacturers responsible for the presence of close substitutes for specific products. Such is a fact of life in many industries. They do hold manufacturers responsible, however, for competition they face from other retailers or from other channels of distribution handling the same product. If manufacturer distribution is very intensive, then, of course, many retailers in each market carry the line. Because volume is spread among so many outlets, profit potentials decrease for individual firms. With this decrease in profit potential comes a decrease in willingness to give the manufacturer promotional support.

Of even greater impact is the threat of interchannel competition. In this situation the retailer is faced with competition from other types of resellers or from the manufacturer himself. It is very difficult for a retailer (say a jeweler) to understand why a watch manufacturer asks for his personal selling support and then distributes through the local discount store which sells watches on a price basis. The less competition retailers face from both within and without their channel, the more willing they are to engage in selective promotion for a specific manufacturer. In general, they hesitate to build demand for specific manufacturers unless they themselves can have a good share of the benefits.

CONCLUSION

In this chapter resellers were examined as promotional resources. A brief attempt was made to explain how their economic roles influence wholesalers' and retailers' ability to engage in selling support. In addition, consideration was given to those factors that influence resellers to allocate their promotional resources to specific manufacturers.

Chapters 18 and 19 discuss how manufacturers might gain reseller support for their programs. It is important to recognize, however, that any attempts to stimulate reseller promotional activity require an understanding of what resellers can and cannot do and how they view their roles as middlemen in the distributive structure.

REVIEW AND DISCUSSION QUESTIONS

1. What is a channel of distribution and how is it related to the structure of distribution?
2. How does channel length and intensity of distribution within the channel affect reseller promotional activity?
3. Why is control over a channel of distribution so important to a manufacturer and how might he gain such control?

4. Why does the development of a promotional program by a manufacturer require an understanding of reseller functions and motivations?

5. Discuss the statement: Wholesaling functions would exist even if there were no wholesalers.

6. In what ways are wholesaler promotional objectives similar to those of manufacturers? In what ways do they differ?

7. What factors influence a wholesaler's ability to engage in promotional effort?

8. What aspect of the wholesaler's economic role makes it difficult for him to support the program of an individual source?

9. Which factors appear to influence the wholesaler's apportionment of his selling support activity to various product lines?

10. Why do wholesalers pay close attention to a manufacturer's policy on direct sale to retailers on end users?

11. Is the margin offered the best indication of product profitability to a reseller?

12. Contrast the reseller segment composed of retailers with that composed of wholesalers in terms of numbers as well as degree of diversity.

13. Why is it useful to classify stores in terms of types as well as ownership?

14. Why is display at the retail level such a valuable tool for promotion? How do retailers allocate their display space to specific products?

15. What is meant by the term "interchannel competition"? How does this type of competition influence retailer willingness to engage in sales-supporting activities for the manufacturer?

18

Price, Margin, and Inventory Policies

MANY OF the factors which influence not only the reseller's ability to engage in promotion but his willingness to allocate his selling support to individual manufacturers are, at least in the short run, outside the control of the manufacturer. The reseller's economic role, the composition of his product line, the character of his market, the service requirements he must meet, certain aspects of his competition, the selling tools available for his use—all are factors the manufacturer must consider as outside his range of influence.

However, there are several important considerations which affect reseller willingness and ability to sell and which are amenable in varying degrees to manipulation by manufacturers in the relatively short run. These include: (1) the role of the reseller in the manufacturer's promotional strategy, (2) the type and extent of competition to be faced by resellers from other sellers of the same product, (3) the size of the manufacturer's margin payments to his resellers, and (4) the amount of inventory resellers must carry to support the line. An additional factor in this category, the type and extent of help offered by the manufacturer to supplement or improve reseller promotional performance, is the topic of Chapter 19.

THE PROMOTIONAL ROLE OF RESELLERS

The first area to be considered covers those manufacturer marketing policies that affect the role to be played by resellers. These policies are an outgrowth of a process in which the manufacturer combines elements of advertising, personal selling, and dealer promotion to achieve

437

his promotional objectives. Given certain product and market characteristics, the optimum blend may leave only a very small promotional role
for resellers. On the other hand, it might require heavy emphasis on
reseller selling effort.

Regardless of the mix, the manufacturer concerned with stimulating
reseller support must know *what the role of these intermediaries is to be
under a given strategy.* Only with this information can the manufacturer evaluate the selling performance of his wholesalers and retailers
and consider ways to supplement or improve reseller performance.

The manufacturer does not develop strategy in a vacuum. He is very
much concerned with the constraints placed upon him by the character
of his product line and the nature of the market to which he sells. A
look at several product-market situations illustrates how manufacturer
adjustment to the situation at hand influences the nature of the selling
task to be performed by wholesalers and retailers.

Adjustment of the Promotional Mix

Under certain product-market conditions, manufacturers place major
emphasis on consumer advertising to stimulate demand. These conditions
might include: (1) a rising primary demand trend for the product type,
(2) an opportunity to develop selective demand for the particular product
on the basis of differentiation, hidden qualities, or strong emotional buying motives, or (3) a turnover and margin combination sufficient to
generate funds necessary to support the advertising expenditure. Products
such as grocery and food specialty items, proprietary medicines, distinctive soap products, and cosmetics lend themselves especially well to
strategy which relies on consumer advertising to "pull" the product
through the channel of distribution.

The greater the manufacturer emphasis on pull-type strategy, the less
the opportunity for resellers to engage in promotion. For example, a
manufacturer of a packaged drug often faces a product-market situation
which offers an excellent opportunity for stimulating sales through the
use of consumer advertising. Here the selling role of wholesalers and retailers is at a minimum. Other than providing availability to drug outlets
and performing the minimum exchange and storage functions, the wholesaler makes no selling effort. The retailer, in turn, is required to do little
more than stock the product. The sale of well-known brands of aspirin is
an example of this situation.

In the above extreme example the manufacturer's policy is to force
the product through the channels at minimum margins for resellers, paying only for the costs of physical distribution. As long as availability is
achieved through retail stocking, there is little that resellers can do to
improve sales that could not be done better by consumer advertising.

Therefore, switching funds from consumer advertising to personal selling or dealer promotion would result in a less effective program for the manufacturer. It should be pointed out, however, that this situation is rare, because resellers usually have a greater part to play in the overall strategy.

The following two cases illustrate more typical situations involving the impact of overall promotional strategy on reseller performance of the selling function.

Soap Manufacturer. A firm produced soap and other toilet articles which were said to contain medicinal properties that would prevent and overcome skin irritations. Products were sold both direct to retail accounts that placed minimum orders of two gross and through wholesalers to users of smaller quantities. The margins to direct accounts were approximately 30 percent of the suggested retail price of 25 cents per bar of soap. Retailers who bought from wholesalers averaged about 20 percent. Wholesalers got a 13 percent markup on their selling price by shortening retailer margins from the 23 percent suggested by the company to about 20 percent.

The manufacturer placed total reliance on consumer advertising to obtain and hold his distributors. Average annual sales were about $2,500,000, of which 30 percent went for advertising. Although 100 percent distribution through 50,000 drug outlets had been obtained, spot checks indicated that retailers seldom displayed the company's brand of soap, keeping it under the counter, and often substituted other brands.

Inquiry disclosed that many druggists shelved the soap because they resented their lower than average margins and the price competition they had from the druggists who bought directly at lower prices.[1] Moreover, there was no personal cultivation of any of these druggists either by the manufacturer's salesmen or by the company's wholesalers. The issue was whether the company could continue to ignore the druggists' point of view. An analysis of the situation indicated that sales could be increased if dealers displayed the soap, brought it to customers' attention, and stopped substitution. It was determined that if, on the average, the sales in each retail outlet were increased from five or six bars per week to seven or eight, the company would derive a substantial sales increase of nearly 20 percent of current volume.

If such a redetermination of the promotional mix is feasible, then what is the impact of this policy change upon the selling task at wholesale and retail? Other than making routine calls upon the druggist and accepting orders, what can wholesaler salesmen do? First, they can inform retailers of the company's new policies. If margins are to be raised

---

[1] As noted, retailers averaged 20 percent on purchases from wholesalers and 30 percent on direct purchases of two gross minimum. Traditional drug margins for this type of product were about 33⅓ percent.

for retailers, the wholesaler salesmen can explain the new schedules to their customers. Wholesaler salesmen can also work to get counter and window display space from drug retailers. Although wholesalers may not be able to do the entire job of gaining retailer support, they are assuredly the first line of attack on retailer lethargy. As for retailers, the object is to get them to display the soap and, in some cases, to recommend it to their customers. Even if no in-store selling support is forthcoming, a reduction in substitution by druggists would be an improvement over past conditions.

This case illustrates the effects on the wholesale and retail selling task when the manufacturer changes his promotional mix to gain an increase in reseller "push." The major implication of the case is that the optimum mix may change, in time, to include a larger selling role for wholesalers and retailers even when emphasis is initially placed on consumer advertising to achieve coverage. The decision to increase the role of resellers must, however, be accompanied by appropriate modifications in reseller discount schedules so that they are compensated for their additional effort. More is said about this subject later.

Appliance Manufacturer.[2]   The Durbin Corporation manufactured a line of refrigerators sold over a fairly wide price range. Advertising expenditures exceeded $1 million annually. The division of the expenditure was as follows: 41 percent to general advertising over the company's name to build prestige and acceptance for the firm's line and 59 percent to stimulate retailer selling efforts (38 percent for advertising over the retailer's name, 9 percent for dealer sales helps, and 12 percent for advertising to the trade). Although there was considerable opportunity to develop brand preference through consumer advertising, company executives felt that personal selling at the retail level was important. The reasons for this view were:

1.   The high cost of an appliance creates a considerable resistance which can be overcome only by persuasive personal retail selling.
2.   The company line incorporated several mechanical features which required demonstration and explanation in order to get the prospect to appreciate its advantages over competing lines.
3.   Because trade-ins had to be considered in many of the selling situations, skilled personal negotiation was required.

The company used independent wholesale appliance distributors to sell to selected retail outlets in each community. It reasoned that the large amount of emphasis placed upon local advertising over the dealer's

---

[2] See "Durbin Corporation" in James D. Scott, *Advertising Principles and Problems* (New York: Prentice-Hall, 1953), pp. 313–18.

name was necessary to get outlet identification so that prospects would know who carried the line. It also considered it necessary to engage in strong direct-action advertising—often using price—to get prospects into the local stores.

Here the promotional role of wholesalers and retailers is both complex and important. First, the wholesaler can be instrumental in screening, selecting, and franchising members of the retail dealer organization, assuming that distribution is made through selected outlets. Second, the wholesaler sales force can call on these dealers and make sure that an adequate assortment of the line is carried by them. Retailers, in turn, can cooperate with manufacturer-sponsored promotions, engage in point-of-purchase display, participate in cooperative advertising programs, and follow up leads on potential customers gained through consumer advertising.

In a program such as described above the need for dealer promotion remains large, although considerable sums are spent on consumer advertising by the manufacturer. When consumer buying habits so specify, the retailer becomes an important link in the selling chain, and both the manufacturer and the wholesalers are concerned with gaining retailer support.

Product Evolution

In addition to the influences of product-market characteristics at any one time, changes in the promotional role of wholesalers and retailers occur as products mature. The process of product aging is described by the concept of the maturity or product life cycle, in which the life of a product is divided into stages. Although in Chapter 22 a five stage product life cycle will be discussed, for purposes of illustrating the impact of the various stages on the promotional mix three basic stages will suffice. These stages have been described as (1) the introductory stage, (2) the competitive stage, and (3) the commodity stage.[3]

In the introductory or pioneering stage the demand for the product with respect to price is generally more inelastic than in the later stages of development. However, the manufacturer must make a considerable investment in promotion in order to educate consumers about the existence and uses of the product. In the competitive stage of the cycle the product is challenged by substitutes produced by other manufacturers. The selling task changes from stimulating primary demand to stimulating selective demand. Price becomes more important as cross elasticity of

---

[3] See Joel Dean, "Pricing Policies for New Products," *Harvard Business Review,* Vol. 28 (November–December 1950), pp. 32-33.

demand (the sensitivity of demand for a product to changes in the prices of close substitutes) increases. The final phase of the cycle is the commodity stage. When a product reaches the point where market shares are relatively stabilized, where brand preference is low or nonexistent, and where price reductions will produce more profitable volume than will promotion, the product is said to have reached maturity. It has, indeed, become a commodity like salt, sugar, calcium chloride, or copper wire, and little need exists for promotion.

Introductory Stage.   In the introductory stage of product development a great deal of special selling effort is required to acquaint consumers with the new product type and to gain distribution at wholesale and retail. Some manufacturers sell directly to retailers in this stage, bypassing wholesalers until the need for special promotional effort has subsided. Other manufacturers use wholesalers but restrict distribution so that each wholesaler will be willing to engage in the special selling required. Distribution at retail may also be on a highly selective basis, to gain cooperation from individual retailers.

Competitive Stage.   As products pass from the introductory stage to the competitive stage, the manufacturer's selling task changes from building primary demand to stimulating selective demand. When the product reaches this stage in the cycle, the manufacturer must recognize that, unless special incentive is provided, wholesalers and retailers have little reason to push one brand of a product type at the expense of another. The reseller's task has changed from stimulating demand for a new product to the routine selling of an established one.

Commodity Stage.   In the final stage of the cycle during which the product reaches maturity, brand preference weakens, physical variation among competing products narrows, and methods of production stabilize.[4] At this stage manufacturer strategy puts a greater reliance on price rather than nonprice competition. As the price spread among different brands of the same type of product narrows, the opportunities for wholesalers and retailers to sell on the basis of their own patronage appeals increase. Therefore, service, delivery, and credit extension become the reseller's important selling points.

Implications of Resellers' Promotional Role

As the promotional programs of different manufacturers vary in response to individual product-market requirements, so does the nature of the selling task at wholesale and retail. In those situations where manufacturer emphasis is on the use of consumer advertising to pull

---

[4] Ibid., p. 35.

the product through the channels, the selling role of wholesalers and retailers is at a minimum and is usually concerned with little more than order taking. As elements of push strategy enter the mix, however, the aggregate selling resources of the reseller family become of considerable importance to the manufacturer's program. Such importance increases in such cases as the appliance industry, wherein retailer appeal to the consumer often is more important than brand and the wholesaler can be the most effective agency to gain retailer support.

It is also important to note the changing nature of the reseller's task as products mature. From heavy need for primary demand stimulation in the introductory stages and selective demand stimulation in the competitive stage, the emphasis shifts to price and patronage appeals as products become established commodities. If resellers are assigned some of the extraordinary selling activities required in the earlier stages of the maturity cycle, the manufacturer must be sure to offer extraordinary profit opportunities. But, on the other hand, if the product has matured, the manufacturer should recognize that the role of resellers in stimulating selective demand is limited.

The wise manufacturer takes the step-by-step approach of first analyzing his own promotional program to identify the selling task *resellers might reasonably be expected to perform in light of this program.* Only then is the manufacturer in a position to formulate policies for improving or supplementing reseller performance.

DISTRIBUTION POLICIES AND THE PROBLEM OF RESELLER COMPETITION

When resellers face excessive competition from other sellers of the same lines, their ability to engage in promotional support is diminished. This is because the rivalry faced from other sources both within and outside the channel of distribution causes the reseller's effective margin to be reduced, to say nothing of reduction in his ability to engage in full functional performance. Similarly, the pressures placed on profitability by competition can reduce the reseller's willingness to give selling support to the lines of specific manufacturers.

Whether the rivalry emanates from the manufacturer's direct selling activities or from other resellers handling the same product, a manufacturer-initiated program to gain greater selling support from resellers must consider distribution policies aimed at reducing interchannel and intrachannel rivalries. Market segregation by means of nonprice criteria is one approach by which channel overlap may be reduced. The manufacturer might also consider a policy of selective distribution to lessen reseller rivalry in specific geographic market areas.

Market Segregation

By defining those segments of the market to be served on a direct basis and those segments to be served by specific types of resellers, the manufacturer may reduce channel overlap and thus diminish the competitive frictions that inhibit reseller selling support.[5]

A manufacturer policy of market segregation can stimulate the reseller's desire to grant selling support by giving him a degree of protection from direct sale or from resellers in other channels. This protection, in turn, reduces the pressure on the reseller's margin. Moreover, the reseller generally is more eager to push a line when he feels that the gains from the promotion will accrue to *him* rather than to the manufacturer, through the direct channel.

It is only in rare cases that overlap between the two channels can be totally eliminated. Some market segments require coverage by multiple channels to satisfy the buying preferences of customers. For example, in the auto parts industry distribution of spark plugs must be exceedingly broad through diverse outlet types. This policy is required because buyers expect to find spark plugs at the auto dealer's, the corner gas station, the auto supply store, and in the mail-order catalog. The overlap areas are not without value, however, for they provide an opportunity for manufacturers to test the relative effectiveness of diverse channels in tapping a given market segment. In addition, the competition, if not excessive, may have a stimulating effect on reseller performance.

Criteria for Segregation. Manufacturers may choose varied criteria by which to segregate their markets. Commonly used bases include customer order size, customer location, or end use of product. By applying these criteria, the manufacturer attempts to define for a given type of reseller the segment of the market that is reserved for him. For example, a manufacturer selling directly to retailers as well as through wholesalers made a study of the order sizes of the products sold by wholesaler salesmen. It was found that a typical order was for a single case of one product, and larger orders were almost nonexistent. The average order written by the manufacturer's salesmen, on the other hand, was in excess of 15 cases. As a result of this analysis, the company established the policy of accepting direct orders from retailers, provided they were for ten or more cases of merchandise. Smaller orders would be accepted by the company's salesmen but shipped through a wholesaler of the retailer's choice. This policy was put in writing and widely publicized by the company among its wholesaler customers. Smaller orders were turned over to wholesalers by the manufacturer's salesmen.

---

[5] An example of market segregation would be a case in which a manufacturer sells governmental agencies or original equipment manufacturers on a direct basis, while serving consumers through the wholesaler-retailer channel exclusively.

This policy resulted in a substantial increase in volume for the manufacturer and an increased degree of promotional cooperation from wholesale resellers.[6]

The Kelvinator Division of American Motors Corporation, a large manufacturer of electrical home appliances, segregated its markets on the basis of both customer type and location. Kelvinator's retail division provided for direct sale to apartment house operators, builders, and trailer manufacturers. Another special staff handled direct sales to governmental agencies. Distribution to retail outlets, however, occurred either through factory sales branches or through independent wholesalers. The criteria for use of wholesalers include (1) the availability of an efficient distributor in the geographic area and (2) the relative profitability of using a sales branch rather than the independent distributor in that area. Once the decision was made, territories were defined and overlap eliminated through mutual agreement among the adjacent distributors, regardless of whether they were independent or company-owned.[7]

Making Segregation Effective.   Although the above illustrations are limited in scope, they do support the view that a policy of market segregation defining the reseller's position and protecting his margin can be a useful strategy in gaining his promotional support. The policy must be based on criteria that are economically justifiable and readily understood by resellers.

The dangers involved in pursuing a policy of market segregation are twofold. First, the manufacturer must consider the effects of diminished coverage. Selling effort must not be purchased by sacrificing so much market coverage that a net reduction in revenue results. Second, the manufacturer must not overlook alternative approaches to solve the overlap problem. There are circumstances, for instance, in which a policy of physically differentiating products for sale in diverse channels, perhaps through a change in package or brand name, might reduce interchannel frictions more effectively than a policy of segregating markets.

Selective Distribution

The manufacturer's policy of selective distribution has effects upon intrachannel competition and thus upon the willingness or ability of individual wholesale and retail distributors to engage in selling activity. Selective (or selected) distribution by manufacturers is a policy by which the product is distributed through a limited number of resellers in

---

[6] Richard D. Crisp, "Analytical Approach to Channel Policies—Sales Analysis," in Richard M. Clewett (ed.), *Marketing Channels for Manufactured Products*, rev. ed. (Homewood, Ill.: Richard D. Irwin, 1954), pp. 427–28.

[7] See Martin R. Warshaw, *Effective Selling through Wholesalers* (Ann Arbor: Bureau of Business Research, University of Michigan, 1961), pp. 115–16.

a given geographic area. It is a form of restricted distribution and, as such, is in contrast to a policy of widespread or intensive distribution. Under the latter policy the manufacturer avails himself of all qualified resellers who are willing to carry the line. Exclusive distribution is a special case of selective distribution in which only one reseller serves each market area or segment.

Although selective distribution usually refers to the number of retail outlets serving each market area, the pattern of wholesale distribution tends to parallel that at retail. For example, intensive retail coverage should be accompanied by intensive distribution at wholesale. When retail distribution is more selective, manufacturers can use either selected or exclusive wholesale distribution. In the industrial market, where the wholesaler is usually the last reseller, selectivity of distribution refers to the number of wholesale distributors serving industrial users in the market area.

The way in which consumers buy the product and the effort they are willing to make to locate it should dictate the retail availability requirement the manufacturer seeks to satisfy. If, for example, the buyer is unwilling to "walk a mile" or considerably less for a pack of cigarettes, for chewing gum, or for razor blades, it is wise to seek widespread market coverage through many outlets for these products. On the other hand, when buyers want a major electrical appliance, or carpeting, or expensive clothing, they tend to seek out the individual store or one of a limited number of stores carrying the brand of their choice; in these instances, selective distribution may be considered.

The effects on reseller promotional performance of restricting the number of resellers carrying a line have been well documented. The consensus is that selective distribution reduces competition between resellers and allows them to achieve a higher rate of gross margin on merchandise of this character than on the rest of the line. In addition, the reduced competition provides an incentive for each to concentrate on the line with a reasonable assurance that he, and not his competitors, will reap the benefits of his aggressive selling efforts. Lastly, it appears that being a selected distributor gives the reseller a feeling of prestige. Indeed, for certain products, as one authority noted, "the policy of selected distribution tends to develop a more enthusiastic and successful dealer organization than would result from a policy of nonselected distribution."[8]

As far as the manufacturer is concerned, market coverage is sacrificed under selective distribution. This reduction, in turn, makes the line more profitable for his resellers. In return for added profitability, however,

---

[8] James D. Scott, "Selected Distribution Defined and Described," in Malcolm P. McNair and Harry L. Hansen (eds.), *Readings in Marketing,* 2d ed. (New York: McGraw-Hill Book Co., 1956), p. 314.

the manufacturer feels entitled to certain benefits. Certainly, he may expect the reseller to increase his selling efforts and to increase his investment in inventory and service facilities if needed.

The limits of a policy of selective distribution are set by the nature of the product and the way in which buyers purchase it. Within those limits, however, most manufacturers may exercise considerable discretion with respect to the number of resellers serving a given market area. In making decisions as to the selectivity of distribution, the manufacturer must recognize that a policy which is highly selective may have a favorable influence on reseller effort only when (1) the degree of selectivity is sufficient to provide a reasonable profit incentive for the reseller, and (2) when the profit incentive is not totally dissipated by demands for extra investment in selling, service, or inventory.

Unfortunately, the balancing of gains accruing from selective distribution versus the losses due to restricted coverage is an area of decision which, like so many others in marketing management, is difficult to quantify. A realistic policy of experimentation may provide some basis for measurement in this area. However, such a practice may be difficult to adopt, since experimentation carries with it the danger of disrupting established relationships with resellers.

PRICE AND MARGIN POLICIES

Manufacturer policies which determine the prices at which resellers can buy the line and which influence the prices at which these items can be resold exert an important effect on reseller willingness and ability to engage in demand-stimulation activities. Manufacturer pricing policies directly affect reseller margins as well as the extent of price competition to be faced by resellers from other sellers of the same products.

Channel Pricing

Few manufacturers can gain the market coverage they require without utilizing multiple channels of distribution (i.e., several different combinations of middlemen). The coverage overlap which occurs when the same market segment is tapped by two or more channels can result in a great deal of interchannel rivalry. The competitive frictions accompanying channel overlap can be especially acute when one channel is the direct one in which the manufacturer sells to end users without using middlemen and other channels are composed of various types of independent resellers. Although resellers dislike interchannel competition, they are especially upset when they find themselves in rivalry with the very sources they are seeking to serve.

Resellers obviously dislike interchannel competition because it results in lower prices and higher costs which reduce their profits. They have a wide range of choice as to how they can allocate their selling efforts, so it is possible for them to direct their efforts to the lines of those manufacturers that protect them from excessive interchannel rivalry.

Manufacturer channel pricing policies can be based on two concepts. The first, often referred to as cost pricing, is based on the premise that the resellers in the channel are end customers and that the only differences in prices charged these customers should be those that reflect differences in costs of production, selling, delivery, and service. The second concept, that of competitive functional pricing, is based on the premise that resellers are only a means of reaching the end user, and these resellers vary greatly in the jobs they perform and with respect to the competitive pressures they face.

Cost Pricing. A cost-pricing policy may be weak in terms of gaining reseller promotional support because it is unrealistic and fails to recognize the diversity of types of resellers in the pattern of distribution. Cost pricing cannot compensate different resellers in terms of the portion of the marketing job they perform or in recognition of the competitive pressures they face.

Price variations to resellers in diverse channels of distribution based only on the differentials in costs needed to sell to those channels can *only by coincidence* provide the payments to resellers needed to gain "full channel support."

Competitive Functional Pricing. Acceptance of the second concept of channel pricing policies leads the manufacturer to engage in competitive functional pricing to gain the support of resellers in diverse channels of distribution. This method recognizes more than the differences in costs necessary to sell *to* diverse channels; it also reflects the costs of selling *through* the channels to the end market. In addition, a policy of competitive functional pricing recognizes that channels of distribution may be supplementary, each bringing in volume that one alone could not tap. At the same time the concept is realistic in that it takes cognizance of the fact that channels rarely serve market segments on an exclusive basis, and multiple channels may be competitive.

The use of competitive functional pricing may well result in the manufacturer receiving different net payments from each channel. In a real sense the manufacturer is *buying distribution;* net receipts are determined by both the functions to be performed by the channel members and the rivalry with other manufacturers for the outlets covered by the channel. Indeed, this is the meaning of competitive functional pricing.

The concept of competitive functional pricing is useful in attacking the problem of gaining selling support from the indirect channel composed of independent wholesalers and retailers. This is because it indicates that the price that must be paid to "buy" cooperation must often cover more than payment for functions performed by resellers. Pricing which is effective in gaining reseller promotional support must take into account the competitive environment in which resale takes place, as well as the rivalry from other manufacturer sources for reseller promotional cooperation.

It also should be recognized that prices required to "buy" distribution and promotion from wholesalers and retailers may be bid up by the competition emanating from the manufacturer's selling activities if he chooses to sell direct also. The question then raised is whether paying the price to resellers or reducing rivalry from direct sales will gain reseller cooperation more economically.

Unfortunately, a policy of differential pricing to multiple channels of distribution may run afoul of the Robinson-Patman Act, passed in 1936 as an amendment to the Clayton act. The basic provision of this act is to make it unlawful to discriminate in price between different purchasers of commodities of like grade and quality where the effect is to tend to lessen competition substantially or to create a monopoly. In other words, it is illegal to vary prices to competing customers provided the goods are of like grade and quality, the goods are sold in interstate commerce, and some form of injury to competition results. The only allowable defenses are that price differentials are based on corresponding differences in costs of serving the customers or that the lower price to one was undertaken in good faith to meet the lower price of a competitor. A strong constraint is thus placed on freedom to vary distributor prices, thus underscoring the need for legal review of the promotional program.

In this instance, the coverage pattern of one channel usually overlaps that of another, and the channels are placed in competition. In addition, as the price differentials needed to buy distribution reflect costs of selling *through* channels rather than *to* channels, they are not readily cost justifiable in the terms required by the Robinson-Patman Act.

The fact that the practice of buying distribution may run counter to current price legislation may limit its applicability but does not invalidate its conceptual value. Indeed, for the manufacturer engaged in concurrent distribution through direct and wholesale channels, the legal problem need not arise, and an attack on the pricing problem in terms of buying distribution from resellers may provide valuable insights.

Pricing to Reduce Channel Overlap

Because market coverage by multiple channels of distribution is rarely achieved without some channel overlap, resellers generally face competition from either their counterparts in other channels or the direct selling activities of the manufacturer, or from a combination of both. The frictions which result from such competition inhibit the willingness and ability of resellers to grant promotional support to the manufacturer. Any strategy which can reduce these frictions will increase the probability that resellers will cooperate with the manufacturer's promotional program. Pricing policy can help reduce channel overlap under certain circumstances.

Pricing to Market Segments. In those cases where the manufacturer uses multiple channels to reach different market segments, pricing policy can be used to minimize channel overlap. Such a policy might involve a discount structure which protects resellers in the indirect channels from the rivalry of a manufacturer who also sells on a direct basis. One such plan made it more economical for small retailers to buy from wholesalers than to order directly from the factory, but large stores and chain retailers which bought in large volume were handled on a direct basis at prices lower than wholesalers could offer. In order for this policy to work, the manufacturer was scrupulous in turning small orders over to local wholesale distributors.

The manufacturer policy of charging different prices to different classes of customers also may divide a seemingly homogeneous market into smaller portions, each of which differs in price sensitivity. This strategy, known as segmenting the market, enables the seller to gain customers whose valuations of the product vary widely. The increased volume hopefully results in greater profitability. A by-product of the policy is the "segregation effect" by which channels of distribution can tap given segments of the market on an exclusive basis. Thus potential interchannel rivalry is reduced or eliminated.

Intrachannel Effects of Pricing Policy

Manufacturer pricing policy has an impact on rivalry within the channel of distribution as well as among channels. This "indirect" competition has an important bearing on reseller promotional activity.

Reseller Population. Manufacturer margin payments to resellers determine, to a large extent, the number of wholesalers and retailers that can afford to carry the line. Thus a margin which is generous in relation to the functional task required and to the competitive pressures which must be met at wholesale and retail will foster a larger number of potential distributors. Conversely, a narrow margin payment will restrict membership in the distributor family to a smaller group of the more efficient resellers. The problem, therefore, is to determine the distributor discount that will provide needed intensity of coverage while at the same time compensating resellers for their performance of the physical distribution and promotional functions needed under varying competitive conditions.

The solution to this problem would be greatly simplified for a manufacturer if all of his potential distributors (1) had comparable expense ratios, (2) performed the same functional task, and (3) operated under relatively similar competitive pressures. Given this situation, the manufacturer could select one discount or margin payment which would optimize the combination of coverage and promotion received from resellers in relation to the costs involved. Unfortunately, the real world is considerably more complex. Resellers do not have the same operating costs; the extent and quality of their functional performances differ widely; and the competitive pressures they face also vary.

Setting Reseller Discounts

To attack the problem of setting reseller discounts in a logical manner requires first an estimate of the coverage requirements imposed by the nature of the product and the way in which it is purchased. The manufacturer of convenience goods will find that his channel objectives are heavily biased in favor of intensive retail coverage at the expense of promotional support by resellers. In contrast, the manufacturer of a consumer durable will find that his marketing mix places considerable emphasis on *both* coverage and promotional push. Once having defined his *minimum coverage goals,* the manufacturer must decide how the total selling task should be borne; he must delimit that portion of the selling job he will perform and that portion he hopes to elicit from his resellers.

The Average versus the Marginal Distributor.   The reseller discount must be set in terms of the two requirements, one of coverage, the other of promotion. The most difficult aspect of the problem is to make one payment cover a wide variety of reseller needs and efficiencies. One possible solution is to set the distributor discount at a figure which will provide adequate compensation for his *average* reseller. Another solution is to set the discount so that it covers the needs of his *marginal* distributor.

Setting the distributor discount to cover both the functional and competitive needs of an "average" reseller who faces an average competitive situation has as its major disadvantage the fact that those resellers in the distributor organization that are below average (perhaps because of higher than average costs or tougher than average selling situations) cannot afford to meet the minimal coverage and promotional requirements expected by the manufacturer. The result may be that this reseller tries to shift such functions as storage back to the manufacturer to reduce his costs. There also is the danger that he will reduce the extent and quality of the performance of the selling function.

Much more acceptable is the alternative of *setting the distributor discount to provide the payment necessary to induce the marginal reseller to perform a full functional job.* The "marginal" reseller may be the least effective wholesaler or retailer whose presence is required to provide coverage, or he may be a key wholesaler or retailer who is providing superior selling effort. If effective margin is reduced because of increased costs of performing the reseller functions or because of the impact of competition on price structures, the marginal distributor may drop the line or may cut back to less satisfactory performance. Either way, reduction in effective margin results in a less favorable combination of selling and coverage.

The proposal that distributor discounts should provide for marginal functional performance is *conceptual*, to be sure. It can, however, help the manufacturer define the objectives of his distributor discount policy. In practice, the concept may be dealt with experimentally. The gains in coverage and selling effort achieved by setting compensation for the least effective reseller must be weighed against the costs of paying a premium to all those who are more efficient than the marginal firm. If the premium payments are converted in some part into premium performances of the selling function at reseller levels, all well and good. If, however—as is usually the case—these extra payments are passed on by the more efficient resellers as price concessions, the net result is a further squeeze on the marginal distributor.

Manufacturers should look with suspicion at any rule of thumb for the determination of discount policy. For example, one writer suggests that discounts to the trade might be set "to cover the estimated operating costs (plus normal profits) of the most efficient two-thirds of the dealers."[9] It would seem that in many cases the optimum number of distributors would fall within this range. But, inasmuch as products at wholesale and retail vary so drastically in market coverage requirements and promotional needs, such a blanket approach is unwise. For a manufacturer of convenience goods, coverage requirements might be especially restrictive. Faced with a need to get costs in line, he could very well be forced to make a downward margin adjustment. In order to retain coverage, however, this reduction would be accompanied by reduction in the *promotional task he assigns to resellers* rather than a reduction in the *number of resellers* in his distributor organization.

Using Distribution Cost Analysis.   Although the concept of setting discounts to allow the marginal distributor to engage in the desired selling support may be helpful to the manufacturer, it does little to satisfy reseller complaints of margin inadequacy. The manufacturer's request for more selling effort is often met with statements to the effect that he is already getting more than he is paying for. What is needed is a device to measure the reality of reseller needs—a method of quantifying the

[9] Joel Dean, *Managerial Economics* (Englewood Cliffs, N.J.: Prentice-Hall, 1951), p. 523.

adequacy of margin payments. Distribution cost analysis, the application of cost accounting techniques to measure marketing costs, may help on two counts. First, its usage might help manufacturers revamp margins and price structures to obtain the desired degree of reseller support. Second, the information gained might help the distributor to see the validity of gross margins which vary among resellers and to understand why he should give the manufacturer his promotional support.

Manufacturers must, however, assume responsibility for introducing resellers to the use of such cost analysis if they want to escape the blanket condemnation of wholesalers and retailers for inadequate margins. If sufficient cost data were collected, the manufacturer could provide figures on average handling, storage, and selling expenses for his product, based on the aggregate experience of the reseller organization. Such data would (1) inform the reseller if his costs were out of line, and (2) indicate to the manufacturer whether his margin was in line with the costs of functional performance and the pressure of competition at reseller levels in the channel.

A typical distribution cost analysis for use by resellers to measure the relative profitability of products carried by them would include the following steps:

1. Products which have similar marketing characteristics are grouped together to reduce the complexity of the analysis. For example, if an analysis were being made of products carried by supermarkets, the individual brands and sizes of instant coffee carried would be grouped as instant coffee.
2. Natural expense items are related to the marketing functions of the specific reseller whose product line is being examined. For example, the natural expense item of salaries and wages is allocated to reseller functional categories such as buying, selling, and administration.
3. After the natural expenses have been "functionalized," they are allocated to the various product groupings on the basis of benefit or causation. If the cost of the selling function is $50,000 per year and product group X receives about 10 percent of selling effort, it would be allocated $5,000 of the total of the functional cost grouping.
4. After as much of the functional cost has been allocated as is possible, a summary is prepared showing the gross margin contribution of each product group minus the total of allocated costs. The residual is the contribution to unallocable overhead and profit. The relative size of the various contributions indicates the relative profitability of each product grouping. A typical summary is illustrated in Figure 18–1.

The advantage of distribution cost analysis for resellers is that it shows up the fallacy of accepting gross margin as the sole criterion for

FIGURE 18–1

Relative Contribution to Profit and Overhead of Product Groups Handled by Typical Wholesale Company

Rank	Group	Gross Margin	Allocated Expenses	Contribution
1 .... N		$167,600	$101,305	$66,295
2 .... P		145,500	111,606	33,894
3 L		133,100	119,149	13,951
4 .... M		103,477	92,500	10,977
5 .... O		95,539	87,500	8,039
6 .... S		110,583	102,700	7,883
7 .... T		97,031	94,200	2,831
8 .... R		89,500	93,700	(4,200)

judging a line. It places emphasis on product profitability, where it rightfully belongs. The analysis is not without its limitations, among which are a possible overemphasis of short-run profit contribution as an indication of the value of a product or a group of products and the difficulty of correctly allocating functional costs to the various products.[10]

Implications of Price and Margin Policies

If the assumption is valid that manufacturers use diverse channels of distribution to tap different market segments in order to increase revenues and profits, then the concept of competitive functional pricing illustrates the nature of the pricing problem. To gain balanced sales from diverse channels and to get reseller support, manufacturers must *buy distribution* from these channels. The price paid must recognize both the costs of selling to the reseller in the channel and the functional mix performed by him. But, in addition, the price must recognize the competitive environment in which channel members operate. Manufacturers must be cognizant of the fact that their own direct selling activities may cause substantial interchannel rivalry. This rivalry, in turn, can mean that premium payments have to be made to buy reseller support.

A proper pricing policy also has the value of balancing the support received from multiple channels of distribution. It can, for example, provide incentives for wholesalers and retailers to cultivate the markets which they are best suited to serve, while reserving other markets for the direct selling activities of the manufacturer.

The marginal analysis seems to provide an alternative *conceptual* approach for setting margins to obtain optimum coverage and promotion

---

[10] For an excellent discussion of distribution cost analysis for wholesalers and retailers see Charles H. Sevin, *Marketing Productivity Analysis* (New York: McGraw-Hill Book Co., 1965).

within the channel. It is admittedly difficult to use in practice, but experimentation with different margins under controlled conditions might well have a payoff.

The distribution cost analysis approach also may offer guidance to the manufacturer who must determine the relative adequacy of the margin he offers on his products. In addition to letting the manufacturer see what profit potential he is allowing his resellers, such information may also allow resellers to compare their operating expenses with those of other similar middlemen.

INVENTORY POLICIES

Among the manufacturer policies which have a substantial influence upon reseller promotional activity are those that affect the size and composition of wholesaler and retailer inventories. These policies are important because of their direct impact upon the cost structures of individual resellers. If, for example, the manufacturer assumes a larger share of the warehouse or inventory cost, the reseller has a greater effective margin available to support his selling activities. The manufacturer may assume a larger share of these costs *directly*, by establishing field warehouses or carrying reserve stocks at the factory, or *indirectly*, by adopting a liberal returned-goods policy.

Stock-Level Policies

In attempting to develop a stock-level policy for resellers, the manufacturer must consider two conflicting objectives. The first is to provide a sufficient stock in a reseller's possession to meet market needs for product availability. Under ideal conditions the manufacturer would like to see his wholesalers and retailers carry sufficient stock so that opportunities for sales are *never* lost. The second objective of the manufacturer is to get as much selling support from his resellers as is possible. The manufacturer's dilemma is that the more he pushes for stocking in depth by resellers (without extra compensation), the greater the likelihood that they will shift part of the promotional responsibility back to the manufacturer so that they can make a profit commensurate with their investment in stock. The solution to the problem inevitably is a compromise between the manufacturer's objective of getting full assortments of his products held by resellers and the reseller's desire to maximize his inventory turnover rate.

Actual stock-level policies tend to be a function of the degree of control the manufacturer can exercise over the market. If, for example, the manufacturer has developed strong selective demand for his product, he can exercise considerable influence on how the line is to be resold.

This "channel control" by the manufacturer enables him to specify certain requirements for resellers, including levels of stock to be carried by them. On the other hand, for those products that do not have strong selective demand or make up a small portion of the reseller's total volume of sales, control is vested in the reseller, and it is he who decides the depth and breadth of assortments to be carried.

Three inventory policy alternatives in descending order of the manufacturer channel control required for their implementation might include the following:

1. A policy of "loading," in which resellers are required to hold stocks in excess of quantities justified by current sales potentials.
2. A policy of requiring resellers to hold "basic stocks" keyed to current sales potentials.
3. A policy of not having any stock level requirements for resellers.

Loading.   The practice of requiring resellers to carry more stock than is justified by current sales expectations is termed "loading." Several reasons for the policy can be suggested. General overcapacity in an industry and the resultant competition for a greater share of a relatively static market may result in resellers being pressured to accept larger and larger stocks. The manufacturer who loads a reseller carrying multiple lines of competing products hopes to freeze out competition; that is to say, he hopes to get his products held in sufficient quantity to preclude the reseller's paying too much attention to the lines of rival manufacturers.

If the distributor is a selected or exclusive agent of the manufacturer, loading also may be a form of pressure aimed at forcing increased selling effort. By loading the reseller with excessive inventory, the manufacturer hopes to stimulate him to increase his sales and promotional efforts in order to move the goods off his shelves. The reseller who refuses to accept the "load" may be threatened with loss of the franchise.

Loading may increase sales in the short run, especially under exclusive agency distribution where the franchise is highly valued. The reseller may fight to turn excess inventory into cash in hopes that in the near future the load will be removed. In the long run, however, it is difficult to see how a policy of loading which is not compensated by extra payments from the manufacturer (e.g., rebates, special bonuses, or special credit terms) can result in anything but diminished reseller activity in behalf of the manufacturer. As resellers rely increasingly on price reductions to unload stock their effective margin diminishes, and with the margin goes the financial means required to engage in promotion of a nonprice nature. When, eventually, the price appeal of a line is all that remains, the wholesaler or retailer becomes merely an order taker rather than an extension of the manufacturer selling force.

Basic Stock Policy. A much preferred policy is to attempt to get resellers to hold *basic stocks*. Such stocks can be designed to fit the needs of the individual reseller and the market he serves. The decision as to the depth and breadth of assortments to be carried can be jointly determined by the manufacturer with his wholesalers. The wholesalers, in turn, can work out basic stock arrangements with their retailer customers. If the setting and maintenance of stock levels is a truly cooperative undertaking, and if these levels are set to reflect the sales potentials of individual resellers, the possibility is lessened that wholesalers and retailers will complain of being overloaded with inventory. As a result more effective reseller support should be realized.

The implementation of such a basic stock policy is, of course, limited to those situations where the demand for the product line is sufficiently strong or the distribution by resellers sufficiently selective to gain the needed cooperation from wholesalers and retailers. Moreover, basic stocks are feasible only when the demand for the product falls into fairly predictable patterns for each reseller and when the costs of holding such stocks are in line with the individual reseller's sales potentials.

No Stock Requirements. An inventory policy which does not place any minimum requirements on stock levels to be held by resellers is generally an admission that a more stringent policy would be unenforceable by the manufacturer. If sales are being lost because of lack of product availability, the manufacturer would be well advised to share some of the costs of holding inventory with resellers to get them to hold more stock. A manufacturer who has the control necessary to require minimum stock levels to be held by resellers but does not enforce such a policy leaves itself vulnerable to resellers' "high spotting" the line —that is, carrying only the fast-moving items. This policy (or lack of policy) can result in lost sales as well as minimal selling effort by resellers.

Returned-Goods Policies

Policies which provide for the return of stock, either for credit or for exchange, have an indirect effect on reseller margins by (1) reducing markdowns due to merchandise obsolescence and (2) stabilizing resale prices by removing the threat of distress selling by individual resellers. Since the margin realized by resellers provides the payment for their functional performance, returned-goods policies can influence reseller ability to sell. The following considerations determine the extent to which the manufacturer might provide for the return of goods by his resellers: (1) risk of obsolescence and (2) adjustments to short-run market fluctuations.

Risk of Obsolescence. If the manufacturer's line is subject to a high rate of obsolescence he might well share some of the risk with his resellers by having a liberal returned-goods policy. Such a policy might allow a portion of the reseller's stock to be exchanged for new merchandise, or it might simply warn resellers of items that will become obsolete in the near future. Regardless of its exact nature, any returned-goods policy which protects reseller margins should increase reseller ability to engage in selling support.

Adjustment to Short-Run Market Fluctuations. If unexpected changes in demand leave excessively large inventories at wholesale and retail, a liberal returned-goods policy might avoid price cutting at reseller levels which could damage the reputation of the product. It also could forestall a loss of promotional support. The manufacturer's problem here, however, is to distinguish between the normal risks of wholesaling and retailing, which involve taking some markdowns, and those abnormal situations that lead to widespread distress selling. Obviously, these topics are beyond the scope of this book.

SUMMARY

This chapter has discussed three areas of manufacturer marketing policy which have an effect on the reseller's willingness and ability to support a manufacturer's promotional program with his own efforts. Because manufacturer policies pertaining to price, margin, and inventory are important in terms of their influence on reseller performance, and because these policies are controllable by the manufacturer in the relatively short run, their constant appraisal is necessary. The wise manufacturer examines his own policies and the mode of their execution before blaming resellers for lack of support. Once the concept of full reseller support or what may be expected from resellers in the context of the specific marketing situation has been defined, then, and only then, can the manufacturer take steps to supplement or improve reseller performance. Some of these steps are discussed in Chapter 19.

REVIEW AND DISCUSSION QUESTIONS

1. How may a change in a manufacturer's promotional mix affect the role of its resellers?
2. Contrast a promotional mix in which the reseller's role is small with one in which the reseller's role is large.
3. How does the product life cycle influence the role of resellers?
4. Describe the effects of competition on the reseller's ability to engage in selling activity. What is the difference between interchannel and intrachannel competition?

5. What is market segregation? How does it act to reduce the pressures on the reseller margins?

6. What is selective distribution? How does it differ from market segregation?

7. What are the dangers of overselectivity in franchising resellers?

8. Why is manufacturer pricing policy so crucial to resellers?

9. What is the difference between pricing "to" channels, and pricing "through" channels?

10. What is meant by buying distribution, and what are the legal implications of such a policy?

11. Explain what is meant by pricing to segment markets.

12. Why is the problem of setting discounts for resellers so difficult to solve?

13. What is meant by pricing to gain the marginal reseller?

14. What are the advantages of using distribution cost analysis to check adequacy of reseller margins?

15. Why do manufacturer inventory policies have such an important effect upon reseller promotional performance?

16. Compare and contrast a policy of inventory "loading" for resellers with a basic stock policy.

17. How do reasonable returned goods policies aid in gaining reseller promotional cooperation?

19

Stimulating Reseller Support: Improving, Supplementing, and Controlling Performance

WHEN THE MANUFACTURER has a clear idea of the role his resellers can be expected to perform, given the overall promotional program, and when he understands the ways in which his other reseller policies can influence wholesaler and retailer willingness and ability to sell, he can consider ways to improve or supplement their activities. With respect to *improving* the selling performance of wholesalers and retailers the manufacturer can consider: (1) training programs for reseller salesmen, (2) setting quotas for resellers, and (3) providing assistance to resellers with respect to their advertising and sales promotion efforts.

In terms of *supplementing* reseller activity the manufacturer might consider: (1) the use of missionary salesmen, (2) provision of display and selling aids, and (3) the scheduling of special sales and consumer deals.

Two means are suggested for *controlling* reseller activity: (1) selection of resellers and (2) vertical integration through ownership of reseller outlets or by means of contractual agreements.

IMPROVING RESELLER PERFORMANCE

Training Reseller Salesmen

One of the most effective methods by which manufacturers can improve reseller performance is to assume part of the responsibility for training wholesaler and retailer salesmen. One writer states bluntly, "Generally speaking you [the manufacturer] will benefit from your distributor relationships more or less in proportion to the effort you put into training the distributor's salesmen."[1] A study made by the National Industrial Conference Board further affirmed the contention that training of dealer salesmen was a profitable undertaking for manufacturers. It was found that well-trained reseller salesmen built goodwill for the manufacturer as well as for their own houses by recommending the right product to satisfy the customer's needs and by keeping customers informed about the advantages and uses of new products. Moreover, well-trained dealers maintained more adequate inventories and had better service facilities than did untrained distributors. Finally, well-trained dealers required less of the manufacturer salesmen's time, so they could make more calls per day.[2]

Training at the Wholesale Level. Although the generalizations stated about the value of training are valid for both wholesaler and retailer selling personnel, there is a difference in the objectives and scope of programs aimed at these two levels. The training programs at wholesale are intended to improve the salesman's knowledge of the line and his selling techniques, and often, to train him in addition, to assume the role of management counselors. For example, one manufacturer of major household appliances has an extensive program to train the field representative of its wholesale distributors. Courses held at the factory are given in such diverse areas as product, business, and sales management; retail selling, handling of used merchandise; service training; and general supervision of a sales territory. There is no charge for the courses, but the distributors must pay transportation and living expenses for their men in the program. Courses run for up to five and one half days, and the trainees are worked hard. Heavy emphasis is placed on visual aids, and after factory training each distributor salesman is equipped with a sound-film strip projector and a wide variety of training films. These films are made under factory supervision and are sold to distributors at production cost for use in their own training programs for retailer salesmen.

Thus the objectives of a program to train wholesaler salesmen may be twofold—first, to provide them with knowledge about the product line and how it may be sold most effectively, and second, to prepare wholesaler salesmen to provide management assistance to retailers. This assistance may include the training of retailer sales personnel.

Regardless of the exact content of the manufacturer's training program, it is clear that a program for training wholesaler salesmen fills a gap which in many cases *cannot be filled by the wholesaler himself.*

---

[1] Carl C. Gauk, "Training the Distributor's Salesmen," *Development of Dealer and Distributor Cooperation for Greater Sales,* Marketing Series No. 80 (New York: American Management Association, 1950), p. 17.

[2] E. F. Higgins and J. F. Fogarty, Jr., *Training Dealers,* Studies in Business Policy No. 48 (New York: National Industrial Conference Board, 1950), p. 4.

Because of either the pressures of day-to-day business or the lack of specialized sales management in smaller distributor organizations, many wholesalers will not or cannot do an adequate job of training. Thus this is one form of assistance rendered by the manufacturer which helps the wholesaler where he cannot help himself. In those cases where the wholesaler does have his own training facilities and personnel, manufacturer assistance can make the program more effective and at the same time lighten the cost load.

Training at the Retail Level. Manufacturers' programs to train sales personnel at retail share many objectives in common with programs aimed at training wholesaler salesmen. Attempts are made to impart product knowledge to those who meet the public, as well as to improve their selling techniques. There are differences, however, because of the great dispersion at retail in terms of store size and location. A further complication is the Robinson-Patman Act, which requires the manufacturer to offer promotional allowances or services (including those for training) to retailers on a "proportionally equal" basis. More is said about this requirement later.

Regardless of the difficulties in developing training programs for retailers, the manufacturer must take the initiative when high-quality retail selling is vital to his success, as in the EMBA case.[3] An association of mink breeders had developed a promotional program encompassing both national advertising and point-of-sale activity. Unfortunately, the point-of-sale efforts were handicapped by a shortage of trained fur sales personnel. Moreover, even the largest retailers lacked the ability to develop a training program for their salespeople.

To remedy the situation EMBA commissioned the development of a retail sales force training program to accomplish the following purposes:

1. To make a retail sales force as competent in selling EMBA mink garments as they are in selling ordinary cloth garments.
2. To dispel doubts in the minds of sales personnel regarding the meaning and significance of the EMBA label.
3. To remove the fear that surrounds the sale of fur garments.
4. To emphasize the EMBA image of quality.

Nine stores agreed to participate in the first training session, which lasted three days and was held on the store premises. EMBA specialists conducted a class for the first 30 minutes of each day and then spent the rest of their time on the selling floor. The program was followed up by the visit of a "mystery shopper" to each store who monitored sales procedures and offered suggestions for change when weaknesses were spotted.

---

[3] See "EMBA Mink Breeder's Association" case in Wayne F. Talarzyk, James F. Engel, and Carl M. Larsen, *Cases in Promotional Strategy* (Homewood, Ill., Richard D. Irwin, 1971).

Another situation of interest is the one faced by the Royal Worcester Porcelain Company.[4] This manufacturer of fine English bone china engaged in the selective distribution of its line through 1,500 jewelry and department stores. Although serving a national market, the company's sales volume could support a relatively small appropriation of $200,000 for advertising and sales promotion. Research studies had indicated that the retail salesperson was highly influential in the sale of china but that most were sadly lacking in product knowledge or awareness of the type of information consumers wanted from them. Moreover, retail sales personnel did not give Royal Worcester very much selling "push."

To improve the caliber of retail selling and to gain greater support for the product line Royal Worcester developed a program for training retail sales personnel. It consisted of a 20-minute sound training film which was presented by Royal Worcester salesmen at meetings held for about 1,000 of their retail accounts. The film discussed fine china in general and was well received by sales personnel. To maintain continued contact with retail salespeople, the company developed a monthly sales bulletin which provides product information, selling tips, and information about sales contests and serves to inform retail salesmen of the national consumer advertising program.

These two examples of efforts to train retail sales personnel show that such a program is vital to the success of the manufacturer's promotional program when the product is of such a type that the buyer must seek information and advice from the salesperson. In addition, it is clear that very few retailers have the means or the volition to initiate training programs for the sale of specific types of goods. Thus the manufacturer must assume the responsibility and the cost of training retail personnel if he desires an improvement in the quality and quantity of retail support. Moreover, this assumption of responsibility must be on a continuing basis because of the high rate of turnover of retail employees.

Quotas for Resellers

The establishment of quotas, if properly planned and administered, is a device which can improve reseller performance. Although the use of quotas to measure the performance of salesmen is quite common in an integrated organization, the application of this technique to independent wholesalers and retailers is somewhat limited. One authority points out that:

. . . not all sellers set quotas for their resellers. This results from one or more causes: failure to recognize that there is an underlying need to measure per-

---

[4] See "Royal Worcester Porcelain Company, Inc.," case in Talarzyk, Engel, and Larsen, *Cases in Promotional Strategy.*

formance; difficulty in setting accurate quotas, especially where sales results may be far removed in time from sales effort, as for instance is often the case with the sale of costly industrial machinery; or lastly a realization of the inability to take any action if the quotas are not consistently met, as would be the case with the manufacturer whose product line would be of little importance to a reseller.[5]

In an interview with officials of a home appliance manufacturer it was learned that quotas were used to measure the relative performance of independent wholesale distributors against sales branches. In addition, quotas were set for each sales division within the territory. Of course, in this situation the manufacturer was granting exclusive agencies and could exert considerable influence in requiring distributors to meet quotas. Persistent failure to make the quota could well mean loss of franchise.

In other cases when the manufacturer's line is less important to his resellers, the manufacturer's ability to encourage resellers to meet their quotas is weakened correspondingly. Even if the manufacturer cannot force distributors to meet quotas, however, the use of quotas to provide information on sales potentials can be a means of improving reseller performance. For example, the Atkins Saw Division of Borg-Warner Corporation makes available to its distributors at no charge a market analysis of distributor territory. The purpose of this service is to aid distributors in accurate measurement of their sales performance, to help distributors establish quotas for retail dealers, and to get the resellers to work for a larger share of the available business.[6]

Advertising and Sales Promotion Assistance

In addition to training of reseller sales personnel and the setting of quotas for resellers, manufacturers can attempt to improve reseller efforts by assisting wholesalers and retailers in the planning and execution of their advertising and sales promotion programs. Such assistance may take the form of: (1) cooperative advertising programs, (2) promotional allowances (3) merchandising the advertising, (4) in-store promotions, and (5) contests and incentive payments for sales personnel.

Cooperative Advertising. A program under which a manufacturer pays a portion of his reseller's local advertising costs is commonly called cooperative advertising. Usually the manufacturer shares the cost of local reseller advertising on a 50–50 basis up to a certain limit, often a percentage of reseller purchases from the manufacturer. If, for example, the

---

[5] Harry L. Hansen, *Marketing: Text, Techniques, and Cases,* 3d. ed. (Homewood, Ill.: Richard D. Irwin, 1967), p. 569.

[6] See T. O. Conger, "Market Service Spurs Distributor Sales," *Industrial Marketing,* Vol. 42 (September 1958), p. 168.

agreement specified a 50–50 share up to 4 percent of purchases, a retailer who had purchased $2,500 worth of goods from the manufacturer would be able to spend $200 on advertising them and would receive a $100 rebate from the manufacturer. Thus the net cost to the retailer for this advertising would be $100.

An advantage of cooperative advertising to the reseller, in addition to the partial defrayal of his local advertising expense, is that under most programs the manufacturer furnishes a good assortment of advertising layouts and stereotype mats for reproduction in the local press.

There are also disadvantages for the reseller. First, there is a tendency to promote a line with more vigor than it deserves simply because the cost is being shared by the manufacturer. Moreover, the nature of the advertisements may stimulate selective demand for the manufacturer's brand without increasing the patronage appeal of the store.

From the manufacturer's point of view a well-planned cooperative advertising program can be useful. First, it involves the reseller financially. The wholesaler or retailer lays some of his own money on the line to promote a given item. Even though the sum expended is matched by the manufacturer, the reseller has made an investment in promotion, and to protect his investment the wise reseller will make sure of three things: (1) that he has a sufficient stock of the item on hand to back up the ad; (2) that the item (or items) receives adequate display at point of purchase and, perhaps, in the window; and (3) that the item (or items) advertised receives in-store selling support from the sales personnel. If a manufacturer's cooperative advertising program can get resellers to follow through in this manner, it is probably worth the trouble and cost of its administration.

A more detailed view of a cooperative advertising program is provided by consideration of the one sponsored by the Palm Beach Company, a manufacturer of men's summer weight suits.[7] In one year, for example, Palm Beach spent about $1 million for printed media advertising, with 60 percent of the budget for company advertising and 40 percent, or $400,000, for cooperative advertising with retailers. The bulk of the company advertising (80 percent) was placed in newspapers, with the remainder going to magazines and to trade advertising.

The cooperative advertising plan paid 50 percent of a retailer's cost for newspaper space, radio and TV commercial time, and billboard and car card space. The dealer could spend up to 4 percent of the net wholesale price of merchandise shipped to him and would be reimbursed up to a maximum of 2 percent.

Palm Beach required that the ads include proper product labels and

---

[7] Neil H. Borden and Martin V. Marshall, *Advertising Management: Text and Cases,* rev. ed. (Homewood, Ill.: Richard D. Irwin, 1959), pp. 261–73.

descriptions and be devoted exclusively to the promotion of Palm Beach products. The company also reserved the right to refuse reimbursement "to any retailer, subject to fair trade laws, who broke a valid fair trade price set by Palm Beach."[8]

The really interesting aspect of this program is the intensity with which the company promoted its cooperative program to the retail dealers. Strategy included the following:

1. A magazine-size booklet informing dealers of the Palm Beach line and promotional program for the coming year was mailed in the spring.
2. In addition, the retailer received a 17 × 25-inch cooperative advertising service book containing descriptive material, ad layouts, reproductions of available mats, and suggested radio scripts. Plates for four-color ads were also available at cost ($20–$35) to retailers who wished to advertise in color.
3. The 50-man Palm Beach sales force devoted a major portion of its time talking to retailers about tying in their local promotion with the Palm Beach national campaign. They also planned balanced promotional campaigns for retailers, including display, direct mail advertising, and newspaper advertising.

As a result of the program Palm Beach reported that 65 percent of available cooperative advertising funds had been used by retailers. Careful records were kept, and salesmen as well as top executives of the Palm Beach Company called on stores whose advertising usage was far below the potential permitted by their sales volume. Every attempt was made to convince these retailers to make full use of the cooperative advertising allowance.

The Palm Beach program illustrates a situation in which a high level of reseller support is vital to reaching the manufacturer's sales objectives. The manufacturer has placed a major emphasis on cooperative advertising to gain the reseller support required. Moreover, the program was carefully planned and coordinated with the national advertising campaign. To make certain that retailer participation in the program was as extensive as possible, the manufacturer engaged in considerable personal selling effort to get retailers to increase their advertising. While there are these advantages, there also are real problems, which are discussed later.

Promotional Allowances. In situations where retail promotion is crucial to manufacturer success, payments may be made for types of reseller support other than media advertising. Such promotional allowances or

---

[8] The legality of this clause is subject to question.

payments are very often used to gain display at retail. Display is of great importance when the product being sold is purchased on impulse or is unable to attract any "push" from retailers because of its limited contribution to overall retail profits.

The Whitehall Pharmacal Company case is a good illustration of how one manufacturer of proprietary drugs attempted to improve reseller support effort for his products through the use of promotional allowances.[9] The company manufactures such products as BiSoDol antiacid mints, Kolynos dentifrices, and Anacin. Sales were over $25 million annually, with over $5.3 million being spent on national advertising. To supplement the heavy "pull" strategy, the company used 100 salesmen to call on retailers.

A research study had indicated that point-of-sale displays using about $2\frac{1}{2}$ sq. ft. of counter space were especially effective in increasing sales. The company embarked on a program to get as many retailers as possible to utilize the special display. The key to the program was an allowance to the retailer of 5 percent of his purchases if certain promotional activities were performed.

Problems faced by Whitehall were of two varieties. First, competitors offered equivalent allowances (or in some cases even higher allowances), and it was difficult to gain retailer support because of the tremendous demand for limited counter space. Second, most druggists took the 5 percent allowance, but not all followed through with the placement of the display. It was evident that some type of action was required to get drug retailers to participate in the display program and to make sure that they kept the display on the counter for as long as they were collecting the promotional allowance.

This case illustrates both the need of a manufacturer to gain display at retail and the difficulties faced in gaining such support. The promotional allowance is one approach to gaining special retailer support, but to insure its success special payments have to be backed up by the manufacturer's sales force. The competition for retailer display or advertising tie-in as well as the general inertia of most retailers required, in most cases, more than a mere payment. On the other hand, "push" from the manufacturer without special payment will not be as effective as "push" with a payment for special effort at retail.

Merchandising the Advertising.   Another approach to improving reseller demand-stimulation effort, especially at retail, can be illustrated by the program of the Speidel Corporation.[10] This manufacturer of metal expansion watch bands and identification bracelets sold its line to about

---

[9] "Whitehall Pharmacal Company" in Hansen, *Marketing*, pp. 615–17.

[10] See "Case 26: The Speidel Corporation" in Borden and Marshall, *Advertising Management*, pp. 802–16.

250 jewelry wholesalers who, in turn, supplied 18,000 retail jewelers. Most wholesalers and retailers carried lines directly competitive with that of Speidel.

Although Speidel was spending over $2.5 million per year on advertising, it did not have a cooperative advertising program for its resellers, nor were there any promotional allowances or payments. The company did, however, give the retailer "every possible aid in selling Speidel merchandise." This assistance included a comprehensive dealer display and dealer advertising program. Twice a year ads were placed in trade publications informing retailers of the availability of the latest merchandise and promotional material. Most important, the retail promotions were keyed to the national efforts in magazines and on radio and television. Eventually, TV became Speidel's major medium, and the company used commercials to sell specific items in the line.

Here is an illustration of an effective strategy to gain retailer selling support which does not utilize cooperative advertising or promotional allowances. It is essentially a strategy by which the manufacturer creates selective demand for his product. Such demand makes the retailer's task easier so that the sale of the manufacturer's product becomes more profitable to him.

In-Store Promotions.   Other types of manufacturer programs to improve reseller demand stimulation support may not be on a continuing basis but aimed instead at reaching limited objectives in a short period of time. The in-store promotion is one program of this type. The Inco "Gleam of Stainless Steel Promotion"[11] is illustrative of the use of such a promotion.

Inco, a leading producer of nickel, felt that nickel usage would be increased if sales of stainless steel consumer products could be stimulated. A program was planned around department stores, because research had indicated that they were the most powerful influence on consumer buying habits in the major market areas. The objectives of the program were: (1) to spotlight stainless steel in the large stores, (2) to generate sales enthusiasm among retail sales personnel, and (3) to increase demand for stainless steel products and thus the derived demand for nickel.

The promotion was timed for February and was first run with 32 participating stores. Inco inserted a four-color, two-page ad in *Look* and *Saturday Evening Post* as well as local newspaper ads featuring the name of the cooperating department store in each of the 32 market cities. In addition, the stores ran 103 newspaper ads featuring stainless steel many devoted key window space to the display of stainless steel

---

[11] See case of same name in Talarzyk, Engel, and Larsen, *Cases in Promotional Strategy.*

items. Several steel manufacturers supported Inco's national advertising effort.

Inco gained retailer cooperation by offering the campaign to each store on an exclusive basis. Nominal cooperative advertising allowances were granted, and each retailer was provided with a complete promotional kit. Sales training sessions provided for retail personnel featured a nine-minute training film produced for this purpose.

The results were so favorable that the in-store promotion was continued for three more years. Modifications in the program were minor, but retailer and industry participation increased greatly in each succeeding year.

A similar type of effort on behalf of Hilton Hotels was seen in the Hilton "Follow the Sun" campaign.[12] Tie-ins were made with airlines and with the leading retailers in 15 target areas. The campaign sought to relate the Hilton Hotels' vacation and honeymoon facilities to the bridal promotions of the retailers. The promotion was built around a contest in which registrants might win a free honeymoon in the Caribbean or Hawaii. The participating stores were given a format around which to develop their bridal promotions and also benefited from the store traffic generated by the chance to win a free honeymoon.

Regardless of the method used by the manufacturer, in-store promotion must offer the retailer a *quid pro quo,* or else it will not succeed. Few retailers will put themselves out to support a specific manufacturer unless doing so promises a reasonable payoff. Given that an in-store promotion does offer a retailer a profit potential worthy of his effort, it still must be carefully planned by the manufacturer, and the execution of the program must be guided through to the end if best results are to be obtained. Once a manufacturer has concluded a successful in-store promotion on a modest scale, it is easier to expand the number of participants the next time it is run. Success breeds success, and retailers have an effective grapevine which informs them of how their counterparts in other markets did with a specific promotion.

Contests and Incentives. To stimulate or improve the selling effort at retail, manufacturers may devise contests or provide special incentives for retail sales personnel. A contest or incentive plan is generally a part of a larger program and is aimed at motivating salespeople to participate in the selling campaign with enthusiasm. In the Royal Worcester case,[13] for example, communication with the salesperson was established through the issuance of monthly sales bulletins. Shortly after the bulletin was first issued it was used to announce a monthly contest based on the theme

---

[12] Described in personal correspondence with one of the authors.

[13] See Royal Worcester Porcelain Company case in Talarzyk, Engel, and Larsen, *Cases in Promotional Strategy.*

"How I Made a Royal Worcester Sale." Prizes were awarded to the senders of the best letters received each month; the grand prize was a trip to England. Retail clerk participation in the contest was unusually high and served to focus the attention of many salespersons on the overall Royal Worcester campaign to gain retailer support.

Contests or incentive payments developed by the manufacturer can get out of hand. Too frequent use of contests can orient the salesperson's attention to a payoff to be received for good sales performance at the cost of making him overlook the merits of the product line itself. Salespeople begin to sell items because *they,* rather than the customers, will profit most from the transaction. This orientation, while perhaps giving the manufacturer a temporary increase in volume, does not necessarily provide a lasting benefit unless the product itself is superior. Too many manufacturers use incentive payments and contests for retail salesmen to "push" products which are inferior to those offered by competitors.

Moreover, contests and incentive payments for retail sales personnel may conflict with the desires and objectives of retail management. Some retailers refuse to allow their employees to participate in manufacturer-sponsored contests or to accept incentive payments from manufacturers because they want to maintain control over their selling activities. For a manufacturer program of contests or incentives to succeed, obviously, it must have the approval of retail management. In addition, the program should serve as an "attention getter" to interest salespeople in the product line and the overall promotional campaign. Finally, it should be viewed as a short-run effort to support the overall program and not as a long-run substitute for product attractiveness or utility.

Legal Problems and Other Issues. The use by the manufacturer of cooperative advertising programs, promotional allowances, and other forms of assistance is not without its problems. Of an especially serious nature are those imposed by law. Sections 2d and 2e of the Robinson-Patman Act have perhaps the most relevance to the area of promotional allowances and services as granted by sellers to resellers.[14]

These sections of the act define, in rather loose terms, the conditions under which nondiscriminatory payments or services can be made to members of a reseller group. Such payments or services are legal if they are granted on a "proportionally equal" basis. That is, the dollar value of the payments or services rendered by a seller to various resellers must be in proportion to the size of their purchases from the seller. For example, a reseller buying $10,000 worth of goods a year from a manufacturer should be entitled to ten times the value of payments or services received from the manufacturer, as compared to the reseller whose purchases totaled only $1,000.

---

[14] Public Law No. 92, 74th Cong., H.R. 8442, June 19, 1936.

Moreover, the seller's program must allow "participation" by all interested resellers. The nature of the seller's promotional strategy must not exclude competing resellers on the basis of size, geographical location, or other characteristics.

Revised guidelines for the use of cooperative advertising were issued by the Federal Trade Commission on June 1, 1969. These guidelines make many new demands on both manufacturers and retailers who use cooperative plans. Key items include the following:

1. All competing customers, whether wholesalers or retailers, must be informed of the availability of a co-op plan. This may be done through notices in trade publications, announcements, or in the container or package. The manufacturer may transfer the responsibility for notification to the wholesaler but must still make spot checks to see that the information is being received.
2. A given co-op plan must be "functionally available" to all competing customers on proportionally equal terms and must include more than one way for various kinds of customers to participate.
3. A section called "third party liability," which deals with double billing, bars any advertising medium from quoting higher rates than are actually charged in order to allow customers to claim greater payments than they are entitled to as part of a co-op plan. Under this section the customer is required to reveal and refund any deferred rebates on the cost of his advertising in newspapers and other media.[15]

Additional legal restrictions on the use of cooperative advertising or promotional allowances are those limitations imposed by reseller misuse. For example, many resellers do not run cooperative advertisements correctly. Poor composition, inadequate copy, and poor timing all mean that funds are not as well used as they might have been if more care had been taken in preparation.

Similar abuses are also common with respect to payments made to obtain display space or to gain in-store promotion. Monies are diverted to margin rather than to specific promotional activities.

Finally, there is a wide variance in reseller attitudes toward cooperative selling ventures which makes the manufacturer's task difficult indeed. In some cases resellers may engage in "blackmail," threatening to buy from another source unless special allowances or services are forthcoming. In other situations they may show little interest in even the most generous program, preferring to push their own private brands over those of the manufacturer.

---

[15] Adapted from *Washington Report* (Washington, D.C.: American Advertising Federation, January 28, 1970).

SUPPLEMENTING RESELLER PERFORMANCE

In those situations where *improving* the quality or quantity of reseller performance of selling activity is not sufficient to reach manufacturer promotional objectives, more direct action must be taken to *supplement* reseller effort. The manufacturer must assume some of the responsibility for selling and sales promotion at wholesale and retail levels. The utilization of missionary salesmen is one method of gaining greater activity at reseller levels in the channel of distribution. Provision of selling aids and price incentives are other methods.

Missionary (Specialty) Selling

The use of manufacturer salesmen to supplement the personal selling activities of resellers is known as missionary or specialty selling. In the sale of consumer goods, missionary salesmen are employed by manufacturers to contact both wholesalers and retailers. They check wholesalers periodically to determine if adequate stocks are being held. They call upon retailers to inform them of new products, to arrange window and in-store display, to provide advice on selling, to answer questions posed by the retailer and, in general, to build goodwill. If they take orders for merchandise they usually turn such orders over to wholesalers for filling.

In the sale of industrial goods, missionary salesmen train distributor salesmen, demonstrate effective selling techniques by accompanying distributor salesmen on their calls, secure introductory orders from users, and assist distributor salesmen in closing those sales that demand greater technical knowledge or selling skill than the distributor salesman has.

Two short case histories will illustrate what missionary salesmen can and cannot do to supplement reseller demand stimulation effort.

Paint Manufacturer.[16] A company which manufactured a broad line of varnishes, lacquers, enamels, and other paint products had a product line consisting of over 250 separate items which was sold to the consumer market through exclusive wholesale distributors, who in turn sold to selected retailers. Thirty-five company salesmen called on the wholesalers and spent a great deal of their time with wholesaler salesmen, performing missionary selling activities such as soliciting orders from retailers for the wholesalers' accounts. Paint company executives felt that the salesmen were providing excessive missionary support and that such activity should be curtailed.

In commenting on this case, it was pointed out that:

The fact that such cooperative sales work was needed to maintain sales when the distributors were granted exclusive territories suggests there was a basic weak-

---

[16] See "Nancock Varnish Company," *Harvard Business Reports,* Vol. 9, p. 266.

ness somewhere in the company's marketing plan—as to just where the weakness lay no clues are furnished by the statement of the case. The weakness may have been in the company's advertising, in the merchandise itself, in the type of retail distribution sought, or in the management of the wholesale distributing firms.[17]

Thus, although the belief of company executives that missionary selling support should be curtailed was probably correct, attention should have been directed to finding out why so much missionary selling support was needed by wholesalers who were exclusive agents.

Cereal Manufacturer.[18] A manufacturer of cereals which distributed through wholesalers to retail grocery stores had a regular sales force which called upon wholesalers and another group of salesmen, known as specialty men, which called upon retailers to solicit orders that were turned over to the wholesalers to fill. Wholesalers were allowed the same gross margin on orders, whether obtained by them or by the manufacturer's specialty sales force.

The primary duty of the specialty salesmen was to expand the market coverage. In many situations specialty men used the orders they received from retailers to "force" wholesalers to stock the line or to carry new products. Wholesalers were antagonistic toward the manufacturer's missionary selling because of forcing but also because they felt that it would be an easy step for the manufacturer to establish wholesale branches and to circumvent the wholesalers entirely.

The board of directors of the manufacturer considered the discontinuance of the missionary selling program, but the general manager was able to persuade the board that such effort was needed to sustain sales volume.

This case illustrates the problem faced by a producer of a relatively narrow line who has to obtain intensive retail distribution. The manufacturer needs wholesalers for their coverage but also requires aggressive selling effort beyond the ability of wholesalers to provide. In this situation manufacturer supplementation of wholesaler personal selling activity by means of a special sales force is perhaps the best solution to the problem.

Implications. Missionary effort is advisable when the product being sold requires more personal selling effort than the wholesaler can afford to give. For example, if a product or product line represents a relatively small portion of the wholesaler's line but yet requires extensive retail distribution, point-of-sale display, or the acquisition of shelf space, the manufacturer can use missionary selling effectively to achieve these

---

[17] Ibid., p. 271.

[18] See "Chickamaugua Company," *Harvard Business Reports,* Vol. 5, p. 450.

objectives. Such a situation was illustrated by the case of the cereal manufacturer.

On the other hand, the use of missionary salesmen probably is not wise when, as in the case of the paint manufacturer, other elements of the promotional program are weak. It is an expensive undertaking for any manufacturer,[19] and its use to cover up defects in other elements of the marketing mix can be an unnecessary financial burden. In addition, excessive dependence on missionary selling can generate wholesaler resentment. When missionaries assume tasks such as routine order taking or delivery that could be performed by wholesalers, the wholesaler may feel that there is just a short step to his total circumvention. The net result is a fall-off in promotional support. Even if circumvention is not the issue, wholesalers may resent the missionary salesmen infringing on the time of their sales forces. A general-line wholesaler carrying the products of hundreds of suppliers may feel that missionary salesmen interfere with the most effective allocation of his salesmen's time.

Certainly, correct use of missionary salesmen can improve or supplement wholesaler selling effort. The problems which arise from missionary selling seem to be caused by using missionaries to *supplant wholesaler efforts where supplementation would suffice,* or from poor management of missionary selling effort. As one authority concludes:

Missionary selling . . . in large measure substitutes direct action on the part of the manufacturer for cooperation, which would otherwise be needed, on the part of wholesalers. Still, unless handled judiciously, such selling can be productive of a lack of cooperation in other selling activities, even of unwillingness to handle a manufacturer's products. Missionary salesmen have often been accused, and with some justification, of overstocking dealers, selling to poor credit risks and then expecting wholesalers to fill the orders, of playing one wholesaler against the other by shifting orders between them, of offering special terms or rebates to certain dealers in the name of the wholesaler, and of other similar activities. Wholesalers may believe that missionary sales work is the first step toward direct sale and that it is just another way of decreasing the wholesaler's independence. Also, when missionary salesmen accompany wholesaler's salesmen on their calls, a conflict of personalities may arise which creates ill will.[20]

Display and Selling Aids

Manufacturer provision of display material for point-of-purchase use, mailing pieces for reseller distribution, dealer identification signs, and similar incentives are other ways to supplement reseller efforts. Manu-

---

[19] It has been estimated that the use of missionary salesmen adds between 10 and 15 percent to the cost of goods sold by them.

[20] D. Maynard Phelps, *Sales Management* (Homewood, Ill.: Richard D. Irwin, 1953) p. 514.

facturer use of these promotional devices has the dual purpose of stimulating demand for the product and getting an increased share of the dealer's promotional effort placed at the manufacturer's disposal.[21]

The manufacturer usually has great difficulty in getting resellers to utilize the display material and selling aids made available. Based on the volume of material distributed to resellers, it appears that manufacturer response to nonuse of material is to double the quantity made available. Because resellers often do not know what to do with this great flood of material, it is not uncommon to find a great deal of it in the refuse box in unopened cartons.

Several approaches are available to the manufacturer who requires some degree of display or other activity by retailers, for example. The payment of promotional allowances for display, the use of the sales force to obtain display and in-store promotion, and charging resellers a total payment for materials are all methods which may help gain better point-of-sale display or selling effort.

Perhaps the most effective approach is that of pretesting dealer aids. An executive of General Foods reported the following:

We made several field surveys . . . on the use to which our point-of-sale material was being put, and we reached some disappointing conclusions. We learned, for example, that on several campaigns last year, only half the material shipped out to the field was being used effectively. . . . It had not been checked with the field to predetermine its acceptance. We now have a continuous program . . . for periodic surveys of the grocery stores regularly contacted by our salesmen. . . . This system afforded us an accurate picture of the types and amounts of material which could best be used in these stores. . . . We are convinced that it is a waste of time, effort, and money to send point-of-purchase material to the field if we cannot demonstrate how it will work for the benefit of the store operator. . . .[22]

The Whitehall Pharmacal Company case noted above illustrates the difficulties of using promotional allowances to gain point-of-sale display.[23] Because research had indicated that a new type of display had increased sales as much as 150 percent in those stores in which it was used during a 60-day period, Whitehall developed a bonus plan for its salesmen. This plan could result in a salary increase of as much as one third for those salesmen who were able to get the stores in their territories to utilize the new point-of-sale displays. The extent of the pay-

---

[21] D. Maynard Phelps and J. Howard Westing, *Marketing Management*, rev. ed. (Homewood, Ill.: Richard D. Irwin, 1960), p. 465.

[22] W. P. Lillard, "Point-of-Purchase Promotion," *Proceedings, 6th Annual Advertising and Sales Promotion Conference*, Ohio State University Publications, College of Commerce Conference Series No. C–65 (Columbus, 1950), pp. 55–57.

[23] Hansen, *Marketing*, pp. 615–17.

ment to salesmen indicates the value of display to the company. This situation is of special interest because Whitehall was spending over $5 million annually, or 20 percent of sales, on national advertising. It appears, therefore, that even with extensive "pull," point-of-sale display is an important element of strategy.

Consumer Deals

When the manufacturer wishes to blend some price promotion into his promotional mix to increase sales at retail, he may offer the buyer a temporary price reduction. Such reductions are known as consumer deals or, more explicitly, price deals. They can be contrasted with deals to the trade in that consumer deals attempt to create "pull," while trade incentives are aimed at getting reseller "push." Regardless of the target, a price deal is an attempt to exploit price sensitivity of demand. The strategy of such deals is clarified in a study of the Chicago market in which the findings included the following:

1. Off-season price reductions seem to be more profitable.
2. A high frequency of price promotions tends to make consumers overly price-conscious.
3. Deals do not seem to be a good way to counter new brands offered by competitors, and they are not necessarily more effective if accompanied by product or package innovations.
4. Price dealing is more effective for new brands than for established ones, and it is almost always more effective if kept in proper balance with advertising.
5. No brand—even a well-established, nondealing, luxury brand—is invulnerable to price-deal competition if it has basic marketing problems, and price-deal promotion is never a cure for marketing problems.
6. When special promotional campaigns fall short of expectations, the manufacturer will do better to question his own planning and policy making than to blame the failure on "intractable" retailers.[24]

The last point above has special relevance to the stimulation of reseller performance because the use of price deals to buyers may hinder rather than help reseller cooperation. Poor scheduling, inadequate trade incentives, excessive frequency of deals, and the like may cause wholesalers and retailers to rebel. Interviews with several retailers indicated, for example, that the pressure on grocery retailers to shift inventories back to the manufacturers has been increased in part by the extra confusion and expense caused by a multiplication of deal merchandise.[25]

---

[24] Charles L. Hinkle, "The Strategy of Price Deals," *Harvard Business Review,* Vol. 43, (July–August 1965), pp. 75–85.

[25] Ibid., p. 82.

CONTROLLING RESELLER PERFORMANCE

The control of reseller promotional performance is considerably more difficult for the manufacturer than is control of his own sales force. First, the chain of command which exists in an integrated organization is replaced with a relatively unstructured network of communication connecting independent intermediaries. Through this network flows a series of suggestions and persuasion rather than commands. (Of course, the greater the selective demand for the products of a given manufacturer, the greater the weight his suggestions will carry with resellers.) Second, resellers are both geographically dispersed and operationally diverse. No two wholesalers (or retailers) are really alike because each serves the market in a unique manner in terms of location, assortments carried, and demand-stimulation mix utilized. Thus the combination of manufacturer loss of direct authority due to passing of title of goods sold to resellers and reseller geographical dispersion and operational diversity makes manufacturer control of reseller activities a most difficult undertaking under ordinary circumstances.

The degree of control over reseller performance which manufacturers can exert is, of course, a function of the importance of the manufacturer's line to the individual wholesaler or retailer. When the manufacturer engages in highly selective or exclusive agency distribution and has limited market coverage to make his line more important to his selected resellers, some degree of control over these resellers may be expected.

Selected Resellers

The control process, as discussed earlier in this text, consists of formulating standards of performance, measuring performance, comparing actual results with the standards, and then taking action to correct substandard performances. If resellers are selected wholesalers or retailers for the line of a given manufacturer, the basis for control may be contained in the franchise agreement. In situations where the manufacturer's franchise is extremely valuable (as in the sale of automobiles), the reseller may contract to supply data on sales volume, inventory levels, and general operating expenses. Such information may be used by the manufacturer to measure reseller performance against a variety of standards. Commonly used criteria include share of market, sales growth over time, and the reaching of goals or quotas. In addition, attention may be given to size of sales force, expenditures for advertising and sales promotion, and similar items.

Once arrangements have been made to monitor the reseller's performance in a quantitative sense (and, hopefully, incorporated into the franchise agreement), attention can be paid to the qualitative nature of reseller performance. This aspect of reseller control does not usually require a contractual arrangement. A perceptive manufacturer's salesman generally can report on how resellers are using promotional materials furnished by the manufacturer or whether resellers have effective training programs for their sales personnel. Moreover, the manufacturer or an independent agency such as the Advertising Checking Bureau can audit the reseller's media advertising for control of cooperative advertising payments or to measure degree of support being provided the manufacturer's line. Similar checking may measure reseller activity in getting point-of-sale display or in setting up demonstrations or special selling events.

Nonselected Resellers

When coverage requirements are such that broad distribution through many resellers is required, the manufacturer's problem of control is intensified. There is a limit to what the manufacturer may expect from any one reseller in terms of furnishing data or following a specific recommendation to improve performance. Measurement and control of reseller performance thus becomes less concerned with individual reseller performance and concentrates instead upon the performance of groups of resellers.

The manufacturer may attempt to classify the many resellers carrying his line by type of institution, location, size, ownership, and other criteria. Then a distribution cost analysis may be made to show the relative profitability to the manufacturer of different groups of resellers. One such study, made by a manufacturer of major electrical appliances, indicated the relative profitability of sales made through diverse channels of distribution and retail outlets. The important lesson to be learned from examples of this type is that, given a situation in which many resellers are used, measurement of reseller performance may help the manufacturer control *his utilization of specific groups of resellers*, rather than the performance of individual resellers.

There are, however, some devices for the measurement and control of resellers under a policy of selective distribution which are also usable with broad, intensive distribution. For example, manufacturer's salesmen may be used to arrange for retailer use of point-of-sale display and to check back with retailers to see if displays have been properly placed. Such a program is seen in the case of Whitehall Pharmacal Company.[26]

Manufacturers may also take elaborate steps to check on cooperative advertising efforts of resellers. They can monitor reseller participation

---

[26] See Hansen, *Marketing,* pp. 498–501.

by means of a special department or use outside agencies to supplement internal activities.

Knowledge of the levels of reseller inventories is vital to many manufacturers who engage in intensive distribution through many resellers. Unable to use their salesmen to take shelf and storeroom counts of goods on hand, the manufacturer may avail himself of the services of an independent research agency to collect data on how rapidly products are moving off the retailer's shelves.[27] Without such information the manufacturer might mistake an inventory accumulation by resellers for steady or rising consumer demand for the line.

Vertical Integration

Because of the limits on the control that manufacturers can exert over independent middlemen, many producers have chosen to vertically integrate their channels of distribution through ownership of either all or part of the channel intermediaries. Through ownership the manufacturer gains maximum control over the manner in which his goods are physically distributed and promoted through all of the channel stages.

Vertical integration by means of ownership can be a very expensive undertaking. Not only are the capital commitments enormous, but unless the producer's product line is broad and sales volume is high, unit distribution costs will generally be greater than if traditional channels were used. For those firms engaging in vertical integration by means of ownership, the higher costs of physical distribution are accepted as a tradeoff against the higher levels of promotional activity and customer service that can be provided by closely controlled resellers.

Only a few firms engage in vertically integrated distribution by owning their intermediaries, but those that do have greatly increased their share of market. Thus the vast majority of firms that do not have the economic capability to own their resellers find themselves in an increasingly severe competitive struggle with their integrated rivals. To counteract the advantages associated with vertical integration and avoid having to make the needed financial commitments, many of these firms are adopting a strategy of "distribution programming," in which an integrated marketing system is developed by contractual agreements between a manufacturer and members of the reseller organization.

Distribution Programming.[28]   The development of a planned, professionally managed distribution system utilizing independent middlemen

---

[27] The A. C. Nielsen Company's Retail Store Audit is the best known of these approaches.

[28] This section is based on an excellent article by Bert C. McCammon, Jr., "Perspectives for Distribution Programming," in Louis P. Bucklin (ed.) *Vertical Marketing Systems* (Glenview, Ill.: Scott, Foresman & Co., 1970), pp. 32–50.

enables manufacturers to increase the effectiveness and efficiency of their distribution activities. Bert C. McCammon defines distribution programming as "the development of a comprehensive set of policies for the promotion of a product through the channel."[29] These policies are formulated as a joint effort between the manufacturer and the individual reseller as an attempt to negotiate a relationship that will give both parties some of the advantages of vertical integration, without the need for the manufacturer to purchase resellers.

Recent investigations have indicated that planned vertical marketing systems are "rapidly displacing conventional marketing channels as the dominant mode of distribution in the American economy."[30] Planned systems are taking over because they avoid the loose relationships, autonomous behavior, and diseconomies associated with traditional channels of distribution. In addition, they do not require the capital investments associated with ownership systems. Yet, these planned systems, being "professionally managed and centrally programmed networks, pre-engineered to achieve operating economies and maximum market impact,"[31] can compete effectively with systems which are vertically integrated through partial or complete ownership of channel intermediaries.

The first step in the formulation of a strategy of distribution programming is the careful analysis of manufacturer marketing goals, manufacturer marketing requirements, and the needs of retail (and wholesale) resellers. These goals and requirements are outlined in Figure 19–1. Note that both the goals and requirements can be stated in quantitative terms, thus eliminating the danger of misunderstanding during subsequent negotiations between the manufacturer and individual resellers.

After the completion of the analysis, specific distribution policies can be formulated. McCammon suggests that the policy alternatives available, although quite numerous, fall into three major categories: (1) those that offer "price" concessions to resellers, (2) those that provide financial assistance, and (3) those that provide some form of protection for resellers.[32] Selected policy alternatives classified under the three headings are illustrated in Figure 19–2.

Using the mix of distribution policy alternatives available, and based on the prior analysis of goals and requirements, a "programmed merchandising agreement" must be developed for each type of outlet

---

[29] Ibid., p. 32.
[30] Ibid., p. 43.
[31] Ibid., p. 43.
[32] Ibid., p. 37.

FIGURE 19–1

A Frame of Reference for Distribution Programming

Manufacturer's Marketing Goals

Based on a careful analysis of:
Corporate capability
Competition
Demand
Cost-volume relationships
Legal considerations
Reseller capability

and stated in terms of:
Sales (dollars and units)
Market share
Contribution to overhead
Rate of return on investment
Customer attitude, preference
and "readiness-to-buy" indices

Manufacturer's Channel Requirements	*Retailer's Requirements*
Reseller support needed to achieve marketing goals (stated in terms of):	"Compensation" expected for required support (stated in terms of):
Coverage ratio	Managerial aspirations
Amount and location of display space	Trade preferences
Level and composition of inventory investment	Financial goals
Service capability and standards	Rate of inventory turnover
Advertising, sales promotion, and personal selling support	Rate of return on investment
Market development activities	Gross margin (dollars and percent)
	Contribution to overhead (dollars and percent)
	Gross margin and contribution to overhead per dollar invested in inventory
	Gross margin and contribution to overhead per unit of space
	Nonfinancial goals

Distribution Policies

"Price" concessions
Financial assistance
Protective provisions

From *Vertical Marketing Systems,* edited by Louis P. Bucklin. Copyright © 1970 by Scott, Foresman and Company. Reprinted by permission of the publisher.

utilized in the pattern of distribution. This agreement, the result of joint deliberation between the manufacturer and a reseller, is essentially a comprehensive plan to distribute and promote the producer's product line for a period of six months or longer. An outline of such an agreement is to be found in Figure 19–3. Of special interest is the completeness of the agreement. After a clear delineation of quantitatively measurable goals, it is concerned with plans for inventory requirements, merchandise presentation, personal selling, and advertising and sales

FIGURE 19–2

Selected Distribution Policy Alternatives

I.   "Price" Concessions
   A.   Discount Structure:
       Trade (functional) discounts
       Quantity discounts
       Cash discounts
       Anticipation allowances
       Free goods
       Prepaid freight
       New product, display, and advertising allowances
          (without performance requirements)
       Seasonal discounts
       Mixed carload privilege
       Drop shipping privilege
       Trade deals
   B.   Discount Substitutes:
       Display materials
       Premarked merchandise
       Inventory control programs
       Catalogs and sales promotion literature
       Training programs
       Shelf-stocking programs
       Advertising matrices
       Management consulting services
       Merchandising programs
       Sales "spiffs"
       Technical assistance
       Payment of sales personnel and demonstrator
          salaries
       Promotional and advertising allowances (with
          performance requirements)

---

promotion. Finally, the responsibilities of both parties are enumerated, together with a schedule of dates when certain performances are due.

In describing the application of such agreements McCammon has suggested that:

> Programmed merchandising agreements are fairly widespread in the following product categories: garden supplies, major appliances, traffic appliances, bedding, sportswear, cosmetics, and housewares. Manufacturing organizations currently [1970] engaged in programmed mechandising activities include: General Electric (on major and traffic appliances); Baumritter (on its *Ethan Allen* furniture line in nonfranchised outlets); Sealy (on its *Posturepedic* line of mattresses); Scott (on its lawn-care products); and Villager (on its dress and sportswear lines).[33]

---

[33] Ibid., p. 48.

Figure 19–2 (continued)

II. Financial Assistance

    A. Conventional Lending Arrangements:

        Term loans

        Inventory floor plans

        Notes payable financing

        Accounts payable financing

        Installment financing of fixtures and equipment

        Lease and note guarantee programs

        Accounts receivable financing

    B. Extended Dating:

        E.O.M. dating

        Seasonal dating

        R.O.G. dating

        "Extra" dating

        Post dating

III. Protective Provisions

    A. Price Protection:

        Premarked merchandise

        Fair trade

        "Franchise" pricing

        Agency agreements

    B. Inventory Protection:

        Consignment selling

        Memorandum selling

        Liberal returns allowances

        Rebate programs

        Reorder guarantees

        Guaranteed support of sales events

        Maintenance of "spot" stocks and fast delivery

    C. Territorial Protection:

        Selective distribution

        Exclusive distribution

From *Vertical Marketing Systems*, edited by Louis P. Bucklin. Copyright © 1970 by Scott, Foresman and Company. Reprinted by permission of the publisher.

SUMMARY

Manufacturers' policies developed from diverse selling strategies influence the role of resellers in the overall promotional program. Inasmuch as personal selling activities make up the largest portion of promotional activity at wholesale and retail (with the exception of self-service stores), the maximum use of reseller potential can be made when the manufacturer emphasizes a push strategy. Regardless of the selling activity expected, if the *quality* of the selling performance by wholesalers and retailers is less than is desired by the manufacturer, he may lend assistance to *improve* reseller performance.

Training programs for reseller salesmen seem to be one effective way

FIGURE 19–3

Outline of a Programmed Merchandising Agreement

1. Merchandising goals
   a. Planned sales
   b. Planned initial markup percentage
   c. Planned reductions, including planned markdowns, shortages, and discounts.
   d. Planned gross margin
   e. Planned expense ratio (optional)
   f. Planned profit margin (optional)
2. Inventory plan
   a. Planned rate of inventory turnover
   b. Planned merchandise assortments, including basic or model stock plans
   c. Formalized "never out" lists
   d. Desired mix of promotional versus regular merchandise
3. Merchandise presentation plan
   a. Recommended store fixtures
   b. Space allocation plan
   c. Visual merchandising plan
   d. Needed promotional materials, including point-of-purchase displays, consumer literature, and price signs
4. Personal selling plan
   a. Recommended sales presentations
   b. Sales training plan
   c. Special incentive arrangements, including "spiffs," salesmen's contests, and related activities
5. Advertising and sales promotion plan
   a. Advertising and sales promotion budget
   b. Media schedule
   c. Copy themes for major campaigns and promotions
   d. Special sales events
6. Responsibilities and due dates
   a. Supplier's responsibilities in connection with the plan
   b. Retailer's responsibilities in connection with the plan

From *Vertical Marketing Systems*, edited by Louis P. Bucklin. Copyright © 1970 by Scott, Foresman and Company. Reprinted by permission of the publisher.

in which manufacturers can upgrade the caliber of wholesaler personal selling effort. Such assistance is especially desirable when the product sold requires demonstration, installation, or a high degree of technical competence on the part of the reseller salesman. Training is not recommended in cases where the volume potential of the manufacturer's line is small in relation to the costs involved in setting up a suitable program.

Providing market information beyond that the reseller can gather for himself seems to help him allocate his selling efforts more effectively. Such information can point out where sales opportunities are not being exploited. It can also indicate to the reseller how his performance measures up against that of other members of the reseller organization.

If the *quantity* of reseller effort is less than is deemed necessary to achieve manufacturer objectives, assistance may be provided in the form of missionary salesmen. These manufacturer efforts have as their objective the *supplementation* of reseller activity. When carefully supervised, such assistance can greatly increase the extent of sales effort aimed at wholesaler customers.

Under appropriate conditions cooperative advertising programs are a very effective form of advertising assistance. They are especially helpful when, as with selected distribution, it is necessary to identify local retail sources of supply. Further, by getting distributors to invest their own funds in the local promotion of the manufacturer's brand, cooperative advertising programs may predispose resellers to carry better assortments of stock and to push the products advertised.

Manufacturer contributions which help resellers to do a better selling job themselves or encourage reseller promotion, such as display material or special deals, must be carefully integrated into the overall strategy, with special attention being paid to making these aids or deals fit the requirements of the *resellers*.

The manufacturer must be careful not to confuse his objectives and attempt to supplement wholesaler performance when efforts to improve it would suffice. Larger than necessary promotional costs are then incurred by the manufacturer. Conversely, if additional selling effort is needed at wholesale or retail, manufacturer programs to improve the quality of current reseller performance will probably not fill the gap.

Manufacturer efforts to supplement or improve reseller performance may grow to take over typically reseller functions. Such functional shifting should not be permitted by the manufacturer unless his analysis and experimentation have indicated that efforts to supplement or improve middleman performance will not do the job. Taking over tasks historically performed by wholesalers and retailers may suggest that the manufacturer is considering their ultimate circumvention. The reseller who harbors such a suspicion is not likely to offer his selling support willingly.

The control of promotional activities by the manufacturer is much easier when the agency being controlled is under the manufacturer's direct supervision. Such is the case with manufacturer control of the sales force. Control becomes more difficult when the agencies performing the efforts are independent middlemen who have purchased the manufacturer's product line for resale. Regardless of the degree of difficulty involved, the control process in either case is identical and consists of setting standards, measuring performance in light of these standards, and taking corrective action where actual performance is substandard.

The extent of control over resellers is a function of the importance of the manufacturer's line to them. Thus efforts to create selective demand through advertising or to reduce intrachannel rivalry by means of selective distribution should result in heightened manufacturer ability to control reseller efforts. If resellers are uncooperative for one reason or another, the manufacturer may use independent specialists to check on their performance. The manufacturer can always control his own channel strategy by careful selection of resellers, even if he cannot control their individual performance.

If a level of control is needed beyond that which can be expected from independent channel intermediaries, the manufacturer may engage in partial or complete ownership of his resellers. Because of the long-term financial commitments associated with vertical integration through ownership, an increasingly utilized alternative is vertical integration by means of contractual relationships between manufacturers and individual resellers. The resulting distribution system provides many of the advantages of a system owned by the manufacturer, without requiring a heavy investment in ownership. It also preserves the independence of the intermediary and allows him to provide the distributive economies which result from his carrying the lines of several manufacturing sources.

REVIEW AND DISCUSSION QUESTIONS

1. Why is it important for manufacturers to assume some responsibility for training the personnel of their resellers? Why must this be a continuing responsibility?

2. Why is it so difficult to enforce quotas for resellers? Of what value might a properly set quota be to a seller?

3. What advantages may accrue to a manufacturer who offers a cooperative advertising allowance to his resellers? What are some possible disadvantages?

4. Why are promotional allowances by themselves usually insufficient to gain reseller cooperation? What else can a manufacturer do to supplement promotional allowances to resellers?

5. When might a contest for retail clerks be useful in furthering a manufacturer's promotional program? Why are many retail managements against contests for their employees?

6. What types of reseller abuse may limit the effectiveness of manufacturer programs to stimulate reseller promotional efforts?

7. Explain the difference between improving and supplementing reseller performance. Why is it so important that the manufacturer make this distinction?

8. What tasks should a missionary salesman perform? What tasks should he not perform? Why do some resellers resent manufacturer missionary activity?

9. Why does so much of the display material sent retailers end up unused in the refuse basket? What steps might a manufacturer take to prevent this waste?

10. What is the manufacturer's strategy in offering a temporary "price deal"? What reactions might he expect from his resellers?

11. What is the principal danger faced by a manufacturer who attempts to supplement the performance of his resellers?

12. Why is control of reseller performance so difficult for a manufacturer?

13. What roles does selection of resellers play in gaining some degree of control over their activities? What factors limit the extent of control that manufacturers can exert over their resellers?

14. What are the advantages and disadvantages of a policy of vertical integration of channels of distribution through ownership?

15. What is distribution programming, and how does it differ from traditional efforts to work with resellers?

16. Mention some of the areas that might be covered by a programmed merchandising agreement. How would you expect that compliance be monitored under such an agreement?

20

Supplemental Communications

THE PRIMARY ELEMENTS in the promotional mix—advertising and personal selling—are supplemented by two other elements in addition to reseller support. These are (1) public relations, which is concerned with earning public understanding and acceptance, and (2) sales promotion, which includes packaging, sampling, price offers, and other means useful in stimulating consumer purchasing and reseller support. Although these factors are considered as supplementary, this by no means indicates the degree of their importance. Often they can be pivotal considerations in promotional success or failure.

The basic managerial problems faced in these two supplemental efforts are similar to those discussed for the other media in preceding chapters. Therefore, here we will provide a general descriptive overview of the media utilized and their roles in the promotional mix.

PUBLIC RELATIONS

Public relations is that communication function "which evaluates public attitudes, identifies the policies and procedures of an individual or an organization with the public interest, and executes a program of action to earn public understanding and acceptance."[1] Its purpose thus is to secure mutual understanding and goodwill, and it can be an important part of the promotional program of an organization.

Figure 20–1 provides an overview of the target markets for public

---

[1] Bertrand R. Canfield and H. Frazier Moore, *Public Relations: Principles, Cases, and Problems,* 6th ed. (Homewood, Ill.: Richard D. Irwin, 1973), p. 4.

FIGURE 20–1

**Target Markets and Representative Objectives for
the Public Relations Function**

Ultimate Consumers
Disseminate information on the production and distribution of new or existing
  products
Disseminate information on ways to use new or existing products
Company Employees
Training programs to stimulate more effective contact with the public
Encouragement of pride in the company and its products
Suppliers
Providing research information for use in new products
Dissemination of company trends and practices for the purpose of building a
  continuing team relationship
Stockholders
Dissemination of information on: (1) company prospects, (2) past and present
  profitability, (3) future plans, (4) management changes and capabilities,
  and (5) company financial needs
The Community at Large
Promotion of public causes such as community fund-raising drives
Dissemination of information on all aspects of company operations with the
  purpose of building a sense of unity between company and community

relations and some of the tasks which can be accomplished through this
form of communication. Communication is both internal within the
organization and external to its various publics. The media utilized can
be any combination of print, oral, or audio-visual. Included are the functions of corporate advertising and publicity.

Because public relations is a communication function, it should be
undertaken to accomplish specific communication goals, using the procedures discussed in preceding chapters. Much of the detail of management problems can be omitted here, therefore.[2] Our intention is to build
an understanding of the role of both internal and external public relations, and to this end several case histories are cited.

Internal Communications

Internal communication is designed to let employees know what
management is thinking, as well as to facilitate communication in the
reverse direction. At one time organizations were sufficiently small that
this could easily be done on a face-to-face basis, but this is no longer
so in most situations, and the need often exists for a formal communication program designed for such purposes as information and morale
building. Failure to provide such a program can have devastating effects
on productivity, morale, and turnover.

---

[2] See Canfield and Moore, *Public Relations,* and E. J. Robinson, *Communication
and Public Relations* (Columbus, Ohio: Charles E. Merrill Publishing Co., 1966).

Because the details of internal communication programs are beyond the scope of this book, only brief reference is made to the variety of media which can be utilized for this purpose. These are itemized in Figure 20–2.

An example of the use of internal communications is the program by which the Atlanta Gas Light Company introduced its new corporate symbol to employees.[3] Following a series of mergers, the company was faced with difficult communications and public relations problems caused by the use of three different names in different parts of the state of Georgia. A need existed to design a company symbol which was so dis-

FIGURE 20–2

Media for Internal Public Relations

Print:
  Management letters to employees, employee newspapers and magazines, bulletin board announcements, annual and interim financial reports, employee handbooks or manuals, management bulletins for executives and supervisors, pay-envelope inserts, booklets explaining policies and procedures, daily news digests, reading racks, indoctrination kits, posters, and policy statements.
Oral:
  Employee and executive meetings, public address systems, open houses, plant tours, family nights, informal talks by key executives on visits to departments, new-employee orientation meetings, employee counseling, panel discussions, grievance and employee-management committees, recordings, and employee social affairs
Audiovisual:
  Motion pictures, color slides and film strips, closed-circuit television, sound slide film, flip charts, easel charts, posters, maps, flannel boards, and product exhibits

  Source: Bertrand R. Canfield and H. Frazier Moore, *Public Relations: Principles, Cases, and Problems,* 6th ed. (Homewood, Ill.: Richard D. Irwin, 1973), pp. 60–61.

tinctive and identifiable that it would immediately identify the "gas company" no matter where or when it was seen. Once the new symbol was designed and adopted it was necessary to inform employees of the program and indicate how they could assist in building a more distinct public image. This took the form of stories in company magazines, letters to supervisors, and personal visits to key executives and operating staff.

External Communications

As a part of the promotional plan, public relations is most concerned with external communications designed to enhance the image of the organization in the minds of its various publics—ultimate consumers, suppliers, stockholders, and the community at large. The image is the

---

[3] Canfield and Moore, *Public Relations,* pp. 63–67.

overall reputation or *personality* achieved by the organization in its public interface.

Image is of great importance for overall promotional strategy because it is the attitudinal background against which all organizational offerings are evaluated. If it is defective in important ways, a considerable competitive handicap results.

There is no denying the fact that many, if not most, business firms are facing a growing public credibility crisis. This has been caused, in part, by the attacks from consumerists, government, and other critics. It is also true, however, that public antipathy has been aroused by

FIGURE 20–3

Media for External Public Relations

Mass Media:
  Newspapers, magazines, radio, television, annual and interim reports, correspondence, booklets, reprints of executive speeches, program kits and study materials for clubs, educational materials, library reference materials, manuals, and handbooks
Oral:
  Meetings with shareholders, consumers, dealers, suppliers; opinion leaders in plant communities, educators, and legislators; open houses; plant tours; business education days; speeches by employees and executives; visits to community institutions and suppliers; radio and television broadcasts; and community social affairs
Audiovisual:
  Displays and exhibits, motion pictures, sound slide films, charts, maps, posters, slides, television broadcasts, models and construction, and demonstration devices.

  Source: Bertrand R. Canfield and H. Frazier Moore, *Public Relations: Principles, Cases, and Problems,* 6th ed. (Homewood, Ill.: Richard D. Irwin, 1973), pp. 60–61.

numerous examples of product failure, outright deception, and various other forms of irresponsibility. The growing "shortage economy" which exists as of this writing only serves to heighten the problem as one firm after another has been shown to produce only high-profit items, regardless of the strength of unmet market demands for less profitable products.

Some firms, of course, by and large ignore their public image. Their numbers probably will increase as long as shortage conditions continue, because these circumstances create a temporary monopoly. Many are quite sensitive to their public interface, however, and make wise use of corporate advertising, customer relations programs, and publicity. Figure 20–3 illustrates the rich variety of media opportunities that is available for this purpose. Of special importance in the external campaign are (1) organizational symbols, (2) corporate advertising, (3) customer relations programs, and (4) publicity.

Organizational Symbols. Organizational symbols and names are significant in identifying the organization and differentiating it from competitors. Each symbol in Figure 20–4 is a type of shorthand stimulus which calls to mind a constellation of meanings every time it is seen.

Concern over corporate image has prompted a rash of symbol changes

FIGURE 20–4

Organizational Image Symbols

in recent years. In part this has been brought about by mergers, as was the case with the Atlanta Gas Light Company. In other situations established symbols were felt by management to project an image which was no longer in keeping with the current environment or current organizational activity. The new Rockwell International symbol represented in Figure 20–4 was launched with a heavy advertising program designed to broaden Rockwell International's image beyond the aircraft industry. The company makes over 100 different product lines.

The symbol must identify the organization at a glance, or it has failed in its intended purpose. All of those in Figure 20–4 meet this criterion well except PPG industries (Pittsburgh Plate Glass), which seems to err in the direction of undue abstraction.

While the identification value of the organizational symbol is obvious, many feel that changes have at times been instituted for the wrong reason. The sums spent for this purpose are often surprisingly high, and the minor changes introduced quite frankly usually do not justify the effort. In the final analysis the primary reason for the symbol change often is simply to gratify the egos of top management. It is not by accident that a symbol change frequently accompanies a major turnover of top-management personnel.

Corporate Advertising. Corporate advertising differs from the types of advertising discussed previously only in that it usually does not focus on specific products of the organization. Its purpose, instead, is to build awareness and favorable attitudes toward the firm. The problems of media selection and message design, however, are virtually identical.

The key question in a corporate campaign is what the company wants to be known for.[4] Corporate advertising can be of real significance in creating a coordinated overall image which can provide the background and setting for all other efforts.

Corporate advertising also is a useful means of reaching the public to fulfill such communication objectives as correcting mistaken impressions, announcing new programs, generating interest among the financial community, or attracting new personnel. In Figure 20–5, the Phillips 66 advertisement is a direct attempt to stave off criticism of the oil industry and the company, in particular during the early days of the energy crisis. The message by the Institute of Life Insurance is an attempt to reduce public apathy toward life insurance and to point out a generally unrecognized point regarding price trends, and the American Wood Council has a similar purpose.

Some objectives for corporate advertising are not at all obvious on the surface. Quite often a campaign will be undertaken to make a company

---

[4] F. E. Webster, Jr., *Marketing Communication* (New York: Ronald Press Co., 1971), p. 617.

FIGURE 20–5

Examples of Corporate Advertisements

Who made the difference between oil that's waiting, and oil that's ready and waiting?

The North Sea. Treacherous. And violent. Beneath it, millions of barrels of crude oil — desperately needed to help solve the world shortage. Finding it was one thing. But getting it out is another. Frequent storms churn the North Sea and make it impossible for tankers to load. So the oil must wait.

Ekofisk One. A million barrel oil storage tank that enables production to continue in any weather. From the bottom of the North Sea, it reaches 36 stories — 130 feet above the water.

Ekofisk One is built to withstand any storm. And it can store all the oil produced until the weather lifts and tankers can load safely.

Who was instrumental in the development of this million barrel marvel? The same company that makes fine products for your car.

The Performance Company: Phillips Petroleum Company. Surprised?

FIGURE 20-5 (continued)

"What's happened to the price of life insurance in the last 20 years?"

It's gone down.

One reason why the price of life insurance is lower is that people are living longer than they used to. Which means that companies can charge less.

Another thing that's helped reduce the price of life insurance is an improvement in the earnings from our investments. An improvement we've applied against the price of insurance.

And finally, we've done our level best to keep down the cost of doing business.

Because of these things, the price of life insurance is actually less today than it was 20 years ago. And these days that's something nice to know about.

We're bringing you these messages to answer your questions.

And here's what we're doing to help you know more.

We're maintaining a field force of over 200,000 agents, trained to answer your questions about life insurance. On the spot.

We'll send you a personal answer to any questions that you may have about life insurance or the life insurance business.

We'll mail you a free copy of our 20-page booklet, "The Life Insurance Answer Book". With helpful answers to the most frequently asked questions about life insurance.

Just send your card or letter to our central source of information: the Institute of Life Insurance, Dept. D-7, 277 Park Ave., New York, N.Y. 10017.

Your life insurance companies.

FIGURE 20–5 (concluded)

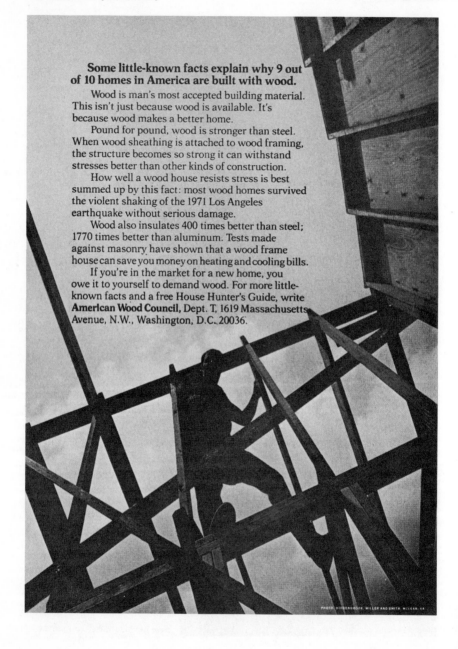

Some little-known facts explain why 9 out of 10 homes in America are built with wood.

Wood is man's most accepted building material. This isn't just because wood is available. It's because wood makes a better home.

Pound for pound, wood is stronger than steel. When wood sheathing is attached to wood framing, the structure becomes so strong it can withstand stresses better than other kinds of construction.

How well a wood house resists stress is best summed up by this fact: most wood homes survived the violent shaking of the 1971 Los Angeles earthquake without serious damage.

Wood also insulates 400 times better than steel; 1770 times better than aluminum. Tests made against masonry have shown that a wood frame house can save you money on heating and cooling bills.

If you're in the market for a new home, you owe it to yourself to demand wood. For more little-known facts and a free House Hunter's Guide, write **American Wood Council,** Dept. T, 1619 Massachusetts Avenue, N.W., Washington, D.C. 20036.

or perhaps an industry appear to be competitive and thereby ward off potential antitrust and monopolistic behavior charges by government. Another purpose is simply to gratify executive egos. This may explain why corporation presidents so often appear in print in full color saying things which might be said more appropriately using other means.

Customer Relations Programs. One response to the pressure of consumerism is the establishment of customer relations programs. These can take the form of corporate advertising such as that by the Chrysler Corporation illustrated in Figure 20–6. The low credibility assigned advertising by large segments of the public, however, makes the success of this type of effort very doubtful.

Other firms have instituted "hot line" programs whereby the customer allegedly can receive prompt response to complaints. A more appropriate strategy probably is to establish stronger guarantees and quality control programs. The toughened consumer satisfaction guarantee of the American Motors Corporation has helped it make significant inroads into the market shares of less responsive competitors.

Publicity. The role for publicity is to present "information designed to advance the interests of a place, person, organization, or cause and used by mass media without charge because it is of interest to readers or listeners."[5] It may come as a surprise that a large percentage of editors stated that up to 50 percent of the publicity material received is valuable for immediate or future articles in their publications, and more than one fourth would like to receive more.[6]

The principal types of publicity are business feature articles, news releases, financial news, new-product information, background editorial material, and emergency publicity. Any of these can be of real value in making the program of an organization known. For example, a series of articles was written about Dr. Kenneth N. Taylor, who paraphrased the *Living Bible* which now has sold over 11,000,000 copies and was the fastest selling nonfiction book of 1973. A study of the influences on the decision to buy indicated that a *Newsweek* article, in particular, proved to be influential in stimulating initial awareness and interest in this new product.

Case Histories of Successful Public Relations

Two case histories which illustrate the basics of strategy and execution in a public relations program are presented here. They concern a professional association and a major airlines.

---

[5] "Public Relations and Publicity," in A. W. Fred (ed.), *Marketing Handbook* (New York: Ronald Press Co., 1965), p. 19–25.

[6] Canfield and Moore. *Public Relations*, p. 117.

FIGURE 20–6

Customer Relations Corporate Advertisement

Used with permission of the Chrysler Corporation.

EXTRA CARE IN ENGINEERING... IT MAKES A DIFFERENCE.

Chrysler Corporation offers 7 important engineering differences that could help you choose your next car.

There are important engineering differences in every Chrysler Corporation car made in this country that are basic to the way we build our cars. You should know about them before you buy your next car. We at Chrysler Corporation think these differences add up to what you want in a new car.

You want an engine that keeps on working:
Electronic engine testing. Every one of our engine plants in this country has Electronic Engine Function Testers to help prevent substandard engines from getting into your car. The testers are designed to assure you of smooth-running, reliable engines by checking for exhaust pressure pulse variations to make sure the engines are assembled and firing properly. It isn't the easiest thing to do, but we feel the results are worth it.

You want to spend less time on service:
What we've done about service. All the carmakers, including Chrysler Corporation, are working to improve service. We're also putting effort into improving our cars so they need less service in the first place. For example, our Electronic Ignition has no points and condenser to replace. And our solid-state voltage regulator has reduced customer-paid replacement by over 90%.

You want dependable starting:
Electronic Ignition. It delivers up to 35% more starting voltage than conventional systems to help you start in any kind of weather. Electronic Ignition also eliminates the major cause of ignition tune-ups because it has no points or condenser to replace. And thousands of test miles have shown the system to work as good as new even after 50,000 miles.

You want electronic advances:
Tomorrow's electronics now. Electronic Ignition isn't the only electronic advancement on Chrysler Corporation cars. We also have a solid-state electronic voltage regulator with no moving parts to go out of adjustment. Then there's our Electronic Digital Clock, standard on Imperial and optional on all our full-size cars, and a factory-installed Electronic Security Alarm System, optional on many of our cars.

You want a transmission that lasts:
TorqueFlite Transmission. While our two major competitors have changed their basic design several times since 1958, we've refined, improved and upgraded TorqueFlite and we feel it is the best automatic transmission on the road. TorqueFlite has no recommended maintenance, under normal driving conditions. Standard on all full-size cars.

You want solid protection:
Unibody Construction. Chrysler Corporation uses over 4,000 welds to join the body panels and structural members into a single, sturdy unit. We think it provides strength and durability.

You want a comfortable ride:
Torsion-bar suspension. Our torsion-bar suspension is a different way of obtaining a comfortable ride and is more easily adjustable for height than coil springs.

Compare Chrysler Corporation's engineering differences. See your Dodge or Chrysler-Plymouth dealer before you choose your next car.

CHRYSLER • PLYMOUTH • DODGE • DODGE TRUCKS

The Ohio Association of Osteopathic Physicians and Surgeons.[7]   The public does not generally recognize that the Doctor of Osteopathic Medicine (D.O.) has the same basic training as the M.D., plus unique training in treatment of the muscular-skeletal systems. As a result, there is an untapped market opportunity for osteopathic medicine.

A study of 619 Ohio residents disclosed that the overall image of the D.O. in the state is low, primarily because of ignorance of his function. Most could not define the meaning of the term osteopath, for example. The least knowledgeable proved to be under 25 years old.

In addition, evaluation of the D.O.'s competence was low, especially as reflected in questions on the type of physician who would be used to treat a back ache and (or) severe stomach pain contracted in a strange city. Not surprisingly, preference for the D.O. was substantially higher among those who are knowledgeable about osteopathic medicine. Also, competence ratings were significantly more positive among those who were aware that the M.D. and the D.O. are equivalent in training, specialization of practice, and available hospital facilities.

These findings pinpointed some needed remedial efforts:

1. People must be informed about osteopathic medicine, especially those in the younger age brackets.
2. Present users are more knowledgeable than the public at large, but they frequently are not aware of the full scope of osteopathic medicine and hence (1) do not make full use of the D.O.'s services and (2) are not a positive influence on others.
3. The use of D.O.s would probably increase if the public were aware of (1) the equivalency of training between M.D.s and D.O.s, (2) the full range of specialization in practice offered by D.O.s, and (3) the excellence of facilities and care at osteopathic hospitals.

While there is not space to review the complete public relations program recommended to the Ohio Osteopathic Association, it centered primarily around a brochure designed with a distinct youth appeal stressing the nature of osteopathic medicine and the full range of services offered. The first target for dissemination of this brochure was present patients. The objective was to make the user a more enlightened patient so that he would utilize the D.O. for a broader range of illness and to provide him with more concrete information so he could inform others through word of mouth.

Another target was the high school student who is tomorrow's patient as well as osteopathic practitioner. Efforts were suggested in the form of

---

[7] "The Ohio Association of Osteopathic Physicians and Surgeons," in James F. Engel, W. Wayne Talarzyk, and Carl M. Larson (eds.), *Cases in Promotional Strategy* (Homewood, Ill.: Richard D. Irwin, 1971), pp. 28–50.

assemblies, programs, and individual counseling to broaden the base of understanding of this form of medicine.

A third suggested target was the community at large. The profession as a whole is derelict in disseminating research findings and hence does not present a scientific image to the public, and this can be changed easily. The individual D.O. was encouraged to make his office and facilities reflect a modern, up-to-date image. He was also urged to be active in community affairs. Increasing his visibility by this means should lead to an increase in patient load, to say nothing of presenting a more positive view of osteopathic medicine.

Notice that no mention has been made of paid advertising. It was felt that newspaper advertisements, for example, would only invite retaliation by the M.D., and costs would be excessive.

While definite quantitative objectives for the campaign were not stated because of the uncertainty of the amount to be funded by the Association, clear benchmarks were provided. Thus it would be quite possible to resurvey a comparable sample at a later period to ascertain changes in awareness and preference.

This case illustrates that public relations is a communication function and hence should be managed to attain communication goals. It is based on consumer research to the same extent as advertising and other forms of promotion. In this case a consumer survey led to (1) an indication of target markets for public relations and (2) determination of the informational content of the campaign. Accountability was facilitated by the utilization of known benchmarks.

Eastern Air Lines.[8] In the early 1960s Eastern Air Lines faced a loss of nearly $20 million, mostly as a result of public antagonism to poor service. In fact, WHEAL (We Hate Eastern Air Lines) clubs had been informally organized by businessmen travelers. Needless to say, the very survival of the airline was threatened.

A new management team instituted many changes, one of the first of which was to commission an image study. The Young and Rubicam agency conducted an attitude analysis of travelers in New York, Chicago, and Washington D.C., the primary service areas of Eastern. It was found, in summary, that the airline had a high awareness level, but its image was seriously deficient. Ratings of specific performance categories were the lowest among the various competitors. Businessmen, in particular, flew on Eastern only because they had to.

One of the first areas for remedial action was to add to the jet fleet and to update all phases of service. An initial specific change was the

---

[8] "Eastern Air Lines: Attitude Change," in Roger D. Blackwell, James F. Engel, and David T. Kollat, *Cases in Consumer Behavior* (New York: Holt, Rinehart & Winston, 1969), pp. 94–102.

design of a new Eastern symbol. Lippincott and Margolis, an industrial design firm, presented a bold new symbol intended to connote speed, modernity, and the jet age. A modern color scheme of "Ionosphere and Caribbean" blue was designed for all planes, and flight personnel appeared in new, smartly tailored uniforms.

Training films stressing the new look at Eastern were developed and presented to employees. The internal communications emphasized the marketing program of total customer satisfaction. Ticket agents and other support personnel were trained to give customers complete satisfaction.

The company also endeavored to be a good corporate citizen. One phase of this program was to improve employee satisfactions through compensation, recognition, pride, advancement, and labor peace. It improved relationships with the regulatory agencies by personal management appointments. The financial community also was the target of public relations through development of timely and factual reports. Improved relationships with society as a whole were achieved through participation in federal, state, and community affairs of all types. The company story was told widely through films and other means.

The extensive changes in the total product of the airline and these public relations activities had succeeded by 1965 in turning the corner and generating a profit. The total communications program clearly stands as an outstanding case history. Unfortunately the 1970s have seen a return to the situation faced ten years before. Deterioration of service and other problems have returned the airline to a crisis situation, and there are signs as of this writing that the WHEAL clubs are being formed once again and even that bankruptcy is possible. It is unfortunate that management did not learn from that wise counselor of nearly 3,000 years ago: "A prudent man foresees the difficulties ahead and prepares for them; the simpleton goes blindly on and suffers the consequences." (Proverbs 22:3, *Living Bible*). Who says that modern management thinking is a 20th century development?

The Image of Public Relations

It is clear that much can be done to improve organization image through external public relations. Unfortunately, often public relations is undertaken as "window dressing" to gloss over and distort the true facts. The result is that the public relations industry itself has a bad image in many quarters, a reputation that frequently is quite deserved. Organizational accountability demands credibility in dealing with the public. To use the vernacular, anything less than this is rightly termed a "corporate ripoff."

SALES PROMOTION

Sales promotion has been defined by the American Marketing Association as encompassing "those marketing activities, other than personal selling, advertising and publicity that stimulate consumer purchasing and dealer effectiveness."[9] Others have utilized widely varying definitions, with the result that it has come to signify in the trade almost everything which cannot legitimately be managed under the headings of personal selling or advertising.

In part this subject has been considered earlier under the topic of stimulating reseller support. The focus here is on those activities that are directed toward the consumer to stimulate buying action, including: (1) packaging, (2) trade fairs and exhibitions, (3) sampling, (4) premiums and trading stamps, and (5) price incentives.

Packaging

The importance of packaging as a form of promotion is underscored by the fact that it is an industry grossing nearly $40 billion annually, and every indication points to continued growth. Apart from the obvious function of provision of physical protection for the product, packages also serve to identify the product and to convey meaning about it.

For products sold through mass merchandising and distribution, the package is especially significant in that it substitutes for personal selling. Often 10,000 or more items compete for the consumer's attention, and the product must stand out in this high noise level if it is to have a competitive chance. Color, unusual shape, and other design variables all play a significant role. One method is utilization of flattering colors to provide background and contrast. Another is to suggest desirable product qualities through package size or shape.

The package also is significant in conveying meaning about the product. White symbolizes purity and freshness and hence is commonly utilized in packaging baked goods to convey the proper image. Green, on the other hand, connotes the values of nature and coolness and hence appears as the background color on the box of nearly all brands of menthol cigarettes. In the same sense shape will affect image. One household cleaning product comes in the shape of a large industrial drum, to reinforce the advertising claim of "strong enough to be used by a janitor."

Another function of the package is to facilitate display. Earlier discussion of point-of-sale advertising emphasized that the display itself is pivotal in calling to mind and reinforcing the advertising message for

---

[9] R. S. Alexander, *Marketing Definitions: A Glossary of Marketing Terms* (Chicago: American Marketing Association, 1960), p. 20.

the consumer. Extremely unusual shapes often cannot be readily displayed and hence will either be removed or deemphasized by the retailer. On the other hand, competitive sameness is self-defeating in that the product will not stand out. The obvious strategy is to avoid either extreme and to design the package in such a way that both distinctiveness and ease of display are attained. Needless to say, this often is easier said than done.

Finally, packages are increasingly used by the consumer as a source of information. Recent regulations by the Food and Drug Administration and other governmental agencies have required the listing of nutritional data and various other types of information which focus on the ways in which the product can affect health. Warnings on cigarette packages are an example of the latter. It is by no means clear that the consumer either expects or utilizes the detailed information which the law often requires, but there is no question that such informative labeling is here to stay in this era of consumerism.

Trade Fairs and Exhibitions

At one time the fair provided the most important market for consumer goods, and it is making a strong comeback today, especially in the high specialty items such as various products used in hobbies and leisure-time pursuits. In the larger metropolitan areas, in particular, it is not unusual to discover many trade shows underway simultaneously. Examples are automotive, photography, electronic, lawn and garden, and home furnishings. Competition among manufacturers can be keen indeed, and great premium is placed on attractive and imaginative booths and displays.

Sampling

House-to-house or in-store sampling is an effective but highly expensive means of introducing a new product. Hence it is most often used by large firms, such as Procter & Gamble and Colgate. Maximum success is achieved when the free sample is part of a coordinated campaign which features introductory awareness advertising, price incentives, and point-of-purchase display. Hopefully awareness will have been stimulated by advertising so that the product will receive a fair trial by an interested prospective consumer. There is no question that the free sample breaks through the noise level and stimulates a much higher degree of new-product trial than would otherwise result. The ultimate measure of success, of course, is sales volume several months later. All too often the sample is tried, discarded, and purchasing habits remain unchanged. Little success will be achieved unless competitive brand loyalty is being eroded for some reason or the new product has a clear and demonstrable difference. If a difference cannot be detected by the prospective user, there is real doubt that the substantial investment required to sample on a large-scale basis will produce sufficient payout.

On occasion sampling will be used for other reasons. There have been some attempts to revive the sales of a slumping product, but the distribution of a sample rarely will reverse the downturn. The cause most often lies in some marketing deficiency which should be remedied first. Also, some large firms use sampling as a defensive weapon to blunt the effects of attempts by competitors to introduce new products through this means. Procter & Gamble, in particular, has utilized this strategy for decades, and its continuing domination in many product classes attests to the influence of its marketing muscle.

Generally the advertiser will not undertake the sampling effort but will retain one of the variety of service firms in this field. One of the largest is the Reuben H. Donnelley Corporation, which distributes samples through mass mailings, handouts, or door drops. It also is possible to confine distribution to more selective audiences through Welcome Wagon and other specialized service firms.

Premiums and Trading Stamps

With premiums and trading stamps the basic benefit offered the consumer is the same—some type of item over and above the product purchased which offers the benefit of getting something extra at little or no extra outlay.

It may be surprising that the premium industry grosses nearly $4,500,-000,000 each year.[10] The purpose of the premium is to induce the consumer to buy now rather than later. The item given may be given free or it may be self-liquidating (the customer pays an extra amount which covers only the manufacturer's out-of-pocket costs). The success depends, however, on making it appear as an unusual bargain.

Experience shows that low price is not necessarily the key to successful use of the self-liquidating premium. Rather, the item itself is most important. Generally the premium should bear some logical relationship to the basic product or service itself, or the consumer may completely disregard it. The offer of a free rose bush with each purchase of a bag of lawn fertilizer, for example, could serve as a real buying incentive.

The danger, of course, is that the consumer will be stimulated to purchase just to get the premium, while basic product preferences remain unchanged. This obviously can be self-defeating. Another danger is that the level of competition is reduced to jockeying for advantage through

---

[10] National Premium Sales Executives, Inc., figures.

offering a better premium than others. When this is reflected heavily in advertising, one cannot help wondering just what is being sold. If the product itself does not have competitive advantage, this type of competition all too easily can prevail. A better strategy would be to place the same resources into product development.

Trading stamps are another way of offering premiums to the consumer. This industry ranked high in popularity from approximately 1955 through the early 1970s. Retailers willingly incurred the extra 2 to 3 percent expense required and found that sales increased sufficiently to offset these costs. When all competitors offered stamps, however, this sales increase no longer was possible. The net result was that the expense was passed along to the consumer in the form of higher prices. As long as the consumer still desired stamps, this did not seem to be a problem, but most careful observers knew that this era would inevitably come to an end.

The trading stamp boom was abruptly halted by the onset of the economy of scarcity accompanied by runaway inflation which began in the 1970s. Retailers saw that stamps offered no competitive advantage and found the dropping of stamp plans one of the easiest ways to reduce costs. As of this writing, few major retail chains still offer trading stamps, and there is little likelihood that such plans will return as long as current economic circumstances prevail.

Price Incentives

A short-term reduction in the price of a product or service is referred to in the trade as a *consumer deal*. The two most common forms are coupons and cents-off promotions. As the previous chapter pointed out, they can provide a substantial payoff in stimulation of reseller support, to say nothing of the consumer buying incentive.

The basic objective, of course, is to increase product trial among prospective customers, and greatest results are attained in those product categories that have relatively low rates of brand loyalty. Where loyalty is high, small price differences are unlikely to overcome the perceived advantage of remaining with a preferred brand. In the first place, brand switching often is seen as having a high degree of perceived risk, with the result that the psychological cost of trying an unknown brand is too high. Furthermore, a price-induced trial may last for only one purchase, and basic brand preferences may remain unchanged. Usually when loyalty is high, relatively large price reductions will be required.

There is always the danger that dealing will become the standard competitive tool, in which case no competitor really benefits. All engage in it for mostly defensive reasons, and the consumer wisely will adopt the strategy of purchasing the brand which offers the best deal at that point in time. No competitor really can gain differential advantage under these circumstances.

The consumer deal most likely will succeed under these conditions:

1. When the price incentive has been used only infrequently and at widely spaced intervals by the manufacturer.
2. When the manufacturer avoids dealing as a strategy to force the retailer to stock in the hopes of offsetting acceptance of a price offer by a competing brand.
3. When the brand is relatively new.
4. When deals are not used as a substitute for advertising.[11]

At all costs, deals should be avoided as a cure-all for declining sales. An ever-present tendency is to resort to the price incentive when the real problem lies elsewhere in deficiencies in the marketing mix. Careful analysis must be undertaken before embarking upon this strategy to ascertain that there is a favorable probability of increasing brand loyalty. Often this will require an actual market test. Great care also must be taken to maintain normal advertising support, and the trade must be approached in such a way that their cooperation is both solicited and maintained. The result otherwise may be a financially abortive strategy or, even worse, the triggering of unnecessary and ruinous competitive warfare.

SUMMARY

This chapter has examined the various forms of supplemental communication. The first of these, public relations, is that communication function by which an individual organization strengthens its interface with its various publics. Some efforts must be directed internally to employees and distributors. At other times it is necessary to address the consuming public, government, education, and others in the external world. The corporate symbol, corporate advertising, customer relations programs, and publicity were all shown to have a useful role in external public relations.

Discussion then shifted to those activities usually referred to as sales promotion—packaging, trade fairs and exhibitions, sampling, premiums and trading stamps, and price incentives. Because the management problems are similar to those encountered in other phases of the promotion mix, this chapter was intended only as an overview.

REVIEW AND DISCUSSION QUESTIONS

1. Differentiate between internal and external public relations; between public relations and publicity; between public relations and corporate advertising.

---

[11] C. L. Hinkle, "The Strategy of Price Deals," *Harvard Business Review*, Vol. 43 (July–August 1965), pp. 75–85.

2. How does corporate advertising differ from regular consumer advertising? Can consumer advertising perform the same functions?

3. Often the public relations department is organized so that it is separate from the marketing department. What justification could you advance for this practice? What suggestions, if any, do you have for change?

4. Based on public attitudes toward business, politics, and other types of institutions at the time you are reading this text, what is your opinion of public response to public relations activities? Can it be strengthened? How?

5. One of the leading manufacturers of portable dictating equipment for home and business use has produced a model which, by experience, has spent more time in the repair shops than on the job. Considerable hostility has arisen toward this otherwise reputable firm. You, as public relations director, are given the assignment of improving the corporate image. What would you do?

6. A leading public relations practitioner made the following statement: "You boys in advertising just don't understand the problems we face. We have to do your dirty work. Whenever you blow it, we have to mop up and make the customer happy again. We have to try to make the company look good in the community. We have to tell them that we are concerned about product quality, water pollution, abatement of slums, etc. Your job is easier. Don't tell me I can set goals for what I do. There just isn't any way we can measure performance." Evaluate.

7. Examine the displays in local supermarkets in such product lines as hand soaps, soft drinks, and breakfast cereals. From this observation, what packaging principles can you derive?

8. The federal government requires a warning on cigarette packages that smoking may be harmful to health. From the perspective of consumer welfare, what effects do you think this type of informative labeling has had?

9. What conditions must be met before a strategy of house-to-house sampling of new consumer products will succeed?

10. The trading stamp industry is now facing a slump because of the dropping of stamp plans by retailers. What explained the success of trading stamps in the past two decades? What environmental changes would be required for stamps to retain their former level of consumer interest?

11. Given the current high rate of inflation, would you recommend that manufacturers increase the use of consumer price incentives? Why or why not?

part six

Coordinating and Integrating the Promotional Program

Having discussed management of the various elements of the promotional program, we will again assume the broader perspective of the framework for promotional strategy. Chapter 21 examines the subject of organization of promotion within the firm. Consideration is also given to the use of such outside resources as advertising agencies and media-buying services. Chapter 22 clarifies the management problems inherent in bringing about necessary coordination as the complete promotional program is implemented. Evaluation and follow-up, the final stages in the promotional planning program, are also discussed in Chapter 22.

21

Organization of the Promotional Program

BECAUSE the organization of promotional activities requires a proper marketing orientation, organizational relationships within the marketing department are the first topic of this chapter. Next is the division of effort between internal resources and outside service agencies. In the case of advertising, in particular, considerable use is made of advertising agencies and other types of specialized services. There are no clear-cut rules and procedures to guarantee an effective organizational pattern, however, and this chapter should be viewed primarily as an overview of the most important considerations.

ORGANIZATIONAL REQUIREMENTS AND STRUCTURES

This section begins with the requirements of a modern marketing organization and then evaluates common organizational patterns as they pertain to marketing in general and to promotion in particular.

The Requirements of a Modern Marketing Organization

Marketing has undergone a rapid evolution from its early position as a secondary business activity to its present status as the basic area for decision making in a firm. The need for an organizational structure consistent with the changing role of marketing in a marketing-oriented company has become apparent.

The following requirements are minimum for a modern marketing organization:

1. *A Systems View of Marketing by Top Management.* Success in today's business environment requires recognition by top management of a systems approach to marketing. Basic to the attainment of corporate goals is the conceptualization of the firm and its activities as a marketing system. Robert Ferber, past president of the American Marketing Association, has stated that:

> . . . marketing activities in the 1970s are likely to become both more integrated and more diversified when combined with recent developments in the field of marketing itself (such as those relating to use of computers, systems analysis, and development of more formal models for decision making). The increasing complexity of the modern corporation means that different parts of the corporation will have to be linked with each other for maximum efficiency in more formal planning systems. Such systems will have to incorporate not only all the usual functions of marketing but many other functions as well.[1]

As a result, a marketing orientation is becoming increasingly common within top management.

2. *The Importance of a Systems Approach to Marketing.* Good marketing performance is seldom achieved when the related functions are placed low in the corporate hierarchy. This means that (a) the marketing activities in a firm must be better organized, coordinated, and managed, and (b) the marketing executive must be accorded a more important role in total company planning and policy making than generally has been true in the past—marketing management is the marketing concept in action. The organizational structure should guarantee that the chief marketing officer reports directly to the primary operating executive.[2]

3. *An Organization Consistent with Marketing Requirements.* No single form of organization is superior for all purposes, but there is a basic criterion underlying all adaptive organizational structures: responsibility must be delegated commensurate with authority to appropriate operating levels, and the capacity for quick-response decisions cannot be hampered by excessive reliance on top-management approval of all action. The capacity to move quickly to meet marketing opportunities is built into the structure through clear-cut, operating delegation of duties.

4. *Marketing Strategy Oriented toward a Systems Approach.* It may seem obvious to emphasize that all marketing efforts should be aimed toward attainment of common objectives, but there appears to be an inevitable tendency for strategy to branch out in unrelated directions. For instance, the advertising manager may sponsor a campaign featuring house-to-house sampling in the expectation of a strong increase in de-

---

[1] Robert Ferber, "The Expanding Role of Marketing in the 1970's," *Journal of Marketing,* Vol. 34 (January 1970), pp. 29 and 30.

[2] William J. Stanton and Richard H. Buskirk, *Management of the Sales Force,* 3d ed. (Homewood, Ill.: Richard D. Irwin, 1969), p. 9.

mand in a given area. The sales manager may be unaware of this strategy, so proper sales force efforts at the retail level are lacking. The problem here is a communication problem which may be due to the fact that the advertising and sales departments are located in different divisions in the firm. Marketing strategy can be unified when related activities are discussed and integrated in the organizational structure.

5. *A Tailor-Made Promotional Program.* Many companies still place the majority of the promotional effort in advertising. The result is that personal selling and reseller support often are deemphasized. Allocation of funds must be related to the tasks to be performed. In discussing what he calls "the promotional blend," E. Jerome McCarthy points out:

> Once the promotion objectives for a product have been established, a marketing manager may decide to use a blend of promotional methods, since some jobs can be done more economically one way than another. Some very profitable promotion blends and marketing mixes have departed from the typical to better satisfy some target market. This emphasizes the blend of the promotional activities within the chosen marketing mix and this is adding to the insight of what is contained in the complexities of the marketing mix.[3]

Moreover, it is common for an imbalance to be reflected in the marketing organization itself, with a disproportionate number of personnel devoted to advertising activities.

6. *Sophisticated Use of Outside Resources.* Finally, it is a rare firm which is totally self-sufficient in all resource areas. For this reason, the advertising agency is used. The specialized agency can augment a firm's own resources in specific areas. Moreover, it can bring an expertise and wealth of experience to bear on marketing promotional problems which may be difficult to match within the firm. In addition, there is much to be gained from the perspective of an outside source which presumably can analyze problems with greater objectivity. The development of a proper working relationship, however, requires considerable effort by both parties. This subject is discussed later in this chapter.

Organizational Structure

Types of Structure. It is, of course, impossible to describe all of the organizational structures traditionally used in the business firm. The traditional form is the so-called *functional* structure illustrated in Figure 21–1. In 1948, this form was in use by 63 percent of *Fortune's* top 500 companies.[4]

---

[3] E. Jerome McCarthy, *Basic Marketing: A Managerial Approach,* 3d ed. (Homewood, Ill.: Richard D. Irwin, 1968), p. 440.

[4] R. W. Ackerman, "How Companies Respond to Social Demands," *Harvard Busines Review,* Vol. 51 (1973), pp. 88–99.

The *product organization* form illustrated in Figure 21–2 originated in the consumer goods industries[5] and has grown until it is the basic pattern of 76 percent of *Fortune's* top 500 companies today.[6] This reflects in large part the significant influence of product diversification since World War II. As Figure 21–2 indicates, it is common for the product (or brand) manager to report to a corporate vice president of marketing, although there are many variations in patterns of lines of authority.

Organization of Promotion. A significant disadvantage of the traditional functional organization is that marketing decisions are made by several functional managers and finally coordinated by one of the mar-

FIGURE 21–1

Common Form of Functional Organization

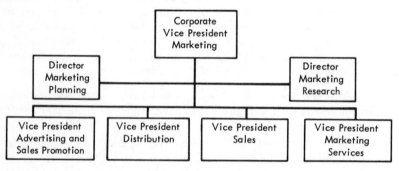

keting executives. This results in imposing too many management levels to be filtered before a final decision can be reached. The product organization is a significant step toward reducing these levels and maximizing the ability of the firm to act and capitalize upon profit opportunities.

The product manager is generally given responsibility for profit performance,[7] but this responsibility, in the past at least, is not always backed by sufficient authority to act.[8] Advertising strategy and execution, for example, often reside with the advertising and sales promotion manager. Obviously this can create an intolerable situation, but there appears to be a trend now toward appropriating both the necessary authority *and* responsibility to the product manager.[9]

---

[5] R. M. Fulmer, "Product Management: Panacea or Pandora's Box?" *California Management Review,* Vol. 7 (1965), p. 65.

[6] Ackerman, "How Companies Respond."

[7] D. B. Lucas, "Point of View: Product Managers in Advertising," *Journal of Advertising Research,* Vol. 12 (1972), pp. 41–47.

[8] B. C. Ames, "Payoff from Product Management," *Harvard Business Review,* Vol. 41 (1963), p. 163.

[9] Lucas, "Point of View."

Recent studies disagree, however, on the *extent* to which authority and responsibility are matched. Darrell B. Lucas reports, for example, that the great majority of the product managers studied from among *Fortune's* top 250 companies have full control over basic promotional strategy and execution for their brands, with the exception of various decisions pertaining to selection and management of the sales force.[10] The vice president of advertising thus performs more of an advisory and coordinating role. This fact in itself gives rise to some concern, because it is inevitable

FIGURE 21-2

Product Organization Form

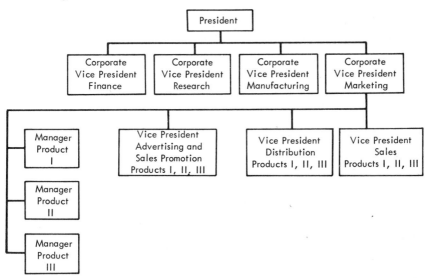

Source: Adapted from B. C. Ames, "Payoff from Product Management," *Harvard Business Review,* Vol. 41 (1963), p. 142.

that the product manager usually will not have the experience in advertising that was contributed by the advertising manager under the more traditional functional organization.

On the other hand, Victor P. Buell, in an extensive study of advertising decision making and control, found that the product manager usually *does not* make advertising decisions.[11] Thus he feels that the myth of full authority at the product management level must be dispelled. The product manager's role is more one of coordination and execution in less important areas of decision, whereas advertising decisions usually are made

---

[10] *Ibid.*

[11] V. P. Buell, *Changing Practices in Advertising Decision-Making and Control* (New York: Association of National Advertisers, Inc., 1973).

at the higher levels. Buell does confirm Lucas's finding, however, that there is a trend to rectify this situation and to institute advertising and promotional staff specialists who provide services at the product management level.

Most agree that there is an uncertain relationship between sales management and the other marketing functions.[12] Often they are located in completely separate organizational levels, with the result that needed coordination and integration are not forthcoming. Furthermore, the public relations function often seems to be in no-man's-land and is found frequently under the control of the marketing manager or the advertising director, or else is centered in a separate department.[13]

Full organizational coordination of promotional activities is a rarity. This is decidedly unfortunate, and it certainly inhibits the ideal of a systems approach to marketing management.

USING OUTSIDE SERVICES

Many large firms are staffed and equipped to perform the full range of their own promotional functions; Procter & Gamble is an example. However, it generally is not feasible for the smaller organization to develop the necessary expertise to do this, and they must utilize various outside services to carry out their promotional program. These include: (1) media-buying services, (2) creative boutiques, (3) research services, (4) consultants, and (5) advertising agencies.

Media-Buying Services

The media-buying service initially appeared in the middle 1960s to provide help for smaller advertising agencies. A period of rapid growth has ensued, largely due to the growing complexity of media buying that has been brought about by the proliferation of specialized media to reach highly segmented markets. Today these organizations service both agencies and clients, who determine their own media strategies so that the sole role of the media-buying service is to execute the plan in optimum fashion. Historically there has been a concentration in broadcast media, but this is rapidly changing.[14] Compensation plans vary, but most consist of some type of fee averaging from 3 to 5 percent.[15]

The media-buying service has provoked controversy, much of it stem-

---

[12] *The Gallagher Report,* Vol. 18 (1970).

[13] *The Gallagher Report,* Vol. 19 (November 2, 1971).

[14] Ibid.

[15] "Client Dealing Cuts at Heart of 15% Plan: Maneloveg," *Advertising Age,* November 30, 1970, p. 63.

ming from the traditional advertising agency, which has seen some departure of clients.[16] Growth of this type of service has continued unabated, however, and it would appear that continued media proliferation will make for a bright future.[17]

Creative Boutiques

The success of the media-buying service has encouraged the formation of specialized agencies whose sole function is to provide assistance in creative planning and execution. Media buying and other activities are left to the client. Compensation is a negotiated fee. The greatest use to this point has been for new-product development, print advertisements, and television commercials.[18] Perhaps the most significant advantage is concentration of talent within one group which can be focused as needed on specific projects. The number of such groups has burgeoned, and continued growth seems assured.

Research Services

The significant role of marketing research has been stressed in this text, and expenditures for this purpose have increased dramatically during the past decade. The demands for technical expertise in this function have grown commensurately. Only a few advertisers have in-house capability for this purpose, and most make use of outside research agencies. These specialized organizations can provide services such as the following: interviewing and field supervision, sampling design, questionnaire construction, data analysis, specialized store audits, and so on.

Consultants

There is some undeniable benefit from outside counsel in the various phases of marketing strategy. The benefit, of course, stems from objectivity as well as experience. Therefore, use is made of consultants which range from individuals such as college professors to highly sophisticated firms which can provide a full range of related services. Probably the role of the consultant will continue to grow in proportion to the increase in complexities of marketing planning. The only caution which need be stated here is that the consultant should never be used as a substitute for managerial expertise. The consultant's role is, at best, supplementary.

---

[16] *Grey Matter,* Vol. 41 (June 1970).

[17] E. B. Weiss, "The 1975–1980 Outlook for Advertisers and Agencies," *Advertising Age,* August 7, 1972, p. 45 ff.

[18] *The Gallagher Report,* Vol. 19 (November 2, 1971).

ADVERTISING AGENCIES

Of all the outside services, the advertising agency is by far the most significant. For example, 96 percent of leading advertisers make at least some use of the advertising agency.[19] The existence and growth of specialized outside services such as the creative boutique have brought dramatic changes in both the use of the traditional advertising agency and management within it. It is no overstatement that the agency business is in real turmoil today, and the "conventional wisdom" which was true just a few years ago is no longer operative.

The nature and operation of the traditional full-service advertising agency is analyzed first. Then, to highlight the significant changes now taking place, the new type of agency which is emerging will be examined.

The Traditional Full-Service Agency

The advertising agency originally was a broker of space for advertising media, but there has been a dramatic change since this beginning over 100 years ago. Today most large agencies, at least, are equipped to provide full counsel on advertising strategy, media placement, research, development of package designs, determination of advertising budgets, the staging and managing of distributor and dealer meetings, design of sales-training programs and advertising presentations for sales meetings, and a host of related promotion functions.

Principles of the Agency-Client Relationship.[20]   Through custom and years of trial and error, four basic principles have been established to serve as the foundation of the traditional agency-client relationship:

1. *Avoidance of a Relationship with Competitors.* It is traditional for an agency to refrain from handling the advertising of a firm which competes with a client. In turn, the client agrees not to engage a second agency. The issue of the agency retaining a competitor, referred to as account conflict, has largely been resolved by avoidance of *directly* competing accounts. Indirect conflicts between large accounts which *may* have some products in common are increasingly being overlooked. Clients, however, commonly retain multiple agencies, some of which handle only portions of the total account. Hence this operating principle has in essence been abrogated.

2. *Client Approval of Expenditures.* The agency is obligated to obtain approval for all expenditures made in the client's behalf. Obviously this is good business practice.

---

[19] *The Gallagher Report,* Vol. 19 (November 2, 1971).

[20] F. R. Gamble, *What Advertising Agencies Are—What They Do and How They Do It* (New York: American Association of Advertising Agencies, 1960), pp. 23 and 24.

3. *Client Obligation for Payment.* The client is obliged to pay its bills for space or time purchased by the agency promptly. The space bill is received by the agency, which then forwards it to the client. If the bill is not paid promptly, the agency must make payment to the media, an unwarranted drain on cash reserves.

4. *Forwarding of Cash Discounts.* Most advertising media offer a small cash discount if bills are paid within a certain period. The agency is obliged to forward this discount to the client because it is, in effect, the client's reward for prompt payment of space and time bills.

Recognition of Agencies by Media. The agency must be recognized by advertising media before orders for space or time will be honored. At one time this practice of recognition was so rigid that agencies were compelled to follow certain practices which were later found to be in violation of antitrust laws. The most troublesome criterion of recognition in terms of the Justice Department was compulsory agreement by the agency to accept compensation only through full retention of a 15 percent commission paid by the media to the agency on the total bill for space or time. In other words, agencies were required to agree not to rebate any portion of the commission. The net effect of this practice was to forbid, by arbitrary dictate, any price competition by agencies. A consent decree was signed by five media associations and several associations of advertising agencies in the 1950s, and commission rebating is no longer prohibited.

Media recognition is presently based on proof by the agency that it possesses sufficient financial resources to pay space or time charges if the client defaults on payment. Media may also request proof that the agency offers adequate personnel and facilities to service clients, but such approval is largely a formality.

As onerous as media recognition became prior to the consent decree, the procedure has been instrumental in improving agency practice. A tightening of standards through recognition led to major improvement in agency performance, and all members of the advertising business were beneficiaries.

Agency Management and Operation.[21] A traditional full-service agency needs personnel in such specialized fields as marketing research, media research, media planning, media buying, creative writing, creative design, and account management. The work usually is demanding, and considerable reliance must be placed on the imagination and resourcefulness of the individual. There are few routine tasks in the usual sense of the word; most agency employees are forced to be "self-starters."

---

[21] A helpful although somewhat outdated manual on agency management is Kenneth Grosbeck, *The Advertising Agency Business* (Chicago: Advertising Publications, 1964).

Many agencies require a master's degree of new trainees. As a result, the pay for qualified personnel is higher than in most other fields.

The agency business has been tagged a "heart attack" business. There is some truth to this; pressure placed on the individual is great and may not be readily apparent. The agency organization chart is not deep; there are relatively few layers of management. The chief manager (called the account executive) for a given product will have several assistant account executives working with him. There are no lower levels of management as such. Tasks and responsibilities placed on most agency management personnel are therefore equivalent to those faced only by *higher management* in most manufacturing firms. Though pressures may be high, rewards are great. Independent, energetic, creative, and talented people are attracted to advertising agency work. Special problems are encountered in the use of minority group personnel, but their percentage in the agency work force is growing.[22]

Agencies are organized in a variety of ways, but two forms are most common: (1) by group and (2) by department.

ORGANIZATION BY GROUP. A group agency, in effect, is a cluster of individual agencies under one management. A complete team is assembled to prepare the promotion program for each large account or perhaps for several smaller accounts. The team typically is headed by a senior account executive with top management stature, as well as several junior account executives. It will include artists, writers, promotion men, researchers, and others to provide needed services.

The group system concentrates efforts and skills on a related set of problems without dilution of managerial talents through assignments to other accounts. A high degree of specialization is thus attained.

ORGANIZATION BY DEPARTMENT. The departmentalized agency provides a separate department for each agency function. Departments for media, copy, art, production, research, traffic (coordination), account service, and promotion each serve all clients. The account service department, composed of account representatives, assumes responsibility for service for accounts. Services of other departments are drawn upon as needed without the assignment of specified individuals on a permanent basis. One writer may be assigned to five accounts. Specialization is discouraged by this form of organization, but individuals can gain a breadth of experience not possible under the group system.

Top-management contact with agency output is paramount, whatever form the organization takes. In smaller agencies, top management can readily evaluate and approve the campaign as it develops. In larger

---

[22] See L. Nadler, "Helping the Hard-Core Adjust to the World of Work," *Harvard Business Review,* Vol. 48 (1970), p. 117 ff.

agencies, day-to-day contact becomes impossible, and "plans boards" are established for periodic top-management review.

While the plans-board procedure may seem to be time-consuming and unwieldy, it serves to detect loose thinking and questionable recommendations prior to presentation of plans to the client. Moreover, the account group benefits from the insights of skilled professionals. There is a danger that the account team, being tempted to prepare the campaign only for plans-board approval, will forgo daring and imaginative recommendations. The board should be viewed as a valuable resource for ideas and guidance rather than as a court for evaluation of the performance of the account group.

Agency Compensation.   Rapid changes are taking place in agency compensation plans. Two basic plans are used: (1) the commission system and (2) the fee system.

THE COMMISSION SYSTEM.   The great majority of advertising media are "commissionable" in that a traditional 15 percent discount is paid to the agency that places the advertising. This historically has provided the compensation for the agency, and 45 percent of leading advertisers are reported to utilize this system with their agencies.[23]

The 15 percent commission is an arbitrary sum. Agreement must be made between client and agency enumerating the services to be provided under the commission and those for which extra fees will be charged. The planning, design, and preparation of advertisements are provided by the agency without additional compensation, but other services, including marketing research and publicity, are performed on a fee basis.

When production charges are billed to the client by the agency, it is customary to add a markup ranging from 17.65 percent for composition, engravings, and electros to 20 percent or more for printing. This markup covers the costs assumed by the agency in arranging for the preparation and guaranteeing that the items are of satisfactory quality. In other words, the agency is providing a service to the client which should be compensated for by a fee.

The agency also will usually add a markup to the costs of marketing research and other services to provide for overhead and a reasonable percentage of profit. A common arrangement is to multiply time costs by a factor of 2.5 or 3.0.

The commission system is defended by some advocates on the basis that it is easy to understand and administer. Moreover, its fixed amount avoids price competition between agencies. The argument is that an idea is difficult to evaluate in cost terms, and agency competition in terms of price is thus impossible. Moreover, it is claimed that the agency is re-

---

[23] *The Gallagher Report,* Vol. 19 (November 2, 1971).

warded in proportion to the use made of its ideas—the more the space or time purchased, the greater the commission in total dollar terms.

Most of these arguments for the commission system dissolve upon close analysis. The critical weakness is that a 15 percent commission may not be related to real services performed by the agencies, possibly being either excessive or too low. Consider the comment by one manufacturer: "The 15 percent system would seem to indicate that an ad running in a $35,000-per-page magazine requires seven times the effort of an ad running in a $5,000-a-page magazine, and the commercials for a $10,000-per-program show. That, as we all know, is not the case. In print advertising, as a matter of fact, quite the reverse is often true."

Another important weakness is that the commission system has provided an excuse for some agencies not to utilize accounting systems to justify their charges. To a manufacturer, on the other hand, the absence of cost accounting is unthinkable.

Yet another limitation is the temptation for agency management to avoid placing dollars in noncommissionable media. Direct mail, point of purchase, and advertising specialties are only three of many useful media an agency may avoid rather than charge a fee to the client. Most agency spokesmen will emphatically deny that commissionable media are favored, but this temptation can be avoided completely through abandonment of the commission system.

THE FEE SYSTEM. The 1960s saw a strong movement toward compensation of the agency by fees, a movement given impetus by the fee arrangement between Shell Oil and Ogilvy, Benson, and Mather (now Ogilvy and Mather, Inc.) in 1960. In this agreement, the agency is compensated by a fee based on agency costs plus an appropriate markup, with all commissions from the media either rebated to the client or deducted from the fee. Of the leading advertisers, 30 percent are now on a total fee system with at least one of their agencies, and another 23 percent use some combination of commission plus fee.[24]

In assessing the benefits of the fee system, one client stated:

> The arrangement calls for the client to decide the kind and extent of services appropriate for each product and, in turn, the agency will be compensated for these services as performed. . . . This new approach well may solve the twin problems of tailoring the amount and kind of service to the needs and stage of development of each product, while at the same time adequately compensating the agency for the services required on new products versus established ones.[25]

The agency also benefits, as one agency executive pointed out:

---

[24] Ibid.

[25] A. J. Vogl, "What's Behind the Big New Test of the Agency Fee?" *Sales Management,* November 15, 1963, p. 37.

1. The agency can be totally objective in its planning and recommend non-commissionable media with no concern over agency compensation.
2. The agency knows it will be compensated for its services, and an incentive thus exists for provision of a total system of communication services.
3. Agency income is stabilized; sudden cuts in commissionable media will not spell financial disaster.[26]

The fee system requires the use of precise cost accounting. Account executives must keep accurate time records which become the basis for charges to the client. These reports provide an excellent record of profitability as well as a structure of costs.

It should be made clear that the fee system is difficult to administer; the exact fee is a matter of negotiation. Nevertheless it is more defensible than the commission basis, for compensation is geared to the tasks performed. A better basis is provided for a productive working relationship between both parties.

The Emerging Advertising Agency

That the advertising agency business is now in a state of turmoil is reported in nearly every issue of every trade publication.[27] In particular, the traditional full-service agency is in real jeopardy unless changes are made. The root cause is that client organizations are shifting various promotional functions out of the agency. To some extent they are being transferred to media-buying services and creative boutiques, as discussed earlier. Furthermore, clients themselves are assuming an increased share of the task. When the entire function is assumed by the client (creative design, media scheduling and placement, and so on) the client is often said to operate a "house agency." Probably a better term is "client management,"[28] because most who do this use some combination of outside services as well as their own staff. Norton Simon, Inc., for example, is serviced by its own advertising-marketing organization, entitled Norton Simon Communications.[29] It started with over $6,000,000 in assignments from the Hunt-Wesson division, but it also makes use of advertising agencies and media services, all of which are compensated on a fee basis for certain products.

There are a number of reasons for this trend toward client self-sufficiency. Most stem from the various pressures for accountability

---

[26] John Elliot, Jr., "The Pros and Cons of the Fee System," address given at the Association of Industrial Advertisers, July 1, 1964.

[27] See for example *The Gallagher Report,* Vol. 21 (April 23, 1973) and Weiss, "1975–1980 Outlook."

[28] Weiss, "1975–1980 Outlook."

[29] Ibid.

which require closer control by client management over all of its activities. These pressures include, for example, increased costs of consumerism; costly documentation of advertising claims brought on by government review; market segmentation, with its requirements for specialized copy and media; and the lack of precise measures of advertising effectiveness.[30] Promotion is increasingly viewed as more than just advertising, and more significance is placed on such facets as improved display, personal selling, and store demonstrations.

What do these pressures mean for the full-service advertising agency? Several major changes appear to be evident: (1) the demise of traditional full-service operations, (2) revised compensation plans, and (3) a new partnership between client and agency.

The Demise of Full Service.   A self-sufficient client will not require all of the services of the traditional agency but will legitimately use only those that cannot be performed adequately internally. If the agency is not prepared to meet these demands, it will be the loser, not the client. The J. Walter Thompson agency is said to have lost the profitable Firestone Tire and Rubber account because the agency president insisted on retaining full-service relationships under a traditional commission compensation.[31] Similarly, the Doyle Dane Bernbach agency lost the $1 million Transamerica account for the reason that agency management allegedly dictated to the client what the advertising strategy and execution should be.[32]

It is clear that the balance of power does not lie with the advertising agency. If a client wishes to purchase only certain services, he is quite free to utilize the media-buying agency, the creative boutique, or the research supplier. In fact, this is a distinct trend which can be expected to multiply unless the agency gives up its insistence on full service.

The key to agency survival is to break away from traditional operations and offer services on a modular or "à la carte" basis. This will require radical reorganization. A large agency with 100 clients, for example, will have to operate in 100 different ways. This cannot be done with traditional departmentalization, plans boards, and so on. The agency probably will be required to break into a number of smaller autonomous profit centers. Some will, in effect, be creative boutiques. Others will be media-buying services or research specialists. For those clients that still wish full service, it is reasonable to offer a consulting service which also will operate as a profit center.

The primary change in agency operation is to break full service into components which can be used or not used, as desired by clients. To the

---

[30] Ibid.

[31] *The Gallagher Report,* Vol. 21 (April 23, 1973).

[32] Ibid.

extent that this is done, the large established agency appears assured of a bright future. Those that do not adapt will be in serious trouble.[33]

Revised Compensation Plans. The modular or à la carte service basis will mean the end of the commission system. In the final analysis, this system has never had much real justification, and there will of necessity be a distinct shift to compensation by fee.

A New Partnership between Client and Agency. There appears to be a trend toward establishing "creative groups" within the client organization. These are not house agencies in the full sense of the word, but they do develop basic strategy and creative ideas and in some cases execute the actual advertisements. Usually the execution of the message and the choice of media are left to an outside service group, however. Under this type of operation, the agency is useful in providing needed services on an à la carte basis. In addition, the role of consultant for strategic planning for marketing in general and promotion in particular becomes significant. It is likely that the agency of the future will take this consultative role more seriously,[34] and this may be the key to survival of the advertising agency as we now know it.

Development of a Productive Working Relationship

Good working relationships between client and agency do not just happen—a real dedication to this end must be manifested by both parties. Experience has established a number of guidelines, some of the most important of which are discussed below:

1. *Maintain a Top-Level Liaison.* Top-level client and agency executives should communicate regularly to air major issues arising as part of day-to-day operations. Most junior executives do not have sufficient status to modify operating policies. Minor misunderstandings can easily become magnified into major difficulties.

2. *Accept Innovation.* The agency is a specialist in marketing communication. Its recommendations should not be constrained by client pressure for noninnovative strategy. The comments of one agency president in this context are:

Don't be afraid to try something new. Expect your agency to keep innovating. Don't feel obligated to continue a campaign which doesn't live up to hopes. Don't expect your agency to be right every time, but be sure that the chances for success are good always. Don't give up something which is good too soon. Don't ask for great ads; insist instead on great campaigns.[35]

---

[33] *The Gallagher Report,* Vol. 21 (August 6, 1973).

[34] P. C. Harper, Jr., "The Agency Business in 1980," *Advertising Age,* November 19, 1973, p. 63 ff.

[35] William Marsteller, "How to Get the Most Out of Your Ad Agency," *Sales Management,* November 31, 1961, p. 36.

3. *View Marketing Communication in Proper Perspective.* One of the danger signs often seen is undue reliance on advertising as compared with other elements of the communication mix. When advertising fails to perform as hoped, the agency frequently must assume blame. Once again, the importance of realistic communication objectives and a balanced promotion mix cannot be overstressed.

4. *Emancipate the Agency from Fear.* As David Ogilvy says:

Most agencies run scared, most of the time. This is partly because many of the people who gravitate to the agency business are naturally insecure, and partly because many clients make it unmistakably plain that they are always on the lookout for a new agency. Frightened people are powerless to produce good advertising.[36]

Some clients have achieved the reputation of being "agency hoppers," changing agencies every year or two. In many such instances the agency serves as the scapegoat for deeper troubles elsewhere in the client organization. In these instances, an agency change is seldom a permanent solution to the difficulties.

Procter & Gamble, one of the world's largest advertisers, rarely changes agencies. Other large firms follow a similar philosophy. It is recognized that all agencies will fail at times to produce great campaigns, and evaluation is based instead on the overall batting average. The agency is encouraged to do its best by knowing that one misstep will not be fatal.

5. *Permit the Agency to Make a Profit.* The operating margin is sufficiently small that most agencies will cut costs and avoid utilizing top managerial talent if a client demands such a volume of services that the agency cannot profit on the account. With no incentive to offer top-quality service, the agency may seek every opportunity to resign the account. The agency and the client must each make a profit. Good service will not be provided if unnecessary impediments are placed in the way of this complementary objective.

SUMMARY

This chapter has explored the subject of organization. The focus first was on organization structures which facilitate coordinated and integrated marketing strategy. Two forms of this organization were analyzed: functional and product. Because the product structure has become more common, greatest attention was paid to promotional management in this context. Then attention was directed to the division of functions between internal personnel and outside services. Five different types of outside

---

[36] David Ogilvy, *Confessions of an Advertising Man* (New York: Dell Publishing Co., 1963), p. 92.

services were reviewed: the media-buying agency, creative boutiques, research services, consultants, and the advertising agency. Because of the historically significant role of the advertising agency, an in-depth analysis was made of the causes and results of an important trend away from full-service operation to what is now known as modular or à la carte service.

There are no clear-cut rules and procedures guaranteeing effective organization. This chapter has offered insight into alternative patterns and the nature of the various outside services that can be utilized.

REVIEW AND DISCUSSION QUESTIONS

1. Differentiate between the functional and product forms of organization. What differences are there in promotion management under each form?

2. It was noted that there is a disadvantage to the product form of organization in that advertising and other forms of promotion are assigned to personnel who may lack the necessary experience and expertise. What can be done, if anything, to minimize this disadvantage? Do the advantages of the product form of organization compensate for this problem?

3. What factors led to the growth of the media-buying service? Why do many experts predict that its role will be even greater in the future?

4. One authority feels that the creative boutique is only a passing fad which will disappear in favor of a return to the full-service advertising agency. Do you agree? Why or why not?

5. Evaluate the commission method of agency compensation. What are the reasons for its use? Is it likely to be replaced by the fee system?

6. It is said by some that the full-service agency as it has traditionally existed must change or it will be forced out of existence. What are the pressures for change? What must the agency do, if anything, to survive?

7. Some full-service agencies are adamant in opposition to offering modular or à la carte services. What reasons could you think of to explain this attitude? If you were called in as a consultant, what would your recommendations be to agency management with this attitude?

8. Some suggestions were given for development of a productive working relationship between client and agency. What guidelines, if any, would you add to this list?

9. Read the article on the 1975–1980 outlook by E. B. Weiss footnoted in this chapter. Weiss assesses trends that will profoundly affect the practice of advertising management in the next decade. What other changes can you see coming in agency-client relationships? Is Weiss correct in his predictions?

22

Coordination, Evaluation,
and Follow-Up

ONCE the first four stages in promotional planning and strategy as outlined in Chapter 3—situation analysis, establishment of objectives, determination of budget, and management of program elements—have been completed, the next stage is coordination and integration of the program. This is the topic of the first part of this chapter, which includes a case history and an analysis of the PERT technique. The second major part considers evaluation and follow-up, the final stages in the promotional plan, with emphasis on the product life cycle.

COORDINATION OF PROGRAM ELEMENTS

Before dollars are actually invested in a program or campaign, a final review must be undertaken to determine whether each element has been properly designed to attain its stated objective. Next the program is scheduled so that each step is implemented as planned, without any activity getting out of phase. Achieving effective coordination is a difficult task, but the success of the campaign can be affected in a major way if it is not attained.

By way of illustration, the first part of this section is devoted to description and analysis of a campaign undertaken to launch the Kahala Hilton Hotel in Honolulu. This case history, which illustrates the way in which the various elements in the promotional mix are combined to attain communication objectives, should make apparent the magnitude of the need for achieving coordination and integration in promotional programs. The Program Evaluation and Review Technique (PERT) is later introduced as a promising solution to some of the difficulties encountered in the coordination attempt.

The Kahala Hilton: A Case History[1]

The Kahala Hilton in Honolulu, Hawaii, is situated on a somewhat remote site a short distance from Waikiki. Although it was destined to be one of the world's great resort hotels, the initial occupancy did not live up to expectations. The need for a crash promotion program became apparent, and McCann-Erickson, Inc., was given this assignment.

Situation Analysis. A prolonged situation analysis was not possible, but several basic issues soon became apparent. First, the Kahala Hilton was not designed to appeal to the mass market. While its prices are not excessive by U.S. standards, its location in Hawaii limits the potential market to those in the continental United States and elsewhere who have considerable discretionary income. Moreover, the costs of travel to Hawaii are least from the West Coast of the United States. Therefore, the market to be reached, for the most part, was greatest among those living in the western part of the United States with above-average incomes.

It was hoped that favorable publicity through word of mouth and other means would soon develop, but awareness of the facilities offered by the Kahala appeared to be low among prospective customers. Moreover, little was being generated in the way of support from travel agents and others who influence travel plans.

Objectives. From the situation analysis, the objectives for the campaign quickly emerged. The target market was designated as prospective users located on the West Coast who, ideally, travel extensively and can afford the expense of a trip to Hawaii from the U.S. mainland. The communication objective was to communicate the advantages offered by Kahala facilities in a striking and unusual fashion so that interest would be generated which was sufficient to bring occupancy figures past break-even levels as quickly as possible. Travel agents were established as a promotional target with the goal of stimulating sufficient interest that they would actively encourage customers to patronize the Kahala.

Budget. The exact procedure utilized to arrive at the budget was not disclosed, but it is known that it generally followed the task and objective procedure using the build-up method discussed in Chapter 10. Basic strategy called for reaching a large mailing list with direct-mail appeals as well as use of selected newspapers, in-store promotions, and other means. To support this program over a period of several months, at least $50,000 was required, and this figure was the final amount allocated.

In this instance, the entire campaign was planned and implemented by McCann-Erickson, whose previous work on similar problems furnished the background necessary.

Program Elements. The promotional program was comprehensive, and prospective customers were approached in a number of ways. These included (1) direct mail, (2) newspaper advertisements, (3) a tie-in with

---

[1] Used with special permission of Hilton Hotels, Inc., and McCann-Erickson, Inc.

FIGURE 22-1

Mailing to Carte Blanche Members on the West Coast

KAHALA HILTON, HONOLULU

July 8, 1964

Dear Friend:

I think you will be interested in the attached letter from Lowell Thomas to Conrad N. Hilton containing comments pertaining to the new Kahala Hilton in Honolulu.

Since we know that many discriminating travelers like to learn about new resort properties before they become generally known, we are sending you an advance proof of a color brochure describing the hotel.

As Mr. Thomas says, the Kahala is "the most stunning and elegant of all." Why don't you pick up your phone and call your travel agent or a Hilton Reservation office and pay us a visit? We'll be very happy to see you.

Edwin K. Hastings
Vice President Pacific
Hilton Hotels International

LOWELL THOMAS
President

MARCO POLO CLUB

July 6, 1964

Dear Conrad Hilton:

Having just come in from my twenty-ninth trip around the globe (far too many I agree), I feel I should salute you for what you have done for the world traveler. Much of the time I am off the beaten path; sometimes giving myself such a beating that later I revel in the luxury you now have provided for us in so many cities.

Recently, when we were filming the Stone Age peoples of New Guinea, in a remote valley we visited a long building, put up hurriedly by the natives — some are still cannibals — a structure to house 3,000 Stone Age men who were taking part in a tribal event. The young Australian patrol officers called it the Mount Hagen Hilton.

Since then, on a second flight to the South Pole, I bunked for several nights on the Antarctic ice, in a specially insulated building that has become a South Polar landmark there on the edge of the Ross Sea, the famous "Ross-Hilton".

I particularly congratulate you for the way you have used local building materials, as with all that beautiful marble in Athens; dressing your attendants in the costumes of the country; serving well known local dishes, and so on.

The newest of your establishments where I have stayed is the most stunning of all, the Kahala Hilton, in Hawaii, just around the bend from Diamond Head and Waikiki.

The Pacific Ocean covers more of this planet than any one natural feature. And over this vast area, the Kahala stands out as the most elegant of all.

Every time I make a long journey, from now on, I hope to include another visit to the Kahala.

Best wishes, aloha, and So Long.

Mr. Conrad N. Hilton,
President, Hilton Hotels
Beverly Hills, California.

IN THE WALDORF-ASTORIA
NEW YORK 22, N.Y.

FIGURE 22–1 *(continued)*

FIRST PROOF

NOT COLOR CORRECTED

For From the Wedding Crowd...

You sun-bathe beside a tropical lagoon where multicolored fish flicker just beneath the surface in the afternoon sun . . . close by, the murmuring surf calls you to a refreshing swim from a white-sand beach . . . around you, cascades of bougainvillea frame the rolling fairways of the Waialae Country Club's golf course . . . and, in the distance, Diamond Head soars majestically toward an azure sky.

There's nothing like it in all the seven seas: you are in incomparable Hawaii . . . in the exotic and elegant playground world of the Kahala Hilton, Honolulu's most distinguished hotel.

Days come and go leisurely, luxuriously at the Kahala Hilton; your every whim is attended in the classic tradition of the world's foremost resort hotels. And, incredible as it seems, this paradise is only a few air hours, or ocean-liner days, from the mainland!

Quiet Elegance

Set apart, in its own special corner of Honolulu's exclusive Kahala residential area, the Kahala Hilton, created expressly for the most discerning vacationers, offers a private resort world of island, countryclub living. The spacious grounds of the Kahala Hilton are beautifully landscaped, with tropical foliage and a profusion of flowers that is echoed within the hotel by splashing fountains, colorful plants and trellised balconies.

Classical Settings

The open-air atmosphere that is sustained in the public rooms and each of the 300 beautifully appointed guest rooms and suites is enhanced by the hotel's elegant decor. The spacious lobby with its magnificent chandeliers sets off the luxurious mood that permeates the entire hotel.

Dining Perfection

Day or evening, dining on the picturesque Hala Terrace is always a treat. You'll enjoy native or international dishes, with the sun, stars and sparkling water as your companions. Gentle fountains grace the stately Maile Lanai Dining Room, where you'll enjoy gourmet cuisine at its finest, following cocktails in the adjacent Maile Lounge. If you're hosting a special dinner party, the Waialae Room, with its magnificent decor of lava rock, is the perfect spot.

First-Class Service

Whether for refreshments in your cabana or poolside or a parasol on the beach, you'll find Hilton service at your beck and call. From breakfast on your private balcony to a nightcap in the Maile Lounge, your every comfort is personally attended to provide the extra special attention that makes a perfect holiday.

Kahala Hilton

HONOLULU

CALL YOUR . . . AXEL AGENT OR HILTON RESERVATION OFFICE
Consult the "Yellow Pages" of your phone book

a steamship company, (4) contacts by Hilton executives, and various specialized promotions.

DIRECT MAIL. Because of the sharply segmented market for this client, considerable waste would occur if the usual mass media were used. To reach the pinpointed potential customers in the western target market, a precisely aimed direct mail campaign was designed. The mailing used appears in Figure 22–1. Lowell Thomas was engaged to write a letter to Conrad Hilton lauding the Kahala as one of the world's great hotels. This letter was then enclosed with a note from Edward K. Hastings, vice president of the Pacific region, telling the recipient that the Kahala is an "unspoiled" resort property not yet discovered by the mass of travelers. This "inside story" appeal was reinforced by enclosure of a four-color brochure describing the Kahala which was stamped "First Proof Not Color Corrected." (Reproduced here in black and white.)

The mailing list included over 150,000 members of Carte Blanche, Hilton's credit card subsidiary. The mailing was sent to all members located in Arizona, California, Colorado, Nevada, New Mexico, Oregon, Texas, Washington, and British Columbia. In addition, delegates to the Republican National Convention in San Francisco were included.

NEWSPAPER ADVERTISEMENTS. While the direct mailing reached an excellent potential market, it by no means exhausted the list of those who might be induced to visit the Kahala. Therefore, it was decided to run a series of small newspaper advertisements (224 lines) on the society pages of daily or weekly newspapers in wealthy communities in California, Arizona, Texas, and British Columbia. The complete media schedule is given in Figure 22–2.

Small space was used for the reason that large display advertisements are not required to attract attention in this type of paper. Moreover, space was purchased on the society page on the assumption that women serve as a kind of "family opinion leader" in formulating family travel plans. In the newspaper copy in Figure 22–3, it will be noticed that the same "inside story" appeal was used. This advertisement was run four times during the months of June and July in most papers, and the total cost was $7,872.54.

TIE-IN WITH MATSON LINES. Matson Lines is one of the leading shipping firms between the West Coast and Hawaii. A tie-in between the Kahala and Matson offered substantial benefits to both.

A mailing was sent to 10,000 customers in the target market states who had traveled on Matson Lines at some time in the past. The copy read as follows:

Here's a little secret—shared only with the private world of Matson travelers. We've joined with another gracious host, the Kahala Hilton, to offer you an elegant new way to travel and enjoy Hawaii. It's a Matson-Hilton holiday—a

FIGURE 22–2

Newspaper Schedule for Kahala Hilton

Publication	Date	Cost
Piedmont Piedmonter	July 3, 10, 17, 31	$143.40
Menlo Park Recorder	July 2, 9, 16, 30	143.40
Burlingame Advance-Star and Green Sheet (includes Palo Alto Times and Redwood City Tribune)	June 28, July 5, 12	383.04
Orinda Sun	July 3, 10, 17, 31	89.60
Ross Valley Times	July 1, 8, 15	80.64
Lafayette Sun	July 3, 10, 17, 31	89.60
San Marino Tribune	July 2, 9, 16, 30	98.56
La Canada Valley Sun	July 2, 9, 16, 30	134.40
Beverly Hills Times	July 3, 10, 17, 31	249.60
Palos Verdes News	July 2, 9, 16, 30	116.48
Arcadia Tribune	June 28, July 5, 12, 26	134.40
Millbrae Sun & Leader	July 2, 9, 16, 30	125.44
San Carlos Enquirer	July 1, 8, 15, 29	125.44
Walnut Creek Contra Costa Times	June 28, July 5, 12, 26	179.20
Fullerton News Tribune	June 29, July 6, 13, 27	134.40
Inglewood News	June 30, July 7, 14, 28	89.60
Los Gatos-Saratoga Times Observer	June 20, July 6, 13, 27	80.64
Newport Beach-Costa Mesa Orange Coast Pilot	June 29, July 6, 13, 27	179.20
Palm Springs Desert Sun	June 29, July 6, 13, 27	116.48
Monterey Peninsula Herald	June 29, July 6, 13, 27	161.28
Pasadena Independent Star News	June 29, July 6, 13, 27	331.52
San Diego Union Tribune	June 28, July 5, 12, 26	752.64
San Gabriel Valley Tribune	June 28, July 5, 12, 26	295.68
San Mateo Times & News Leader	June 29, July 6, 13, 27	206.08
San Rafael Independent Journal	June 29, July 6, 13, 27	197.12
Santa Barbara News Press	June 28, July 5, 12, 26	197.12
Santa Maria Times	June 29, July 6, 13, 27	134.40
Sunnyville Mt. View Standard Register Leader	June 29, July 6, 13, 27	107.52
Ventura County Star-Free Press	June 29, July 6, 13, 27	152.32
Whittier News	July 1, 8, 15, 29	134.40
Midland Reporter Telegram (Texas)	June 28, July 5, 12, 26	125.44
Dallas News (Texas)	June 28, July 5, 12	423.36
Houston Chronicle (Texas)	June 28, July 5, 12	501.90
Phoenix Republic Gazette (Arizona)	June 29, July 5, 12, Aug. 9	562.24
Tucson Star Citizen (Arizona)	June 28, July 5, 12, 26	358.40
Vancouver Sun Province (B.C.)	June 28, July 4	537.60

world apart, where comfort and good taste come first. Minutes from the frivolity of Waikiki, the quiet elegance of the new Kahala Hilton beckons discerning visitors. A secluded, pristine beach is your doorstep to the blue Pacific. Sunning, dining, cocktails—the life is an easy one.

The perfect complement to these elegant days is your Lurline cruise in the Grand Manner. You know the good life on Matson's Pacific. It's better than ever. Isn't it time to slip away again? To enjoy Hawaii in a refreshing new way. With Matson. And Kahala Hilton. Send us the reply card, and we'll send you complete information.

A four-color brochure was enclosed describing the services and facilities of Matson and the Kahala.

CONTACTS BY HILTON EXECUTIVES. It was felt that the Kahala would profit most through word-of-mouth advertising. Therefore, Hilton executives around the world were asked to write personal letters to their friends and relatives or to contact them in other ways to announce the Kahala and its services. Over 1,200 letters were written, and the response was felt to be excellent.

THE NEWLYWED MARKET. The Luce Clipping Service was retained to collect all announcements appearing in West Coast papers during the promotion, beginning in August. Each bride-to-be received a letter mailed from Hawaii inviting her to honeymoon at the Kahala. An unusually receptive market was thus reached in an efficient manner.

IN-STORE PROMOTIONS. It was agreed that in-store promotions would provide excellent communication exposure. A complete store package was prepared, and personal selling was utilized to solicit the cooperation of fashion department stores and specialty shops in a number of leading cities on the West Coast. This promotion got under way in August, with 30 cooperating stores as the target.

FIGURE 22–3

Newspaper Advertisement for the Kahala Hilton

Be sneaky

Don't tell a soul, but there's a wonderful new place in Honolulu called the Kahala Hilton. A gorgeous estate, right on the beach. Bordered on three sides by the golf course and tennis courts of the Waialae Country Club. It's only 15 minutes from the bustle and bazazz of Waikiki, but hardly anybody's found out about it yet. So please keep it that way . . . just steal away from the crowd and be prepared for pampering. Fabulous food, sumptuous suites, superlative service. A wide sweep of coral-free beach. An enormous swimming pool. A lovely lagoon to sip cocktails by. And nobody to bother you.

The cost? Surprisingly low. From $12 a day per person for a double room that's twice as big as normal.

So don't breathe a word. Save it for when you get back and tell your friends what they've missed. They'll *hate* you.

See your travel agent, or call any Hilton Hotel or Hilton Reservation Office, or call Los Angeles MA 8-6231

HONOLULU

The basis of this promotion was display of a 22″ × 28″ poster costing $2.50. If a store agreed to use the display in a high-traffic window or in an inside department, a complementary gift of six nights at the Kahala was offered to management. Cooperation by a retail store beyond this specified minimum, of course, would result in a more lucrative reward. Display suggestions appear in Figure 22–4.

FIGURE 22–4

Display Suggestions Provided for the Kahala Campaign

WINDOW DISPLAYS

Order these full-color
Kahala Hilton posters
for your own office
and display windows.

Each poster measures 28" wide
by 22" deep.

Bright, colorful parasols,
made of translucent paper,
show off smart swimwear
fashions. The poster is
in the foreground. On the
floor is an easel-backed
card which carries the
selling message. Fanned-
out Kahala Hilton brochures
are also shown.

The "big catch" of this window
design is travel luggage, shown
caught in a fisherman's net
suspended from a fishing hook.
Pineapples and tropical fruit,
sand and sea-shells, carrying
out the Hawaiian feeling,
surround the selling sign.
The poster is in the foreground.

CONTACTING COUNTRY CLUBS. The West Coast country club set was felt to be another promising market segment. Direct-mail solicitations were sent to 900 golf pros at various clubs and to 1,100 club officers during August. Stimulation of word-of-mouth advertising was the objective of this mailing.

STIMULATING TRAVEL AGENT SUPPORT. The travel agent, widely used by international travelers, was a prime target for personal selling by the

Hilton International Division sales staff. Frequent calls were made by Hilton representatives, and each agent received a monthly sales letter including hotel brochures and selling tips.

The agent received the letter in Figure 22–5 along with a kit containing the full direct mailing sent to the Carte Blanche list. He was

FIGURE 22–5

Travel Agent Promotion for the Kahala Campaign

Hilton Hotels International

CONRAD N. HILTON, PRESIDENT

| CABLE ADDRESS | | TELEPHONE |
| HILTELS,NEW YORK | THE WALDORF-ASTORIA · NEW YORK 22, N. Y. | 212 MURRAY HILL 8-2240 |

Dear Travel Agent:

We've been talking directly to <u>your</u> clients and prospects about the stunning, new Kahala Hilton Hotel in Honolulu, Hawaii.

How? We've pinpointed that segment of the traveling public in <u>your</u> area that represents the best market for the Kahala Hilton -- and you! Yes, we've been pre-selling <u>your</u> clients and prospects on this fabulous new resort with a unique advertising and promotion program. This program included:

* Special mailings of the First Proof of the colorful Kahala Hilton brochure, with a reprint of a rave review by Lowell Thomas, to select lists of the top travel prospects in <u>your</u> community.

* Special window display program in key department stores and fine specialty shops throughout four western states.

* Special series of two advertisements directed to women, on the society pages of small community newspapers reaching high-income families in 39 markets in the West.

This entire promotion was directed to the best travel prospects in your area. They now know that the completely air-conditioned Kahala Hilton is a superb, secluded resort ... yet it is only a twelve-minute drive to Waikiki by free and frequent shuttle service ... that it is truly the pearl of the Pacific. Many of these prospects will be planning a Kahala Hilton vacation soon.

So take advantage of this tailor-made market for Pacific travel. Order the Kahala Hilton material contained in this folder in the quantities you need. Use the Lowell Thomas letters and "first proof" spread for your own direct-mail promotion ... the magnificent, full-color brochures for your other mailings and rack use ... and the beautiful, full-color poster for your office and display windows. Just fill out the postage-paid reply card and mail today.

Remember, they've all been planned to help you make the Kahala Hilton your <u>first</u> resort ... for profit!

Cordially,

HILTON HOTELS INTERNATIONAL

William F. Prigge
Director of Sales

WORLD PEACE THROUGH INTERNATIONAL TRADE AND TRAVEL

asked to publicize the Kahala to his customers through use of the hotel brochure and display material. Over 23 percent of agents returned the reply card requesting these items—an excellent response. Moreover, all agents whose cooperation was judged to be good were visited by Hilton sales representatives.

The Matson-Hilton tie-in was promoted to the travel agent through direct mail and personal selling, although it was not begun until the above efforts had been completed.

CONTACTING AIRLINES. The Hilton sales force also called regularly on airlines and other transportation companies. Every attempt was made to motivate airline sales offices to publicize the Kahala with brochures and display materials.

The Outcome.   The total expenditure for the promotion was approximately $50,000, the largest part of which was invested in direct mail advertising. Results of this direct mail effort are difficult to measure. On the basis of initial occupancy figures, predictions for the first year would not have exceeded 20 percent. Occupancy reached nearly 50 percent of capacity during and immediately following the campaign. Moreover, the payout over the long run should be considerable from vacation trips stimulated by the promotion.

Analysis of the Kahala Program.   This campaign was an apparent success for many reasons. Of primary importance was the fact that the situation was analyzed effectively in a short time, the market target was pinpointed, and realistic communication objectives were established and followed. To Hilton's credit were lack of rigid budgetary limits and willingness to invest in promotion necessary to reach the objectives.

Media selection was such that the target market was reached economically. The glamor of mass media was bypassed for face-to-face communication, in-store promotions, and interpersonal relations with travel agents and airline personnel.

An advertising message was formulated based on awareness of the motivation of international travelers to avoid tourist spots and to frequent hotels and resorts which do not appeal to the masses. The "inside-story" appeal clearly capitalized on this preference and presented the Kahala Hilton effectively. The brochure marked "Not Color Corrected" gave the reader the feeling that he was part of a unique group getting the inside story in advance of others. This same appeal was played up to a lesser extent in newspaper advertising.

Point-of-sale communication through travel agents and in-store promotions was handled effectively. The response of travel agents was further evidence that campaign objectives were attained, for many apparently recognized and capitalized on a profitable opportunity.

Finally, the entire campaign was well coordinated and integrated. It was underway in all phases just three months after its inception, with no activity out of phase with any other. The direct mailing and news-paper advertising were timed to coincide, and displays were in position and travel agents' offices were aware sufficiently in advance to generate enthusiasm to follow through on the response to advertising by prospective travelers.

PERT: A Method for Coordinating Campaign Elements

Coordination obviously is necessary for campaign success, but it can be difficult to achieve in practice. A campaign is a complex undertaking in which many elements run simultaneously. Although the Kahala program was not an extensive one in terms of investment, duration, or geographical reach, it nonetheless was sufficiently complex that difficulties were encountered in meshing the various parts of the plan so that none fell out of phase with others. It was a task, for example, to ensure that all travel agents had received direct mail kits and had been called on prior to the starting date.

There is no substitute for a master planning schedule which spells out in detail what is to be done, who is to do it, and when it is to be done. Management then has an analytical tool which provides a complete picture of the campaign and facilitates a review of its progress at any point in time. The use of such an analytical method has been greatly enhanced since the advent of electronic computers. One such method, PERT (Program Evaluation and Review Technique), offers real potential in promotional planning.

PERT was first used in 1957 to guarantee that the Polaris missile program remained on schedule, and the U.S. government now requires its use on all defense projects. It is finding increased use in marketing for several reasons, including the following:

PERT, as currently developed, is a proved advanced approach to planning and control, which can be applied in marketing as well as other fields. It is particularly effective for complex projects involving many interrelated and interdependent tasks and where completion time is critical. PERT provides a *graphic picture of the entire project* so that management can plan effectively. Using PERT, management can realistically compute project completion time, identify critical activities, and determine the effect that delays in each activity will have on the project as a whole. As work progresses, PERT provides for evaluation of progress, reestimation of completion dates, pinpointing of anticipated trouble spots, and the pretesting of alternative ways to get the project back on schedule.[2]

---

[2] John F. Stolle and Jack C. Page, "Out of Polaris: A Space Age Technique to Launch New Products," *Sales Management,* July 3, 1964, p. 24.

There are a number of detailed manuals for the application of PERT which are recommended to the interested reader.[3]

The Nature of PERT. The foundation of PERT is a graphic representation of activities and events required to accomplish a given task, with explicit attention given to interdependencies and interrelationships between activities. A sequential network of activities is constructed, and analysis centers upon realistic estimates of the time required for completion of necessary activities. This provides a comprehensive plan for program completion wherein the effects of delays in the completion of any activity upon the whole program immediately become apparent. This information provides the necessary data for realistic rescheduling.

A PERT Network. The PERT network is a flow diagram consisting of activities and events required to accomplish stated objectives in which

FIGURE 22–6

The Activity-Event Relationship

the interdependencies are graphed. An event is considered as a specific accomplishment which is apparent at a given point in time. Activities are defined as tasks which utilize available resources and lead to the events. Activities are the work to be done and the personnel and materials needed, and events are specific accomplishments or finished activities.

On a PERT network diagram, activities are represented by arrows between the events depicted numerically within circles. One such relationship is shown in Figure 22–6. Events 4 and 7 are functionally related. The activity connecting these events cannot take place until event 4 is finished, and, in turn, event 7 does not take place unless the connecting activity is completed. If several activities lead up to an event, all activities must be completed before the event comes into existence.

In Figure 22–7 the beginning activity in planning part of a campaign in an advertising agency is shown as the product group meeting. This meeting gives rise to three separate activities which lead to media, budget, and creative plans. These plans must be executed before the complete preliminary strategy statement (the final event) can be prepared.

---

[3] For a thorough introduction see James E. R. Kelley and M. R. Walker, *Critical Path Planning and Scheduling—An Introduction* (Fort Washington, Pa.: Mauchly Association, 1959); and *PERT Fundamentals*, Vol. III (Washington, D.C.: PERT Orientation and Training Center, 1963).

Time Estimates. Promotional planning and scheduling seldom is routine, and realistic time estimates present a real problem. PERT usually requires the following three time estimates for each activity:

1. *Optimistic time*—the least amount of time required to finish an activity.
2. *Most likely time*—the time which seems most probable as estimated by those responsible for completion of the event.
3. *Pessimistic time*—the maximum amount of time the activity could take if "the worst happened."

FIGURE 22–7

PERT Network Diagram

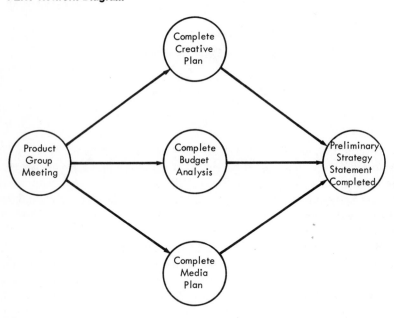

These three estimates are combined to derive "expected time," which is computed as follows:

$$T_e = \frac{a + 4m + b}{6}$$

where

T_e = Expected time
a = Optimistic time
m = Most likely time
b = Pessimistic time.

The Critical Path. Assume that a PERT network has been graphed (with events numbered in circle) and expected times have been computed for each activity (indicated on lines connecting circles). At this point the greatest managerial usefulness of PERT becomes apparent, for it is possible to isolate the most time-consuming path or paths. This is referred to as the "critical path." Since the ending event cannot occur until all activities leading to it are completed, the critical path clearly controls the ending time for the entire project. A major advantage of PERT is that trouble spots are identified ahead of time, and special efforts may then be allocated to overcome various bottlenecks and delays in the entire project.

In the PERT network represented in Figure 22–8, the critical path

FIGURE 22–8

PERT Network Representing a Critical Path

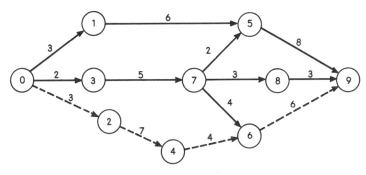

is depicted by broken lines. There are nine events, and the expected time in weeks is indicated by the numbers above each arrow. The critical path is determined by adding the numbers of each possible path of activities between events 0 and 9. The path with the *greatest* amount of time required for completion is the critical path.

In this example there are five possible paths, with required times ranging between 13 and 20:

$$
\begin{array}{ll}
0, 1, 5, 9 & \ldots\ldots\ldots\ldots\ldots 17 \text{ weeks} \\
0, 2, 4, 6, 9 & \ldots\ldots\ldots\ldots\ldots 20 \text{ weeks} \\
0, 3, 7, 8, 9 & \ldots\ldots\ldots\ldots\ldots 13 \text{ weeks} \\
0, 3, 7, 5, 9 & \ldots\ldots\ldots\ldots\ldots 17 \text{ weeks} \\
0, 3, 7, 6, 9 & \ldots\ldots\ldots\ldots\ldots 17 \text{ weeks}
\end{array}
$$

Here path 0, 2, 4, 6, 9 is the critical path, with a total elapsed time required of 20 weeks. Therefore it is the path that requires the greatest attention if the project is to be completed in less than 20 weeks.

Another way to view the critical path is to state that it has the least slack. By "slack" is meant, in effect, open or free time between the time required to finish the activities along a given path and the latest allowable time for these activities. Computation of PERT times using the concept of slack can be done using a standard computer program. One of the advantages of PERT is that resources can often be interchanged whenever slack exists along some path or paths in the network. That is, resources can be "traded off" and applied to the critical path to reduce the total time required for its completion and hence speed up completion of the entire project.

Application of PERT to Promotional Strategy. If a systematic planning approach has been followed for a promotional program, it is a relatively simple step to utilize PERT in scheduling and controlling. All that PERT involves is graphing these interrelated events, specifying the connecting activities, and computing expected times. Although the resulting network can be quite complex, the critical path or paths are easily isolated using computer procedures. The complexity of resulting networks should not be a deterrent to the use of PERT, for these complexities are a function of the *promotional requirements*, and they exist regardless of whether or not PERT is used. The advantage of PERT is that it enables management to depersonalize the complexities and bring them under objective, realistic control.

A study of new-product introductions indicated that 13 percent of the companies surveyed had used PERT for this purpose.[4] Moreover, promotion is almost always part of new-product introduction. One example of the use of PERT for this purpose appears in Figure 22–9. Notice that there are five network paths between events 1 and 12:

A. 1, 2, 5, 7, 8, 10, 11, 12
B. 1, 3, 6, 9, 12
C. 1, 3, 6, 8, 10, 11, 12
D. 1, 3, 4, 6, 9, 12
E. 1, 3, 4, 6, 8, 10, 11, 12

If the time values along each of the paths are added, the following results:

A. 8.8 weeks
B. 10.4 weeks
C. 8.0 weeks
D. 11.5 weeks
E. 9.1 weeks

The critical path is thus path D, requiring 11.5 weeks.

---

[4] Stolle and Page, "Out of Polaris," p. 24.

FIGURE 22–9

PERT Application to Promotional Strategy

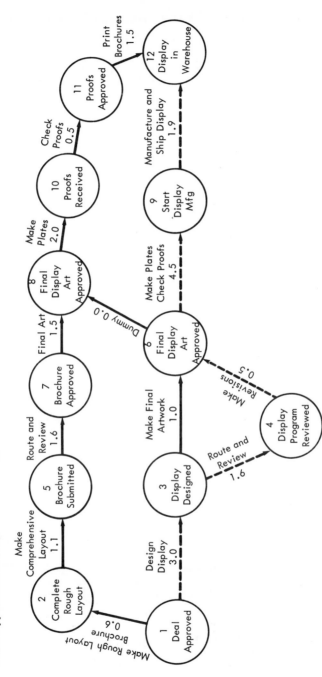

Source: Reproduced with special permission from John F. Stolle and Jack C. Page, "Out of Polaris: A Space Age Technique to Launch New Products," *Sales Management*, July 3, 1964, pp. 26 and 27.

If this critical path time of 11.5 weeks would mean that the project will exceed its programmed finished time, then efforts may be aimed at speeding up performance along path D. For instance, it may be possible to reduce the activity time between events 6 and 9 by asking the plate maker to work overtime. The costs, of course, would be increased, and it must be determined whether or not the reduction in time is worth the increased costs.

PERT can be a truly valuable management tool, and *it is a logical extension of a systematic approach*. Thus it offers these advantages:

1. Systematic planning is guaranteed. PERT requires a systems approach to planning, and the technique imposes discipline on management thinking.
2. Responsibilities are clarified. The PERT network clearly defines what is expected from individuals responsible for each activity and with whom each manager is expected to coordinate his work.
3. Decisions can be pretested. Alternative networks can be graphed and expected times computed. Thus the outcomes of alternative approaches can be isolated with a clarity not previously possible.
4. Delays can be evaluated. Without PERT or its equivalent, management is prone to apply crash programs to all activities to speed up those few that are really critical. Crash programs on network paths with slack, however, are highly wasteful. PERT avoids this waste through isolating the critical path or paths, so crash programs can be applied only at the trouble points.

It seems apparent that this valuable management technique will rapidly find increased use.

EVALUATION AND FOLLOW-UP

There are two final stages in promotional planning and strategy which follow execution of the coordinated program. The first of these is measurement of effectiveness, which has been discussed in other chapters and will not be stressed here except as it contributes to the final stage, *evaluation and follow-up*. The steps in evaluation and follow-up are: (1) assessment of results against objectives, (2) postmortem appraisal, (3) assignment of accountability, and (4) assessment of future implications.

Assessment of Results against Objectives

It has been stressed that objectives must be *measurable*. If they have been stated in vague terms, evaluation and follow-up are impossible. Assume, for example, that the communication objective is "to interest people in buying the *Living Bible*." There is no way that results, no matter how precise, can be compared against this objective. Assessment is possible, however, if the objective is stated as: "to stimulate awareness so that 60 percent of those interviewed will mention *Living Bible* when asked 'What are the names of the versions of the Bible you are familiar with?' " An appropriately designed pre-post analysis permits an accurate indication of whether or not this second goal has been attained.

Postmortem Appraisal

In the postmortem stage the question asked is: What did we learn from the results of this campaign? Assume that an actual advertising program fell 15 points short of the 60 percent awareness specified for the *Living Bible*. An analytical look then should be taken at the campaign, step by step. Perhaps the message was unclear, inappropriate media were chosen, or the 60 percent awareness objective was unrealistic. In any case, the goal is to pinpoint the causes for the results.

Common sense would specify that the results of the postmortem analysis be written down and used in later planning. Chapter 9 described how difficult, if not impossible, it is to set objectives without some basis of experience. The postmortem thus provides invaluable data for the future.

Unfortunately, most organizations completely neglect the postmortem. In his study of leading advertisers, Victor P. Buell lamented that managers were repeatedly "reinventing the wheel" and making the same mistakes, both of which could have been avoided by relying on properly digested experience.[5] The obvious solution is to codify experience and extract the operating principles that emerge. One of the great managers of all time stated that "The wise man is glad to be instructed, but a self-sufficient fool falls flat on his face." (Proverbs 10:8, *Living Bible*).

Assignment of Accountability

One result of the postmortem should be assignment of accountability to those who are responsible for the program's success or failure. One of the most pervasive human tendencies is to use every possible device to escape accountability. Anyone who has worked in complex organizations could find evidence of the effects of this practice. The senior author, for example, was a consultant for several years for one of the large oil producers of North America. It became obvious that postmortem analyses were never held, and each manager, once he was promoted and left his job, was careful to leave his desk and files clean. Thus there was nothing tangible which could implicate him with failure and tarnish his career

---

[5] V. P. Buell, *Changing Practices in Advertising Decision-Making and Control* (New York: Association of National Advertisers, 1973).

opportunities. Not surprisingly, rewards seemed to be given to those who "played it safe," and incompetency was apparent at top-management levels.

Such situations must be avoided *at all costs*. A simple step is to assign precise job descriptions to each manager and measure his performance against these standards. If the product manager has failed to meet his objectives, and *this pattern is repeated over time,* the obvious step is to take some sort of remedial action. Similarly, success should be promptly rewarded. Only then is it possible to get maximum benefit from systematic promotional planning.

Assessment of Future Implications

Throughout this book, the perspective has been on the short-term program or campaign by necessity, because most management decisions are of this nature. Evaluation and follow-up, however, demand that a broader viewpoint be taken to encompass the longer term. In particular, the focus must be on the *product life or product maturity cycle,* or that period of time during which the product will offer commercial payout sufficient to warrant its continued existence.[6]

A model of the generalized product life cycle is given in Figure 22–10. It has the following phases:

1. *Development*—that period prior to the time the product is brought to market during which situation analysis and production tool-up are performed.
2. *Introduction*—usually a period of slowly growing sales, during which the costs of introduction are greater than the return (refer to payout planning discussed in Chapter 10, which takes account of an explicit period in which a loss is deliberately incurred to launch a product).
3. *Growth*—demand accelerates, and the promotion problem shifts from stimulating awareness to stimulating trial of the product over those of competitors, which are now appearing.
4. *Maturity*—the market is now saturated by competitors, and competition shifts more to maintenance of "share of mind" (see Chapter 12) and price competition.
5. *Decline*—the product is losing appeal and is a candidate for deletion.

Thus the role for promotion changes over the product life cycle. The introductory campaign usually will require a larger than normal budget and will utilize high levels of both reach and frequency to build aware-

---

[6] See R. D. Buzzell, "Competitive Behavior and Product Life Cycles," in J. S. Wright and J. Goldstucker, (eds.), *New Ideas for Successful Marketing* (Chicago: American Marketing Association, 1966), pp. 46–67.

FIGURE 22–10

The Generalized Product Life Cycle

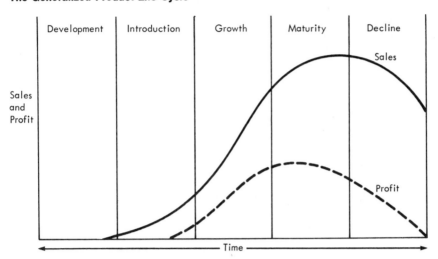

ness and initial interest. Competitors usually appear quickly, however, and the emphasis shifts during the growth stage to stressing competitive superiority. Once maturity is reached, there usually are few if any real product differences. Hence the objective is to prevent share of mind from decreasing, and increased resort will be made to various forms of price competition. In the decline stage, active promotion usually ceases other than to guarantee that appropriate distribution still is achieved. The product is continued, other things being equal, only as long as it makes a contribution to profit.

The timing of the life cycle varies from product to product, but it is inevitable. As a result, management must be sensitive to signs that the present marketing program, and promotion in particular, is "wearing out." Often it is necessary to introduce product changes or to stress in promotion hitherto untapped benefits in order to delay the onset of maturity and decline. An ability to sense the need for these changes and the appropriate timing is often what differentiates a consistently success-ful firm from an "also ran."

When sales and profits are leveling off or turning down, however, it should not automatically be assumed that the problem lies in advertising or other aspects of promotion. It could be due to a number of other factors, and there is an inherent danger in changing a campaign and thereby sacrificing the awareness and momentum which have been built up. Dial soap, for example, has retained its position as the top deodorant bar in the business for over 20 years without changing its fundamental advertising proposition.

SUMMARY

From the perspective of the total promotional program, this chapter has considered the coordination of the various program elements to meet the objectives of the plan. A case history illustrated the importance of coordination and integration, and it was shown how PERT analysis can be a powerful assist at this phase. Then attention was directed to evaluation and follow-up, which take place after the campaign has run its course. It was stressed that this is the appropriate time to learn from what has succeeded or failed, to codify this experience for future use, and to assign accountability to those responsible for performance. It was also pointed out that the evaluation phase should move from the short-run perspective to a longer run view which encompasses the total product life cycle and the changes in promotional strategy which must occur as a product approaches maturity and decline.

REVIEW AND DISCUSSION QUESTIONS

1. Review the Kahala Hilton case history and prepare a PERT network of its various phases.
2. Would PERT analysis have helped management in the Kahala campaign? If so, how? What difficulties, if any, would be encountered in its application?
3. What is the significance of the critical path in a PERT network?
4. It was pointed out that the results of a postmortem analysis should be codified for use in future planning. What, in particular, should be written down and used? Be as specific as you can, using the Kahala case as an example.
5. Why does management seem to avoid accountability? What would you do if you were hired as marketing director and assumed responsibility over a group of product managers who had been permitted to escape accountability for many years? What problems would be anticipated?
6. What stage of the product life cycle do you think the following products have attained? Dial soap, Pepsi-Cola, Amana Radar-Range ovens, knit clothing, Vitalis hairdressing?
7. How would the promotional strategies of each of the above products differ? What factors account for your judgment?

part seven

Epilogue

The man who knows right from wrong and has good judgment and common sense is happier than the man who is immensely rich! For such wisdom is far more valuable than precious jewels. Nothing else compares with it. Have two goals: wisdom—that is, knowing and doing right—and common sense. Don't let them slip away, for they fill you with living energy, and are a feather in your cap.

—Proverbs 3:13–15; 21–22, *Living Bible*

The discussion to this point has largely been from the vantage point of managerial strategy, although frequent reference has been made to broader social issues. Many questions remain to be examined, however, for no manager can escape the social, moral, and economic consequences of his actions. In this sense, Chapter 23 may well be the most important segment of this book. The authors have attempted to take a fresh look at opposing points of view without resorting to the defensive platitudes and self-serving value judgments so often advanced when marketing is placed under social scrutiny.

It will become apparent that we hold an unswerving conviction that our way of life is threatened to its core. While the causes by no means can be laid entirely at the feet of the business firm, there are some serious issues which, at their very heart, reflect managerial irresponsibility. It is hoped that this epilogue will provide a perspective which can shed light rather than heat, and can at least point the way to some solutions.

23

The Economic and Social Dimensions of Promotional Strategy

IN THE PAST it was customary for textbooks on advertising and selling to devote one chapter to social and economic considerations, mostly because it was felt to be the proper thing to do, not because anyone was really interested. A body of "conventional wisdom" thus took shape which was dutifully quoted and rarely challenged. Today, however, the social justification of promotion has become a primary concern. Many are advocating radical change, even to the point of abolition of the profit motive and business as it is now known.

The authors have not hesitated to discuss these broader dimensions throughout the text. There are some as yet unaddressed issues, however, which touch upon very sensitive nerves and which affect the ultimate survival of a way of life.

This chapter begins with a review of the traditional justification of promotion. Reference is made most frequently to the economic and social role of advertising, for the reason that it usually represents the front line of critics' fire. It should become apparent, however, that the points of controversy underlie all forms of promotion in common. Then these traditional arguments are challenged, and the need for some drastic revisions in basic premises is made evident. The chapter concludes with an assessment of the fundamental meaning of socially responsive promotional management in a rapidly changing world.

PROMOTION IN A FREE ENTERPRISE ECONOMY

Two fundamental and highly significant premises underlie any discussion of the role of promotion in a free enterprise economy. First, and probably most important, it is assumed that a *high and rising standard of living is a valid social goal.* Second, *profit is assumed to be an accurate measure of the extent to which a business organization has succeeded in meeting consumer desires and thereby contributing to a rising living standard.* Promotion then becomes defensible to the extent that it performs the following functions: (1) motivation of the consumer to increase his standard of living and provision of useful information toward that end, (2) provision of a stimulus for firms to produce new products at lowered prices, and (3) prevention of monopoly and strengthening of competition.

Each of these points will be examined. The effects of the three basic functions of promotion will be discussed first, followed by reevaluation of the two basic premises regarding the role of promotion in our present economy.

Effects on Consumer Behavior

Motivation to Increase Standard of Living. It is assumed that motivational influences on the buyer are not sufficient to induce people to work, to produce, and to distribute the necessary goods. Some stimulus is required to influence buyers to attain higher incomes and to spend these funds on a rising inventory of goods and services. Leo Bogart defends advertising in this way:

Apart from what a specific advertising campaign does for a specific product, there is a broader combined effect of the thousands of advertising exhortations that confront every consumer in America each day, a constant reminder of material goods and services not yet possessed. That effect at the level of individual motivation is felt as a constant impetus toward more consumption, toward acquisition, toward upward mobility. At the collective level, it is felt in the economic drive to produce and to innovate which fuels our economic system.[1]

There is no denying that promotion (advertising in particular) performs this role, yet its impact should not be overstated. Advertising is not a major *causative* factor in the remarkable level of affluence in Western societies. The original settlers in America were forced to conquer a hostile environment, and this work orientation was perpetuated and reinforced through the doctrine of individual effort inherent in the Protestant religion (the Puritan ethic). In addition, a unique orientation toward the future resulted from a conscious revolt against the traditions of parent countries. Therefore, striving toward improvement of standards of living is intrinsic in this country, and it is doubtful that such a desire is in any

---

[1] L. Bogart, "Where Does Advertising Research Go from Here?" *Journal of Advertising Research,* Vol. 9 (March 1969), p. 10. Reprinted from the *Journal of Advertising Research,* copyright 1969, Advertising Research Foundation, Inc.

way established by advertising. It is more probable that advertising reinforces these values and directs them toward specific products and services so that their production and sales become feasible. Therefore, demand-stimulating activities do indeed exert an indirect effect on national income, as alleged, but it should not be concluded that advertising and selling are the cause of high and rising living standards.

Provision of Buying Information. It is the traditional defense that advertising offers benefits to the consumer through providing information which is useful in buying decisions.[2] One economist claims that:

. . . advertisements provide the information that the brand advertises. This is useful information for the consumer to have. Advertisers have an incentive to advertise winners rather than losers. In consequence simply by responding to advertising the consumer can expect to get a better product than he would get otherwise. . . . Advertising helps consumers by directing them to the better brands.[3]

Certainly it is true that advertising *can* provide useful information, especially when a deliberate effort is made to discover the buyer's evaluative criteria and to build awareness along these dimensions. This role becomes especially significant in a world characterized by rapidity of change. An apt illustration is provided by the study which documented that educated housewives spending more than the average amount of time in shopping failed to pick the most economical item almost 50 percent of the time.[4] They were unable to make the best choice because there were so many models, sizes, and choices. Hence, the consumer must be helped in the choice process, and advertising can be of real value in this regard.

The actual performance of industry in meeting the information needs of consumers, however, falls far short of the ideal. Consider this example, which is just one of hundreds which could be cited. Naturalist Euell Gibbons was retained by General Foods in 1973 to advertise its long-established product, Post Grape Nuts. Gibbons claimed that "natural ingredients are important to me . . . its naturally sweet taste reminds me of wild hickory nuts. I call Grape Nuts my back-to-nature cereal." The unfortunate fact is that Grape Nuts is fortified with vitamins and minerals and hence does not qualify as a true natural food, in contrast to recent offerings of competitors. But what will be comprehended by the consumer? It should be obvious to the reader, as Weiss points out,

---

[2] See George J. Stigler, "The Economics of Information," *Journal of Political Economy,* Vol. 69 (1961), pp. 213–25.

[3] P. Nelson, "The Economic Consequences of Advertising," unpublished paper, State University of New York at Binghamton, 1973, p. 2.

[4] E. B. Weiss, "Markets Fiddle while Consumers Burn," in J. R. Wish and S. H. Gamble (eds.), *Marketing and Social Issues* (New York: John Wiley & Sons, 1971), p. 276.

that this is a subtle evasion of fact.[5] This can hardly qualify as advertising which "helps consumers by directing them to the better brands."

This is just one example of the type of competitive behavior which has given rise to the consumerism movement. What has the response of business been to the pressures generated by Ralph Nader and others? Some light was shed by A. G. Woodside's study of advertisers' willingness to document their advertising claims when queried.[6] Most manufacturers were unwilling to provide any justification whatsoever. Only a minority replied affirmatively, leading Woodside to conclude that a typical response was "We do not propose to debate our advertising with you." There were some outstanding exceptions, however, such as the following reply from Charles Hearnshaw of the 3M Company with respect to advertisements in *Time* for Scotch Brand cassette tape:

As the manufacturer of a quality product, we welcome the opportunity to provide our customers with information of a nature more detailed than that which could be included in a one-page ad. Being proud of our accomplishment, we are eager to share the full story of its superiority. Our only regret is that we so seldom are given the opportunity to completely explain the details of the product's excellence to a willing ear.[7]

In a broader study of company response to consumerism, F. E. Webster, Jr., reports that planned, coordinated programs of response to these pressures are the exception rather than the rule.[8] The usual response is more one of tokenism, and there seems to be a widespread tendency to regard consumerism as a passing fad which "affects the other guy."

Given the pervasiveness of public disenchantment with business veracity today,[9] one is not likely to win a debate by taking the affirmative on the informative role of advertising. All that can be concluded is that advertising *can* and *does* perform this role when it is managed responsibly and is conditioned by a genuine consumer orientation. Unfortunately the exceptions speak so loudly that the public is concluding that the advertiser's "walk does not match his talk."

Effects on New Products and Price

New-Product Development. It is claimed by the apologist for advertising that buyer interest does not attain sufficient intensity in the

[5] E. B. Weiss, "Does Consumerism Show Signs of Giving up the Ghost?" *Advertising Age,* April 30, 1973, p. 47.

[6] A. G. Woodside, "The Documentation of Advertising Claims," *Scan,* Vol. 21, No. 4, p. 18.

[7] Ibid.

[8] F. E. Webster, Jr., "Does Business Misunderstand Consumerism?" *Harvard Business Review,* September–October, 1973, pp. 89–97.

[9] See for example T. P. Hustad and E. A. Pessemier, "Will the Real Consumer-Activist Please Stand UP," Paper No. 345, Herman C. Krannert Graduate School of Industrial Administration, Purdue University, March 1972.

absence of promotion to justify investment by manufacturers in new products. Advertising, it is said, provides this stimulus, along with a quick and economical way of reaching a mass market with product information and persuasive communication. It is contended that the rapid rate of new-product development that is so characteristic of the American economy would be substantially reduced without advertising.

Does advertising, in fact, influence the rate of product development? Most would answer in the affirmative. Buyer adoption of new products is slow and, as a result, advertising and selling contribute to the quick establishment of large-scale demand which is necessary to serve as a profit incentive for the producer.

Advertising stimulates product development in other ways as well. Producers in oligopolistic markets compete largely on a nonprice basis, and competitive advertising can be self-defeating unless the producer can somehow claim his product is superior. Such pressures provide incentive for product differentiation and improvement.

Mass selling contributes to product quality in yet another (often overlooked) manner. Producers seldom enter the market for a one-shot, hit-and-run sale. The profitable manufacture and sale of an advertised brand requires continued satisfied use by a mass market of buyers, and maintenance of quality is essential for repeat purchase. The buyer is not likely to repurchase unless his demands are satisfied. Therefore, both the buyer and the producer can be served simultaneously. This relationship is not unique to Western societies; it was found, for example, that the incidence of shoddy merchandise and buyer deception declined sharply in the Soviet Union after producers were encouraged to identify their products.[10] Customer loyalty cannot be generated unless quality is maintained.

Effect on Prices.   One of the alleged economic contributions of promotion on a mass scale is to lower the costs of production and distribution through facilitating economies of scale. According to this argument, promotion permits producers to offer goods to the public at lower prices than would otherwise be possible. Advertising can affect price also by reducing distribution margins on brands. This can happen for two reasons: (1) goods are caused to turn over so rapidly that they can be sold profitably at a smaller markup, and (2) product identity is created which permits the public to compare prices between stores, thus setting a limit on the retailer's pricing freedom.[11]

There is, in fact, no current definitive evidence to contend that ad-

---

[10] Marshall Goldman, "Product Differentiation and Advertising: Some Lessons from Soviet Experience," *Journal of Political Economy,* Vol. 68 (August 1960), pp. 346–57.

[11] R. Steiner, "Does Advertising Lower Consumer Prices?" *Journal of Marketing,* Vol. 37 (1973), pp. 19–26.

vertising either lowers or raises price.[12] It should be pointed out, however, that production and selling costs can be reduced only when firms have excess capacity which can be utilized if sales volume is expanded. When this does not exist, there are no economies of scale to be generated. This fact may help explain some of the ambiguities in the evidence. But even if costs are reduced, it is by no means clear that the gains will be passed on to buyers as lower prices. While the most intensively advertised product categories have, in fact, shown smaller increases in price than their less heavily advertised counterparts since World War II, the differences in price levels are not large.[13]

It is also possible to argue plausibly that advertising can *raise* prices. In the first place, some contend that advertising is inherently wasteful for the reason that rival appeals cancel one another.[14] The only price effect of advertising then is to add to the costs of each firm, and ultimately to the level of prices. It is undeniable that this argument has a substantial measure of truth. When competitors are advertising to gain market share, efforts often are offsetting. No competitor will succeed unless one has some skill or product advantage not possessed by the others. This can, of course, be a powerful incentive for product innovation.

Others allege that advertising affects price adversely by encouraging competition to achieve product differentiation, which enables the firms to develop a high level of brand loyalty. This brand loyalty in turn renders demand less responsive to changes in price, with the result that firms thereby avoid price competition and, at times, charge higher prices than would otherwise be possible.[15]

While advertising can affect brand loyalty as the critics claim, it is dangerous to argue that brand loyalty in itself permits a firm to engage in anticompetitive behavior. The evidence supports an opposite conclusion, because brand-share stability is often lower for the most heavily advertised product categories.[16] In reality, high advertising levels frequently result from the introduction of new products to counteract consumer dissatisfaction with existing brands. Therefore, advertising outlays often are the result of brand *disloyalty* rather than *loyalty*. Advertising itself is incapable of maintaining consumer acceptance of an unsatisfactory product.

---

[12] Ibid.

[13] Jules Backman, *Advertising and Competition* (New York: New York University Press, 1967), p. 144.

[14] See Donald F. Turner, "Advertising and Competitors," address to Conference on Federal Controls of Advertising-Promotion (1966).

[15] See for example Colston E. Warne, "Advertising: A Critic's View," *Journal of Marketing*, Vol. 26 (October 1962), p. 12.

[16] L. G. Telser, "Some Aspects of the Economics of Advertising," *Journal of Business*, Vol. 41 (April 1968), p. 169.

It is true that price competition is avoided in certain industries, but once again it is false to assign the causative role to advertising. The industries usually referred to by critics are oligopolies characterized by a few large firms producing similar products. As William Fellner has pointed out, it is not economically feasible to engage in price competition because price changes are promptly met by competitors.[17] The net result can be ruinous for the entire industry. Therefore, it is to be expected that nonprice competition will prevail.

Granted that nonprice competition is prevalent in many industries, this does not necessarily mean that advertising under such circumstances is socially detrimental. First it must not be overlooked that few markets are truly static. There always are new customers entering, so advertising can perform a broader function than merely shifting the boundaries of market share. Moreover, it should be apparent to any observer of the economic system that companies seldom succeed under oligopoly if an unchanging product-service mix is maintained for long. Powerful incentives exist to expand market share through product improvement, and the companies remaining on top do so through innovative marketing. The buyer, of course, is a beneficiary.

To mention yet another point in rebuttal, there are powerful counter-effects to the long-run avoidance of price competition. Distributors quickly enter mature markets with private brands at lower prices. Furthermore, firms past the peak of a product life cycle seldom can reverse the downturn with advertising, and, as a result, turn to price as an alternative.

Effects on Competition and Market Structure

The defender of mass promotion often bases much of his argument on the premise that it facilitates and strengthens competition. Incentive is generated for product improvement so that the firm has unique benefits to feature in its advertising. By this means any given competitor is deterred from attaining a monopoly position. Without this incentive for innovation it is contended that market shares of existing firms would stabilize, and there would be general stagnation insofar as product improvement is concerned.

The issue of competition and market structure has long drawn the critics' fire. Two types of rebuttal to the argument of the beneficial effects of promotion are offered: (1) large companies drive weaker competitors out of business through sheer financial power, and (2) the necessary volume of advertising creates barriers for entry of new firms into a

---

[17] William Fellner, *Competition among the Few* (New York: Alfred A. Knopf, 1949).

market. Many feel that large firms have acquired such a degree of advertising power that competition is eliminated and market shares are concentrated within a limited number of firms in the industry. The U.S. Supreme Court, arguing from this point of view, ordered the Procter & Gamble Company to divest itself of the Clorox Company on the grounds that Clorox had gained an unfair advantage over competitors. The FTC has since followed this same line of reasoning in several other cases.

If advertising truly reduces competition in this manner, as contended, then there should be high levels of advertising in those industries in which leading firms have a large share of the market, and vice versa. While this is true in some industries (soaps, cigarettes, and others) it is untrue in others such as drugs and cosmetics.[18] Furthermore, advertising power alone does not ensure permanence of market share; in fact only 13 of 50 industries had the same top four companies in both 1947 and 1958.[19]

Insofar as the second argument is concerned, the following is a typical statement from those who contend that high level of advertising expenditure creates a barrier which prevents the entry of new firms into the market:

. . . the second most disturbing feature of advertising . . . lies in the area of monopoly power it has placed in the hands of the most substantial spenders (that is, investors in advertising). The national advertising outlay is not evenly divided among contenders for customers. It bulks with a very heavy weight at the top. It appears difficult, if not impossible, today to launch a new brand of food or drug without the outlay of as much as $10 million. If this is true, then what we face is a fantastic tax upon freedom of market entry.[20]

It is futile to deny that the heavy marketing investment necessary to survive in most markets today is a deterrent to entry. Moreover, existing firms have built brand loyalty, which prevents newcomers from finding an easy foothold. Once again, however, advertising is assigned a burden which it does not bear alone. Large capital outlays, investment in inventories, the establishment of distributive networks, and other components of successful marketing all are deterrents to entry. In fact, high concentration in many industries developed *without* advertising. Perhaps it is more realistic to state that the requirements of a large scale of operation are the fundamental deterrent to entry, and advertising is only one manifestation.[21]

If advertising does create barriers to entry, this should be demonstrated by a correlation between levels of advertising and profit rates. The evidence on this point is mixed. The strongest negative evidence comes from

---

[18] Telser, "Aspects of Economics of Advertising," p. 169.

[19] Backman, *Advertising and Competition,* p. 113.

[20] Warne, "Advertising: A Critics View," p. 12.

[21] Backman, *Advertising and Competition,* p. 79.

the food industry, where it was found that profits are highest among the heaviest advertisers.[22] This was not found in an analysis of the 100 leading advertisers, however.[23]

Even if advertising does help to contribute to entry barriers, this does not necessarily imply absence of competition within the industry. As Jules Backman points out: "That competition is both vigorous and intensive among companies already in the market is clearly apparent from the marked increases in the number of products available and the significant changes that continue to take place in the market shares in most industries."[24]

To sum up, available evidence does not support the case of either the advocate or the critic of the influence of advertising on market structure. There is undoubtedly a complex of other causative factors, of which mass promotion is only one.

The Validity of the Fundamental Premises

It is difficult indeed to make a strong case for large-scale advertising and selling using the traditional arguments. The case has not been conclusively disproved by its critics, but neither has it been proved by its advocates.

However, consider the implications of a successful challenge of the two fundamental tenets stated above, that a high and rising standard of living is a valid social goal and that profit is an accurate measure of business performance. The effects of the three basic functions of promotion could become almost irrelevant, because the foundation of the case would have been removed. This section, which questions the validity of these premises, therefore deserves careful consideration.

Is a High and Rising Standard of Living a Valid Social Goal? The basic premise contends that society should work toward the goal of a continually higher standard of living. William Lazer, for example, asks:

In our society, is it not desirable to urge consumers to acquire additional material objects? Cannot the extension of consumer wants and needs be a great force for improvement and for increasing societal awareness and social contributions? Is it not part of marketing's social responsibility to help stimulate the desire to improve the quality of life—particularly the economic quality—and so serve the public interest?[25]

This premise is the target of a formidable challenge. In part it comes from the fact that the world has awakened to the fact that its basic re-

---

[22] *Advertising Age,* May 11, 1970, p. 1 ff.

[23] Backman, *Advertising and Competition,* p. 154.

[24] Ibid., p. 8.

[25] William Lazer, "Marketing's Changing Social Relationships," *Journal of Marketing,* Vol. 33 (January 1969), p. 6.

sources are not inexhaustible.[26] The energy crisis is just one manifestation. Continued unrestrained striving for economic growth can, within a very few years, drain the world of its irreplaceable resources. D. H. Meadows et al. use the analogy of a pond which contains a crop of lilies that doubles in quantity every two days and will totally consume the pond and cause it to die in 30 days.[27] On the 29th day, the pond will only be half covered, but there is just one day remaining to prevent disaster. In their opinion, the world is now approaching or at the 29th day.[28]

The prospects are frightening indeed, but warnings that were given much earlier were ignored. Consider the farewell address of President Dwight D. Eisenhower, for example:

As we peer into society's future, we—you and I, and our government—must avoid the impulse to live only for the day, plundering, for our own ease and convenience, the precious resources of tomorrow. We cannot mortgage the material assets of our grandchildren without risking the loss also of their political and spiritual heritage. We want democracy to survive for all generations to come, not to become the insolvent phantom of tomorrow.[29]

Western societies, the United States in particular, have proceeded as if air, water, minerals, and other resources were free goods that could be used without restriction. Ownership of these resources has been viewed as a common property right to be used by all, with the costs to be borne by society as a whole. W. C. Engs urges that we regard our planet as a closed system with limits on growth and make our economic principles compatible with these concepts.[30] It is time, he argues, to call a halt to shifting the costs of unlimited growth and technological progress to the public and to make these costs internal to the responsible firms. If accepted, this proposal would greatly increase the operating costs of business organizations which, up to this point, have viewed basic resources as being free. It would also provide a powerful incentive for conservation and restraint.

A second type of challenge may, in the final analysis, be more devastating. This challenge comes from the careful student of history. There is no convincing historical precedent that an increase in standard of

---

[26] D. H. Meadows, et al., *The Limit to Growth* (New York: Universal Books, 1972).

[27] Ibid.

[28] It should be noted that there is strong disagreement with many of the predictions of Meadows, et al. See for example Carl Kaysen, "The Computer That Printed Out W*O*L*F," *Foreign Affairs*, July 1972, and Rudolf Klein, "Growth and Its Enemies," *Commentary*, June 1972.

[29] Dwight D. Eisenhower, "Farewell Radio and Television Address to the American People," January 17, 1961, in Wish and Gamble (eds.), *Marketing and Social Issues*, pp. 175–77.

[30] W. C. Engs, "Needed: New Rules for Industrial Managers," in Wish and Gamble (eds.), *Marketing and Social Issues*, pp. 228–32.

living means true social progress in any basic sense. Quite to the contrary, a generalized quest for personal wealth and economic attainment often has been symptomatic of a society in the last stages of decay. Consider the observations of Will and Ariel Durant:

Caught in the relaxing interval between one moral code and the next, an unmoored generation surrenders itself to luxury, corruption, and a restless disorder of family and morals, in all but a remnant clinging desperately to old restraints and ways. Few souls feel any longer that "it is beautiful and honorable to die for one's country." A failure of leadership may allow a state to weaken itself with internal strife. At the end of the process a decisive defeat in war may bring a final blow, or barbarian invasion from without may combine with barbarism welling up from within to bring the civilization to a close.[31]

It may well be that present-day Western societies mirror ancient Rome's free-living days before its ultimate fall that was generated by decay from within. As materialism and economic achievement were carried to extremes they contributed, along with other factors, to the eventual collapse of one of the most advanced civilizations to date.

Opinion polls are reflecting growing public doubts about the materialistic course of free enterprise societies. The young, in particular, are expressing great concern over the by-products of a rising gross national product.[32] It would not be fair to assign undue blame to the business system, but a grave challenge is imposed. In the final analysis it could well be that *promotion is only accentuating the very forces which are bringing our civilization to its knees.* In light of this very real possibility, Lazer's assertions about the social desirability of increased and unrestrained materialism seem incredibly naive at the very least, and perhaps even destructive if they are taken seriously.

What is the ultimate answer? No one can say at this point, and the issues are presented here with their full implications so that the reader can be a part of a responsible national consensus which must emerge.

Is Profit a Valid Measure of Business Responsibility?   It has traditionally been held that profits are an objective measure of the social values of ideas and that the national consensus is found in market performance.[33] In other words, motivation to attain a long-run profit results in service to society because profit will not result unless buyer needs and desires are served in a satisfactory manner. If this contention is true, profit will be the reward of the firm that has been most successful in following the marketing concept which embodies at its heart adaptation to the desires of the consumer.

---

[31] Will and Ariel Durant, *The Lessons of History* (New York: Simon & Schuster, 1968), p. 93. Reproduced with special permission.

[32] See the evidence cited in Chapter 5.

[33] Joel Dean, *Managerial Economics* (Englewood Cliffs, N.J.: Prentice-Hall, 1951), p. 10.

For most of the period since World War II, there has been some validity to this point of view because on the whole the firms that have been most successful have been those with the most responsive marketing programs. *Assuming a high and rising standard of living to be valid,* the consumer has been served materially by the firm which continually strives to gain a competitive edge through marketing innovation. It was quite acceptable in 1960 to allege that "A manager can say he is putting 'fairness' or 'the good of society' ahead of profits, but the suspicion arises that he is merely escaping from accountability into the realm where there are no checks on his power."[34]

The 1970s, however, have seen a shift away from an economy of excess supply over demand to an economy of scarcity. In the former environment, the business firm had little choice from a monetary perspective but to adapt to the consumer in order to achieve competitive gain. In an economy of scarcity, such a motivation is no longer necessary. At this writing trade press accounts read as follows: "Steel firms avoiding structural steel needed in construction and say profit is insufficient"; "newsprint scarcity looms as paper industry says it is no longer profitable"; "cutback in flight service causes ticket lines to burgeon as service deteriorates." In essence, companies in all industries characterized by an excess of demand over supply are shifting their resources to their most profitable products, *regardless of consumer desires.*

What has happened to the marketing concept? The truth is that the marketing concept and profit motivation are likely to be compatible *only* under circumstances in which there is an excess of supply over demand. There now is ample evidence of this point, for the first time on such a wide scale since World War II. As one business statesman points out:

. . . we are failing as marketing institutions . . . we are failing to recognize that the purpose of every institution is to meet the needs of its customers. Instead, we increasingly place our primary emphasis upon internal activities, upon the utilization of our resources, upon being properly organized, on doing many things that are not designed to improve our position with the public, with our customers and potential customers, and to do so profitably.[35]

Kenneth Boulding is quite correct when he observes that there is a marked distinction between the profit system as an organizer of economic life and the profit motive in the "bad" sense of unadulterated lust for selfish gain.[36] Many now agree that the profit system functions success-

---

[34] "Have Corporations a Higher Duty Than Profits?" *Fortune,* August 1960, p. 108 ff.

[35] H. M. Williams, "Why and How We Are Losing the Free Enterprise Battle." *Advertising Age,* November 26, 1972, p. 34.

[36] Kenneth Boulding, "Ethics and Business: An Economists' View," in Wish and Gamble, (eds.), *Marketing and Social Issues,* pp. 91–97.

fully only if the profit motive is tempered by altruism or by a sense of public responsibility and identification with the individual in a larger community.[37] In the final analysis, profit must be defined to encompass more than mere financial attainment. Without such a broadened conception, business practices may be considered justifiable which, from the perspective of history, might be counter to the public interest. In reality, the premise underlying profit orientation is that business must be *accountable* for its performance—accountable to owners and stockholders in the traditional financial sense but also to consumers and to society at large.

In an economy of scarcity, profit in the sense of narrow financial gain is a highly fallible measure of service to the consumer and to society. It is high time that this fact is recognized and a halt is called to the traditional defense of profit. To maintain this defense in a changed environment can only result in hypocrisy.

THE DILEMMA OF A SYSTEM IN CRISIS

It should be apparent that the conventional wisdom regarding the economic and social role of promotion is open to real challenge. The most serious challenge, of course, comes from growing recognition that continued striving for economic growth will only hasten the end of our way of life. What is the role of advertising under these conditions? There are few, if any, answers to be found in the conventional wisdom. A variety of solutions have been proposed, ranging from radical social change to more moderate means to make the present system work.

Is Social Revolution Necessary?

An increasing number of voices are uniting to advocate some sort of radical change in the free enterprise system. All involve some form of constraint on traditional economic forces motivated by profit.

John K. Galbraith, for example, has long been concerned with the viability of an economic system that operates with unrestrained self-interest.[38] His writings have evolved over the years, and he now advocates an equalization of power between planning and marketing systems.[39] He calls for a freeze of prices, costs, and incomes. The wealthier members of

---

[37] See for example Williams, "Free Enterprise Battle," and Engs, "New Rules for Managers."

[38] In his earlier writing, Galbraith contended that advertising does nothing more than build a system that cannot meet its basic survival needs. See John K. Galbraith, *The Affluent Society* (Boston: Houghton Mifflin Co., 1958).

[39] John K. Galbraith, *Economics and the Public Purpose* (New York: Houghton Mifflin Co., 1973).

the "technostructure," for example, would not be permitted to grow more affluent, and the gains from economic productivity would go largely to increasing the incomes of poorer segments of the population. Profit motivation as well as individual materialistic acquisition thus would be sharply curbed in the interests of restoring a balance of power between the various economic groups and entities. Presumably greater income equality and a better quality of life would evolve.

Those of a Marxist persuasion will go well beyond the relatively mild proposals of Galbraith and others. They see profit as the major factor underlying the excesses of materialistic striving. Various solutions are advocated to remove the profit motive through drastically increased governmental intervention. The end result is to place ownership of the factors of production (land, labor, capital, and management) in the hands of the "people" (under governmental control) and to provide for central direction of the allocation of economic resources. There would be only a small role, at best, for demand-stimulating functions. When the incentive for personal selfishness is thus removed, over time there should be a growing change within people. A true Marxist envisions an end-point utopia characterized by real love between people, equality, and peace. If revolution is necessary to achieve this end, the means are justified.

There is some undeniable appeal to these proposals, especially given the excesses and abuses discussed above. Yet, it is necessary to consider some basic premises of this viewpoint. Would man and his materialistic striving change if the economic and social environment is radically changed? There is an all-important yet unexpressed assumption that man enters the world with no inherent predisposition to become self-centered and hence materialistic, and these strivings are shaped by the environment in which he lives.[40] If this premise about the nature of man indeed is true, then the logical solution lies in changing the environment through radical reform if necessary. Man himself then will change, and a more utopian world can be achieved.

There is, however, a diametrically opposed view of the nature of man which would lead to quite a different conclusion as to the most appropriate course of action to be taken in order to achieve social change. After a lifetime study of history, the Durants conclude that:

. . . the first biological lesson of history is that life is competition. Competition is not only the life of trade, it is the trade of life—peaceful when food abounds, violent when the mouths outrun the food. . . . we are acquisitive, greedy, and pugnacious because our blood remembers millenniums through which our fore-

---

[40] This is the widely accepted point of view articulated most convincingly by B. F. Skinner. See *Beyond Freedom and Dignity* (New York: Alfred A. Knopf, 1971).

bearers had to chase and fight and kill in order to survive, and had to eat their gastric capacity for fear they should not soon capture another feast.[41]

They go on to point out that this basic nature of man does not change: "nothing is clearer in history than the adoption by successful rebels of the methods they were accustomed to condemn in the forces they deposed."[42]

According to this view man is constrained by human nature to live a self-centered life, according to the dictates of his ego. Thus excessive materialism, war, moral decay, and so on are *symptoms of a problem inherent within man himself,* with the result that a change in the environment would not strike at the heart of the problem. This is also the Judeo-Christian view, which proceeds from the premise that man is incomplete within himself, that he is a sinner and cannot bring about fundamental internal change apart from a faith in a personal God and total commitment of one's life to Him. Thus man is urged

. . . as an act of intelligent worship, to give God your bodies, as a living sacrifice, consecrated to Him and acceptable by Him. Don't let the world around you squeeze you into its own mould, but let God re-mould your minds from within, so that you may prove in practice that the plan of God for you is good, meets all His demands and moves towards the goal of true maturity.[43]

Each individual must decide for himself which point of view he adopts. A look at history, however, provides some interesting insights. If the first hypothesis is true about the nature of man, then it should be possible to point to historical examples where environmental changes brought about the desired result. Perhaps the best starting point is with Communist Russia, because it is the country where socialism has been adopted longest with the goal of achieving the utopian state envisioned by Karl Marx. Yet Russia has been forced to institute profit as the basic business incentive, as well as advertising, branding, and other forms of mass marketing.[44] The basic reason for these drastic changes in policy is that per capita wealth has risen to the point that Russian consumers now can afford more of the luxuries of life and hence are demanding that these desires be met. The economic system, in turn, has been unable to adapt without a consumer orientation similar to that evident under capitalism. In Russia, it appears, a *striving for material achievement has not been removed by a radical change in the economic system.*

The Durants, proceeding from their premise about the acquisitive and

[41] Durant and Durant, *Lessons of History,* p. 19.

[42] Ibid., p. 34.

[43] *The New Testament in Modern English,* trans. by J. B. Phillips (New York: Macmillan Co., 1960). The passage here is Romans 12:1–2.

[44] See L. E. Ostlund, "A New Concept," *Journal of Advertising Research,* Vol. 13 (1973), pp. 11–20. Also see Goldman, "Product Differentiation and Advertising."

competitive nature of man, have concluded that profit is an inevitable necessity:

The experience of the past leaves little doubt that every economic system must sooner or later rely upon some form of the profit motive to stir individuals and groups to productivity. Substitutes like slavery, police supervision, or ideological enthusiasm prove too unproductive, too expensive, or too transient. Normally and generally men are judged by their ability to produce—except in war, when they are ranked according to their ability to destroy.[45]

If the Judeo-Christian view is true, then the changes must come from within man himself as a result of the exercise of his volition, *not* from changes in the environment. How such a change takes place, of course, raises spiritual questions which are beyond the scope of this book.[46] A real dilemma thus faces the individual. Each reader must decide the issue for himself as he takes his place in a complex world.

Can the Present System be Made to Work?

The authors do not believe that radical social reform is necessary, for we feel that the system can be made to work. We agree with Boulding when he says that there is nothing inherent in the profit system per se which requires a narrow selfishness and lack of identification with the broader concerns of mankind.[47] The key is to adopt a proper attitude with respect to social and ethical responsibility.

Social responsibility is less demanding in that it embodies accepting an obligation for the proper functioning of the society in which a firm exists. It involves accountability for those activities through which the firm can reasonably be expected to contribute to the society. Often it requires little more than obedience to existing laws and norms.

More is required than social responsibility, however, as one businessman colorfully points out:

If the law as written gives a man a wide-open chance to make a killing, he'd be a fool not to take advantage of it. If he doesn't somebody else will. There is no obligation on him to stop and consider who is going to get hurt. If the law says he can do it, that's all the justification he needs. There is nothing unethical about that. It's just plain business sense.[48]

In this context, a produce manager in a supermarket who gets rid of a lot of half-rotten tomatoes by including one with its good side exposed in every pack is doing nothing socially improper. After all, it *is* legal.

---

[45] Durant and Durant, *Lessons of History*, pp. 54–55.

[46] See for example Elton Trueblood, *A Place to Stand* (New York: Harper & Row, 1969).

[47] Boulding, "Ethics and Business."

[48] A. C. Carr, "Is Business Loving Ethical?" in Wish and Gamble, (eds.), *Marketing and Social Issues*, p. 107.

This kind of short-sightedness cannot contend with the current critical challenges to our way of life. Whether he likes it or not, the businessman must also wrestle with *ethical responsibility*—determination of *how* things should be, pursuit of the right course of action, and doing what is morally right.[49] This responsibility requires a finely developed sense of values which provides a real code for behavior. It must be assumed that one choice is better than others when many options are available. The major perplexity is to develop a value system so that the best choice is made, given the complex of influences on management today.

ORGANIZATIONAL RESPONSE TO A CHANGED ENVIRONMENT

The pressures on today's manager are multifaceted. Decisions must be made which satisfy not only traditional monetary profit criteria but also the pressures from consumers, labor, government, and a host of other sources. Old rules are obsolete; times have changed. The question is no longer whether changes *will* occur in business practice but rather *how these changes will occur and what form they will take.* Those who long for an earlier more comfortable era and cling to "business as usual" have no place in today's world.

Appropriate response must be forthcoming from the organization itself in terms of the design and implementation of its mission, from multiple organizations in cooperative programs, and from the individual manager who, in the final analysis, holds the key to adaptation to the changed environment. The unresolved question is whether *voluntarism* can bring about the necessary adaptation or whether broader roles must be assumed by government. There will probably be a new meeting ground between both forces, and it is hoped that it will not be necessary to substitute governmental regulation to compel behavior which should be forthcoming from a proper attitude of social and ethical responsibility.

The Organizational Mission

It has traditionally been assumed that profits are an objective measure of the contribution of a business organization to society. The shortcomings of this point of view were explored above. Profit is just one form of *accountability;* as Peter Drucker points out, all institutions must now hold themselves accountable for the quality of life and must make fulfillment of basic social values, beliefs, and purposes a major objective of their normal activities.[50]

---

[49] James F. Engel, David T. Kollat, and Roger D. Blackwell, *Consumer Behavior,* rev. ed. (New York: Holt, Rinehart & Winston, 1973), p. 618.

[50] Peter F. Drucker, "Management's New Role," in Wish and Gamble (eds.), *Marketing and Social Issues,* pp. 24–28.

Financial Accountability. Frequently the financially successful firm is viewed as suspect, especially if it has gained at the expense of its competitors. It must be recognized, however, that buyer desires for new and improved products are met through competition, and firms cannot compete without some emerging as victorious and others suffering losses. Moreover, it is often overlooked that successful businesses are managed to enhance the long-run survival of the organization. The firm, especially if it is incorporated, outlives any individual set of managers, and successful management must of necessity be oriented toward survival on a money-making basis. It cannot afford to extract a momentary gain from shoddy merchandise, because reliance must be placed on repeat sales. Repeat sales, in turn, will not be made to dissatisfied customers, so the firm is forced to serve the customer's interests.

Accountability to Consumers. A "Guide to Consumerism" stipulates that the consumer is entitled to "(1) Protection against clear-cut abuses . . . (2) provision for adequate information . . . (3) protection . . . against themselves and other consumers."[51] Consumerism has arisen because management has been guilty of *one-way communication with the buyer; it is not listening to what is being said in reply.* Of course, most firms give lip service to the marketing concept, but does it really pervade their corporate missions? A survey of 250 leading corporate executives revealed that over two thirds of them are having difficulties with consumer activists, but the vast majority feel that the cause is *failure of business to publicize its good side!* And nearly 80 percent evidenced a belief that the current negative attitude toward business is not justified.[52]

It is difficult to sympathize with the kind of shortsighted management that cannot grasp the true causes of consumerism. The fact is that business is falling short of a consumer orientation. No amount of publicity will correct this situation. If service to the consumer is not a part of the organizational mission, a commitment backed up by action, then there is little hope that voluntarism will work. Government must step in to compel the firms to ensure the legitimate rights of the buyer.

Accountability to Society as a Whole. "It is increasingly recognized that business must divert some of its profits to help solve social problems or it may face upheavals as serious as those which have swept the college campus." These are the sentiments of the president of Hunt-Wesson Foods, in a speech made to an industry group[53] Hunt-Wesson is acting on these convictions in many ways, such as improved medical care fa-

---

[51] G. S. Day and D. A. Aaker, "A Guide to Consumerism," *Journal of Marketing,* Vol. 17 (1970), pp. 12–19.

[52] *The Gallagher Report,* Vol. 20 (November 20, 1972).

[53] Quoted in *Advertising Age,* February 23, 1970, p. 191.

cilities in the ghetto. It is only one of a number of companies that recognize a broader responsibility, beyond that of financial returns to stockholders. Indeed, survival, the basic goal of any business enterprise, may demand expenditures and efforts directed to basic social problems.

While some businesses have taken accountability to society quite seriously, others have ignored this responsibility. The following quotation from William Geissman, manager of technical services at the National Lock Company in Rockford, Illinois, is not unusual: "Taking care of water pollution is money down the drain. It adds nothing to the product, and about all you get out of it is a little goodwill in the town . . . They also know they can't put us out of business because 3,000 people depend on us for a living . . . we're trying to hold back as long as we can hoping to find a more economical way."[54] Such a statement is totally reprehensible in that it reflects a lack of concern about basic survival issues. Fortunately the mood of the public is now such that firms operating under this type of philosophy will be forced through various forms of pressure to change. Hopefully the days of such calloused management are drawing to an end.

It is obvious from this discussion that profit, in the narrow sense of financial return, can no longer be a complete measure of the contribution of a firm to society. Accountability, on the other hand, is a more realistic criterion, because it encompasses financial return as well as contributions to broader social issues. As this point is recognized and acted upon responsibly by management, there is reason to hope that many of the most flagrant abuses will be corrected and steps taken toward solution of unresolved social problems.

Phasing Accountability into Strategy. Most organizations now assign reward to individual managers on the basis of sales performance, regardless of how much publicity they give to social responsibility. As H. M. Williams notes:

Such an environment does not encourage any activity that does not maximize current profits. Nor does it recognize or penalize shoddy but temporarily profitable marketing and advertising practices. We do not make, nor in many cases do we know how to make or desire to make, estimates of the non-quantifiable or of the social and political implications of achieving plans.[55]

This is accentuated in the product form of organization, which decentralizes corporate and divisional responsibilities.[56] Social concerns tend to be centralized at the headquarters level but do not find their way to those levels at which decisions really are made and implemented. The

---

[54] Quoted in *Business Week*, October 14, 1969, p. 120.

[55] Williams, "Free Enterprise Battle," p. 34.

[56] R. W. Ackerman, "How Companies Respond to Social Demands," *Harvard Business Review*, Vol. 51 (1973), pp. 88–99.

solution is for top management to initiate appropriate social and ethical considerations, to make compliance a part of the reward and punishment system, and to provide staff help in implementation at decentralized levels.

There also is real value in a periodic social audit.[57] At the moment, only 14 percent of the major firms have instituted such a measure.[58] Most of these have an executive officer who is responsible for overseeing such actions as response to consumer complaints and supervision of various social action programs.

Cooperative Efforts

Because social and ethical responsibilities will never be met completely by individual organizations, a need exists for cooperative efforts. Certainly as a very minimum an industry should provide a means for curbing false advertising as well as practices which are deceptive or unethical. Unfortunately there are numerous codes of practice that represent nothing more than unenforced platitudes. Such superficial efforts, often undertaken to keep government at bay, do more harm than good in the final analysis, because they are nothing more than a band-aid placed over an open wound.

It is sometimes said that it goes against the grain of free enterprise to make cooperative codes of ethics compulsory, and to an extent we must agree. Nonetheless, it must not be overlooked that the mass media are intended for public use and are not the sole province of the advertiser. Government can present a convincing case for expanded activity to protect the public interest if self-regulation does not suffice. As never before, the advertising industry is faced with a challenge in this respect which cannot be ignored.

Cooperative efforts have taken the following forms: (1) Better Business bureaus, (2) policing by advertising media, (3) cooperative improvement efforts, and (4) public service.

Better Business Bureaus. Local Better Business organizations are sponsored by business firms to eliminate unfair methods of competition. They work with the national Better Business Bureau, which, among other things, publishes *Do's and Don'ts in Advertising Copy* to help advertisers steer clear of legal and ethical hurdles.

Individual customers or business firms initiate complaints to Better Business Bureau offices, and the action taken varies from publicity to

---

[57] R. A. Bauer and D. H. Fenn, Jr., "What *Is* a Corporate Social Audit?" *Harvard Business Review,* Vol. 51 (1973), pp. 37–48.

[58] *The Gallagher Report,* Vol. 20 (November 20, 1972).

legal action. The volume of advertisements and sales claims investigated each year is said to substantially exceed that processed by governmental enforcement agencies.

Policing by Advertising Media. The media also have taken some positive steps in the form of industry self-regulation. Magazines and newspapers frequently turn down advertising which in their opinion violates good taste or is deceptive in its claims. Examples are the *New Yorker's* refusal to accept certain types of lingerie advertisements and the rejection by the *Milwaukee Journal* of a lucrative space purchase from Hadacol even before the product was banned from further sale.

Most of the larger television and radio stations belong to the National Association of Broadcasters (NAB). The NAB issues a seal of approval to stations subscribing to the NAB Code of Good Practice. This code is fairly rigorous in its provisions; it bans, for example, payoffs, rigged quiz shows, and deception regarding product characteristics. This is not to say that all areas of public responsibility are comprehended in this code. There have been numerous attempts to establish the NAB as a more definitive voice within the industry, and support for such an action may be growing.

Cooperative Improvement Efforts. Industry associations of various types attempt to induce their members to adhere to ethical codes. The Proprietary Drug Association of America, for instance, enforces a code of ethics for its members, who handle over 80 percent of all packaged medicines sold in the United States. Similarly, the Toilet Goods Association operates a board of standards to which members submit advertising copy. The board ensures that the copy is consistent with provisions of the Food, Drug, and Cosmetic Act and other legislation.

One encouraging cooperative effort is the National Advertising Review Board (NARB) sponsored by the Council of Better Business Bureaus and other organizations. Its membership is composed of leaders from the advertising industry and representatives from the public. The mandate is to screen advertising and to cite those that deviate from reasonable standards of truth and good taste.

The council's national advertising division receives and evaluates complaints against advertising. If an agreement cannot be reached, reference is made to the NARB for study by a panel. In its first year the NARB had 20 complaints referred to it, and of the first 18 decisions handed down, half were decided against the advertiser. There is no legal sanction to these decisions, but the weight of adverse publicity can serve as a powerful corrective force.

Some have contended that NARB efforts have been too few and that its machinery grinds too slowly. There may be merit to this criticism, but hasty judgments also would be unwise. Further assessment of the NARB record must await longer service.

Industry Public Service.   Some members of the business community have long been sensitive to their role in serving the public sector of the economy. The War Advertising Council was the first formal manifestation of this awareness; it was set up during World War II under the sponsorship of advertisers, agencies, media, and trade associations. The primary purpose was to stimulate the sale of War Bonds, and this objective plus others was given a real assist by the industry. This organization was later superceded by the Advertising Council.

The variety of public causes given support by the Advertising Council is impressive. Among the better known organizations and social issues given backing are: (1) aid to higher education, (2) the American Red Cross, (3) United Community appeals, (4) the Radio Free Europe Fund, (5) the Youth Fitness program, and (6) the Smokey the Bear campaign to stamp out forest fires. Costs are underwritten by advertisers, media, and agencies, for the council has only 50 full-time employees.

Further Cooperative Efforts.   There are many additional unmet needs which require cooperative efforts, one of the most crucial being research directed toward a greater understanding of the process of promotion. The barriers of limited information which hinder the effective management of advertising and promotion have been noted throughout this book. Steps have been taken in recent years to dispel these barriers, but they are only a beginning. Basic research is needed into all phases of promotional decisions. Because the pressures of day-to-day management virtually preclude the necessary research efforts by individual firms, a cooperative industry research program is required.

In addition, industry can continue to meet its obligations through expansion of its activities on behalf of public causes. The tools of mass communication are ideally adapted to stimulating public awareness of unmet needs, and the Advertising Council has done excellent work in this respect.

Finally, industry codes of ethics must become more than just platitudes stated for public consumption. Unless real enforcement provisions are established, little purpose is served. If business is serious about cleaning its own house, it must do so through incisive action.

The Individual Manager

If the spirit of social and ethical responsibility discussed here is to be made operative, a commitment to this end is required of individual managers. This commitment, however, often requires a type of personal courage and sacrifice that many are not prepared to give because too many obstacles must be faced.

A 1973 study by the American Management Association found that a majority of the almost 3,000 executives questioned felt under pressure to compromise personal standards to meet company goals.[59] Pressures for profitable performance have been markedly stepped up rather than abated. It is small wonder that 85 percent of all managers face a deep personal conflict when they discover that their youthful ideals and goals run counter to business operations that seem to be low on principle and high on expediency.[60] This conflict is most severe between the ages of 34 and 42, and it often is manifested by unwillingness to take on new problems and a desire to minimize the total demands of a job on one's life.

What is the individual to do when he finds his own personal goals are in conflict with organizational expectations? Researchers at the California Institute of Technology gave this advice: "take a tranquilizer, conform to the system, and realize that there are problems beyond your ability to solve."[61] In other words, cop out and conform. This is also the advice of an executive who noted the contradictions he faced but concluded that it is necessary to "play by the rules of the game" if one is to accumulate much money or power.[62]

Are increased salary and advancement really worth that sacrifice? More and more are answering a resounding no to that question and dropping out of the system rather than compromising their convictions. This is sometimes a necessary action, but the end result if all who are similarly in conflict drop out could be disastrous.

Obviously, ethical concerns can no longer be swept under the rug; they must be acted on if a way of life is to survive. This demands people who *dare to be different*—who are willing to seek solutions and act upon their convictions regardless of personal cost. When such a spirit of innovation is absent, there is little basis for optimism about the survival of a way of life whose vitality stems from the exercise of individual initiative.

There are increasing examples of managers who indeed are daring to be different. Creative people in advertising agencies are demanding factual backup of advertising claims from their clients. Younger managers are not hesitating to voice their dissatisfaction with insulting advertising. Executives at all levels are refusing to give in when forced to behave illegally or unethically. The authors are personally familiar with a number who have successfully taken their stands. Others, unfortunately, have taken their stands and paid the price of dismissal, but their personal integrity remains intact.

It must be assumed that each individual has arrived at a workable code of ethics. Some see no problem with subtle deception and other

---

[59] *Business Week*, September 15, 1973, p. 178.
[60] *Sales Management*, May 1, 1969, p. 20.
[61] Ibid.
[62] Carr, "Is Business Loving Ethical?"

forms of legal but basically immoral business behavior. This speaks volumes about the content of their ethical codes. Far too many conclude that they will do what is necessary for themselves, regardless of the consequences, as long as they do not get caught. This is not the kind of ethical code which will make a real difference in today's world.

Ultimately everyone must come to grip with the eternal question of whether or not there are standards of truth which can govern behavior. Some say no—that truth is illusive and behavior should be based on the whims of the moment. Others place their roots deeply in religious conviction and guide their lives accordingly. Is religion out of place in the business firm? Some may say yes, but others are coming to a commitment that real ethics and morality pervade *all of life,* including life on the job.

Those who have found themselves—who have a workable philosophy of life—have a place to stand from which they can dare to be different. Those who have not come to this point have little choice but to cave in when the pressures become great.

Will Voluntary Self-Regulation Work?

The issue of voluntarism versus governmental control which was raised at the outset of this section must be addressed again. Hopefully, business people, individually and collectively, will be able to meet the challenges of today without intervention by government. Quite honestly, the authors join those who express their doubts. Over half of 1,000 advertising executives indicated that they do not feel the industry can effectively regulate itself.[63] Few advocated more governmental restriction, but they seemed to be without any suggestions for necessary change.

All that need be said in conclusion is that the pressures for sweeping change will not abate. If the industry does not respond, it has only itself to blame when government steps in.

CONCLUSION: A PERSONAL NOTE

The authors have worked closely together now through three editions of this book. Our backgrounds are quite different, as well as our styles of life. We are united, however, in expressing our deep concern about the survival of a way of life. We have not hesitated in this edition to speak out against practices we do not find defensible. We feel that the examples of business hypocrisy cited here are deplorable, but we also recognize that there are many instances of responsible behavior. However, we do not see the progress necessary to reverse the forces that are undoing the very fibers of Western society.

---

[63] *The Gallagher Report,* Vol. 20 (June 5, 1972).

More than ever before, this has been a difficult book to write. Quite honestly, we fear that it could be utilized in the business world in such a manner that today's shortcomings are only perpetuated. If that is the result, we have failed in our obligation.

Let it be clearly stated that we are diametrically opposed to a "business as usual" attitude. We feel that consumerist pressures are completely warranted and that their very existence reflects a failure to implement the marketing concept which is so piously mouthed in public statements. We condemn those forms of management that ignore legitimate pressures for social and ethical responsibility.

Our concluding wish, indeed our prayer, for the reader is that he or she realistically wrestle with the issues raised here. Take consumer orientation seriously. Recognize the role for business which now transcends narrow financial profitability. Find your own operative value system which will enable you to have a place to stand and dare to be different.

SUMMARY

This chapter has been devoted to a critical analysis of the economic and social role of promotion. The criticisms of this economic activity are far-reaching, and the pros and cons were discussed in terms of their effects on prices, competition, consumer choice, and standards of living.

For the most part, the claimed social benefits of promotion are based on the premise that a high and rising standard of living is valid. Once this premise is disavowed, the issues become more sharply focused, because the materialistic society of today's Western world may be sowing the seeds of its own destruction. It was pointed out, however, that the economic system is merely a reflection of the basic motivations of its members, and the ultimate solution lies outside of business itself.

Nevertheless, there is much that can be done through a philosophy of business management which stresses financial accountability to owners and stockholders as well as accountability to consumers and to society as a whole. Some suggestions were given which centered around the corporate mission, collective activities, and the role of the individual manager.

REVIEW AND DISCUSSION QUESTIONS

1. Many critics of marketing claim that advertising creates impediments to workable price competition. The premise is that greater price competition would enhance consumer welfare. Do you agree?

2. Is the absence of price competition a sign that a business firm has established a monopolistic position?

3. Can the blame for development of economic concentration within a few firms in an industry be attributed to advertising? Why, or why not?

4. In the early 1960s a detergent in tablet form, Vim, was introduced for a short period and then removed from the market because of unsatisfactory sales. Assume that the company could come into posession of unlimited financial resources. Could increased advertising expenditures have saved this product?

5. A well-known student of consumer affairs made the following statement to a group of home economists at a national meeting: "One of the greatest problems consumers face is lack of adequate information in making a purchase decision. They lack the know-how to be rational buyers, and business is not about to do anything to help them. The only hope is for government and other agencies to step in and give the consumer the information she needs." Comment.

6. Are the mass media, in your opinion, influenced by advertisers to present editorial content compatible with vested interests? If so, what suggestions can you make for change?

7. William Lazer has argued that marketing should work toward the end of helping the consumer to accept self-indulgence, luxurious surroundings, and nonutilitarian products. Do you agree?

8. Many proposals are advanced to reform the practice of advertising. Some have as their intent the elimination or reduction of the volume of advertising and hence a reduction of the socially detrimental effects of undue materialism. In your opinion, will this type of reform be a meaningful step in solving the basic underlying problems?

9. What is consumerism? What are some of the ways that business can adapt meaningfully to the pressures being generated?

10. The president of Hunt-Wesson Foods proposes that business must divert some of its profits to help solve social problems. However, this may serve to reduce the financial rewards to stockholders, thus giving rise to what might become a conflict of interest. Can this conflict be resolved?

11. In what sense are many criticisms of promotion really a criticism of poor management?

12. Congress has enacted into law safety standards for automobiles. Should this legislation have been necessary, or can cooperative industry efforts suffice for such purposes?

Appendix

Designing and Producing the Mass Communication Message

INTRODUCTION

THIS SECTION is written for those who are charged with the responsibility for doing the creative work required for the production of a variety of mass communication messages. It is for practitioners and students who have to put together the various components of the creative mix and eventually have to look at the messages and say yes or no.

There are several objectives for this appendix. First, it is the intention of the authors to bring together various types of production treatments from a number of sources. Second, sets of operational guidelines have been outlined at numerous points to suggest techniques, procedures, or methods for managing the creative aspects of advertising messages. They should not be considered as rules made for the obedience of fools but rather as suggestions for the guidance of men of wisdom in the advertising business.

The language of advertising is very much like the language of war: campaigns are "launched" for new products, messages are "aimed" at "target" audiences, and advertising "strategies" employ certain "offensive" and "defensive" "tactics" in order to reach marketing goals. In this respect the process of producing advertising is akin to the one generals might employ in working out battle plans or determining goals for the achievement of military objectives.

In discussing the design and production of the mass communication message we will not repeat the materials presented earlier which suggest the ways in which a product or service is positioned. This takes into account the various parts of the marketing mix that help determine the marketing strategy and the tactics to implement its execution. In various chapters suggestions were given on how to build different strategies and the steps that can be taken to carry them out. Here is a summary:

1. State the marketing objective or objectives.
2. Make the strategy or strategies fit the marketing plans.
3. Put the strategies in writing.
4. Make the objectives and strategies reasonable.
5. Be single-minded; great plans can be carried out when they are not fragmented by multidirectional goals.
6. Check your competition.
7. Determine whether your increased business may come from someone else's business.
8. Understand your target audience.
9. Make a meaningful promise to the buyer.
10. Support your promises with convincing evidence.
11. Make your product unique; set yourself apart.
12. Agree on what is most important about your product.
13. Think ahead, don't underestimate your competition.
14. Keep your strategy up to date.
15. Have a good product or service to offer.

THE HEADLINE

The headline is often considered to be "what would be said if only one or two lines of space were available for the message." It must put forth the main theme or appeal in a few words. Considered in this context, there is no reason to make it less than a powerful selling message.

Without doubt the headline shoulders a large part of the task of attracting the reader's attention. It should tell the whole story, including the *brand name* and the *promise* to the buyer. Otherwise the advertiser is wasting his money. Research shows that four out of five readers never get farther than the headline. The illustration also aids in attracting and holding attention, but readership studies repeatedly demonstrate that the headline is the major component in attracting attention. If it is not powerful, many good prospects will never get far enough into the ad to read the message.

Classifications of Headlines

Headline information serves various purposes. It may (1) provide news, (2) state product claims, (3) give advice, (4) select prospects, (5) arouse curiosity, or (5) identify product or company name.

News. This type of headline plays a role similar to its counterpart in the news story, for it often summarizes the point of highest interest in the copy. To command attention and arouse interest, such a headline must be pertinent and timely. It dispenses with cleverness and gimmicks and uses a direct, straight-selling approach. "Chevrolet Wins the Mobil Economy Run" is an example.

Product Claim. Featuring a product claim can be a good attention-getter in that it appeals to the reader's self-interest. The claim should be significant and believable. A headline that says "This Tire Will Give You Good Mileage" would have less impact than one that says "This Tire Gives 30% More Mileage Than Competitively Priced Tires." One might expect many brands of tires to give good mileage, but 30 percent more is something worth looking into.

While there are many examples of successful headlines that make claims, the use of this approach has been somewhat weakened by advertising that makes irresponsible statements. You should proceed on the assumption that the reader will be dubious. To ensure believability, care should be taken to provide ample supporting evidence in the copy.

Advice. Advice given in a headline may be followed by a promise of results from product use. Such a headline is "You Owe It to Yourself to Try Slimmo Reducing Tablets," with a secondary headline featuring a claim: "Use Slimmo Ten Days and Lose Ten Pounds." A properly conceived advice headline appeals to the reader's self-interest in that it is aimed at helping him solve a problem or prevent its occurrence.

Prospect Selection. Because very few products are of interest to everyone, the advertisement should appeal only to potential customers. The headline is a principal device in the process of selecting prospects from among readers. Copy striving to reach everyone is usually so generalized that its effectiveness is lost. A headline that says "New Drug Aids Those Who Suffer from Asthma" would be a combination of *news* and *selectivity*. In other situations the headline may be purely selective in purpose, as in the headline that says "Attention, June Graduates." The great majority of headlines are selective to some extent, regardless of emphasis.

Curiosity. Sometimes referred to as the provocative approach, the curiosity-oriented headline attempts to arouse interest through appeal to the unusual. It is hoped that the reader will be stimulated to read the copy text to find the answer to a "riddle" that is posed.

The curiosity approach can be used when some aspect of the product is of such genuine and timely interest that the reader is predisposed to seek information. A headline that asks "Are You Protected from Atomic Pollutants?" would arouse interest on the part of many people and induce them to read the text for more information. Volkswagen has made effective use of this approach. In one of the most memorable advertisements in its campaigns the headline read, "Lemon." Then the copy proceeded to explain the quality control procedures which prevent the customer from getting a "lemon."

The curiosity headline gives the copywriter great freedom in the use of his imagination, and its use can be tempting. However, some experts caution against the use of this approach in situations in which a direct-selling headline would be more appropriate. The curiosity type of headline too often is used for the sake of novelty alone, and, as was pointed out in Chapter 13, novelty without meaning is not creativity.

Product or Company Name. Occasionally the name of the product or company is used as the headline. This approach might be effective when the product is of such timely interest that the mere mention of the name is sufficient to arouse interest. In World War II a headline reading "Tires" would have attracted real attention from consumers in a market of scarcity. Substantial interest among many ethnic and racial groups can be obtained today by giving recognition to integrated racial relationships.

Some Guides for a Persuasive Headline

A fair amount of published research is available which delineates the characteristics of headlines that are effective in attracting attention. Although there is general agreement on certain of these characteristics, they can be violated successfully in many situations. There is a real difference, however, between violating a known criterion intentionally and violating it through ignorance.

Researchers at Marplan have found that confining the headline area to a small portion of the advertisement and using only one or two lines of type will produce the highest readership.[1] In addition, David Ogilvy mentions the following criteria:

1. On the average, five times as many people read the headline as read the body copy. If you haven't done some selling in your headline, you have wasted 80 percent of your client's money.
2. Headlines should appeal to the reader's *self-interest,* by promising her a benefit. This benefit should be the basic promise of the product.
3. Inject the maximum news into your headlines.
4. Include the *brand name* in every headline.
5. Write headlines which force the reader to read your subhead and body copy.
6. Don't worry about the *length* of the headline—*twelve*-word headlines get almost as much readership as three-word headlines. Headlines in the six-

---

[1] "Basic Readership Factors," internal publication of Marplan Division of the Interpublic Group of Companies, Inc., New York.

to twelve-word group get the most coupon replies. Better a long headline that sells than a short one which is blind and dumb.

7. Never change typeface in the middle of the headline; it reduces readership.
8. Never use a headline which requires readership of body copy to be comprehensible.
9. Never use tricky or irrelevant headlines.
10. Use words to select your prospects—like MOTHER and VARICOSE VEINS.
11. Use words which have been found to contain emotional impact.

KISS	DARLING	INSULT	HAPPY
LOVE	ANGRY	MONEY	WORRY
MARRY	FIGHT	FAMILY	BABY[2]

It is also generally accepted that the headline must be simple and easily understood. Moreover, it must join with the other message elements in presenting a unified and coherent message.[3]

COPY

During construction of the headline, ideas flow toward the next step—writing the body copy. An idea put aside as inadequate for the headline often becomes a subhead, a copy block lead line, or the lead for successive copy paragraphs. The copy reinforces the headline and delivers the sales message.

Whatever writing form the copywriter chooses to express the selling points, he will find that there is an ever-increasing demand for facts. It is a naive copywriter who does not include hard information on the product and its benefits throughout the message.

Classification of Copy Approaches

It is useful to classify copy approaches by manner of presentation.[4] In *direct-selling news* copy, for example, the message is presented in a straightforward manner similar to the informative content of newspaper articles. New-product messages are typical examples. In contrast, *implied suggestion* gives the reader an opportunity to draw his own conclusion from the facts which are presented to him. Usually the facts are obvious enough to direct the reader to a favorable conclusion about the product or service.

---

[2] David Ogilvy, "Raise Your Sights! 97 Tips for Copywriters, Art Directors and TV Producers—Mostly Derived from Research" internal publication of Ogilvy, Benson, & Mather, New York. Reproduced with special permission.

[3] Hugh G. Wales, Dwight Gentry, and Max Wales, *Advertising Copy, Layout and Typography* (New York: Ronald Press Co., 1958), p. 155.

[4] Ibid., pp. 189–200.

In *narrative description,* the copywriter starts with an account of some human experience that presents a problem and the solution in terms of favorable orientation toward a product. In a related copy type, the *story form,* human experience also is used in a straightforward account of product use by a purchaser. It also may involve an analogy between a storybook use and the product itself.

One effective approach is to use *monologue* and *dialogue.* The monologue is a single subject, such as a person (or an animal) reporting on his reactions to certain goods and services. The dialogue presents a conversation between two persons (or animals) who elaborate on the merits of the product. This often can be in the form of a *testimonial message.* One benefit of the testimonial is the implied opportunity for the reader to emulate or imitate the person giving the testimonial. The testimonial is also employed to provide a means of stating authoritatively that certain benefits can be found in using a product or service by following the exemplary behavior of the person or persons giving the testimony.

Humor can be very effective if the entertainment value of the presentation has real selling appeal to those who are exposed to the message. Messages that deal with food, drinks, and entertainment generally find this an appropriate form. More is said shortly about the use of humor.

Finally, some use can be made of the *comic strip* or *continuity* forms. These have found growing use because of the popularity of children's television programming and fictional characters, but its effectiveness is limited by mechanical problems in production of the comic strip.

Some Copy Problems

The Use of Humor. As mentioned above, considerable use is made of humor, but this should not be regarded as an index of its effectiveness. Many agree with Ogilvy's statement that "Humorous copy does not sell. It is never used by the great copywriters—only by amateurs."[5]

Others would not take such a strong stand, but research findings seem to support the conclusion that humorous commercials generally are less effective than their nonhumorous counterparts. The Schwerin Research Corporation reports that commercials featuring *all* humor (less than 4 percent of all advertisements) seldom prove to be as effective as other approaches. However, some use of humor, in general, will help the commercial to perform better than a commercial with no humor whatsoever.[6] The conclusion, then, is that humor at its best is used sparingly.

The purpose of advertising is *not* to entertain. Few advertisements

---

[5] Ogilvy, "Raise Your Sights!"

[6] *Schwerin Research Corporation Bulletin,* Vol. 10 (October 1964).

can entertain and sell simultaneously; both elements are combined only through use of great skill.

Answering Competitors' Claims. Perhaps it is human nature for an advertiser to react defensively when attacked by a competitor. While direct competitive derogation is seen infrequently, many advertisers indirectly attack competitors through their own strong claims of superiority.

There is real danger in a direct counterattack. If a competitor makes the claim, for example, that his make of automobile is the "quietest on the road," he has in effect appropriated that claim for himself. If it is answered by a counterclaim stating that "we also are quiet," his earlier statement is reinforced. Lindley Frazer has concluded from his study of propaganda in World War II that propaganda always must be offensive, not defensive.[7] If an appeal is answered, this lends credence to it.

Direct-Action Copy. Much advertising copy is designed to activate those in the final stages of their decision-making process as they move toward purchase. Similarly, the copy may serve to lead those now preferring a brand to purchase it more frequently and in greater quantities.

Among the many direct-action approaches are samples, contests, coupons and price offers, premiums, and combinations of related products. Some of the objectives to be attained are:

1. To obtain new triers and convert them into regular users.
2. To introduce new or improved products.
3. To increase brand awareness or awareness of a new package.
4. To increase readership of advertising by using coupons as attention-attracting devices.
5. To stimulate reseller support.

Success with the direct-action approach is most likely where brand loyalty is low. A buyer may actively seek a special incentive to buy, such as a price reduction. In addition, the direct-action method can be highly effective when the product or service being advertised possesses no distinct competitive advantage. For this reason, coupons and other incentives are a basic competitive tool among manufacturers of soaps, breakfast foods, cake mixes, and other items where no single firm can claim uniqueness and where brand loyalty is not especially strong.

The direct-action or "forcing" approach must be used with caution. When all competitors use this type of stimulus the result cannot help but have a diminishing effect for any individual firm. Moreover, the person may buy only for the incentive and return to a preferred brand later, in which case a costly promotion has failed.

Experience indicates that the forcing approach should seldom be used

---

[7] Lindley Frazer, *Propaganda* (London: Oxford University Press, 1957), p. 99.

when strong appeals can be made to product superiority. The Scott Paper Company abandoned couponing for this reason and was successful in its stress on the product line itself and its unique advantages for the buyer.[8] Moreover, a strong stimulus to buy will have a lasting effect through increasing market share only if the product clearly demonstrates its differentiation in use. Many new products have been successfully introduced by direct-action means (Procter & Gamble's Salvo is an example), but sales of an existing product with no apparent superiority are not likely to be affected greatly.

The direct-action stimulus clearly has a legitimate role when it has been indicated through research that a significant number of buyers require an additional stimulus for purchase action. The danger is that it may be used simply as a competitive fad. Thus the importance of sound product strategy based on consumer research is again apparent.

Slogans.   A slogan is a small group of words combined in unique fashion to embody the selling theme. In general it will be short and to the point and feature the product name whenever possible. Through repetition it hopefully becomes associated with the product and its benefits, thereby provoking prompt recall of the advertising message.

Some slogans emphasize product performance, and the mention of the generic name is all that is needed to bring a powerful association to mind. Others are designed to emphasize product quality, such as the ageless slogan for Ivory Soap: "99 and 44/100 Per Cent Pure." A manufacturer may employ a slogan to minimize substitution of a competitor's product and stress confidence in quality. "You Can Be Sure if It's Westinghouse" became a well-known quality slogan.

Legal protection for slogans was granted in the Lanham Act of 1947. If the slogan is registered and certain additional requirements are met, legal protection is ensured. The detailed requirements of the act are explained in most basic marketing texts.[9]

Some Guides for Persuasive Copy

Imagination, of course, must be disciplined to generate creative and persuasive copy. While there is no universal set of steps to be followed, there is substantial agreement with many of the following points mentioned by Ogilvy:

1.   Don't expect people to read leisurely essays.
2.   Go straight to the point; don't beat about the bush.
3.   Avoid analogies—"just as, so to."
4.   Avoid superlatives, generalizations, platitudes. Consumers discount them—and forget them.

---

[8] "Coupons: ANA Study Cites Dangers," *Printers' Ink,* May 18, 1962, pp. 25–28.

[9] For a summary see Theodore N. Beckman, William R. Davidson, and James F. Engel, *Marketing,* 8th ed. (New York: Ronald Press Co., 1967), ch. 3.

5. Be specific and factual.
6. Be personal, enthusiastic, memorable—as if the reader were sitting next to you at a dinner party.
7. Don't be a dull bore.
8. Tell the truth—but make the truth fascinating.
9. Use testimonials. Celebrity testimonials are better than anonymous ones.
10. Don't be afraid to write *long* copy. Mail-order advertisers never use short copy—and they know exactly what results they get.
11. Make the captions under your photographs pregnant with brand names and sell.[10]

One could, of course, disagree with some of these points. Some advertisers never use testimonials. Notice the several important basic criteria that are set forth. Persuasive copy should be (1) specific, (2) interesting, (3) believable, (4) simple, and (5) relevant.

If the copy surrounding an illustration or several illustrations does not make it apparent as to what the product's use or contribution to the buyer's benefits may be, a caption must be included underneath it. Research has generally found that the readership effect of a series of pictures with captions can be twice as great as body copy.

Nothing can lose a reader's attention more quickly than a general claim insufficiently supported by specific facts. "Chevrolet gets good gas mileage" is much less effective than "Chevrolet delivers 23.9 miles per gallon in the Mobil Gas Economy Run." Furthermore, the copy must contain relevant, meaningful information if it is to interest the reader and not bore him. Even interesting copy generally should not demand complex mental reasoning by the reader. It is much more effective if it focuses on a single theme.

The wording has much to do with the effect of the message on the recipient, for clumsy wording can violate the criterion of simplicity. Such words as "new," "wonderful," "powerful," "time-saving," and "finest" have lost their impact through overuse by advertisers, and the consumer is likely to reject them as being irrelevant. Good copy in most advertisements should amplify the headline, offer proof of what the headline claims, explain the product's advantages, and make clear what the reader is expected to do. It should in most cases end with an appeal to action, such as "visit your dealer now."

VISUAL ELEMENTS

The visualization of the basic theme is of such importance that one authority has suggested it be prepared before any other elements.[11] According to this view, the most graphic, poignant, and appealing pic-

---

[10] Ogilvy, "Raise Your Sights!"

[11] Beatrice Adams, "What's the Big Idea?" *Creativity—Methods and Techniques,* Proceedings, American Association of Advertising Agencies, 1958, pp. 1–20.

ture should be made of the theme; then the words are added. This is substantiated by a number of studies that demonstrate that the illustration is of critical importance in attracting and holding attention.[12]

A number of methods can be used in creating the illustration—line drawings, cartoons, photographs, and artistic renderings of subjects. Photographs provide the most realism, but an artist's drawing may create a subtle mood or highlight an attribute of a product in use which may not be possible with photographs. In large part the choice of the method will be made on a subjective basis by the creative team.

Classification of Visual Forms[13]

Visual forms can be classified according to their features or techniques.

The Product Alone. Perhaps the simplest form of illustration is one in which the product is shown without background or setting. This method may prove powerful when the product has intrinsic characteristics which command attention. Precious jewels, high-priced automobiles, and similar distinctive items can attract attention without the use of background. At times, in fact, a background may distract from the product's impact.

The Product in a Setting. Not many products are of such distinction that they can be shown without background. The setting is chosen to show the product to advantage and, in many instances, the objective is to have the reader associate the quality of the setting with the product. In other situations the setting may imply the pleasant and satisfying uses of the product; Figure 1 is an example.

The setting must be chosen carefully, for an incongruous background can lead to violation of the important criterion of believability. The low- or medium-priced car, for example, should not be shown in exclusive surroundings, because the product would seldom be found in such an environment.

The Product in Use. This is perhaps the most widely used method of visualization. The power of suggestion is stimulated by this means, because the reader immediately identifies himself with the product user and becomes the recipient of its benefits. Figure 2 provides an excellent example of this approach.

Benefits from Product Use. This method features the positive results derived from product use. It is hoped that the reader will project himself

---

[12] "Why People Will Read Ads Through," *Printers' Ink*, December 6, 1963, pp. 23–29.

[13] Much of the discussion here is drawn from Wales, Gentry, and Wales, *Advertising Copy, Layout and Typography*, pp. 110–21.

FIGURE 1

Distinctive Attributes Enhanced by Background

FIGURE 2

Use of Product Coupled with Benefits Derived

as one who can benefit equally, especially if he has an acute need for the product. The reader with a headache clearly could grasp the benefits from the remedy advertised in Figure 3.

Dramatizing Need. Frequently the need satisfied by a product is obvious, and little would be gained by illustrating it. In fact, such an illustration could be a trite and irrelevant visual treatment. In other situations, the potential customer may not be aware that a need for the product exists until it has been illustrated. Moreover, effective visualization may dramatize an obvious and known need and thereby spur the reader to take action. Scouring pads, for example, are used mostly on pots and pans, but they also can be used to clean white-sidewall tires. The reader may have experienced difficulty in cleaning white sidewalls and may never have associated the use of scouring pads for this purpose. A dirty tire being made white through this product use can thus be a powerful illustration.

Explaining Product Uses. The illustration of a scouring pad in use serves another purpose—to dramatize multiple product uses. Frequently there is limited market knowledge of product capabilities, and customers may refuse to buy because they don't know how to use the product. If

FIGURE 3

Showing the Benefits from Product Use

FIGURE 4

Highlighting Product Details

they do buy they may use the product incorrectly and get poor results. The visual treatment can be helpful in showing details of methods of use or the procedures to be followed.

Featuring Product Details. Often the advertising theme will center around an improvement in some detail of the product or its operation. The detail may be dramatized by changing the perspective to make one

FIGURE 5

Dramatizing Evidence Supporting Product Claims

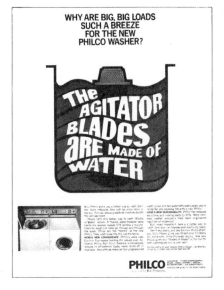

FIGURE 6

Dramatization of the Headline in the Illustration

part proportionately larger than others or by presenting the product from an unusual angle to call attention to that part. Other methods are to show a cross section of the product or print parts of it in color. Product details are clearly highlighted in the advertisement in Figure 4.

Dramatization of Evidence. Evidence is often the lifeblood of effective advertising. Unfortunately, advertising too frequently has been handicapped by the use of unsupported claims. Many effective illustrations are created to support claims with factual evidence. Figure 5 provides an example.

The Comparison Technique. This method may be used to point out certain product attributes that have competitive superiority. One variation is to show the results of using the product as compared to the situation existing before product use. The removal of carbon from engine valves after using a brand of gasoline for 6,000 miles is an example. Another method is to compare the results of using one product with the results obtained from another.

Dramatization of the Headline. The headline and illustration are usually closely related, and the illustration can effectively strengthen the headline by communicating in a picture what the headline states in words. This technique is effectively used in Figure 6.

The Use of Symbolism. The winged feet of Mercury symbolize speed; Uncle Sam signifies patriotism. Advertising may make effective use of such symbols to associate the product or service with the basic idea conveyed. Notice how often the cross is used in advertising products with Christian religious significance.

Some Guides for Persuasive Visualization

Studies on the use of visual elements to attract and hold attention have disclosed that greatest effectiveness results when:

1. The illustration is placed in the upper part of the page instead of being positioned below the headline.
2. The illustration is the dominant element in the layout.
3. Photography is used instead of art work.
4. People or things are pictured in proper proximity.
5. The colors used are vivid.[14]

In addition, Ogilvy offers the following suggestions which can generally increase the probability of attracting and holding attention:

1. The average person now reads only four ads in a magazine; it is becoming increasingly difficult to find readers. That is why it is worth taking great pains to find a GREAT illustration.
2. Put "story appeal" in your illustration.
3. Illustrations should portray reward.
4. To attract women, show babies and women.
5. To attract men, show men.
6. Avoid historical illustrations; they don't sell.
7. Use photographs in preference to drawings. They sell more.
8. Don't deface your illustration.
9. Use captions that are written the way people talk.
10. Don't use a lot of illustrations—they look cluttered and discourage a reader.
11. Don't crop important elements in your illustration.[15]

Some advertising artists would disagree with certain of these points; others would state different ones. Each would react according to his own experience and working knowledge.

The Use of Color. There is no question that using color adds to costs of space or time, printing, and production. Advertisers have found, however, that the extra cost is well rewarded, for a number of reasons:

1. The attention-attracting and attention-holding power of the message may be increased sharply.

---

[14] "Basic Readership Factors."
[15] Ogilvy, "Raise Your Sights!"

2. Contemporary social trends have encouraged experimentation in color in all phases of life, ranging from the factory to the home. Thus people have become responsive to innovative color stimuli.
3. Most products look better in color, especially food.
4. Color can be used to create moods ranging from the somber appeal to the freshness of greens and blues.
5. Color can add an image of prestige to the advertisement, especially if most competing advertisements are in black and white.
6. Visual impressions can be retained in memory, hence resulting in greater message recall.

Numerous studies have demonstrated the attention-attracting power of color. It is, for example, the one outstanding factor in stimulating high readership of newspaper advertisements.[16] The data in Table 1 are

TABLE 1

Comparison of Readership of Black and White Advertisements and Color Advertisements by Size

			Black and White Advertisements					
		Average Size Lines (rounded		Men			Women	
Range of Size Lines	Number of Ads	to nearest 5 lines)	Noted	Seen-Assoc.	Read Most	Noted	Seen-Assoc.	Read Most
140–289	847	195	7%	6%	3%	26%	22%	11%
290–389	409	315	9	7	4	33	30	14
390–589	403	475	10	9	4	38	35	14
590–689	329	605	13	11	5	44	40	17
690–974	206	830	15	14	5	47	43	17
975–1089	341	1000	15	14	5	50	47	17
1090–1289	148	1200	20	18	6	51	47	17
1290–1589	45	1480	21	19	4	57	53	17
1590–2399	40	1940	26	23	7	54	51	16
1 page	20	1 page	37	34	10	60	58	20
		Color Advertisements *Black and One Color*						
1000–1089	262	1005	22	20	7	54	50	20
1090–1289	70	1205	24	21	7	57	54	25
1290–1589	47	1485	26	24	6	55	52	20
1590–2399	19	1875	30	29	8	59	57	20
1 page	36	1 page	40	39	11	64	64	23
		Full Color						
1000–2399	57	1160	31	29	9	59	56	21
1 page	119	1 page	42	38	11	72	68	29

Source: *1968 Starch—Million Market Newspapers Adnorms Report,* Daniel Starch & Staff, Inc., Mamaroneck, N.Y.

[16] "What Stirs the Newspaper Reader?" *Printers' Ink,* June 21, 1963, pp. 48–49.

representative of the findings of many newspaper advertising studies. In television, color commercials have been found to be 55 percent more effective than black and white.[17]

Skillful use of color also can set the mood for the advertisement. Connotations of various colors include:

RED: Anger, action, fire, heat, passion, excitement, danger
BLUE: Sadness, cool, truth, purity, formality
YELLOW: Cheerfulness, spring, dishonesty, light, optimism
ORANGE: Fire, heat, action, harvest, fall
GREEN: Calm, wet, spring, youth, nature, ignorance, immaturity
BLACK: Mystery, mourning, death, heaviness
WHITE: Cleanliness, purity, virginity

Color reproduction techniques have reached a high degree of refinement in magazines, and newspapers have made major improvements in its use. Increasing use has been made of preprinted inserts for newspapers, and real advances are seen daily in standard newspaper color procedures (run of press color). Inks have been standardized so that the advertiser can order certain colors and expect the same result anywhere the message is run. Moreover, production improvements have served to lower costs significantly, and the differential for the addition of color is now from 5 to 10 percent in newspapers. There is little doubt that it will be used in increasing amounts in a wide variety of newspaper ads.

TYPOGRAPHY

An important element in the printed advertisement is the type to be used. There are few areas of the graphic arts of more interest historically and of greater importance in the development of civilization and culture than the creation of type printing surfaces, first used in printing the Gutenberg Bible in 1456. The first movable type was hand carved and crude in outline and impression, but its impact on literacy was startling as reading matter became available to more than a privileged few.

In place of the hand-carved, wood-block, one-design typefaces of medieval days, there now are hundreds of typefaces in many sizes. They are available as foundry type to be set by hand and matrices, which are brass-type molds from which single pieces of type, large or small, may be cast by machines operated by hand or computer and ejected as single letters, words, or lines of type.

---

[17] *Are Color Television Commercials Worth the Extra Cost?* (New York: Association of National Advertisers, 1966).

‚These days even more type faces are available from sophisticated typewriter-like equipment, machines that compose type photographically, and even devices that electronically create type on the face of a cathode ray (TV) tube at phenomenal speeds.

Type Structure and Measurement

Figure 7 represents a single piece of foundry type and labels its components. Notice that each piece of type includes a face, neck, shoul-

FIGURE 7

Foundry Type Characteristics*

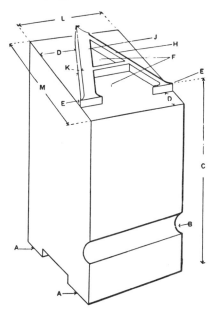

A. Feet. Type that is loosely spaced and leans over when printed is called "off its feet."
B. Nick. Helps compositor to place type right side up in stick. Keeps him from using wrong font.
C. Type-high, or height to paper, .918 inch or approximately $11/12$ inch.
D. Shoulder. Nonprinting area surrounding a character.
E. Serif.
F. Counter or void.
H. Thin stroke of face.
J. Thick stroke of face.
K. Neck, beard, or drive. Made in matrix while casting, rest is made in the mold.
L. Set or set width.
M. Point size.

* In modern production methods, instead of foundry type, phototype methods are used.
Source: David Hymes, *Production in Advertising and the Graphic Arts* (New York: Henry Holt & Co., 1958), p. 66.

ders, and feet. The face is the design of the letter or symbol. It may contain serifs (the little lines at the top and base of the letters), but some forms of type do not have this characteristic and are called sans serif (without serif).

There are various classifications of type, according to:

1. *Type groups*—type families with similar characteristics. Such a group is Old Style, which has serifs. Another is more modern, without serifs, such as Helvetica. This book uses Helvetica in all headings.

2. *Type families*—typefaces with similar characteristics. These may carry the same name as their designer, as in Bodoni, or signify mood, as in Futura.
3. *Type series*—the typefaces designated on the basis of their size. Each type family has many series within it.

It is important to learn the terms used in designating type series. The following are of special importance:

Point = 1/72 of an inch.
Pica = 12 points.
Inch = 6 picas or 72 points.
Em = Area occupied by a capital M. A 12-point em is 12 points wide and 12 points high and is equal to one pica in its linear measurement.

FIGURE 8

Point Method of Type Measurement

The letters in Figure 8 have 72 points to an inch, but the point measure does not reflect the exact size of any single letter. Rather, point size measures the height of a line of type, or the distance between the *descenders* and the *ascenders*. The width of a letter is measured by the pica, the pica unit equaling one sixth of an inch.

The standard unit for measuring the depth of a block of copy is the agate line. The line equals one fourteenth of an inch. Remember that the agate line or the column inch is the standard means of quoting newspaper space rates.

Selecting the Type

Selection of the most appropriate typeface or faces can be a demanding task. The two most important factors in this decision are legibility (readability) and mood. The connotations of typefaces are clearly different. You would not, for example, want to use an old-style face in advertising a new-model automobile.

There are other factors to consider as well:

1. *Type size in relation to use.* Headline type will be larger and perhaps of more weight than the type used in the reading matter.

2. *Number of words in the headline to be capitalized.* Words in the headline to be in all "caps" should be in typefaces whose capitals are easy to read, but it should be remembered that it is easier and more natural to read words set in "caps and lower case" (capitals and small letters).

3. *Number of words or word units in the headline.* The length of the headline or subheads will help determine the size of type to be used, as well as the number of words in each word group.

4. *Design of type in relation to use.* The design of the typeface may set the right mood, but script designs, for instance, tend to be more difficult to read than other faces.

5. *Amount of copy and amount of space available in the layout.*

6. *Uncontrollable factors.* The reader's ability to read cannot be controlled, but it would be folly to use very small type for older persons. The larger the type size the easier it should be to read under most lighting conditions.

The current trend in type size in magazine advertising is toward body type set in a size large enough so that the whole advertisement can literally be read with one sweep of the eyes. It may be that 24-point type will replace 12-, 13-, and 18-point for this purpose.

Greater reader interest can be assured by using space between the lines of set type. This is called leading; it can be done automatically in typesetting or by hand. The lines of type in the body of this text are leaded 2 points.

THE PRINTED ADVERTISEMENT

Layout

The layout is an arrangement of all elements of the advertisement in an integrated whole. Each element may be excellent by itself, but the finished advertisement will be unsatisfactory unless the elements are carefully blended in terms of the probable reaction of the reader.

Steps in Preparing a Layout. The elements of the layout are first assembled into what is usually referred to as the "rough." As can be seen in Figure 9, lines are drawn in for the copy and the picture is only sketched. As rough as this first layout is, it permits an evaluation of the manner in which the elements combine to create a pleasing effect. The copy at this stage is usually prepared on separate sheets.

The layout then is refined into "semicomprehensive" form. The elements are drawn in with sharper clarity, and it is possible to pretest the message at this stage to derive a preliminary indication of its probable effectiveness. If pretesting evaluation is favorable, it is common to

for the holidays

store name

FIGURE 9

Illustration of a Rough Layout

Source: Taken from *Advertising Copy, Layout, and Typography* by Hugh G. Wales, Dwight L. Gentry, and Max Wales. Used with permission of the Ronald Press Company.

prepare a final version referred to as the "comprehensive." Copy is not yet inserted, but the lines representing copy blocks are drawn precisely to represent the exact size of the space for copy. The layout at this stage is ready for approval by management, and a final buyer pretest may be necessary.

Roughs are made in miniature in the same proportions as the final advertisement. The reduction is one to two—the dimensions of the miniature sketch are one half the dimensions of the finished layout. An easy way to determine this size is to draw a full-dimension layout area and bisect it with a diagonal, as in Figure 10. The line through A (the midpoint) drawn parallel to the top of the layout will strike the diagonal at D. A line dropped from the intersection D to the bottom of the layout, parallel to the vertical edge of the advertisement, will complete the miniature. Elements of the rough made in this reduced size will appear in the same proportions when the advertisement is produced in actual size.

Criteria of an Effective Layout. The layout of a printed advertisement usually is formalized along the lines of certain principles which recognize that the situation of the reader is more stable than that of the listener to the television or radio commercial. There is time for him to feel the presence or absence of unity, balance, good proportion, judicious contrast, harmony, and eye direction. The television viewer or radio listener, however, is exposed to the message for only a short time, and his attention

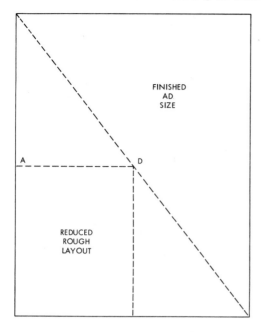

FINISHED
AD
SIZE

A — — — — — — — — — D

REDUCED
ROUGH
LAYOUT

FIGURE 10

**Method for Determining
Proportions in the Rough Layout**

may be fragmented. Layout principles of printed advertisements include
(1) unity, (2) balance, (3) proportion, (4) contrast, (5) harmony, and
(6) eye direction.

UNITY. Each element is first designed as a separate unit, but the
completed layout should create a feeling of oneness. The headline should
not stand out unduly from the remainder of the message, any more than
the roof of a building should dominate the structure. Consistency in
typeface, overlapping elements, and the use of such connecting devices
as lines and arrows may serve to enhance unity.

BALANCE. Balance has to do with the way an advertisement "feels,"
whether it is formal or informal. Balance occurs when elements of equal
weight or substance are placed in proportion in reference to a given
point. The focal point is the optical center—a point slightly above the
center and to the left. The eye is most likely to be attracted to this
spot at first glance.

When elements are placed in equal relationship on both sides of a
center point, the resulting layout is said to be in formal balance. An
example of formal balance is given in Figure 11. If elements are placed
at different distances from the center, the layout is in informal or asym-
metrical balance. Figure 12 is an example.

Formal balance obviously can create a somewhat uninteresting effect
if it is carried to extremes. On the other hand, it does connote dignity
and conservatism. Informal balance can be more interesting in its visual

FIGURE 11

Advertisement with Formal Balance

FIGURE 12

Advertisement with Informal Balance

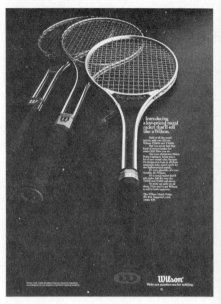

impression and create an impression of excitement. Carried to extremes, however, it can appear unnatural to the reader.

PROPORTION. This principle is closely related to balance; it refers to the division of space among the elements to create a proper optical effect. Yet proportion also requires creating emphasis in terms of the size and shape of each element. There are some sales points or copy elements that deserve more weight and space than others, and proportion calls for allocation of space in these terms.

CONTRAST. This attention-getting device is vital when an advertisement is competing with many others for the reader's attention, particularly among several advertisements on a magazine or newspaper page. Dramatic use of color, for example, may cause an advertisement to stand out. Also, the background may be left uncluttered to create large areas of white space. White space is utilized effectively in Figure 13 to create an unusual effect.

HARMONY. Harmony, like unity, has to do with the impression the whole advertisement makes on the reader. It is the reader's feeling that all is right in what he sees—the parts of the layout are related. There is

FIGURE 13

Effective Use of White Space

FIGURE 14

Placement of Elements to Create Eye Movement

Source: Used with permission of Eastman Kodak Company.

nothing incongruous or unmatching, or, if incongruity is introduced, it has been so skillfully accomplished that the reader is not jolted into a negative reaction toward the presentation.

EYE DIRECTION.   As noted earlier, the reader's eyes are generally attracted to the optical center of the advertisement. From that point they may move in any direction, and it often is useful to employ various devices to direct this motion in a desired manner throughout the message.

The eye might be attracted from the optical center through heavy emphasis on color in other parts of the layout. In addition, arrows, lines, or other mechanical devices might be employed. Perhaps more common is the placement of elements so that the angle of the dominant elements will lead the eye in the desired direction naturally. Notice how the eye is drawn downward into the copy in the advertisement reproduced in Figure 14. In addition, the direction of gaze of dominant figures depicted in the layout can be used for this same purpose. The use of gaze motion is illustrated in Figure 15.

Layout Styles.   Just as artwork, photography, typeface choice, and hand-lettering design have gone through periods of "in" and "out," so

FIGURE 15

Gaze Motion and Good Space Management

Even she knows what tastes good

There's much <u>more</u> <u>flavor</u> in
THIN KRISPY crackers

Source: Used with permission of Sunshine Biscuits, Inc.

has layout. The trend in the 1960s and early 1970s has been toward the space-dominating close-up of a model or the product, coupled with a headline and selling message set in the same type style, the headline often being the lead sentence in the copy and the size of the type diminishing only slightly after several lines. This style allows a sweep of the eye to catch almost the complete pictorial and written sales message. Figure 16 is an example.

There is also the "Mondrian" style, which was inspired by the delicately related size of rectangles in the style of the Dutch painter, Piet Mondrian. The area is divided by intersecting sets of parallel lines, and the elements of the ad are assigned to the various areas created by the intersecting sets of parallel lines. This style is the least costly for the illustrations used because each is finished as a rectangle. It is a style that is infallible in its dependency on the sound relation of spaces, but it has the inherent advantages and disadvantages of the standardized format. Limitations may be imposed by its inflexibility.

FIGURE 16

Space-Dominating Close-Up Visualization and Layout Popular during the 1960s and Early 1970s

Frank Young's "white fence" method utilizes white space as a separation element. One element touches only once on all four imaginary borders of the page, and each point is not equally spaced in relation to the others. Such conscious use of white space recognizes white space for what it is—an element of layout, to be dealt with as an element rather than as ample space to be filled up. Used as a design element, white space is particularly important in newspaper advertisements, where it is worth every bit as much as the space occupied by the illustration or the copy in its ability to isolate the elements of an advertisement from competing with news and other advertising matter. It can be an element of direction for eye movement, an element of control, and an element of contrast or emphasis.

Modern art has in no small way been responsible for some imaginative approaches to design in the graphic arts, industrial packaging, and advertising design. The informality of modern art has created its own formality—the dignity of unbalanced use of space. Its contrast with the formal pattern of spacing and weight of elements and the only slightly less inflexible informal balance that has prevailed has meant new horizons for creative talents in advertising. It has been felt in photography and in type, in the use of color and paper texture, and in an open discovery approach to layout elements and their relationships.

Producing the Finished Advertisement

Printing Methods.   The basic printing methods are: (1) letterpress, (2) lithography, (3) gravure, and (4) silk screen.

LETTERPRESS PRINTING.   Use may be made of a platen press (two flat surfaces), a flatbed press (flat and curved surfaces) or a rotary press (two curved surfaces). Platen and flatbed presses are used for the printing of direct mail and product information enclosures as well as some smaller newspapers.

The majority of printed advertising is reproduced through the letterpress method. It is the oldest printing method, originating with the printing of the Gutenberg Bible. In the letterpress method, the impression of the type on the paper comes directly from the face of the type itself and from other typographical elements. The type may be set by hand, by a mammoth linotype machine that has a manually operated keyboard similar to a typewriter, or by a computer-controlled facility.

The traditional letterpress method uses hot, molten lead in which lines of type are cast. The main headline and subheads are often set by hand. The type which has been set is then assembled with the other elements, as outlined in a later paragraph.

One of the trends in the field of type composition replaces hot-metal casting with fast cathode-ray tube (CRT) phototypesetting. The unit may or may not be computer controlled, but in larger installations it is always either tape operated or computer controlled. With the increase in phototypesetting, the use of hot metal is decreasing, as it has for the past decade. Hot metal will probably continue to be used, but its percentage of use will undoubtedly decline year by year.

Even newspapers are turning to photocomposition, a natural method for papers printed by web offset. (Web offset refers to a lithopress which prints on both sides of a web or roll of paper in one operation.) Many of the letterpress newspapers are also moving to photocomposition. In such a case, the output of the phototypesetter is "stripped up" (the act of positioning or inserting copy elements in negative or positive film on a unit negative) to make a full newspaper page, which is then photographed to produce a negative. The negative is used to make a relief plate that is mounted on the press. A pattern plate is produced from the negative by using an emulsion on the plate. The plate is then used to make mats (a papier-mâché reproduction of the page), the mats are used to produce stereos (metal plates cast from the mats), and the stereos are attached to the cylinder or bed of the press so that printed copies can be produced.

The first step in letterpress printing is the marking of the printed materials and layout to give details of how the advertisement or printed page is to be set up and printed.

The compositor will assemble the type bars and illustrations and fasten them securely in a metal frame; he will pull a proof to permit corrections, make the corrections, and place the corrected metal frame in a page form which is the size of the finished page. If the copy is computer-set and assembled, all these steps are performed automatically. The last stage is to prepare the papier-mâché mat to be cast into the plate. The printing surface receives the ink, which is transferred to the paper under regulated pressure at high press speed and accuracy.

LITHOGRAPHY. This is literally "chemical printing." The most common form of lithography is referred to as offset. The process basically involves impression of the design onto a metal surface, application of ink, transfer of the message to a roller, and final printing onto paper. The offset method provides high-quality reproduction of direct mail sales messages, catalogues, and booklets and is especially good for four-color reproduction.

A plate is prepared of the entire advertisement, including type and visual elements. The images on the plate are in the form of a greasy coating. Then the plate is dampened with water. The greasy images repel the water, while the uncoated or blank portions of the plate retain it. Then the plate is coated with an oily ink. The dampened, uncoated portions of the plate repel the ink, while the greasy image retains it for transfer to the paper.

GRAVURE. This method of printing is often found in the special sections of Sunday newspapers featuring four-color advertisements. In addition it is widely used in printing magazines. The gravure procedure lays a heavy coating of ink on the paper, and it can always be felt by running a finger over the surface.

Printing is done from an engraved or depressed surface. Small cups are etched into the surface of a cylinder, representing type, pictures, and other elements. Acid etches the metal to sufficient depth to reproduce the tonal values. (Hence gravure which provides an infinite variation in tone and color reproduction is excellent.) The paper is then placed in contact with the printing cylinder, and ink is transferred to the paper in the desired pattern.

SILK SCREEN. The silk-screen process is widely used where printing runs are small and when other methods would be too costly. No plates are required; printing is done from a silk screen stretched in a frame over the surface. A stencil is placed on the screen which blanks out areas that are not to take a printing image. Then ink is pressed through the uncovered areas of the screen and transferred to the printing surface.

Silk-screen printing is useful in color reproduction. It also is economical in print runs of less than 10,000 copies, for it eliminates the costly stages of preparation of plates. In addition, it can be used in combination with the letterpress or lithography methods.

Producing the Illustration. Reproduction of the visual elements of the message is a fascinating part of the graphic arts. Advertising agencies may use their art departments for hand-lettered renderings and for the rough layouts, but the comprehensive or finished layout is often sent out to art studios which are staffed and equipped to prepare illustrations for printing.

Line drawings, consisting of black lines and white space, with no greys or shading, are the simplest form of drawing to reproduce. A picture is taken of the copy. The film is then processed as a negative and is laid upon a thin metal plate. The plate is coated with an acid-resistant emulsion which clings to the areas which are photosensitive and is washed away from those that are not. When submerged in an acid bath, the unprotected areas are etched out, leaving raised areas which are the lines of the drawing. When ink is applied directly to this plate the lines of the drawing will print, and the areas around the lines will not.

If shading is required it can be done on the original drawing through skillful use of black and white. Or it can be done on the finished copy through use of the benday method. Bendays are line and dot shadings available in many varied patterns that can be added directly to the original negative to produce the desired effect.

Photographs are reproduced by a different process called halftone. The picture is placed on a copy board before a camera, but a direct exposure is not made as it is in reproducing a line drawing. Instead a screen or grid is placed between the camera lens and the film. The result is that the mass of the picture is broken down into thousands of tiny dots, the fineness of the dots being determined by the printing requirements. For newspaper printing a 60-line screen is used, with 3,600 dots per square inch. The result can easily be seen with the naked eye. Newspaper stock is somewhat porous, so a fine screen cannot be used because the dots will blur together and ruin the reproduction.

Magazine reproduction demands a finer 120-line screen, giving 14,400 dots per square inch. The finished picture is reproduced with much greater clarity. If color is to be used an even finer set of screens is employed. Tonal values are broken down into 57,600 dots per square inch.

If the picture requires both line-drawing and halftone treatment, a combination plate is made of the line-drawing negative overlaid with a halftone negative. The engraving process is the same for both methods. Hand finishing may be required to make the picture sharper in detail or to highlight areas of the picture by removing some of the dots, leaving pure white space to "highlight" the objects.

Color Reproduction.   A refinement of the halftone process is used for this purpose. A separate negative must be made for each of the primary colors (red, yellow, and blue) and one for black (to give depth and perspective). A negative is made for each of the four colors by using filters which block out unwanted colors. Each color is photographed with a different screen, and the screen is turned a specified number of degrees so that the dots of each negative will fall beside those of the other negatives rather than pile on top of them. Individual plates are made, each of which prints its own color, and the plate must be perfectly placed on the press so that each dot will fall precisely where it should. The human eye then takes over, and the illustration will appear to be solid color.

Producing the Complete Advertisement Using Letterpress.   In the engraver's composing room the elements of the advertisement are "locked up." A wax mold is made by placing a metal plate coated with wax over the type form and applying pressure that implants a deep and sharp impression in the wax. The wax sheet is placed in an electrolytic bath where by electrolysis copper is deposited on the wax to a required thickness. The copper is stripped from the wax, backed with additional metal, and mounted on a wood base to bring it to the proper height for printing purposes. The result is a finely etched plate called an electrotype.

Four-color process work utilizes lead instead of wax. The original plates are set, and the lead is molded under the pressure of hydraulic presses. The lead later receives the copper deposit, and the finishing process is the same from this point on. The resulting plate may be sent to the newspaper or magazine for direct use in their presses, but it is more common to use mats for this purpose.

LAYOUT AND PRODUCTION OF THE BROADCAST ADVERTISEMENT

Layout and Design

Layout in broadcast media seldom is formalized by utilizing principles such as those discussed for the printed message. There was greater formality in the early days of radio, when an opening commercial, two program breaks, and a closing commercial were commonly used. It was assumed that listeners were sitting at home with ears tuned to the radio. The informality and casualness of radio programming and radio listening habits has changed this, and the form of the broadcast advertising message has become quite varied to adapt to the nature of the listening situation.

The customary format of radio programs today provides a substantial number of hours devoted to music recordings during the 24-hour broadcast schedule. Often 12 minutes of each quarter-hour segment are given over to music, with from two to three minutes of news or weather. During this 15-minute music-news-weather segment, there will be different radio commercials of varying lengths. Radio stations also schedule interview programs, which may be educational or entertainment segments.

The television message is somewhat more formalized, but the viewing of television is also casual. Thus there are few principles of layout per se to be followed in broadcast advertisements, other than to specify the importance of harmony among elements. Obviously, one element, such as the audio portion, should not dominate other portions if this can be avoided.

The layout of the television commercial usually is developed through use of "storyboards," although a script may be used without direct rendering of the visual elements. The radio commercial uses only the audio script. The storyboard differs little in its nature from the rough layouts developed for printed advertisements, except that individual rough layouts are made for each major scene in the commercial. An example of a storyboard appears in Figure 17. Notice that the audio elements are written beside a rough rendering of the visual ones.

Production of the Commercial

Radio commercials usually are produced in final form by the script department of the advertising agency, by an agency specializing in such script and dramatic writing, or by staff members at a radio station. The message elements are combined carefully and reproduced on tape. The "live" radio commercial is confined mostly to local radio advertising today.

The production of a television commercial entails greater complexity. For this reason, storyboards or trial commercials should be pretested before the finished commercial is made. The costs of production can be considerable—often $30,000 or more—and few companies can afford the risks of producing the commercial and *then* testing it.

A 16-mm motion picture documentary has been prepared by video station KTAR of Phoenix, Arizona, which gives the operational details involved in producing a very low-cost TV commercial. The claim is made by KTAR that their station can produce and tape a TV commercial for $1,000.[18]

Commercial production is largely the province of specialized firms. The commercial may be shot in a studio if the visual background permits the use of fixed sets. The costs, of course, are greatly minimized if this is possible. Often, however, it is necessary to "go on location" and make the commercial under natural settings. The costs then become considerable, especially if color is used.

Once the films are shot, the designers of the commercial spend considerable time viewing the film (often referred to as the rushes). Unusable footage is cropped out, and the finished commercial is then made by combining the visual and audio elements at appropriate places.

Until recently all television commercials were reproduced on 16-mm film. Substantial use is now being made of video tape.

MEDIA REQUIREMENTS AND THE ADVERTISING MESSAGE

Many of the topics discussed above require modification and qualification from medium to medium, for the media themselves impose requirements on the creative task. Requirements of the various media are discussed below.

Newspapers

Copy. Newspaper advertising often attains a high degree of readership, for it is frequently used as a source of buying information. Because much newspaper copy is oriented toward stimulating visits to dealers and other forms of direct action, there is need for concise wording using such appeals as economy and urgency.

Production. A newspaper is severely limited in quality compared with other printed media. Layouts cannot depend for their effect on fine-

---

[18] This instructional film can be obtained by writing to TV Station KTAR, Phoenix, Arizona 85026.

FIGURE 17

Television Storyboard

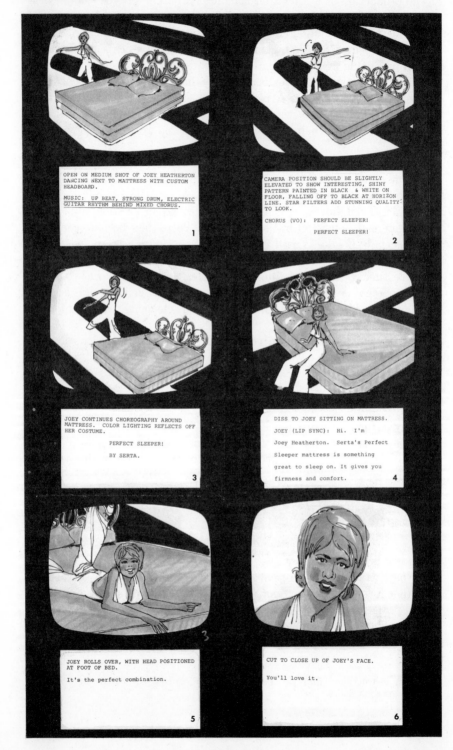

OPEN ON MEDIUM SHOT OF JOEY HEATHERTON DANCING NEXT TO MATTRESS WITH CUSTOM HEADBOARD.

MUSIC: UP BEAT, STRONG DRUM, ELECTRIC GUITAR RHYTHM BEHIND MIXED CHORUS.

1

CAMERA POSITION SHOULD BE SLIGHTLY ELEVATED TO SHOW INTERESTING, SHINY PATTERN PAINTED IN BLACK & WHITE ON FLOOR, FALLING OFF TO BLACK AT HORIZON LINE. STAR FILTERS ADD STUNNING QUALITY TO LOOK.

CHORUS (VO): PERFECT SLEEPER!

PERFECT SLEEPER!

2

JOEY CONTINUES CHOREOGRAPHY AROUND MATTRESS. COLOR LIGHTING REFLECTS OFF HER COSTUME.

PERFECT SLEEPER!

BY SERTA.

3

DISS TO JOEY SITTING ON MATTRESS.

JOEY (LIP SYNC): Hi. I'm Joey Heatherton. Serta's Perfect Sleeper mattress is something great to sleep on. It gives you firmness and comfort.

4

JOEY ROLLS OVER, WITH HEAD POSITIONED AT FOOT OF BED.

It's the perfect combination.

5

CUT TO CLOSE UP OF JOEY'S FACE.

You'll love it.

6

FIGURE 17—Continued

DISS TO JOEY ON FLOOR. ONCE AGAIN TO
FINISH CHOREOGRAPHY AND SONG.

JOEY (LIP SYNC):

NOW INSTEAD OF COUNTING SHEEP
YOU CAN COUNT ON A GOOD NIGHT'S SLEEP.

7

SLOWLY PULL BACK WITH REVERSE FOCAL
LENS FROM VERY ROOF OF STAGE SO TO
REVEAL JOEY, DANCERS AND MATTRESS
ARE ON GIANT "SERTA" LOGO PAINTED
ON FLOOR.

BE A PERFECT SLEEPER
BUY A PERFECT SLEEPER

8

CONTINUE PULLBACK

PERFECT SLEEPER

9

MOVE BACK OPTICALLY TO REVEAL SERTA
LOGO.

BY SERTA.

MUSICAL EFX:

10

PERFECT SLEEPER

D'Arcy/Chicago

PIC RECEDES TO CENTER OF FRAME. IT'S
NOW THE STANDARD "SERTA" LOGO. POP
ON TITLE "PERFECT SLEEPER" ON BLACK
FRAME.

MUSIC: UNDER FOR :08 DEALER TAG.

11

CLIENT: Serta, Inc.
TITLE: "Giant Logo" (:50 + :08 Tag)
CODE #: _____ DATE: 7-10-73
COPYWRITER: XSWP4950
ART DIRECTOR: _____
SA-T-780 7/20/73

screen reproduction, for example. Under no circumstances should a plate used for a magazine illustration be used in newspapers, or vice versa. Line drawings may prove to be more effective because they offer greater clarity and eye appeal.

All reading matter must be designed to attain high legibility. Newspapers, as a rule, are read quickly, and there is competition from other advertisements and editorial matter. Moreover, distracting typographical elements should be put aside in favor of layouts that provide highly controlled eye movement. The directional movement created by judicious placing of elements plays a large role in overcoming the distracting effect of competing advertisements and news features.

Magazines

Copy. Magazine copy frequently can be longer than newspaper copy, for the reader generally spends more time on each page and may be exposed to the message more than once. The elements must combine to separate prospects from nonprospects, and a heavy burden is placed on the copywriter to produce a headline that will successfully generate reader selectivity. More time is probably spent on writing the headline than on any other element of the message.

Because the magazine will typically reach a relatively select audience by the nature of its editorial content, copy must be closely tuned to the motivational determinants of the prospects. The selected audience frequently is a critical audience, not likely to be satisfied with a general claim that might be successful with larger consumer groups. In addition, the audience of a special-interest magazine (say a photography magazine) is likely to be sensitive to the product and highly interested in important facts. The copy may, as a result, be more technical and take more space. More illustrations are often used to depict details of product construction or use.

Production. Most magazines offer colors, high-gloss paper for fine-screen halftone reproduction, placement on certain pages, and a wide range of typefaces. Even though it may add to costs, it usually is advisable to make the total advertisement as much in character in all respects with a given publication as the budget will allow.

A decision must be made on whether or not to use "bleed"—the technique of laying out photographs or other materials in such a way that they will extend to the edge of the page without the usual white border. Bleed usually costs 15 percent extra, but it often is necessary for proper visualization of the product. Frequent use is made of two facing pages to provide more space for arranging the elements in a dramatic combination.

Billboards

Copy. The poster depends almost entirely on the power of the illustration to attract attention. Color and size are two of the most widely used devices to attract attention, as are animation and various illumination devices. Copy usually will be brief, and it may be in the form of a slogan. The fleeting moment for reader attraction and attention requires the use of highly legible type in very large sizes.

Production. Poster space is usually referred to in terms of "sheets," ranging in size from 82 × 48 in. to 104 × 234 in. The finished layout will consist of many sheets which are printed by silk screen or lithography.

Direct Mail

Copy. Much effort is devoted to creating a personalized message. Procedures exist so that what appears to be a hand-typed letter can be reproduced by mechanical means, personalized, and sent to a large list of potential customers. It is human nature to be flattered by personal attention, and the object is to make the reader become personally involved in the mail piece.

The headline or lead paragraph bears the burden of holding attention unless an illustration or graphic feature is used. The advertiser may want the person to read a letter or accompanying enclosure; the person may be urged to send in a coupon or make some other form of direct response. In any event, direct mail usually calls for the reader to do something and do it now before he puts the mailing down, even if it is just to mark the calendar for a coming event.

Direct mail copy by its very nature will be more personal than any other form of advertising writing. Often this personalization requires a unique skill, and it may be wise to use specialists for this purpose. In any event, authorities have offered these useful suggestions:

1. Know exactly what you want your mailing to do for you. What are you trying to accomplish? Do you want an order? Or an inquiry? Or a chance to have one of your salesmen call?
2. Address each mailing piece (correctly) to an individual or company who can buy the product or service you have to sell. . . . The mailing list is the absolute foundation of successful direct mail. Solicit your list as often as it pays off.
3. Write your copy so that the recipient will know what your product or service will do for him! Have you appealed to his or her selfish interests or have you used all your white space talking about yourself, your president and your beautiful new factory?
4. Make the layout and format of your mailing tie in with your overall plan and objective. Have you used black-and-white when four-color printing is

indicated? Have you used a typewritten letter when mimeographing would fit the picture better? . . . The appearance of your mailing must be in keeping with the overall job you're trying to do.

5. Make it easy for your prospect to send you an order or an inquiry. Have you included in your mailing an order form for direct business, have you listed the places where your product is available?

6. Test every mailing you make. Never take anything for granted in direct-mail advertising or selling. Don't even trust your own experience. . . . Test everything—even the ideas that seem sure to fail as well as the ones that are bound to succeed. Test media. Test ad size. Test position. Test color against black and white.

7. Tell your story over again. Very few salesmen make a sale on their first call. Even the best of them call back many, many times before turning a prospect into a customer, and it isn't reasonable to expect a single mailing to produce a large return.

8. Include several pieces in any direct mail package, such as advertising about several products, coupons, and certificates. Every product offered should be measured in terms of profit. The weak must go—or at least take less space in the catalogue or sheets. For example, every year over 200 new items are tested in separate mailings by the Shell Oil Company as candidates for inclusion in the Shell Merchandise Catalogue.

9. Don't be afraid of long copy. If your headline or mailing selects the audience and offers them a worthwhile promise, they will read on—and frequently buy. For example, a six-page letter for Mercedes-Benz sold approximately 1,000 diesel cars in one month. Since this model sold at $4,400 each, the letter produced over $4 million in sales.[19]

Layout and Design. The form of the direct mail piece will determine its layout in part. The usual form is a letter, but it also may be a card or catalogue, to mention only a few possible variations. Direct mail is unique in that for a moment or longer it may have the sole attention of the reader. There is no competition from news or other media stimuli. Special burden is thus placed on the layout and visual elements to hold attention. Type is varied, and color is introduced at various points to hold and direct the eye through the entire message.

Radio and Television

Copy. The discussion to this point has been concerned with printed advertisements. It is to be expected that broadcast advertising differs in certain details. Radio has become perhaps the most informal of all media, and this informality has permeated its advertising requirements. Frequently the commercial is not written down word for word, but an

---

[19] Edward N. Mayer, Jr., "7 Cardinal Rules for Direct-Mail Success," *Printers' Ink,* May 30, 1957, p. 38, and David Ogilvy, "Raise Your Sights!" Reproduced with special permission.

outline is given to the announcer, who then provides his own words and style. Heavy use may also be made of humor and whimsy.

Ogilvy makes these suggestions for the television commercial:

1. It is easier to double the selling power of a commercial than to double the audience of a program.
2. Make your *pictures* tell the story. What you *show* is more important than what you *say*. If you can't *show* it, don't say it.
3. Try running your commercial with the sound turned off. If it doesn't sell without sound, it's a feeble commercial. Words and pictures must march together, reinforcing each other. The words must say what the pictures are showing. The words in your titles must be identical with the words spoken.
4. In the best commercials the key idea is forcefully demonstrated. But in the poorest commercials there is little or *no* demonstration.
5. The best commercials are built around one or two simple ideas—*big* ideas. They are not a hodgepodge of confusing little ideas; that is why they are never created in committee. The best commercials flow smoothly, with few changes of scene.
6. The purpose of most commercials is to deliver the selling promise in the most persuasive and memorable way. State your promise at least twice in every commercial.
7. The average consumer sees ten thousand commercials a year. Make sure that she knows the name of the product being advertised in your commercial. Show the package loud and clear. Repeat the brand name as often as you can. Show the name in at least one title.
8. Good commercials rely on simple promises, potently demonstrated. But promises and demonstrations can be made tedious and indigestible by logorrhea [excessive talkativeness]. Don't drown your prospect in words.
9. Make the product itself the hero of the commercial.
10. In *print* advertising you must start by attracting the prospect's attention. But in television the prospect is *already* attending. Your problem is not to attract her attention, but to *hang on to it*.
11. *Start selling in your first frame.* Never warn the prospect that she is about to hear a "friendly word from our sponsor." Never start your commercial with an irrelevant analogy. Never start with an interrupting device.
12. Dr. Gallup reports that commercials which set up a consumer problem, then solve it with the product, then prove it, sell four times as much merchandise as commercials which simply preach about the product.
13. Dr. Gallup also reports that commercials with a news content are more effective than the average.
14. All products are not susceptible to the same commercial techniques. Sometimes there isn't any news; you cannot always use the problem-solution gambit; you cannot always demonstrate. Sometimes you must rely on *emotion* and *mood*. Commercials with a high content of emotion and mood can be very potent indeed.
15. To involve a person emotionally you should be human and *friendly*. People don't buy from salesmen who are bad-mannered. Nor do they buy from phonies or liars. Do not strain their credulity. Be believable.

16. Movie screens are forty feet across, but TV screens are less than two. Use close-up pictures instead of long shots. You have a small screen; get some *impact* on it.

17. You cannot bore people into buying your product. You can only *interest* them in buying it. Dr. Gallup reports that prospects are bored by "sermon" commercials, in which the announcer simply yaks about the product.

18. Television commercials are not for entertaining. They are for *selling*. Selling is a serious business. Good salesmen never sing. The *spoken* word is easier to understand than the *sung* word. Speech is less entertaining than song, but more persuasive. Persuasive commercials never sing.

19. The average consumer sees more than two hundred commercials a week, nine hundred a month, ten thousand a year. For this reason you should give your commercial a touch of singularity. It should have a *burr* that will cling to the viewer's mind. But the burr must not be an irrelevance. And it must not steal attention away from the PROMISE.

20. Whenever you write a commercial, bear in mind that it is likely to be seen by your children, your wife—and your conscience.[20]

Design and Production. Production procedures were discussed earlier and will not be repeated here, other than to stress the growing importance of film and videotape over live commercials. Most network telecasting now is in color. There is no question but what the greater realism pays off in strengthened ability to hold attention. In addition, many feel that the persuasive effectiveness of the commercial is greatly sharpened.

SMALL SPACE: A SPECIAL CREATIVE PROBLEM

Small space is a relative term: a quarter page or less in a magazine; a few column inches in a newspaper; the ten-second commercial; the two- or three-foot highway sign; the direct mail piece of less than standard letter size. Small space offers a special challenge to creativity, for it is usually easier to say what you have to say in large space. Nevertheless, small space also offers unique advantages.

The short commercial (often called the "ID") is growing in popularity on radio and television because prime time may be purchased at a much lower cost per commercial. Research has shown that viewers much prefer the shorter commercial. The persuasive effectiveness (based on the Schwerin measure discussed in Chapter 14 is nearly as great as the 60-second message, brand name recall is virtually identical, and playback of specific sales points from the 20-second spot is 71 percent as effective as playback from its 60-second counterpart.[21] In addition, many

---

[20] Ogilvy, "Raise Your Sights!" Reproduced with special permission.

[21] Robert M. Hoffman, "The 20-Second Commercial," *Media/Scope,* July 1963, p. 74.

feel that the "shorty" can do almost any advertising task. One television expert puts it this way: "There is hardly a product that cannot be successfully advertised with 20-second commercials. We've found that's time enough to allow for adequate demonstration and good registration of the product name. And, a 20-second announcement can be made just as colorful and exciting as a longer one."[22]

Research data also document the effectiveness of small space in printed advertising. While larger advertisements do produce a greater number of readers, the gain in readers is not in direct proportion to size.[23] Unique creative use of the small space can more than offset the advantage of the larger unit.

The emphasis, of course, is on brevity. The headline may carry the entire burden, and there seldom is space or time enough to develop lengthy copy. As a result it is common to take one selling idea at a time and develop it over time through a series of integrated messages. Each advertisement in the campaign will have common elements such as visual treatment, slogan, or background music. Integrated ten-second commercials for Sprite utilized a common background jingle effectively, and many other examples could be given of this technique.

SUMMARY

This appendix has focused on design of the various message elements, with special emphasis on the printed advertisement. Most of the discussion, however, applies to advertising in *all* media.

While a number of guides or criteria were advanced, it cannot be emphasized too strongly that there is no universal set of rules. These criteria were included to provide the foundation for proper disciplining of the imagination to produce a persuasive message. To these would be added many more gained from experience and research. Moreover, they must be modified and adapted to fit each individual situation.

Many technical details of design and production have only been highlighted. However, the complexity should be apparent. Art and production specialists are employed for these various tasks, and the interested reader is encouraged to consult appropriate books to augment his background.[24]

---

[22] Ibid., p. 74.

[23] "What Is the Best Size for a Newspaper Ad?" *Media/Scope,* July 1965.

[24] One useful source is Wales, Gentry, and Wales, *Advertising Copy, Layout and Typography.* Another is Hugh Wales, John McNamara, and Hal Johnson, *New Product, Brand Name, Consumer Packaging and Advertising Philosophy* (DeKalb, Ill.: Northern Illinois University, 1972).

Index

Index

*This book is set in 10 and 9 point Modern #21,
leaded 2 points. Part numbers are 24 point
(small) Helvetica Medium and part titles are
24 point (small) Helvetica. Chapter numbers
are 30 point Helvetica Medium and chapter
titles are 18 point Helvetica. The size of the
tpye page is 27 x 45½ picas.*